EUROPE IN TRANSITION

EUROPE IN TRANSITION

From Feudalism to Industrialization

ARVIND SINHA

MANOHAR
2026

First published 2010
Reprinted 2026

ISBN 978-81-7304-853-1

Published by
Ajay Kumar Jain *for*
Manohar Publishers & Distributors
4753/23 Ansari Road, Daryaganj
New Delhi 110 002

Printed and bound in India

To my mother

LATE CHANDRA PRABHA SINHA

Contents

Illustrations

MAPS

GRAPHS

Tables

Acknowledgements

Teaching has given me much pleasure and satisfaction for many years and I owe a great deal to all my students and colleagues, past and present, in the writing of this book. I express my sincere thanks to the entire team of my publishers, especially Ramesh Jain, Ajay Jain, B.N. Varma and Siddharth Chowdhury for convincing a lazy person like myself to write a textbook on early modern Europe, and for enduring the delay; and to Suresh Prasad for going through the manuscript and making suggestions. Anupam Anand of Geography Department, University of Delhi and Shweta, made their contributions in this book by preparing maps and graphs. Finally, I take this opportunity to thank my family for their care, patience and encouragement.

ARVIND SINHA

Introduction

This volume is an attempt to help the students to understand the process of change leading to the creation of modern Europe in the right perspective. It covers a wide range of topics analysing developments over almost three centuries. This period represented a crucial phase in the transition from the mediaeval to the modern world.

Capitalist society in Europe was formed following the developments through the sixteenth, seventeenth and eighteenth centuries, transforming the feudal order into a merchant and monetary society and then into industrial capitalism. It witnessed changes in the economic organization, social classes and in the forms of government. The expansion of the European economy into new regions leading to the creation of colonial empires and the expansion of mental horizons were accompanied by new social attitudes, cultural patterns and a scientific outlook. Scholars usually describe this period as 'pre-modern' or 'early modern' for many reasons. Crises in centuries-old traditional values developed and created an atmosphere for change. One can observe the seeds of modernity germinating at different levels in these three centuries, which paved the way for rapid and fundamental changes in the European pattern of life. A blind faith in religion was gradually replaced by a rational approach. Explorations in the unknown territories resulted in physical and geographical expansion of the world. The discovery of gunpowder completely changed the nature of warfare. It equipped the Europeans with powerful arms and weapons with which they successfully subjugated the New as well as the Old World. The successful discoveries of new sea trade routes by Columbus towards the west and by Vasco da Gama towards the east marked the beginning of the European colonial empires in the far-flung territories of the globe. Astronomical studies brought about inventions of new instruments. It led to better understanding of the natural world. Centuries-old explanations of natural phenomenon were replaced by modern scientific attitude. Speculative studies gave way to experimentation and formulation of scientific laws based on mathematics and physics. The publication of Copernicus's *De Revolutionibus Orbium Coelestium* in 1543 marked the beginning of the modern scientific age. All these changes helped in the dawn of the industrial age in which technology progressed from windmills to the stage of steam-driven machines for mass production. The economic progress caused vast social and cultural changes. Some of the decentralized and fragmented units gradually made way to strong centralized states. These unified states owed their power to the bureaucratic structure, reformed judiciary, improved military and naval organization, centralized taxation and unified market structure. Expansion of market structure and progressive urbanization promoted the interests of the middle classes and thereby challenged the feudal social organization. The loss of ecclesiastical unity brought about sweeping changes through new ideas, secular literature and science-based philosophies. In short, most parts of Europe were slowly moving out of the feudal structure and were entering the capitalist mode of production. This has led many scholars to describe these centuries as a period of transition. An attempt has been made to present this vast subject matter in a concise and lucid manner which can be understood by all levels of readers.

This book has been divided into fourteen chapters. It is not possible to follow a simple chronological approach as most of the topics run parallel to each other and are at times interrelated. Besides, within the dimension of a book of this size, it is difficult to combine in-depth analysis with chronological details. To overcome this problem at least partially, a table giving the brief sequence of events has been provided at the end of each chapter.

As already stated, the book concentrates on the study of economic history. Nine out of the fourteen chapters have detailed discussions on economic themes. Hence a fusion of economic and social factors is evident in this study. The first chapter contains a compact survey of the socio-economic life in different parts of Europe at the end of the fifteenth century. After a long period of social formation and a slow pace of change, the pace of progress hastens. There are three other chapters with diverse themes related to the sixteenth century. Chapter 2 'The Renaissance and Society' is taken up at different levels to develop an overall historical perspective of this period. The origins of the Renaissance is explained by showing how it was a break from the past and, at the same time, discussing in what ways it had elements of continuity with roots in the past. The methodology adopted is based on regional study, highlighting its chief characteristics by means of comparison and contrast between different regions. The major achievements are discussed under separate headings placing them in proper social context.

Chapter 3 examines the factors which promoted sea voyages and explorations and the creation of early colonial empires under Portugal and Spain. It also includes a detailed discussion on the structure of the empire and the impact these discoveries had on the colonial and European populations. Chapter 4 discusses the Reformation which, along with the Renaissance (Chapter 2) forms a preface to modernity. It includes a discussion on the origins of this movement, the principal ideas of some of the religious reformers, a brief survey of its progress in different regions and the political, cultural and economic consequences. The last part includes a short debate on the relationship between the Protestant ethics and the rise of capitalism in Europe to make the reader understand the significance of Reformation thought in the creation of the modern world.

Chapter 5 'The Rise of Absolutist States' is a study of the relationship between the structure of changing societies and the evolution of the state. It attempts to examine the theoretical issues pertaining to the transformation of feudal and fragmented principalities into sovereign states under powerful monarchies in several parts of Europe. The main theme of debate among historians is whether these central states emerged within the parameters of feudalism or were they the outcome of the rise of capitalism. This discussion is followed by case-studies of some European States.

The sixth chapter examines the economy of Europe during the sixteenth century. This was a period of population growth, expansion of the market and monetary economy, price rise and the development of commercial institutions. It witnessed the rise of western Europe along the Atlantic coast and the decline of the Southern States along the Mediterranean Sea. A detailed analysis is provided of the factors responsible for this reversal. Two other sub-topics in this chapter – The Price Revolution and Commercial Revolution – discuss the plausible causes and the role of these events in the transformation of the European economy.

Chapters 7 to 10 are related to the historical developments of the seventeenth century. The seventeenth-century crisis is approached from several different angles along with various interpretations of the issues involved, as reflected in the different schools of history. The impact of the crisis has been discussed region and class-wise. From the point of view of scientific outlook and new perceptions of the world, the seventeenth century is regarded as a turning point. Chapter 8 presents a study of the debates and major controversies on the relationship of modern science with religion and society. Chapter 9 takes up the issues raised in the English Civil War of 1642, culminating in the Revolution of 1688. The entire process of political change in England is explained through social analysis to enable the readers to understand and appreciate the complexity of the revolutionary situation. The chapter also highlights the political and constitutional progress in England along with socio-economic advancement. The triumph of the bourgeoisie is the most important step in the rise of capitalism.

The rise of mercantilism in Europe was not confined to the economic policies but also formed an essential part of the state-building process. Chapter 10 brings out the principal tenets of mercantilist ideas and narrates the practice of such ideas by the governments of the European States and also highlights the finer difference between them. Chapter 11 examines the nature and extent of colonial rivalry among the European States, the trade structure and studies the relationship between the colonial empires of Britain and France and the process of industrialization, discussing the role of overseas trade in the primitive accumulation of capital in Europe. There is a brief discussion of the slave trade as well.

Chapter 12 deals with the ideas of enlightenment as an intellectual movement and evaluates its impact on the policies pursued by some of the rulers of central and eastern Europe. Chapter 13 is important as it discusses the economic progress achieved by the end of the eighteenth century in the fields of agriculture, trade and industry, creating ground for the Industrial Revolution in Britain and subsequently in other states of Europe.

Chapter 14 takes up all the alternative views and debates on why and how European feudalism began to disintegrate. It also explains the nature of transition from feudalism to capitalism taking up various theoretical aspects of the debates and their respective models.

The book covers diverse subjects of vast magnitude. Effort has been made to present the subject matter in a simple and concise form without distorting the balance of the whole. Any such comprehensive work of this nature has to be dependent on the research of other scholars although some portions are based on the original sources. References are given only for direct quotations and on points of special indebtedness. Attempt has been on analysing the events and hence narrative has been kept to the minimum. Several maps and graphs have been provided to enable the readers to have a better understanding of parallel events. The book gives a brief annotated bibliography at the end of each chapter. This should prove useful to those who wish to have access to deeper knowledge of specific themes.

However, before starting with the chapters, it would be useful to know in brief about the schools of history which have made contribution to our understanding of this period. The two most important schools comprise of (a) the Marxist writers and (b) the Annales group of scholars. The Marxist approach to history holds the most important position in the writing of history as it provides a socio-economic explanation that was virtually non-existent in the earlier writings.

Friedrich Engels gives all credit to Karl Marx for starting a new theory of history that is given the name the 'materialist conception of history' or commonly called 'historical materialism'. Before Marx, Hegel had conceived human civilization as a dialectical progression (that meant a struggle of opposites – thesis and antithesis – eventually achieving resolution in a higher synthesis). Whereas Hegel believed that ideas are the motive force in human history, Marx and Engels considered material conditions of a society or the method of production play a deterministic role. For Marx the most important factors that shape human history are: the economic level of development of society under consideration, changes in the mode of production, the social divisions within the society and the nature or the stage of class struggle.

For Marx, the simple truth that gives meaning to history is the fact that man must eat to live. His very survival depends upon his ability to produce what he wants from Nature. Production therefore is the most important of all the activities of human beings. The material production for Marx meant the ways in which means of subsistence are produced by individuals and groups working together that involve some degree of division of labour. As work or production is central to the daily life of human beings, social relations assume a material base. How people work helps mould any given society. This view is called the materialist interpretation of history and was elaborated in *The German Ideology* by Karl Marx and Engels. They contend that history could best be understood by the realization that the economic structure was the ultimate, though not the only basis of human history. The totality of the relations of production constitutes the economic structure of society, the actual foundation is called the 'base' or the substructure. Upon this is built a 'superstructure' representing law, politics, philosophy, religion, culture and 'definite forms of social consciousness'. Marx and Engels suggest that state and social consciousness are part of the superstructure that corresponds to society's economic base. The economically dominant class became the politically dominant class and used state as their instrument. However, they also concede that at times, the state may attain a certain degree of independence from the propertied ruling class, as had happened in the absolutist states of early modern Europe. Most of the times, according to them, the social relations of production and their hierarchies change as the material forms of production change. Marxist writings emphasize the role of the 'mode of production' (comprising the evolving relations between forms of material production, the division of labour and social structure) in the periodization of history into the ancient or the slave mode, the feudal mode and the capitalist mode of production respectively. The mode of production conditions the general process of social, political and intellectual life. In all the modes of production, the class, which controls the forces of production, dominates the rest, thus perpetuating tensions and conflict. The structure of each society is dependent on the mode of production, i.e. as Marx put it, the hand-mill gives you society with the feudal lord while the steam-mill makes the industrial capitalist.

Another important aspect of Marxist writings is the theory of class conflict. The concept of class holds a special place in Marxist theory. The emergence of classes is related to their economic interests. This is not to say that men, consciously or unconsciously, act only from economic motive. It is only to suggest that while other motives exist they are subordinate to economic factors. Nor does it mean that religious, metaphysical, ethical or literary ideas have no role whatsoever and all these are completely reducible to economic motives. Marx had attached great importance to production, which was seen as a collective act that led to the conclusion that man as an individual has little role in human history. In the *Communist Manifesto* Marx wrote that the history of all hitherto existing society is the history of class struggle. However, the concept of class was mainly applied to the capitalist society. Yet, his writings imply that at every stage of society, a particular class gets control of the means of production and exploits the rest. Changes in the means of production would give rise to new social forces and a revolutionary situation would be produced. A struggle between the new and the old dominant class would lead to the class war. As to what caused the revolutionary situation to emerge, Marx and Engels suggest that it was the result of incompatibility between the forces of production and the relations of production. The forces of production include technology, raw materials, and sources of energy, land utilization and the skill of a workforce. The relations of production imply the relations of property or social relations that existed between the direct producers and the owners of the means of production. Although the idea of class war had been there in the writings of the French scholars St Simon and

Giuzot, Marx applied it in union with Hegel's Dialectic. This implied that with increasing exploitation each dominant class necessarily develops its opposite, and from this class struggle a new ruling class emerges till finally a classless society emerges. The rise of the bourgeoisie in a feudal mode of production results in the overthrow of feudal nobility through the bourgeois revolution, paving the way for the capitalist mode of production. This revolutionary situation does not happen till the mode of production reaches a definite stage of maturity and finds the existing relations of production becoming 'fetters' in its further growth. Thus, the first part of the *Communist Manifesto* brings out the pattern of historical change from the ancient world to industrial capitalism.

The last few years have seen the emergence of divergent views even within the Marxist framework as Marx had left certain ideas ambiguous, thereby leaving lot of scope for interpretation. This is evident in the Marxist explanations of the nature of the absolutist states, of the English revolution and the decline of feudalism. Some of the present-day Marxists do not accept the dominant role of the productive forces and the writings of Christopher Hill and Robert Brenner reflect different approaches. On the question of the role of foreign commerce in the emergence of capitalism, there has been an intense debate even within the Marxist school, though Marx had emphasized the influx of gold and silver from South America, the exploitation of the Asian societies and the slave trade as being among the forces which contributed to the conditions of capitalist development. Much of the criticism of historical materialism has centred on the subject of interpretation of base and superstucture. Many scholars argue that it is impossible to locate a pure economic level of society separate from politics, law and various forms of social consciousness. Base and superstructure are no longer seen as separate institutions. Similarly, the Marxists themselves such as Régine Robin and Althusser have modified the class-conflict explanation of the French Revolution raising doubts about the existence of class conflict in eighteenth-century French society. Thus, in the twentieth century, different variants of Marxism emerged.

In the writing of history, the influence of Marxism had been crucial and deep. A large number of historians throughout the world adopted this approach in their method of historical investigation. Marxism provided a different view of long-term changes in society. Materialist interpretation and class-struggle explanation has helped the historians to see the political institutions and social protests in their broader social context. Among the notable Marxist historians one can mention the names of Maurice Dobb, Rodney Hilton, Christopher Hill, George Rudé, Eric Hobsbaum, E.P. Thompson, Robert Brenner, J.S. Cohen, P. Anderson and many others. Most of these names will be appearing frequently in subsequent chapters.

The second important school of historians is called the Annales. It developed in France and attracted global audience because of its novel approach of studying and explaning history. It was a major shift in history writing from the point of view of methodology and intellectual content. This is based on interdisciplinarity that has opened new styles of investigation and presentation of historical facts. The Annales era from the 1930s to the 1970s dominated historical research and came to be called *La nouvelle histoire* or the New History. The Annales School owes its name to the journal *Annales*, initially called *Annales d'histoire ecomique et sociale.* It was founded in 1929 by Marc Bloch and Lucien Febvre. They brought the economic and social sciences together in an interdisciplinary and collaborative framework. After Febvre's death in 1956, Fernand Braudel took over its editorship till 1969. Several other scholars such as Jacque Le Goff, Immanuel Le Roy Ladurie, Marc Ferro, Pierre Chaunu, Pierre Nora, Mona Ozouf and many others contributed to this new writing.

Marc Bloch is considered the founder of the Annales School. Bloch believed that history must be problem based. In his writings, he drew widely from geography, collective psychology and sociology. His book *The Royal Touch* is a seminal work of historical anthropology. It presents kingship in a wholly novel way. It deals with the popular belief in France and England during the Middle Ages that the king had the power to cure scrofula (a skin disease called the king's evil). It is different from other historical writings as it is a work of comparative history, it deals with the problem of collective illusions and made significant contribution to the field of religious psychology. Bloch's another major contribution to historical studies is his *French Rural Studies*. This pathbreaking work is concerned with long-term developments from the thirteenth till the eighteenth century based on new type of sources. The most well-known work of Marc Bloch is *The Feudal Society*. It covers a period of four centuries and includes a wide range of topics like servitude, liberty, economy, social organization and the entire culture of feudalism. Unlike the Marxist class analysis of feudal society based on economic exploitation and antagonistic relationship between the lords and the serfs, Bloch presents an intra-class approach and explains the interrelationships of various groups, individuals, the state and the peasants, all seen as a society. He expressed the totality of the feudal experience. Lucien Febvre also worked on historical geography. In his *Religion of Rabelais*, Febvre studies the problem of unbelief in the sixteenth century and thus presents the history of collective mentality, a subject on which many others worked subsequently.

Among the scholars who had a deep influence in our understanding of early modern world, Fernand Braudel holds a special place. His *The Mediterranean and the Mediterranean World in the Age of Philip II* has been described by Peter Burke as an 'extraordinary book' and many consider it as the most remarkable historical work to have been written in the twentieth century. This work revealed new possibilities of history writing. This work is considered remarkable because it embodies Braudel's conviction that history can be divided between three 'durations' or *durée*. Braudel distributed the history of the early Mediterranean across these units of time. This he calls the tripartite model of historical explanation. The long duration implies the time of geographical structures, the environment, the sea, the mountains and the climate, the so-called biological and geographical determinant forming 'immobile history'. The medium duration is the socio-economic conjunctures of ten, twenty or thirty years. These are the economic and social fluctuations of regionally or nationally defined populations, price fluctuations, institutional and military trends, etc. The short duration consists of individual, political and cultural events of specific groups and individuals. Thus *The Mediterranean* is divided into the study of (a) the geography, (b) the society, and (c) the individual. Braudel's another major and exhaustive work is written in three volumes under the title *Civilization and Capitalism.* It offers the economic and social history of the world from the Middle Ages to the coming of the Industrial Revolution. This is also based on historical experience of human civilization. The first volume, *Structures of Everyday Life* includes demography, biological regimes, 'daily bread', food and drinks, architecture, clothes, technology, sources of energy and patterns of life in towns and cities. This volume deals with infrastructural and timeless features, the daily routines which is linked to primary preconstraining reality of population trends. The second volume, *The Wheels of Commerce* gives attention to the markets and exchanges, from pedlars and merchants to fairs, market halls, and stock exchanges that were responsible for the emergence of world economy. The third volume, *The Perspective of the World* deals with the world economy based on the division of space and time, although many of the subjects like politics, wars, dynastic rivalries and religious conflicts is left out. Braudel's work was hailed as 'a revolutionary work that best encapsulated the aims and the spirit of Annales' by Febvre and many others. According to Lynn Hunt, Braudel combined both institutional and intellectual influence in an extraordinary fashion. His real originality can be seen in his study of relationships shaping structures of *longue durée*, climate, biology and demography as fundamental determinants of society. He was blamed by some for presenting a relatively static geo-history rather than a more dynamic economic history.

Some of the most imaginative writings of Annales historians deal with rural histories and study of climatic changes by scholars like Le Roy Ladurie (*Peasants of Languedoc* and *The Territory of the Historian*) and Pierre Goubert on Beauvais, family life and women by Christiane Klapisch, Michèle Perrot and Georges Duby, and the study of festivals by Mona Ozouf. Gordon Manley has presented three centuries of climatic readings in thermometric series. New tools have been used by Annales historians to reconstruct history that includes climatic data, dendrochronology (study of a tree's rings giving its age), phenology (study of annual data of flowering and fruiting of plants), glaciological method, geomorphology (study of moraines), palynology (study of marshes and peat bags situated downstream of glaciers), nuclear biology to date C-14 and the role of many non-human factors in the study of human society. This has led Lyn Hunt to observe that no other group has made more valuable contribution to historiography and historical method than the Annales School. In French history, Annales has become a standard point of reference. It has contributed to new methodology by adopting regressive, interdisciplinary, global and comparative studies. The term 'regressive method' is associated with Bloch, particularly his presentation of rural history in which historical study begins from present and moves backward. The use of quantification method and structural method has helped in the preparation of demographic studies on a scientific basis. Annales presented an almost boundless range of topics and methods of study. While Marxism insisted on primacy of the economy and society over political and cultural formations, the Annales paradigm itself did emphasize on change, conflict and rupture in the long-term tendencies. In recent years, the Annales School has been criticized on several grounds. It is argued that in Braudel's conception of history, space, time and man were the three ruling abstractions but in reality, the Annales writings have turned man into vehicle for the long-standing repetitive interactions between space and time and his role has been made negligible. Second, the overemphasis on statistical data has turned historians into mere gatherers of quantifiable information. In this method, historical change is liable to be ignored or go unexplained. It is asserted that the purpose of history is to explain change. Third, the Annales writings show an ambiguity of relationship between social science and history. The role of the historian, in the language of Ladurie, is becoming that of a programmer. Yet, the writing of Annales School has immensely contributed to our understanding of the structure and functioning of pre-modern European societies. The seventeenth-century crisis can be better understood with the study of Annales literature.

Arvind Sinha

CHAPTER 1

The Face of Europe in the Late-Fifteenth Century

Geographical Frontiers

The face of Europe at the end of the fifteenth century was still medieval in many respects. Although the mountains, hills, plains and rivers were the same as they are today, man's dependence on these geographical features was much greater then. There were other differences as well. The course of the rivers has now changed just as the forest cover has been greatly reduced. The rivers were flooded more readily then and the pattern of demography has changed immensely.

Europe in the late-fifteenth century could be divided into different regions on the basis of its geographical features, as can be seen in Map 1.1. The economic variations to some extent were influenced by the relief features, climate and natural resources. Unlike other continents it has practically no desert and hence contains a greater proportion of land suited to agriculture. It enjoyed considerable mineral wealth, especially coal and iron – two most important pre-conditions for industrial development. In respect of disposition of the main expanses of land and water, Europe had been fortunate in being placed in the middle of the land hemisphere. It is surrounded by waters on three sides and combines the advantages of the mid-land position with easy access to other parts of the globe by sea. In the north-west and south, Europe is bound by the sea. With economic expansion, this factor contributed to the strength of the navy of the European powers, whereby the Europeans could reach distant regions and establish their political and economic supremacy. In the east, Europe merges with the

Asiatic mainland, and here its boundaries remained artificial. The Ural Mountains stretching from north to south could not form a convenient boundary as it could be easily crossed in many places. Thus in the absence of a permanent political boundary and with the possibility of frequent invasions, this region remained a source of conflicts and rebellions. The presence of the Black and Caspian seas encouraged Russia to expand in the west to establish its supremacy over the smaller states of this region, to resist the expansion of the Ottoman Empire and to control the Asian trade. The triple division on the basis of vegetation – coniferous, deciduous and steppe influenced the living patterns of the people. The Muscovite state was situated in the deciduous region where rye, barley, oats and wheat were grown. The towns were situated far apart and most of the northern region was covered with snow, and Russia therefore could not develop due to sparse population in that region. Till the late-fifteenth century, Russia was closer to Asia than to Europe. The effort to reach the sea, especially an ice-free sea, had been an important objective of Russia since medieval times. Russia's long and historic remoteness from the sea may be seen as a major reason for her aloofness from western Europe. On the south, Tatars and Turks barred the way to the Black Sea; on the west, Lithuanians, Swedes and Finns checked Russia from acquiring the Baltic. The great northern forests prevented the Russians from finding a way to the White Sea and it was an Englishman, who showed this route to the Russians in the mid-sixteenth century. Pressure from the west had the effect of directing Russian expansionist movements eastward. The Russians had reached the Pacific coast as early as 1639, almost half a century before they could obtain their first base on the Baltic coast. The distance from western Europe, where feudal structure was showing signs of disintegration with the expansion of trade, had left Russia unaffected. The geography of this region contributed to the continuation of serfdom for a very long time. Even the growth of trade took place within feudal control, and instead of becoming an agent of dissolution, it strengthened feudalism.

Another geographical zone was central Europe consisting of numerous big and small states like Poland, Prussia, Brandenburg

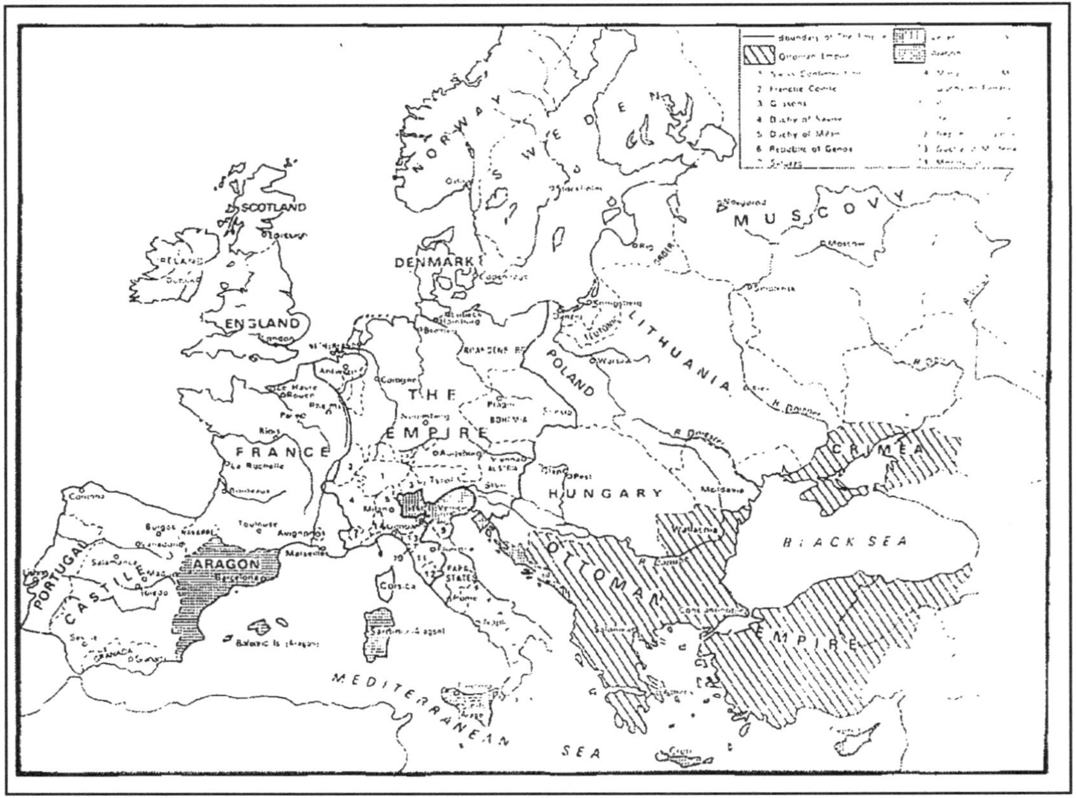

Map 1.1: European States in about 1500

and many others. The region did not possess any structural unity. There were wide divergences in the form of physical features and ethnic groups. The northern region to glaciated lowland, the middle has mountains and basins and the lower regions consist of plains. central Europe was indeed a transitional region between the east and west, north and south and was, therefore, more varied within than the other main regions of Europe. Climatically it covers the marginal zone – between the wet changeable weather of western Europe and the stable, dry and extreme climate of eastern Europe. There were numerous small and a few large states that remained independent till the nineteenth century when they formed the powerful German Empire. Surrounded by the Alps in the south and the Baltic and North Seas in the north with several navigable rivers, this region was well linked through international trade routes. Though lacking political unity, this region was the hub of manufacturing, commercial and intellectual activities. It was known for its silver, copper and iron, and its arable and pasture lands. In the middle ages, central Europe had a number of cities and towns but the feudal structure had remained very powerful.

Northern Europe consisted of the Scandinavian peninsula that included Sweden, Norway, Finland and the Low Countries. The highlands of Scandinavia (and Scotland in the British Isles) had experienced periods of glaciations – the 'Great Ice Age' – and the intervening interglacial warm periods. Geological history reveals that at many times in the past, ice caps similar to the present Greenland and Antarctica had developed over Scandinavia and pushed their way out across the North Sea and Baltic into Russia and north Germany and Poland, seriously affecting the lives of the people. The countries situated near the North Sea did not have any expansion of agriculture in the fifteenth century, and instead had reached its limits and recession had set in. The chief features in the first half of the sixteenth century were the abandoned holdings and depopulated and deserted villages and the prosperity that one notices in the later period had not begun. However, in the subsequent period it developed into an important centre of dairy production and industrial activity. The other region adjacent to Holland was the Baltic Sea area, which had been developing into a centre of cereal production. An interesting feature of the Low Countries was that large portions of coastal regions were below sea level and the process of land reclamation through dikes had started. It emerged as a highly productive region during the sixteenth century. In the middle ages, the Low Countries exhibited the most precocious development of the city life and it was an important centre of textile industry. Later it led the way in the agrarian development and enjoyed numerous commercial advantages that were exploited from the sixteenth century onwards.

The southern region of Europe formed the Alpine territory, extending from the Spanish peninsula to the Black Sea coast and on to Asia Minor. The Alpine mountains provided the most significant barrier to transport and communications between the northern and the southern Europe. The Alpine area provided a great range not only of terrain but also of climate and soil. Crop farming remained restricted to the valleys and slopes and pastoralism was predominant. Southern Europe consisted of three important peninsulas – the Iberian, Italian and the Greek. Together, it has been described by Braudel as 'the Mediterranean zone'. The climate and its vegetation provided a strong unifying element to the region and tended to evoke a common agricultural response despite internal disunity and diversity. The entire Mediterranean coastline had a common physical feature in the form of hilly and mountainous land while Italy was separated from the rest of Europe by the Alps and the Iberian peninsula was cut-off from France by the Pyrenees. The difference between the Mediterranean climate and the rest of Europe is striking. The scanty rainfall in the summer months and relatively heavier rainfall in the winter months with mild temperatures influenced the pattern of vegetation in this region. The Mediterranean coast did not specialize in grain cultivation because of its poor soil and climatic factors. Unlike the dense deciduous forests of central and western Europe, Mediterranean forests grew in open formations although turned into scrub. The regions specialized in wine and olive production although certain areas could produce corn. These three products have been called 'the Mediterranean triad' and formed the basis of their rural economy. The use of Latin had been spreading over the great plains of northern Italy from classical times. The rise of Venice and Genoa, the leading trading ports, facilitated the spread of the Latin culture in several parts of Europe across the Alps. The Iberian peninsula too had poor soil with mountains and valleys breaking the central plateau. High mountains all along the Bay of Biscay coast made the interior region arid. Thus Spain concentrated on sheep farming. The Moorish population in the twelfth century promoted a pastoral economy where a guild of shepherds came into existence called *Mesta*. They were able to introduce a type of sheep called Merino, the best in the world. An interesting feature that emerged from this economy was a system of special highways that was created by the sheep and the shepherds. These highways were created by the migratory sheep farmers who travelled distances up to 350 to 450 miles. The highways were protected by state regulations. Spanish wool was transported to Flanders for manufacturing cloth and Medina Del Campo had become an important centre of wool trade. The regular migrations caused clashes between pastoral and agricultural groups and it also adversely affected the forests in that region and did not encourage agriculture.

In the fifteenth century Italy was divided into more than a dozen principalities and states constituting an important part of the Mediterranean zone. The main feature of the northern Mediterranean coastlands was the high proportion of hilly and mountainous land. It did not stop foreign invasions but prevented the coming together of people into a single entity. The wild and vast blocks of mountains between scattered areas of fertile land created an obstacle to unity and promoted separate 'city states'. This region had witnessed some great civilizations in the past that were either overthrown by foreign invasions or fell relentlessly into decay due to disunity although Latin had provided a unifying force to the plains of northern Italy. Till the beginning of the sixteenth century, the economy of the city-states was to a great extent dependent on the trading and manufacturing activities of the urban centres. There were important cities such as Milan, Venice, Genoa, Florence, Siena, Rome and several others. Many of these states encouraged mulberry cultivation to promote the production of silk. Silk manufacturing industries had come up in different parts of the Italian peninsula and the introduction of sheep farming promoted woollen textiles. Towards the closing decades of the fifteenth century, the transoceanic discoveries and the expansions of the Turks in the east was turning the Mediterranean into commercial back waters, and threatening the economies of the Italian states that had prospered till now. From this period the commercial activities moved from the Mediterranean and started concentrating in north-west Europe. Moreover, the Italian states had become embroiled in wars which lasted from 1494 till 1538. The economic glory of the Italian states was nearing the end with the beginning of the sixteenth century.

Western Europe in 1500 consisting of France, Britain, Belgium and Holland, was emerging as the most important geographical zone, experiencing the first signs of economic transformation. This was a maritime region with sufficient rainfall and fertile tracts of land. In northern France, the Seine basin near Paris with Picardy, Beauce and Caux constituted an important agricultural region. The land was extremely fertile because of the river deposits and superficial deposits of clay made the region particularly suitable for cereal production.

Northern France in the middle ages had shown outstanding prosperity but the Hundred Years War (1337–1453) had destroyed this. The war caused significant population losses. However, in southern France the devastation was followed by the introduction of grape cultivation for the production of wine. Agricultural production in western France started reviving towards the end of the fifteenth century after a period of long recession. Attempts were made to utilize the marshland while enclosures in a few regions promised consolidation of landholdings by replacing the open fields.

As southern France falls in the Mediterranean zone it developed its own lifestyle, having its own language *Languel'oc* as opposed to *langue d'oil* of the north. While northern France was adopting customary law (*droit coutumier*), southern France had been practising the Roman law (modified into *droit écrit*). In the southern France stood the Central Massif with fertile valleys exhibiting prosperous agriculture. Further south, coastal France excelled in wine production. However, the potential of these regions could not be achieved and France remained a strong feudal state till the eighteenth century.

In England also, agriculture started showing signs of recovery and some of the regions witnessed the conversion of open fields into enclosures for sheep farming. The relative geographical isolation from the rest of Europe encouraged internal development and political centralization after a period of destructive wars. From the late-fifteenth century, rural cottage industry was emerging and foreign trade was beginning to show distinct growth and prosperity. The signs of feudal decay were visible in this part of Europe.

Feudal Structure in Europe

Before discussing the major changes in the economic life of Europe, which began with the sixteenth century, it is necessary to understand the economic and political organization of Europe, which had grown over a period of centuries under the feudal system. Without entering into a debate on the definition of feudalism, it will be useful to know how that feudal order organized the economy and society of Europe.

The downfall of the Roman Empire in the west led to the formation of the Frankish state in the late-fifth century AD. The fertile plains, land, cattle, weapons and horses attracted the Frankish nobility. This period marked the growth of large landed estates and control over the peasants was secured by providing protection to them in return for their services. This marked the beginning of feudal organization – a fusion of Roman villa and German village community. With the passage of time it developed into a form of economic and social organization. The feudal society in western Europe developed into a hierarchical form, in which every person was assigned a place according to a graded order. The king stood at the top of the hierarchal order. He bestowed land (fief or estate) on a number of subordinates known as dukes and earls. They were called feudal lords and they themselves bestowed a portion of their fief to the lesser lords called the barons. These grants were conditional and were given in return for military service or other forms of assistance. The dukes and earls were the vassals of the king while the barons were the vassals of the dukes and earls. Below the barons were the knights. The latter did not have any vassals under them. Every feudal lord, except the knight, was a vassal of his superior and himself a lord as well. The peasants constituted the lowest segment of the society and were divided into mainly three categories – the free holders, villeins and serfs. The free holders received lands from the lords which they used and managed on their own. They did not work for the lords and paid taxes. The villeins gave part of their produce from their allotted land and gave their labour free for a fixed number of days to their lords. Otherwise, they were free. The bulk of the peasants consisted of serfs who were allowed to use the lord's land for cultivation on a set of conditions imposed on them by the feudal lords. This relationship of duties and obligations of the serfs for their master-lord constituted the most important aspect of feudalism.

Feudalism in Western Europe has been studied and presented in different ways. A number of British and German scholars emphasize the aspect of military organization along with the legal and customary principles on which the feudal relationships were based. John Critchley emphasizes the military tenure dimension of feudalism – a view that has been commonly accepted. He points out to the close personal bond between the lord and the vassals, which was based on an oath of fealty by the vassal. Other scholars like Rushton Coulborn suggest that feudalism was basically a method of government rather than a type of economic or social system. Its essential characteristic was the relationship between the lord and the vassals, in which political authority was treated as a private possession – personal in nature rather than institutional. From the political point of view feudalism was essentially a system of extreme political decentralization where the authority was parcelled among the feudal lords. At the same time one cannot ignore the existence of the king, however, weak he may be. From the late-fifteenth century political centralization under these rulers had started in many of the larger states.

An important contributor to the study of feudalism is Marc Bloch, the well-known French scholar. He considers feudalism as system of human relations and studies it from the point of view of social order. According to Bloch, the fundamental features of European feudal organization consisted of a subject peasantry; widespread use of the 'service tenement' (i.e. the fief) instead of salary, supremacy of a class of specialized warriors, ties of obedience and protection and fragmentation of authority due to decentralized power structure. For Marc Bloch, feudalism coincided with a profound weakening of the state, particularly in its protective capacity. The feudal system meant the vigorous economic subjection of a host of humble folk to a few powerful men. 'It involved a far-reaching restriction of social intercourse, a circulation of money too sluggish to admit of a salaried officialdom, and a mentality attached to things tangible and local' (Bloch, *Feudal Europe*, p. 443). Thus we find that Bloch did not attempt a definition of feudalism, rather he provided a description and concentrated his attention on European feudalism. He also points out that feudal Europe was not all feudalized in the same degree and it was nowhere feudalized completely. In no country did the whole of the rural population come entirely under the bonds of personal and hereditary dependence and the concept of state never absolutely disappeared.

Marx and Engels did not describe feudalism in terms of class organization but their theory implied that class provided the fundamental foundation of feudal society. The class relations (nobility–serf) based on landed estate determined the feudal organization. Feudalism is shown in the nature of an estate organization with little or no division of labour, with primitive conditions of production. However the most important analysis of feudal organization is provided by Marxist writings. Feudalism is seen as a mode of production based on appropriation of feudal rent by the feudal lords from the peasant tenants in a primarily agrarian society. Marx distinguished feudal rent from the capitalist's ground rent and said that the level of feudal rent was determined by the ability of the feudal ruling class to impose non-economic forms of compulsion. Non-economic compulsion means that the rent had been extracted through the superior force exercised by the landowners. The institution of serfdom legitimized this force. The peasants did not enjoy property rights and they were not legally free though they were given the right to use the land on certain conditions. One important element of feudalism was the lord–vassal relationship. It was based on the concept of fief. The word feudalism comes from the word feud, feudal or fief. This was a form of property mentioned in the law books of medieval times and the feudal law was the law of fief, as distinct from the law dealing with other kinds of property. The classical fief was a piece of landed property held by a vassal from a lord in return for military service and other forms of assistance. The relationship of lord and vassal was expressed by the oath of fealty. However, it was not a universal form of feudal society. This type of feudalism mainly developed in central Europe and in Norman England. The relationship between the lord and vassal was important in a period when the state powers had fragmented because of the localized nature of the economy in a state of poor communication. It was also exercised through the institution of feudal courts. The lords exercised power in feudal society by holding court for their vassals, and settled disputes and ordered punishments. This court also functioned as an administrative organ for levying taxes and raising military forces. Jurisdictional power was also necessary to maintain a lord's control over the peasants. The decentralization of authority under feudal lords led to the imposition of obligation over the villagers by the lords such as forcing all inhabitants to grind their corn in the lord's mill, press their grapes in the lord's wine press, bake their bread in his oven and each time they did so they had to contribute a part of their product either in kind or in money. Free labour service was extracted mainly in the *demesne* (the personal farm of the feudal lord that contained arable lands, meadowlands, vineyards or *le clos* and sometimes water mills, breweries and inns) and the size of *demesnes* varied from one lord to another. Many historians consider the labour services rendered in the *demesne* land as an essential part of feudal rent, a method, by which the ruling class appropriated surplus labour. These writers suggest that the development of rent in kind and in money was a sure sign of the breakdown of the feudal mode of production in western Europe, while the continuation of large *demesnes* and servile labour rent in eastern

Europe from the sixteenth to the eighteenth centuries suggests the continuation and strengthening of feudalism there.

There are different views on the impact of market expansion on the feudal economy. It is true that in most parts of Europe, the greatest part of social product (like foodstuff) was not meant for the market and most of the local production was consumed within the peasant household or taken away by the lord through forced appropriation. The produce of *demesne* farming was consumed to some extent within the aristocratic household but part of it went to the market. The disposable surplus varied considerably depending on different factors such as war natural calamity, etc. The feudal ruling class also had special needs related to the market. The market demand of the feudal lords included luxury items such as silk, spices, wines, ornaments – small in bulk but high in cost. These items were not produced by the local economy but brought from distant regions like Asia or Africa. The feudal ruling class needed money to purchase them and this money was obtained through rent and jurisdictional profits. Thus the administrative and political centres of the kings and their vassals created a demand for the high-priced luxury goods at the centres of feudal power, including the seats of religious officials, who were associated with the feudal organizations. Hence, in the period of high Middle Ages, the process of urban growth, marketing and manufacturing activities expanded and started affecting the European feudal order. At the same time it is important to note that the medieval cities presented no fundamental threat to the feudal order. There was a fusion of interest rather than a conflict between the early merchant capitalists and the feudal lords. The bourgeois families in northern Italy provided loans to the feudal rulers and aristocrats. The real antagonism in the feudal society existed between the class of feudal nobility and the serfs. The use of political means to appropriate economic surplus made Perry Anderson stress the point that feudalism was neither strictly an economic system nor strictly political. Its chief features consisted of vassalage, the fief and as Anderson puts it – the 'parcellized sovereignty' and thereby feudalism combined land-lordship with military services in which authority was fragmented and de-centralized among the lords.

Impact of Black Death on Agrarian Economy

The economic expansion of the High Middle Ages in Europe ended by the beginning of the fourteenth century. The growth of population and the increase in agricultural production was brought to an end between 1310 and the 1340s when European society experienced a period of scarcity. This was followed by the spread of the Black Death – a devastating plague which spread over Europe by the littoral way from Constantinople and eastern Mediterranean (1347) to Italy, Spain and France (1348), then to Switzerland, Austria, Germany and the Low Countries (1349) followed by Scandinavia and Poland (1350). It transformed the feudal crisis (declining returns from land in the absence of modern technology) into a serious demographic catastrophe. It resulted in immense demographic loss. It is estimated that the loss of population varied from about 12 to 60 per cent depending upon the region. The average loss of population is estimated at 40 per cent. The loss was so great that it took over a century to recover from it. Subsequent feudal wars continued to adversely affect the European economy till the end of the fifteenth century.

From the beginning of the fifteenth century, new economic patterns began to emerge. The prices of foodstuffs declined with the improvement in production, and because of demographic losses through plague, there were fewer mouths to feed. There were price fluctuations in certain years but the overall prices throughout the century remained not only low but stable. This trend resulted in fresh specialization in the agrarian sector. The demand for other types of food items such as dairy products and meat began to increase. There was a definite shift towards specialized products particularly in regions which had poor soil or unfavourable climate. Hence specialized regional economies began to emerge – parts of England specialized in wool production, France developed wine production, northern Europe promoted dairy farming while the Baltic region emerged as the chief centre of cereal production. The agrarian crisis caused by the Black Death also resulted in an increase in the relative significance of towns and cities due to mass exodus from the countryside. A large number of smaller towns came up and the importance of towns like Antwerp, Florence, Venice, Barcelona, London, Lyons and many others grew. The growth of trade encouraged formation of trading organizations like the Hanseatic League (a German institution that mainly traded with the Baltic and the North Sea) and the Merchant Adventurers (of England with monopoly rights to trade with Flanders). By the late-fifteenth century the Italian cities in southern Europe were becoming the focal point of commercial economy.

For agriculture and feudal organization, the economic crisis and the demographic losses brought about fundamental changes in the land relationship in different regions of Europe. In certain regions there was considerable loosening of the ties between the feudal lord and his servile labour. Citing the case of Normandy in France, Guy Bois described the social changes after the Black Death as a crisis of feudalism, while others like Wilhelm Abel termed it as an agrarian crisis. After the initial period of declining population, fallen grain prices and rise in real wages, which had put the feudal lords in a difficult position (particularly in the prolonged conflicts like the Hundred Years War) and caused drastic increase in the feudal rent, the situation began to improve slightly after 1460. The response of the feudal lords to the changing situations varied greatly from one region to another. In England feudal rents declined, the long-term grain prices also fell and with it the income of the manorial lords came down sharply. Several feudal lords introduced sheep farming by enclosing their lands in order to increase their income. In such regions, the peasants were evicted from the land while in other regions there was a tendency to commute feudal rent payment into money or kind. The three-field system which prevailed in most European states, allowed alternative use of land and thereby helped in retaining land productivity.

In the urbanized territories of northern Italy such as Lombardy, the agrarian situation was not too bad. The burghers of the town invested some of their income in agriculture and thus promoted crop specialization. The government in the cities promoted irrigation system, which contributed to greater productivity. However, this was not the situation in other parts of Italy. In

Germany and in eastern Europe the nobility went in for agricultural development. The feudal crisis had strengthened the process of refeudalization. The scope of exploitation by the feudal lords widened considerably. They resorted to their local judicial powers and succeeded in imposing extensive service conditions on the peasants and utilized the compulsory labour to form their own estates. The liberty of the peasants to move from one place to another was restricted and they were pushed to hereditary subjections. While in western Europe there was a relaxation of ties of peasant dependency. The seigniors of eastern Europe extracted higher dues from the peasants to keep the wage costs of their household servants down. In the regions east of the river Elbe, the feudal nobility resolved their economic problems through different ways. As the territorial rules were weak, and the nobles enjoyed greater power through their representative assemblies, they could easily subject the peasants to their own rule and enlarge their estates by controlling judicial authority as well as by receiving ecclesiastical patronage. In the two important states of eastern Europe – Poland and Lithuania, the feudal crisis resulted in the introduction and strengthening of serfdom. The legal and political powers of the nobility in relation to the peasant and townsman increased immensely through the laws of the Polish Diets. The feudal magnates totally controlled the *Segm* (Parliament) and thus imposed their will on the peasants. They succeeded in not only controlling but also profiting from the grain trade. In the other eastern territories such as Bohemia, Moravia, Hungary, Romania and Russia, the process of feudalization hastened and the peasants became more like personal properties of the feudal lords.

Many scholars, like Robert Brenner and others, provide an explanation for the existence of two types of agrarian systems in early modern eastern and western Europe. They focus on the different patterns of the historical evolutions. In the states of western Europe, like England and France, the rulers had succeeded in establishing their predominance over the nobility by the sixteenth century, while in the countries of eastern Europe with the exception of Russia, politics was dominated not by the kings but by the noblemen. The eastern rulers needed the support of the nobility to remain in power and were forced to grant concessions to the feudal lords to subjugate the rural population. The Polish ruler in 1518 gave a pledge to the representative assembly of the nobles that he would not accept appeals from the peasants against their masters. The weak urban centres and the virtual absence of an urban bourgeoisie gave the nobility much greater powers than that enjoyed in western Europe. Western Europe also started moving towards the conversion of feudal dues into feudal rent. The expansion of trade and the growing monetary transactions began to break the old structure of feudalism, leading to a division of labour between the town and the country. The growth of cities created greater demand for foodstuff. This transformation was particularly visible in the case of *demesne* lands, which were the chief centres of servile labour. The feudal lords replaced compulsory services such as *corvée* (compulsory labour rendered to the master in return for the use of land), boon work (to be performed in certain seasons, assigned in the form of task rather than fixed number of days) with monetary dues. The status of the peasants improved in some parts of western Europe but every peasant community did not equally profit from these developments.

The most significant change observed in the late-fifteenth century was the rise of absolute monarchies. In western Europe, the feudal structure was preserved under the absolute monarchs but the state's control was established over the peasants without altering their traditional status. Absolute rulers started assuming powers that were exercised earlier by the feudal lords. The states began to appropriate surplus from the peasants. However, the gradual decline of the manorial system and the institutions of serfdom led to the rise of hired labour, as the feudal lords showed greater interest in receiving money instead of service. *Demesne* land was farmed out to peasants in exchange of money rent rather than *corvée*. Many of these men climbed the social scale and became wealthy peasants or yeomen and some achieving the status of gentlemen. Gradually the landholding relationship started changing and farmers became *métayers* or sharecroppers (those who received land on rent from the feudal lords and paid them not with their labour or money but with fixed share of their crops).

Thus by 1500, the rigid rural life within the feudal structure started breaking down in certain parts of western Europe while at the same time the feudal organization in eastern Europe and in most of central Europe was strengthened by the efforts of the feudal nobility. The expansion of trade along the Atlantic coast promoted commercialization of agriculture and a growth towards capitalism while the rest of Europe took another two to three centuries to break the feudal structure. The different levels of agrarian development caused an uneven economic development in Europe.

Crafts and Industry

After a long period of demographic decline, there were signs of recovery from the 1460s. Although the growth of population varied regionwise, the biggest increase could be noticed in the towns and cities. Antwerp, which emerged as the chief commercial town of Europe during the sixteenth century, experienced a population growth from 20,000 in 1440 to about 50,000 in 1500. Similarly, the population of Sicily and Naples almost doubled between 1460 and 1600, and that of Rome increased to 1,00,000 from 50,000 in roughly the same period. This population increase in towns created significant demand for not only foodstuff but also for manufactured commodities. More significantly, this increase helped in the creation and expansion of craft and industry – the sector that experienced the fastest growth in the sixteenth century. An important urban organization that controlled the manufacturing activities was the urban guild.

In the medieval towns and cities the guilds were the most distinctive forms of economic and social organizations. They were professional associations whose main function was to protect and promote the manufacturing and trade interests of their members. The guild played a positive role in the world of artisans as it provided unity and rendered help to its members and their families in times of sickness and distress. There were merchant guilds and craft guilds.

The merchant guilds primarily maintained a monopoly of the local market for its members. They imposed strict conditions such as restricting foreigners from trading in the city, thus protecting its members' interests. They also controlled the prices of products. Similarly, the crafts guilds controlled the production side and supervised the entire process of production. Each guild was controlled by a master-craftsman who was an expert in his specialized field. Another category of members of the crafts guilds were the journeymen who had learned their trade but still worked under the masters and the apprentices. Each apprentice had to spend a fixed number of years to learn the art from the master and could only become the master of a guild by producing a 'masterpiece', which had to be approved by all the master craftsmen. These guilds retained monopolies over their products and prevented competition by not allowing outsiders to enter the trade. They fought for minimum wages and determined the market price of their product and also controlled each stage of production and the quality of material used. They were extremely powerful in most of the urban centres of Europe. Till the end of the fifteenth century the guilds continued to dominate production of manufactured products. From the end of the fifteenth century it was the textile sector that experienced the most dramatic change in its organization and total production, thereby contributing to the expansion of the European economy. In some parts such as Flanders, England and Netherlands, textile-manufacturing activities had starting moving out of urban workshops towards the countryside. This was done to escape the strict regimental control of the guilds in order to produce on a larger scale and at lower prices. On the other hand the urban workshops and the urban cloth markets in the Italian cities were controlled and dominated by the guilds. The guilds maintained the quality of their textiles but they also controlled the market. This meant they could command high prices for their products and maintain huge profit margins. To avoid being controlled by the guilds many craftsmen moved to rural areas where they could produce light and cheap woollen textiles. This shift away from the guilds made the textile industry dynamic and prosperous. The economic prosperity of England and Netherlands during the sixteenth century was greatly promoted by the rural textile manufacturing.

The textiles sector constituted the most important economic area for employment and production. Textiles constituted the biggest industry but its organization was complex. Throughout the fifteenth century, the Italian states enjoyed a pre-eminent position in textile production. However, by the end of the fifteenth century the old centres were beginning to decline while some new centres were emerging. Florence was one of the most important textile-manufacturing centres. It produced 1,00,000 bolts of woollen cloth annually in the fourteenth century but by the early-sixteenth century it had declined to 30,000 bolts. This did not imply an industrial decline for Florence because the decline of woollens was offset by silk production. The old woollen textile industry of Netherlands at Ypres, Ghent and Bruges had started declining but within Netherlands production of new types of woollen fabrics had begun. They were lighter, cheaper and catered to the demand of the population outside the nobility. In the fourteenth-century England was essentially an exporter of raw wool. During the fifteenth century she began to export woollen products of good quality and by the middle of the sixteenth century England became one of the chief producers. The economic transformation in England was in fact bound with the production of woollen textiles. The export of wool continued to decline while the export of cloth showed constant growth. Between 1503 and 1509, England exported 81,835 bolts of cloth and 5,000 sacks of wool. Between 1540 and 1548, the annual exports of cloth had gone up to 1,22,254 bolts. A crucial factor in the growth of the English cloth industry was the availability of water power, which enabled the manufacturers to use the new mechanical fulling mills. It enabled the artisans to manufacture more cloth than they could by the traditional method. Rural manufacturing was not only less expensive but it also provided part-time employment to the farmers and their family members during slack periods. An important feature of textile production was that the cloth manufacturing activity in many places such as England, the Netherlands and Germany gravitated towards the countryside away from the towns. It led to the rise of rural cottage industry that was relatively free from guild control on quality and technique. Consequently the cost of production was much lower than in other European towns.

Another industrial activity was mining and metallurgy. Usually small enterprises of four or five workers cooperatively produced iron, copper, silver and coal. However, as the demand for such metals increased, more machinery was needed to exploit deeper seams in the mines and new processes were developed. Primitive forms of capitalist organizations came into being to manage larger units employing greater number of workers. Cities located in central Europe, particularly in the German states, began exploiting iron, silver and copper mines on a large scale. Ore was mined at a depth of about 300 metres that required more developed forms of organization and equipment. Ore was becoming expensive to mine and needed huge investments and some big merchants started investing in this field. The reorganization of mining started in the fifteenth century when the merchant capitalists took control of production. So long as mining was carried out to extract minerals lying closer to the surface, it did not require advanced technology or heavy finances. Deeper mining needed the installation and maintenance of expensive equipment. This change was evident in the silver mines of the Harz Mountains in Bohemia, copper mines of Tyrol in the Alps and the gold and silver mines of Hungary. Free workers were converted into wage labourers and their number multiplied as the drilling operations went deeper. New technology was adopted to pipe out water in the form of pumping machines driven by horse power. The nobility and the rulers in that region gained from the prosperity of the inhabitants. The heavy investments prevented individual merchants from carrying out the operations alone. A form of joint stock operation came into existence in which the stock of the mine was divided into shares called *kuxen* in the multiples of 64 or 128. In 1580, Augustus I of Saxony owned 2,822 *kuxen* (Braudel, *The Wheels of Commerce*, p. 323). However, during the sixteenth century, the heavy cost of mining activity, the declining returns, labour problems (as it developed in Hungary in 1525–6) and the growing competition from America resulted in the withdrawal of capital from several mines. The exception was of

Schwaz in Tyron, where the Fuggers controlled copper and silver mining, with over 12,000 workers under them and another 500 to 600 labourers employed to pump out water from the tunnels (Braudel, *The Wheels of Commerce*). The territories along the Rhine Valley and upper reaches of the Danube emerged as the chief production centres of metals. This region also had a developed textile industry that gradually shifted towards the countryside.

The other flourishing industries of the late-fifteenth century included glass manufacturing and printing. During the 1430s and 1440s, Johann Gutenberg of Mainz in Germany carried out experiments that resulted in the invention of the printing press by about 1453. Although block printing and paper printing through wooden blocks was known in China for centuries. Gutenberg, who belonged to a family of goldsmiths, had developed a moveable metal type. Two other names are also associated with this invention – Johann Fust and Peter Schoffer. The printing press was a major event in the commercial and academic world and it began to spread in different parts of Europe, particularly in the Italian cities. Book production increased manifold by the end of the fifteenth century. Although most of the European cities had their own printing presses, the most important centre was Venice, where about 150 printing presses existed.

Shipping and arsenals (dockyards) were the emerging commercial fields in parts of Europe. Till the fifteenth century shipbuilding had developed in the southern parts of Europe, particularly in Venice – the chief commercial centre, before the trading zone shifted towards the Atlantic coast during the sixteenth century. Although construction work of naval dockyard had started much earlier, its extension seriously began in 1476. The Venetian arsenal built, repaired and equipped ships on the capitalist lines. About 1,000 workers were engaged at one place and it was considered the largest industrial establishment before 1560. The site of work and its operations were controlled by the Lords and Commissioners of the arsenal and were placed directly under state control. Many of these officials were paid salaries and given houses by the state. The workers employed there were masters in their own profession and were members of the craft guilds but they also worked for the private ship builders. There were ironsmiths, carpenters, sail-makers and pulley-makers. However all the ships in Venice did not belong to this state-run arsenal. The bulk of the merchant fleet was actually constructed and owned privately. The late-fifteenth century also witnessed the rise of shipping industry in Portugal and Spain with the creation of colonial empires.

Trading and Commercial Activities

The late-fifteenth century was a turning point in the European economic history, as it marks the beginning of the long-distance trade and the establishment of colonies in the far-flung regions of the world. This aspect has been taken up in another chapter in greater detail but at this point the focus is on the nature of trade and the scale of business organization that existed in the late-fifteenth century. Within Europe, important forms of exchange were growing in scale that included raw materials, food and manufactured products and several luxury products.

Though the beginning of international trade cannot be ascribed to the sea voyages and explorations because Europe was already receiving luxury products from Asia and Africa through the land routes or through the Mediterranean Sea, this period is significant because of the expansion in international trade, particularly the maritime trade across the oceans. In the fifteenth century, the growing economic strength of the towns of southern Germany and Bohemia challenged the Italian dominated Mediterranean trade and the North Sea trade of the Hanseatic League. The Hanseatic merchants had acquired monopoly rights of trade in the northern routes from Lithuania to the Baltic Sea through political and military means but the south German traders adopted the Italian methods of monopoly trade to establish and expand their influence throughout central Europe. The Merchant Adventurers of England was another state protected monopolistic institution that had extended its influence into Flanders and had successfully challenged the position of the Hanseatic League. The old commercial and financial centre was located in Bruges in Belgium. The English, the Italian and the Hanseatic merchants frequently visited this town carrying goods in bulk such as wool, grain, fish and spices. By the end of the century, Antwerp, an important port city of the Spanish Netherlands, was fast replacing Bruges as the commercial epicentre of Europe. It was not the international trade, however, but the local and regional trade of Europe that provided the initial thrust for market expansion.

During the fifteenth century most of the towns in Europe had developed their own local markets where products from the neighbouring regions were bought and sold. Some of the larger towns had developed markets to handle and organize trade. These market-towns received or sent products to more distant parts within Europe. A few markets in Europe dealt with the exotic products from the east. Most of this trade was local, regional or intra-European. Although a major part of Europe was still under the impact of feudal organization and as mentioned earlier, the scale of trade remained limited under feudalism. Yet European regions were coming closer with the expansion of inter-regional contact. The bulk of the business dealt with common local products that were bought and sold or exchanged by the local people. Cloth, food products and cattle were the chief products and the exchange took place through local fairs such as the fair of Cologne, a purely rural event held three or four times a year. A similar kind of fair was held at Medina del Campo. It was a shepherds' fair under the patronage of the Castilian rulers. As the size of towns grew and populations increased, the demand for food products like cereals, vegetables and wine increased. It had to be met not only from the immediate neighbourhood but also from distant regions. Similarly, the rise of universities, Cathedral cities and administrative centres began to attract large populations. In such places the markets expanded and assumed a permanent form. Here, wholesalers and retailers, merchants and traders grew in number. Many of these markets imported products of daily consumption, which were stored and sold in proper shops. Products of local industry were sold or exchanged with products that were not available in the neighbourhood. Thus Spanish wool was sent to Netherlands and Italy in exchange for the Baltic goods such as cereals and forest products. Hungarian copper was sent to Germany and France, English woollen was sent to northern Europe and the Baltic states in exchange of agricultural products like salt, wine, fish, vegetables oils, fruits and dyestuff from southern and western Europe. There was a huge demand for salt which was produced in many parts of the continent but in small quantities. It was at Luneburg, south of Lubeck, where an important salt industry developed. Salt produced in this region was marketed to distant places and it became an important source of earning for the local people. With the expansion of the shipping industry, timber became a commercial product. In short, it can be said that in many places the traditional fairs – the chief means of exchange – were being replaced by regular markets in cities. Usually a merchant began to specialize solely in trading activity while retail trade was left to the shopkeepers.

In the fifteenth century, land transport remained seriously limited because of bad roads. The mode of transport had not changed much for centuries. Under these conditions, the use of inland waterways, river navigation and convoy of carts and domesticated animals facilitated the trade. Inland trade faced many serious problems from bandits, wars among the states or among the feudal lords, unfavourable weather conditions (floods, intense winter) and heavy tolls as each region was divided into numerous small states. This can be seen in the case of the Rhine Valley where the number of tolls had doubled from thirty-five to about seventy within a period of hundred years. The rise of centralized absolute states greatly facilitated the growth of trade by providing political stability and greater security to the traders. The late-fifteenth century witnessed a major advance in the art of shipbuilding. The tonnage capacity increased and with it the capability of undertaking longer journeys. The Portuguese led the way in this direction. With the construction of bigger and faster ships, improvement was also made in navigational equipments. The freight costs proved lower in the case of sea journeys compared to land transportation and thereby reducing costs greatly.

The expansion of trade enlarged the scale of business organization. In the Italian states, there already existed a long tradition of business enterprise and techniques of commercial organization. However, these organizations were not modern capitalist systems because the capital infrastructure had not yet fully evolved. There was no corporate organization beyond partnership. The Italian merchants, specially the Florentines, possessed a large reservoir of liquid capital for investment. These merchants provided capital for real estate, traded in commodities, manufactured cloth and arms, spent money on developing mineral resources and even invested in military campaigns or in the purchase of ecclesiastical posts. Great sums of money were accumulated by Italian families in Piacenza, Asti, Sienna, Lucca and in Florence. A striking feature of this banking activity was its organization into companies or *case* (house). There were many temporary trading corporations such as *commendas* or *societas*. These were a type of partnerships in which the investors provided two-thirds of the capital while the factors or agents provided the rest. The factors managed the market aspect and were responsible for the collection of payments. The profit was divided equally between the investors and the factors. According to Henri Lucas (p. 162), such types of trading corporations could be seen in the twelfth century in Genoa and in many other Italian towns. Another type of business organization was called *accommodatio*, in which the investors provided all the capital while the factors merely acted as agents for selling goods and collecting payments. For this they received a quarter of the share of profits. All these were temporary organizations and were formed for a single or for a fixed number of voyages.

With the expansion of trade in the late-fifteenth century, important forms of credit instruments had already developed in the Italian states to handle the large volume of exchange. These included instruments like letters of credit and exchange, *lettres de foire* (letters of exchange which were popular in the business circle of Flanders, Brabant, Artois, Champagne and in the Italian states). The Italian merchant families had perfected the art of business and company finance by developing the system of bookkeeping, first the single-entry system and subsequently the double-entry system, which is used even today. Luca Pacioli made double-entry bookkeeping popular in his book *Suimma of Arithmetic Techniques* in 1494. It was a basic work on commercial arithmetic. In this, the transactions were entered twice under assets and liabilities. However, the origin of the double-entry book is a subject of debate. Many scholars have rejected the old view that it perhaps originated in Genoa around 1340 and it is now believed that it developed almost simultaneously in several Italian centres. According to R. De Roover (M.J. Kitch, *Capitalism and Reformation*, 1968, p. 75), the three factors that contributed to the progress of accounting were partnership, credit and agency. This period also witnessed the emergence of the concept of insurance. It first started in the field of marine activities and was later introduced in other trading spheres. In Italy a body of insurance laws grew, which was later controlled by magistrates and consuls.

The structure of business, particularly in Italy and Germany, revealed certain pre-capitalist features. Florence had a large number of merchant banks. These were not like modern banks but were essentially local financial institutions that accepted deposits and extended loans. Their chief business was to handle foreign exchange such as transfer of credit and exchange operations. They also functioned as moneychangers and established branches in different cities of Europe. These were usually family organizations. There were several merchant-banker families such as the Medicis, Frescabaldi, Filippo Strozzi, Bardi, Peruri (all from Florence), Capponi in Lyons (France) and Fuggers in Augsburg (Germany). The house of Medici in Florence was the most well known among the merchant-bankers. We come to know of their scale of operations from a record book of tax declarations called *Catasto.* The house of Medici was one of the greatest banking families in Europe with branches in cities like Geneva, Avignon, Bruges and London. The Medici family became wealthy by lending money to the Popes and the Cardinals at exorbitant rates of interest (which could be as high as 50 per cent). They also lent to the rulers in order to become their tax collectors. They had commercial dealings with the rulers of Burgundy, England and Milan. The Medicis also bought and sold bills of exchange, the most common method of handling commercial credit. This family had a long experience of handling international commerce and through their wealth they were able to establish their political domination. The Medici family also managed the Tolfa alum mines from 1466–76. Alum was used as a raw material in the expanding textile industry. Cosimo de Medici

(1389–1464) developed a series of bilateral partnerships between firms in other parts of Europe. This solved the problem of unlimited liability, which had caused huge losses earlier. The commercial and political connections with the Pope and other influential political families helped the Medicis retain their position till the early part of the sixteenth century. Jacques Coeur was another banking family that existed in France. It maintained close connections with the merchants in other cities, including those in Barcelona, Bruges, Paris and in cities in the eastern Mediterranean. Through his wealth he became the financial adviser of King Charles VII and made a fortune by managing the French royal mint. He restored the dwindling financial conditions of the French ruler. In Germany Fugger was the most important merchant-banker family. The first Fugger known to historians was Hans, who was a weaver and came to settle in Augsburg in southern Germany around 1380. He imported cotton from Venice and was involved in the manufacture and sale of fustians, a fabric made of flax. His son Jacob I expanded the family business after 1469 and began to deal in silks, woollens, linen, fustians, brocades and in spices, jewels and textiles. They established business connections with the chief merchants of Italy, the Netherlands, Silesia, Poland and Hungary and assumed the role of official bankers of the Pope by handling all forms of money transfers between Germany and Rome. Their wealth increased fourfold between 1470 and 1500. The climax of glory came when their loans enabled Charles V of Spain to become the Holy Roman Emperor in 1519. They also exercised some control over the copper and silver mines in Germany and were the leaders of the Tyrolean silver mining industry. Thus these banking houses and the business families created a commercial structure which gave way to the more developed forms of business and commercial organizations and paved the way for the modern banking system. This is studied in greater detail under Commercial Revolution.

The Christian Church

With the decline of the Roman Empire and the formation and extension of the feudal system the European church had split into two branches – the Papal church was in Rome while the Greek

Orthodox church was established in the eastern region of Europe under the Byzantine empire. The church under the Pope became an important bond for European society and strengthened the feudal structure in western Europe. The demarcation between the ecclesiastical and lay society was not very rigid. In theory, the clergy was not a hereditary class and was recruited from all levels of society, although the upper sections of society had greater representation in it. During the High Middle Ages, the position of the clergy altered gradually from pressures created by money economy and rising prices. The expansion of trade and growing expenditure on luxury items demanded more income. The higher clergy holding superior posts in the church adopted new devices to supplement their income. The feudal crisis had adversely affected the fiscal resources of the church as most of its income came from *tithe* (a tax imposed by the church on land income that constituted 10 per cent of the total income), which had been showing diminishing returns because of the economic and demographic crises mentioned earlier. The gap between the higher and the lower clergy increased as the position of the latter deteriorated. The higher church officials held powerful positions in the state administration, while simultaneously retaining their ecclesiastical posts. Cardinal Wolsey in England and Cardinal Ximénes in Spain are a few examples of persons holding the highest temporal and spiritual positions together. The priests of country parishes were often poorly educated and badly paid and led a life which differed little from that of their flocks. The growing evils of plurality of posts held by a single priest resulting in absenteeism, nepotism and financial exactions reached the highest level under Pope Innocent VIII.

The institutional crisis in the Papal church started from the fourteenth century and passed through three significant phases. The first was the Babylonian captivity of the Papacy (1305–78) when the Papacy was located in Avignon in France instead of Rome and remained subservient to the interest of the French crown. The second phase witnessed the Great Schism (1378–1417) that resulted in rival states competing with the opponents for the post of Pope – one led by the French group comprising the states of Scotland, Castile and Aragon recognizing the claims of Clement, while the rest of Europe pushed the claims of Urban VI. Even the European monastic orders were divided into Roman and Avignon camps. The crisis was resolved in 1417 by the Council of Constant. The third crisis was related to the nature of church government (1417–1517), in which the Conciliar movement played an important role in determining the relationship between the papacy and the European rulers. Although the Pope had won the spiritual position by the late-fifteenth century through the support of the European rulers, there was a growing tendency among the European states towards the establishment of national churches. The Pragmatic Sanction (1438) of the French ruler had resulted in the creation of Gallican church largely independent of Papal influence. It was followed by the grant of Inquisition to the Spanish rulers and the English Crown's breach with Rome. The Pope was compelled to accept these compromises. All these events demonstrate the signs of Papal decline. These cracks were symptomatic of the coming peril.

The most important trait of the Christian church in the late-fifteenth century manifested itself in the form of Renaissance Papacy. The Papal authority had to re-establish itself against the centrifugal forces of the Conciliar movement. There was popular resentment against the church policies and a growing demand for reforms. The Pope was able to rehabilitate himself in Rome by 1450 after much hostility. Once secured, subsequent popes began rebuilding the church and the city of Rome. The first step in this direction was taken by Pope Nicholas V (1446–55). A Renaissance Pope, he was keen to restore the former glory of Rome. He and his successors began patronizing art, established lavish courts, spent huge sums of money on new buildings and projects. Following the Renaissance humanists they acquired ancient manuscripts to demonstrate the intellectual and religious superiority of Rome over other cities. The church employed the famous Florentine architect, Alberti, who wrote a masterpiece on architecture titled *On Architecture* (1452). Several urban projects were undertaken such as the construction of beautiful public squares, bridges and roads reflecting the revival of classical antiquity. Attempts were made to restore the great buildings. Pope Sixtus IV undertook the construction of the Sistine Chapel in the Vatican Palace in 1475. The great artist of that period, Michelangelo painted its ceiling. Sixtus employed some of the best artists of Renaissance, but he was unpopular for his violent and extortionist policy and for his territorial ambition. Many others, including the cardinals and secular families also patronized Renaissance artists and architects. One of the well-known patrons was Chigi. He did not belong to a noble family and was ennobled by Pope Julius II for his construction of Villa Farnesina. Rome by the end of the fifteenth century had become a grand city. Its population grew rapidly from only 17,000 in 1400 to about 85,000 by 1517. It had become one of the major European cities and this strengthened the church's standing in the Christian world. However, the temporary glory and artistic splendour had pushed spiritual matters into the background and the growing resentment against the church was not noticed by papal officials till the coming of Luther's revolt.

The Political Map of Europe

European political structure in the late-fifteenth century was essentially feudal in character. It presented a very complex picture because it varied from one region to another and even within the same region it assumed numerous forms. The political map of the European states and principalities displayed a combination of hereditary, elective or even joint monarchies. Besides, there were broad or narrow form of oligarchies and some semi-independent or independent confederacies. There was also an emperor, who ruled over large territories of Europe but without any effective control. He was called the Holy Roman Emperor. In short, the people of Europe were governed in a variety of ways.

Most parts of Europe had decentralized political systems. The feudal nobility enjoyed vast powers in political, judicial and administrative spheres. There were exclusive sovereignties but at many places overlapping and constantly shifting lordships restricted these. Dynastic policy played an important role particularly in matters of marriages and hereditary claims in determining the fortunes of the rulers. The lords were constantly engaged in small skirmishes but on many occasions succession disputes transformed them into large-scale wars. However, in certain parts of Europe the process of centralization was going on. Towards the end of the fifteenth century states like France, England, Spain and the Muscovy (Moscow) experienced the emergence of strong centralized monarchies.

France was the richest, the most populous, and territorially the largest of the European kingdoms in the fifteenth century. With a population of nearly twelve million people and its territory stretching from the borders of the Low Countries in the north to the Mediterranean coast in the south, France displayed economic and cultural diversity. After a long period of war with England under the leadership of Joan of Arc, the French were able to recover sizeable lands from the English. The process of unification of France continued but was checked by certain smaller but powerful states like Burgundy, Brittany and Anjou. Charles the Bold ruled the Duchy of Burgundy. The kingdom of Burgundy included the richest territories of the Netherlands and Franche-Comté. Bruges had developed into not only an important trade centre but a strong cultural centre. Its court displayed French culture and art of that period. After the death of Charles in 1477, the heiress of Burgundy married Arch Duke Maximillian, the son of the Holy Roman Emperor, who succeeded the throne in 1493. The northern part of France was ruled by the Valois dynasty but there were many independent principalities or fiefs such as Guienne under the English king, Flanders under a Count and Brittany under a Duke. They all resisted the French efforts of unification. However, under Louis XI (1461–83), Charles VIII (1483–98) and Louis XII (1498–1515) France was able to establish her supremacy over Burgundy, Anjou, Maine, Provence and Brittany. All of northern France was unified except Calais, a port town which remained in English hands till the mid-sixteenth century. In France, the rulers provided a reasonable level of political stability as most of them ruled for fairly long periods and the change over, from one ruler to another, was relatively free from succession disputes unlike in many other states. The rise of absolutism in France did not alter the position of the peasants. The personal bondage under serfdom gave way to economic dependence. The dual control of the state as well as of the feudal lords made them very vulnerable. Moreover, the peasants were expected to pay to the church a tenth of their income in the form of *tithe*. The protection of the legal property of the peasants by the state on the one hand and the excessive exploitation by the nobility on the other prolonged the misery of the French peasants.

In England the strength of the monarchy was growing for over a century. A prolonged war with France stretching for over hundred years and an internal war called the War of the Roses lasting almost thirty years till 1485 paved the way for the Tudor dynasty in England. The cumulative effect of these wars was the weakening of the feudal nobility. England made rapid strides in the social and constitutional sphere. The knights were among the first of the feudal elements to lose the status of an armed military class. During the fifteenth and early-sixteenth centuries, they merged themselves with the gentry. The landed families in England began to socially intermingle and even enter into matrimonial relations with the leading merchant families. This marked a steady social transformation in England. Richard III and Henry VII laid the foundations of a despotic form of government that was slowly centralized and made effective. The establishment of Tudor dynasty led to a period of a prolonged stability. The Tudors contributed to the rise of parliament as a representative institution. This period witnessed significant progress in the socio-economic and political domains in England.

Spain was another state that showed signs of growing importance and domination over the European states. The process of transforming small autonomous states and principalities into a unified whole began with the union of the crowns of Castile and Aragon. The heiress of Castile, Isabella and Ferdinand, the prince of Aragon were married in 1469. The future of Spain was built on this marriage. By the Agreement of Segovia in 1475, Isabella handled the internal government of Castile while Ferdinand looked after foreign affairs. They jointly participated in the administration of justice. There were many reasons that led to the supremacy of Castile over other states of Spain. Castile was the largest territorial state in that region. Furthermore, it enjoyed a distinct advantage of a large population and material resources over other states. The representative institutions in the form of *Cortes* was given an increasingly reduced role in state matters and the powers of the church were used through the *Inquisition* (a religious tribunal established to suppress heresy) to strengthen the powers of the Spanish monarch. Although a complete political unification was achieved only in 1716, Spain began to play an increasingly dominant role in European affairs by the end of the fifteenth century. An important factor in the rise of Spain as an imperial power was her acquisition of several colonies in the New World. In the process, Spain became the chief supplier of silver and many other products to Europe.

The emergence of a strong centralized state could also be seen in eastern Europe. The rise of Russia as a centralized state under a strong and ruthless monarchy began in the period of Ivan III (1440–1505). From a small principality under the suzerainty of the Mongol rulers, Ivan, began absorbing the neighbouring territories. By refusing to seek permission from the Mongol rulers, he successfully resisted their powerful invasions and thereafter, this 'grand prince of Moscow' ceased to be a vassal of the Mongols. He set in motion the Russian expansion and conquered the powerful mercantile republic of Novgorod, subdued the ruler of Tver, Vyatka and purchased the principality of Yaroslavi and some part of Rostov. He transformed the independent landed aristocrats into service nobles and imposed several conditions on them. The rise of Russia was accompanied by the introduction and strengthening of serfdom. Unlike in the western states of Europe, where serfdom as an institution was either weakening or transforming into a new form of tenurial relationship based on money rent, Russian political structure strengthened feudalism.

While some parts of Europe were developing absolutist forms of political structure, the states in northern Europe were either decentralized or were still to be unified. Since 1397, the Scandinavian countries comprising Sweden, Norway and Denmark were jointly ruled by a single monarch under the Union of Kalmar. It was a series of personal unions from 1397 till 1524 under Margareta Valdemarsdotters. Cracks started appearing in it from 1430s. Strong movements had developed against this union in

Sweden, joined by nobles, free peasants and the miners. These reflected the sentiments of aristocratic hostility towards a strong monarchy. The administration of the rulers of Denmark could never become effective within Sweden. The pressure from a strong aristocracy created constant obstacles in the rise of absolutism. However, a strong monarchy within Sweden was emerging through an alliance with the Estates of *Riksdag* against the traditional organ of aristocrats, the *Irksrad*. This resulted in a long contest between absolutism and noble oligarchy. The ruler Gustavus adopted a combined policy of ruthlessness and pragmatism by introducing populist measures and strengthened his financial position by exploiting iron fields and forests. He succeeded in developing an absolutist government but only for a brief time. During this period, Sweden became an important power and actively participated in the European political and economic conflicts.

The Netherlands was a part of the Low Countries situated near the North Sea. It consisted of seventeen states and included the present territories of Belgium, Luxembourg and the Netherlands. Each province of the Netherlands had been governed by its own constitution, traditions and customs. This region lacked not only political unity but there was total absence of social and economic homogeneity, rather, it reflected racial and linguistic disunity. It escaped the full impact of feudalism because of its geographical proximity to the sea and also because of its autonomous social organization.

Central Europe contained numerous small states ruled by kings, dukes or even church officials. The southern German states, despite their individual rivalries, formed the *Swabian League* in 1488 to contain Swiss inroads and to prevent the expansion of Bavaria under Duke Wittelsbach. In Germany, the separatist tendencies were so strong that they did not wish to be controlled by any imperial government. Many of the German states were constituents of the Holy Roman Empire. In the late-fifteenth century Maximillian I (1459–1519) ruled the Holy Roman Empire. The idea of Holy Roman Empire was medieval in character as it was an attempt to bring the rulers of smaller kingdoms under one nominal organization. Its chief objective was to defend and promote the

Roman Catholic Church under the Pope against the possible threats from outside or from within Europe. However, by the fifteenth century, the empire was becoming redundant and losing its purpose of existence. The Holy Roman Empire had existed at two levels. The Emperor at the top was assisted by a feeble administration within an assembly of estates called Diet, representing the elites of Germany, Bohemia and some provinces of the Netherlands. Within it there was a house of seven 'electors' and these chosen princes elected the Holy Roman Emperor. The lower level consisted of the House of Representatives, representing 300 members of varying ranks and position, consisting of kings, electors, dukes, margraves and even some knights enjoying landed property. The Holy Roman Empire stretched across vast territories of Europe and included Austria, the German states, Bohemia, the Netherlands, the Low Countries and some of the states from northern and central Italy. Despite having such vast stretches of land across Europe under his jurisdiction, the powers of the Holy Roman Emperor remained nominal rather than real. This was because of the policy of dynastic alliances between the ruling families of Europe. Maximillian I was able to acquire the Duchy of Burgundy, the seventeen provinces of the Netherlands, Artois and the Franche-Comté through his marriage with Mary, the princess of Burgundy. He found it rather difficult to control the Netherlands as it had an extremely decentralized form of government dominated by the urban nobility and commercial aristocracy. He married his son, Philip to the daughter of Ferdinand and Isabella of Spain. With the addition of Spain and Portugal, the empire became ungovernable and could not have any effective control even over the German states. The Germans always resisted and felt suspicious of the designs of the Habsburg rulers, who came to rule the Holy Roman Empire. The dynastic ambitions and territorial rivalry led to a prolonged war in the Italian territories known as the Habsburg–Valois Struggle, i.e. the war between the emperor and the French rulers. It resulted in the French invasion of Milan causing great embarrassment to Emperor Maximillian, who suffered numerous failures. It was a prolonged war and its participants kept changing with every fresh campaign.

Unlike Russia, where centralized form of state absolutism was developing, the rest of eastern Europe had a political organization that was rather weak and complex. It included the kingdoms of Poland-Lithuania, Hungary and Bohemia. These kingdoms were linked together loosely by dynastic ties. The crowns of Hungary and Bohemia were united and that of Poland had a close relationship with the Hungarian king. All these rulers belonged to the house of Jagiello of Poland and Lithuania. The family ties of the ruling houses, the elective nature of the kingship in Poland, Hungary and Bohemia, and the near absence of the class of professional administrators restricted the possibility of administrative continuity. This region faced insurmountable difficulties in forming strong centralized states as the destinies of these countries were completely decided by the personal interests of the nobles. The constitutional structure of Poland was even more primitive than that of Hungary. Poland was constantly engaged in foreign wars. *Szlachta* was a class of lesser nobles that had successfully risen to the position of equality with the king in the conduct of states affairs. They had also expeditiously increased their powers over the towns and the peasant population. The introduction of commercial farming by the traditional landlords in order to export cereals via Danzig transformed the free peasants into bonded labour through a series of laws passed between 1496 and 1511. These laws prevented the peasants from leaving the land without the consent of the master. This caused a degradation of the legal status of the peasants. The situation in Hungary was even worse. The power of the crown had been virtually eliminated and in the absence of an effective political force, the doors were opened for a bitter struggle between the lesser nobility and the big landed magnates. This caused immense deterioration in the status of the Hungarian peasants. Bohemia had become an aristocratic republic for all practical purposes. As was the case in Hungary and Poland, the nobles in Bohemia were left with vast political powers and constitutional freedom while the remaining classes were pushed to servitude, deprived of all benefits. The position of the Bohemian peasants also underwent a similar decline. The nobles in Bohemia pursued offensive measures against the towns, which were further aggravated by religious and national antagonisms. The town's burghers were forbidden to trade in the country districts and merchants were even arrested on the roads. They were also excluded from the Diet by the constitution of 1500. A fierce struggle among the magnets pushed the country into almost a civil war. However, the burghers were able to recover some of the lost ground and got back the right of representation in 1517. This entire region remained a source of trouble for the neighbouring states. In the initial years it was the Polish–Lithuanian combine which carried out constant raids in the outer regions, including parts of Russia. The political weakness of this region subsequently invited the stronger states to attack the weaker ones and reap benefits. Towards the end of the eighteenth century Poland became one such example. She was partitioned among the three powerful neighbours – Russia, Prussia and Austria.

Italian City States

The most important region of Europe for economic activities and cultural advancement was the peninsula located south of the Alps Mountains. It consisted of the Italian states representing a variety of political forms. During the first half of the fifteenth century, this region witnessed prolonged warfare involving territorial and dynastic ambitions. Italy was never fully developed into a feudal organization and the Italian towns did not decay when feudalism swept across Europe, north of the Alps. The economy of the Italian states continued to survive on commerce, trade and industry while agriculture played a relatively minor role. The rise of the Italian states was primarily linked with the expansion of towns and cities. The period of High Middle Ages saw the Italian peninsula divided into three major zones, (a) *Regnum Italicum* consisting parts of northern and central Italy forming an integral part of the Holy Roman Empire, (b) central Italy, including Rome ruled by the Pope, and (c) the southern Italian states and kingdoms mostly ruled by foreign dynasties such as the French, Aragonese, Germans and the Normans.

Society north of the Alps was still organized on a rural and feudal basis, but the Italian city states greatly influenced the evolution of urban institutions. The *signory* of aristocrats ruled most of the city states and developed new mechanisms for government and administration. Each city had its own *podesta* (mayor) and each district was ruled by Captains of the Guard. The prolonged wars among the Italian states resulted in the emergence of five important states displaying roughly equal powers and thereby maintaining a form of balance of political influence with no single state dominating the others. Interspersed among these five major states were a multitude of smaller territories enjoying reasonable autonomy but subjected to the influence of larger states. These included Milan, Venice, Florence, the Papal states comprising extensive territories in central Italy and Naples. Everywhere in Italy, these leading cities gained at the expense of lesser ones. The five states remained at peace after the Peace of Lodi in 1454 till the French invasion of 1494. Although these states were very different in terms of size and character, their political influence was well balanced. Milan, under the control of the Visconti family, was a Duchy and held a strategic position. Here, the leading citizens formed a council consisting of 900 members. The city was located on an important trade route to France and western Germany, and had flourishing industries in metallurgy and textile. It had put a check on the territorial expansion of Venice, because it had a strong standing army and a well-trained cavalry. The expansion of irrigation increased agricultural output and this helped in the growth of the silk industry. The Visconti dukes developed an efficient central administration, particularly after 1447 when some experiments were made in the direction of republicanism but they failed. Soon after, Francesco Sforza became the Duke of Milan. A good administrative organization contributed to the military strength of Milan. This was a period of cultural glory but it also marked the beginning of political troubles.

Naples and Sardinia displayed all the characteristics of a feudal state in the fifteenth century. They retained the traditional organization imposed on them by the Norman conquerors. The nobles of foreign origins possessed large landed estates and lived almost like kings. They functioned virtually independent of the monarchy, which was in the hands of a dynasty from Aragon. These states

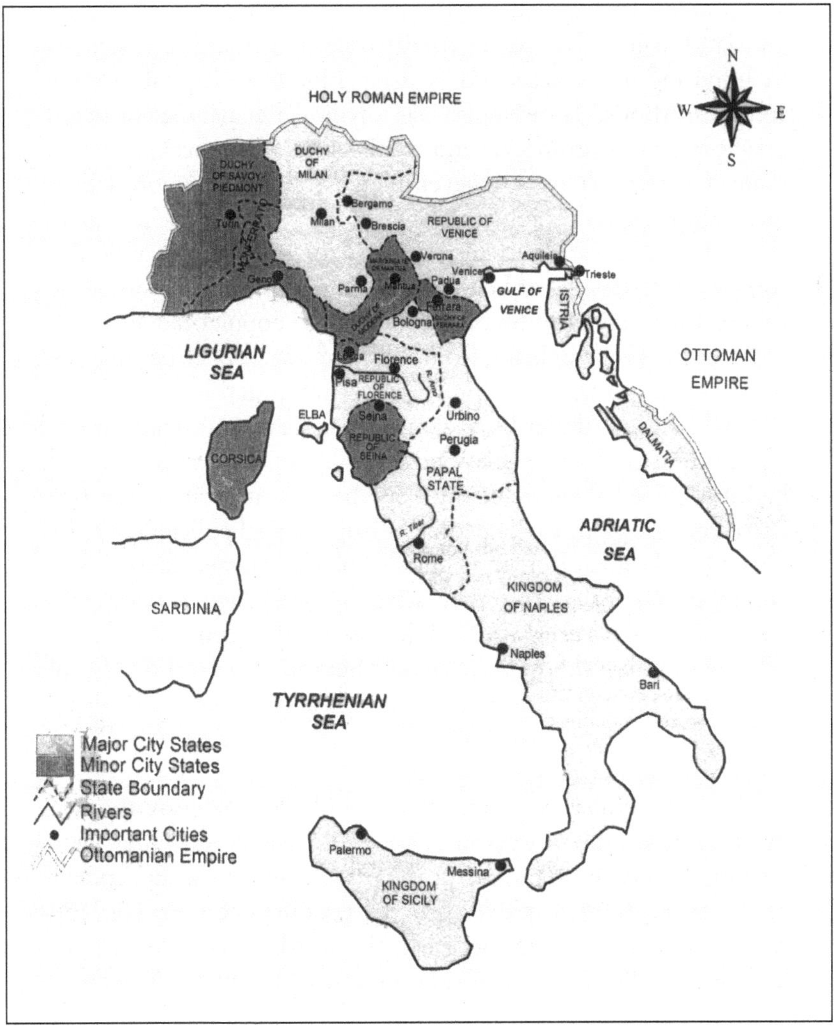

Map 1.2: The Italian City States in Late-Fifteenth Century

had a long historical tradition of parliamentary government based on the English model. The Parliament acted as a court of judgement and promulgated laws and was represented mainly by rich nobles and landowners. The rulers tried to develop financial resources by imposing heavy taxes and by using Florentine capital in trade ventures. Alfonso II of Naples was a typical Renaissance prince, a great patron of learning, art and architecture. His court patronized many talented artists. However, Naples remained embroiled in internal and expernal problems. Its relations with the Pope remained tense on the question of territorial suzerainty. Naples was also contesting the designs of Venice in the Adriatic Sea. In the domestic sphere, the heavy taxation of the state led to popular rebellions.

After the Great Schism, Rome and the Papal states became the ecclesiastical principality. The Pope was interested in bringing all Italian territories under his suzerainty and he encountered various hurdles in this. Rome was essentially a republican city although it had recognized the seat of the Pope because it brought prestige and economic gains to the people of Rome. Papal policies could be resisted by the great Roman families who owned large mansions and landed estates and had representatives in the College of Cardinals. Papal cities like Perugia and Bologna, and the ruling houses of other places were almost independent, but they were afraid of Papal authority for fear of excommunication and also because of the Papal influence over their own subjects. Politically and culturally Rome remained an important city in Italy.

Of all the Italian city states Venice and Florence were the two most economically prosperous, although in many ways they were a contrast to each other. The prosperity of Venice was dependent on its trade monopoly over oriental products coming via land routes through Constantinople. In the words of Braudel, Venice had become the centre of world economy by the fifteenth century as all-important trade routes merged at this point. The northern route linked Venice to the Netherlands passing through Augsburg, Vienna, Nuremberg, Vasle, Strasbourg, and Hamburg. The western trade route linked Venice with Bruges and London and the eastern route to Levant. From the thirteenth century Venice was involved in a bitter rivalry with Genoa, another Italian city. Venice was an expanding state, full of territorial ambition. By the end of the fourteenth century, it occupied Corfu, considered as the gateway of the Adriatic. A ring of towns, territories and a chain of forts protected it from the rest of Italy. By the late-fifteenth century it almost became an empire dependent on commercial and strategic interests along the route to Levant. Its frontier stretched from the Alps to the Po and from the Adda to the Isonzo. The political authority of this city state was in the hands of an oligarchy of merchants – a *Council of Ten*. Other cities under the jurisdiction of Venice were treated equally. The lower classes also shared the benefits of Venetian long-distance trade and gained from the government policy of light taxation. The nobility realized the advantages of a strong government and although it participated in the monopoly of political power, the wealth was not allowed to be concentrated in the hands of a single family through government regulations. So there was better distribution of wealth and the interest of every class was protected and this contributed to the political stability to a large extent. Before 1560, Venice had the largest arsenal, which was considered to be the biggest industrial establishment of that period on a pre-capitalist pattern. The Venetian economy was thus equipped with institutions like markets, shops, warehouses, the arsenal and the mint. Moneychangers and bankers, carried out transfer of money and transaction of goods. The function of the stock exchange was carried out by the *Rialto* that fixed commodity prices and fixed interest rates on public loans. It also fixed premiums for maritime insurance. The profits from trade were accumulated in a variety of places from where the money was invested and reinvested. Oliver Cox commented that Venice provided the first example of capitalism, a view which is not fully shared by Fernand Braudel. The Venetian mint at Zecca was another important economic centre, producing about 2 million *ducats* of gold and silver coins annually. The merchants of Venice effectively controlled all the major commodities of trade in the Mediterranean such as pepper, spices, Syrian cotton, grain, wine and many others. Foreign merchants were asked to stay in a segregated area, a little away from the city in *fonduks* (a street of buildings). They were forced to buy goods for an amount equal to what they had brought from outside. The Venetian states adopted a system of trade intervention called *Galere da Mercato* and also provided state vessels to the export merchants. It was a state policy – a combination of state enterprise and private association. The *galere* was a kind of consortium of export merchants who were interested in reducing their transportation costs to remain competitive against their foreign rivals. The concentration on trade does not imply that Venice did not have its own industries. It included printing, woollen, silk, paper, glass and mirror industries. As Miskimin points out, the Venetian industry prospered during Italy's darkest period. There were two worlds of labour in Venice – the guild workers constituting two-thirds of the labour force, and the so-called 'free' or unregulated labour constituting the remainder. The 'proletariat of the sea', in the words of Frederick C. Lane, included porters, oarsmen, seamen, stevedores, while the *arti* or guilds organized different trades. According to Braudel (*The Perspective of the World*, p. 133), in 1586, the city had a total population of 1,50,000 inhabitants. Of this 34,000 were workers.

Florence unlike Venice was essentially an industrial centre. It became the cradle of the Italian Renaissance. The Arno River flowed through it and was navigable from the Mediterranean port of Pisa. This port was a centre of textile production but was conquered in 1406 by Florence. This enabled Florence to become a maritime power. The political history of Florence was chaotic and full of interruptions caused by political uprisings, unlike the stable political history of Venice. The Medici family dominated the political power and the government revealed its commitment towards republicanism. Yet the rivalry between working classes and rich families prevented the government from functioning effectively. The members of the greater guilds and the merchants involved with textile production formed the dominant classes of the city and displayed strong commercial interests. They had established control over seven out of nine places in the *signoria* (chief magistracy). It was a form of corporate polity in which even the members of a guild of middling status (like small shopkeepers and artisans) occupied seats in the magistracy and voted in the council, but all the major decisions and policy formulations were left to the merchant oligarchy. However, their frequent quarrels and clash of interests made the government weak and ineffective and enabled political opponents to exploit the situation. Although the Medici family provided an element of continuity to the government and brought certain constitutional changes to strengthen their control over the state (the three important leaders – Cosimo, Piero and Lorenzo de Medici remained fairly popular), they could not have the last say in every matter.

The concentration of wealth in Florence stemmed from its industrial activities. The economy was dominated by a large number of merchant-banker families. The Medici family along with Strozzi, Giovanni, Morelli, Bardi, Peruri, Frescabaldi and many others had their own branches across major European towns. These were considered to be the most important banking houses of that period and they displayed the pre-capitalist spirit existing at a time when a greater portion of Europe was under a state of feudalism. Tuscany in Florence was a centre of banking and large firms. Important capitalist elements could be located in the commercial practices like the use of cheques, the existence of trading companies, the use of double-entry bookkeeping and simplified procedure for maritime insurance. As Braudel states, it was Florence which developed industry to the maximum and moved unequivocally into what can be described as the manufacturing phase (*The Perspective of the World*, p. 128). However, despite the concentration of wealth and industries the existence of a large urban proletariat with their wage problem created political disturbance and political instability.

The city states of Italy played an extremely important role in developing the modern rules of international relations and sophistication in the art of administration and diplomacy. The leading families and social elite developed efficient state bureaucracies in their respective states. In the late-fifteenth century all power was concentrated in the hands of rulers. Each prince tried to turn the *de facto* power into something more legitimate and Italian courts became the centres of politics. The immense powers wielded by these rulers came to be called *stato*, a model emulated by many European rulers. The Renaissance princes of Italy made a distinct contribution to the idea of 'resident diplomacy'. This was reflected in the regular practice of appointing resident ambassadors in the courts of foreign states, forging offensive and defensive alliances, non-aggression pacts and commercial treaties and state declarations of guarantee and neutrality. It was through these measures that the Italian states perfected modern techniques of international relations. Similarly, the Italians perfected the techniques of business organization.

The practice of stationing permanent representatives abroad was followed by the weak states in order to develop partners in international relations. The Venetian court nursed its interests through such ambassadors. The ruler of Milan, Sforza showed a great deal to the diplomatic skills by appointing permanent ambassadors in France. Sometimes ambassadors were exchanged with foreign states to cement an alliance. Ambassador provided news service to guide governments in their foreign policy. Most ambassadors were expected to send reports of important happenings in the states where they were appointed. The self-interest of these states and the attitude of watchfulness led to the development of the principle of standing diplomacy. By the late-fifteenth century all Italian states had representatives as ambassadors at each other's courts. All major European countries subsequently adopted this practice. Occasionally, this assumed a form of shadow diplomacy with secret agents, spies and informers, and the Italians often used merchants and bankers for this purpose. The practice of sending secret instructions to the ambassadors also started during this time. The aim of the diplomat was to outwit and deceive his opponents to succeed in the international sphere. These principles of international relations played a significant role in the history of pre-modern Europe.

Finally, an important contribution of the Italian city states system was to develop the principle of balance of power in international relations. This principle was also adopted within a state as a *politique* formula for managing rival factions. Each Italian state tried to preserve its own territory and defend its own interests by ensuring that no single state became strong enough to enslave the other and to this end, each state paid great attention to even minor political events or changes. The Medicis and the Venetian *signoria* hired mercenary armies to defend themselves as well as to carry out territorial expansion. Unlike medieval rulers who led their own campaigns, the Italian princes generally hired a professional military commander who was given a contract called *condotta* for an assigned campaign. This example was later followed by the larger states of Europe such as France, Spain and England.

Thus the political and socio-economic changes by the late-fifteenth century were transforming the face of Europe leading to the emergence of modern Europe. Geography provided a stimulus to the maritime nations of Europe. The introduction of gunpowder and its use in firearms was vital to the success of European overseas expansion. The discovery of distant regions, formation of colonial empires and new trans-oceanic trade routes provided a spur to the coastal economies of western Europe. New trading and commercial organizations were creating conditions for the rise of capitalism. Not only did the pace of social and cultural transformation gained momentum, but the rise of centralized monarchies in some parts gave new forms to state structure. These absolutist states provided security to trade and private property. Technological changes in the art of navigation and shipbuilding, improvement in the manufacture of artillery, armaments and military organization ensured European domination over the rest of the world and marked the first stage of global integration.

Suggested Readings

Abel, Wilhelm, *Agricultural Fluctuations in Europe: From the Thirteenth to the Twentieth Centuries* (tr. Olive Ordish), London: Methuen & Co., 1980. Thoroughly researched work on European agriculture and has rich statistics on the subject.

Bath, B.H. Slicher van, *The Agrarian History of Western Europe, AD 500–1850*, London: Edward Arnold, 1963. Discusses the political and economic dimension of feudalism and also includes a brief historiography.

Bloch, Marc, *The Feudal Society*, 2 vols., London: Routlege and Kegan Paul, 1965. A classical work on feudalism and is a must for all students of European feudalism.

Braudel, Fernand, *The Mediterranean and the Mediterranean World in the Age of Philip II* (tr. Sian Reynolds), London: Fontana, 1972. A classical work on the Mediterranean economy and the geo-political aspects representing the Annales School of historical writing.

Critchley, J.S., *Feudalism*, London: George Allen & Unwin, 1978.

Dobb, Maurice, *Studies in the Development of Capitalism*, London: Routledge and Kegan Paul, 1963. A scholarly work on the decline of feudalism that started a long debate in the academic circle.

Goldthwaite, Richard A., 'The Medici Bank and the World of Florentine Capitalism', *Past and Present*, 114, 1987, pp. 3–31. Useful article on the Italian banking system.

Kula, W., *An Economic Theory of the Feudal System: Towards a Model of the Polish Economy 1500–1800,* London: New Left Books, 1976. This is considered a path-breaking work as it analyses the serf-run estates of early modern Poland and contains some useful hints for locating similar estates in medieval western Europe.

Lucas, Henry S., *The Renaissance and the Reformation*, New York: Harper & Row, 2nd edn., 1960. Very good discussion on the Italian state systems and the pre-capitalist features in Europe.

Miskimin, Harry J., *The Economy of Later Renaissance Europe 1460-1600*, Cambridge: Cambridge University Press, 1977. Provides a comprehensive account of the European economy. Rich in statistical details.

Najemy, John M., ed., *Italy in the Age of the Renaissance, 1300–1500*, Oxford: Oxford University Press, 2004. Contains twelve essays by leading specialists on the Renaissance with a comprehensive introduction.

Pettegree, Andrew, *Europe in the Sixteenth Century*, Oxford: Blackwell, 2002. An interesting presentation of the history of Europe covering various dimensions like time, space, winds of change, etc. Good for the religious wars, Reformation and the Dutch revolts.

Pounds, N.J.G., *An Historical Geography of Europe 1500–1840*, Cambridge: Cambridge University Press, 1979. Presents a narrative of European events and relates it to the relief features of the region.

Potter, G.R., ed., *The Cambridge Modern History of Europe*, vol. I, *The Renaissance 1493–1520*, Cambridge: Cambridge University Press, 1981 (1st edn. 1957). Classical presentation, particularly of the Renaissance. The first three chapters are good.

Postan, M.M., ed., *The Cambridge Economic History of Europe*, vol. I, Cambridge: Cambridge University Press, 1966. A detailed dicussion can be found on the economy of the European states in the early years of the pre-modern period.

Rice Jr., Eugene F., *The Foundations of Early Modern Europe, 1460–1559*, London: Weidenfeld & Nicolson, 1971. Good basic reading for the earlier part of pre-modern Europe.

Rosener, Werner, *Peasantry of Europe*, Oxford: Blackwell, 1994. Covers a vast geographical region and particularly good for studying peasantry under feudalism.

Ruiz, Teofilo F., *Spanish Society, 1400–1600*, Harlow: Longman, 2001. Takes up popular culture, festivals and carnivals.

Strayer, Joseph R., *Medieval Statecraft and the Perspective of History*, New Jersey: Princeton University Press, 1971. Has an elaborate discussion on the meaning of feudalism and a good account of the development of feudal institutions.

Wiesner-Hanks, Merry E., *Early Modern Europe*, Cambridge: Cambridge University Press, 2006. Covers European history from the coming of the printing press till the French Revolution, particularly strong on gender and social relations.

Wolf, John B., *The Emergence of European Civilization: From the Middle Ages to the Opening of the Nineteenth Century*, New York: Harper, 1962. Useful work for beginners as it provides a wide-ranging study of political institutions, socio-economic patterns and changing trends in intellectual activities.

CHAPTER 2

The Renaissance and Society

In simple terms, 'Renaissance', means 're-birth'. In historical context, it implies a momentous cultural movement marked by revival of interest in the classical age of the Romans and the Greeks. It aimed at rediscovering the cultural accomplishments of the classical period and rescuing its arts and literature in order to revive and recreate a new culture, free from medieval bondage. It was not the discovery of the ancient past but, more significantly, the application of that classical knowledge of arts, literature, social values and political life in accordance with their own concept of social order that constituted Renaissance, which they believed was dramatically different from the contemporary world. Thus, roughly between 1300 and 1600 major attempts were made through a series of movements in many parts of Europe, mainly in the Italian city states, to reshape and recreate social values. It became a period of intense creativity in the field of thought, literature, arts, architecture, politics and practical sciences. This movement was extremely complex and assumed varied forms according to the social climate of each region. It is difficult to give a universally acceptable meaning to Renaissance. The nature and significance of this movement has been the subject of changing viewpoints and interpretations. The whole subject of Renaissance has drawn the attention of a large number of historians ever since the movement began.

The beginning of the Renaissance can be traced to the time of the 'Black Death' or even earlier in the fourteenth century, and its end to the early-sixteenth century. This entire period of nearly two centuries witnessed grave political turmoil, ravages from incessant warfare and natural calamities. Yet, in the history of the Italian states as well as in some parts of Europe, it was an extremely fertile period for culture.

Meaning

The concept of Renaissance and its place in history has undergone changes because of a variety of interpretations. The origins of the term 'Renaissance' go back to the writings of Giorgio Vasari (1511–74), an Italian art theorist, who used the term *rinascita* to describe the preceding two centuries. About the same time, the French naturalist Pierre Belon (1518–64) used the term 'renaissance', implying classical antiquity in a new spirit. The Italians called the movement *Rinascimento*. It was seen as an unexplained phenomenon that coincided with the restoration of classical literature. Théodore de Béze ascribed this to the fall of Constantinople in 1453 that caused the flight of the Greeks to Italy. This view took root in later centuries but is no longer accepted because it has been proved beyond doubt that the movement began in the early-fourteenth century. The idea of rebirth or revival began to gain ground in Italy from the period of Giotto. The achievements of Renaissance artists or poets were often compared to the ancients before they were exalted. The writers of the Renaissance displayed a strong dislike of the culture of the Middle Ages by describing it as the 'dark ages' or 'barbaric darkness'. Renaissance has been seen as the line dividing modern Europe from medieval Europe. Many Italians knew that in the distant past Rome was the centre of the civilized world but the power and glory of the Roman Empire was destroyed by the invasion of Germanic tribes, the Goths and the Vandals. The classical age, to which they looked back with pride, was followed by a long period of the so-called Middle Ages. They considered it as a time of unrelieved darkness, blind faith, economic stagnation and constant fighting. Italians believed that during this time art and literature had fled Europe. It marked the death of the high culture of the past. It was through Renaissance that they sought to transform all aspects of life – intellectual, social, cultural and political. The intellectuals spoke of the art of the Middle Ages as Gothic, implying a barbaric character. The scholars of the Renaissance were critical of the intellectual movement that preceded the Renaissance, known as scholasticism – a view that influenced subsequent writings. This has led Alister E. Mcgrath to observe that scholasticism was probably one of the most despised intellectual movements in human history. Scholasticism was an academic movement that flourished between 1250–1500. It laid great emphasis on the rational justification of religious belief. The University of Paris became its main centre, although the movement had succeeded in many other parts of northern Europe. This led to the establishment of a number of theological schools and theological debates. This movement tried to systematize and expand Christian theology and sought to provide a theory or method to religion by developing a philosophical system of its own, based on Aristotelian presuppositions. The scholastic writings were usually long and argumentative and were based on logic, philosophy and theology. Humanism, a movement within Renaissance, made sustained attacks on scholasticism.

The age of Enlightenment (another cultural and intellectual movement of Europe during the eighteenth century that preceded the French Revolution) renewed and sharpened the prejudice towards the Middle Ages. The writers of the Enlightenment described the medieval period as a period of blind faith and superstition that was brought to an end by the rationalistic spirit of the Renaissance. Voltaire, a prominent Enlightenment scholar, stressed the intellectual content of the Renaissance and believed that it promoted the spirit of independence, and brought about the rebirth of vernacular literature and fine arts. Voltaire, in his *Essay on Manners* (1756), wrote that the sixteenth century was a time when nature produced some extraordinary men in almost all fields, above all in Italy. According to Peter Burke, the writers of the Enlightenment gave two reasons for this phenomenon – liberty and opulence of the Italian states. Shaftesbury believed that the revival of painting was because of the existence of civil liberty in the free states of Venice, Genoa and Florence. This liberty was considered important also by Sismondi. He stressed that the development of Renaissance lay in the importance of wealth and freedom of the Italian towns. The Enlightenment writers believed that liberty encouraged commerce that in turn encouraged culture, and commerce and all forms of art were considered companions.

This view of assigning transcendent importance to the Renaissance in the development of modern civilization remained fashionable for a very long time, though the concept of the Renaissance underwent changes in historical literature. Jacob Burckhardt's *Die Kultur des Renaissance in Italien* (1860) is still regarded as the best analysis of the Renaissance despite some criticism. It was an attempt to relate culture to society. Burckhardt analysed societies in terms of the reciprocal interaction of three 'powers' – the state, culture and religion. He broadened the concept of the Renaissance from the arts and belles-lettres to the world of society and history. To Burckhardt, the Renaissance ushered in attitudes that initially transformed Italy and then the whole world. It inaugurated the 'modern' world with fresh attitudes to natural phenomena, moral and religious questions, to public affairs and towards the creative world of arts and letters. It also brought an age of individualism. This view of the Renaissance still persists in the general sense. Denys Hay divides the critics of Burckhardt into two broad categories. The first were those who argued that the Renaissance, which began in Italy in the fourteenth and fifteenth centuries, was only one of several such episodes in the cultural development of Europe. Hence, the Renaissance should be considered as a generic name for successive but disparate returns to Classical Antiquity. The second form of criticism insists that the Italian Renaissance cannot be regarded as something special and important and it does not deserve to be treated as a separate event. The first view has validity because studies in medieval culture bring out the significance of the 'Carolingian' Renaissance and the 'twelfth-century' Renaissance. In these movements many people were involved in the search and preservation of ancient manuscripts. However, it must be admitted that these movements did not appeal to the wider public; as was the case with the Italian Renaissance. Nor did they enjoy widespread patronage. Burckhardt gave credit to the Renaissance for its role in the birth of individualism that later replaced corporate forms of identity. Many scholars criticize him for the excessive weight he placed on the death of the corporate world of the Middle Ages. According to them, the institutions he assumed to have died – the guilds and the church – continued to play an important social role even in sixteenth-century Italy.

The derogatory picture of the Middle Ages, as presented by the writers of the Renaissance, was not based on facts. Modern research of the medieval period establishes beyond doubt that the High Middle Ages was not the 'death' of classical learning. In fact, Western attraction to the Greek culture began in the Middle Ages itself. Men like Robert Grosseteste and Roger Bacon helped in the revival of the study of Greek grammar and translated the works of Aristotle. St Thomas Aquinas showed keen interest in Aristotle. There were several humanists such as Trebizond, Theodore Gaza and Jacque Lefevre d'Etaples, who were great admirers of Aristotle. The revival of Latin classics was first centred around Cicero – the most esteemed scholar and writer of the Middle Ages. There was a steady revival and later maturing of Gothic art mainly in the north after an initial period of turmoil. According to E.H. Gombrich, Italians were less aware of this gradual growth and the unfolding of art than the people living further north. Hence, they saw the achievements of Giotto as a great innovation.

Karl Marx and Engels saw the Renaissance as a relation between the arts and the economy, i.e. between cultural production and material production. They suggested that the economic 'base' shaped the cultural 'superstructure'. In the Italian Renaissance whether an individual like Raphael could succeed in developing his talent depended wholly on demand, that in turn depended on the division of labour and the conditions of human culture resulting from it. Engels believed that this movement constituted a great turning point in the history of the West. Treating the sixteenth century as a period of diverse events such as the formation of a new culture, new religion, economic formations, the New World and the new science, Engels argued that it was the greatest 'progressive revolution' that mankind had so far experienced (Karl Marx and F. Engels, *Selected Works*, vol. 2, F. Engels, *Dialectics of Nature*, p. 30). Alfred Von Martin, while emphasizing the themes of individualism and the origins of modernity, also stressed on the economic basis of Renaissance by calling it a 'bourgeois revolution', where the noble and the cleric were replaced by the rise of the capitalists as the leaders of society. Many others do not wholly support this view.

Some scholars not only reject the importance given to the Renaissance but contend at the same time that there never was any such thing as the Renaissance. Etienne Gilson argued that the formation of the modern world was based on physical science but the humanists did not show interest in it and hence the belief that the Renaissance helped create a modern world cannot be accepted. Lynn Thorndike in *A History of Magic and Experimental Science* argued that the true Renaissance actually occurred around the twelfth century – that medieval Latin and scholasticism possessed great merits; that Gothic paintings had been neglected just as Gothic architecture and sculpture had been ignored and that democracy and popular education declined rather than advanced in the early modern times. Writers like H.O. Taylor and Helen Waddell suggest that from the twelfth century both classical and Christian traditions continued simultaneously and that the medieval poets were equally influenced by classical models. Johan Huizinga in *The Waning of the Middle Ages* speaks of the Renaissance as the 'autumn of the Middle Ages', just as W.K. Ferguson in *The Renaissance in Historical Thought* locates its roots and origins in the Middle Ages. Many recent writers hold the view that medieval men were as concerned with the discovery of the world as their Renaissance successors.

Among the important writers who provided a social interpretation of Renaissance, one can include the names of E. Garin, Michael Baxandall, Hans Baron, and Paul Oscar Kristeller. Friedrich Antal argued that industry and international trade gave Florence an unusually developed bourgeoisie. The Renaissance art mirrored the vicissitudes of the elite and that there was a direct relationship between the artist and the patron. Baxandall came out with the thesis that painting was an indication of social relationship between the patron and the artist in which the former played a determining role – a view shared by many others. There are also several writers who present the Renaissance in a socio-economic context.

Thus the meaning and significance of the Renaissance are open to several interpretations. The Renaissance is no longer seen as a distinct period of history or an epoch dividing the Middle Ages from the modern era. A deeper and wider study of medieval period helps us to see this period as one of transition in which the elements of both periods were present. It was not a completely separate period by itself, rather a part of continuous historical development. The Renaissance marked the fulfilment of medieval promise and not simply a return to classical antiquity. The socio-economic forces of that period caused the break-up of medieval society and the feudal system along with the universal church, since they were all interrelated. The revival of commerce and industry was accompanied by the growth of towns and money economy. The medieval society based on land tenures and agriculture could not have continued indefinitely. The cumulative social, economic and political changes created conditions in which fresh ideas emerged, which not only created high standards, renewed interest in arts and literature, but also influenced the attitude of the ruling elite. This greatly influenced the culture of the Europeans and gave them a fresh vision of society that they were trying to create.

Social Basis

The Renaissance as a movement was the product of an urban environment. It grew and prospered in the regions which had important cities or towns. As mentioned in the last chapter, Italian city states were the most urbanized centres of Europe. The Renaissance culture was the product of an interesting and curious world of Italian city states, in that the revival of the ancient world and its application to the present society came to reflect the civic needs of that time. The most common question raised is why did the Renaissance flourish in Italy. There were several reasons for it.

The Renaissance in Italy sprang from the urban environment that existed in the cities of northern and central Italy. Northern and central Italy had an exceptionally large number of towns where urban life was more dynamic and sophisticated than any part of Europe. The social structure of these towns was far from egalitarian. The principal social groups, particularly in Florence, consisted of three categories. At the top of the social strata were the richest men called by various names like *nobli, principali, grandi* or 'the first citizens', who monopolized political power and kept all the principal official posts with themselves. Members of this group were well-educated, widely travelled, experienced and lived in magnificent houses in the heart of the city. Below the *nobli* were the category of *mezzani* or *populari,* who were men of moderate means and were shopkeepers, bakers, wine sellers, druggists, artists, lawyers, notaries, civil servants and teachers. They functioned within their respective guilds. There was a distinct gradation of guilds based on hierarchy. The top four guilds of cloth merchants (the *calimala*), the wool manufacturers (*Arte della lana*), the silk manufacturers (*Arte della seta*) and the bankers (the *cambio*) were virtually monopolized by the *grandi*. The *mezzani* were a propertied class of people but their participation in government functioning was extremely limited. Though they had narrow intellectual interest they could read and write and depended on arithmetic for their accounts. The lowest strata comprised the poor people (*poveri*) or the masses. One-third of this category in Florence belonged to the guild of cloth manufacturers. A large section consisted of domestic servants and manual workers. They were almost excluded from political power. The upper section of the society brought about the Renaissance and quite often the wealth was provided by the second category.

The concentration of wealth in the Italian cities and their very active civil life created a more worldly view of life. No ruler by himself could control the variety of intellectual and cultural experiments. The Italian Renaissance was the product of a century of civic autonomy. The peace treaty of Lodi (1454) created a situation in which no individual ruler could assert complete political authority over the other city states. At the same time no individual could fall prey to an aggressor. This was an important factor in the development of the Renaissance. The presence of many self-governing city states prompted them to culturally and politically compete with each other. For Denys Hay it was the polity of the Italian states that acted as the stimulus for cultural changes. It resulted in a remarkable diversity of cultural and intellectual activities that was not seen in the rest of Europe. It provided multiple sources of patronage, and a constant competition to hire the most talented people to work for the development of their own cities.

This competition elevated the standards of perfection and flooded the Italian cities with personalities of high reputation and accomplishments.

Economic growth laid the material basis for the Italian Renaissance. For centuries Italy had been an important region for business and manufacturing. The phenomenal commercial and financial developments, population growth and an increasing level of production promoted certain pre-capitalist features in some areas of the Italian economy. The Italian merchants, particularly in Florence, possessed a large reservoir of liquid capital for investment which was utilized in real estate, trading and in cloth manufacturing, arms and industrial goods, mineral resources, funding military campaigns or even on art projects. From the end of the thirteenth century, Florentine merchants and bankers acquired control of Papal banking and became its tax collectors. Soon they began dominating European banking on both sides of the Alps and earning huge profits. They possessed knowledge and expertise on capital investment that enabled them to reap maximum gains. Three centuries of international trading, banking and industry fostered what could be called a 'mercantile' or 'bourgeois mentality'. It displayed an ability to quantify – a mathematical knowledge to keep the accounts accurate – as urban society required accuracy in economic dealings. The art of measurement and the value of time were important ingredients of the mercantile mentality. The continuous warfare among the Italian states had created a demand for military and hydraulic engineers. The large number of officials required proper civic education to equip themselves with urban affairs, and the large-scale construction work due to the accumulation of wealth created a demand for quality architects and painters. Hence, the cities in Italy provided a suitable climate for the Renaissance.

The Italian aristocrats, unlike those in the rest of feudal Europe, preferred to live in the urban centres and involved themselves in the civic affairs of their towns. Instead of living in the rural chateaux, they built palaces in the cities. Unlike the kind of segregation between the landed nobles and the urban merchants that existed in feudal Europe of the north, the Italian landed classes were increasingly drawn into town life on equal terms with leading commercial and industrial families. It was this integration of rural society with the world of merchants and industrialists that separated Italy from the other regions of Europe. The nobles made their town house the centre of their social life. There was virtually no major distinction between the aristocracy and the upper bourgeoisie. The amalgamation of these two important sections of the Italian nobility and leading commercial and industrial groups led to the formation of a relatively integrated civil society in which the balance gradually drifted away from the knightly element and the medieval tradition of chivalry. At the same time, an aristocratic ethos had been created that reflected the impulse of the elite to spend lavishly for private purposes. The social and economic supremacy of this elite was fortified by its control of the government in states like Florence. The association of the aristocrats with the merchants provided civility and Italian social life became increasingly aristocratic, most notably in Milan where a courtly society had developed, while in republican states, the elite began to behave more like the court aristocracy. By the early-sixteenth century what was expected of the noble or an aristocrat was best illustrated in *The Book of the Courtier* (1528) by Baldassare Castiglione. He mentioned some basic attributes which every courtier was expected to possess. He was expected to be endowed with impeccable character such as noble birth, grace and talent. These were considered fundamental. Besides, he was expected to have traits of refinement which were to be cultivated through humanist or classical education, knowledge of the arts, music and painting, and perform physical exercises to have a well-developed personality. He was also expected to follow certain code of conduct, such as tactfulness and diplomacy, needed in civic affairs. This book brings out those ideals which the great patrons of the Renaissance tried to achieve. Burckhardt suggests that Castiglione's work is reflective of the merging of the upper and middle classes as a result of their living together in cities.

The presence of wealth in the Italian towns was another important factor in the emergence of the Renaissance. By the thirteenth century, the Italian economy, because of its large-scale commercial activities, had become the most prosperous region in the whole of

Europe. The heavy and intensive investment in culture from the late medieval period was probably due to urban pride and the concentration of per capita wealth. Many historians believe that public support for culture first came in Italy by the middle of the thirteenth century. On the other hand, scholars like Robert Lopez and Carlo M. Cipolla question the link between economic prosperity and cultural progress. For them the period between 1330 and 1530 was one of economic depression. It witnessed diminution in the value of land, demographic decline caused by the Black Death, reduction in profit margins of the feudal lords and lowering of interest rates. However, it appears that they agreed to an inverse relationship between economic condition and cultural development. In this period of economic depression, the political elite and businessmen competed with each other for patronage, power and prestige, thus turning culture into an economic venture. Somehow, this viewpoint has not gained much support from historians. According to another explanation, the presence of a large number of princes ruling so many Italian cities provided greater possibility of patronage and employment. The great princes such as Visconti and Sforza in Milan, the Medici in Florence, the Este in Ferara and the Gonzaga in Mantua made major contribution to the Renaissance by patronizing art and literature in their respective courts. Even the lesser aristocratic families made similar contributions as did the popes in Rome. Popes Alexander VI, Julius II and Leo X were popularly called the 'Renaissance Popes' because of their contribution to the field of art and architecture.

From the middle of the fourteenth century, a conscious reaction started against the form and content of chivalrous poetry as well as scholastic learning of the Middle Ages. It began to change the taste of the readers and promoted classicism and aggressive power. Cicero's writings began to furnish new standards and gave new meaning to the ideas of ancient patricide. The *humanitas* of Cicero provided the watchword for an education that claimed to free man from social conventions and the narrow-mindedness brought by professions. It became a guide to the interpretation of antiquity. Besides, the attitude of adoration and reverence for the ancient world of Rome had existed throughout the Middle Ages. The

Italians looked back nostalgically to the classical world of Rome and Greece. Several attempts were made at recovering the past before the humanist movement of the Renaissance emerged. It is also argued by historians that the ruins of the Roman Empire that existed around the city states, particularly near Rome, drove the imagination of the Italians to recreate their past glory. It is said that Brunelleschi, the greatest architect of Renaissance, frequently travelled to Rome to measure the ruins of temples and palaces. He made sketches of their forms and the ornamental details to create new models. The intellectual and cultural activities in Italy were greatly influenced through the sources of antiquity which were transmitted from the Byzantine Empire through the scholers, theologians and the merchants of Venetia and Genoa. This resulted in a grand union of Greek and Roman cultures. There were many channels of Greek penetration into Italy. Venice had strong commercial links with the Byzantine Empire but Greek knowledge also reached indirectly through a number of Greek envoys and fugitives such as Cardinal Bessarion of Nicaca, who donated his library to the humanist scholars. The Florentine expansion in the east also brought them closer to the Greeks, particularly after the conquest of Pisa in 1406. Men like Manuel Chrysolaras taught Greek and young scholars and intellectuals who displayed receptiveness towards humanist ideas surrounded him.

The political rivalry among the Italian cities led to different intellectual reactions, as was the case in Florence. In 1494, the popular party and the republicans with the help of the French army overthrew the rule of the Medicis, which had opposed the march of the French ruler, Charles VIII to Naples. This led to a fierce struggle in Florence between the republicans and the princely authority. This was at a time when Florence was the pivotal centre of Renaissance. The intellectual reactions to these struggles proved extremely important. The prolonged struggle saw the Medicis return to power with the help of the Papal and the Spanish army but only for a short period. It was against this background that Machiavelli wrote his famous treatise *The Prince* which led to a detailed political dialogue and the study of Florentine history by the intellectuals of that region. Many of the elite privately met in the Oricellari Gardens to analyse the problems of the republican city and to discuss contemporary politics and literature. Republicanism formed the majority opinion in this group. The intellectual climate in this era promoted discussions and led to the formation of fresh ideas on the question of city constitution and the nature of government. During this period some talented persons were employed in the service of the state. In 1512, Michelangelo, the great genius of the Renaissance period, himself supervised the fortifications.

Patronage too played a part in the origins and maturing of the Renaissance. Individual artists, architects and scholars generally did not possess the funds needed to carry out projects on a large scale. Most of them had to depend on patrons for financial security. Some scholars believe that the principal factor for the revival of classical art and literature was the fact that the towns could offer an entirely fresh source of patronage. Earlier, art works were commissioned by corporate bodies and by the church. This practice continued throughout the period of the Renaissance. Along with this, another source of patronage developed in the form of individual bankers, merchant princes and various groups interested in commissioning works of art. In recent years, historians have emphasized or denied the role of patrons in setting the standard of art during the Renaissance and the role they played in the selection of themes. The desire to achieve social fame and immortality were the main reasons for the patronage. Some of the patrons wished to be identified with the works of art they had commissioned. This was clearly revealed in the writings of Cosimo de Medici and Giovanni Rucellai, who built palaces and churches to establish the glory of Florence and of their own names. In fact, aristocrats and wealthy merchants competed with each other to become patrons of the arts. Peter Burke identifies three motivations behind this – piety, prestige and pleasure. The church was one of the greatest patrons of art as was the Medici family. According to Vasari, sometimes even artisans, tailors and members of craft guilds commissioned works of arts.

This competition led to the employment of artists and architects within the Italian cities on a much larger scale than ever before.

While many patrons treated sculptors and painters as men of mechanical skill or merely skilled artisans, patrons like Cosimo de Medici considered them as men of genius. Earlier, very few artists were recruited from the lower middle-class for major projects but slowly individual genius gained recognition. For example, Michelangelo could dictate his own terms to the patron. Thus, we find that in the earliest period of the Renaissance, patronage was dominated by urban public support because of the concentration of wealth in the cities and because of the popularity of republican ideas. It would be wrong to suggest that religion had no part to play in the emergence of the Renaissance. Many of the gigantic buildings were the combination of piety, civic pride and religious patronage. The City Council of Siena decided to rebuild its Gothic cathedral of St. Mary, a decision that was prompted by a religious urge but was also bound up with civic values. The governments of the city states built city halls to promote civic pride. In a spirit of competition, town councils also built or renovated streets, public squares, lodges and public buildings to beautify their cities. Public institutions played a major role in the first phase of artistic activities in the fourteenth century. The city of Siena demonstrated the use of art to communicate political ideas. In Florence, public art was often organized and funded by various guild organizations. Some major guilds commissioned sculpture for the Chapels of Or San Michele, which was the famous shrine in the grain market. The guild of the cloth merchants paid for the frescoes of St John the Baptist, whilst the guild of silk merchants designed the hospital building. These guilds enjoyed significant political influence in the city administration. However, during the fifteenth century most of the Italian city states became victims of the hereditary rule of princely families and the princely aristocracy monopolized patronage. Hereafter, Renaissance flourished only in the courts of Italian rulers and in the Papal courts. The Renaissance popes began to implement specific ideological programmes from the late-fifteenth century to emphasize their role not only as spiritual leaders of Christianity but also as temporal lords of the central Italian states.

From the mid-fifteenth century, the chief patrons of the Renaissance in many parts of Italy were wealthy individuals. Some of the families of the Italian towns built individual palaces or villas in the countryside which became summer retreats. They hosted and entertained high officials and peers in these palaces, gardens and villas. The interiors were decorated with beautiful paintings, portraits, gem collections and their libraries displayed a vast collection of ancient manuscripts and famous works. The competitive spirit of the Italian city states was also revealed in the construction of chapels and basilicas with elaborate and beautiful ornamentation. At the same time, it must be remembered that the Renaissance was a cultural movement that was confined to the upper classes of society and was by no means democratic or popular. Its social base remained limited to the ruling elite. For the vast majority of the poor, illiterate and marginalized rural Italians, there was no Renaissance. At the same time, the urban environment was an essential condition for the emergence of the Renaissance and it could not have achieved the scale and magnitude it did in a rural or a feudal society.

The Italian Humanism

The Renaissance in Italy consisted of two important phenomena: a renewed interest in classical Latin and Greek which came to be associated with humanism; and the visual arts that attained the pinnacle of glory in this period. Modern writers debate the relationship between humanism as a group of academic disciplines and the culture of the Renaissance as a whole. In opposition to Burckhardt and George Voigt who looked upon Renaissance humanism as a phenomenon inextricably linked with Italian politics and society, scholars such as P.O. Kristeller and Augustin Renaudet have detatched humanism from this social context. They consider humanists an academic group which was mainly concerned with the traditional humanist subjects. The term owes its origin to the Latin word *humanitas*, used by Cicero and others for those cultural values which were derived from liberal education. The term *umanista* was an academic jargon used by the Italians to describe a teacher or a student of classical literature and the arts associated with it, including the one of rhetoric. Subsequently, it assumed the nature of an academic movement of the educated elite and the intellectuals and came to be known as Humanism.

Humanism as a cultural movement came to be involved with the rediscovery and study of ancient Greek and Roman texts, their restoration and interpretation and the collection and assimilation of ideas derived from those texts. The range of interest of a humanist varied from archaeological studies to a detailed philological study of written records, from philosophy to epic poems of the past, translations and commentaries of original manuscripts and included a wide range of subjects such as creative and visual arts, jurisprudence, medicine and mathematics. In fact, humanism became a vehicle of cultural transformation of western Europe.

The interest in classical literature was neither confined to Italy nor to the men of Renaissance. Writers like Nicholas Mann point out that twelfth-century French culture was permeated by classical material and even vernacular literature came to bear its influence. By the end of the century three romances, *Roman de Thèbes, Eneas* and *Roman de Troie* besides many other short published works, were based on the ancient text. John of Salisbury was an outstanding English scholar of that age and possessed some knowledge of Latin literature. He praised eloquence and defended liberal studies – the themes which later became extremely popular among the Italian humanists. However, such early attempts at the revival of classical literature neither became popular nor assumed the character of a movement. The feudal and agrarian society of that region was the greatest barrier to the development of an intellectual movement. The Italian states had a large urban population consisting of educated laymen, lawyers and civil servants. It was this class of people which promoted the ideas of humanism. While the French classical study that continued till the fourteenth century was confined to grammar, in Italy, it was put to varied use by its urban populace. The Italian humanists used their knowledge of classical literature to raise the standard of eloquence. Rhetoric served them as an art of public speeches, for writing business and official letters, in legal profession, and in diplomatic dealings as many of the humanists held positions of influence as teachers, secretaries or chancellors to rulers and communes, as diplomats of the states in foreign courts or were actively involved in the affairs of the state. As a class of elite they wielded great influence over state matters. They were largely secular and many of them were laymen rather than clergy.

There were many centres of humanist learning all over Italy in the fourteenth century, such as Florence, Padua, Vicenza and Verona. The court of Naples witnessed a revival of Greek studies. Another centre of humanist activities was situated in France that had great bearing on Italian humanism. This was the Papal curia at Avignon. During the period of the so-called 'Babylonian captivity' of the popes, the capital of the Pope was temporarily shifted to Avignon under French protection. The result was the transformation of Avignon into an important diplomatic and cultural centre. The Pope not only provided patronage to scholars and men of letters but also developed an important library consisting of classical texts and manuscripts. The most well-known intellectual figure to emerge from this court was Francesco Petrarch (1304–74), often described as the father of humanism. His father wanted him to study law at the University of Bologna but after his death, Petrarch decided to pursue studies in literature. He was an outstanding scholar and an original writer. He was a great admirer of Dante Alighieri (1265–1321), the famous poet and scholar, and author of the extraordinary work, *Divine Comedy*. This work was full of wit and subtle criticism of the existing society. Dante represented the transition in literature from the medieval to the Renaissance period. While his philosophy of life was rooted in religion, his writing reflected his deep interest in all aspects of human life. Although Dante was an eminent scholar who could write in Latin, French and German, he chose to write in Italian and thereby expanded the cultural horizons of the subsequent humanist world.

But it was Petrarch who developed a craze for the classical authors. He successfully mastered the art of rhetoric from the ancient works and developed a love for poetry that had great bearing on his writings. Petrarch promoted a secular world and remained active in public life as a politician and diplomat. Petrarch spent a major part of his early life at Avignon, where he was introduced to

Dante Alighieri (1265–1321)

the cultural and intellectual world of the curia. There he found numerous manuscripts. He successfully pieced together and restored the text of Livy's *History of Rome*. It was Petrarch's passion for the search of classical texts and manuscripts that influenced the subsequent generation of scholars and study of texts became one of the chief activities of all humanists. He influenced his friend and disciple Giovanni Boccaccio as well. Petrarch is best known for his vernacular poetry and his great sonnets, the *Canzoniere*. The influence of Roman poets is evident in this work. However, his reputation as a humanist rests on his Latin works. He revealed a great love for learning and an unbound enthusiasm for classical studies. He was highly critical of the society in which he lived and was disgusted by urban violence and wars. It was he who popularized the expression 'Dark Ages' that separated the classical world from his own times. He showed the way to others by highlighting the value of classical literature as a vehicle of reforms. He demonstrated that the study of classical literature was only the means to an end and not an end itself. His programme of reforms involved first reconstruction of classical culture followed by a careful understanding and imitation of the classical heritage. Finally, instead of merely copying ancient values and styles, he suggested a series of changes and reforms. Till his end, like many future humanists, Petrarch remained a Christian but he was mentally torn between contemporary Christianity and pagan antiquity.

Petrarch's reform programme greatly inspired the Italian intellectual life and contributed to its subsequent transformation. He attracted a number of young scholars who were involved in discussions on literature, philosophy, politics and education. His method of historical and literary investigation of the ancient world became the basis for future studies carried out by the humanists. His programme became popular among the wealthy oligarchs of Florence. He was the first to condemn the scholastic philosophy of the Middle Ages as its scholarship was based on rigid application of logic and became highly technical in terms which could seldom be enjoyed. The humanists led by Petrarch gave importance to rhetoric or the beauty of language, which was considered more important than a series of logical proof. The subsequent generation of humanists continued to attack scholasticism. This has led some historians to believe that humanism was the antithesis of scholasticism. According to Frederick B. Artz, the main weakness of Petrarch was his conventionality of mood – alike of dreams, of ecstasy and of poetic melancholy that took the place of worldly reality. However, his poetic verses had set a pattern and many poets borrowed from his vocabulary, his figure of speech and his methods of analysing emotions.

Giovanni Boccaccio (1313–75) was another important humanist and was known for his work the *Decameron*, a collection of over a hundred stories. Boccaccio was ahead of Dante and Petrarch in the search for ancient Latin manuscripts because of his knowledge of Greek. He made new discoveries in style, in Latin scholarship and in vernacular prose and poetry. He wrote some excellent works on classical mythology, history, geography but the most important of all was his *Genealogie* (a genealogy of pagan gods). He provided a new insight to scholars, artists and musicians. Like Petrarch, he considered poetry to be a vehicle through which truths could be presented symbolically. He was a fine story-teller, possessed remarkable wit and had a sharp eye for the finer details. Boccaccio's work as a humanist showed many new fields for literary and artistic treatment. He was widely read and had considerable influence on a number of writers and poets of the later generation.

The humanist programme as propounded by Petrarch and developed under Coluccio Salutati, the Florentine Chancellor (1331–1406), along with a group of intellectuals led to the ideology of civic humanism. Cicero also served as a source of inspiration in the development of civic humanism. These men believed that one must lead an active life for one's own state and that everything, including wealth, should be considered good if that increased one's power of action. An active life in civic matters does not put hurdles in the development of intellectual strength but actually stimulates it. They argued that through participation in state affairs an individual grows to maturity, both intellectually and morally. The civic humanists wrote letters, orations and history, displaying the classical virtues of city life. Like Cicero, the civic humanists believed that moral and ethical values were hidden within public life and therefore participation in public life was seen as an exercise in virtue. The civic humanists saw their task as preparing men who would promote public virtue and through them make the government and administration promote republican qualities. Leonardo Bruni (1370–1444) recreated the history of the Roman republic in his writings and suggested that the virtues of the Roman state should be adopted by Florence. Although civic humanism first emerged in Florence, it soon spread to other cities of Italy. It reflected the values of an urban society. This movement increased the involvement of the humanists in government activities and the knowledge of rhetoric, which they had gained from the ancient world, was put to the service of the state. The greatest rhetoricians became successful diplomats.

During the period of the High Renaissance from about 1490

to 1530, there was a growing interest in classical models in literature as in art. Some of the classical works of Plautus (dramas), Terence (comedies), Seneca (tragedy) and Horace (known for his satire) were copied and adapted by the humanists. Ludovico Ariosto (1474–1533) emerged as the greatest literary genius since Petrarch. Most of his life was spent in the service of the House of Este. He wrote in Latin as well as in the vernacular. His writings revealed perfection, excelling not only in character analysis but also in the invention and handling of plots. His satires revealed grace, elegance and simplicity and were influenced by the style of Horace. Ariosto was entrusted with the job of writing comedies for the court theatre. His greatest work was a romantic epic, the *Orlando Furioso.* He revealed deep insight into human behaviour. Another outstanding prose writer of this period was Count Castiglione (1478–1529). In his portrait made by his friend Raphael, he is seen as an urban aristocrat. His *Book of the Courtier* became extremely popular among the ruling classes. He wrote in Latin as well as in Italian.

A large number of humanists displayed their individual qualities in the service of the state. They tried to seek eminent positions through official posts or through writings. They also revealed a diversity of interests. As P.O. Kristeller suggests, the early humanist did not have one single coherent philosophy or attitude towards life. What gave them a semblance of unity was their enthusiasm for the rediscovery of Latin and Greek classics and the immense values they found in them for literature and morals. Despite their varied conclusions, they laid emphasis on elegance of writing, speech and morality by stressing the uniqueness of man, his feelings and his potential. They believed that the Romans knew how to say things. Many humanist writers adopted the Latin model because of its beauty of expression. Greek on the other hand had less impact on style but perhaps more on ideas.

Love for beauty constituted the most important attribute of humanism. A striking aspect of the humanist culture was its emphasis on table manners, style (which was considered more important than the size), decoration and appearance. The word *humanitas* was used not only for human kindness but also for the refinement of taste, education and mental cultivation. In fact, humanism was a remarkably heterogeneous movement which varied with regions. In Naples, Urbino, Mantua and Milan, it assumed a courtly complexion. In Rome, the ancient ruins worked as the source of inspiration for the humanists but there was little interest in Greek till the period of Pope Leo X. After that humanism gravitated towards the Papal court. The House of Medici in Florence provided the chief patronage and the ruling elite here was itself greatly involved in the movement. There was a strong bias in favour of Greek studies in Venice and the pursuit of humanities was confined to some members of the nobility and within a group of scholars. Many of them were engaged in school education or were learned men associated with publishing activities. Within humanism, there were divisions between the followers of Latin and the supporters of Italian, between the supporters of the ancient and those of the modern, and within the classicists themselves – between Ciceronians and anti-Ciceronians, i.e. between the imitators and the re-interpreters. The chief hallmarks of Italian humanism included individualism and dignity of man, secularism, revival of Latin and Greek, promotion of vernacular literature, study of history and a new approach to philosophy.

The Dignity of Man

Italian humanism seems to emphasize on the dignity of man – the privileged position of man in the world. This was represented not only in the writings and literature of scholars like Alberti but even in the works of arts. Many of them emphasized the relationship of harmony which they saw between man and the universe. As Alberti stated 'beauty is the harmony of all parts'. Man was seen as the best creation of God. The focus was on the uniqueness of man and his potential. So in the eyes of God, the perfect man was the microcosm in relation to God and the universe was the microcosm. The humanist writers tried to relate man and the world in which he lived to the new ideal of a harmonious cosmos. They placed great stress on human dignity aimed at realizing individual potentiality.

Individualism and secularism were the other significant aspects of humanism. The renewed emphasis on the individual's ability created new social ideas. Many of the humanists such as Nicolaus Cusanus or Nicholas of Cusa (1401–64) believed that the whole universe was not only created but also permanently sustained by God. Thus, the study of nature, for some humanists, was directed at a search for the God. This search later got focused on man, as he was perceived as the highest form of creation on earth. As Heinrich Decker suggests, the efforts towards a religious understanding of the world and humanist strivings towards education were not merely two parallel trends; they merged and became one. The fact that the saviour of mankind, Jesus Christ appeared as a man and was the centre of Christian religious belief was absolutely compatible with the humanist ideas. However, instead of ascribing everything to God, the humanists believed that God had laid down an irreversible programme for the universe and that man was responsible for his own good and evil acts. The human will and human morality was, therefore, not controlled by God but by man himself. They believed that active public life benefitted others and was more praiseworthy than a strictly private monastic life. Humanists wanted to create an environment in which the potential of man could be fully exalted and his mental faculties could reach its full potential. In this way they paved the way for secularism in which civic life was freed from ecclesiastical domination.

Revival of Antiquity

The humanists made available the recovered and restored classical literature in the purest form. So their first task was to recover those classical manuscripts which the medieval scholars had overlooked or ignored. They began their search for ancient manuscripts single-mindedly and some of them had provided financial resources for the acquisition of original texts. It is believed that Niccolo de Niccoli (1364–1437) sold his farms and parental property to build his collection of books. Besides acquiring manuscripts, the humanists made copies for their patrons, edited them or added commentaries to establish their authenticity. Lorenzovalla (1407–57) provided literary criticism of ancient texts and placed them in original form as different from medieval Latin. Bracciolini (1380–1459) who had served as a papal secretary for many years was an avid collector of classical manuscripts. There was an unusual craze for obtaining ancient documents. The method of obtaining these original manuscripts varied from copying, buying and sometimes even stealing. Guarino de Verona after a long journey returned from Constantinople in 1408 with over 50 manuscripts. In 1422, Giovanni Aurispa brought back 238 manuscripts. The possession of ancient manuscripts became a status symbol for the humanists.

Greek Revival

The humanists had great attraction for Latin works and their interest in Greek studies developed slightly later. It is believed that Petrarch was fascinated by Greek literature and possessed a copy of *Iliad*, though he did not learn the language. It was Manuel Chrysoloras (1350–1415), arriving in Florence in 1397 from Constantinople who introduced Greek studies in Italy. Guarino of Verona was another celebrated scholar who contributed in making Greek studies popular. Many scholars argued that the Renaissance was an age of Platonism whereas the study of Aristotle was confined to the period of scholasticism. It would be wrong to presume that the study of Greek was confined to the works of Plato. It is true that the humanists were great admirers of original texts in the study of Plato but their interest in the ideas of Aristotle also continued. The discovery of Latin texts was important but the beginning of classical Greek studies was the real success of the humanists. They were greatly aided by the cooperation of many Byzantine scholars who had come to live in Italy during the fifteenth century. These experts in Greek texts provided impetus to the Greek studies, including the writings of Plato, Sophocles, Euripides, Thucydides and many others. Famous humanist intellectuals such as Marsilio Ficino (1433–99) and Giovanni Mirandola (1463–94) helped Cosimo de Medici in Florence to set-up the Platonic Academy. Many such academies were subsequently created in other parts of

Italy. Members of these societies were scholars who studied and interpreted the works of Plato, paid tribute to their hero by celebrating Plato's birthday through holding banquets, gave speeches highlighting Plato's political ideas and translated his works. The political ideas of the Greek philosophers had great influence on some of the humanist scholars. Through Cicero, another eminent scholar who held a special place in the humanist writings, the humanists found in the ancient Greek literature an ideal wisdom. The study of Greek was important for individual and collective life. Greek ethics contained a distinctive set of assumptions. The induction of rules from Greek experience provided a means of ordering chaotic events of human life and showed the way to political theory and eventually to sociology. The growing enthusiasm for Greek philosophy was not confined to Plato and Aristotle but included the Stoics, Epicureans and Eclectics.

The Platonic Academies that developed in the fifteenth century in Florence made significant contribution to ideas and activities in the public sphere. They helped to legitimize the position of the Medicis and offered justification for the increasing professionalism in government. They also placed great stress on education and search for knowledge. They expected that literary studies would lead to philosophy and subsequently to a change of mind. Marsilio Ficini (1433–99) translated Plato's works into Latin in the context of Christian traditions by highlighting the dignity of man. For him, scientific observation and logic was not so important as true wisdom and experience, love and contemplation all of which lead to human dignity. For him, everything was hierarchical, from the lowest matter to God, and the human soul was placed somewhere in the middle of this hierarchy. These ideas of hierarchy of beings were further extended by Pico and these were shared by many other humanists forming the school of *Hermeticum*. The translated texts of the Hermetics suggested mutual influence of mind, material and celestial worlds. It gave rise to Hermetic magic (based on the magical texts of the first century), astrology and alchemy and gave certain controversial ideas on the reciprocal relationship between the natural world and the cosmos that persist even today in some parts of the world. The study of Greek and Arabic authors of science on the one hand contributed to independent mathematical and empirical reasoning (the humanist learning in Italy helped the formation of revolutionary ideas on the nature of the solar system of Nicolaus Copernicus), but on the other hand it also strengthened the occult and magic traditions that placed obstacles to scientific progress.

Vernacular Literature

Vernacular literature had already developed in the Middle Ages but was limited in form. The humanists' emphasis on classical Latin led to its widespread use by scholars, theologians and lawyers. Latin literature had an influence on vernacular style and to some extent it elevated and purified it but at the same time it developed a type of writing that was too self-conscious, too imitative of classical models, rhetorical and often artificial. However, the role of humanists in the promotion of the vernacular cannot be denied. It was Petrarch who wrote in both Latin and the vernacular. Some of his unfinished and lesser-known works such as *Africa* and *The Second Punic War* marked the emergence of Italian as a language of the people. He wrote in Italian, which evolved mainly from the old Tuscan language. Thereafter a strong interest in Tuscan language in the Florentine academic circle in the late-fifteenth century transformed it into Italian language under the influence of Lorenzo de Medici and his court as it gained greater acceptability. Petrarch's poems became accessible to his admirers as he also expressed his ideas in Tuscan. The cultivation of artistic verse and prose in Tuscan in the upper and middle layers of Florentine society contributed to the cause of vernacular literature. Petrarch was followed by a period of Greek and Latin scholarship that lasted almost a century. The knowledge of classical literature and civilization spread with the preparation of grammars, dictionaries and handbooks. Italian vernacular literature of a very high quality emerged in the later half of the fifteenth century.

Humanism and History

One of the first illustrations of an impending break with medieval historiography took place during early phase of the Renaissance in the fourteenth century. Theological interpretation of history and the supernatural element in history were replaced by a new secular interpretention without directly attacking Christian authority. Petrarch's *Lives of Illustrious Men* in fact set this trend. In the search for the ancient world, a great number of Latin poems, histories, biographies and ovations were written and distributed in printed form from the middle of the fifteenth century. Humanists introduced the concept of periodization of history – ancient, medieval and modern. In the literary genre, the humanists made an important contribution in the writing of history. The concept of universal history in the tradition of Augustine and Orosius was dropped and rejected by the humanists. Instead they introduced the idea of natural causation in history and showed the way for proper use of source material. Italian humanists established modern historical scholarship. They created the idea of liberal education and founded some new disciplines like numismatics and epigraphy. The humanists led the way in rewriting the history of Italian cities. It was based on a new sense of chronology with a secular outlook in which the writing of history was no more seen as a process in the divine sphere. Their models were from the Greek and Roman historians, especially Livy. Among the humanists, the *History of the Florentine People* by Leonardo Bruni and *History Since the Decline of the Romans* by Frario Biondo (1388–1463) were some of the earliest works of history. Biondo presented a long view of history and revealed critical handling of sources which is considered a milestone in modern historiography. Bruni adopted the utilitarian approach to history. His writings were analytical in method and constructive in reasoning. Hence, he is called by some scholars as the first modern historian. The chief limitation of classical historians was that they had confined themselves chiefly to the political events and largely ignored the economic aspects. As historians they tended to over-simplify the characters of the chief historical figures. There are two views among the scholars on Renaissance being the beginning of modern history writing. Some writers (e.g. Hans Baron) argue that the writing of modern history began with Bruni from around 1400 while another view (F. Gilbert) suggests that it had not started till the sixteenth century. Writings on history, according to the second viewpoint, began with the writings of Niccolo Machiavelli (1469–1527) and Francesco Guicciardini (1483–1540). The latter revealed great interest in political analysis and examined the consequences of the wars of 1494 on Florence. It was the study of history in his *Discourse on the Forgery of the Alleged Donation of Constantive* which led Lorenzo Valla to reject the authenticity of a document on the basis of which successive generation of popes had defended their right of political domination in central Italy. Valla argued that it was a forgery and not a real document. Guicciardini projected the diversity of human nature and strove to provide a broader interpretive framework.

The Humanist Education

Humanists considered education an important means to propagate a new view of man. According to Peter Burke, rhetoric was stressed because it was seen as a good training for political life. Renaissance humanism introduced certain changes in the educational curriculum which influenced not only Italy but also other parts of Europe. The humanists considered the study of classical literature, particularly the content and style of ancient Greeks and Romans as the best form of learning. As humanism started as an elitist movement, classical learning became part of intermediate and advanced education. It influenced the middle and the upper-middle class male population in Italy, France, England and Germany and was not meant for the masses and served only the elite. Many of the private, municipal and provincial schools adopted humanist educational programmes. Humanist teachers in the Italian cities and courts created schools in which the students were taught Latin, grammar, rhetoric, Roman history, political philosophy, including Greek literature, and philosophy. The humanists considered education in the classics as the best form of education to pursue political careers as advisers to princes or diplomats, such an education prepared the pupils in the art of speech, arguments, public writing in the civic spheres so that they could develop into good public or civil servants. In their attempt to provide examples from many classical authors and ancient personalities, humanists produced an extensive biographical literature of princes, scholars, philosophers and sages. Many scholars give credit to the Italian humanists for their reform in handwriting. The Gothic script, characterized by angularity and compression was replaced by the humanist cursive script. Niccolo di Niccoli and Salutati revived the Caroline minuscule.

The humanists produced treatises on educational theory and developed secondary schools, e.g. as developed by Vittorino at Mantua. They showed that education could break the barriers which had been created by the medieval scholastics. Poggio Bracciolini discovered a treatise on education in 1416. It brought a new understanding of language, philosophy and religion. Another humanist, Lorenzo Valla, laid emphasis on education in the form of historical-textual research and he lectured at the courts and universities in different parts of Italy. The humanists in their educational programme laid stress on the value of liberal arts in order to teach the secrets of true freedom. They emphasized physical education as well, as they believed in the idea of a sound mind in a sound body. Private education, like wealth, lineage, public post and family connections, had become a status symbol not only in Florence but also in other cities of Italy. The biggest limitation of these educational programmes was that girls were not included in it although the Italian humanists had been propagating the idea of freedom and fullest development of individual personality.

Political Thought

It is true that the humanists did not make any major contribution to the development of political philosophy as compared to the Greeks. The humanist movement could not boast of great figures like Plato or Rousseau. The only name that stands out among the humanists in the sphere of political thought is that of Niccolo Machiavelli. The Renaissance humanists were not involved with the subject of political theory. Their writings were mainly for the liberally educated people such as rich merchants, aristocrats and professionals. Although they did not produce any major work of political philosophy, they fundamentally changed the intellectual world within which political thought existed. They contributed not by producing a system of thought but by creating a climate of thought.

The Platonic Academy became an informal group of scholars patronized by Cosimo de Medici. He commissioned Marsilio Ficino (1433–99) to bring out a translation of Plato's dialogues. Ficino was given a life endowment so that he could concentrate only on this work. Though the Platonic Academy did not become a formal educational institution, the translation of Plato's philosophy called 'Neoplatonism' became an important intellectual system. Ficino's work synthesized Christianity and Platonism into a single system based upon two primary views – Neoplatonic hierarchy of substances (the long chain of beings from the lowest form of matter to the highest spirit in the form of God) and the theory of spiritual love. It was an attempt to fuse the material world with the spiritual world. This theory of spiritual love had a great influence on Western literature, as it revealed that just as all parts of the universe are bound together by God, people are also bound together in their humanity through love. Hermenticism was another form of intellectual movement based on Ficino's translation of a Greek manuscript by the name of *Corpus Hermeticum*. One aspect of this manuscript emphasized the occult sciences like astrology, magic and alchemy. The other aspect stressed the theological and philosophical beliefs and speculations. The Hermentics argued that God existed in all forms of nature, in earthly objects as well as in the heavenly bodies. The universe was portrayed in organic and animistic terms. Thus, for the Hermentics the world was a living entity and was in constant movement. So they offered a new view of mankind, that human beings were endowed with divine power and in order for them to regain their original divinity, they must search for knowledge in nature and utilize the powers of nature fruitfully.

One of the important philosophers of the humanist movement was Pietro Pomponazzi (1462–1525). He was a renowned Aristotelian of that period and was a professor of philosophy in Padua University. He relied on Aristotle's view of physics but could not prove the existence of an independent soul. He wrote *On the*

Immortality of the Soul (1516) in which he did not deny the immortality of soul but argued that since the question was insoluble a theory of ethics could be established based on the concept of rewards or punishments after death. Distinguishing between faith and knowledge, he pointed out that what could be true for a philosopher may not be true for a theologian. His work was destroyed on the orders of the court of Inquisition.

Machiavelli was a controversial thinker whose writings aroused contrasting reactions. They were the product of political chaos caused by prolonged warfare beginning with the French invasion of Italy in 1494. In a series of works, Machiavelli wrote what he claimed to be a new Science of Politics. He was born in Florence and was a student of a well-known teacher-scholar of Latin, Paolo da Ronciglione. After the fall of the Savonarola regime in Florence, a new city government was elected. With it Machiavelli rose to prominence. He became head of the Chancery and Secretary to the Foreign Relations Committee of the Republic. He served the Florentine Republic for fourteen years and led several diplomatic missions. He wrote numerous reports and remained in touch with important political leaders. This gave him an opportunity to analyse their politics in his most famous work, *The Prince* (1513). His aim was to show the Medicis the path to greatness. Machiavelli believed that political action depended on three forces – *virtu, necessita* and *forturna*. He did not use the term *virtu* in the same sense as the Christians had done. For him, *virtu* denoted the strength and vigour needed to construct a politically successful society. *Forturna* was shown as the element of chance. He believed that it should remain within the confines of human endeavour and not to be treated as God's providence and must be harnessed to political life. For Machiavelli this meant a struggle to control unpredictable events and for this *virtu* was considered necessary. He regarded political life as a constant struggle in which the opportunities must be exploited by the use of *virtu*. He strongly believed that politics had its own rules of behaviour and that one should counter evil with good. Machiavelli seems to suggest a separation of politics from the Christian faith and religion. For him religious morality does not apply to rulers and that a prince must exploit the weaknesses of his opponent. In fact, no other thinker did more than Machiavelli to overturn all earlier views on the ethical basis of politics. He subordinated morality to political ends. He believed that his contemporary leaders paid little heed to the lessons of history. His other well-known work was his *Discourses On Livy.* It was a treatise on military organization in which he praised the ancient Roman republic as the model for all times. Unlike his contemporary humanists, Machiavelli rejected the method of imitation of great men of the past. He believed that governing is a process that requires different types of skills at different times. Petrarch, an early humanist, had fully believed in the powers of classical wisdom to transform contemporary society. Machiavelli while admitting the value of classical wisdom, emphasized that the rulers must adopt actions in tune with the times.

Christian Humanism in the North

The humanist spirit did not remain confined to the Italian city states. Across the Alps, it travelled to different European cities, particularly those which had kept their doors open to the south. It can be said that the ideas of humanism spread to northern Europe through the trade routes originating from Italy. However, the nature of humanism assumed a different character outside Italy. The northern humanism is often described as the Christian humanism unlike the civic humanism of Italy. In regions outside Italy, the new learning was synthesized with basic Christian beliefs. It is called Christian humanism because at most places, the church, popes and Christian scholars officially sanctioned it. Not only did the church provide patronage, but the subject of study was usually related to Christian themes. Here the rediscovery of man did not necessarily mean abandonment of God and ultimate search for perfection. It focused on the spread of Biblical study and criticism of medieval theology. At most of the centres attention was given to scriptures. The classical learning and Biblical study, according to the humanists outside Italy, would lead to greater harmony between faith and intellect.

The printing press played an important role in the spread of the new learning. From the 1450s there rose a 'print culture' in Europe. Till the invention of printing with movable lead type, the humanists had to copy manuscripts by hand. The introduction of printing provided a practical way to produce books. Johann Gutenberg had developed the printing press at Mainz in Germany and printed about 200 copies of the Bible in 1452–3. It was soon followed by other forms of editions like Psalms, scriptures, devotional books, abridged collection of lives of the saints, theological texts, classical writings and popular literature. The technology of the printing press began to spread in several parts of Europe and it is estimated that by 1500 there were over 1,000 printing presses. The impact of printing was felt everywhere in Europe and print shops became important vehicles of cultural exchange and communication. It marked the end of the competition among the humanists to procure the original manuscripts as multiple prints began to be available at different places. Printing also promoted the cause of the new learning. Famous printers of that time like Aldus Manutius in Venice and Johannes Froben in Basle were closely associated with humanist activities. Several humanists visited their printing shops for editing and proof-reading. Print shops became popular centres for the clerics and laymen to get acquainted with the new humanist ideas on subjects like law, theology, philosophy and science. Multiple copies of texts of even rare manuscripts were made available and the printing press acted as an important tool of the humanist propaganda.

The origins of Christian humanism can be seen in the Low Countries of the north, particularly in the Netherlands. Christian studies provided the impetus. It originated from the mystical spirit of the laymen who were associated with Christian Renaissance. The most famous was the movement of *devotio moderna.* It taught the Christian ideas in the form of spiritual communion with God through Christ. For them Christian life was more important than Christian doctrine. Although it was an orthodox movement, it did not break with the church or deny its role but challenged the scholastic method of reaching religious truth. The order of laymen was founded by Gerard Groote (1340–84) and subsequently influenced by men like Thomas à Kempis (1380–1471) and Wessel Gansfort (1419–89). Members of the *devotio moderna* established schools in different parts and spread Christian ideas based on classical studies and the study of scriptures. It was from such schools that the most famous humanists emerged. The greatest figure among the Christian humanists was Desiderius Erasmus (1466–1536).

Desiderius Erasmus wielded great influence all over Europe through his writings and scholarship. He placed his faith in education rather than the common practices of the Christian church. To his contemporaries he exemplified the humanist effort of making Christianity more purposeful for men on earth. He believed that Christian life had been perverted through unnecessary emphasis on religious observations and dogmas. The influence of Erasmus reached different corners of Europe, and particularly affected the educated people of the sixteenth century, and it was he more than anyone else who reflected the essence of northern humanism to subsequent generations. He provided an intellectual character to Christianity by fusing together learning and piety. Piety for Erasmus was an essential part of humanism. It was an element of the human spirit but was not a part of formal religious observance. He believed that learning was essential to an understanding of theology. He was not so much of a reformer as an intellectual and a critic of contemporary society. He had friends and followers all over Europe from England to Poland, in the Scandinavian countries and Hungary and from Spain to Italy. His role has been variously estimated. His toleration and moderation has been interpreted differently and he has been described as a precursor of the Enlightenment of the eighteenth century. His personal life reveals the tension that existed between his interests and his vocations. He was pushed into monastic life and ordained as a priest. This experience he bitterly regretted as it curbed all opportunities for intellectual activities. His secular taste did not suit the prevalent ideas of the church, nor did his attacks on the church highlighting the distinction between Christian living and Christian doctrine.

The Praise of Folly (1509) was the most widely read book of Erasmus. It made him the 'Prince of Humanists'. This book greatly benefited from the invention of printing. Important printers of that time invited him but his most productive years were spent with Johannes Froben in Basle. This work was written against scholastic pedantry and dogmatism and also against the ignorant and superstitious masses. His other book *Colloquies* raised the subject of religious practices through satire and criticism. It was a collection of popular stories mainly for the students that provided moral lessons and also exhibited brilliant language. It was against superstitious rituals and magic. Another prominent work was *Handbook of a Christian Knight* (1501) which stressed on the value of piety. There were many other works of Erasmus such as *Adiges*, a collection of proverbs from Greek and Roman sources, *Complaint of Peace* which highlighted Christian pacifism, but the most impressive literary production was *Notes on the New Testament* (1505). He spent ten years studying and analysing the early Greek Biblical manuscripts to produce an authoritative text. His explanatory notes and his own Latin translation is regarded as one of the greatest Biblical scholarship of all times. All these works reflect the many-sided intellectual that Erasmus was. He displayed a startling style of Latin prose and wit and dazzled his readers with his verbal expression. His works demonstrate his skill of writing which deftly used irony, sarcasm, symbolism and sharp criticism. His ideas attracted the Catholics as well as Protestants of that time. The extraordinary influence of Erasmus was exerted not only through his brilliant writings but also through his frequent travels and long sojourns in Italy, France, England and Germany.

Cultural developments began in the late-fifteenth century but actually flowered after 1510. English humanism developed as an intellectual and artistic movement with impulses coming from the European Renaissance. Humanism in England assumed the form of 'new learning' and began to influence the field of education and literature. The new humanist learning and the literary activities created a strongly nationalistic literature. It developed after the coming of the Renaissance in France. In fact, the period of High Renaissance in England emerged after a gap of several years. The decade's greatest humanist writer in England was Thomas More (1478–1535). The two great humanists, Erasmus and More, became close friends when the former visited England. However, the two adopted very different paths despite their common interests. More shared with Erasmus a concern for popular piety and a strong disgust towards the corrupt society. While Erasmus came out with a Christian philosophy, Thomas More was a Christian humanist but was not very optimistic about the contemporary society.

Unlike Erasmus, More pursued a public career and served the English state in the highest position as a Chancellor. He was a lawyer by education and wrote a humanistic history of Richard III in the course of his public career. His most famous work was *Utopia* (1516). It was a description of an ideal society on Utopia (an imaginary island). It is about a meeting between an Englishman Morus and an unknown traveller Hythloday. In the course of their discussion, Thomas More is able to present a powerful critique of the contemporary political society and the problems of a humanist in the court of a powerful ruler. In his *Utopia* the state carried out through rigorous discipline, a society which tamed man into ideal members. Interestingly More was trying to find a solution to the ills of an autocratic court by creating an equally dominating state. The essence of the good society for Thomas More was the evolution of money economy and private property. This imaginary picture of an ideal community was a commentary on the glaring abuses of the time such as poverty on the one extreme and idleness and unearned wealth on the other, religious persecution, the senseless wars and an oppressive government. The *Utopia* of More was to provide common goals and larger intellectual pursuits to its members to enable them to practice the natural virtues of wisdom, justice and moderation. In this, Christian life was presented not merely as a personal matter but as an essential part of community living. While More's writings were extremely critical of political values and religious practices, yet he never acted on these utopian principles and remained attached to the public life of the state. When he was the Chancellor of England, his political career came to a sudden halt with the divorce question of Henry VIII and the subsequent break with the papacy. He refused to acknowledge

Henry as the temporal head of the state as the supreme head of the English church and resigned his post. He was eventually imprisoned and executed. However, Thomas More exerted great influence on contemporary scholars and his *Utopia* continued to inspire fellow humanists. Like the Florentine humanists of a century earlier, Thomas More also emphasized the sense of community. He remained a staunch Catholic till the end. There were several other Englishman who showed keen interest in the new learning based on humanist ideas.

Oxford and Cambridge universities became the chief centres of literary activities. In the early period, the emphasis was on literature and instructions. The main fields of English literature of the early-sixteenth century included books of instruction, guides to courtly behaviour and good manners, devotional literature and educational works. John Colet was another well-known figure in the English literary circle. He founded St Paul's school. He undertook a journey to Italy and was greatly impressed by Italian humanism, especially Neoplatonic philosophy. On his return, he emphasized the role of education and became the central figure of the English humanist movement.

Erasmus also influenced Grocyn who tought Divinity and Greek in Oxford and Linacre the English humanist and physician. Many educational works promoted the new learning. These included Sir Thomas Elyot's *Boke Named the Governour* (1531) and Roger Ascham's *Toxophilus* (1545). These publications were based on historical themes. Many of them were in chronicle form, such as Edward Hall's *Union of the Two Noble* and *Illustre Famelies of Lancastre and Yorke*. Edmund Dudley's *Tree of Commonwealth* was a criticism of the contemporary society.

After a gap of almost half a century, there was a sudden revival of English literature from the 1570s, when poetry and drama of exceptional quality began to appear. Hooker emerged as a great prose writer, while Wyatt and Surrey started the new literary movement in the mid-sixteenth century. Their visit to Italy and the influence of the writings of Dante, Petrarch and Eriosto brought new trends into English literature though not without controversies. Surrey was a gifted poet but was executed for treason at the young age of 30. Italian influence on his writings is visible. He successfully introduced the use of blank verse in the English poetry. However, the new trends introduced by Wyatt and Surrey did not bring about immediate change. The great period of Elizabethan literature began with the publication of Edmund Spenser's *Shepheardes Calender* and John Lyly's *Euphues*. Spenser was one of the most gifted poets of the Renaissance period. He had received humanist education and had a deep understanding of classical Italian and French literature. He had complete mastery of English poetry and reflects the fine pastoral scene of the period. He worked continuously for over twenty years for his incomplete masterpiece *The Faerie Queene* (1579) which laid the poetic tradition in England. English literature under the influence of humanism developed drama. Dramas became extremely popular with the people of London and the nobility and the great public demand for dramas explains the sudden outburst of plays in the late-sixteenth century.

The political climate of sixteenth-century England was conducive to literary creations. Christopher Marlowe was a highly gifted poet who turned to writing popular plays. He used history as a source material for his plays and effectively used blank verse for his dramas. Marlowe is regarded as the most talented of the pre-Shakespearean poet-dramatists who made an outstanding contribution to the development of English tragedy. Thomas Kyd was another famous writer. *The Spanish Tragedie* of Kyd was an instant success, capturing the hearts of the sixteenth-century audiences. This story of revenge is well-constructed and adapted to popular requirements. Robert Greene, John Lyly, Ben Johnson, John Fletcher, Thomas Dekker and many others made valuable contributions in the sphere of English literature.

Among the many writers, though not strictly in the category of the humanists, was William Shakespeare. He used historical themes and romantic figures in his literary creations. His spirit and style reflected the spirit of Renaissance. He revealed his genius through his poetry, sonnets and plays and is regarded by many as the greatest literary figure of England. His works revealed an amazing variety. He showed his competence as a playwright of comedy as well as tragedy, sentiment and fantasy. He selected historical figures and made imaginary figures real. Shakespeare is believed to have written as many as thirty-six plays but each play was distinct on grounds of subject and characters. Through history, he reveals a vision of the nation itself rather than the rulers. The sway of the Renaissance ideas on English education was quite deep. This is evident from the views of Roger Ascham, one of the foremost educationists of that period. He was tutor to princess Elizabeth and transformed her into one of the most cultivated, widely read and multi-lingual sovereigns of her age.

France was more familiar with the ideas of the Italian Renaissance and with its scholarly artistic work than any other part of Europe. This was mainly due to the French military invasions of Italy which brought thousands of French men in direct contact with Italy. This effect influenced to some extent the style and subject of French literature. Though French humanism remained essentially Christian as distinct from the civic humanism of the Italian states, French literature proved more receptive to the Italian influence. In France, it was Lefèvre d'Étaples who showed his concern for society by directly addressing it with his scholarship. Another important humanist figure was Guillaume Budé, a contemporary of Lefèvre. He studied at the university of Paris and later visited the Platonic Academy at Padua. He was interested in the works of Aristotle. He was a peculiar mixture of Christian mysticism of the Middle Ages and the classical learning of Plato and Aristotle. His major work *Quintuplex Psalter* (1509) presents a unique combination of classical and Christian elements. The greatest French poet of the Renaissance period was Rabelais. He was a physician by profession but in his youth he had accumulated vast knowledge of classical and Italian literature. Another major work of that time was *Defense and Ennoblement of the French Language* written by Du Bellay. It ran into several editions and translations. There were a number of scholars who followed the literary style of the Italians. This book of Du Bellay called for the restructuring of the French poetry based on the study of classical and Italian verse. Ronsard was a leading young poet of the *Pléiade* a name given to a group of sixteenth-century French Renaissance poets. He wrote poetry in many forms but he could not complete his epic work. In the beginning people laughed at his original style but subsequently they began to not only appreciate but follow him.

In Spain, Boscan and Gacilaso de La Vega popularized Italians sonnets and introduced new forms of classical Latin poetry. The humanist movement in Spain remained an orthodox form of Christian humanism and was led by Cardinal Ximenes de Cisneros. Ximenes studied law and theology at the University of Salamanca and began his career as an ecclesiastic. He soon rose in position in the Spanish church. He was involved in the new learning or the Renaissance philosophy of education. He founded the university of Alcala that had provided trained candidates for higher positions in the church. His education programme concentrated on theology, natural philosophy, law, Latin, Greek and Hebrew. There were some other scholars familiar with humanist ideas such as Lucio Marineyo, Siculo and Martin. Humanism in Spain assumed an orthodox form and was primarily used to improve the content of education of church officials to restore the prestige of the church and to improve the intellectual calibre of the priests. In other words, the aim was to raise the stature of the Spanish church. The greatest work from Portugal in this period was *The Lusiads*, an epic poem by Luis Vaz de Camões. It was a form of epic poem.

Unlike humanism in England, France and Spain where it remained basically a movement for new learning and educational reforms and was led by important scholars and leaders of the church, German humanism assumed a distinct character. In the western states of Europe, the humanist programme continued within the inherited framework of church and society but in Germany it developed an anti-Roman character. Germany lacked an effective central authority and the church in every state enjoyed relative economic and political strength. The golden age of medieval universities came quite late in Germany compared to France or England. The universities had developed a strong scholastic tradition that influenced intellectual and religious life. On the origins of German humanism, there are two different opinions. One common viewpoint is that attempts at religious reforms began with movements in the form of *devotio moderna* and schools of *brotherhood* that tried to concentrate on piety. The grounds for humanist movement were prepared by them while the source of humanist ideas came from Italy. The second view is presented by some recent writers (Robert Black, p. 17) who contend that although by 1500 humanism had penetrated almost all the universities of Germany and had successfully reduced the educational domination of medieval scholasticism, its success was not built on indigenous foundations of movements like *devotio moderna*. For them, German humanism was an Italian import, introduced by scholars and patrons who had themselves studied in the Italian centres. The progress of German humanism is linked to the spread of Reformation and the role of secular authorities. The German humanists had closer connection with university life than they had in Italy. These ideas spread faster because of the existence of printing presses in the important cities of Germany. The humanist ideas found support at the courts and among the bishops. However, the emergence of humanism in the German states converted the universities into battlegrounds between scholastic and humanist ideas. Germany had already become a storm centre of religious controversy with the coming of Martin Luther. This was followed by a period of civil war. The conflict between the scholastics and the supporters of humanism was sharpened because of these events. The University of Heidelburg became the centre of humanist learning where the indigenous model of reform was introduced. Two important branches of intellectual activities developed. The first was led by Johannes Reuchlin (1455–1522) at Wurttenberg. To study the Christian sources in original, he embarked on the study of Jewish mystical writings. He was supported in his efforts by the humanists. Johannes Pfefferkorn, a Dominicon priest who opposed Reuchlin's use of Jewish traditions in the study of Christian theology, led the second branch. This became a battle between the humanists and the scholastics. Among the earliest of the famous German humanist scholars was Johannes Wessel. He received his humanist training in Italy and began teaching Greek at Heidelburg. He was succeeded by Rudolph Agricola and was considered the father of German humanism. During the sixteenth century, a group of humanists centred round Konrad Mutian at the University of Erfurst. This centre produced a great number of younger humanists. The humanists at this place hardly did anything academic nor were they involved in formal teaching but they created a critical attitude towards the church establishment. Thus German humanism arose out of a decentralized political system and had support from a large number of people in the cities and towns who had suffered because of socio-economic changes. The humanist movement increasingly concentrated on reforms of political society and attacks on the papacy, thereby creating a congenial atmosphere for religious reformation.

Humanism in northern Europe was different from the Italian civic humanism. The cities of northern Europe, although considerably rich and prosperous and involved in the international trade, could not enjoy the kind of autonomy which cities like Florence or Venice had enjoyed. The cities of northern Europe remained subordinate to state authority and did not enjoy civic pride. The dominant feudal structure of the northern states had increased the role of the church in social life. The church was the centre and patron of education and could tolerate only specific reforms. Hence, the northern humanism tended to specialize in theological and scriptural studies. Moral and religious reforms formed the core of the movement. It gave stimulus to indigenous cultural movements, and as such its impact appears to be more durable. They were more interested in building educational institutions and promoting learning in accordance with local customs and history. The prosperity of the Italian cities and the strength of its urban society kindled a secular spirit and created a favourable environment for the promotion of art and literature. Italian humanism was therefore much broader in scope and range of humanist activities.

The humanist movement on both sides of the Alps, i.e. in the Italian cities as well as in the rest of Europe, created new attitudes and broadened mental horizons of the people but their immediate influence was confined to a limited section of society. Even in the hearts and minds of many individual humanists the old and the new existed side by side. A person of the stature of Lorenzo de Medici had written ribald drinking songs on the one hand, and mystical poems of religious devotion to the saints, on the other. This led many to believe that humanism was a germinal period of modernism. John Stephens goes to the extent of saying that the humanists were noisy and self-important officials and had little concern about ideas. They worked for the princes and the civic governments and their chief work was to draft letters and speeches, write moral treatises and histories to express civic consciousness. They had not yet found a system of scientific concepts and were suspended between faith and knowledge. Recent studies of humanism have brought out the darker side of its character such as the belief in magic and views on women.

While discussing the achievements of the humanists, one must admit that many humanists displayed extraordinary skill as professional scribes and copyists and reformed the script to its modern form from the Gothic that dominated Europe in the thirteenth and fourteenth centuries (Robert Black, p. 76). By introducing cursive writing, the humanists created the modern Italian script. However, their efforts to revive Latin did not achieve full success. Some of the humanist writings, particularly the philological study of the classical texts of Leonardo Bruni, applied critical techniques to historical study. In the field of grammar, the humanists of the fifteenth century changed the Latin curriculum of the Middle Ages in a relatively short period of about fifty years and brought about an academic revolution of great significance. Recent writings on this subject emphasize that this transformation was not so sudden, rather it was much more complex and gradual. The humanists through their activities promoted civic culture that was more secular and human, though not necessarily less religious. Whether this was an age of human dignity or that of misery of human conditions as portrayed by Fazio and Poggio, remains an inconclusive debate.

Humanism and Women

Some historians believe that the status of upper-class women declined during the Renaissance. A study of their role in society in the High Middle Ages and in the fifteenth and sixteenth centuries, the nature of work they performed, their rights to property, and their political powers indicates that women in the age of Renaissance enjoyed fewer rights than they did in the earlier periods. It is interesting to note that the advocates of reform and human dignity showed little concern for women. Their attitude towards women and their education remained ambivalent, although they did not openly deny the usefulness of good education for women. At the same time, they never wished that women should achieve those standards which they suggested for men. The pursuit of virtue recommended for man was not considered desirable for women because it was believed that this would drive them away from family responsibilities. Throughout Europe very few women got a chance to contribute to the humanist movement and they usually belonged to the ruling families—Princess Mary Tudor and Elizabeth of England, Marguerite of Navarre and Catherine de Medici of France. Even the princesses were not expected to participate fully in the humanist programmes. The Italian humanists prohibited women, including the rulers, to study rhetoric and other humanist subjects. They believed that all studies should stop once a woman was married. If she still wished to continue her studies, the only avenue left for her was to join a convent or lead a life of seclusion. Humanists of the stature of Thomas More emphasized Christian reading for women instead of pagan classics because the study of satires and comedies contained immoral ideas. All these restrictive views, however, did not deter some enthusiastic women from participating in humanist learning and excel in some of the humanist virtues. At the same time, it must be remembered that their number was very small and most of them belonged to the highest strata of society.

In Italy, during the fifteenth century, Christine de Pizan, daughter of an Italian physician was encouraged to learn classical languages by her father and later by her husband. After their death, she focused her attention on academic writings. She lived at the French court where she wrote on Joan of Arc and a book on education. But her famous work was *The Book of the City of the Ladies* (1405) in which she counters the arguments of men that women were inferior to men and were incapable of delivering moral judgement. Christine argued that lack of education in women was the root cause of their inferiority. Isotta Nogarola of Verona was another humanist. She possessed great literary skill and was a gifted writer but the reaction of contemporary male humanists towards her works was not only discouraging but extremely harsh.

In England, the daughters of Thomas More, the great humanist scholar, were considered highly educated and cultured. They acquired knowledge from their tutors and their father and through self-study, as they could not enter humanist academies. Humanist ideas in England came from Italy and influenced a small group of women, mainly from elite families, who began receiving humanist education. They searched for works on philosophy, theology and poetry and studied translations of the ancient books. Margaret wrote a number of original Latin orations besides poems and treatises. Through her English translation of Erasmus's work she gained great respect and reputation but she never made any public statements or published her original works. On some issues she had strong disagreement with her father, Thomas More.

The French humanist women displayed their learning and qualities publicly despite general skepticism on the part of men. Marguerite of Navarre, sister of the French ruler Francis I, developed her own court where she promoted the education of women. She espoused the cause of religious reforms in her writings. A few humanist women attended her court and participated in intellectual activities. They included English noble women such as Mary, Anne Boleyn and the future queen of France, Catherine de Medici. She wrote *Heptameron* which contained seventy-three stories. It was published after her death and was later translated into English. Although she did not advocate women's education nor demand better social status for them she did criticize the traditional institution of marriage. Some feminist writers like Hélisenne de Crenne, Madeleine Neveu des Roches and Marie Le Jars Gourney insisted on the importance of women in any given society but regarded the institution of marriage as a threat to their independence. Boccaccio in his *Concerning Famous Women* provided a collection of 104 outstanding women from antiquity as models for contemporary women. It was a humanist treatise drawn from the writings of ancient Greek and Roman literature. These women were admired for their traditional virtues like chastity, obedience, etc. Marguerite, like Boccaccio, also adopted the dialogue form with male and female speakers each having an equal share in the narration. However, Christine de Pizan wrote a strong riposte in her *The Book of the City of the Ladies* (1405) and highlighted the contributions of women to the intellectual and political life of Europe. Among the other French women who displayed humanist traits were Jeanne d'Albret, Renée de France, Jacqueline Longwy and Duchesse de Montpensier. There were a few radical types such as Louise Lavé who urged women not to restrict themselves to the domestic setting. She published a collection on romantic love and showed familiarity with classical literature and rhetoric. The great Protestant reformer John Calvin made derogatory remarks against her. The writings of women scholars suggest that Isabella, the Duchess of Mantua, was another woman who had a number of humanists and artists in her court. However, there was a general belief among men that women could not produce literary or artistic works of great quality. Women were discouraged to display virtues of civic humanism. Some women did try to learn classical languages and philosophy but they were exceptions rather than the rule.

Basing her argument on the French experience, Cathleen M. Bauschatz suggests that the introduction of the printing press in the late-fifteenth century brought books and reading material to upper class homes. The latter were earlier confined to castles and monasteries. As some of the wives and daughters of printers were active in the printing business, humanist ideas penetrated their homes despite the exclusion of women from the humanist education programme (Sonya Stephens, ed., *A History of Women's Writing in France*, 2000). However, the role of women in the Renaissance remained extremely restricted because they rarely received the education that would encourage them to write. Moreover, they were not encouraged to perform public roles as bureaucrats, administrators or professors. The pre-modern society placed a complete check on their participation in the public domain. Very few women could follow professional careers in art as it required residential apprenticeship with an established master. The guilds also discouraged women to enter its membership. Only those women with artist fathers or brothers, such as Susanna Horenbout of Ghent, Fede Galizia of Milan or Elisabetta Sirani had limited opportunities in the world of art. Among the prominent categories of women, the Renaissance courts mention the role of courtesans. This depiction brings out the darker side of the Renaissance society. Prostitution seemed to have flourished in the Italian courtly society to provide serevices to wealthy and rich men. Some contemporary records suggest that sex workers constituted nearly a tenth of Venetian population and perhaps more in Rome (*Encyclopedia of Women in the Renaissance*, p. 102). Many Renaissance paintings portrayed these courtesans in nude or semi-clothed visuals and artists used them as models. They were admired by some but they faced indignities and humiliation as well. They were the most visible women in the Renaissance society.

The Visual Art

Visual art was popular in Renaissance Italy as it was considered a symbolic language. It was seen as a medium of communication with social, spiritual and political values. During the Renaissance it possessed an inner power and became a matter of civic pride. The exterior of the urban centres came to be measured in artistic terms. According to Peter Burke, the arts between 1350 and 1550 were transformed in two ways – through a return to nature and through a return to antiquity. The former influenced the field of painting while the latter determined the trends in architecture.

Humanism as a cultural movement had great impact in creating interest in art, architecture and music. The aim of humanism was to perfect all forms of art and scholarship. The emancipation of man and the focus on the dignity of men created an atmosphere of intellectual freedom and individual expression. The recovery of the secular and humane philosophy of Greece and Rome not only led to individualism but promoted new trends and styles in the sphere of art. The architects, sculptors and painters broke away from the Byzantine Gothic patterns and indulged in sweeping, independent inner expressions. The craze of classics and the love of beauty became the most striking features of Italian Renaissance.

The beginning of some new styles in Italian art can be located in the works of artists like Giotto di Bondone of Florence (1267–

1337) in the late-thirteenth and early-fourteenth centuries. Boccaccio described him as the founder of a new art. The illustrious poet Dante cited Giotto in his *Divine Comedy* as the greatest living artist. His reputation spread rapidly and he came to be described as the founder of Renaissance painting. He revived the beauty of classical art by abandoning the conventional and the rigid forms of Byzantine art. Instead, he tried to capture the appearance of the world as he saw it. Compared to the late fully-developed form of art during the High Renaissance, Giotto's block like figures and rudimentary landscapes did not look very realistic. What was original in his work was his ability to extract from nature its essential forms and reproduce them in a simple and expressive way. He was in great demand in his time and was patronized by prosperous bankers like Peruri, Bardi and by King Robert of Anjou. Among his important works were the frescoes in the Upper Church of the Basilica of San Francesco d'Assisi, Arena Chapel in Padua, Florence Cathedral and his paintings included the *Massacre of the Innocents*, the *Monument of Truth*, the *Lamentations*, the *Betrayal of Christ* and the *Death of Saint Francis*. All these works displayed his power of expression of human emotions and that of presenting narrative details.

The art that developed after Giotto successfully established a more realistic relationship between figures and landscapes. Florence became the most important centre of artistic creations. In no other city was the feeling of confidence and hope more intense than in this city of wealthy merchants. The revolutionary trends seen in the artistic developments during the Renaissance is evident from the works of Lorenzo Ghiberti (1378–1455), Filippo Brunelleschi (1377–1446), Masaccio (1401–28) and Donatello (1386?–1466). Their sculpture, architecture and paintings were based on experiments and in the process they brought about visual representation of space through the laws of perspective. This experimental trend during the Renaissance went in two directions. The first emphasized the mathematical side of painting such as working out laws of perspective, organization of outdoor space and the use of light and shade. Perspective implies representing three-dimensional objects on a two-dimensional plane. It is based on the formulation that as parallel lines recede into the distance, they seem to converge. The second involved the investigation of movements of the human anatomy. Antonio painted a realistic portrait of the human body under stress.

Ghiberti was commissioned to design the door panels of a baptistery in Florence. On the bronze doors he presented stories from the New Testament and the Old Testament by using a new technique of linear perspective and created a sense of space in his classically inspired figures. His work gained instant fame. Michelangelo describes those doors 'as the Doors of Paradise'. In this work, Ghiberti had succeeded in securing the commission by ousting another famous sculptor, Filippo Brunelleschi, who left sculpture to become the greatest architect of the Renaissance period.

Masaccio's trinity in the Florentine church depicts a new style of painting experimenting with linear perspectives. He was followed by a number of new artists who raised the art of painting to new heights. Sandro Botticelli (1445–1510) added classical symbolism in his famous works – the *Birth of Venus* and *Springtime*. These were painted for the house of Medici and were based on Neoplatonic symbolism of truth, beauty and humanity.

Among the young Florentine artists and architects, the name of Filippo Brunelleschi (1377–1446) stands out. After Giotti, Brunelleschi showed his brilliance in imparting a sense of orderly coherence. He was employed to complete the cathedral of Florence, a Gothic structure. The Florentines had wanted their cathedral to be crowned by an imposing cupola which no artists had been able to do as it required spanning the immense face between the pillars on which this cupola was to be created. Brunelleschi successfully devised a method for this. He devised new styles in architecture in which the classical models were freely used to create new forms of harmony and beauty. It is said that he travelled to Rome and personally studied the ruins of the temples and palaces and made sketches of their ornamentation and forms. For the next few centuries, architects of Europe and America adopted his classical forms – columns and pediments. At the same time, his work was very different from the past as it combined columns, pilasters and arches in his own style to produce an effect of light and shade. His framing of the doors clearly show his mastery of the ancient structures. His architecture was not mere imitation of the past. His use of the law of perspective was based on mathematics by which it was shown that the size of the object diminishes as they recede in the background. Brunelleschi's experiments and creations demonstrated the significance of proportion. His studies on perspective proved vital to the development of Renaissance art.

Just as Brunelleschi was the pioneer architect, Donatello was the greatest sculptor. His work broke new grounds. His creations were full of energy and spirit. There was realism and vigour as is evident from his bronze statue of David. Donatello tried to replace the gentle refineness of his predecessors by a new and vigorous study of nature. He encouraged the study of anatomy and he also believed that beauty was a matter of proportion. This attitude of the Renaissance artists towards beauty was one of the key features of Renaissance art.

High Renaissance

The last decade of the fifteenth century marked the beginning of major developments in the field of Italian art. The period from about 1490–1520 is described as the 'High Renaissance'. In early Renaissance, the art of the ancient period was imitated naively and was held up as a source of beauty and accurate representation. In the period of the 'High Renaissance' this art was scientifically and critically analysed. The new ideas were particularly understood and appreciated by the educated humanists and the elite of the city-states. In fact, the change particularly in the field of painting is noticeable from around 1450s. The different disciplines such as the 'universal man' of the humanists' philology, technique of art and scientific theory, anatomy, the use of geometry to express a sense of proportion, antiquity and rhetoric were getting interlocked and became the hallmark of the Renaissance period.

Art and architecture in the period of the 'High Renaissance' concentrated on visual as well as theoretical conquest of nature. It expressed the skill and genius of the individuals such as Leonardo da Vinci, Michelangelo, Raphael, Bramante and many others. Recent interpretations of Renaissance art have brought out two divergent views. The first emphasizes the truly classical quality of this style, which combined the Greek art of the fifth and fourth century BC with the spiritual and formal dignity, harmony and equipoise that had never been equalled in the history of post-classical art. It showed individual interest of the artists in worldly beauty represented in human forms along with a reliance on classical models. The second view emphasizes that fields like architecture never reproduced the ancient models. They showed greater awareness of reality of their age than the scholars of humanism. They were willing to develop past traditions not as imitators but as creators. Although architecture of this period was based on classical principles, the ornamentation was done according to contemporary tastes. According to art historian A. Wittkower, the sources of important motifs of Renaissance architecture were taken from antiquity, medieval and Byzantine periods. The arches on columns were borrowed directly or indirectly from the Christian basilicas, which in turn were dependent on the art of late-classical structures. The cylindrical exteriors in northern Italy in the centrally planned arches were adopted and transformed from the tradition of medieval baptisteries. The typical Renaissance vaults, the high domes and the transition between square crossing and circular shape of the domes were influenced by the Byzantine style. The chief ideals of Renaissance architecture were reflected in the perfection of varied sources through symmetry and regularity of simple geometrical shapes, integrity of isolated masses and clarity of articulation (see figs., p. 125). City planning and garden design were the two architectural forms which developed during the High Renaissance. The tradition of Alberti was maintained though the use of the rules of proportion. Harmony and balance was a striking feature of the Renaissance art. In the sphere of painting, because of the absence of past models, art subjects were developed from Greek and Roman mythology and from historical themes. Renaissance paintings used a few decorative details but these were in no way imitative. Paintings reflected maturity and elegance that had come through continuous experiments and intensity of expression.

Renaissance Architecture

An Italian sixteenth-century villa: the Villa Rotonda near Vicenza.
Designed by Pallidio, 1550.

High Renaissance in Italy (1490s–1520s) was dominated by the works of three great artists – Leonardo da Vinci, Michelangelo and Raphael. They created new standards in the world of art. Leonardo da Vinci (1452–1519) was the first such figure, probably the greatest artist produced by Florence, who represented the period of High Renaissance. He is regarded as the most versatile genius who personified in himself the diverse qualities of a painter, architect, engineer, musician, mathematician, military and hydraulic engineer, poet and scientist. He came from a low social background and began his life from an artist's shop but succeeded in obtaining the patronage of Lorenzo de Medici. He continued the tradition of experimentation initiated by the earlier artists, particularly Brunelleschi. His work was based on an intensive study of human anatomy and large-scale experiments that included dissection of the human body. His creations are divided into four separate periods. He began his career in Florence and worked there till 1482, and then he moved to Milan and stayed there till 1499, when the French forces invaded the city. He returned to Florence and worked there till 1506, had a short stay in Milan before finally accepting the invitation of the French king, Francis I, where he lived and worked till his death. He believed in the most accurate imitation of nature and he himself created his works on the study of nature. His analysis of human anatomy was remarkable as it was based on his personal experiments of dissection of human corpses. His love for nature was close to worship. Among his masterpieces were the *Virgin of the Rocks*, the *Last Supper* and *Mona Lisa* (*La Gioconda*, also written as *La Joconda*). His creations depicted not only his extraordinary technical skill and his understanding of science but also his sense of geometrical composition. The smallest object in a painting is presented with accurate detail. The *Last Supper*, was painted on the walls of a refectory in Milan. Every character in this painting reveals an emotion as the painting concerns the betrayal of Jesus Christ. *Mona Lisa* has become a legendary painting and a thing of eternal beauty. The treatment of main and secondary characters, the sense of composition and the use of light and shade are the hallmarks of da Vinci's art. As an architect, he built the Medici residence and the Milan cathedral. In 1883, a notebook was discovered containing the sketches of human anatomy and some other drawings. It depicted his scientific mind as it contained blueprints and plans of looms, spinning wheel and even an aeroplane (see fig., p. 128).

Another figure of great stature of the High Renaissance period was Michelangelo Buonarroti (1475–1564). Like da Vinci, he was also from Florence. Where da Vinci was a naturalist, Buonarroti was an idealist and preferred expressing abstract truths. He was a Tuscan, belonging to a family of bankers and was proud of his lineage. He was also a multifaceted genius – a painter, sculptor, architect and a poet – and possessed an extraordinary power of understanding the unseen truth.

Michelangelo beautifully expressed the humanist fascination for man's potential. He depicted human figures, particularly the male as strong and powerful character. Princes and popes outbid each other to obtain his services. The city authorities of Florence honoured the two greatest legends – Leonardo and Michelangelo, by inviting them to paint a story from the city's history on the walls of the council chamber of the Town Hall. It was a great moment in the history of art but soon Michelangelo had to leave for Rome on the invitation of the Pope to make a gigantic mausoleum. Michelangelo was temperamental and short tempered which became worse with age. He was admired and feared for his temperamental outbursts and unrestrained independence. He was commissioned to build the Pope's tomb but the work was constantly disrupted due to his other commitments. His work on the tomb lasted nearly forty years, affected by the Sack of Rome and the Reformation. He left the work assigned to him by Pope Jullius II but was subsequently convinced by the Pope to return after a gap of time. Hence his work represented two different artistic styles and presentation of human condition due to frequent interruptions. His greatest achievement in painting was the ceiling of the Sistine Chapel (1508–12). It depicted a scene from the Book of Genesis, presenting a concentration of paintings at a single location. While maintaining his commitment to the Greek style, he retained the principles of harmony, solidarity and dignity. His famous art piece in the form of the *Last Judgment* was a fresco on the altar wall of the Sistine Chapel. It placed Michelangelo at a height that no artist

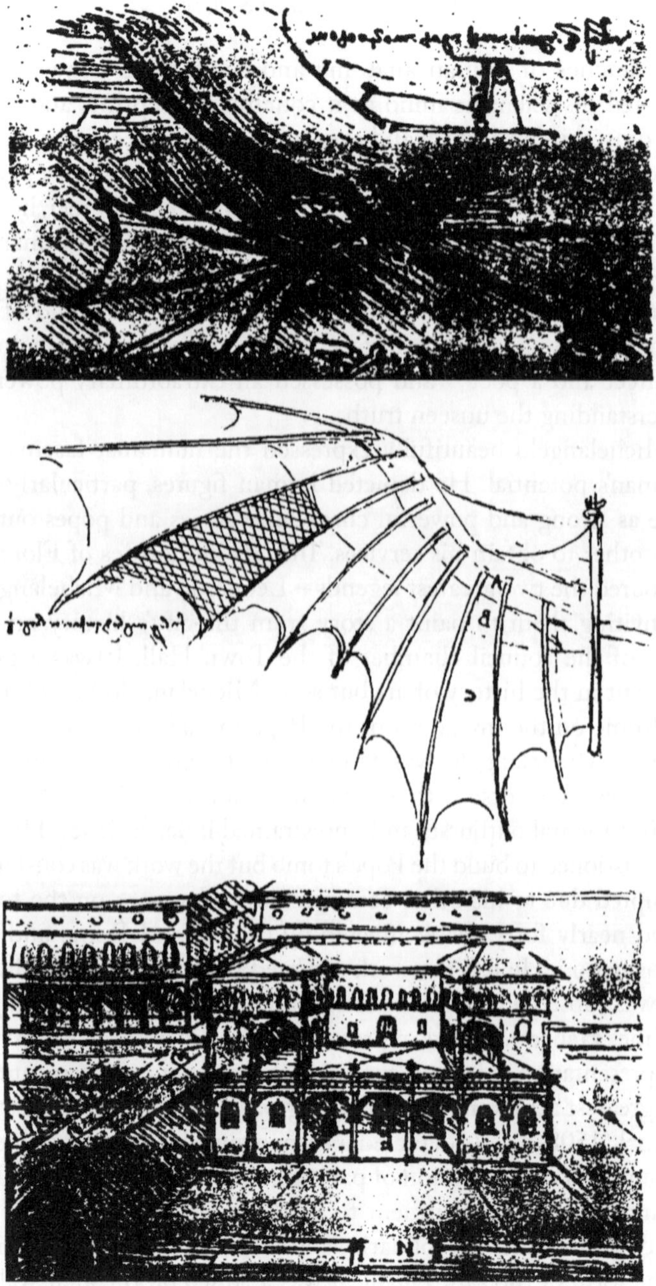

Sketches of Leonardo da Vinci

had reached before. Changes in his life and mood seem to have had enormous effect on his work. However, he could never complete the tomb that had brought him to Rome. Financing such a gigantic project as St Peter's Church needed massive funds. Pope Julius appealed to monarchs, nobles and bishops for funds throughout Europe and sold indulgences to create funds. It is an irony that this issue lighted the spark of Protestant movement. Besides, Michelangelo's project was seriously interrupted in 1527 by the invasion of Rome by Charles V, the Holy Roman Emperor. It caused complete devastation of the city and created financial problems. Michelangelo is also remembered as a talented poet. He wrote a large number of poems, particularly love poems consisting of 343 sonnets, madrigals and capitoli (satirical pieces). As a sculptor, his greatest creations were the *Rebellious Slave* and *David*. The latter is a statue 5.5 meter in height and presents the best possible expression of beauty of the male figure. It was placed in front of the Florence City Hall to display the humanistic values of the city. The other creations included *Madonna of the Stairs*, *Battle of Centaurs*, *Madonna and Child*, *Apollo*, *Moses* and *Victory*. As an architect he created the Chapel of Leo X and St Peter's Dome.

When the two great artists of Florence, Leonardo and Michelangelo, were competing with each other, another great artist had emerged from the city of Urbino. He was Raphael Sanzio (1483–1520). He was a pupil of the 'Umbrian School' and had learned his art from a well-known artist of that region Pietro Perugino. He had attained mastery in painting altar pieces. In a short span, Raphael created an important place for himself in the world of art. He liked painting characters, which were beautiful, intelligent and noble. Raphael died at the age of thirty-seven but his short life is full of diverse and great artistic achievements. He designed many buildings and studied the ruins of Rome. He established contacts with the great dignitaries and scholars of his period, and was greatly respected in the Papal court. He painted a fresco in the villa of a prosperous banker Agostino Chigi based on a verse from a Florentine poet. His art reflects not only the quality of composition but also the beauty of figures, a sincere portrayal of nature. He is also known for his Tapestry cartoons and Madonna paintings. Madonna del Granduca was a painting based on classical form and was regarded by several generations as a standard of perfection. It reflected the tender feelings of the artist as he painted the child Christ. He also decorated the walls with frescos and painted the ceilings of various rooms in the Vatican which displayed his perfect mastery of design and balanced composition. His paintings present a synthesis of classical learning and experimentation.

Thus the great Italian masters represented concrete achievements by the discovery of scientific perspective, the knowledge of anatomy to create beautiful human forms, a knowledge of classical forms representing dignity and sense of proportion, and frequent use of geometry in artistic creations. One of the most noticeable features of the Renaissance paintings and sculpture was the creation of nude human forms because humanists considered man to be the greatest and the most beautiful creation of God.

Renaissance Art Outside Italy

As humanism in northern Europe developed its own characteristics, the artistic developments outside Italy were often influenced by Italian art but the peculiarities of different regions also determined the style and the subject of artistic creations. Gombrich in his work, *A Crisis of Art,* suggests that in northern countries such as Germany, Holland and England, the artists were confronted with a real crisis – the question whether painting could or should be continued at all. This crisis was brought about by the Reformation as many Protestants objected to pictures or statues of saints in the church because these were considered symbols of popish idolatry. As a result artists lost an important sphere of patronage. The staunch Calvinists objected to all forms of display and decoration, even in the form of art. Moreover, even the style of buildings in the north was not suited to the large fresco decorations, as developed in the Italian palaces. Artistic creations outside Italy, therefore, were restricted to paintings. However, the development of art prior to the religious turmoil of the sixteenth century attained high standards in certain parts of Europe.

An important centre of art and the Renaissance culture developed in the court of Burgundy. It was a small duchy which was trying to free itself of French control. During the mid-fifteenth century, a number of courtiers and scholars, artists and musicians visited this court. The Burgundian dukes invited a number of great artists and architects. A Dutch sculptor, Claus Slutar (1350–1406), was commissioned to decorate the Convent of Champmol. The most famous artist in this court was Jan van Eyck (1390–1441). He was particularly known for his portrait paintings. He painted a number of courtiers and even Italian artists appreciated his work. However, he was not as concerned with perspective or figures as were the Italian artists.

Another centre of art developed in the Netherlands. Jerome Hieronymus Bosch (1450–1516) was a famous painter who exhibited astonishing imagination and even in his religious subjects, he focused not on the holy figures but on the mass of ordinary things. He created caricatures of human sinfulness and depicted the cruelties of selfishness. A well-known artist of the Netherlands was Rembrandt van Rijn (1606–67). As this was the period of Dutch resistance to the Spanish rule and the time of bourgeois victory, the artistic themes also depicted this aspect of political life. Merchant oligarchs dominated the region. This Dutch artist was overwhelmed with orders but he concentrated on depicting ordinary people, their character and emotions, and religious themes. He earned a name for portrait paintings and is also believed to have made nearly a hundred self-portraits.

Albrecht Durer (1471–1528) was another great artist of the northern Renaissance. He was the son of a distinguished master goldsmith who came from Hungary and decided to settle in the city of Nuremberg in Germany. He displayed an amazing gift for drawing and specialized in woodcut illustrations. He travelled to distant regions, including Basle in Switzerland, to perfect his art. Nuremberg was an important centre of book trade and he made woodcuts for some books. He made woodcuts and exquisite engravings of religious themes. He also undertook a trip to northern Italy to acquire technical knowledge. Durer not only gained inspiration from the Italians but he himself influenced them through his engravings and woodcuts. His technique of engraving was greatly influenced by Marcantonio Raimondi (1475–1534), the famous engraver. His landscapes inspired several Italian painters. Durer experimented in many media and is known for his beautiful water colour paintings of animals and plant life. His art is a blend of northern and southern traditions, a combination of melancholy and divine passion. He made several self-portraits by looking into the mirror and his famous paintings includes *Virgin and Child, Adam,* the *Fall of Man,* the *Feast of the Rose Garden* and the *Self Portrait.* The woodcut technique was already popular in Germany but it reached new heights of expressiveness in the works of Durer. His figures had a three-dimensional thrust which was not seen in earlier woodcuts. It seems he borrowed the use of perspective from the Italians. Like Italian artists he displayed a fascination for human nude forms but his nudes were depicted with fig leaves respecting the conservative traditions of northern Europe. His treatises on proportions and perspective appeared in, *Teaching of Measurement,* in 1532, which was later translated into Latin. Probably the Christian ideals of Erasmus had a strong influence on his style.

Among the second generation of Renaissance artists, one can include the name of Hans Holbein (1497–1543), a German artist who left Germany because of the religious turmoil of the Reformation. He settled in London, and became the court painter of Henry VIII, and died there of plague. In England, his artistic scope remained limited. The task of the court painter was not to paint Madonnas or objects of natural beauty. His job was to design jewellery and royal furniture, costumes and suits for pageantries, decorate royal palaces and its halls and to display art patterns on royal weapons. Holbein was an astute and ambitious painter. He concentrated on portrait painting, which was a popular form of art in England. He had developed close friendship with Erasmus on whose recommendations he stayed with Thomas More. He made portraits of both these personalities. He was a skilled miniature painter as well and achieved almost photographic realism in his paintings. Among his famous paintings were *Thomas More*, the *Ambassadors* and *King Henry VIII.*

The Renaissance in France assumed a distinct character of its own. Louis XII and Francis I were outstanding patrons of scholarship and art. In 1515 Francis had led an army to Marigneno and conquered Milan. This gave him an opportunity to see the great masterpieces, including da Vinci's paintings. Next year he sent an invitation to the ageing da Vinci. The great Italian master was promised 7,000 pieces of gold and a palace of his own choice in any region of France. Francis succeeded in inviting a large gathering of artists and architects. The Dutch portrait painter John Clouet also lived in France to add to the French art collection. Francis brought many other Italian painters – Andrea del Sarto, Benvenuto Cellini, Il Rosso and Francesco Primaticcio – to decorate the walls of his palace with frescos. The distinctive architecture in France was reflected in the chateaux built along Loire River. Francis and his nobles constructed the famous Chateaux of Amboise, Chambord and Chenonceaux. These structures combined the gothic, which was extremely popular in late medieval France, with the new Renaissance architecture stressing on classical horizontality. On the other hand, the new royal palaces of the Louvre in Paris (designed by Pierre Lescot) and Fontainebleau near Paris were some magnificent examples of Renaissance structures. The Louvre displayed a close resemblance to the Italian classical style of architecture. The life in a chateau (castle) created an ideal courtly society of rich culture that Castiglione had envisaged.

During the Renaissance, attention was paid to gardening and horticulture. Crescenzio, a senator of Bologna, wrote on rural affairs and gardening in the early part of the fourteenth century that was published in Florence in 1471. The first botanical garden was made at Pisa in 1543 and another at Padua in 1545. Although, the art of gardening developed first in Italy, it attained perfection in Holland. The garden of Leiden began in 1577 in which new plants were introduced. The captains of outward-bound ships were directed to bring seeds and plants from all parts of the world and soon the garden boasted of 6,000 species of plants. A few years later, France had also developed a grand garden at Montpelier.

Music

While Italy was a source of inspiration in the field of art and architecture, the trend was quite opposite in the sphere of music. The development of music set up new standard in northern Europe, particularly in Flanders. In the pre-Renaissance period experiments in music were carried out in Italy and France by composers such as Francesco Landini (1324–97) and Guillaume Machaut (1300–77). They had created a school of music called *Ars Nova*. However, between 1450 and 1600, great strides were made in polyphony. The flow was from northern Europe towards Italy. The rising interest in music was not confined to any single place but could be seen in several courts of northern Europe. Subsequently it spread to the Italian states where the northern music was not only admired but also developed through experiments and new techniques.

The technique of polyphonic music was developed by a group of Flemish masters during the second half of the fifteenth century. It came to be known as the second Flemish school. The first had developed at the court of Burgundy. Dufay was another leading composer, greatly admired by the Italians, who played at the council of Constance. He established in the Netherlands a tradition of polyphony (a graceful and intricate style in which several voices followed their own melodic path independent of each other). His most famous pupil was Ockeghem.

The famous names of the Flemish school were of Jean Ockeghem (1430–95) and Jacob Obrecht (1430–1505). The former had been a tutor to the French kings. He made a significant contribution in the field of music through technical experiments. Obrecht's musical talent was developed at the cathedral of Antwerp. At one time he was a music teacher of Erasmus. His music was spontaneous and melodious and was based on a form that was called 'vocal orchestration'. His melodies were extremely popular. Unlike the visual arts where the study of ancient objects and literature stimulated the artists and the architects, the evolution of music was independent of such ideals. By the beginning of the sixteenth century, the Flemish composers began to have links with the musicians of the other regions, particularly of France. From there they spread to the courts and cathedrals all over Europe. It was the cathedral schools of the Netherlands that taught music to the rest of Europe.

There was another famous school of music that was based on the principle of 'imitation'. This could be found in the works of Ockghem. Music historians compare him with Donatello for discovering a new form of music just as the latter had discovered a new style of sculpture. In this style of a polyphonic music individual voices commence not simultaneously but follow one another. Experiments were carried out by the composers of that period to create intricate forms of polyphonic music. Another distinct trend was the gradual elimination of instruments from vocal music that led to the creation of pure unaccompanied style. The focus was now on individual melody. Throughout the late-fifteenth and early-sixteenth centuries, the major centres of music were concentrated in the Low Countries. The court of France too, became a significant place for musicians. Here, the various trends of music were amalgamated by Josquin des Prés (1450–1521). He made his music more expressive than others by basing them on sentiment and mood of the words. His fame spread to distant courts of Europe and his influence on music and musicians of other regions continued to grow. He is described as 'The Prince of Music' and the first modern composer. His work reflected a formal balance.

Music also developed and flourished in England during the sixteenth century. The Tudor monarchs, particularly Henry VIII and Elizabeth I, provided patronage to music with great enthusiasm. The English musicians not only adopted the madrigal from Italy but also perfected music in the form of songs and instrumental creations. William Byrd (1543–1623) was a famous master in England who could be compared favourably with great composers of the Netherlands and Italy. In the Elizabethan period, music became considerably secularized, which was earlier solely for the church. Its popularity could be seen in the homes of the nobility and in social gatherings.

In Italy, two centres of music were located at Rome and Venice. While the Roman school of music remained conservative and traditional, the Venetian group of musicians believed in experimentation. The Roman centre concentrated on the religious choir and adopted a tone of absolute devotion and seriousness. Giovanni Pierluigi da Palestrina (1525–94) was among the great music masters of Rome, who was known for religious melodies and printed many of his compositions consisting of madrigals, masses and motets. As Venice was a large cosmopolitan city in northern Italy, the music reflected the vibrant character of the population. The music composers of Venice developed a brilliant form of choral music and made colourful use of instruments. The influence of Josquin can also be seen in Venetian music.

Music in Europe reached a new height as a form of artistic expression. Although every geographical region had developed its own group of musicians and musical style, yet music travelled extensively along with the musicians and made spontaneous impacts outside the region of its origin. As such it emerged as a European art. The two different trends of music compositions – secular and the sacred music – gained considerable popularity and reflected the typical Renaissance spirit of learning and experimentation.

Thus, the Renaissance is seen as much as a period of revival of antiquity as the formation of new ideas. It brought to the fore a vast range of human pursuits from literature, education, and writing of history to art, architecture, music and civic virtue. It recaptured classical models, analysed political institutions and created fresh interest in human society. This period presents divergent voices and talents with a critical attitude towards the contemporary world. By encouraging experimentations and artistic expressions, the movement set diverse cultural trends. Though the Renaissance was not a distinct movement and had its roots in the medieval past, there is no denying the fact that it contributed in the emergence of modern world.

The post-Renaissance art branched out into two different movements: Mannerism in the sixteenth century and Baroque during the seventeenth and eighteenth centuries. Mannerism, a term derived from the Italian word for style, was a reaction against the idealist perfection of classicism. In order to emphasize the emotional effect of the painting and the emotional expression of the painter, the art displayed distortions of light and spatial frameworks and created a heightened scale of emotional presentation.

Important Events of the Renaissance

1300–21	*The Divine Comedy* written by Dante
1304–14	Giotto paints the famous frescoes of Arena Chapel at Padua
1304–74	Petrarch, father of Italian humanism. Crowned poet laureate in Rome.
1350	Boccaccio writes *The Decameron*
1373	Salutati is made Chancellor of Florence
1385–1400	*Canterbury Tales* by Chaucer
1400	In *Panegyric on the City of Florence*, Bruni writes the history of the Roman Republic
1401	Lorenzo Ghiberti is commissioned to construct the doors of the Baptistery in Florence
1419	Brunelleschi completes his famous structure 'Founding Hospital' in Florence
1425–52	The famous 'Eastern Bronze Door' completed by Ghiberti
1434	Jan van Eyck paints *Arnolfini Wedding*; Cosimo Medici comes to power in Florence
1452	Leonardo da Vinci born in Florence
1453	End of the Byzantine Empire with the capture of Constantinople by the Turks
1455	Publications of Gutenberg's Bible and Psalms
1469	Marcilio Ficino publishes his *Platonic Theology*
1478	Botticelli's *Springtime*
1484	Botticelli paints *The Birth of Venus*
1494	Charles VIII of France invades Milan. Other states join and the Italian war lasts till 1538. Republican government restored in Florence
1497	Leonardo da Vinci completes his painting *The Last Supper*
1499	Coming of Bramante to Rome from Milan marked the beginning of the cultural primacy of Rome
1500	Michelangelo sculpts *Pieta* in Rome. Erasmus publishes *Adagia*
1501–4	Monumental figure of *David* created by Michelangelo
1506	Da Vinci paints *Mona Lisa*
1508–12	The Sistine Ceiling at Vatican by Michelangelo
1511	Erasmus publishes *Praise of Folly*
1513	Machiavelli wrote *The Prince* (*Il Principe*)
1514	*Galatea's Triumph* by Raphael
1516	Thomas More's *Utopia* is published
1518	Raphael's *Cupid and Psyche*
1527	Sack of Rome by Emperor Charles V of Spain
1528	Castiglionne publishes *The Book of the Courtier*

Suggested Readings

Artz, Frederick B., *From the Renaissance to Romanticism: Trends in Style in Art, Literature and Music, 1300–1830*, Chicago: Chicago University Press, 1962. Extremely useful book for the cultural achievements and novel features of Renaissance.

Baron, Hans, *The Crisis of the Early Italian Renaissance*, Princeton: Princeton University Press, 1966. Classic discussion of the rise of civic humanism and the relationship between diplomacy and intellectual life.

Baxandall, Michael, *Painting and Experience in Fifteenth Century Italy: A Primer in the Social History of Pictorial Style*, Oxford: Oxford University Press, 1972. Explains the development of the Renaissance art lucidly and scientifically.

Black, Robert, ed., *Renaissance Thought: A Reader*, London and New York: Routledge, 2001. A must for all, as it include articles by all well-known scholars on diverse aspects on the subject.

Brucker, Gene A., *The Civic World of Early Renaissance Florence*, tr. S.G.C. Middlemore, Princeton: Princeton University Press, 1977. An excellent analysis on the city's physical, economic, social and political features and cultural triumph.

Burke, Peter, *Popular Culture in Early Modern Europe*, 2nd edn. Aldershot, Hans, 1994. A refreshing account of the social aspect of the Renaissance.

———, *The Italian Renaissance: Culture and Society in Italy*, Princeton: Princeton University Press, 1999. An analytical account of the creativity, style and influences that contributed to the richness of Renaissance art.

Burckhardt, Jacob, *The Civilization of the Reaissance in Italy*, Oxford: Oxford University Press, 1981 (1st edn. 1860). A nineteenth-century path-breaking interpretation yet the most acceptable scholarly work till date on the subject.

Cereta, Laura, *Collected Letters of a Renaissance Feminist*, tr. Diana Robin, Chicago: The University of Chicago Press, 1997.

Chastel, André et al., *The Renaissance: Essays in Interpretation*, London: Methuen, 1982. A collection of essays of known writers on Renaissance presenting diverse and lesser studied aspects.

Gilmore, M., *The World of Humanism 1453-1517*, New York: Harper Colophon, 1952. A well-written work in the nature of survey, especially on humanism.

Gombrich, E.H., *The Story of Art*, New York: Phaidon, 1951. An important work of an art critic.

———, *Symbolic Images: Studies in the Art of the Renaissance,* 3rd edn., Oxford: Phaidon, 1985. Work of an expert on Renaissance art.

Hale, J.R., *Renaissance Europe: The Individual and Society 1480–1520,* Berkeley: University of California Press, 1971. The focus of this book is on people and not on events.

Knecht, R.J., *Renaissance, Warrior and Patron: The Reign of Francis I,* Cambridge: Cambridge University Press, 1996.

Kristeller, P.O., *Renaissance Thought: The Classic, Scholastic, and Humanistic Strains,* New York: Harper Torchbook, 1961. A scholarly and original work on humanist ideas providing fresh insights on the theme.

Martin, John Jeffries (ed.), *The Renaissance World,* New York/London: Routledge, 2007. Lavishly illustrated and multi-disciplinary volume, offers new perspectives on artistic, cultural, political and intellectual achievements of the Renaissance society.

Mignolo, Walter D., *The Darker Side of the Renaissance: Literacy, Territoriality and Colonization,* Michigan: University of Michigan Press, 1995. Argues that all aspects of Renaissance period was not glorious and that the society revealed some dark aspects as well.

Robin, Diana, Anne R. Larsen and Carole Levin (eds.), *Encyclopedia of Women in the Renaissance: Italy, France, and England,* California/ Oxford, ABC Clio, 2007. Offers over 135 revealing biographies of Women artists, scientists, doctors, writers and other extraordinary women based on the latest research.

Ruggeero, Guido, ed., *A Companion to the Worlds of the Renaissance,* Oxford: Blackwell, 2002. Has a rich collection of articles on various aspects of the Renaissance world including the negative aspects of Renaissance society and the achievements and limitations of the movement.

Stephens, John, *The Italian Renaissance: The Origins of Intellectual and Artistic Change Before Reformation,* London: Longman, 1990. Explains the changes in the realm of culture, Latin letters and arts and brings out the Italian legacy.

CHAPTER 3

Explorations, Discovery and Colonial Empires

The beginning of international trading and the enlargement of the European commercial economy were closely linked with the maritime activities like geographical explorations and search of unknown lands. This process started slowly but intensified in the last decade of the fifteenth century and resulted in the colonization of America, Asia and Africa. Portugal and Spain were the first to develop colonial empires in distant regions. Subsequently, the north-western European states established their own colonies in various parts of the globe. Colonial rivalry caused numerous wars till recent times. The creation of colonial empires was a decisive step in the ascendancy of Europe and its subsequent domination over the rest of the world.

Until the fifteenth century, the European states had established trade links with the East via overland routes. Spices including pepper, cinnamon, cloves and mace as well as silk and cotton cloth were all brought from the East, from India and beyond and trans-shipped to Europe by the Italian merchants of Venice or Genoa. These items reached western Europe through the Levant. Similarly, some parts of Africa sent gold and precious metals in exchange for European goods. With the rise of the Ottoman Empire during the fifteenth century, Europeans began to face difficulties in their land route to Asia. This fact, along with the religious antagonism between the Christians and the Muslims resulting in crusades against the Muslim states promoted search for sea routes to Asia. The Portuguese and the Spanish provided the incentive by promoting and patronizing voyages to unknown lands.

The Portuguese dominated sea voyages and ocean sailing for almost the whole of the fifteenth century. The Portuguese sailors and navigators made persistent and prolonged efforts to acquire practical knowledge of the wind currents that took them to the neighbouring islands and the uninhabited lands. For a long time it was believed that the Portuguese provided the leadership in the field of navigation because they were poised for expansion after reconquering their territories from Islam by the mid-fourteenth century. The efforts of Prince Henry the Navigator, an enthusiastic patron of the voyages of discovery, pushed Portugal ahead of other nations. The traditional view about Portugal has been that the country was cut-off from the rest of Europe and was poor in natural resources. It is said that the population of Portugal in the early-fifteenth century was less than a million; that there were very few towns, which were far apart; and that the commercial middle class was very small but it dominated the Portuguese trade. The peasants constituted the largest section of the population and toiled on poor quality soil. The landholdings were small in the northern region like Minho and there was overcrowding, while the southern provinces like Algarve and Alentejo which had become free from the Moors had large agrarian estates. The Portuguese nobility was led by the House of Aviz that was war-like in attitude but gave importance to trade and commerce. Historians wonder how this so-called backward region provided the leadership in the early era of sea voyages and in the creation of a large colonial empire.

The Portuguese had embarked on wars with the Moors on the north-African coast, which were perceived as crusades, but the fact is that these were also fought for economic gains. The Portuguese mariners had explored the west-African coastline with the ultimate aim of capturing the supplies of gold coinage from the south of Sahara – one of the principal sources of the Moorish wealth. With greater experience of prevailing wind systems of the African coast, weather conditions and improvements in navigational techniques, the Portuguese penetrated further south. According to H.V. Livermore, between the capture of Ceuta in 1415 and the death of Henry the Navigator in 1460, the Portuguese had acquired leadership in nautical science, naval construction and the methods of exploration and colonization. They had made their way down into the western coast of Africa within 8° of the equator. Ralph Davis argues that neither ideological causes and crusading spirit nor the technical changes alone were responsible for the Portuguese interest in exploration. The real reasons were the complex interaction of economic stresses, internal politics and personal factors. Braudel also emphasizes the fact that Portugal was not such a poor region in the late-fifteenth century as has been depicted, nor completely cut-off from the rest of Europe. Her economy was neither primitive nor elementary. The Mediterranean type of climate enabled her to produce a variety of products like oil, cork, fruit, wax and honey, which she supplied to the northern states of Europe and imported corn from outside. The external trade helped in the development of navigational activities and promoted shipping interests. The role of Prince Henry cannot be minimized as he collected a galaxy of scholars and navigators in his court and despite many failures, he continued to encourage sea voyages. There appear to be several motives in the early Portuguese efforts. The shortage of capital to finance such expensive voyages was overcome by the loans provided by foreign merchant bankers such as the Fuggers of Germany and the merchant bankers of Genoa. They invested in these voyages not only to share in the potential gains but also to counterbalance the trade supremacy of the Venetians. The African trade brought wealth to the traders, to the crown and to the members of the aristocracy. The Portuguese began to sell luxury items like gold and ivory to the European market and earned huge profits. In the second half of the fifteenth century, seamen from Andalusia and explorers from Castile began to compete with the Portuguese in the search for new territories and sea routes to India and China. The Portuguese succeeded in occupying the Canaries which led to a fresh wave of explorations in the third quarter of the fifteenth century.

Motives Behind the Early Voyages

It is extremely difficult to assign precise motives for sea explorations and distant voyages. When Europe was dominated by a feudal social order, a few states like Venice and Genoa had amassed wealth by establishing their monopoly over the luxury trade between Asia and Europe. Most of the Asiatic products passed through land and then brought to Europe through the Mediterranean Sea. Countries located on the Atlantic coast wanted to break this Italian monopoly and looked for alternative sea routes to Asia. A beginning was made by the Iberian powers – Portugal and Spain.

The traditional explanation for the early explorations by the European sea voyagers mentions three factors – God, Gold and Glory. God signifies the role of Christianity in such voyages. The term 'Gold' generally refers to the economic motives while the term 'Glory' implied those individuals who played a crucial role in the search for new territories. For a long time it was believed that the Turkish advance in the Middle-East and their occupation of Constantinople in 1453 blocked the trade route and the flow of oriental products from the Red Sea. However, this argument does not hold ground now. In fact, the Portuguese voyages had started in real earnest long before this date. Nor did the Turkish expansion disrupt the trade route because till the end of the fifteenth century spice imports from the Middle-East were rising and their prices were falling. Furthermore, the Ottomans did not conquer the chief distributing centres in the Levant until the opening decades of the sixteenth century. Thus, it can be said that the Turkish rule did not cause lawlessness and disorder, rather it facilitated the oriental trade.

Some of the early sea voyages near the west-African coast were mainly crusades against the Muslim population. This crusading spirit soon acquired a military form under the leadership of Spain. The Europeans wanted to have contact with Christians in distant land, for they believed that there were Christian communities outside Europe. This led to an upsurge in missionary zeal among the Franciscans, who also promoted voyages. Moreover, as the Pope was the supreme religious authority throughout Europe, his decisions had great weight. Many sea-voyagers and their patrons sought his blessings for the spread of Christianity into the new lands.

In the Middle Ages, some individuals and members of the nobility had developed a keen interest in sea voyages. In 1256, Marco Polo had set-off from Venice to China and Japan. He spent fourteen years in the court of the Mongol emperor, Kublai Khan. He wrote a glowing description of the cities in China. When he was imprisoned in Genoa in 1298, Marco Polo dictated his account to his companion, Rusticello of Pisa, in his famous book *Livre des merveilles du monde*. From 1307, his book was copied, translated and distributed all over Europe and remained popular till the seventeenth century. Marco Polo's visit to the east and his return via the sea route and his spirit of adventure inspired several explorers and voyagers. Another Venetian, Niccolo Conti, visited Asia around 1400 and gave a detailed picture of the eastern riches. His work was also widely circulated. However, it was Prince Henry (1394–1460), fifth son of John I of Portugal, who has been credited by writers and historians with initiating and patronizing early sea voyages. It is difficult to point out his exact motive but his personal interest and his desire for glory might have been the reasons. Prince Henry embodied much of the crusading spirit of the Portuguese discovery in the fifteenth century. He was a generous supporter of research in cosmography, astronomy, cartography and the techniques of sailing. He obtained funds to send out well-organized expeditions at frequent intervals. Under his direction, the Portuguese made rapid strides in exploring unchartered lands by using the latest research and sailing methods. Navigators were sent by him along the west-African coast who discoverd the Madeira islands, Sudan and Senegal. He came to be known as Henry the 'Navigator', although, he had never undertaken a sea voyage himself. Historians have given him a laudatory role in shaping the historical process of his time.

The emergence of strong centralized states under powerful rulers also contributed to sea voyages and the creation of colonial empires. Some of the rulers took personal interest in promoting geographical explorations and in search of new territories, which later proved to be of immense value to them. The contribution of Isabella and Ferdinand of Spain clearly demonstrates the role of absolute monarchs in the early phases of empire building. In Portugal, the establishment of the Aviz dynasty, with the help of the bourgeoisie instead of the traditional nobility, created new interest in sea voyages to seek economic gains. However, all these could be considered contributing factors.

While emphasizing the role of economic factors, Scammell (*The First Imperial Age*) argues that gold was not the initial motive for the Portuguese because commercial economy had not developed to such an extent that it needed gold in large quantities. The Portuguese interest in gold developed much later. It was the Catalans and some Italians states which desired sea routes to the gold-producing regions. Portugal was not economically developed to such an extent that it had to carry vigorous search for gold. Braudel (*The Perspective of the World*, p. 140) does not accept this argument and suggests that the Portuguese economy was neither primitive nor elementary. For centuries Portugal had established contact with the Muslim states like Granada and had developed a reasonable level of monetary economy, which existed, to some extent, on wage labour. There were strings of seaside towns and villages populated by sea-farers and fishermen. The semi-collapse of the landed aristocracy and the rise of the bourgeoisie contributed to the development of the trade network. At the same time, it is true that foreign merchants were greatly involved in the early sea voyages. The Italian city states like Florence and Venice had concentrated huge wealth through their commercial and financial skills and invested large sums of money on these voyages. The availability of capital also played a part in the early phase of sea voyages and discoveries.

There is some disagreement among the historians on whether the growing population played any role in these voyages and discoveries. It is argued by some that the European population was far greater than what the continent could support at that time. The search for new territories is often seen as an outcome of an urgent need for land and food. This need grew with the expansion of the Turks, who blocked the European advance towards the east and denied them access to land and sea resources of the eastern Mediterranean. However, historical facts present an opposite picture. When the Portuguese sea voyages began in the early decades of the fifteenth century, Europe had just passed the phase of demographic crisis in the form of Black Death and showed no signs of overpopulation. Even the acquisition of Cape Verde Islands suggests that the people were not prepared to go and settle in new territories. However, the growth of population in Europe became evident towards the close of the century. From the late-fifteenth century, the population had started swelling and this led to an increase in the demand for certain commodities. A steady growth of population and an increasing volume of trade probably created a shortage of gold and silver and other forms of metal currency. Till 1400, silver was mined in Bohemia in large quantity but the supply of gold remained short. Africa was the chief supplier of gold dust but not of the base metal. There is no doubt that most of these early sea voyages were conducted in search of gold and silver and that their success was determined by the potential economic advantages of the discovered land. Columbus was able to get financial support for his next two voyages once he produced proof of the availability of silver in the regions he had discovered. Historians hold divergent views on the role of food requirements in promoting sea voyages. Herman Cortés who conquered Mexico, openly confessed, 'We Spanish suffer from a sickness of the heart for which gold is the only cure.' Historians hold divergent views on the role of food requirements in promoting sea voyages. On the one hand, it is pointed out that the Iberian states were dependent on other states for their food requirements and this must have played a role in their search for new territories. It is argued that the first prey of Portugal in North Africa was a grain-producing region. On the other hand, it is argued that the Portuguese were more interested in other trade products rather than foodstuff. It was only after discovering the new territories that they realized the value of cultivating crops like sugar.

In the fifteenth century the demand for spices as a preservative for meat and food products was constantly growing. Contemporary accounts suggest a marked increase in meat consumption. However, the quality of meat was poor and it could be made palatable and preserved only by adding plenty of spices that mainly came from Asia. It is quite evident that Vasco da Gama's original motive was to reach the source of spices in Asia, and when he reached India he

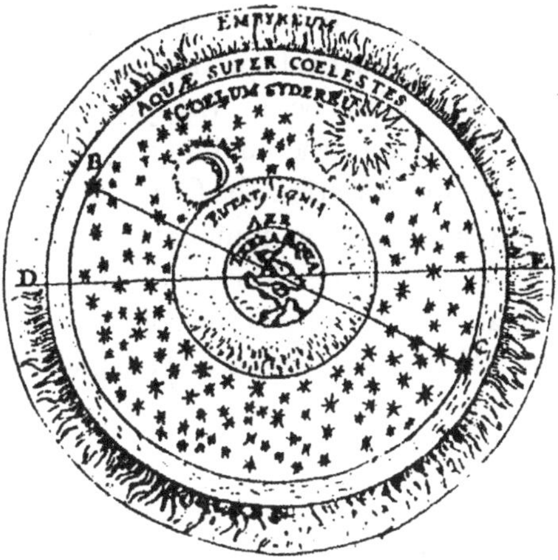

Medieval Concept of Universe.

found the pepper price in Calicut much lower than that prevailing in Venice.

The advantage of controlling the lucrative slave trade was another reason that contributed to the emergence of colonies outside Europe. Since the Black Death in the fourteenth century, most European states faced an acute shortage of labour. As a result an extensive market for slaves developed in Portugal by the mid-fifteenth century. Every year about 1,000 slaves were brought there and slavery became a common feature in the well-to-do Portuguese and Spanish households. It is estimated that by the end of the fifteenth century, slaves constituted 10 per cent of Lisbon's population. So the demand for slaves must have also contributed to the quest for colonies along the African coast from where most of them were procured.

Thus, while maintaining the overall preponderance of the economic factors, the territorial discoveries and the creation of colonial empire can be attributed to the combined efforts of the rulers, the bourgeoisie and the aristocracy. The aristocracy was in search of new lands and new opportunities to extend their power and to excel in military ventures by first extending the *Reconquista* to Morocco and subsequently to develop agrarian interests in the recently acquired regions. The promotion of sugar cane is a reflection of their interests. The bourgeoisie was interested in making profits through new products and actively participated in promoting these products on both sides of the ocean. The interest of the rulers was to expand their influence in the far-flung areas, to increase their revenues and to become powerful. The Christian missionaries used this opportunity to increase their number through conversion after their early success in the crusades. Many individuals also contributed to achieve personal glory, because of their thirst for knowledge and spirit of adventure. With the emergence of colonies, further motives gradually evolved.

Improvement in Geographical Knowledge and Navigational Technology

A series of writings since the ancient period describe the land-masses across the sea. Ptolemy's *Geography* and many works of Strabo and others were translated into Latin by the humanists. Cardinal Pierre d'Ally wrote *Imago Mundi* in 1410 in which he suggested that Asia was accessible by a long eastward journey. All these works had some basic errors but they created a renewed interest in the search for unknown lands. Educated people in the middle ages believed that the world was round, but there was considerable disagreement on what lay on the other side of Europe. The Europeans had no knowledge of the American continent. Pliny, an ancient geographer, believed that the equator constituted an impassible barrier and all those who tried to cross it would be scorched to death. Even Ptolemy thought that the Indian Ocean was land-locked, while Strabo had projected India into the Atlantic. It was Toscanelli who asked Columbus to sail westward from Lisbon on the same latitude to reach Asia. All these limitations in their notion of geography did not deter them from believing that the ocean was not a barrier to their journey. The success of the early sea voyages was bound up with the skill of map-making and navigational techniques. Greater understanding of geometry and arithmetic provided the essential foundation of the art of navigation, cartography and surveying. Maps and charts which had been used since the thirteenth century, owed very little to academic science.

Ptolemy's System.

Mathematicians and astronomers like Martin Behaim and Gemma Frisins provided theoretical basis to scientific navigation while sailors like Columbus and Cabot provided a practical demonstration. The Portuguese made major contributions in the field of navigation and cartography. Zuane Pizzigano prepared the nautical chart in 1424. It depicted the entire region of the north Atlantic that included Ireland, England, western Europe, the Iberian Peninsula and north-western Africa. Gabriel De Valseca's famous chart of 1439 included the Black Sea, the Mediterranean Europe, the Atlantic islands on the African coast comprising Cape Bojador and the nine islands of the Azores. The Portuguese navigators adopted the altitude-distance method instead of using the Pole Star to determine longitudes. The first recorded use of stars to estimate latitude was made in 1462 and the use of midday sun to calculate the latitude began in 1484. Abraham Zacuto, a Portuguese Jew, who later became the royal astronomer in Lisbon, prepared a table of the sun's height. In 1514, Joao de Lisboa made use of the magnetic compass for determining magnetic declination. This was a major step in bringing the two fields together – academic science and practical skills. In 1569, the Flemish cartographer Gerard de Cremer, popularly known as Mercator, devised a method of projecting on a flat piece of paper an accurate picture of the curved earth. This came to be known as Mercator's projection. It made it possible for navigators to chart a course by drawing straight lines. The study of maps and map-making increased and facilitated sea journeys. An important cause of the Portuguese success was their use of charts, which was kept as a close secret and was not shared with the outsiders. The earliest of such surviving charts dates back to the first half of the fourteenth century. It is called the Portolan chart and is made on a tanned animal hide. However, by the sixteenth century, the science of navigation was becoming international with the cooperation between the mathematicians and the navigators.

The long-distance sea voyages required improvement in the techniques of ship-building. The ships, which were built in the sixteenth century, were called *cobs* and were heavy, broad, tube-like and clinger in design. The *cobs* were replaced from about 1430 by the *caravels* which were slimmer, lighter and more durable. They were faster and were based on Arab technology. Later a combination of techniques produced *caravela redonda* which proved particularly useful because it could carry naval guns. The Dutch also developed *fluyt,* which was based on better technology. It was lighter than the *caravel* and kept the operation cost very low.

The Renaissance and Sea Voyages

On the relationship between the early sea voyages and the Renaissance, there are two schools of interpretation. The first may be called the Renaissance School as it suggests that the spirit of the Renaissance influenced the early sea voyages. The humanists in the second half of the fifteenth century first used the word 'discovery'. It implied the finding of ancient texts and culture and the discovery of new territories by sea voyagers beyond Europe. Poggio compared the achievements of Henry the Navigator to that of Alexander the Great and considered his achievements greater. Luis de Matos' noteworthy work on Latin literature also included the theme of discovery. He wrote: 'Renaissance man's enormous curiosity about the discovery of new worlds is an undisputed fact.' The invention of the printing press by Gutenberg caused a sudden spurt in the Latin and vernacular works. Between 1481 and 1610, the catalogue of books dealing with the geography of countries outside Europe consisted of 524 titles.

One can easily find some common features between the Renaissance and the early sea voyages. The participants in both these events were aware of their own historic roles. They both possessed a common appetite for fame and glory. It is believed that the great Portuguese epic of Luis de Camoes, *Lusiads* had great influence on Vasco da Gama and that Columbus was advised by Toscanelli to follow certain directions. It is also argued that the discoverers behaved like scientists to convert cosmographical theory into practice. As J.R. Hale writes, 'the first scientific laboratory was the world itself'. The followers of the Renaissance School argued that the overseas explorations were based on curiosity and experiments that were the guiding force of the Renaissance movement. It is also suggested that many of the mariners and early voyagers of Portugal and Spain were from Italy – the seedbed of the Renaissance. Columbus came from an Italian city, Genoa. However, it must be pointed out that Genoa, unlike other Italian cities, hardly demonstrated active Renaissance culture. There is no denying the fact that some aspects of classical geographical knowledge was acquired by the Renaissance humanists from Italy which encouraged some early sea voyagers. But the relationship was not as close or as direct as has been suggested.

As opposed to the Renaissance School, a large number of scholars believe that the overseas expansion came from the medieval preparations. The single most dominant motive for the oceanic journeys was economic, e.g. the quest for Asiatic luxury goods which were greatly prized in medieval Europe. The Islamic merchants were actively involved in the chain of exchange from Asia to Europe. The process of sea voyages and the creation of colonial empires had started in the medieval period itself. As early as 1291, Vivaldi brothers of Genoa had sailed out on the Atlantic wishing to reach the East Indies by westward route. They lost their lives on the way but their attempts continued to inspire Portuguese mariners who later succeeded in reaching the Azores.

The leading states of Italy, which had vehemently patronized the Renaissance had no direct links with the voyages of discovery. Similarly, the discoverers and sea voyagers had little or no interest in the world of Renaissance scholarship. For the humanists, the rediscovery of ancient worlds and civilizations was far more important than the new world which the Europeans saw. The geographical base of the two events was quite different. The Renaissance was centered in the Italian states and Burgundy, while the sea voyages were undertaken from the Iberian states of Portugal and Spain. The Renaissance was primarily concerned with the cultural aspect of society while the sea voyages had direct religious and economic motives.

The Early Sea Voyages

The Portuguese provided the leadership in early explorations and sea voyages. The Atlantic archipelagos of the Canaries, Madeira and Azores were found, explored and then colonized by the early-fifteenth century by the Iberians. Between 1415 and 1475, after the conquest of Ceuta, Cape Bozador, Cape Verde and Sierra Leone in western Africa, the geographical boundaries of medieval Europe were broken. The main interest was sugar that was procured and cultivated in these islands, followed by African gold, and then malaguetta pepper. It was after 1460 that political and religious incentives came into operation. The discovery of the islands led to their exploitation. It was the strong sugar interest, according to Braudel, which caused the exploitation of these islands. Subsequently, the availability of labour in these islands saw the beginning of slave trade between Africa and Europe.

The accession of John II to the Portuguese throne in 1481 marked two important voyages. Diego Cao explored a long stretch of coast from the equator to Cape Cross, which is present Namibia. His voyages revealed the inhospitable nature of Angola and Namibia where little food was available. He is believed to have crossed the Cape of Good Hope twice without sighting it. Bartholomew Diaz was another important explorer who went further south and found a Cape which he termed the Cape of Storms, but King John renamed it as the Cape of Good Hope (1488) because it promised an assured route to India. Among the sea voyagers, the most well known was Christopher Columbus. He was born in Genoa in 1441 and showed extraordinary interest in sea voyages. He gained the knowledge of the Atlantic in his voyages to England and Ireland, and perhaps to the African coast. He had experience of staying in the Madeiras, on the north-west coast of Africa. Here he studied Atlantic sailing charts and learnt of Western voyages. He conceived the plan of his journey to India during this stay and even approached John II of Portugal but could not get his approval. After the death of his wife, he along with his young son Diego, went to Spain in 1484 to seek royal favour. He made a number of friends in the influential royal court. According to J.H. Parry, 'Columbus's ability to thrust himself into the circles of the great was one of the most remarkable things about him.' He had an illegitimate son, Ferdinand, who became his father's great biographer. Christopher Columbus had acquired practical rather than academic qualifications in the field of navigation. He had a difficult time convincing the European rulers to sponsor his trip to India through a westward journey. He is believed to have approached the rulers of Portugal, England and Spain to help him undertake the voyage. Finally, the Spanish rulers were persuaded to sponsor his journey while the Genoese bankers provided loans to him in the hope of future gains. As the important ports of Spain, Cadiz and Seville were choked with Moors leaving for Morocco, Columbus was forced to begin his voyage from Palos, a small harbour very close to the boundary of Portugal, on 3 August 1492. He finally landed on a tiny island of the Bahamas. His strong will power and optimism had given him strength to achieve his goal, despite the strong resistance of his crew. It was at sunrise of 12 October 1492 that his famous ship *Pinta* sighted land. The land was given the name of San Salvador that means Holy Savior. From there he explored some other islands, which included Cuba and Hispania. There he could visualize the availability of gold by observing the jewellery of the local population as well as future store of manual labour for his European masters. The Spanish Crown assured him of a reward. He made three more voyages but could not reap the real benefit of his efforts. On his fourth voyage he sailed with four ships from Cadiz in 1502 and explored the coast of Honduras, Nicaragua and Panama. In Jamaica, he faced mutinies and shipwrecks. After his return in 1504, he spent the rest of his life in legal battles and in sending petitions to the Crown in an attempt to receive honours, power and wealth that had been promised to him at the time of his first voyage. He lived in poverty in his last years and subsisted by borrowings. Before his death on 20 May 1506 he wrote to his old and faithful friend, Diego de Deza, 'It appears that his majesty does not think fit to fulfil which he, with the Queen, who is now in glory, promised me by word and seal. For me to contend for the contrary, would be to contend with the wind . . .' (R.H. Major, *Select Letters of Christopher Columbus, Four Voyages to the New World*, London: Hakluyt Society, 1847).

Columbus reflected two contrasting traits, a man of the Middle Ages, as well as a man of the Renaissance. His theoretical background, his philosophical and theological viewpoints and the premises of his scientific concepts were medieval but his spirit of

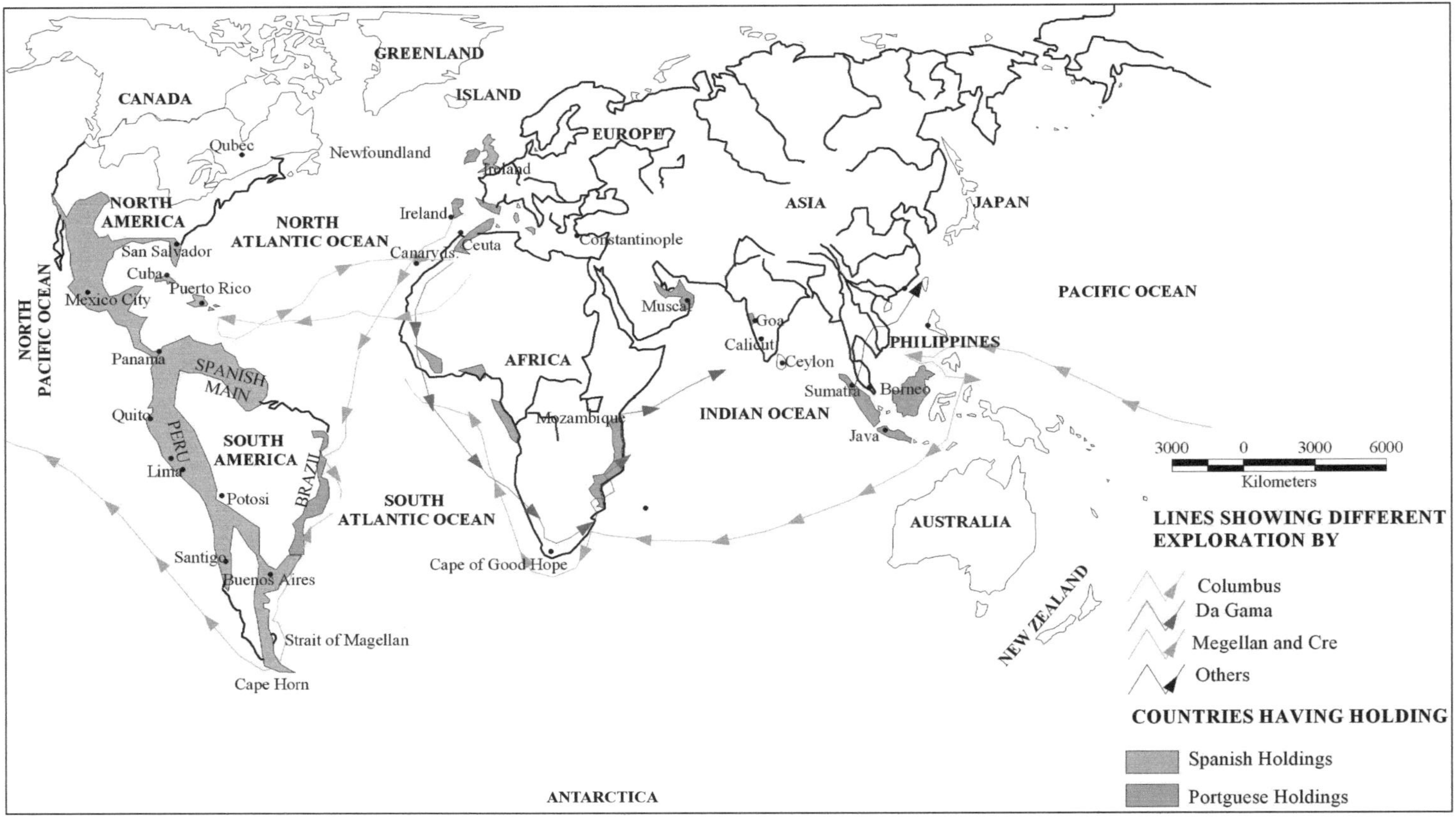

Map 3.1: Overseas Explorations in the Fifteenth and Sixteenth Centuries

enquiry, his capacity to face hard facts and problems, all belonged to the age of the Renaissance. Columbus proved to be an inept administrator of the colony he established at La Isabela (now called the Dominican Republic). He ruled for three years by brutal force and antagonized his own subjects who rebelled against him. Till his death, he continued to believe that he had reached India and he referred to the inhabitants of Central America, whom he had discovered, as Indians. It is argued that Columbus added a fourth part of the world for the Europeans – the Americas. It was left for his successor Nicolas de Ovando to introduce African slaves in 1502 to fully exploit the newly discovered region. These lands were later called the Americas after the name of an Italian explorer, Amerigo Vespucci, who was a very influential person among the European rulers. The importance of Christopher Columbus is not that he discovered America. The real significance of his voyages is that it marks the first stage of global integration in which Western man extended his influence to the far-flung areas.

Many recent historians do not project Columbus as a hero or a great discoverer. Rather, he is described as a symbol of exploitation and imperialism. His biographer of the nineteenth century, Justin Winsor casts a cold light on the dark side of his character. He strongly criticizes Columbus's proposed canonization by Roman Catholics. It is now suggested that this so-called 'age of discovery' was marked by a new epoch of imperialism and destruction. Even the discovery was meant only for the Europeans since these lands had always existed for centuries. Historians of the present generation now view European inroads into America in a new perspective and address the consequences of European colonization from perspective of the native Americas. They speak not of the discovery but the 'encounter' or the 'contact' between Europeans with the American world.

According to Pierre Chaunu, three kinds of expeditions contributed to the birth of America. The first were the voyages of the Spaniards to the American coasts and islands along the route followed by Columbus. The second was in the form of voyages towards the north-west passage made mostly by the non-Mediterranean people, for example, John and Sebastian Cabot from

Vasco da Gama

England, who discovered Newfoundland. The third included the voyages of explorers from the newly acquired bases in the West Indies, which ultimately contributed to the creation of the colonial empires.

Another pioneer among the great explorers of that period was Vasco da Gama, who found the sea route to India. He was the son of an admiral in Portugal and had followed the voyage of Dias round the Cape of Good Hope. He was lucky to get proper assistance from the Portuguese ruler. The expedition of Vasco da Gama was a planned armed trading venture and his first voyage (1497) is regarded as the most famous. He was lucky enough to receive the service of a famous Arab navigator, Iben Mejid, who piloted his squadron in 1498 across the Indian Ocean to Calicut on the west coast of India, an important centre for the pepper trade.

He was totally bewildered by the religion of the people and the social practices. The ruler of Calicut was the Zamorin, an urbane and tolerant ruler. Da Gama had mistaken Hindus for some kind of Christians and the temples as churches of India. His presents for the local Indian ruler were far inferior to what was available and became an object of laughter for the court officials. On the other hand, Vasco da Gama himself was a ruthless and cruel man. During his second voyage, he captured a shipload of Muslim pilgrims coming back from Mecca and set them on fire for not paying suitable tribute. At another place he ordered the severing of limbs of a number of fishermen and sent them to the coast of Calicut to terrify the Zamorin, in order to get his demands accepted. Nevertheless, his journey represents one of the greatest navigational achievements of that period. It was much longer journey than that of Columbus and he had to cross several latitudes southward and negotiate a variety of ocean currents and wind systems. His success resulted in the establishment of the first European sea-borne empire in Asia, which was based on naval gunnery. In fact, this was the beginning of the European enslavement of Asia that continued for the next four centuries. The Portuguese empire in the Western hemisphere was developed in Brazil, discovered by Cabral (1500) when his ship was blown off course by a storm from the west coast of Africa to the east coast of South America.

Along with Columbus and Vasco da Gama, Ferdinand Magellan is regarded as the third greatest explorer of that age. He was the son of a nobleman and had taken part in the Portuguese empire building expeditions in the Indian Ocean. He served under Albuquerque and helped in the capture of Malacca in the Malay Peninsula. He was wounded in a battle and became lame for the rest of his life. He left the Portuguese service and led an expedition for the Spanish ruler, Emperor Charles V to the Moluccas. Magellan was entrusted with this job as he was familiar with that region. However, he had to follow the westward route because of the terms of the Treaty of Tordesillas (see below for explanation). Magellan sailed across the Atlantic against all odds, into the Pacific Ocean in 1519 (he named it Pacific because it was more peaceful and calm compared to the Atlantic). It was Vasco Nunez de Balboa, a Spanish adventurous sailor, who had reached the Isthmus of Panama Canal in 1513 and saw the Pacific Ocean across the land. His crew endured fourteen weeks of thirst, hunger and scurvy while crossing the Pacific Ocean. Magellan travelled through the dangerous passage (Strait of Magellan, named after him) in the extreme south of South America and reached the Philippines. Earlier, under Portuguese service, he had travelled eastward to the Moluccas and had served the Portuguese governor. His journeys demonstrated his great skill as a navigator. His voyages confirmed that the world is round. The vastness of the Pacific Ocean was realized for the first time because of his efforts. He was killed along with his forty men in a local war at Mactan island. But despite his death the expedition returned to Spain in 1522 under Sebastian del Cano via Cape of Good Hope, making him the first man to circumnavigate the earth.

Several sea voyagers and pioneers from different countries also contributed to the knowledge of geography and the concept of the world, thus extending European control over unknown regions. John Cabot (1450–99) was an Italian born English explorer who sailed to North America and discovered Newfoundland (1497), although he had set out to find an Atlantic route to the Far East. The merchants of Bristol provided the capital in order to enjoy the monopoly of the new trade. Sebastian Cabot (1470–1557) probably the son of John Cabot was a navigator and cartographer under the Tudors, the English rulers. He also carried out long voyages in search of a north-west passage to Asia. He later joined the service of the Spanish Emperor as Pilot Major. In his last years he was the first Governor of the Merchant Adventurers of England (1551) and Muscovy Company (1555). The Frenchman Jacques Cartier navigated the St Lawrence River in North America (1535) thus establishing a French colony in Canada. Champlain Marquette discovered Quebec while Joilet and La Salle explored the Mississippi River leading to the creation of New France in North America. Henry Hudson, an Englishman, employed by the Dutch to find a north-west passage to Asia, discovered a river which was named after him. Francis Drake and Hawkins of England were also involved in many sea voyages.

Rise of Colonial Empires

The rise of colonial empires began with the discovery of new territories. In fact, the discoveries were merged into conquests and the conquests led to colonization and the colonial empires of Portugal and Spain were created. As Braudel states, 'The conquest of the high seas gave Europe a world supremacy that lasted for centuries.'

The Portuguese domination stretched across the entire Old World from the European Atlantic to the Indian Ocean, the East Indies and the seas bordering the Pacific and is commonly linked to the interests of the merchant class who stood to gain by the trade outlets. However, the initial motivation for the colonial empire came from the nobility, particularly the so-called notorious 'younger sons' lacking their share in land ownership. Once the colonies emerged, the role of merchants and missionaries increased. The traders played an important part in the development of the far-flung colonies. The Portuguese colonization began in the east and was largely planned and carried out as a royal enterprise. The early Portuguese attempts after 1415 had inevitably resulted in the success of Vasco da Gama's voyage to India and the building of *India Portugueza.* The Portuguese success in the Indian Ocean, according to Dan O' Sullivan (p. 20), was because of their tenacity of purpose, naval gunnery and timing. At that time no single maritime power existed in the Indian Ocean. As a result, the Portuguese established their domination over the land-masses in Asia and successfully intruded into the existing sea traffic of Asia. Their commercial success was based on their powerful navy and their control of important commercial seaports. Their earlier attempts along the African coast were dominated by interest in sugar and the demand for slaves. In Asia, the Portuguese dynamism was exhibited in their efforts to monopolize the spice trade.

The Portuguese expansion on the African continent began in 1415 with the conquest of the Moroccan city of Ceuta, facing Gibraltar. The fort of La Mina was the first European construction in the tropics, on the Bay of Guinea. Fortifications to build a commercial post started in 1481 by the orders of King John II. It became an important place for gold and ivory as well as the slave trade. The process of empire building immediately followed Vasco da Gama's voyage to India. Along the Malabar coast, there were several states but they proved ineffective in resisting Portuguese domination. Similarly, on the east coast of Africa, Egypt and Persia there were powerful states yet they did not post permanent fleets in the Indian Ocean. This made the task of the Portuguese much easier. The Portuguese knew that the trading cities of the Mediterranean had grown rich from their control of luxury goods coming from Asia through intermediaries. The Portuguese undertook the long and hazardous voyages round Africa into the Indian Ocean with the object of eliminating the middlemen and trade directly with India and the Spice Islands. The Portuguese continued to dispatch ships and men after their success in 1498. The success of da Gama and Cabral revealed that the Malabar ports could be wrested by force. In 1505, King Manuel sent Francisco de Almeida as the first Viceroy for India. The Portuguese exhibited a new strategy of creating a sea-borne empire by controlling certain key ports. Their aggressive approach led to the acquisition of some very busy commercial ports in Asia. In western India, Diu which was a large harbour, was secured. During the term of the next Viceroy, Alfonso de Albuquerque (1509–15), Goa was captured from the ruler of Bijapur. He was the second Viceroy of the Portuguese empire in Asia and contributed in the process of empire building. He carried out many naval expeditions in different parts of the Indian Ocean and pursued a clear policy of wresting the trade monopoly of spices from the hands of the Asian merchants. Albuquerque pursued a policy of eliminating potential rivals that included not only the small Asian powers but also the Spanish encroachment from the east. He kept the Portuguese away from local Asian politics and instead concentrated on developing a network of safe sea routes for the Portuguese merchants. These routes were policed by naval squadrons and managed by the naval bases scattered along the Indian Ocean over a wide area. Goa was a very significant port with a large population that was dominated by the merchant community. The capture of this territory not only provided an important commercial base to the Portuguese but also gave them the advantage of controlling the entire western coast. This was the first and the foremost important chain of ports that the Portuguese had set up. Malacca in the East Indies, particularly known for its spice trade was captured in 1511. By 1515, Ormuz was taken over by the Portuguese on the northern part of the Persian Gulf. His successors gained major territories in different parts of Asia, like Ceylon, which was the principal area for certain types of spices and precious stones. Thus the Portuguese established their total monopoly over the Europe-bound spice trade which included pepper from Sumatra, cinnamon from Ceylon, camphor from Borneo, nutmeg from the island of Banda, and cloves from the Moluccas.

During the sixteenth century, the Portuguese were the only organized European commercial and maritime enterprise in the Indian Ocean. This enterprise was called the *Estado da India* or India House at Lisbon. It consisted of a factor, treasurer and three writers in the beginning but the number of officials continued to increase. It functioned like a department of overseas trade which discharged the functions of a huge store-house and served as a custom-house. It used every possible means at its disposal to control and influence the traders of the spice market of Europe. The naval tradition of the Portuguese that included piracy, privateering and sea wars was carried into Asia and served as an instrument of maritime expansion. Its naval superiority gave the Portuguese commerce the much-needed protection. The *Estado da India*, as Neils Steensgaard suggests, did not depend on territorial power but on its mastery over the open seas and the resulting claim to sovereignty (*The Asian Trade Revolution in the 17th Century*, p. 89). For Sanjay Subrahmanyam, the nature of Portuguese intervention in the Indian Ocean is represented in their initial commercial and subsequently military presence in the form of the construction of a chain of forts – Kilwa, Hormuz, Goa, Cannore – and the establishment of their first factory at Calicut in 1502. The system of factories and fortresses was destined to impose perfect monopoly on the spice trade of Asia. In Asia, the Portuguese crown was directly involved in trading ventures and confined its entire interest to trade. The crown never undertook the responsibility of territorial acquisition unless it contributed directly to their treasury. K.M. Mathew gives credit to the Portuguese for creating an organizational structure in India that served as a guideline for the future colonizing powers. Before 1800, Portugal was the only state whose sovereign directly controlled the Asiatic dependencies. The Viceroy headed the Portuguese system established on the Malabar Coast and centred at Goa. As a representative of the Portuguese king, he entered into commercial treaties with the local rulers and supervised the entire operation of the Portuguese trade in India. The Captains-General, assisted the Viceroy. Every fort was placed under a captain who also supervised the administration of justice. However, the administration in Asia was corrupt and showed extreme intolerance of the local population. The administrative efficiency remained low because of poor salaries and the authority showed no concern for the welfare of regions under their control.

The profits of the Portuguese commercial enterprise in the Indian Ocean attracted the Dutch merchants and bankers. They began procuring spices from the Portuguese but when in 1580 the Habsburg rulers inherited the Crown of Portugal, the Dutch began trading directly with the east by creating their own settlements. The Dutch attacked the Portuguese through a private merchant company. By providing armed protection to the local rulers in Java and the Spice Islands, the Dutch retained trade monopoly in that region. The Dutch political involvement in the Indian Ocean was not the result of any imperial design of the Netherlands but grew out of local circumstances. Thus the Portuguese and the Dutch ventures in Asia were based on economic and strategic means that enabled them to control important trade posts along the coastline in the Indian Ocean.

In the Western hemisphere, the Portuguese advance was stopped in the beginning itself. There was a serious conflict between the Portuguese and the Spaniards over new territories. Pope Alexander VI issued a series of bulls in 1493 on a Spanish request that assigned all the islands and mainlands, discovered or yet to be discovered, to the Crown of Castile – those which were located on the western side of a line drawn at 100 leagues of the Cape Verde island. The Portuguese protested against this decision and ultimately the two

Iberian powers negotiated a bilateral treaty at Tordesillas in 1494 that moved the line of demarcation 270 leagues farther to the West.

The Portuguese discovery of Brazil and its subsequent colonization forms an interesting study of the process of empire building. The origin of the Portuguese empire in Brazil is shrouded in controversy. Some scholars suggest that Cabral carried secret instructions of the Portuguese king to establish his claim on this territory while the general view is that Cabral, in order to avoid the Doldrums, lost his way and accidentally reached Brazil. He soon dispatched a report of his discovery to the ruler in Lisbon. The process of colonization commenced soon after, although very little was known of the land. This region revealed a distinct rural character. A large number of slaves were brought to develop the agricultural resources in this region and many new crops were introduced such as tobacco, coffee, cocoa, cotton and sugar. There was complete lack of availability of metals and hence the Portuguese were satisfied with the exploitation of the Brazilian agricultural wealth. As the local Indian population proved unsuitable for plantation labour the Portuguese control of the slave trade in Africa helped them in procuring outside labour. According to J.H. Parry, by 1580, Brazil had some sixty sugar mills. In 1570, Brazil's sugar production was about 2,915 tons, by 1600 it had risen to some 19,434 tons. The increased production of sugar in Brazil had serious repercussions on the sugar cane producing regions at Sao Thome and the Madeiras, which had flourishing sugar production in the earlier period. As a result, sugar cane cultivation was replaced by sweet wines. The Portuguese population was about 20,000 while the slaves constituted a population of about 14,000. The Portuguese in Brazil hastened in the 1530s to counteract the French attempts to colonize it. Brazil was divided into twelve captaincies, each assigned to proprietary landlords known as *donatarios*. They were expected to settle in the new territories and defend their land at their own expense. In return, they were given extensive administrative, judicial and fiscal powers over such colonists whom they could induce to settle. The Portuguese policy in this region was less ambitious and less effective than that of Spain. The captaincy

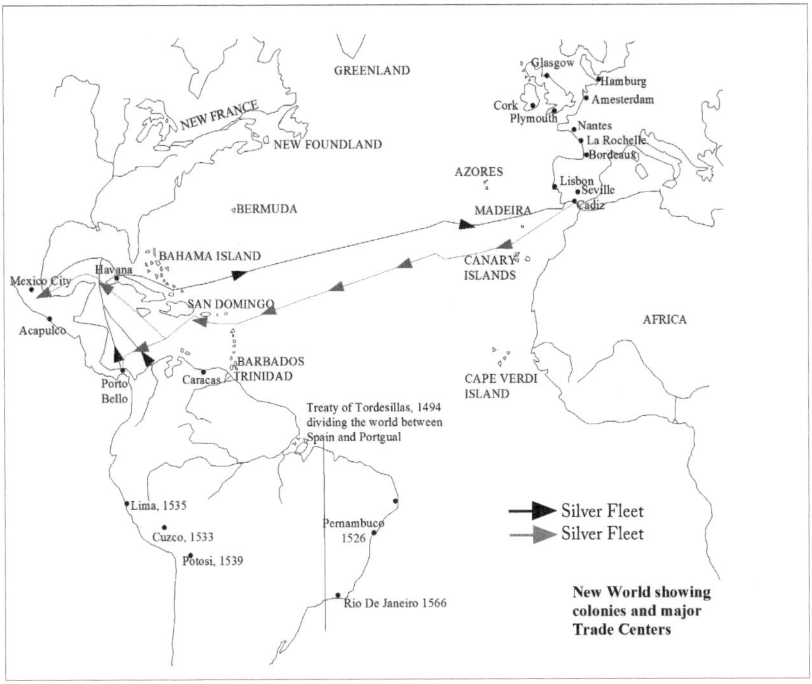

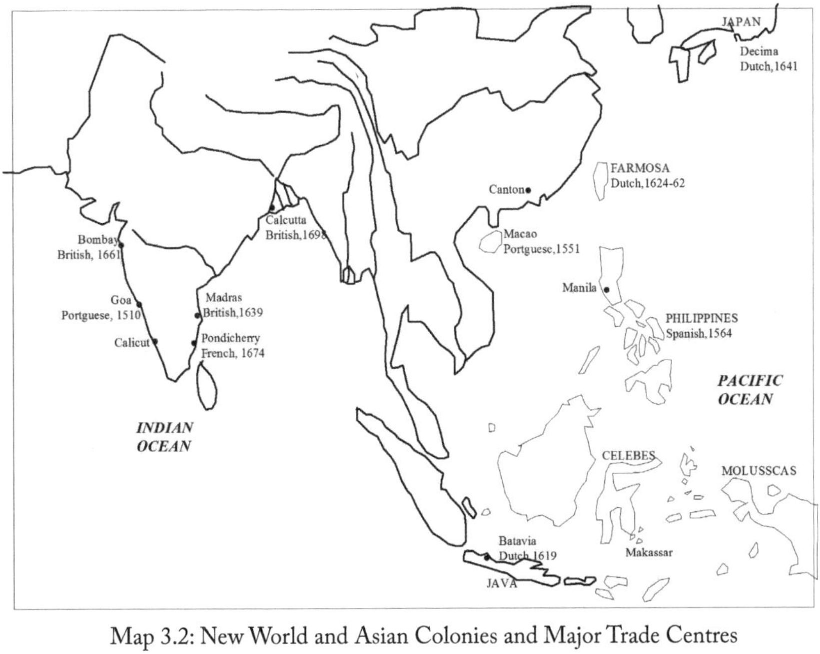

Map 3.2: New World and Asian Colonies and Major Trade Centres

system revealed the weakness of royal authority and inefficient organization.

The Portuguese colonial society was based on three criteria: purity of blood, social rank and marital status. Those born in Portugal (called *reinoes*) formed the highest rank. Those born in Asia (called *castios*) and in Africa (*mulattoes*) formed the second layer and the native Christians formed the lowest strata. The Portuguese population in the colonies was divided into the familiar threefold estate basis. It comprised the ecclesiastics (officials of the church), nobility and ordinary married and unmarried men. An unmarried man was called a *soldato*. He had to render military service and live on the charity of *hidalgos* (minor nobility). Till the *soldato* got married, he did not receive any regular salary. The *soldatos* virtually formed the private army of the nobles though their appointment was for colonial administration. As such the *soldatos* were elements of a feudal militia with meagre remuneration and divided loyalty.

The Spanish Empire

The Spanish colonial empire centered in the western hemisphere after the discovery of America by Columbus. Except for the Philippines in Asia, the Spanish colonial empire was spread in large territories of Central and South America and the West Indies, described as the 'New World'. The Spanish population in this region did not include peasants and manual labourers against whom the Spaniards displayed extreme prejudice. There were a large number of officials, lawyers, notaries, landowners (*encomenderos, ranchers*), mine owners, clergy, besides merchants and shopkeepers. It was essentially an urban empire confined to the territories which were known for mines and metals.

The Spanish colonial empire revealed several general characteristics but the most important was its urban character. The settlements were widely dispersed but had an underdeveloped urban network and revealed peculiar concentration and dispersal of population. These centres were controlled by administrative authority with strings in Spain. Unlike the Portuguese empire where

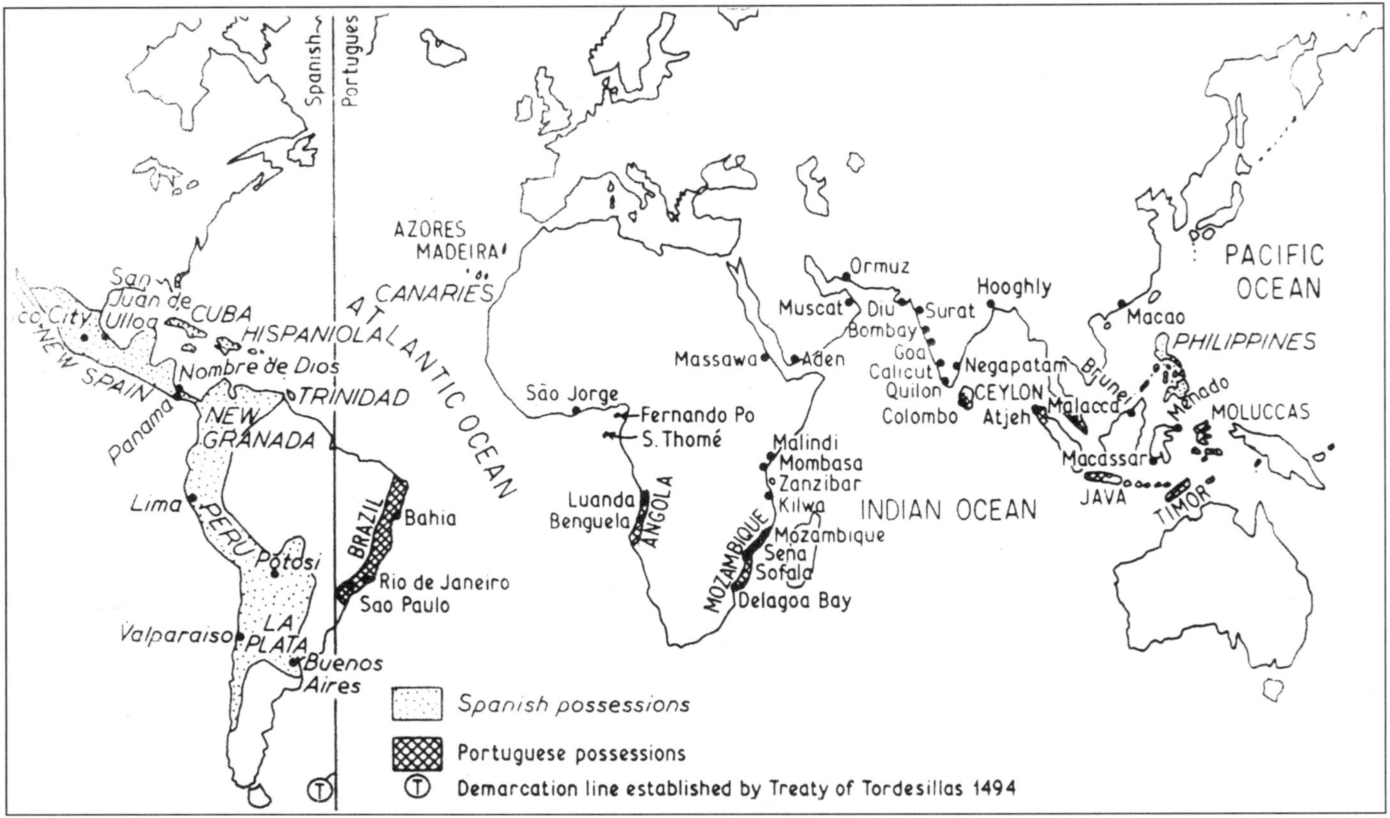

Map 3.3: Spanish and Portuguese Empires in the Sixteenth Century

the crown was directly involved in the process of empire building from the beginning, the Spanish empire was initiated by private efforts and subsequently the Crown of Spain established its control. Immigrants from varied backgrounds went to the Spanish colonies in the New World. Individuals and families immigrated to the New World with diverse motives such as winning a fortune for higher status or to escape the Spanish laws, while several missionaries came to spread Christianity in order to increase the number of its followers. But a majority of them desired gold and silver or wanted to establish their own political power. Of these, the most well-known group to contribute to the Spanish empire building was the *conquistadors.*

The Age of the Conquistadors

The discovery of new land by Columbus and gold samples he brought back led to rumours that infinite riches could be procured from the new land. The most ambitious and adventurous men from Spain began to leave their motherland in search of territories that they could claim for their own. With this started the age of the conquistadors. Such people acquired most of the American territories. They were professional explorers and their explorations in the new territories between 1520 and 1550 brought vast tracts of unknown land under their control. This process of conquest was started in 1519 by Hernando Cortés. With mere 600 men he was able to subjugate the entire Aztec empire. Cortés was from an aristocratic background from south-west Spain but was not well off financially. He had a short experience of the New World in the West Indies in 1504, where he worked under the governor of Cuba. He was asked to search for a rich territory in the New World but was forced to leave Cuba, as the Spanish authorities did not trust him. From there he left as a rebel for Mexico with a small army at his command. Cortés was highly ambitious, brave, well-educated and possessed administrative experience. He had a complex character and is described by his contemporaries as a cunning personality. A lot has been written on him and his adventures. He landed at a place in Mexico in 1519, which he named Vera Cruz.

He began his operations by first destroying the ships in which he had arrived. By this he brought to an end the wish to return to Cuba of the malcontent element in his army. He took the sailors of the ships along with his army. He also laid the foundation of a municipality. He surrendered his commission received at Cuba to the magistrates of Vera Cruz. From them he received a new commission as the representative of the Spanish crown in Mexico and then secured the confirmation from the emperor. By this act he established his own independent command. The arrival of the Spaniards had brought devastating smallpox that affected the local population. Cortés found this an appropriate opportunity to strike. On his arrival, he met a Mexican woman, Dona Marina, who became his interpreter and mistress. She knew the inner weaknesses of the Aztec empire and the geographical surroundings. The Aztec ruler, Montezuma sent ambassadors with gold, silver and other gifts on hearing that the Spaniards were about to reach Tenochtitlan. This was done not with the intention of accepting the superiority of the aliens (the Spaniards) but to demonstrate his superiority through the display of wealth. Cortés, however, maintained that it was an act of accepting his supremacy. This was also conveyed to the Spanish ruler. With the help of many local Indians, who were unhappy with the rule of Montezuma and had turned against him, Cortés invaded the Aztec empire. He not only defeated the Aztecs and their emperor Montezuma by treachery but also destroyed their beautiful capital – Tenochtitlan. His associates described the city as extraordinary and very beautiful. It had almost 60,000 houses all painted in white and encircled by a vast lake. The city was captured and destroyed and a new one was built, which is now called Mexico City. Cortés became an absolute ruler of a territory, much bigger in size than Spain. Emperor Charles V of Spain made him the Governor of the 'New Spain' in 1522.

Another famous conquistador was Francisco Pizarro, who left Spain with just 180 men. Unlike Cortés he was illiterate, lacked administrative ability, was in his late fifties but was tough, full of enterprise and endurance. He served in Balboa's army and was involved in slave trade. He was also involved in founding Panama City. Here he held a small land grant and came to learn of the Inca civilization on the west coast of South America. He received the support of some Amerindians who wished to overthrow the Inca rule. A situation of civil war had already existed because of a dispute over succession. Taking advantage of this internal trouble, Pizarro overthrew the Inca rule and established his own government in Peru. In 1533, he plundered the Inca empire which was known to possess a vast quantity of gold. The Spaniards eventually discovered silver mines of Potosi in this region, which proved to be an important source of silver supply to Spain. Charles V made him Governor even before he had conquered the area. There were others like him such as Alvarado, who conquered Guatemala, and Quesada, who established his power over New Granada. There were many others, who had added great semi-independent territories to the kingdom of Spain, men like Pedro de Alvarado, Cristobal de Olid and Sebastian de Belalcazar. In fact, the first important conquistador on the American mainland was Vasco Nunez de Balboa. He had sailed in 1500 and founded the city of Darien. His success over the local population of the Isthmus rested on a strategy that included force, threat and diplomacy. It is suggested that in 1513 he crossed the dense forest and reached the shores of the Pacific. It was Balboa, who provided the knowledge of the existence of a narrow strip of land that separated the Atlantic from the Pacific. However, he could not reap the benefit of his discovery because his reports reached the crown very late and by that time Arias de Avila had already been appointed the royal governor of Darien. The victories of the conquistadors might have been courageous and successful but they were destructive and based on treachery and cruelty. They fought only for themselves and not for Spain. When the Spanish Crown realized the value of these territories (such as silver mines), it immediately decided to establish governmental control over them.

The conquistadors pushed their way into all the chief centres of American Indian civilizations at a remarkable speed and their successful territorial gains can be compared with the Portuguese mercantile advancement in the east. However, the Spanish conquests were far more enduring and changed the entire European relationship with the outside world. This also had a profound impact on the European society. The conquistadors faced serious problems but their brief rule created greater hardships for the Amerindians through misrule and exploitation. The conquistadors had gone to the Americas at their own expense, faced real hardships and carried out warfare without the help of their own government. The conquistadors added territories, which were much larger in size than their own country.

The Spanish institution that became a subject of serious controversy in their official and unofficial circles was the *encomienda*. Though initially King Ferdinand had approved it, the Spanish rulers because of its abuses and oppression finally disapproved it. In 1509 Ferdinand gave legislative consent to a decree which provided that on completion of any new conquest, the governor or *adelantado* might divide the natives of the area among the conquerors. This institution assigned groups of Indians to a Spaniard who could employ their services in any manner he so desired. A powerful lord in the Spanish colonies was called an *encomendero*. He was conferred a grant or *encomienda*, comprising a certain number of people or tribes. They were expected to work under the *encomendero* on land and in the mines. In theory, the *encomendero* was to protect these conquered people, civilize them and convert them to Christianity. Those Indians who voluntarily agreed to become Christians were to be treated as free men. However, the conquerors treated all the natives as their personal property. Cortés claimed 115,000 people in Mexico under him while Pizarro claimed his right over 20,000 men in Peru. The condition of these people was wretched and often pathetic, particularly those who worked in the mines. The Indians were placed under permanent personal servitude to individual Spaniards. There were serious objections against it in the New World as well as within Spain because it was considered to be worse than slavery and regarded inhuman in every possible way. It caused severe hardships to the Indian population and their number started dwindling rapidly. The masters continued to ill-treat the survivors in their mad hunt for gold. The officials in Spain and the Dominican missionaries who had come from Spain carried out propaganda against this exploitation. It is believed that the Mexican population in central parts was about 10 to 12 million in the pre-conquest period, and dropped to about 6 million in the mid-sixteenth century and further declined to less than 1 million by the early-seventeenth century. In the Caribbean island, the Amerindian population fell so rapidly that the plantation economy had to import a large number of slaves from Africa. The number of slave labourers increased sharply and many of them had to work in the mines of Honduras. The Spanish king tried to check it through the laws of Bargos in 1512 but it did not succeed. An attempt was made to define the rights of *encomenderos* over their Indian subjects and these rights were increasingly restricted. In the important ordinances between 1526 and 1529, the revised *encomiendas* were expected to treat the Indians as free persons and they were not to be ill-treated or hired to a third party.

The Spanish crown faced numerous challenges in the colonies. It not only needed to supervise the vast bureaucracy and the native population apart from the newly arrived Spaniards but also had to control the activities of many adventurers, who had become the masters of the newly acquired territories in the name of the Spanish crown. The most important objective of the crown was to fully exploit the riches, especially silver and gold, of the new territories. The Spanish king headed the colonial administration and tried to curb the activities of the private adventurers. Some historians suggest that Isabella was initially opposed to the enslavement of the Amerindians and even disapproved of the nature of religious conversions but the influence of the crown was seriously limited because of the distance and the virtual defiance of the local Spaniards in the New World. In such a situation, the local administration played a vital role in the lives of the people. The Spanish colonial administration gradually emerged by 1535 and the basic structure was modelled on the institutions that had developed in Spain during the *Reconquista*. To counter-balance and weaken the *encomienda*, the crown created an institution in the 1530s, called *Corregimientos de Indios*. All the natives were placed under *corregidores*, the royal officials. The labour services and tributes of the natives were thus utilized for the king through the royal officials in place of *encomenderos*. These officials also provided justice in their respective *corregimientos*. The chief advantage of this institution was to check the influence and power of the *encomenderos*.

The Spanish king tried unsuccessfully to prevent the *encomienda* system in Mexico and other mainland colonies in 1520s and 1530s. He opposed the system because it had led to the creation of a feudal nobility with an independent power base and income who challenged royal authority and revenues. From the 1540s, the Spanish crown began to show greater interest in controlling the territories acquired by private Spaniards and tried to give an effective organization to the colonial empire. By this time the Spanish empire included territories like Mexico, Texas, Peru, Chile, Cuba, Hispaniola, Trinidad, Florida and a large part of South America. In 1542, the colonial code known as the New Laws of the Indies, carried effective curtailment of the settlers' privileges. The Spanish settlers were shocked and astonished to see a major change in the policy of the state. It was perhaps the reports of violence and anarchy after the capture of Peru that compelled the crown to enforce royal authority with greater vigour. The new laws formed a comprehensive code. Articles 31 and 35 abolished the *encomienda* system but it was again recognized in New Spain and Guatemala in 1549. To enforce these new measures, special commissioners were sent to major centres of colonial government with enormous powers to remove those officials who resisted such orders. They were called *visitador*.

The colonial structure of Spain, as it emerged by the mid-sixteenth century, consisted of a hierarchy of institutions strictly controlled by the mother country. It consisted of two levels of authority. One that was created in Spain, in the form of controlling councils and the other that emerged in the New World. In central America and the West Indies, there developed a system of municipal administration based on the interplay of royal and private interests. Municipalities provided the only method of organizing vast territories, distributing land and other resources and bringing the unruly conquerors to accept royal authority. The municipal government was also the first and the basic unit of territorial jurisdiction. The legal and enrolled householders were called *vecinos* who elected twelve *regidores* and from them two *alcaldes* or municipal magistrates were elected. The royal government sent residencies which carried a formal review of the judges and the working of senior administrators and judicial officials. The *visitador* carried out secret inspection of the whole province and of individual officers. Spanish colonies were divided into viceroyalties or governorships assisted by Captains and *Corregidores*. All these institutions were controlled by the supreme colonial authority in Spain called the Council of Indies which was created in 1524. It cooperated with another council called *Casa de Contratacion* which had been created in 1503. These two institutions directed every aspect of colonial government including fiscal organization and appointments. They functioned as legal and trade bodies, controlling all exports and imports between Spain and the New World by creating total monopoly over trade and shipping.

The Spanish rule in the colonies displayed on the whole an urban character. In the initial years it appeared to be unstable. Some important centres like Santo Domingo, Guatemala and San Salvador experienced several natural calamities like epidemics and floods. The Spanish administration was greatly affected in these regions. As Spanish territories consisted of regions of extremely high altitudes, thick jungles and vast expanses of land the chief administrative centres were dispersed and isolated. The distances that separated the urban settlements and the many geographical barriers created problems of communication. Only a few cities had large clusters of population, and on the whole the Spanish colonial empire had widely dispersed settlements with a concentration of aristocracy in the urban centres. There were different patterns of conquest and political formations in the New World. The rule of the Spanish king was established more effectively in Mexico, while in Peru the pacification and development of the administrative structure lagged far behind the conquest. Similarly, different patterns could be seen in the case of the West Indies. The effectiveness of the Spanish rule and the nature of control varied according to the geographical features as well as the economic potential of each region. This is evident from the Map 2.3.

The Impact of the Colonial Empires

The European explorations and discoveries of vast regions in the late-fifteenth and early-sixteenth centuries was an important turning point in human history as it led to the ultimate colonization of many parts of the New World. It was navigational superiority along with knowledge of firearms that had led to European success. It established European influence and power in distant regions but Europe, too, was deeply affected by its contact with the rest of the world.

The historiography on the discovery of the New World has undergone many significant shifts in the last five centuries. The immediate impact did not appear to be so dramatic as is generally believed. The death of Columbus was hardly mentioned in any of the important circles. It would be difficult to visualize any sudden change in the perception of the common people of the world outside. The importance of the new territories was felt with the coming of bullion in large quantities and gradual familiarity with the new products. Several historians emphasize the beneficial impact of the discovery of the new regions, particularly America. Walter Prescott Webb, an American historian, suggests that the success of Columbus led to subsequent European progress. It opened a 'New Great Frontier' for Europe. In 1500 Europe had a population of about 100 million, occupying and exploiting about 1,000 million hectares of land. The New World suddenly presented another 5,000 million hectares of land, thereby creating fresh opportunities for the Europeans. It resulted in a boom for the next four centuries. However, this view ignores the internal dynamic elements within Europe that enabled the European economy to grow. Pierre Chaunu also stresses the point that the discovery of new lands stimulated the growth of a wide range of European industries. Wallerstein and Andre Gunder Frank and many others emphasize the role of colonial trade in the emergence of the world capitalist economy. Even Karl Marx had stated that the modern history of capital dates from the creation of a world embracing commerce and a world embracing market in the sixteenth century. Although the colonial empires alone cannot take credit for the subsequent European progress, one cannot deny their role in hastening the process of capitalist development and weakening the feudal structure. The emergence of the colonies caused the decline of the Mediterranean economy and gave rise to the economy of the Atlantic coastal belt in north-western Europe.

Two major schools have developed among historians on the discovery of America. The first, called the Bardic school, was the product of narrative writings that glorified the great achievements of the European voyagers like Christopher Columbus. This school includes the names of eminent historians like George Bancroft, William Prescott, Francis Parkman and Samuel Elliot Morison, Alfred W. Crosby ('The Columbian Voyages, the Columbian Exchange, and Their Historians', in Michael Adas, pp. 141–64). Their writings were mainly biographical in style and full of admiration for the conquerors. They ignored the negative side of the conquest and praised the role of the conquistadors. The local populations of Mexico and Peru was described rather contemptuously as 'savages' and 'barbarians' in these works. The second group, called the 'Berkeley school' follows an inter-disciplinary approach to study the impact of the discovery of unknown regions. It includes scholars from varied disciplines like geographer Karl O. Sauer, physiologist Sherburne F. Cook and the historians of Annales School as well as some others such as John L. Stephen, Lesley B. Simpson, Du Bois, and Melville Huskovits. They rejected the notion that the Indian civilizations in the newly founded territories consisted of savages or uncivilized people. The roots of European imperialism were traced to the Mediterranean age of the crusades, where the organizational structures and exploitative techniques were developed and later imposed on other territories outside Europe. These scholars emphasized the triangular trade that developed between the Iberian countries, the trans-Atlantic lands, the Azores and the Canaries. Pierre Chaunu describes it as the 'Mediterranean Atlantic'. With experience, the sailors of southern and western Europe learnt the patterns of the oceanic winds and thus sailed to Asia and America. They became land seekers in Madeira because of sugar cultivation and in the Canaries they replaced local aboriginal population, the Guanches. With imported slave labour tropical crops were produced for the European market. These techniques were subsequently adopted in the distant regions of America and the West Indies.

The discovery of new territories had a significant economic impact on the lives of the Europeans. The most important result of the colonial empires of the Iberian states was the shift of an economic balance from the Mediterranean states to the Atlantic countries. Although the Portuguese control over the spice trade did not abruptly cease (the Mediterranean trade through Egypt and Arabia), it certainly reduced its profitability. The most dominant and economically powerful states of Italy lost their grip over the Asiatic trade and gradually experienced a steady decline. On the other hand, a number of seaports emerged along the Atlantic coast and played a larger role in the economic life of Europe. Cadiz, Seville, Lisbon and Antwerp were among the first few ports to gain importance in the sixteenth century. Lisbon, a relatively insignificant port commercially, became the third largest city in Europe with a population of over 1,65,000 once the colonies were established.

The long-distance trade contributed to Europe's shipping industry and gave immense stimulus to the merchant mariners. The Europeans brought to America firearms and weapons. Spain provided the lead with a large fleet of well-equipped ships capable of handling trans-oceanic trade. The whole of the important shipping industry came to be located on the Atlantic coast, although the real advantage was reaped by the two relatively new Atlantic states – Holland and England.

Exchange of Crops and Diseases

Historian Alfred W. Crosby has examined the biological consequences of the European arrival in America. He believes that the exchange of plants and animals between these continents was beneficial and led to globalization of biology, but there were also devastating and catastrophic consequences like the spread of diseases. The discovery of new regions with immense resources altered the nature of trade between Europe and the outside world. It introduced to the Europeans new agricultural products that were rich in food value like potatoes, tomatoes, cocoa (out of which the Aztecs made cold drinks), tobacco (known for medicinal properties), maize, peanuts, vanilla, rubber and kidney beans. One can imagine how these must have transformed the diet of the Europeans and subsequently of the other regions of the world where they were introduced and consumed. Two crops, maize and potato, were able to solve to a large extent the problem of feeding the growing European population. The arrival of many plants and their adaptation and dispersion in Europe had important nutritional results. The process of adaptation was very slow as tastes had to be developed and the suitability of the land had to be determined. From Spain and Portugal the imported crops spread to northern parts of Europe. Maize displaced rye and millet. After the mid-sixteenth century it was introduced in the Italian states of Lombardy and Piedmont. From there it reached eastern Europe. Sweet potatoes became a popular crop in the gardens of Spain and Portugal during the sixteenth century. It was introduced as a staple crop in Europe but it became extremely popular in Ireland and Poland, where it was grown extensively. It greatly altered the diet pattern in those societies. In regions where the plots of land were small, the peasants found that these new crops gave higher nutritional yield per acre than cereals. During the eighteenth century, white potatoes became an important crop of Germany. Initially, the poor peasants consumed it but gradually it reached the royal kitchens. Another American food, tomato, slowly became popular in southern Europe during the sixteenth century. It also transformed the menu of the Europeans. It was not welcomed in France and was totally rejected in England but gained ready acceptance in India, Italy and North America. So was the case with red pepper. Both these products have low caloric value but are rich in vitamins and flavour. Apart from food the Portuguese also introduced delicate and coarse varieties of textiles from Asia. The upper classes in Europe began to develop a craze for the superfine variety of cotton from India. For the first time Europeans began to use cotton underclothes and handkerchiefs.

Thus, the early colonial empires promoted exchange of products of daily consumption from one part of the world to another. Asian ginger, rice and pepper reached the New World, maize travelled to Africa and corn, quinine, and turkey, were taken from the New World to other continents. The new agricultural products and the development of plantations promoted certain types of industries in Europe, particularly along the Atlantic coast. The pre-Columbian Indians of America had no domesticated animals except dogs and llamas. The Spaniards introduced various animals, horses, cattle, sheep, donkeys, goats, pigs, water buffalo and fowl. This had great bearing on the American life, including their food content.

Until da Gama's voyage, the chief income from the overseas empire came from African gold, slaves and malagueta (cheap substitute of pepper). Asian spices like black pepper, ginger, cinnamon, cloves, nutmeg and mace became the most important source of state revenue of Portugal, accounting for 27 per cent of the royal income in 1506 that rose to 39 per cent by 1518 (McAlister, p. 252). The real centre of spice trade was Antwerp where foreigners earned substantial profit from it. Around 1520, some 6,000 tons of pepper is believed to have been shipped from Asia to Portugal. The exchange of products, raw materials and food from the New World in return for industrial products, proved extremely useful to Europe and in the long run led to European hegemony over other continents.

Demographic Consequences

Fernand Braudel, Eric R. Wolf, Wallerstein and William Mcneill have highlighted the significance of population migration in the spread of various diseases. There is disagreement among specialists on whether some diseases existed in America before 1492. It is argued that yellow fever could be African or it could have been endemic among the American monkeys. Many other diseases are believed to have been exported from Europe to the Americas such as smallpox, measles, whooping cough, chickenpox, bubonic plague, malaria, diphtheria and influenza. A historian describes this as 'bacteriological warfare'. However, the most deadly killer of Amerindians was the smallpox. From Renaissance to the nineteenth century, it remained one of the most widespread and fearsome diseases of the European continent. It first appeared in the West Indies in 1518, spread to Mexico with the inroad of Cortés and then swept across Central America. It is believed to have caused demographic losses from a quarter to at least one-third of the population. The valley of Mexico had fifty devastating epidemics between 1519 and 1810 (Crosby, p. 149). These diseases had a lethal impact on the Amerindian population.

The creation of colonial empires resulted in large-scale migration of population from Europe to the New World. As McAlister states, 'the discovery merged into conquest, and conquest blended into colonization'. While the scope of migration to Africa and Asia hardly existed as they were already well populated, the vast stretches of American land and the West Indies offered plenty of opportunities. Countless Portuguese migrated to Brazil, where they developed agriculture on large farms. The Spaniards moved in large numbers to exploit the riches of the New World. These were basically the result of individual initiatives and the policies of the crown. The individuals left for many reasons: to make a fortune in the new lands, to improve their status, at times to escape the harsh rules and the oppressive administration, to free themselves from religious tyranny, or to make profits from the trade; the Christian missionaries moved there to proselytize the local population. The state also encouraged the migration through grants of land or exemption from taxation in the early part of the settlement with the object of receiving greater revenue. It was keen to send the immigrants to less favoured regions that faced shortage of manpower. It is difficult to make a definite estimate of the number of immigrants to the New World, through the official Spanish figure (in the registers of the licenses) show that 15,480 men migrated to the new lands between 1509 and 1559 appears to be rather small. Many of the vessels, which left for America, did not register with the *Casa* in Seville, as they did not have regular licenses. Moreover, the figures for some years are missing from the register and this has led historians to believe that the number was much higher. For example, Boyd Bowman on the basis of available data estimates that 45,374 persons left Europe between 1493 and 1579. But he accepts that this was probably one-fifth of the actual number of immigrants. So the number must have been about 2,26,870 persons (McAlister, pp. 110–11). Of these, 95 per cent were from Castile alone, and the rest from Aragon, Navarre, Andalusia, apart from the Portuguese and Italians.

The Italians had close links with Spain because of the Aragonese rule over the Italian kingdoms. Besides, they were good navigators and wealthy merchants and enjoyed considerable influence over the Spanish crown. The new territories offered vast opportunities to the Europeans. This migration appears to be one-sided as we do not hear of the American local population migrating to Europe in sufficient numbers. It is argued by some scholars that countries like Spain were deprived of productive population – due to vast migration to the New World. However, the loss was much greater for the Africans and the Americans. The Spanish conquistadors and their men destroyed prosperous and large civilizations like the Aztec and the Inca. It is estimated that almost 70 million people died because of the European conquest. According to Sherburne F. Cook and Woodrow Borah, the population of Amerindians in central Mexico was about 25 million in 1520; it came down to 11.2 million by 1532, 4.7 million in 1548, 2.2 million in 1568 and 8,52,000 by 1608. In Peru, according to David Noble Cook, the Amerindian population went down from 9 million to 5,98,026 by 1620. It is aptly said that 'Columbus was the advance scout of catastrophe for Amerindians'. Attempts were made to offset the decline by other methods such as the import of African slaves and through marriage between the Europeans and the local women. Their offspring were called *creoles*. They played a significant role in perpetuating Spanish rule in the New World. By the end of the seventeenth century, African slaves were carried to almost every region where the Europeans penetrated. It is interesting to note that, at the time of the American independence, 19 per cent of the total population consisted of blacks. These population shifts changed the ethnic character of the population of the western hemisphere.

Art and Literature

The impact of the early colonial empire on art and culture may not have been very profound in the initial years but some indirect influence is discernible in course of time. Information about the New World began to reach Europe slowly through Spanish sources

Images of the New World.

Images of the New World.

as well as through sea voyagers, missionaries, pirates and traders. This made the Europeans wonder as the extent and variety of the world and the alien works of nature and man. It began to interest not only the governments, rulers and court officials but also cartographers and educationists and it became a source of inspiration for many writers and artists. The assimilation of information on the New World proceeded very slowly as educated Europeans were involved in their own activities and traders were blindly pursuing profit from the enormous expansion of trade. Few people in the academic world were excited with these new discoveries. The adventurous journeys to the new lands and to the unknown civilizations stimulated the ideas of only a few writers. The navigators and sailors popularized medieval legends, as many had believed that somewhere in the unknown region lay El Dorado, the seven cities of Cibola and many other mythical places. The famous English writer Edmund Spenser's unfinished masterpiece *The Faerie Queene*, and William Shakespeare's *The Tempest* were not just fantasies but also had substance. They suggested that the restraints of the Old World restricted human potential whereas men could achieve their potential in a free world, implying the newly discovered regions. Even *Utopia* of Thomas More was the creation of an ideal state, an imaginary republic, created by reason. Men could live in civil and religious freedom in a place where the inequities of private property did not exist.

Many poets and playwrights found inspiration in subjects ranging from shipwrecks in far-flung waters, piracy, to the fall of Amerindian empires. Men like Francis Drake and John Hawkins captured popular imagination as the most adventurous and successful sea pirates. The first conscious attempt to capture the atmosphere and characters of the oriental world could be seen in *Travels* (1614) by Fernao Mendas Pinto. Ramusio of Italy and Hakluyt of England provided fresh knowledge of the New World in their writings. The French writers like Michel de Montaigne during the sixteenth century pleaded for the acceptance of diverse human customs, as were found in different parts of the world. Another poet Pierre de Ronsard of the same period, urged that the Brazilian Amerindians should be allowed to live undisturbed.

Although the influence of exotic themes and subjects of America and Asia could be seen in the arts and architecture of the conquistadores, the impact was not so profound in literature. Some influence can be noted in the creations of Dutch painters like Albert Ecknout (1607–65), Frans Post (1612–80) Andrea Manteana and Cristovaode Morais. Some of the paintings used images of black slaves as symbols of empire-building. It was during the eighteenth century that the interest in oriental art actually developed. In the field of literature, writings based on colonial pictures greatly enriched the literature of early modern Europe, particularly in Spain, by the imagination drawn from the outside world.

The discovery of new routes and new lands had a significant impact on the knowledge of geography and cosmography. Many centuries-old beliefs and theories were proved wrong by adventurous navigators like Magellan. His circumnavigation of the world destroyed the earlier concept of the flat earth. The discovery that there were two oceans, thousands of miles wide separating land masses, broadened the horizon of the Europeans. The sea voyages revealed that the circumference of the earth was much wider than what the ancient scholars believed. There was now a thirst for the new knowledge of oceanography, cartography and the problems of distances and directions. The earth was presented more accurately on the basis of latitudes and longitudes. Gerardus Mercator, the Flemish-born German cartographer successfully projected the spherical surface of the earth into a geometrical plane. However, the information on the interiors of the continents reached the Europeans very slowly. The new knowledge made immense contribution to the biological and zoological sciences. It introduced Europeans to several new species of plants and animals. The first most widely-read work on these plants appeared in 1569, by Spaniard Nicolas Monardes.

The Economic Impact

There is no doubt that the colonies had a great bearing on the economic life of Europe. The European settlers undertook the organization of production in the colonies. They used the indigenous peoples and the Africans as slaves for primary production in mines and fields. In the East, the situation was different. In Asia, the Europeans met well-developed economic and social systems of production and marketing of goods. The Europeans desired these products and here they remained as merchants and not as primary producers.

The economies of the New World presented two different characteristics concerning the organization of production and trade. One was based on money and was geared towards European benefits. Its chief exports were precious metals, hides, cochineal and sugar. Other secondary items of exports consisted of forest products and dyewoods. In exchange, the inhabitants of the New World received cloth, hardware items, wines, olive oil, mercury for silver mining, some luxury items and most important of all, the slaves. The second aspect was related to mercantile economy based on mines and plantations. It was concentrated along Zacatecas, Mexico City, Potosi, Lima, Panama and Havana. The production depended mainly on the system of forced labour in which the black slaves supplemented the Indians and those of mixed blood descent, particularly in the mines of Mexico. This second aspect is described as a proto-capitalist's structure in which, according to McAlister, the New World faced economic dependence on Europe. The New World as well as the oriental empires brought huge wealth into the European economy. The Spanish mining in America and the Portuguese commercial ventures led to the exploitation and extraction of riches. Along with this, forced labour from the Indians certainly contributed to the long phase of European growth during the sixteenth century. It marked the beginning of colonization of distant regions by the European powers that lasted through to the twentieth century.

The growing demand for certain agricultural products led to the creation of plantation economy. Large-scale production of cash crops in the colonial possessions was carried out as it was not possible to grow these crops on such a scale in Europe because of the unsuitability of soil and climate and the non-availability of land. The formation of the colonial empires promoted plantation economy in the newly-acquired territories. This plantation system had been profitably tried out in the Atlantic islands near western Africa, particularly sugar cultivation. The success of the earlier efforts led to its introduction in tropical America and the Caribbean islands. Such plantations required heavy capital investments. The Dutch developed plantation farms during their brief occupation of Brazil. When the Portuguese ousted them they introduced the plantation culture in the West Indies. The Dutch introduced the art of making rum and molasses to the English and the French West Indies. A small number of landed magnates of European origin began to control vast stretches of mainland and made fortunes through slave labour. The Europeans exploited the local labour and when their number started dwindling, they began importing slaves from Africa. Sugar was converted from a highly priced luxury product to a commodity of common consumption. It became a part of international commerce and as it needed huge capital investments, the sugar industry of the New World got linked to the money market of Europe. The ultimate beneficiaries were the banking families of Amsterdam and London. It also influenced the coastal belt of the Atlantic Europe, where a large number of sugar refineries sprang up, particularly on the Atlantic coast of France and England. Tobacco cultivation too gained popularity among the European settlers. No indigenous crop of the New World could rival the success of tobacco. It was grown in the Spanish and Portuguese colonies, and was soon introduced to western India. From Spanish America it was taken to Virginia and Maryland in North America ruled by the British. It made an immense contribution to the tobacco industry of Yorkshire and Glasgow. Tobacco made worthwhile contribution to the treasuries of the European powers. The cotton plantations in the West Indies and subsequently in North America were also dependent on slave labour from Africa. It later helped the textile industry of the European nations. Sugar, cotton and tobacco became a chief source of profit for the European settlers who exploited slave labour. The expansion of the plantation economy transformed the commodity pattern of trade: commodities of mass consumption replaced luxury items.

A far-reaching impact of the colonial empire was related to silver imports from the New World. The entire process of empire building had started with the objective of controlling the sources of silver and gold and the Spaniards had achieved tremendous success in it. The Spaniards first discovered the silver deposits in 1545, when a 2,000 feet high silver mountain was discovered at San Luis Potosi in modern Bolivia. This was followed by successive discoveries on the Mexican mountain chains at Zacatecas in 1546, Guanajuato in 1548, Taxco in 1549, Pachuca in 1551, Sombrerete and Durango in 1555 and Fresnillo in 1569. The opening of the famous silver mine at Potosi had a great bearing on the fortunes of not only Spain but also other states of Europe. This has led many historians to believe that the price revolution in Europe during the sixteenth century was caused by the influx of silver bullion from America. The result of the price revolution has been discussed in another chapter but it must be mentioned here that the rising prices must have brought about major social dislocation. The vast volume of trade also had an impact on the commercial institutions of Europe, which experienced major transformation and growth. Closely associated with the Price Revolution was the expansion in the volume of trade covering different continents which needed elaborate organization and management and required better techniques of credit instruments, insurance, banking and many other commercial institutions to handle transactions and regulate trade. By the second half of the sixteenth-century Europe experienced the Commercial Revolution. Although the entire credit for the Price Revolution and Commercial Revolution cannot be assigned to the colonial empire, yet its contribution to the development of the European economy cannot be minimized.

The most notorious trade practices promoted by the Europeans with devastating consequences was the trade in African slaves. In the words of Urs Bitterli, 'The Atlantic slave trade is among the most monstrous and brutal projects undertaken by humankind to subjugate fellow human beings in the entire course of history.' Slavery as an institution had existed for centuries in almost every part of the world. From the thirteenth to the mid-sixteenth century, merchants from Genoa often purchased captives from Scandinavia, and Slavs from Russia and the Balkans. A slave market had emerged near Crimea. From mid-fifteenth century, the importance of

Genoan and Venetian slave merchants diminished with the rise of the Portuguese and the Spanish trade. At the beginning of the sea voyages, male slaves were used in the production of sugar and women as domestic slaves in the Mediterranean region. Anne Marie Jordon provides examples of black slaves at the court of Queen Catherine at Lisbon working as musicians, cooks, housekeepers, servants, gardners, etc. In the courts of south European states, black slaves were considered sign of social prestige and distinction (Thomas F. Earle and Kate J.P. Lowe). Earlier, slavery existed on a limited scale but the rise of the colonial empires made it voluminous in which human beings were turned into commodities and were shipped to distant continents to reap huge profits. On many occasions, slaves began to be exchanged for commodities of the other regions. Both Catholic as well as Protestant countries like Portugal, Holland, France and England were deeply involved in this trade. The Spaniards had virtually converted the local Indians into slaves through the institution of *encomienda*. Gradually the African slaves replaced the Amerindians and Jamaica emerged as the chief centre of slave trade. African slavery was strongly geared to European demands. The Portuguese began to acquire slaves from the African coasts and started supplying them not only to the European markets but also to Brazil, Spanish America and the Caribbean islands. In Brazil, the indigenous population proved unsuitable for plantation labour which was either destroyed or decimated by diseases. Thus, the African slaves were in great demand in every part of the world where plantation economy had developed. After 1600, Spanish America acquired about 3,000 slaves a year while Brazil nearly 5,000. In Asia as well, the Dutch started using the slaves to work in gold mines in Sumatra and to grow nutmeg in Amboina. Many Chinese were taken there as slaves. The Dutch and the Portuguese in Sri Lanka and other European colonies made use of Indian slaves from the subcontinent. The Portuguese and Dutch suppliers met the Spanish demand in the New World for black slaves. Several Africans were procured by the Portuguese entrepreneurs and brought to Spain for reshipment. From the 1520s, the slaves were sent directly to the New World. A group of contractors formed a monopoly for supplying slaves and came to be called *Asiento* and for some time they were very active in this trade. Later, the Dutch broke the Portuguese monopoly. The establishment of a colonial empire in the New World resulted in the rapid growth of slave traffic and the emergence of triangular trade, linking Africa, Europe and the New World. In response to the demand from the European planters, gold and silver miners and the towns of the New World, Africa sent huge consignments of slaves, about 9 lakh in the sixteenth century and 37.5 lakh in the seventeenth and between 70–80 lakh in the eighteenth century! This had repercussions throughout the African continent. On the one hand, it weakened and sapped the power of the inland states like Monomofapa and Congo and, on the other side, it encouraged a host of small and weak states to emerge along the coastal belt supplying European merchants with slaves and trade products. This opened the passage for the colonization of Africa. The Portuguese were the first to penetrate the African trade through the Gulf of Guinea and Angola in the western region and Mozambique in the east. They were followed by other European states.

Impact on Spain

The colonial empire appears to have had both positive and negative impact on Spain. Her colonial possessions certainly increased both power and prestige of the Spanish crown in Europe. The physical and administrative resources expanded enormously. It also derived vast patronage in the New World. The Spanish empire created a vast bureaucracy – the Council of the Indies, *Casa de Contratacion,* judicial structure, viceroys, *audencias*, the naval fleet and additional subjects. This raised the stature of the crown. In fact, the expanded bureaucracy in the long run became unweildy and burdensome. The crown also acquired ecclesiastical patronage and Charles kept the right to collect *tithes* with himself. He created new bishoprics and the Christian population in the New World owed allegiance to him. As many as twenty-two bishoprics and archbishoprics were established to regulate the lives of the Christian subjects there.

The Spanish and the Portuguese colonial policies were based on strict vigilance of the trade routes and the creation of trade monopolies (under state supervision) while the import of bullion led to mercantilism. For the first time, trade became a matter of national concern, as J.H. Parry suggests, 'a rising preoccupation with a single purpose'. Every state tried to be economically independent. They adopted policies for granting charters and privileges, monopolies and protection, control over foreign trade, encouragement to the navy and an overriding consideration to the accumulation of bullion by means of trade regulation. All these aspects became the chief tenets of mercantilism. Richard Hakluyt observed that Spain gained by transferring its unruly population to the new lands and pleaded with the English ruler to pursue a similar policy. The arrival of treasures made Seville one of the chief ports of Europe. The colonial trade promoted shipbuilding activities in northern Spain as there was a growing demand for merchant ships. However, this prosperity lasted only for a brief period. In the long run, the impact of the American Empire on Spain was far from beneficial. The Spanish decline is often associated with her colonial possessions and stemmed from the gross misuse of resources and false belief that bullion meant wealth and prosperity.

The Spanish economy was backward at the time it started acquiring colonial empires. The economic base was weak as agriculture was not well developed because of large infertile lands and because of the importance given to sheep farming. The industrial base too was fragile. As such, Spain could not properly utilise the riches that came from the New World, although industries like shipping did benefit. As the American demand for European goods increased with mass immigration of Europeans, Spain was incapable of exploiting the situation. Even after marshalling all her men, and materials like oil and wine of Andalusia, cloth from industrial towns, Spain proved unequal to the task of meeting the colonial demand. The rest of Europe seized this opportunity and the Spanish colonies came to be exploited more by merchants of other states than by Spain.

One of the negative aspects of Spanish colonialism was its total focus on the exploitation of bullion, and hardly any attempt made to diversify trade. To meet the increasing demand in her colonies for food and manufactured goods, Spain was compelled to arrange cargos from other countries, particularly from England, France and the Flanders. The Spanish colonies specialized in mining precious metals. In 1594 the Spanish cargo from America to Europe mainly consisted of bullion – 95.62 per cent of the total cargo consisted of treasure, 2.82 per cent of cochineal, 1.16 per cent of hides, 0.29 per cent of indigo and the rest were other small articles. In 1609, treasures still held 84 per cent of the share. As Scammell points out, the silver-bearing lands of the Indies became the heart of Spain's American empire and the governments of Mexico and Peru became the prime concerns of the Spanish rulers. The over-exploitation of the local population led to their virtual extinction and subsequently blacks from Africa had to be purchased. The two chief mines – Zacatecas and Potosi officially exported about 25,000 tonnes of silver to Europe between 1500 and 1660, while the annual unofficial exports may have constituted a larger volume. Mercury replaced lead in the Spanish exports. Andean mining alone employed nearly 13,000 workers. Several countries gained at the expense of Spain and received a vast portion of silver bullion by supplying manufactured items of their own industries. Holland, France and England entered this field of trade and caused serious damage to the Spanish interests. The activities of the French privateers caused havoc to the Spanish trans-Atlantic trade. It was Spain that extracted, imported and re-exported vast quantities of bullion but the gains went to the north-western European states.

Most historians blame the Spanish crown for squandering away the advantages of this prosperous trade. The Spanish rulers, Charles V (1516–66) and Philip II (1556–98) indulged in an adventurous foreign policy involving Spain in numerous wars. The Habsburg – Valois struggles, actions against Lutheran reformation, wars against England, the Netherlands (the War of Independence lasting several decades) and against the Turks, ate up not only the Spanish revenues but also the profits of the colonial enterprises. J.H. Elliott argues that Charles's imperialism was made possible by deficit financing and it was the lure of American silver, which provided an important inducement to the great financial houses to advance money to the Spanish ruler on such a massive scale and for so many years. Thus, the New World helped to sustain Europe's first great imperial adventure of the sixteenth century. The Spanish rulers had over-estimated their income from bullion. The fact was that the royal share of the treasure constituted only 11 per cent of its total income (John Lynch). It was based on the percentage of the output of bullion – one-fifth in the beginning and later coming down to one-tenth. The royal shares were used to pay huge interests to foreign bankers for the loans they had provided to the crown. Besides, a substantial portion of the bullion was spent to pay for the foreign goods which had been taken to the New World. The Spanish army in the Netherlands, sent there to suppress the rebellion, also consumed a good portion of American treasure. So in real terms, Spain experienced not a surplus of bullion but its acute shortage. As the silver supply began to decline, the Spanish rulers had to debase their currency several times. The decline in royal revenue led to a search for alternative income. The taxes that were raised hit the peasantry, manufacturers and commercial men. Historians like Elliott have placed the phenomena of Spanish decline in the wider context of the Atlantic world. Between 1621 and 1641, the Spanish Atlantic empire was beginning to collapse. This was partly caused by a fall in silver remittances from the Indies and the fresh international conflicts involving Spain. The New World was increasingly drawn into the European struggles of the 1620s and 1630s and the power struggle of Europe acquired a trans-Atlantic character. Thus the grandeur of the empire may have been impressive to contemporary Europeans but it rested on a fragile economy.

The atrocities committed by the Europeans in the newly acquired territories, particularly by the Spaniards, caused indignation only in a small circle of Europeans. The Spanish jurists initiated an intellectual debate on the legal status of the native Americans. William Penn suggested that the Quaker principle of religious toleration be practised in dealing with the Indians. Las Casas was the first person in that period to raise the question of the rights of conquered non-Western peoples. The atrocities of the Spanish officials and private individuals gave a terrible picture of the European conquest. The initial admiration gave way to serious criticism. Las Casas's *Brief Account of the Destruction of the Indies*

(1552) and Girolamo Benzoni's *History of the New World* (1565) provided a negative propaganda to the Spanish power. It was under Casas' influence that the Spanish monarchy abolished the slavery of the Amerindians although it could not enforce it. In *Apology* (1581), William of Orange presented a vivid picture of the destruction of 20 million Indians as an evidence of the innate propensity of the Spaniards to commit acts of unimaginable cruelty. Even the Catalans carried out a pamphlet campaign against Castile, projecting the sufferings of the Indians. Las Casas's major contribution was ideological rather than legal. It was the first major work on human rights. He provided the concept of the 'noble savage'. It was probably in France and England that the concept received attention as the inhabitants of the New World were presented as innocent people corrupted by the Europeans. Some thinkers and writers began to receive inspiration from the pre-Columbian civilizations and their society was seen as natural and pure as opposed to the luxurious and artificial society of Europe. It was against this background that Thomas Hobbes in his *Leviathan* presented the picture of a natural society prior to a society based on social contract.

What began as an exploration and search for new territories beyond Europe resulted in the acquisition of new lands for commercial and strategic gains. Slavery was promoted to exploit the potential resources of the new territories to reap higher gains. These encounters often caused collision in which the weaker side was subjugated by sheer naval and military power and turned into a colony for economic gains. The transformation of contact into collision, causing virtual destruction of local population in some regions, can be clearly seen right from the first voyage of Christopher Columbus and carried forward by the Spanish conquistadors.

Thus we find that in the years between the voyages of Columbus in the late-fifteenth century and Captain Cook in the late-eighteenth century laid the foundation of the modern world. Widening of knowledge, perception and exchanges of goods of commercial value transformed the nature of subsequent encounters. These encounters represented a struggle for empire building in which most of the European powers participated.

Major Events

1400	The Azores were chartered
1406	Ptolemy's *Geography* translated into Latin
1415	Portuguese take Ceuta
1418	Henry the Navigator begins to patronize the Portuguese voyages. Exploration of Madeira Islands
1434	Gil Eannes rounded Cape Bojador
1444	Cape Verde Islands discovered. Nuno Tristam reaches Senegal River
1451	Birth of Columbus
1460	Death of Prince Henry, the Navigator
1475	Zacuto's Tables of Sun's declination
1482	Diego Cao's first voyage
1488	Bartholemew Dias rounded Cape of Good Hope
1492	Columbus sails from Spain and discovers the New World
1494	Treaty of Tordesillas
1496	John Cabot's first voyage
1498	Da Gama reaches Calicut
1499	Voyage of Amerigo Vespucci and Hojeda
1499	Voyage of Gaspar Corte Real to Greenland
1500	Voyage of Cabral to Brazil
1502	Vasco da Gama's second voyage
1502	Columbus's final voyage
1508–11	Conquest of Jamaica and Puerto Rico by Spain
1510	Capture of Goa by the Portuguese
1511	Capture of Malacca by the Portuguese
1513	Balboa sights Pacific Ocean
1519–22	Magellan's Voyage to Malacca through the southern hemisphere
1519–21	Cortés acquires Mexico
1524	Verrazzano's voyage to North America
1531–33	Pizarro conquers Peru
1534	Cartiers's first voyage; organization of The Society of Jesus by Loyola
1542	Charles issues New Laws for the New World
1545	Opening of silver mines at Potosi

Suggested Readings

Adas, Michael, ed., *Islamic and European Expansion: The Forging of a Global Order*, Philadelphia: Temple University Press, 1993. The chapters by William H. McNeill, Alfred W. Crosby and Philip D. Curtis are extremely useful for the study of sea voyages to America, the Atlantic slave trade and historiography on exchanges and provide fresh insight on sea voyages and their impact.

Bethencourt, Francisco and Diogo Ramada Curto, eds., *Portuguese Oceanic Expansion 1400–1800*, Cambridge: Cambridge University Press, 2007. It is an extremely valuable contibution using unexplored sources and examines the relational dynamics between groups and regions within the Imperial Complex in economic and religious terms.

Boxer, C.R., *The Portuguese Seaborne Empire 1415–1825*, New York: Hutchinson, 1969. A standard account of the Portuguese trading activities and the nature of their empire.

———, *Four Centuries of Portuguese Expansion,* Berkeley: California Press, 1972. A well-written narrative of the development of the Portuguese empire.

Chaunu, Pierre, *European Expansion in the Later Middle Ages*, tr. Katherine Bertram, Amsterdam: North Holland Publishing Company, 1979. Based on exhaustive research on the trade between the New World and Spain.

Crosby, Alfred W., *Ecological Imperialism: The Biological Expansion of Europe, 900–1900,* Cambridge: Cambridge University Press, 1986. Good for cultural exchange, population migrations maps and illustrations.

Curto, Diogo Ramada and, Francisco Bethencourt, eds., *Portuguese Oceanic Expansion 1400–1800*, Cambridge: Cambridge University Press, 2006. The essays treat a wide range of subjects – economy and society, politics, institutions, cultural figurations and provide a broad understanding of the Portuguese Empire having a global dimension.

Davis, Ralph, *Rise of Atlantic Economies*, Ithaca: Weidenfeld and Nicolson, 1973. An analytical presentation of not only the colonial activities across the Atlantic but the regional economies of Europe.

Donald, F. Lach, *Asia in the Making of Europe*, vol. II, *A Century of Wonder*, Chicago/London: University of Chicago Press, 1970. Good for Asian discovery including art, handicrafts, curiosities and iconography.

Earle, Thomas F. and Kate J.P. Lowe, eds., *Black Africans in Renaissance Europe*, Cambridge: Cambridge University Press, 2005. Contains articles on the presence of African blacks in Europe during the fifteenth century based on archival sources and iconography.

Elliott, J.H., *The Old World and The New, 1492–1650,* Cambridge: Cambridge University Press, 1970. Brief but good presentation of the relationship between Spain and her colonies.

McAlister, Lyle N., *Spain and Portugal in the New World, 1492–1700,* Oxford: Oxford University Press, 1984. An exhaustive explanatory presentation of the emergence, nature and consequences of the early colonial empires.

Mathew, K.S., *Portuguese Trade with India in the Sixteenth Century,* New Delhi: Manohar, 1983. Provides an Indian perspective to the Portuguese empire.

Parry, J.H., *The Age of Reconnaissance,* London: Weidenfeld & Nicolson, 1963. An excellent survey on European navigation and expansion in the early phase.

———, *The Spanish Seaborne Empire,* New York: Knopf, 1966. Good narrative presentation of the Spanish colonial activities and the structure of their empire.

Phillips, William D. and Carla Rahn Phillips, *The Worlds of Christopher Columbus*, Cambridge: Cambridge University Press, 1992. Takes up all aspects of Columbus, including his voyages, conquests, colonization and the post-Columbian world.

Scammell, G. V., *The First Imperial Age: European Overseas Expansion 1400-1750,* London: Unwin Hyman, 1989. Good detailed account of origins of empires and their impact on either side of the continent. The author has placed European trading activities in a wider perspective.

Schwartz, Stuart B., ed., *Implicit Understanding, Observing, Reporting, and Reflecting on the Encounters between European and other Peoples in the Early Modern Era,* Cambridge: Cambridge University Press, 1994. Contains nineteen articles by different scholars on the European vision of the newly discovered territories. The book discusses the cultural encounters and includes implicit ethnographies.

Subrahmanyam, Sanjay, ed., *Sinners and Saints: The Successors of Vasco da Gama,* New Delhi: Oxford University Press, 1998.

———, *The Portuguese Empire in Asia, 1500–1700*, London: Longman, 1993. Scholarly work with a fresh approach on the subject.

Taviani, Paolo Emilio, *Christopher Columbus: The Grand Design*, 2 vols., London: Orbis, 1985. The first volume includes a biography of Columbus and a discussion on his ideas and motives and the second volume includes a series of extended notes and documents.

CHAPTER 4

The Reformation

The Reformation in the conventional sense implies the schism or break within the Roman Catholic Church that functioned under the Pope in Europe for centuries and the creation of a separate Protestant Christianity. This break-up of the unity of Christendom was only one part of the Reformation. It led to the creation of several radical and moderate folds within Christianity such as Lutherans, Calvinists, Puritans, Anabaptists, Anglicans, Presbyterians. There was also the efforts of some Catholics to reform their church through the counter-reformation. More significant were the profound changes in the religious sensibilities and attitudes of the people towards social and economic issues. The Reformation embraced a number of areas – reform of both the morals and structures of church and society, re-interpretation of Christian spirituality and the reform of its doctrine. The popularity of Reform movements cannot be properly understood purely in religious light. Rather these have to be placed in their historical, political, social and economic context. The Reformation was far more than a movement directed against the abuses in the Roman Catholic Church. It was the culmination of a complex situation with roots deeply buried in the medieval past.

Prelude

The Christian church was effectively unified till the mid-eleventh century. However, western and central Europe came under the control of the Pope while the Byzantine church emerged under the influence of the Patriarch of Constantinople. There were bitter conflicts between the two heads on the question of supremacy and church incomes. In AD 1054 a split in the Christian Church occurred. Since then the Western church came to be called Catholic (means universal) and the church in the Byzantine empire came to be known as the Orthodox Church (means the 'right faith') or the Greek Orthodox Church in some parts.

The Catholic Church was a strong bond which provided religious uniformity to the numerous feudal units. In the absence of political unity, the church helped in the stabilization of social relations. The Pope was the head of Catholic Church which owned vast amount of wealth and property. All the ecclesiastical (an adjective pertaining to church matters) appointments throughout Europe were made by him. He lived in Rome and had an elaborate hierarchical establishment with splendid rituals, magnificent cathedrals and a vast organization to control education and charity. He raised his own army and his own ambassadors were appointed in distant states. The rulers and princes found it difficult to disobey the Papal edicts (the orders of the Pope having the force of law). The popes interfered in the internal, political and financial matters of the rulers.

During the thirteenth century, several rulers became vassals of Pope Innocent III. About one-third of all cultivated land in western Europe was under the control of the Catholic Church. It owned cattle, granaries and cellars. The bishops, abbots and the various church officials differed little from other feudal lords. In a way the Catholic Church provided unity to European feudalism. The weakening of the feudal structure from the late medieval period was bound to have repercussion on the church as well.

Origins of the Reformation

The Catholic Church in the fourteenth and fifteenth centuries faced institutional problems because of the failure of the Papal authority to provide spiritual leadership. This was at a time when religious sensibility of the people had heightened; when wars, epidemics, diseases and crop failures had created such chaos for which the only explanation for the common people could be the wrath of God. Contemporary writings unquestionably indicate a state of increasing ecclesiastical corruption and inefficiency. The church leaders showed their inability to satisfy the people's longing for personal piety.

The economic changes and the feudal crisis had led to pre-occupation of the Papal courts with financial and political matters. The entire financial burden of growing expenses of the church usually fell on the ordinary people. The Roman Catholic Church charged its members for various services that included marriages, baptisms, confessions and burials. Appeal against the priest had to pass all the way to Rome and that involved heavy legal expenditure. The financial burden of the Catholic Church was one of the important factors leading to the mounting criticism of Papal authority. The political entanglements inevitably created financial demands. It was the style of collecting funds to meet the growing demands, which created bitterness and hostility against the church and provided the immediate background to the Reformation.

The papacy had developed its own extensive bureaucratic structure and fiscal system. It required huge funds to carry out crusades against the Turks and the Italian war (Pope Alexander [1492–1503], Julius II [1503–13], Leo X [1513–21] were all actively involved in the Italian War with their political alignment with France or Spain). They also needed funds for the lavish buildings and basilicas made during the Renaissance, to maintain a vast bureaucracy and army and to pay for the luxurious lifestyle of the church officials. The traditional methods of extracting revenue were intensified. The clergy collected *tithe* (about a tenth of the income) from the population. The latter also had to pay to the church for wedding ceremonies, baptism of the children, *dispensation* for uncanonical marriages and for many other services. The Pope received various types of subscription from officials of the far-flung churches. These included Tenths (one-tenth part of the income was to be sent to Pope), First Fruits (offering connected with the beginning of the harvest), Annates (the first year's revenue benefice paid to the Papal Curia) and Peter's Pence (a yearly tax of penny on every household). The most controversial of all the subscriptions was the sale of indulgences (cards of pardon from a grave sin on huge payment to the church). The papal revenues showed signs of diminishing returns and the new ways of collecting wealth had become extremely unpopular, particularly among the rising social classes. Most of the cardinals (the Pope's representatives in distant states) also enjoyed the highest political power in their respective countries, e.g. Cardinal Wolsey in England, Cardinal Ximenes in Spain, etc. The church officials tried to accumulate as many church offices as possible to enhance their revenue. This practice of pluralism (holding of several church posts simultaneously) in fact led to the problem of absenteeism. As one person could not perform the duties of so many posts, the church office holders neglected their episcopal functions and delegated their duties to underserving persons who had little knowledge or interest in performing those duties. Naturally the standard of church administration started falling.

The economic problems of the church led to an increasing separation between the upper and the lower clergies. The higher officials like cardinals, archbishops, bishops and abbots who came from the nobility vied for church positions and accumulated huge wealth, while the lower clergies (the parish priests) remained poor and came from among commoners. Social discontent among the lower clergies grew for whom the avenues of promotion remained blocked. The lower clergy were also unable to provide right religious and moral guidance. Growing social discontent was directed against the various views of the church officials, their avarice and rapacity, the ignorance and poor quality of clergies and priests. Demand for reforms also emanated from an increasing number of women who devoted their life to God. Though they could not be ordained as priests nor could be included as members of the secular clergy, these saintly women or divine mothers as they are sometimes called, wished to purify religion by spiritual reforms.

Growth of Popular Religion

The demand for reforms in the religious organization does not necessarily imply a rise in anti-religious sentiments. Works (like the one by Bernd Moeller's 'Piety in Germany Around 1500' in S. Ozment, ed., *The Reformation in Medieval Perspective*, 1971, pp. 50–75) indicate that the failure of Papal church led to a craving for a purposeful religion and ideas of definite salvation. There was a distinct growth in popular religion in Germany and some other centres on the eve of the Reformation. A crisis of the authority was accompanied by the rise of doctrinal pluralism.

Popular religion implied efforts to convert the abstract views of theologians into concrete social practices. 'Popular piety' reflected the forms and modes of expression shared by large social groups perceiving themselves within a Christian context. This piety remained tied to the traditional ideas of hope and prophecy, the desire to be redeemed, fears of death and ideas of purgatory and eternity.

One common form of religious piety in the fifteenth century was to undertake pilgrimages to holy centres and making donations out of reverence at religious relics. By such contributions it was believed that the period of purgatory (the condition after death in which the soul is purified in preparation for heaven) could be drastically reduced.

Other forms of religious piety were the popular mystical movement – *the Modern Devotion*, the Brothers and Sisters of the Common Life founded by Gerard Groote in Netherlands. The most noteworthy name in this form is that of Thomas à Kempis who is believed to have written the mystical classic – *The Invitation of Christ.* It suggested that the path to salvation was not through dogmas and speculations but by strictly imitating the moral and ethical conduct of Christ. That God's judgement is determined not by words but by deeds. The Bible was regarded as the true guide to Christian life. Although nothing was said against church practices and beliefs, popular mysticism reduced the importance of the formal church in the lives of the common people. The movement of popular mysticism was led by Wessel Gansfort. Later, Luther himself shared ideas similar to Gansfort's, especially his idea of viewing true Christianity as a spiritual communion with God.

According to Alister E. McGrath, almost a century before the Reformation, a crisis of authority was surfacing in the Christian world. To enforce orthodoxy and check that were energing among the people radical views, Papal authority needed greater centralization. The central church found it difficult to define Christian orthodoxy and enforce it because of two emerging trends in the late-medieval church. One was *the Great Schism* (1378–1417) which led to the division of the Western church. After the death of Pope Gregory XI, there were three rival claimants for the post – Gregory XII, Benedict XIII and John XXIII, a situation in which the authority to settle disputes was handed over to a council. The Council of Constance (1414–17) selected Martin V as its candidate for the post of Pope and advised him to bring about religious reforms. Two rival theories of authority developed – those who believed that the real authority to decide doctrinal disputes resided in a general council (called the conciliarist position) and those who held that this authority resided in the person of the Pope (the curialist position). Second, the demand for church reforms aggravated this crisis of authority. The Counciliar Movement through the councils of Pisa (1409), Constance (1414–17) and Basle (1431–9) made attempts to persuade the papacy to delegate authority. It was an attempt to bring changes within the church through the efforts of individuals, monastic orders and general councils.

Individual attempts for reforms were made by men like John Wycliff (1320–84) in England and John Hus (1374–1415) in Bohemia. Their followers came to be called Lollards and Hussites respectively. In England, it was a simple Biblical egalitarianism calling for the dis-endowment of the church. Wycliff stressed the role of faith – a free gift of God to everyone. It did not depend on participation in the church's rituals or following its sacraments. Initially the English nobility that disliked the economic power of the church supported his views. However, the support rendered by the peasants in the revolt of 1381 adversely affected Wycliff's position because it meant losing the support of the gentry, as their interests clashed. The Lollards failed to get support of the English gentry and the movement remained confined to the small academic world of Oxford University where Wycliff had taught in the 1360s and 1370s. The Hussite movement in Bohemia was more complex. Hus was a university theologian who later denied Papal supremacy. He conceived the church in exclusive terms as the community of faithful obedience to Christ's law and attempted to create a utopian religious society. He was declared heretic by the Pope and was burnt alive at the stake in 1415. These were localized protest movements against the powerful papacy challenging its doctrinal and spiritual leadership in Christendom. However, the academic influence of Wycliff and Hus on the outside world remained slight and weak. The Bohemian nobility played an important role as the patrons and protectors of this radical movement, a feature later seen in the aristocratic societies of the Puritan era. Similar efforts to reform the religion by forming separate organizations outside the Roman Catholic Church such as Albigenses and Waldenses also failed and were suppressed by the papal authorities. However, these attempts of reforms form the background to the sixteenth-century Reformation. These above-mentioned movements clearly suggest that initially there was some hope that the church could be reformed from within and when such hopes clashed with the adamant attitude of the church officials fresh attempts were made to impose reforms through an appeal to the secular authorities. Bohemia remained a religious battleground between the authorities and the people well into the seventeenth century.

A question that is often raised by scholars is why these earlier attempts failed while the attempts of religious reforms succeeded in the sixteenth century. There are several plausible explanations.

Firstly, after the feudal crisis, strong centralized states began to emerge in several parts of Europe under absolute monarchies. The middle ages had witnessed disputes between the church and the states on some core issues. The judicial jurisdiction claimed by the Pope and the assertion of political sovereignty by the rulers had been a source of contention. Machiavelli had very ably demonstrated the evil effects of religious interference in politics. The church with its own legal and fiscal organization across national boundaries had become a hindrance in the path of royal efforts to achieve centralized administrations. The kings and the princes desired complete supremacy over their own states – control of the subjects as well as their pockets. Greater control meant larger revenues. Henry VIII of England completed the break with the Roman Catholic Church with popular support on grounds of nationalism.

There is sufficient evidence to suggest that there existed a powerful anti-Roman feeling in Germany, which lent support to the Lutheran reformation. Protestant reformers allied themselves with civil or state authorities to carry forward their views on reform. Martin Luther sought the support of the German nobility while Zwingli in Switzerland appealed to the city councils of Zurich for implementing his reform programme. European Reformation progressed mostly with an alliance between the reformers and the civil authorities. The Reformation often took the form of a movement led by individual rulers to achieve their freedom from the Roman Catholic Church. At the same time, we must remember that the institutional breakdown of the Catholic Church and Christendom was not confined to only those areas that opted for Protestantism. The Catholic Church lost its hold on episcopal appointments and a resistance by the local princes and lay authorities to the universality of Canon law (the legislation which governs the faith, morals, and organization of the church) and Roman ecclesiastical courts had started much before 1517.

Second, the Reformation in the sixteenth century was possible because of the technological innovation such as the printing press. Though not wholly dependant on the printing press, the Reformation did contribute as an agent of change in the intellectual climate. The printing press replaced the painstaking process of copying manuscripts by hand. The multiplication of the original copies and its availability in different parts of Europe made great impact in the academic world. The printed works could easily spread the ideas of religious reformers. As McGrath points out, the greater influence of Protestantism at Cambridge than at Oxford was partly because of the former's proximity to the continental European ports from which the Protestant books were obtained. Lutheran books were more popular amongst the English upper classes by the third decade of the sixteenth century because these classes were literate and had the money to pay for the printed books. The Reformation focused on the original sources – the Bible and the works of the Christian theologians of the first few centuries. These theologians were usually referred to as the 'Patristic Writers'. The coming of the printing press helped in the preparation of more accurate editions of their works. The Humanists immensely contributed to this process. The writings of Augustine (a Scholastic writer), the publication of the New Testament and the production of the Greek New Testament first published in 1516 by Erasmus made such sources widely available and helped in the spread of Reformation ideas in different parts of Europe. In the absence of a printing press, Wycliff's ideas were hardly known but the printing press enabled Luther's views to spread speedily beyond Germany. The Reformation drastically increased the availability of reading material and widened the book market. Within Wittenberg alone seven shops sprang up, printing exclusively the writings of Luther and his associates (Carter Lindberg, 1996, p. 37). At the time of Luther's death in 1546, as many as a million copies of the Bible had been printed. The Reformation propaganda included tracts, pamphlets, translations, pictures and cartoons.

The third significant factor which contributed to the cause of the Reformation, was the rise of Renaissance humanism. It created an intellectual climate, which was lacking in the days of Wycliff and Hus. Although humanism as a movement was not directly related to religion or church organization, it provided tools of criticism and raised several issues that at times were related to the religion preached and practised in those days. It can be said that the challenge to papal supremacy that culminated with the Protestant Reformation would have been unthinkable without the contribution of Renaissance humanism.

Christian humanism was an attempt to rediscover man through the search and study of original manuscripts. The classical learning when applied to Biblical study could provide a greater harmony between faith and intellect. In certain parts of northern Europe, Biblical research was accompanied by scathing attacks on scholasticism. Scholasticism was an academic movement of the late medieval period in which Christian theology was developed by an appeal to the philosophy of Aristotle, Thomas Aquinas and Duns Scotus. They tried to establish the inherent rationality of Christian theology based on logic. This had made the religion too vague and complex for the common people. A bitter confrontation between humanism and scholasticism in the late-fifteenth century created fresh grounds for the Reformation to develop. Erfurt University in Germany was one such centre where Martin Luther's theological ideas took shape in reaction to scholastic theology. The critical analysis of the original texts by the humanist scholars removed several misquotations of the patristic writers, including Augustine's writings, and placed them in relevant context.

No other humanist figure had such powerful influence on the reformation leaders (like Zwingli, Bucer, etc.) as Erasmus of Rotterdam. His writings are considered to be the best example of Northern Humanism. Desiderius Erasmus (1466–1536) tried to make Christianity meaningful for the people. His influence spread throughout the sixteenth century and his views are at times described as the 'Erasmian Reformation'. It was Erasmus who laid stress on the role of the scriptures, which needed to be taken away from the monopolistic control of the theologians. Practical piety for him was a matter of spirit rather than formal observance. He discouraged unnecessary religious practices like the worship of saints or obsession with pilgrimages. He emphasized humanist education, which would lead to a just society under an educated prince and on the true path of Jesus Christ. His work *Enchiridion Militis Christians* (Handbook of the Christian Soldier), was the most influential humanist writing of that period and was first published in 1503. It gained Europe-wide popularity after 1515 when its third edition came out. He wanted the Christian religion should be based on the original scripture, the philosophy of Christ to provide a form of morality and the New Testament be treated as the law of Christ, which Christians must obey. His typical humanist stress upon inner religion stirred the ideas of several later reformers. He believed that there was no need to confess one's sins to a priest when it could be done directly to God. Nor did he believe that religious life was the highest form of Christian life. Erasmus strongly believed that the future of Christianity lay with the laity rather than with the clergy.

The impact of humanism on the Swiss Reformation was quite pronounced. The city of Zurich in which Zwingli started a programme of reform that was broadly based on humanist ideas of corporate church and the primacy of scripture. Here humanism provided an intellectual plank based on the views of Erasmus.

In Germany also, humanism was an important force that directly challenged scholasticism. The universities in the German states had become the battlegrounds between the two groups. German university circles played a great role in the rise of humanism and some of the princely patrons focused on the new education propagated by the humanists. As A.G. Dickens suggests, it is difficult to describe German humanism as a movement because apart from the common love for the ancient world, the humanists in Germany exhibited a wide variety of convictions. The chief humanists – Rudolf Agricola, Brant Wimpfeling, Mutian, Celtis, Hutten and many others had their own set of programmes and views. Most of them quite often revealed anti-Papal tendencies. They were strong critics of papal abuses and reflected strong national feelings and popularized folk legends. They contributed immensely to the growth of vernacular literature and acted as 'midwives to the Lutheran Reformation' (A.G. Dickens). Folk poems reflecting anti-Papal sentiments such as the 'Blind Leading the Blind' and the popularity of plays like 'Of the Rise and Fall of Antichrist'.

Millenarianism

Millenarianism was a belief among the Christians that some time in future the world would come to an end and christ and his saint shall reign for a thousand years upon the earth. Goodwill will triumph and historical wrongs will be rectified and injustice and exploitation of poor would end. These ideas were derived from the *Book of Revelations* and perhaps received acceptability from the official church. It was believed that the duration of this glorious reign of Christ and his saints on earth would be of one thousand years. Hence it was called millennium while the future kingdom called 'millenarianism'. The social and economic inequalities led medieval reformers, particularly from the poorer strata of society, to interpret this doctrine to mean that Christ would condemn the rich and establish a new world for the poor. They believed that for a thousand years, the poor would rule Christ's kingdom. It was a radical interpretation that gave its believers a justification to attack established institutions and corruption prevalent within them. This made them argue that the medieval church was ruled by an anti-Christ, described as the 'whore of Babylon' mentioned in the Bible. When the reformers of the sixteenth century led by Luther, called the Pope an anti-Christ, they were actually perpetuating this old tradition of protest and systematic attacks on the church. Even Chaucer highlighted the corruption among the church officials in *The Canterbury Tales* in which the two clerics were made objects of scorn and disgust because they sold indulgences and were extremely corrupt.

Recent studies by historians, sociologists and anthropologists suggest that millenarianism was a wide trans-cultural phenomenon having an element of religion. It was responsible for some early-modern revolutions. It can be seen as a form of salvation representing collective mentality. However, not every Christian held this belief and there were several others who disowned the millenarian belief and the excesses of their followers.

Social Context of the Reformation

Scholars have variously explained the religious upheavals of the Reformation that destroyed the outward framework of the society under a single church. As Lawrence Stone points out, there are two ways of looking at this crisis. The first view lays stress on the religious emotions and faith, that could be seen in the popular undercurrents of the movement. The Reformation is seen as a series of responses from leading men and institutions who faced popular pressures and demands. This view, in fact, emphasizes the ideological tensions and clashes that were already at work in late-medieval Europe. The second view lays great stress on the outstanding personalities and their use of power and the might of the state to impose their ideas on the people. This determined minority imposed its views on Christian doctrines on a docile or at times reluctant majority by use of force like the Calvinist rule in Netherlands and the Anglican reforms in England.

As regards the beginning of the Reformation, one interpretation (going back to the writing of Henri Hauser) suggests that it was effective in those areas of Europe that were victims of violent economic and social dislocation. The growth of population caused rise in prices. The fragmentation of rural holdings, rising rents and declining wages caused rural people to migrate to towns, leading to unemployment and a widening gap between the rich and the poor. The artisans and the peasants were particularly affected by the stagnant or lowering wages, rising prices and increasing taxation. Hence, it is suggested that the success of Luther and Calvin was due to poverty, resentment and social discontent of the masses. However, this view cannot be accepted without qualifications, as there is very little evidence of such population pressure that could cause social dislocation on such a scale and get people directly involved with the Reformation. This interpretation cannot be applied to all the regions because Germany, where the Reformation took off, was a reasonably developed region while Scotland, another centre of Reformation, was quite backward.

Marx and Engels suggests that the Reformation was related to the rise of the bourgeoisie. The Reformation is seen as 'revolutionary' because it represented the challenge of a new class to feudal order. Also, in the long run, the overthrow of the old church opened the way to a gradual secularization of thought among the literate classes, with religion being viewed as a purely private concern. Engels explains that the Reformation was possible because of Germany's economic development and its growing share in the international trade. In his article 'The Great Peasant War' Friedrich Engels wrote that the years between the beginning of the Reformation and the end of the Peasant War formed the early Phase of the bourgeois revolution in Germany. The Peasant War is seen as an expression of a socio-economic conflict of which the Reformation was an ideological expression. For the Marxists, the revolutionary terminology of social prophets was a device to enlist the masses and thereby the reformers became the unwilling agents of social revolution. It is believed that the growing commercial activity contributed to the wealth and size of the merchant community and that Luther, Calvin and Zwingli made direct impression on this influential social group in the free cities. However, it can be doubted whether (a) the increase in wealth of the bourgeoisie was as fast as that of the new aristocracy which benefited from the rise in rent and landed incomes or the rise in economic strength of the princes who had acquired wealth by seizing church property and augmented state revenues through new taxes (see Chapter 9). How can one explain the success of the Presbyterian religion in Scotland which was an extremely poor and backward region. There hardly existed a class of bourgeoisie to promote the new ideas. In fact, the Reformation leaders appealed to the princes, nobility and the city councils rather than the bourgeoisie.

The sociological explanation of the Reformation has gained ground in recent years. According to this view, the clergies were discredited for their failure to discharge spiritual and administrative functions and the new educated elite from the laity showed its eagerness to take over these functions. This is discernible at all stages of the Reformation. The path to salvation as practised and administered by the ill-reputed priests was losing its appeal. The anti-clerical feelings were greatly strengthened by the humanist movement while the New Testament contributed to the destruction of priestly authority. Taking advantage of this situation, the princes and nobles in certain regions seized church property and its power. The Reformation had a special appeal to certain groups who were likely to gain from this movement – for the princes it was an ideal instrument for state building; for the oligarchs the teachings of Zwingli and Calvin helped them establish their control over city population; and the growing middle class got a chance to free itself from the shackles of old religious practices, while the lower classes believed that their tax burden would be relieved with the destruction of Papal control. The growing sentiments of nationalism (e.g. in some of the German states, Zurich, England, etc.) also contributed to the quick success of the Reformation.

Thus, the Reformation arose, as Alister McGrath points out, from a complex heterogeneous matrix of social and ideological factors. The rise of nationalism, the growing political power of the south German states and the Swiss cities, the emergence of individual personalities, intellectual movements and theological awareness at the time of growing crises in the church gave way to the Reformation movement, though it varied from one region to another.

The German Reformation

The politics and socio-economic condition of Germany was conducive to the emergence and spread of Protestant Reformation. The German economy was developing quickly, particularly in the fields of textile, paper and glass manufacture in the Rhine and the upper Danube region. The production of iron and copper recorded a steady growth. A few families had established their control over mining ore and the smelting process. They invested in expensive equipments to exploit the mines and employed a large number of the poor as miners. Augsburg and Nuremberg saw the rise of a few families. The most phenomenal was the rise of the Fugger family, from mere weavers to banking princes of Europe. They had diversified their activities into commerce, lending to kings, princes and the church at high rates of interest, and had obtained monopoly rights over silver and copper mines. Other rich banker families were the Ehingers and Schads in Ulm and Hochstetters and Welsers in Augsburg. Although the economy made impressive advances in the sixteenth century, the benefits were not evenly distributed. Max Stienmetz suggests that Germany's economic position was characterized by an upturn in commercial production yet feudalism in the countryside remained strong. The clergy often played the role of landlord fuelling a spirit of revolt among the peasants, and the Catholic Church still owned a substantial portion of land in Germany. The Rhine was the most fertile region under church control and was often referred to as 'the priest's road' and Archbishops and some Bishops had become virtual rulers of church-controlled lands. A strong feeling began to develop against church exploitation by the late-fifteenth century. Hence, anti-papalism and anti-clericalism became the two main characteristics of German region.

A.G. Dickens lays stress on the impact of humanists and pamphleteers during the years after 1500 in stirring up German nationalism, and the encouragement of anti-Italian and anti-Papal sentiments, by providing new weapons to the old campaign against the church. Anti-Papal prejudices had grown between the empire and the popes because of the conflicts on the issue of investiture from the eleventh and twelfth centuries. Lupord, the Bishop of Bamberg in his *Tractate on the Laws of the Kingdom and the Empire* wished to see the German empire independent of the control of Papal authority. Conrad of Megenberg also enthused the German humanists through his literary writings and asserted the authority of the General Council over Pope. Konrad Celtis and Gregor Reisch and many other writers further strengthened patriotic sentiments and put forward their criticisms of Papal power. Gregor made similar charges of corruption and financial exploitation against the papacy and incited political discord within the German empire as Luther had done. In his writings he highlighted the contrast between the actions of the papacy and the teachings of Jesus Christ.

Martin Luther listed Papal and clerical abuses in his famous reforming treatise of 1520 – *An Appeal to the German Nobility*. The rise of humanism emphasized the idea of individual consciousness and human individuality, which raised new interest in the doctrine of justification – how human beings could enter into a relationship with God. However, the humanist effort at reform was elitist in character and found limited popular support. He achieved practical success because of his moderate approach and the popular resentment against the prevalent practice of the sale of 'indulgences'. The rise of humanism in Germany had already prepared the ground for him.

Pierre Chaunu (*Le Temps des Réformes*) mentions three factors that were favourable to German Reformation: Distance from Rome, widespread literacy in that region and fragmentation of political power. He insists that it was the Rhineland corridor rather than the Saxony of Luther that brought together all the circumstances required for a religious change.

Before studying Martin Luther's ideas, it would be useful to know what was an indulgence. It began as a gift of money or donation as an expression of thanks for forgiveness. Later it became an important instrument of income for the church. Initially, indulgence meant relaxation of the punishment imposed by the church for a moral sin. Later it became a remission of punishment in purgatory by God and not the church alone. Thus God's grace was commercially sold through Pope's agents via Albrecht of Brandenburg and the banking house of Fuggers. Indulgences became popular as people feared purgatory and they then bought not only for their own preservation from divine punishment but also for others. It is believed that Cardinal Albrecht of Brandenburg successfully accumulated a remission of purgatorial penalties reckoned to total 3,92,45,120 years (McGrath). The German reformation under Luther was a direct reaction to the church's exploitation of popular piety and the misrepresentation of religious doctrines.

Martin Luther and the Protestant Reformation

Martin Luther (1483–1546) was from a peasant background although his father raised himself into the ranks of lower bourgeoisie by working in the mines. His father provided him with a good education and wanted him to become a lawyer. His mother came from a burgher family and showed an intense piety that must have made Luther close to the German popular religion. While studying Law, Luther showed strong religious inclinations and in 1505 he decided to become a monk. He entered the monastic order in Erfurt much against his father's wish. There are many interesting stories on why Luther became a monk. It is said that Luther was haunted by many fears and when a bolt of lightening and thunder in a forest frightened him, he prayed to God and took a vow to become a monk. Another view suggests that Luther's unexpected encounter with death made him enter the cloister.

Lutheran Reformation had its beginning in a simple question often asked by Christians – what must be done to seek the forgiveness of God. Luther's answer did not fit into the traditional practices of the church and so he decided to split with the Papal church and provided his own solutions and became a popular reformer.

Luther was a professor of Theology at the university of Wittenberg. He showed keen interest in education, displayed a flair

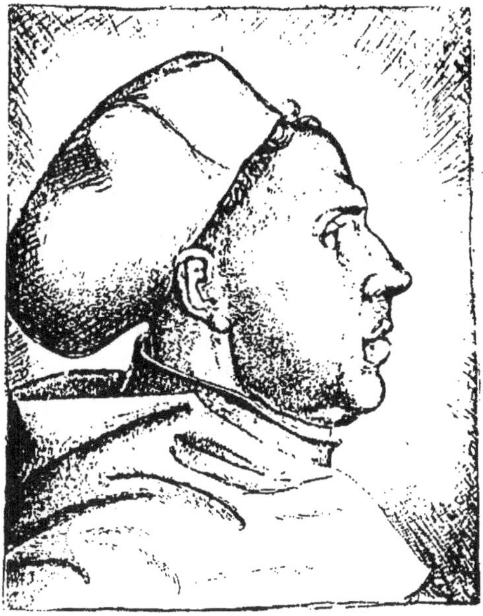

Martin Luther

for languages and had good knowledge of history. These qualities, along with his views on scholasticism brought him closer to the humanists. Yet he maintained a constant distance with the other humanists of his time.

Luther's primary concern as a monk was focused on the assurance of salvation. The prevalent beliefs and practices of the Roman Catholic Church failed to provide any satisfactory answer to him. The traditional chruch had advocated adherence to Catholic sacraments, and make confession in front of a priest as the chief means of receiving God's grace and forgiveness for the sins committed. The other course was to buy the indulgence, which was suggested as a short-cut. In 1517, Martin Luther nailed his *Ninety Five Thesis* on the church door in Wittenberg and directly challenged the sale of indulgences as means of seeking god's forgiveness. His actions immediately attracted the attention of all Europe. Engels described Luther's revolt against the Roman Catholic Church as 'Luther's lightning struck home'.

Luther's protest in 1517 was not aimed against the main fabric of the established church and its doctrine, rather against the elaboration of a dogma that was still controversial. It was only a criticism not defiance of certain church practices. His theological development progressed in the three subsequent years till he finally rejected the claim that the Pope was the sole 'institution' to interpret scriptures. When the Pope issued a bull (a Roman Catholic Church proclamation) of excommunication, Luther publicly burned it. He published a series of pamphlets in which the Pope and his whole organization was openly condemned. In *The Freedom of the Christian Man* (1520), Luther advocated true spiritual freedom through faith in Christ. In 1521, the Holy Roman Emperor asked Luther to appear before the Diet (parliament) at Worms to face trial. Luther refused to recant his position and thus was outlawed by the highest civil authority in Germany. He remained under a sentence of death throughout his life but was shielded and supported by the Elector of Saxony – Frederick, who personally did not like Papal interference in an academic centre. While in hiding Luther translated the New Testament. The supporters of his views came to be called the Lutherans or the Protestants.

Luther escaped the fate of the previous religious rebels for a number of reasons. Pope Leo X was busy organizing a crusade against the Turks while Emperor Maximilian was preoccupied with his succession issue. He died in 1519 and there was an intensive campaign to elect his successor. No prospective candidate could afford to offend Frederick of Saxony, as his support was crucial in the election. By the time the election was over and Charles of Spain became the Holy Roman Emperor, Luther's ideas had spread rapidly and the nobility in Germany started accepting his position. Frederick's support to Luther was the key to Luther's success. Humanist Chancellor, George Spalatin also supported Luther at the court. Luther's Protestantism was adopted as the state religion by Philip of Hesse and was subsequently supported by the rulers of Brunswick, Wurttenberg, Brandenberg, and many other states and by the imperial cities of Strasberg, Augsburg and Nuremberg. Frederick arranged for Luther to stay in secret in Wartburg castle to protect him against the punitive measures of the Pope and the emperor. The imperial free cities were the chief centres of printing and humanist activities and these factors contributed to the initial spread of Luther's views. These urban centres were already resisting the privileged position of the church and Luther's stress on the equality of the clergy and laity gave an excellent opportunity to establish the supremacy of a secular authority. Luther's ideas were also appealing to the middle orders in the towns – the petty burghers, small merchants, tradesmen and artisans. Thus the town governments began to secure their own autonomy over the church to gain economic advantages and establish control over social institutions.

Luther and the Peasant War

Luther's confrontation with the Papal church inspired the German peasants to open rebellion in 1525. About 40,000 peasants participated in this and were joined by the town's people and low-paid miners. Though the Peasant War was not a coordinated rebellion and had several leaders, Thomas Munzer successfully led the movement for a brief period. He organized the struggle against the feudal lords and church exploitation. Their 'Twelve Articles', a programme for action, was quite moderate and did not seek to destroy the feudal system completely. Nor did they ask for a division of all estate lands among the peasants. While the peasants were distributing pamphlets of the Twelve Articles, burning castles and monasteries, seizing lands and taking away cattle, attacking officials of the Catholic Church, the townsmen of Heibronn on the other hand demanded stronger powers for the emperor, introduction of uniform currency and abolition of duties to facilitate trade. In Thuringia, the peasant movement was most successful and widespread. The movement was finally crippled by brutal force of the nobles.

Although an elaborate discussion on the nature of the peasant War in Germany is not possible within this chapter it is well to remember its relation to the Reformation. Marxist writings (Engels, Kautsky, Belfort Bax, M.M. Smirin) suggest that the Peasant War was an expression of socio-economic conflict and formed an early phase of bourgeois revolution while the Reformation was its ideological expression. Steinmetz argues that it was a national movement precipitated by Martin Luther, bringing all the classes (except the ecclesiastical princes) under the leadership of the middling bourgeoisie against the Papal church. It represented the first attempt of the masses to create a unified state from below. Peter Blickle on the other hand, suggests that the Peasant War was an attempt to overcome the crisis of feudalism through a revolutionary reshaping of social and seigniorial relations. The torch-bearer of the revolution was not the peasant (who dominated only the first phase of the rebellion) rather it was the common man – peasants, miners, citizens of towns and the politically dis-enfranchised citizens of the imperial cities. The social aims of the Peasant War were 'Christian Gospel' and 'brotherly love' but failed because of its incompatibility with the Reformation.

Though the Peasant War was inspired by Luther's brave confrontation with Papal power, Luther did not want to lose the support of the nobility who were threatened by the peasants and so he vehemently attacked the rebellious peasants. Luther's theory of political authority developed against the background of the Peasant War. In his doctrine of 'Two Kingdoms' he drew a distinction between the 'spiritual' and the 'worldly' government. God's spiritual government is effected through the word of God and the guidance of the Holy Spirit through the gospel in which there could be no coercion. God's worldly government was delegated through kings, princes and magistrates by the sword of secular authority. On the question of the right to oppose the state, Luther adopted a conservative stance. He condemned all forms of rebellion as means of settling grievances. He argued that a true Christian should suffer the wrong and endure evil rather than fight the authority of the king. Hence, Luther's views were supported by a large section of the ruling class.

Luther's Religion

Luther's reformation began on the question of what an individual must do in order to be saved. From this developed his doctrine of justification by faith. Luther believed that the church had misunderstood the gospel and the true essence of Christianity by adopting practices such as the sale of indulgence. Luther's views were concerned with the question of how it was possible for a sinner to enter into a relationship with a righteous God. According to Luther, when the sinner realized his need for grace he called upon God to bestow it and God was under obligation to grant it. This grace could not be bought or sold. As Alister E. McGrath points out, it marked a new theology of forgiveness, threatening the vested interests of the Pope, clergies and many others.

Luther also criticized the views of the Catholic Church on 'sacraments' that included seven sacraments – baptism, the Eucharist or Mass, marriage, penance, confirmation, holy orders and extreme unction. Luther reduced them to just two – baptism and the Lord's Supper (Eucharist). (Baptism is a ceremony for admitting an infant or a non-Christian into Christian fold and giving him a Christian name while Eucharist is a holy communion of the Christians where bread and wine is taken to experience the presence of Christ amongst them). He held that the medieval sacraments gave totally unjustified priority to the priests. For Luther, the two essential characteristics of a sacrament were the word of God and an outward sign. For him the doctrine of transubstantiation was an absurdity put forward to rationalize wrong practices. In the name of miracle the priests collected money from the innocent people. The idea of priests making offerings or sacrifice on behalf of the people was regarded by Luther as going against the scriptures. Sacraments to him were for the nourishment of faith of the people and not commodities to be bought or sold.

Luther's religion was given an organizational structure and a definite shape by his fellow Professor Melanchthon. He helped Luther prepare three Tracts and establish a new sect of Christians. This new group of Christians called Lutherans believed in the supremacy of faith which destroyed the exclusive position of priests along with their mystical functions. Luther declared that each Christian was to be his own priest. For Luther the external order of the church was of secondary importance. Liberty was an inward faith and not an outward social and political freedom. He abolished the hierarchy of church officials from popes down to priests.

Christianity was made simpler and confined to the basic teachings of the Bible with the scriptures as the sole authoritative source of Christian dogma. The religious service was seen as a communal action and the symbol of participation was the hymn. For this, Luther published Evangelical hymn book for his followers. He abolished monasteries and the practice of celibacy by the priests. Luther himself married a former nun defying Papal rules of conduct for the clergy. He thus brought about a distinction between religious and socio-political matters and destroyed the all-pervasive hold of religion. He translated the Bible into German language so that all the people may have direct access to it. The printing press played a crucial role in this.

The Lutheran movement brought about a sharp division within the Christian church and destroyed papal supremacy. Several German princes saw in Luther a chance to secure greater freedom from the church and Emperor Charles V.

A prolonged fight between the Catholics and Protestants ended with the Peace of Augsburg in 1555. Each of the over three hundred German princes got the right to choose his own religion and the subjects of each state had to abide by his choice. Lutheran Reformation made rapid headway in the Scandinavian countries of Norway, Sweden and Denmark and also spread to Baltic provinces.

Bohemia

The Protestant movement in the Bohemian lands gained widespread success during the sixteenth century. As mentioned earlier, it was the centre of radical reforms of John Hus which transformed the religious situation in Bohemia. The vast majority of Bohemians had been drafted into the Hussite Ultraquist Church with an administrative and dogmatic system independent of Rome. The secular estates of the nobility and the cities effectively directed it. Several groups of Hussites emerged as the opinion varied on the question how radical the protest should be. One of the dissident groups consisted of a voluntary congregation of powerful nobles – the union of the congregation of the Bohemian Brethrens, the radical wing of the Hussite movement. They rejected priesthood and espoused a Christianity based on the Bible. It was against this complex background of religious diversity that the German Reformation of Luther made inroads. The spiritual leaders in Prague, Jan Poduska and Vaclar Rozd supported Luther's work. Even Luther initially showed enthusiasm towards the Bohemians. He made contacts with the Ultraquists but because of doctrinal differences he sought cooperation with the Union of Brethren. Luther's appeal was mainly among the German-speaking Catholic population. However, there were a series of disconnected reformations under individual feudal lords. It was for this reason that a number of radical groups came and settled here leading to serious religious strife and a civil war.

Huldreych or Ulrich Zwingli

Ulrich Zwingli (1484–1531) was a contemporary of Luther who carried out religious reforms in the Swiss confederation of Zurich. Zwingli's Reformation was based on humanist views. His short stay at Basle and his familiarity with the works of Erasmus gave Zwingli a different perception of Christianity. This was not the case with Luther, who did not have that kind of relationship with the humanist movement. Zwingli was essentially a humanist and was greatly inspired by Erasmus. He had studied the Bible in depth, which made him question some of the teachings of the Roman Catholic Church. He presented new views in the course of his preaching. His actual reformation started in 1520 and was completed within five years. It spread from Zurich to five other cantors of Switzerland while the remaining five held on to the Catholic religion.

According to Jean Wirth (*Religion and Society in Early Modern Europe, 1500–1800,* ed. K.V. Greyerz, 1984), Zwingli was an acculturative (the process by which the culture of a particular society is instilled in a human being from the infancy stage) reformer. He depended on the support of the dominant classes to impose a rigorous reform. Under his influence, the bourgeois authorities in Zurich imposed on the people, without having converted them to the cause, a form of ecclesiastical life that was at odds with their traditions and sensibility. It appears that Zwingli preferred an ordinary evolution of reformation but was overwhelmed by the groups comprising opponents of all forms of images of saints-iconoclasts. Zwingli's influence became evident only after September 1523, when the town council of Zurich gave him full backing.

The Swiss Reformation under Zwingli stressed upon the corporate nature of the church. It believed that clergy and laymen formed a 'holy community'. Zwingli also raised the subject of celibacy and set an example by getting married, much to the indignation of the priests and the clergy. The Council of Zurich decided against the practice of exacting fees for baptism, Eucharist and burial. Under the reformed religion, the clergy was to preach only from scriptures and the original Bible was to be read in the churches. Preaching formed an integral part of the church. The images and relics were removed from the church, processions disallowed and the use of candles and holy water abandoned.

The Reformation in Zurich had a great social impact. The monasteries were abolished and monastic charity became a communal concern. The monasteries were converted into poor houses and hospitals; their wealth was utilized to support the poor. The jurisdiction exercised by the Bishop was transferred to the civil body. A new court was established to deal with marriage disputes and to bring moral discipline into society. The church and moral discipline was to be jointly supervised by the church and the state. Together they were to form the 'holy community'. Church attendance was made compulsory in 1529. The power of the magistrate was combined with that of the clergy thus bringing a complete fusion of the church and the state. It came to be known as the 'magisterial reformation'. It was essentially doctrinal and liturgical reformation and was more radical than that of Luther. After Zwingli's death at the battle of Kappel (1531) where he accompanied the army as chaplain, his successor, Bullinger, continued the reforms.

There were some similarities between the Lutheran Reformation and that of Zwingli. Both rejected medieval sacraments and emphasized the word of God. They both retained the traditional practice of infant baptism but for different reasons. The two leaders met at Marburg in 1529 to strengthen the cause of a unified

Reformation. They made an attempt to resolve their differences and agreed on almost all points except on the question of the 'Lord's Supper'. For Luther, Christ was actually present at the Eucharist whereas for Zwingli, he was present only in the hearts of believers. Zwingli treated the occasion as a memorial while Luther insisted upon its literal sense and rejected Zwingli's proposal of brotherhood by saying 'your spirit is different from ours'. While Luther had separated the kingdom of God from the secular order, Zwingli tied the two together.

John Calvin

John Calvin (1509–64) of France was from the second generation of reformers. He is regarded as the most influential reformer because of his powerful impact on different parts of Europe. Calvin was highly learned and possessed a logical brain. Many of his views were derived from the Bible but he was also influenced by St Augustine.

Calvin was forced to leave France because of the religious prosecution carried out by the rulers. In the course of his journey, he came in contact with William Farel, who was waging a lonely battle in Geneva to reform the church. Calvin was persuaded by Farel to stay in Geneva and help in the work. The Genevan Reformation was closely associated with the armed struggle of the city for independence against the Dukes of Savoy and the Bishops of Geneva. Geneva allied with the Swiss cantons of Berne and Fribourg but became a part of Switzerland only in 1815. Within Geneva, a struggle was going on between the Libertines, who wanted mild reform placing the magistrates over the clergy, and, Farel and Calvin, who advocated radical changes and ministerial control. Calvin and Farel had to leave Geneva in 1538 but made a successful return in 1541. Calvin's efforts bore fruit and soon Geneva became the chief centre of Protestantism. Men from distant regions went there to study the new ideas and gain intellectual experience. Calvin trained a new generation from Protestant reformers from different nationalities, thus making Geneva the chief centre of international Protestantism.

Calvin was greatly influenced by Erasmus and other humanists of his time. It is generally believed that Calvin switched from a mild humanist to a radical reformer in 1533 or early 1534. He shared with Luther the belief in salvation by faith alone and supported the doctrine of direct communication of man with God. His emphasis on the absolute sovereignty of God gave a unique character to his teachings. This sovereignty of God was to be exerted through the church. The church was considered a divine institution by Calvin, largely independent of state power.

Describing God as omnipotent, Calvin argued that God is without any limitation of time or place. He believed that man belongs to God and it is man's duty to sacrifice himself to God and that the path to salvation was set forth in the scriptures. He felt that the sacraments were merely external signs of faith. The key to salvation was the Bible – the supreme source of trust and that all should submit to it. The followers were assured of their possible salvation through three presumptive tests prescribed by Calvin himself – the first was an open profession of faith, the second recommended a decent and godly life, and the third asked the men to participate in the sacrament of baptism and communion. For Calvin, the true marks of the church were to rightly preach the word of God and administer the sacraments properly. His rituals were even simpler than that of the Lutherans. The worship consisted essentially of preaching, praying and psalm singing. Like Luther he also retained only two sacraments – baptism and the Eucharist. Calvin's first edition of *Institutes of the Christian Religion* (1536) became the most influential work of Protestant theology and reflected his sharp intellect and legal mind. It was originally written in Latin but its publication in French in 1541 contributed to the development of French Vernacular literature. It was altered and enlarged subsequently till it got its final shape in 1559.

Calvin's biggest contribution to Reformation was through his views on church structure and discipline. His structure of Genevan church had four major institutions. The pastors preached the word of God. The doctors were the scholars who studied and wrote the different portions of Bible. These two formed the upper layer of the church officials. Deacons and Elders constituted the lower ranks to look after the social behaviour and moral standards of people.

They imposed strict disciplines on dress, sexual mores, church attendance and severely punished adultery, fornication, prostitution and other sinful acts. Though Calvin's church is charged with excesses and too much regulation, it was greatly appreciated by the prosperous merchants and shopkeepers for its rigid discipline, which contributed to Geneva's prosperity and checked the indiscipline of the unruly masses. The structure of Genevan church created by Calvin became a model for other reformers throughout Europe.

The doctrine of predestination constituted the most important element of Calvin's social thought. One of the main functions of this doctrine was to emphasize the grace and lore of God. Like Luther and Zwingli, Calvin argued that salvation comes from God's grace. But he believed that God predetermined each individual's salvation or damnation even before his birth. For Luther, God's graciousness was reflected in his granting salvation to any person who prayed for it. For Calvin, salvation was predetermined irrespective of man's merits or demerits. Although this doctrine was not central to Calvin, it became the focal point of later Reformation thought. The success of Calvinism is located in its effective organization and clarity of thought. Its church could operate effectively either with the state cooperation or as a self-contained unit.

Calvin's social thought is believed to have indirectly promoted commercial activity. Money was not regarded as an evil but as a necessity for the support and sustenance of society. He warned that the use of money should not be governed by the lust for profit or wealth but according to the laws of justice and equity. Calvin allowed nominal interest on loans if lent for productive purpose and certainly condemned usury. Calvin in fact, linked economic activity to the needs of the community.

The Spread of Calvinism

Calvin played an important role in the spread of his teachings in several parts of Europe. He was an extraordinary leader and organizer who sent missionaries to France, the Netherlands, Scotland and other parts of Europe to carry forward his reforms.

The Genevan Academy, created in 1559, provided the training for the leaders of the reformed Protestant movement. Calvin sincerely believed that some day France would become a truly Christian commonwealth and he worked for this.

France

It is argued by some scholars that the heterodox elements of the early French reform were not favourable for producing the kind of leadership that was needed for the organized churches. The three individuals – the Bishop of Meaux, Guillaume Briçonnet, the famous humanist figure, Jacques Lefèvre d'Ètaples, and the king's sister, Marguerite d'Angoulême, could have provided this leadership but none did (Mark Greengrass). Lefèvre (1450–1537) was a great Biblical scholar of the early sixteenth century. In 1509, he published his first edition of the Scriptures, beginning with the Psalms. It was one of the most admired works in Europe at that time. This was translated into vernacular French in 1523 followed by the translation of the Bible into French in 1530. In his last years, he went into self-imposed exile and died in the court of Marguerite d'Angouléme. Marguerite was a remarkably talented lady and received the adulation of many scholars. She demonstrated her creative qualities in her famous poems, *The Mirror of the Christian Soul* (1531), *Pearls from the Pearl of Princess* (1547), and the posthumous work the *Heptaméron* (1559), an evangelical collection.

Till the spread of Calvinism, there was no famous figure in France to prepare the ground for reformation. Leading humanists in France also believed in 'justification by faith' (man can be re-deemed from his sin by his faith in God) but they were not prepared to go very far. Lefèvre's pupil Briconnet, the Bishop of Meaux, undertook the reformatory work and even invited preachers holding reformed views but even he was not prepared to break with Rome, the seat of Papal authority. These three reformers were unwilling to create a new religion or a new church by means of reformation and were not ready to provide leadership in such an attempt. Thus, those who were interested in such activities in France turned to the German Rhineland, especially Strasberg and Basle. The French reformers of the earlier phase owed a great deal to Strasberg. The attitude of the French kings towards the Reformation remained hostile. They feared anarchy and civil war as had happened in Germany. Thus, the laws of heresy were tightened and rigidly enforced to drive out the French Protestants called the Huguenots. Though always in minority, the Huguenots (the French Protestants) began to emerge as a political and religious group especially in the former Albigensian lands and in the major urban centres.

Protestantism arrived late in France. The French rulers prevented its spread through various measures. The papacy had made a series of concessions to the French kings during the fifteenth century, which were codified in the Concordat of Bologna in 1516. Through these the French monarchs had obtained the right to make ecclesiastical appointments and gain a firm control over church finances. Thus, Lutheranism was seen as a threat to the privileged position of the rulers in ecclesiastical matters. It was the success of Calvinism that began to divide French society on religious grounds. The progress of Calvinists and their persecution can be seen best in France. The Affair of Placards in the autumn of 1534 in Paris led to a clear-cut policy of prosecution of the Protestants. On Sunday, 18 October a large number of Protestant placards were placed on several walls of the city, entitled 'True Articles of the Horrible, Great and Insufferable Abuses of the Papal Mass'. It was later thought to have come from the hands of Antoine Marcourt, an exiled Protestant. It appears that this event was significant in transforming the French Protestant movement into a clearly defined religion of rebels (Greengrass, p. 26). The rulers decided to stamp it out. After 1542, cases of heresy were strictly judged and the definition of heresy was greatly widened. The edicts of Chateaubriant in 1551 and Compiègne in 1557 included clauses against individuals who were either corresponding or had any association with Geneva. By 1560, Calvinism had obtained significant foothold among the nobility. It spread among the highest court and aristocratic circles, including the House of Bourbon, and made strong inroads among the provincial nobility, the merchants, lawyers, urban dwellers and aristocratic women. By 1559, the Huguenots constituted about a tenth of the total population with about a thousand congregations concentrated in large provincial towns. The aristocratic women formed its most receptive audience. They provided shelter to the fledgling congregations of the Calvinists despite vigorous persecution by the catholic monarchs. The religious issue pertaining to freedom of worship and the rights of establishment came to the forefront after the sudden death of Henry II (1559) (Valois) in a jousting tournament. The monarchy came into weak hands and Catherine de Medici, Henry II's widow who during the reign of her sons exercised the real power. This marked the beginning of a prolonged period of religious wars.

Parallel to the religious issues was the struggle for power between the crown and the powerful nobles to control the king. The important Protestant leaders were Louis I de Condé, Gaspard de Coligny and Henry of Navarre (later Henry IV). The Catholic faction was led by the House of Guise. A third group called the *Politiques* consisting of moderate Catholics agreed with the Protestant demands. The Protestants were strong in the south and west of France while the Catholic strength lay in the northern parts and in Paris. The Protestant cause was taken up by the Bourbon family, which also claimed the royal throne. Catherine was interested in securing peace as any war was likely to weaken the state and would have affected loyalty to the monarch. She failed in her negotiations with the Bourbons and had to depend on the Guises. In the meantime, both Protestants and Catholics alike had raised their own armies to fight for their respective cause. In 1562, civil war erupted between the Catholics and Huguenots. The Genevan leaders rendered all assistance to the Huguenots. A solution to the fight became almost impossible when a Protestant fanatic assassinated Duc de Guise in 1563. The young king, Charles IX, issued the Edict of Amboise in 1563, allowing free worship for all his subjects. The Catholic leaders defied this order by attacking and slaughtering Protestant leaders and their congregations. The war physically divided France and made the role of the monarch insignificant. With least concern for the French rulers, the Guises sought support of Spain, while the Huguenots hired Swiss and German mercenaries to fight for their cause. The announcement by Catherine of her plans to marry her daughter Margaret with

Henry of Navarre (Bourbon) raised hopes of reconciliation. The marriage was fixed for August 1572 and was seen as a big event in France with prospects of unifying the Valois with the Bourbon and thus inaugurating an era of peace. The situation took a tragic turn. That year (1572) on St. Bartholomew's Day which falls in August, thousands of Protestant men, women and children were slaughtered in the most gruesome manner. A large number of Huguenots had gathered to participate in the wedding. The massacre soon spread to the provinces and continued for several weeks. It caused intense hatred between the two Christians factions. The massacre on St Bartholomew's Day is regarded as the bloodiest event in France till the Revolution of 1789. The massacre prolonged the religious wars. The Huguenots wanted retaliation to avenge the slaughter of their relatives and began to plan resistance against a king whose actions were in direct violation to the divine commands. Huguenot writers began to justify rebellion against a king who prosecuted their faith taking cues from Calvin's ideas. The Huguenot rebellion was justified by Languet in his *Defence of Liberty Against Tyrants* in 1579. The massacre also led to the defection of some Catholic noblemen from the court. The Duke of Anjou tried to bring about reconciliation between the two factions. Those Catholics who desired settlement came to be called the *Politiques*. It was this group that allowed the Protestant Henry of Navarre to become the new king by right of succession after he renounced his Protestant faith and became a Roman Catholic. In 1598, Henry issued his famous Edict of Nantes to end the religious strife in France and bring national unity. The Protestant minority was granted limited toleration. This was the first document in any European state that attempted to provide a degree of religious toleration. It gave religious peace to France for nearly a century till the edict was revoked in 1685.

The real legacy of the French Wars of Religion was perhaps the rise of absolute monarchy under Louis XII and Louis XIV during the seventeenth century. By concentrating power through new institutions and by reorganizing existing institutions, the Crown tried to restore peace in France in place of chaos and disorder caused by the religious wars. However, it is important to note that religion alone was not the only cause of the French civil wars. There were other factors like the weak monarchy after 1559 after two strong rulers and the growing ambition of aristocracy to share power.

Scotland

In Scotland, Calvinism became popular in a short time through the efforts of Patrick Hamilton. He was a nobleman who had studied at different universities. He prepared the ground for Protestantism in Scotland. On the orders of the Primate – Charles Beaton, he was burnt alive at Stake for spreading new ideas which were contrary to the beliefs of the existing church. However, the demand for religious reforms could not be crushed. Another Protestant preacher George Wishart made journeys all over Scotland and influenced some important landed nobles. John Knox (1505–72) became the most influential leader of the Scottish Reformation. Knox studied at Geneva and was greatly influenced by the ideas of Calvin. Knox's activities extended to the English court of Edward VI. He went beyond Calvin in the approval of armed resistance to ungodly rulers. He became a leading Protestant preacher and aroused popular passion against Rome. In England, he helped Cranmer in the preparation of *42 Articles of Religion* and the *Second Prayer Book*. The Scottish Presbyterianism was very similar to Calvinism. His sermons inspired the Lords of the Congregation – the rebel Protestant nobility. John Knox played a decisive role in it and became an inflammatory leader of the Scottish Reformation arousing the Protestant nobility to revolt.

The Netherlands

Calvinism in the Netherlands penetrated through the French-speaking population in 1550s. The struggle between the feudal nobility and the monarchial absolutism of the Spanish rulers Charles V and Philip II, the sharp rise of the middle class in towns which had strong links with commercial and maritime activities, the efforts of the guilds to retain their traditional privileges against the rising tide of capitalism, were all mixed up with the struggle for independence from the Spanish Imperial rule imposing Catholic religion on the people. The proximity of Dutch towns to the Lutheran centres in Germany and the commercial and political links had already made the people receptive to the Protestant ideas. The implementation of heresy laws and the vigorous policy of suppression through the Duke of Alva led to resistance under William of Orange. William was a powerful leader and politician from the high nobility of the Netherlands. He was aware of the existence of numerous Protestants as well as Catholics groups. While fighting against the tyrannical Spanish rule over the Netherlands, he also raised the questions of religious toleration and political freedom. For this he organized diplomatic military aid from the enemies of Spain that included Germany and England. Thus the spirit of patriotism was fuelled by the revolutionary Calvinist ideology leading to the establishment of the Calvinist Church in the Netherlands. The rise of Calvinism, especially among the burghers of Amsterdam, Rotterdam and Leiden, provided a basic reason for a split between the Catholic provinces in the west and the United Provinces in the east.

Calvinism also spread into central and eastern Europe. In several German states both, Lutherans and Catholics opposed Calvinism. The Elector of Palatine, Frederick III in Germany was converted to the Calvinist faith in 1563 and this was a great achievement for the Calvinists. It enabled the formation of the German Reformed Church. Calvinism also gained popularity among the nobles of Poland, Lithuania, Hungary and Bohemia. The Hungarian city of Debrecen came to be called 'the Calvinist Rome'. Calvinism proved strong in regions like Transylvania and the Duchy of Cieszyn. It also spread to some of the territories in north America through the English Puritans, the Dutch Reformed Church and the Scottish Presbyterians. Together they formed associations like the Congregationalists, the Presbyterians and the Baptists.

The English Reformation

One view suggests that the English Reformation came from above and the changes were enforced from the centre by deliberate governmental action beginning with Henry VIII's action (G.R. Elton, Peter Clark, etc.). The second explanation suggests that the Reformation had religious rather than political roots and arose from below (A.G. Dickens, Claire Cross). These writers see links between the Lollards in the time of Wycliff and the early Protestant reformers and suggest that the atmosphere for reforms created by them led to rapid advance of the Protestant movement at the popular level.

The origins of the English Reformation can be traced back to the Middle Ages. The followers of John Wycliff and Lollards started a movement of religious and social dissent, which remained underground. They had openly opposed the doctrine of transubstantiation (miracle of turning wine and bread into Christ's blood and flesh by the priests) as blind faith. From the time of Wycliff there had developed a tradition of heresy and anticlericalism in England. The spread of Christian humanism (Colet, Linacre, Grocyn, Fisher, etc.) had created an atmosphere of academic criticism. Bishop Miles Coverdale had translated the Scriptures into English. Dudley in his book, *The Tree of Commonwealth* (1510) written in prison and kept suppressed, suggested religious reforms. Thomas More, a very close friend of the famous humanist, Erasmus wrote his classic *Utopia* in this period only. Stephen Gardiner and Edward Fox warned Pope Clement VII of growing religious schism and the possible danger to the English church but it was ignored by him. The Protestant ideas had started reaching the coastal towns through the printing press, travellers and merchants. The establishment of Tudor rule marked the process of centralization and despotism in which the secular forces began to play an important role. How far the Protestant ideas spread in the first quarter of the sixteenth century is difficult to say but all these factors helped in the spread of the Reformation in England.

Another view suggests that the Reformation in England was political in character as it was imposed from above. The movement was initiated not by any religious reformer but by the king himself with the support of the Parliament. It is an irony that the English Reformation was initiated by the same ruler – Henry VIII (1509–47), who was a strong critic of Martin Luther's reforms. His work

Defense of the Seven Sacraments, earned him the title, 'Defender of the Faith', from Pope Leo X. Henry VIII wanted to divorce his wife Catherine who was a Spanish princess but the Pope could not grant it because divorce was not allowed in the Catholic Church and also due to the fact that the troops of the Spanish Emperor were in control of the city of Rome and the Pope could not go against him. Henry became desperate after waiting for three years, and decided to take matters into his own hands. Through a subservient Parliament (also called the Reformation Parliament) which sat from 1529 to 1534), he severed all relations with the Pope. Under the guidance of Thomas Cromwell, the Parliament passed several Acts against the Papal authority by picking up all those abuses of the church that were unpopular (such as mortuary and succession fees, pluralism and absenteeism and the power of the chantries). The Act of Annates prohibited the English church from sending any part of their income to the Pope, and the Act of Appeal removed the English church from the jurisdiction of the Papal courts. In 1534, with Parliament's approval, Henry declared himself the supreme head of the English church. However, it is worth noting, as A.G. Dickens points out, the divorce suit did not create either Protestantism or smoothen the path of anti-Papal forces. Such forces were quite diverse and laid deep in the English society and by the 1530s, they had already reached a critical stage of eruption. In 1536 and 1539 all the monasteries were dissolved and their property seized. It is estimated that the wealth seized was roughly three times the royal annual income. This property was distributed or sold to Henry's loyal supporters who belonged to the lesser nobility and landed gentry. Henry thus turned the Reformation into a national movement by involving Parliament and the gentry.

Henry's Reformation began as a political act for personal reasons and was in no way Protestant. The Six Articles of Religion of Henry retained all the Catholic doctrines and practices but denied Papal supremacy. Protestants as well as Catholics who refused to recognize Henry's supremacy were severely persecuted. The famous humanist Thomas More was punished for the same reason.

Protestantism made startling progress during the brief reign of Edward VI (1547–53) – Henry's only son. The English church became almost Calvinist when Protestant Archbishop Cranmer drew up the *Book of Common Prayer* and imposed the *Forty Two Articles of Religion* implemented through the Act of Uniformity. The supporters of radical Protestantism were called Puritans who believed in the purified version of Reformation teaching. Their number gradually increased. The Protestant Reformation in England received a major setback in the reign of Mary Tudor (1553–8), daughter of Catherine and Henry VIII. She restored the Catholic religion, asked and received Papal forgiveness for her people and ordered hundreds of Protestants to be burned alive, including Archbishop Cranmer. Her persecutions were extremely unpopular and it hurt the cause of the Roman Catholic religion.

The reign of Elizabeth (1558–1603) began with the threat of religious wars in England. The fear of a Spanish invasion and Papal threat heightened a sense of national identity. Elizabeth's religious settlement established the Anglican Church in England. It was a midway approach bordering on conservative Protestantism. Cranmer's *Book of Common Prayer* was adopted again but with slight modifications and *Thirty-nine Articles* replaced *Forty-two Articles of Religion* eliminating the controversial doctrinal points. The celibacy of the clergy was rejected, two sacraments of baptism and Eucharist were retained and the Episcopal system (church governed by the Bishops) was adopted. Church attendance was made compulsory and the dissenters were heavily fined. The exact nature of English Protestantism became an issue of dispute. The chief advantages of the Elizabethan Settlement were well analysed towards the close of the queen's reign by Richard Hooker in his *Laws of Ecclesiastical Polity*. The church of Elizabeth represented a middle path by accommodating English traditions. A great majority of the English people accepted the Anglican settlement but two groups, the Puritans and the Roman Catholics, continued to oppose it. The Catholics were discredited because of their attempts to stage a coup with foreign support. The Puritans were essentially the Calvinists who were associated with the radical wing of the Protestants. Their number was not too large but they played a significant role in English politics, especially during the period of the Stuart kings. As the English Reformation was achieved through political means, the Puritans attacked the crown and the Anglican Church by using Parliament as a political stage to influence the government and the public mind. Their opposition intensified during the reign of James I (1603–25) and was reinforced by theoretical denunciation of absolutism in the time of Charles I (1625–49). Religion became an important issue along with many separate grievances causing civil war in England (1642–9).

The Reformation helped in strengthening the English monarchy and in creating a national church. As Christopher Hill says, the Reformation not only subordinated the national church to the king, it also subordinated parishes to squires. The English monarchs had gradually increased their powers called prerogatives which were independent of parliamentary control. The king's prerogatives expanded under the Tudor rulers with the setting up of the Council of North and the Council of Wales (to suppress religious revolts), Court of High Commission (to punish dissenters of the official church) and creating new courts in 1540 – Court of Augmentation to control new land revenue and the Court of Ward (to administer land of the minors) was given a new form. At the same time, the Parliament gained importance, experience and organization because of the frequent sessions to handle important subjects like the king's succession or determine the religion of the state. The House of Commons started the tradition of the writing the daily proceedings of the house called the Parliamentary Journal. The Reformation in England also brought about changes in composition of the Parliament because the influence and number of religious men like abbots declined rapidly and the influence of lay elements increased. The process of land transfers hastened after Henry VIII's Reformation. Whether it led to the rise of a new landed class or the fruits of profits were reaped by the aristocracy is a subject of debate. The Reformation brought new problems in dealing with the poor. The government passed several Poor Laws to deal with it that the people found very harsh. The dissolution of monasteries and chantries gave an opportunity to establish a system of national education which led to the mixing of different social stratas.

The Reformation in England created a distinct Protestant literary tradition, which became more evident during its radical phase in the reign of Edward VI. William Tyndale, Simon Fish, John Bale were among the first generation of Protestant scholars but the influence of Protestant ideas can be clearly seen in the writings of Edmund Spenser, John Donne, George Herbert and Milton. A touching account of religious martyrs was given by John Foxe in his *Book of Martyrs*. Similarly, the reputation of English Church music reached its climax in the period of Elizabeth. The anthems and services of William Byrd, Thomas Tallis, Thomas Weelkes and Orlando Gibbons still appear in many Cathedrals and minster choirs.

Thus we can say that the English Reformation was quite different from other countries as here the rulers for personal reasons took the initiative to introduce it. It was implemented through political means. It helped the rulers to establish a despotic form of state by expanding the prerogative powers of the rulers and by creating a national church under state control. Leading Lollard evangelists prepared the ground for the acceptability of Protestant ideas. The Anglican Church Settlement (1559) was an attempt to avoid the extremes and adopt a midway path between Protestantism and Catholicism.

The Radical Reformation

Apart from the Protestant Reformation in different parts of Europe, there emerged numerous splinter group of religious orders advocating radical reforms such as the Anabaptists, Spiritualists, Antitrinitarians and other religious bodies – all 'radical groups' of Protestants. The biggest threat to the establishment of an orthodox Protestant church came from a group called 'Anabaptists', a term of abuse to discredit them.

The Anabaptists rejected the doctrine of infant baptism and believed that the true Christian is one who was re-baptized as an adult. They believed in the doctrine of justification by faith and contended that only those who firmly believed in God could become members of the true church and excluded all others. As infant

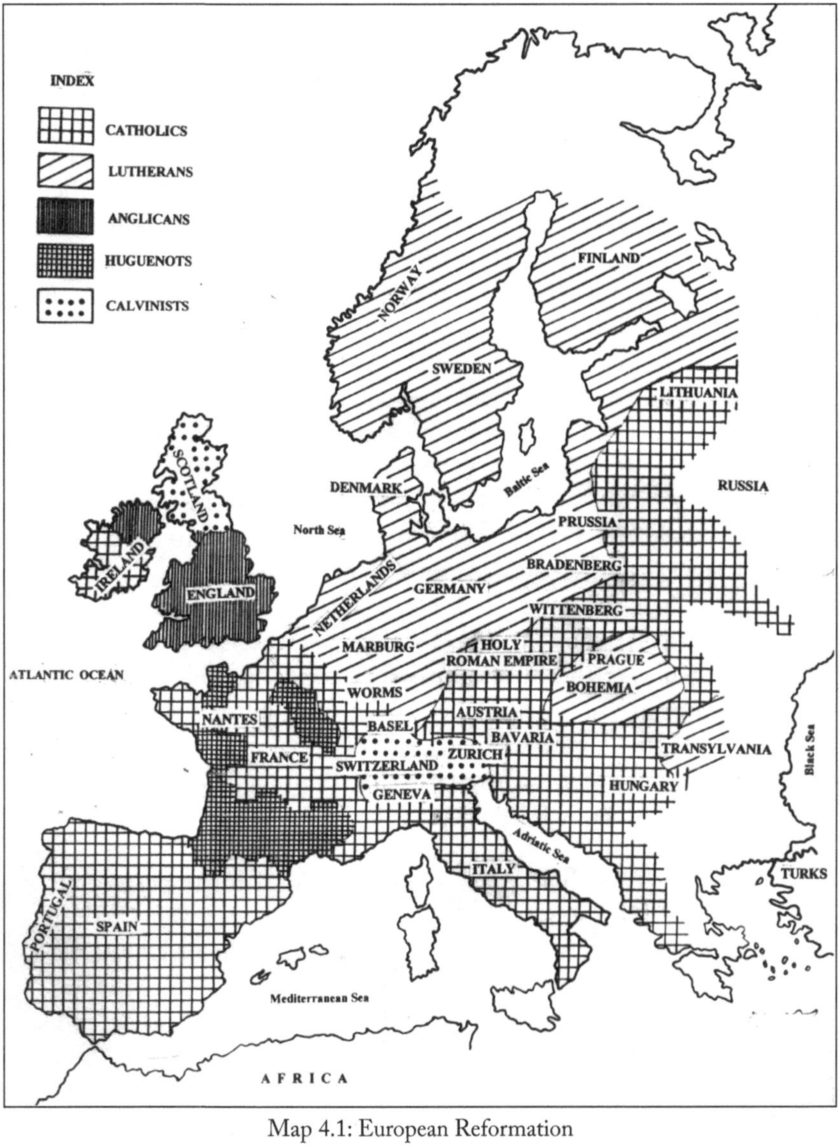

Map 4.1: European Reformation

baptism was considered a sacrament both by the Protestants and the Catholics, the arguments of the Anabaptists posed a threat to their doctrine. In fact, Luther, Calvin and Zwingli, all believed that infant baptism had its origin in the Bible and that unbaptized dead infants could not enter heaven. These views had great relevance in a period of high infant mortality. Moreover, the Anabaptists refused to recognize or participate in civil government, take oaths of allegiance or serve in the army and refused to pay taxes to the government. They argued that the true Christians should never use sword or go to law courts or perform magisterial functions. This group reflected the aspirations of the poor people and wanted social reforms of all the institutions in preparation for Christ's second coming. But not all Anabaptists were from a poor background as is the case of Conrad Grebel, who was a humanist from an upper class family of Zurich. Some of the Anabaptists argued for communal property and regarded private property as a social evil. There were others who picked up literal passages from the Old Testament and recommended the practice of polygamy and promiscuity. They also practised a shared economy. Strong activists like Thomas Muntzer and John of Leyden set up a violent dictatorship in Münster in north-west Germany in 1534. Their followers seized the property of non-believers and burnt all books except the Bible. The most influential and successful leader of the Anabaptists was a Dutch priest, Menno Simons. His followers organized themselves as Mennonites. Luther, Calvin and other Protestants as well as the Catholic reformers strongly condemned the social doctrines of the Anabaptists.

Wherever the Anabaptists settled, the local rulers persecuted them, Protestants drowned them in water and ordered them to be stoned to death while the Catholics burned them alive. Many of the Anabaptists despite all their sufferings and persecution, settled in groups in Germany, Switzerland, Bohemia, Hungary and Poland. Their principal leaders like Balthasar Hubmaier and Jacob Hutter had converted some nobles to their faith, but in the end they met torture and death. Independent groups survived prosecution in England and throughout north-west Europe. They resurfaced in England during the English civil war and failed. But their tradition

Anabaptist's Cage at Münster, 1535

of democratic thought and economic equality remained. Another group in the Anabaptist tradition was the Society of Friends founded by George Fox in England in the seventeenth century. They were commonly called Quakers. They were Christians who held informal meetings without priests and were active throughout western Europe and later in the United States of America.

The Catholic Reformation

The Catholic Church had always faced criticism of its institutional degeneration and corruption. These have already been discussed at the beginning of the present chapter. Wycliff and Hus were treated as heretics. The Waldensian (a medieval religious movement that desired to reform the Roman church which they found extravagant, corrupt and propagating doctrinal errors) and the Albigensians (were followers of a sect in the town of Albi in Languedoc in southern France that acquired immense popularity but was declared a group of heretics by the Council of Toulouse and crushed) in the twelfth and thirteenth centuries were also ignored. It was only in the beginning of the sixteenth century that serious efforts were made to reform the church from within. There was an acute shortage of competent priests and many bishops did not reside in their diocese. They had virtually become administrative officers with more political than religious responsibilities. Some of them became chancellors to princes. The orders of mendicant friars had stepped in where regular clergy failed and they emphasized direct contact with the people. Most of the reformers discussed this aspect. Some efforts were made in this direction through the *devotio moderna* (modern devotion). In these, the laymen took the lead and were joined by some priests and friars. The brotherhoods also devoted themselves to piety and sanctification. The Oratory of Divine Love in 1517 took up the task of remedying the deficiencies of the regular clergy by concentrating on preaching and on the cure of souls through prayers, confessions, etc. There was a general awareness of the church's decline that led to efforts to check it even before Protestantism made inroads. In the late-fifteenth century, an attempt was made to bring about a wide-ranging reorganization of the Spanish religious order by Jiménaz de Cisneros. He had served as Inquisator-General of the Spanish Inquisition. His reforms were a combination of piety and humanism. He tried to convince the clergy to explain the gospel to the parish population and to instruct the children in church doctrines. His own religious house, the Franciscan order, were asked to initiate reforms. His reforms took away the sting of Protestant attacks in Spain and the Catholic religion remained safe from the Protestant inroads. Catholic reformation started around the same time as Protestant reformation, only later it was pushed ahead at an accelerated speed by the Protestant challenge and came to be known as the Counter Reformation.

With the success of Protestant Reformation in the central and northern Europe, it looked in the 1530s that Europe may turn Protestant. The Catholic Church became conscious of its disintegration and took immediate action to reform itself and a century later the picture was reversed. Catholicism re-conquered lost territories showing a vigour and dynamism that was lacking in the orthodox Protestantism.

There seems to be two aspects of Catholic revival in the sixteenth century. The first dealt with the internal reforms to eliminate the well-known abuses that had given rise to the Protestant movement. These internal reforms, which took the form of spiritual revival or institutional improvement, came to be known as the 'Catholic Reformation'. The second aspect reflected the militant character through which they not only recovered the lost grounds but also succeeded in revitalizing the Catholic religion. This aspect was regarded as the 'Counter Reformation'.

The process of revival through inner regeneration gained momentum in the sixteenth century through the activities of religious orders and individuals. In Italy, there were a number of new orders like the Capuchins, the Barnabites and the Ursulines besides the Oratory of Divine Love in Rome. St Ingnatius Loyola (1491–1556) led the field in Spain. He founded his activity through the Society of Jesus (1534) and its members were known as Jesuits. Under the vigorous leadership of Loyola, the Catholic religion was on the road to orthodoxy that was to provide a strong foundation to the Catholic reformation.

Ignatius Loyola was born in a wealthy, noble Spanish family. He was injured in a war against France. While convalescing, he underwent a spiritual transformation. He began reading on the life of Christ and spent a year in a cave at Manresa, where he spent his time in prayers and looking after the poor and the sick. He even undertook a long journey in Europe and in the Holy Land in 1523 to convert Muslims to Christianity but failed in this mission. However, he proved to be a successful Catholic reformer.

Loyola was greatly influenced by the religious fervour of native Spain and was also touched by the mystical as well as humanist influences. He developed the conviction that man could experience God everywhere through his senses. Despite his orthodoxy, Loyola did not join those who wanted to purify the church from the conversos for the purpose of unity of faith and purity of blood, which the Spanish Inquisition attempted. He suggested that in order to reach God, spiritual exercises were needed to train and

Ignatius Loyola

discipline the human will. Selfish thought and temptations of the flesh must be eliminated for the sake of obedience. He felt that private judgement must be set aside in favour of the Order. He recommended that each member practice these exercises based on discipline, mysticism and devotion, for four weeks annually. Even Calvin had stressed the need for physical and spiritual discipline.

The greatest strength of Loyola's reform was its flexibility of approach and methods, which attracted men of character and calibre like Peter Canis of Germany. The Jesuit Order worked in two spheres. First, they worked with rulers as confessors and diplomats and exercised great influence over them. Second, they emphasized educational reforms by establishing new schools and universities. The aim was to train elite young men who would be dedicated to the faith and restore the prestige of theological studies. The Jesuits were successful in creating some of the finest primary and secondary schools in Europe. They tried to develop all aspects of education – games (which had been frowned upon), dancing, play acting, etc. –

and aimed at directing human passion to harmony with Catholic doctrines.

In Italy, a number of new orders were created, the most noteworthy being the Capuchin Order in 1529. It stressed the importance of poverty and austerity and tried to make the church more relevant to the common people. The Capuchins laid emphasis on the virtues of humanity and charity.

Attempts at reforms in the Catholic Religion were made in the first quarter of the sixteenth century but little had been achieved. The tutors of Charles V – Hadrian VI and Leo X made a small beginning. The year 1527 is regarded as a landmark. Rome was sacked by the troops of Emperor Charles V who were not paid their salary. This had a profound psychological impact on the Roman Catholics. They realized the need for urgent reforms. The first major step in this direction was the creation of a Reform Commission of Cardinals by Pope Paul III. The Commission suggested changes from above, and how to accomplish the reforms. The church suggested the old solution of calling a church council. The Pope dreaded such councils as the council of Constance and Basle had asserted its supremacy over Papal authority. Charles V pressed for the council and the Council of Trent was convened thrice in 1545–7, 1551–2 and 1562–3.

According to N.S. Davidson, the Catholic Council of Trent, which first met in 1545, was not intended to achieve a reconciliation with the Protestants. Its main aim was to secure Catholicism in areas, such as Italy where Protestantism had not yet become well established. Its doctrinal purpose was plain and was limited to the beliefs disputed by the Protestants. The reforms recommended by the councils included a ban on the use of monetary indulgences, fresh attention to the education of the clergy and a close examination of the duties and responsibilities of bishops. It clearly rejected religious individualism.

Before the Council of Trent, a liberal section of the Catholics tried to reach a doctrinal compromise (till about 1541) to win back the Lutheran converts. When these attempts failed, coercion was adopted. This was the main characteristic of the Counter Reformation. Attention from internal reforms shifted to the problem of separatism and for this a more militant approach was adopted. The third council fully restored the absolute supremacy of the Pope. The Spanish Inquisition was imported into Rome in 1542 to suppress the religious minorities as the Holy Office. It also rejected any form of conciliation and suggested stringent measures against heretics. Lutheranism was wiped out from Italy. Strict control was established on the publication of religious and secular literature from the printing presses. Paul IV published an Index of Prohibited Books (*Index librorum prohibitorum*) in 1559 to prevent Catholics from reading heretical texts. While Spain provided the influence for both reform and counter offensive, Rome provided leadership and institutions.

The Jesuits played an important role in re-establishing Papal supremacy. Their intellectual discipline and powerful organization provided a strong challenge to the Calvinists. The Jesuit membership increased rapidly from about 1,000 by the time of Loyala's death in 1556 to almost 16,000 half a century later. They created an effective infrastructure in the form of schools, and had preachers and diplomats to counter their opponents. Outside Europe the Catholic missions carried out the policy of converting local populations into their own fold. They did not achieve success everywhere. In many parts of the world the pagan religions and traditions continued and survived alongside the Catholic religion. At some places they faced strong opposition from the local populations. Some individual missionaries tried to adopt a more patient and deliberate approach to the preaching of Gospel by adopting the culture of the local people. They adopted the local lifestyle, dressed in local clothes and remained careful not to hurt the sentiments of the people. This policy of making friends among the local population can be seen in the actions of Francis Xavier, Alessandro Valignano, Matteo Recci and Roberto De Nobili in Japan, China and India during the sixteenth century. The Catholic missionaries were very effective particularly in the New World where Spain and Portugal had vast colonies.

In Europe, the policies of enlightened education, effective preaching, impressive church buildings, persecution of dissenters and vigorous censorship brought back thousands of people in

Germany and Bohemia back to the Catholic fold. The Jesuits became the greatest teachers in Europe. Under them, Catholic religion became aggressive and dynamic.

The Impact of the Reformation

The European Reformation of the sixteenth century was a complex and heterogeneous movement, with direct or indirect ramifications on the political, and the socio-economic life of Europe. Since Christianity was associated with the lives of the rulers, it was bound to have some impact on them.

Political Consequences

The Protestant Reformation produced different perceptions of the relationship between state and church. In most of the Protestant regions, the Reformation hastened the emergence of absolute states by establishing a national church. Monarchs and magistrates gained at the expense of religious institutions. Rulers in these regions rejected the temporal power of the Pope and established their own supremacy over the church and its property. In the Catholic states, the church supported the monarchy to face the challenge of Protestantism. It would be wrong to say that Protestantism created the modern state but it did free the state from religious domination. It promoted the formation of secular states in Europe by strengthening city councils and other secular institutions. At the same time, the Reformations also introduced the problem of 'pluralism' into Western culture—religious, social and cultural—which still confront modern states.

One of the first consequences of the Reformation was the breakdown of the Catholic Church into many divisions. Each community established its own identity (sometimes called Confessionalization) that was highly organized and laid down strict norms of political, moral and social behaviour. Each group developed a rigid identity that intensified conflicts. Social attitudes towards the poor and charity began to change because of the influence of Puritanism. The rulers had taken the property and wealth of the church away but paid no attention to the relief of the poor till the problem became menacing. Elizabeth's Poor Law opened the road to social legislation that had religious sanction.

Protestantism indirectly contributed to the idea of political liberty. Both Luther and Calvin preached political freedom. Luther insisted that subjects must obey the command of their rulers while Calvin had created a theocratic state in Geneva in which the life of the subjects was closely supervised. Calvin separated church and state and assigned the state the role of maintaining peace and order. Yet he hinted, that in an exceptional situation, obedience to a ruler might mean disobedience to God. Here the subjects must follow the Biblical order to obey God rather than man. This resistance, according to Calvin, was not to be attempted by private individuals but by the representative assemblies. This was immediately used by the Calvinists to justify armed rebellions in France, Scotland, the Netherlands and England against the rulers. Calvin's idea stirred political upheavals and revolutions. The nobility and the elite in many places became increasingly associated with the dissident religious movements that had political ramifications. These leaders could not be easily suppressed or tamed. In France the Huguenots and in the Netherlands the Calvinists entangled religious matters with political action against the Catholic kings. In Flanders and the Low Countries, mobs assaulted priests and plundered churches, and destroyed the symbols associated with the Catholic faith. These violent activities displayed a strong symbolic character. At many places the Calvinists exhibited political activism. In France and the Low Countries, Huguenots became the religious nuclei of revolutionary parties headed by the nobility. In England, the Puritans forged a political bond against the government of Charles I. Thus religion began to cause discord and tension within the state–society relationship. Religion became a new issue for political conflicts.

Luther's statement that every man was his own priest and his views on direct relationship between God and man were major steps towards individualism. His reforms emphasized submission to divine revelation and with the publication of the New Testament, diversity of thought was encouraged. Calvin's church provided no such freedom and even the Catholics, especially in the Council of Trent, categorically denounced religious individualism.

It is also argued by some historians that Protestantism marked a mature development of European nation states. They have found connections between the authoritarian structures of the German territorial state and the political ideas of Luther, and between the democratic structures of the urban reformed communities and the ideas of Zwingli and Calvin. The development of the English state and its relationship to the English Protestantism has been explored in recent years. Protestantism has been interpreted as both a product of the rising nation state concept as well as a catalyst to emerging national identity.

Family Life and Women

Marriage existed as a sacrament in the Roman Catholic religion. But the church regarded abstinence and celibacy as a higher state of holiness than marriage. The Lutheran reformers placed family life above celibacy. Luther himself married Catherine in 1525 who made a significant contribution to Luther's life. Luther and Calvin suggested that celibacy should be practised only by those who could control their desires. Both Protestants and Catholics began to advocate the positive side of family relationships. The Protestants placed family at the centre of human life and stressed on mutual love between husband and wife. The family was considered very important by them because they had rejected the idea that any special holiness was attached to celibacy or monasticism. Lutherans gave a new kind of dignity to marriage in daily life. This not only strengthened traditional patrimony, it also enhanced the prestige of parenthood. To Ozment (1980, p. 381), the marriage of Protestant clergy proved conducive to new social attitudes. The medieval dualism of sacred and secular work was rejected by the new view of vocation or calling. Anything that helped the human community was considered a way of pleasing God. In the Protestant world, the role of monastery as the route to heaven, was gradually being replaced by the home and marriage.

The Reformation enabled religious practices to move from the public to the private sphere. Protestant reformers advised men and women to read the Bible and participate in religious services together. Indirectly, though this encouraged the education of girls so that they could read the Bible and religious literature they never visualized equality of social classes or the sexes.

Whether the Reformation made any difference to the lives of women, the answer is not positive. Luther did encourage greater sharing within the household between the husband and the wife but we do not see anything in his writings which can be termed as reforming ideas to elevate the condition of women. Like Calvin, Luther also saw women as pious wives, mothers, managing household duties and living under the authority of their husbands. Piety as an expression of Christian act became increasingly associated with the social role of women. Even schools founded specifically for girls offered them only the ability to read religious texts and train them in household duties. The attitude of religious reformers including Luther, towards women remained reactionary. Luther described a woman like a nail driven into the wall – nailed to the home and household affairs.

The destruction of monasteries by the Protestants meant the end of several women's religious orders. This was one of the few occupational choices for women in the sixteenth century. No comparable alternatives were provided to them. It was only among the Quakers that women got a public role as preachers late in the seventeenth century. In the Catholic Church, women's organizations like Ursulines provided some chance to play an active role within the church organization. The city council of Zwickare established a girls' school in 1525 but it was only meant for imparting moral education rather than promoting intellectual growth. It did little to improve the position of women.

Noble women in certain parts of Europe provided strong appeal to the Protestant ideas. Marguerite of Navarre (1492–1549), sister of Francis I, had created her own court in southern France where both Humanists and Protestants were patronized. Her devotional poem, *Mirror of the Sinful Soul* was a source of inspiration for women reformers. Even Elizabeth was greatly impressed by it and she got it translated into English. Mary of Hungary (1505–58) played a similar role in the Holy Roman Empire. She acted as a patron to the reformers in Hungary. Luther paid special tribute to her by dedicating an edition of Psalms to her. However, these were exceptions. The ordinary woman could not play such a role in the Reformation movement.

Education

The Protestant Reformation and Jesuit missionary activity had an important impact on the rise of literacy in some parts of Europe. But there were a variety of factors responsible for it and no one causal explanation can be provided. Renaissance humanism had already altered the content of education. The Protestant reformers successfully used and implemented humanist methods in their schools and universities. Unlike the humanist schools, which admitted children of elite families, the Protestant schools catered to a wider population. Martin Luther advocated education for all children, the expenses to be provided by the state, and he advised the cities and villages to contribute funds for the schools in Saxony. His fellow reformer Melanchthon received the title of 'The Teacher of Germany' for his education scheme. The famous *gymnasium* or secondary schools were established in Germany where liberal arts and humanist teachings were combined with religious instruction. Strasbourg School (1538) became a model for others. Luther and Melanchthon made definite contribution to the development of the medical faculty at the University of Wittenberg. Max Weber and many others emphasize the contribution of Protestantism in the rise of modern science (see Chapter 9). Calvin founded the Genevan Academy, consisting of private schools or gymnasiums and public schools. These schools were divided into seven classes. It eventually became a university preparing qualified teachers to spread Calvinist ideas in Europe. John Knox and his followers had drawn up a national system of education for Scotland. Similarly, the Catholics also placed a lot of stress on good education. The Jesuits played a pioneering role in the field of education, particularly outside Europe. There was rapid growth in education and a network of colleges arose between 1550 and 1630 when nine colleges were founded in Bavaria alone. The Jesuits came to use theatre as a popular tool for providing moral and religious education. Their education included music and dancing in its curriculum. Psalm singing was popular both among the Catholics and Lutherans. But they showed hostility to organs, polyphony and choristers. They believed that music must edify and not distract. While the Jesuit Order was more concerned with schooling pupils from the upper classes to train them for the influential posts, the Puritan education developed a stronger theory of vocation than had existed in the pre-Reformation era. This helped in the rise of individual confidence. With the Reformation came a greater stress on the individual's relationship with God as the central aspect of Christianity. Puritanism is seen in historical literature as one of the great factors leading to modernization.

The Reformation aroused interest not only in the existing religion but also in the history of religion. The first comprehensive history of the church was written at this time in thirteen volumes under the general editorship of Matthew Flacius, an associate of Luther. His *Magdeburg Centuries* presented the Pope in a negative light. The Catholic Church responded by printing *Ecclesiastical Annals* under Caesar Baronius. Indirectly these works contributed to the studies of historical criticism. The rise of a national church in each state promoted national literatures and the vernacular Bibles played a role in this.

Popular Culture

From the medieval times religion played an enormous role in the everyday lives of most Europeans. In most of the places the clergy enjoyed moral authority and viewed itself as a necessary institution for the salvation of souls. They monopolized the power of conducting sacraments (important rituals on births, marriages and deaths) and confessions that included penance and forgiveness of sins. Ordinary Christians believed that without the clergy, salvation could not be achieved. The calendar year included several religious holidays. Popular religious festivals played an important role in determining the daily lives of the people. In fact, popular culture was greatly shaped by Christianity, particularly after the Reformation.

Both the Protestant and Catholic Reformations played an important role in transforming popular culture, including popular rituals and festivals. Carnivals were the highlight of popular culture, particularly in southern Europe. It was great fun for the masses as they ate and drank, tossed eggs and flour on each other, played games, performed plays, danced and enacted caricatures of nobles, clergy and kings and queens. At many places during the sixteenth-century European society witnessed a conflict between the popular carnivals and church authorities. Some of the contemporary paintings reflect this conflict between Carnival and Lent, the latter term representing the church side. Peter Burke uses the phrase 'the reform of popular culture' to describe the systematic attempt by the clergy and educated men to reform or suppress many of the semi-religious popular festivities like May Day, harvest feasts and the Feast of the Fools. This attempt varied from one place to another and from generation to generation even within one religious fold. Sometimes, the attempt was to suppress the traditional practices or oppose it while on other occasions the attempt was to purify particular practice of popular religion. Certain forms of popular culture such as mystery and magical plays, festivals on saints' days, cards, fortune-telling, sermons by laymen, dancing, gambling, bull-fights, drinking and witchcraft, were opposed by the religious reformers and state officials. Many of these objectionable festivities were found in carnivals and hence carnivals became their chief targets. The struggle between tradition and regulation commenced with the coming of the Reformation, although it had existed on a smaller scale even earlier.

Religion and magic had remained closely interwoven in popular imagination for centuries. The church had been unsuccessful in untangling the difference between prayer and goodluck charms in popular mind. In the medieval times, the clergy often took part in popular festivities but now with the reformations they were moving away from such activities. The 'twirl', a dance in southern France was banned because it exposed the dancer's body when her partner tossed her up in course of the dance. In Italy, market-place comedies were strongly condemned by the Jesuits. All dancing came under attack but some folk-dances received special condemnation. The reformers did not tolerate popular preachings because they felt that these were based on ficticious stories and full of crude colloquial language to entertain the audience. Such preachers were accused of making blasphemous comparisons of divine subjects. Some of the popular entertainments modelled on Christian liturgy, like the Charivari in France were seen as mockery of the sacrament of marriage. Most of the reformers objected to popular customs because these were seen as pagan survivals that promoted superstition. Pagan gods and goddesses were considered demons and were seen opposed to Christian faith. There were two main religious objections to carnivals – first, because these contained traces of paganism and second, these led to over-indulgence. Similarly, magic was also seen as a form of pagan belief. There was also an attempt to get rid of charms and spells. The attack on popular culture was also made on grounds of morality. It was alleged that such festivities were the cause of sins and moral degradation. The participants were exposed to drunkenness and lechery. Dances, songs and plays, according to reformers, aroused physical desires and led to indecency and violence. Popular songs made heroes out of devils. Some books like *The Ship of Fools* and *Discourse Against Carnival* reflected the views of the church. The reformers attempted to separate sacred religion from popular religion.

Peter Burke argues that the Catholic reformers were fighting on two fronts in the early modern period. On the one side they were facing the Protestants while on the other front they were fighting immorality and superstition of the traditional culture. The battle was fought through reformed rituals, reformed images and reformed texts (Burke, 1978, p. 230). Burning effigies of Protestant leaders and public burning of heretical books began to replace bonfires at carnivals. At some places, forbidden plays replaced organized procession. The Catholics did not indulge in total attack on popular culture but only opposed those aspects which they thought were excesses. They tolerated the cult of saints but were against the seeking of worldly favours like cures. They were interested in purifying festivals but not in abolishing them. The popular imagery of St George was accepted without the dragon. They also objected to wasting of sacred time into festivity of worldly pleasures. They rejected the popular tradition of arranging plays or dances in the premises of a church, a holy place. The clergy were forbidden to participate in carnivals, watch dances or plays and bullfights. Sermons became an important means of reaching out to people and some used visual aids to make them interesting. As Burke suggests, reformed Catholics, unlike Protestants, continued to have a religion of images rather than a religion of texts. Perhaps, one of the reasons for this was that Catholic areas had lower literacy than the Protestant regions. Partly, it was the strategy of the Jesuits and Counter-Reformists like de Nobili and others to adopt more accommodative approaches towards local popular culture. The visible shift in the Catholic areas was the coming of new saints like St Ignatius Loyola, St Teresa and John Nepomuk. New emphasis was laid on the cult of Eucharist in reaction to the Protestant rejection of transubstantiation and the role of the clergy. Confession and the importance of sacraments were stressed and translation of the Bible was done in several languages and devotional books were printed at cheaper rates.

Protestants and Catholics views on popular culture were not identical. While the Protestants wished to abolish popular rituals and festivities, the Catholics tried to modify many of them. Many Protestants like Zwingli launched a vehement attack on fasting, celebration of holy days in the name of saints, religious processions, wedding rings on every finger and all forms of magic and charms. Zwingli, Calvin and other radical thinkers were more aggressive towards popular culture than Martin Luther. In Zurich all the images of saints were removed and destroyed. In some places in the Dutch Republic, ringing bells to collect young people to celebrate and sing carnal songs was condemned. In England, Puritans opposed popular recreations like May Games, Christmas feasting, bear-baiting, cock-fighting and staging popular religious drama. Most of them also disagreed with the ideas of pilgrimage. Among the Protestants, Luther was more tolerant to popular culture – images, saints and festivities. He himself promoted music by writing hymns. The burning of the Papal Bull by Luther led to a gathering of students that culminated into a carnival on 10 December 1520 in Wittenberg. R.W. Scribner provides many illustrations of Luther's immediate supporters organizing processions and singing satirical songs against the Pope and clergy. In Munster clergy, monks and nuns were yoked to a plough which was pulled in a carnival procession through the streets by local students. However, Luther's followers were less tolerant. The impact of the Reform on popular culture is difficult to quantify but it is noticeable in some areas and it was certainly not uniform. The traditional religious and mystery plays slowly disappeared as the church placed strict restriction on staging them. The state and provincial authorities also placed similar prohibitions on them. The Protestant reformers tried to introduce radical changes in social attitudes and religious practices though many of them did not succeed. They sought abolition of customary practices like indulgences, worship of relics and saints, pilgrimages and monasticism. The end to the veneration of saints reduced the number of religious or holy days. In Protestant centres, religious ceremonies such as processions were replaced by simple form of worship at private, family or collective levels. All forms of decoration at places of worship were discouraged. Pictures and statues of the Virgin Mary were removed from the Puritan churches. Popular occasions like religious carnivals, saints' days and traditional games and plays were abolished or discouraged. Some Dutch Calvinists tried to end the popular culture of giving gifts on the feast of St Nicholas, but the tradition of folk culture was so strong that it could not be totally eliminated.

The reformers knew that they had to build a new culture to replace the traditional one in order to provide something of value to the people. The Bible was made available to ordinary men and women. According to Peter Burke, the publication of vernacular Bibles was a major event which greatly influenced the language and literature of the countries concerned. According to Scribner, the German Regormarion was the first great age of mass propaganda. An important form of Protestant popular culture was catechism (a booklet providing basic information of religious doctrine) presented in question-answer form. It succeeded in not only providing religious knowledge to ordinary pastors but also played part in the lives of the laymen. Sometimes the catechism was prepared in verses so people could learn them by heart. At places, the knowledge of catechism became essential condition for admission to mass. Religious music also became a part of Lutheran popular culture. The use of images in woodcuts and paintings had some impact on popular mind. Woodcuts and broadsheets became important methods of reaching out to the people. They not only amused ordinary people but influenced popular ideas. Before the Reformation it was a common belief that anyone who looked at an image of Saint Christopher would not die that day. The new art production was becoming closer to the social attitudes of the local population. Erhard Schon became one of the most popular woodcut artist during the Reformation era.

The Reformation also stimulated new compositions in art and music. Luther lavished praise on art and placed music next to the word of God. His famous hymn 'A Mighty Fortress Is Our God' is still well known. Buxtehude and Bach continued Luther's traditions of musical form of worship. However, Zwingli and Calvin in Switzerland were against it. They considered music to be a source of distraction and stressed on a purified form of worship. Instrumental and organ music was thus banned in the Genevan churches. Arts also suffered in these places because the Calvinist church opposed all images, sculptures and idols. The clergy condemned the prominent role played by women and youth in carnivals and other festivals of lay confraternities (voluntary organizations like cultural clubs). Carnivals were virtually eradicated by Protestant churches.

The Catholic Reformation became an important source of patronage to the new style of art called 'baroque' that developed in the post-Renaissance period. This art style complemented the Catholic Reformation through flamboyance, monumentalism and extravagence. It is often seen as the revival of spiritual life in the Catholic Church. Baroque represented irregularly shaped ornamentation. It was a decorative style that gained popularity from early seventeenth century in many states of Europe like Austria, Germany, the Flanders and many Catholic countries. It merged with the classical style of beauty in Protestant England and made an attempt to revive architectural designs of the Greek and Roman forms.

The Church in Rome remained an important source of patronage and promoted religious themes to impress and to highlight emotion. This art stressed the metaphysical aspect of humanity and the physical experience. Baroque art displayed great love for details and its palaces and churches had richly ornamented and exuberant curves in ceilings, murals, altars and statues. The best example of this style can be seen in Rome – the Gesu Church of the Jesuits – with its colourful ceilings and false cupola. The most famous artist of baroque was Gianlorenzo Bernini (1598–1680), a sculptor of Venetia and he represented the spirit of the Catholic Reformation. Baroque art sometimes appeared overtly gaudy. It developed into a more richly decorated form in Rococo style during the eighteenth century. Many baroque artists served the powerful rulers like Louis XIV of France and because of his emphasis on grandeur, baroque art is often seen as absolutist in nature.

Thus, one can say, as Jacques Le Goff suggests, that there existed two cultures in medieval Europe: the 'learned' culture or the culture of the clergy and the 'folkloric' or popular culture. Though the two cultures were very different and popular culture could not be entirely eliminated despite the efforts of the church. For the clergy to become acceptable by the common people, certain aspects of popular culture had to be accommodated. The change in popular religion was never dramatic. One could see the continuation of belief in signs, rituals, prophecies and miracles but the extent varied from one region to another.

Witchcraft

It is worth mentioning at the beginning that the widespread practice of witchcraft was not a part of the Reformation culture and its practice pre-dates the religious movements of the sixteenth century.

The term 'witch hunt' implies a search for scapegoats or of finding pretext to blame someone else for a disaster. Today, with the help of scientific knowledge man has solved many of the

Execution of the witches

mysteries of nature. People in the medieval world were apprehensive of many natural phenomena and lived in perpetual fear – fear of diseases, famines, floods, storms, wars, taxes, and of unexplained deaths. They feared unknown diseases, those that had come from the New World. Then there were family problems such as impotency, infertility and infant deaths. As in some parts of the world today people believed in supernatural powers of the Satan and demons. For all these problems, the blame was put on evil spirits brought upon by witchcraft. Witches came to symbolize the superstitious mentality of popular religion. In the Middle Ages, there was a store of folklore of superstitions among the peasants – spells, evil spirits, magic – and many believed that witches had the power to fly or change shape and they formed a part of a satanic conspiracy to undermine Christianity and Christian beliefs. Witch-craze grew alarmingly during the sixteenth century. Women in particular, in both Protestant and Catholic regions, became the victims of witch hunts. A large number of old and rural poor women were prosecuted and many put to death for practising witchcraft. In 1486, two Dominican inquisitors, Heinrich Kramer and Jacob Sprenger wrote a book *The Hammer of the Witches* with the backing of Pope Innocent VIII. Women, according to medieval writers, were weak and had weak libidos and were lured easily by the devil who had sex with them. Women were definitely more prone to evil. Sex orgies were seen as a part of witchcraft. It is believed that nearly 1,00,000 people were tried and about 60,000 were executed for witchcraft. The largest trials and prosecution took place between 1560 and 1660.

Historians of the sixteenth and seventeenth centuries find the European witch hunt a perplexing phenomenon as the period after Renaissance was a period of progress. The phenomenon of witchcraft has been variously explained by scholars from different disciplines. It is seen by the social-anthropologists as a consequence of emotionally grounded religious and mythical beliefs including the notion of magic. Scholars like Caro Baroja suggest that men and women in the early modern period suffered from collective fears and anxieties caused by social and cultural changes. Those who practised witchcraft were basically irrational. The psychologists see it as a product of collective psychological trauma and hallucination. One recent view suggests that the growing practice of witchcraft during the sixteenth century was possibly due to the impact of syphilis on the European society. Recent works on the subject treat it as a cultural phenomenon based on social reality.

To what extent did the Reformation contribute to it cannot be said with certainly because the practice dates back to centuries. Jeffrey Burton Russell's anthropological analysis contends that witchcraft existed in pre-Christian Europe. According to him, witchcraft in the fifteenth century combined elements of magic and the ancient pagan traditions displaying a spirit of opposition and defiance against orthodox Christianity and society, and assumed the form of heresy. Norman Cohn presents an opposite viewpoint. For him, witchcraft, based on devil-worship did not constitute popular culture and remained confined to a small group of clerics. These ideas began to penetrate society in the sixteenth and seventeenth centuries. Many of the church officials and theologians started believing in the cult of Satan and witches and saw them as a threat to the Christian order. According to Cohn, the four separate and independent elements – folklore, witchcraft, ritual magic and devil-worship – were all grouped as religious dissenters by intellectuals and theologians. The concept of black magic and devil-worship assumed a menacing form by the late-fifteenth century. Catholic leaders and legal scholars began to advance theories but in the seventeenth century, both Catholic and Protestant elite projected a witch as not only someone who might cast harmful spells but also as a heretic. The authorities conducting the trial, even if they found no proof, believed that devil-worshipping was practised by the accused and that Satan was in their midst. The legal procedures of that period allowed the use of torture to extract confessions. The worst form of torture compelled the accused to say what the captors wished to hear. More than 80 per cent of those convicted and executed, often burnt alive, were women. Christian dogma and contemporary writings portrayed woman as morally weaker than man and the poverty of the common people, particularly single and old women, made them more vulnerable to the charges of devil's enticements and witches. By the late Middle Ages, witches came to be seen as the servants of the devil. It was alleged that witches cast spells of misfortune, caused abortion in animals and human beings, raised storm and created havoc. Several theologians and judges tried to show that witches embodied the kingdom of the devil. Burckhardt in his work on the Italian Renaissance provides interesting information on magic and other forms of superstition. According to him, witchcraft had a German origin and that witchcraft was commonly practised in rural Italy while sorceresses were seen more in urban places. The practice of witchcraft was not confined to the Catholic countries. The Puritans in England were actively involved in hangings. Many people, like the Witch-finder General, Matthew Hopkins, made large fortunes from witch-hunting. In England, witchcraft remained a crime against the church. The famous French peasant woman, Joan of Arc played a leading role in repulsing the English forces during the Hundred Years War. She appeared in men's clothes and led the French forces of Charles. She was captured by the English, accused of being a witch, and was condemned and burnt at the stake. In Germany, Martin Luther and Melanchton firmly believed in the power of spells. Luther spoke of the devil's power and held the belief that through witches, he could seriously harm human beings and animals and cause storms. Interestingly, some of the scientists of that period also believed in the power of magic and supernatural beings.

This degrading social practice almost died out by the end of the seventeenth century as the social and intellectual climate shifted away from religion to scientific thought. Some individuals like the German Jesuit, the Friedrich and French scholar F. Bouvot protested through their writings against the practice of witch-hunting and many scientists highlighted the irrationality of such practices. Voltaire in his typical satirical style ridiculed this practice and saw it as a means of alleviating the boredom of the nobility during the long winter nights. Noble et al., write (in their *Western Civilization: The Continuing Experiment*) that the witch hunts are both the last chapter in the history of the Reformation and the first chapter in the history of modern state.

The Economic Impact of Reformation

The Reformation is sometimes seen as a revolutionary event because it represented the challenge of a new class to feudalism. The overthrow of the old church opened the way to a gradual secularization of thought among the literate classes. The Lutheran view that all believers were masters of their own spiritual destiny contributed to the origin of an individualistic ethic. According to some historians, this religious individualism was a counterpart to the intellectual individualism of humanism and it encouraged the growth of capitalism.

The relationship between Calvinism and the economic development of Europe has remained the subject of heated debate among scholars of Europe. The question whether Calvinism was responsible for an emergent capitalism or whether a connection already existed between business and religious zeal remains a major issue of contention in academic circles.

In the course of the debate scholars have raised a number of questions. Did Protestantism zeal spark capitalist expansion while the reformed Catholicism discouraged it? Was it a coincidence that the most dynamic businessmen lived in Protestant Holland and Anglican England, the most industrialized regions at that time? Why did the Huguenots as a businesss community dominate Catholic France? Why was the Protestant Brandenberg – Prussia under the leadership of the Calvinist Elector the only German state in the seventeenth century to experience prosperity? And why did Catholic Italy, Portugal or Flanders – all flourishing regions before 1559 – begin to regress in the seventeenth century and witness a startling economic collapse? Such questions have been constantly discussed among twentieth-century scholars.

In the middle of the nineteenth century, Karl Marx suggested that Protestantism succeeded because it gave expression to the new capitalist values of thrift, hard work, self-discipline and rationality. Frederick Engels also, argued that Calvinism more mature, more fully urban, and republican in temper compared to Lutheranism. It was a faith suitable for the boldly aspiring bourgeois or early capitalist groups (*Introduction to Socialism: Utopian and Scientific*).

The real controversy began in 1905 with the publication of Max Weber's *The Protestant Ethic and the Spirit of Capitalism*. E. Troeltsch further took this up in his work *The Social Teaching of the Christian Churches*. Weber's contention was that the Evolution of modern capitalism was encouraged by the prevalent social ethos. For him, capitalist form of enterprises existed before the Reformation but the capitalist spirit was lacking. There were many individual capitalists during the Middle Ages and during the Renaissance but these businessmen had not been able to instill a profit-making ethos into European society. An intellectual revolution was needed to develop it. This was brought about by the Protestant Reformation. Weber believed that the early Protestants, especially Calvin and his followers, strongly influenced the development of capitalism in the sixteenth and the seventeenth centuries. Weber defined the capitalist spirit as a rationally calculated, highly systematized pursuit of profit rather than an irrational greed for gain, power or glory. Weber did not find this rational capitalism among the pre-

Reformation merchant-bankers like the Medicis or Fuggers. They exhibited greed in their loans to Kings and Popes and lavishly funded extraneous political projects. Weber traces the beginning of the modern capitalist spirit to the small-scale merchants of England and Netherlands of the sixteenth century. They were greatly inspired in the business practices by the ethical teachings of Calvin. Protestantism gave to capitalism a special dynamism and that the Protestants made the best capitalists because of their doctrine of predestination.

Max Weber laid stress on the Protestant idea that every man's worldly 'calling' was assigned to him by God. Calvin's doctrine produced among his adherents, trails of discipline in work, asceticism and drive. The emphasis on self-discipline and hard work were virtues that contribute to orderly business procedures and to success in business, fostering the spirit of modern capitalism. Moneymaking was no more regarded with opprobrium as was done earlier. For the Calvinists it was a method of fulfilling one's 'work ethic' and carrying out a sacred trust. Thus, for Weber, the rise of capitalism was most rapid in those regions which adopted Calvinism. Weber's thesis evolved in opposition to the Marxist views (who emphasize only on the economic and material factors as the instruments of change). Weber stressed the importance of mind, ideas and environment. However, in the course of time his thesis became a subject of debate and criticism.

Weber's arguments have certain obvious limitations. His thesis, according to M.J. Kitch, is more passionate than others but confused. He begins with an unacceptable notion that the capitalist spirit was contrary to human nature and that left to themselves, all men would want only enough to maintain them in the condition in which they found themselves. Many do not accept this viewpoint. Weber equated capitalism with the continuous pursuit of profit by means of rational enterprise. This description seems to apply to only reasonably advanced economies. Though the impact of the Reformation on European business activities and economic climate cannot be determined very precisely, yet Weber's views initiated an interesting debate.

Felix Rachfahl in a series of articles launched his criticism of Weber that was later taken up by number of writers. Rachfahl considers the idea of an ethical and religious motivation affecting or influencing economic actions as dubious. The driving force could be several other factors. He further argues that Calvin had stressed the importance of commerce and industry and in practical terms he was more enlightened than other Catholic preachers. On the subject of interest on loans he laid down severe ethical conditions, often just as restrictive as those of the Catholic Church. Free-for-all capitalism was not tolerated even in Calvinism. Rachfahl also questions Weber's view on the geographical distribution of Protestantism. Amsterdam was under the allegiance of Catholic Spain for a long time. Antwerp was also a Catholic centre but an important trading centre as well. It can be added that during the days of greatest prosperity of the Dutch Republic as a whole, the provinces with the largest Calvinist population shared the least in capitalist growth – the two most Calvinist provinces, Friesland and Groningen, failed to compete with Holland. However, in his conclusion Rachfahl endorses the major contention of Weber. He concludes that Protestantism's economic lead derives in essence from the absence of obstructive forces, which the Catholic church abounded in, blocking the road towards economic expansion.

H.M. Robertson argues that capitalism and capitalist spirit existed long before the Reformation. He dwells upon the phenomena of Italian merchant cities. Robertson points out that Catholicism also fostered the capitalist spirit. For this he gives the example of the thrift of the Franciscans. Robertson rejects the importance of 'calling', which he argues existed in the Catholic church also. If there was any change in outlook on economic activity, it was in the second half of the seventeenth century when industry, thrift and labour became godly duties.

Lujo Brentano, an eminent German economist and social reformer, also blames Weber for giving a very narrow definition of capitalism that can be applied only to the Puritan societies. Furthermore, he argues that capitalism and the desire to make money existed long before the Reformation in the Italian cities.

When the economic centre shifted from the Mediterranean to the North Seas, the Catholic merchant families also migrated to participate in the colonial trade but continued to practise the Catholic religion. Brentano suggests that the concept of 'calling' was not alien to the Catholics and could be located in the Latin version of the Bible. He also emphasizes the role of the Roman law and its attitude to business conduct. The revival and extension of the supremacy of the Roman law was independent of Catholic or Protestant faith.

A well-known non-Marxist scholar and a Christian socialist, R.H.Tawney, argued that capitalism was nothing new in the sixteenth century nor was it so exclusively Protestant. He underlined, though in a much milder way than Weber, the importance of Calvinism and emphasized more strongly than Weber the difference between Calvin and Luther. Tawney saw the nascent capitalism as the prime factor which conditioned Calvin's attitude to enterprise and accumulation of wealth, not vice versa. The ground was prepared in Spain, Italy and Portugal. The spirit of capitalism, according to Tawney, is as old as human history. In the sixteenth and seventeenth centuries, the economic change was accompanied by religious change and the change in the religious outlook was made more pronounced by the Puritans.

Thus, Tawney turned the thesis round and argued that Calvinism in the seventeenth century adapted itself to the bourgeois and the capitalist ethos of the commercial classes and offered encouragement to entrepreneurship. Men did not become capitalists because they were Protestants, nor became Protestants because they were capitalists. In a society, which was already becoming capitalist, Protestantism facilitated the triumph of new values. Where capitalism already existed, it had a freer scope from now. To Weber, capitalism was one of the glories of Protestantism and he praised the vast material expansion that resulted from it. Tawney attacked not only capitalism for its failure to provide social justice but also Protestantism for perverting the Christian message of poverty and charity into a gospel in which success sanctified the work and profit equalled godliness.

Christopher Hill argues that there was nothing in Protestantism that automatically led to the rise of capitalism. Its importance was that it undermined obstacles that the more rigid institutions and ceremonies of Catholicism imposed. In a society already becoming capitalist, Protestantism facilitated the triumph of the new values.

A number of recent historians have claimed that the rise of capitalism had nothing to do with religion at all and that it existed throughout the middle ages – in Italy, south Germany and Zantine. The leading capitalists of the Reformation era remained faithful to Rome. Even Calvin had very reluctantly agreed to charging a very nominal interest in 1545, but he was against all forms of greed. In the Reformation and in the post-Reformation Protestantism there was no approval of moneymaking as something pleasing to God. The essence of the doctrine of 'calling' was merely to show that men need not leave the world in order to serve God but never suggested that they should follow their daily task in the sole pursuit of profit. It is also contended that commercialism was entrenched in the Netherlands long before Calvinism reached there, and in Catholic France Jacques Coeur and in Catholic Germany the Fugger family prospered.

P. Gordon Walker asserts that the acceleration of capitalism was more due to the price-rise, which hastened the arrival of the Industrial Revolution.

Calvinism is said to have influenced the development of finance, industry and commerce. Stephen J. Lee suggests that it was mainly due to the fact that the Calvinists as a minority group found themselves discriminated against by the law of the land or by social isolation and were prevented from entering professions. They were forced into private enterprise of trade or manufacturing. They spread their wings along the trading centres, which were more prosperous than the countryside. They were welcomed in the Netherlands and England where they contributed to the economic development.

Finally we can conclude with E. Geoffrey French's view that there is no good reason for linking Protestantism with capitalism. Neither the view that the outburst of material improvement and commercial enterprise which characterized the centuries after 1600 in some way emanated from the new cast of mind which had also produced Protestantism (Weber), nor the view that capitalism exploited the peculiarities of the Protestant form of Christianity to free itself from all restraint (Tawney), is borne out by facts.

Major Events

1381	Peasant revolt in England and its support to John Wycliff
1415	John Hus burned at the stake for his religious views
1414–18	The Council of Constance
1431–49	The Council of Basel
1504	Publication of the *Enchiridion Militis Christians* (*Handbook of Christian Soldier*) by Erasmus
1509	Erasmus writes *Praise of Folly*
1517	Martin Luther writes his *Ninety-five Thesis*
1520	Pope Leo X excommunicates Luther
1521	The Diet of Worms called by Charles V to condemn Luther
1524–6	The German Peasant War
1520–5	Zwingli's Reformation in Zurich
1530	Diet of Augsberg. Emperor Charles V invited both the Catholics and Lutherans to bring them together to strengthen the Empire but failed.
1529–34	The English Parliament carries out Henry VIII's Reformation. A series of acts led to a breach with Rome and the supremacy of Henry over the English church
1534	Henry VIII declared head of the English Church; Francis I of France declares Protestants heretics; Loyola founds the Society of Jesus; Radical reformers, Anabaptists, capture Munster in Westphalia.
1535	Calvin publishes *Institutes of the Christian Religion*; Henry VIII dissolves monasteries and seizes their wealth
1536–64	Calvin's Reformation
1545–63	The Council of Trent
1555	The Peace of Augsburg; Lutherans get the right to reform their own states
1559	The Anglican Settlement under Elizabeth I of England
1562–98	Wars of religion in France ended with the Edict of Nantes in 1598

Suggested Readings

Barry, Jonathan, Marianne Hester and Gareth Roberts, eds., *Witchcraft in Early Modern Europe: Studies in Culture and Belief*, Cambridge: Cambridge University Press, 1996. An important work on the subject covering diverse regions.

Burke, Peter, *Popular Culture in Early Modern Europe*, London: Harper, 1978. He describes and interprets the popular culture of the 'subordinate classes' of Europe from 1500–1800 in a masterly way.

Cameron, Evan, *The European Reformation*, Oxford: Clarendon Press, 1991. An important work on the subject. It highlights the common elements of the religious reformers.

Clark, Stuart, ed., *Languages of Witchcraft, Narrative, Ideology and Meaning in Early Modern Culture*, London: Macmillan Press, 2001. An important work on the subject with a comprehensive introduction that has historiographical discussion in it.

Cross, F.L and Livingstone, *The Oxford Dictionary of the Christian Church*, Oxford: Oxford University Press, 1974.

Davidson, N.S., *The Counter Reformation*, Oxford: Basil Blackwell, 1987. A remarkable survey of the relations between popular religion and the authorized church.

Davis, Natalie Zemon, *Society and Culture in Early Modern France*, California: Standford University Press, 1975. Pathbreaking work on mentality, particularly good on attitudes towards women.

Dickens, A.G., *The English Reformation*, New York: Schocken, 1964. A standard and well-documented work.

———, *The German Nation and Martin Luther*, London: Edward Arnold, 1974.

Diefendorf, Barbara B., *From Penitence to Charity: Pious Women and Catholic Reformation in Paris*, Oxford: Oxford University Press, 2004. Provides an entirely new approach to women's participation and leadership in the Catholic Reformation in France, highlighting the role played by aristocratic and bourgeois women in Paris.

Elton, G.R., *Reformation Europe, 1517-1559*, London: Fontana, 1968.

———, ed., *New Cambridge Modern History of Europe*, vol. II, Cambridge: Cambridge University Press, 1990. Chapters by Bindoff, Scribner, Betts, Spooner, Elton and Stayer cover almost all aspects of the Reformation.

Greengrass, Mark, *The French Reformation*, Oxford: Basil Blackwell, 1987. A well-researched work on the religious issues in France.

Greyerz, Kasper von, ed., *Religion and Society in Early Modern Europe, 1500–1800*, London: George Allen, 1984.

Hsia, R. Po-chia, ed., *Cambridge History of Christianity*, vol. 6, *Reform and Expansion, 1500–1660*, Cambridge: Cambridge University Press, 2006. Provides a comprehensive analysis of the development of Christianity in all aspects including theological, social, political, regional and cultural.

Jones, Norman, *The English Reformation: Religion and Cultural Adaptation*, Oxford: Basil Blackwell, 2002.

Kitch, M.J., ed., *Capitalism and the Reformation: Problems and Perspective in History*, London: Longman, 1967. Good for the discussion on the relationship between Protestantism and Capitalism.

Koenigsberger, H.G. and George L. Mosse, *Europe in the Sixteenth Century*, London: Longman, 1968. Very good discussion on the Reformation and on the Price Revolution.

Lindberg, Carter, *The European Reformations*, Oxford: Basil Blackwell, 1996.

McGrath, Alister E., *The Intellectual Origins of the European Reformation*, New York: Basil Blackwell, 1987.

———, *Reformation Thought: An Introduction*, Oxford: Basil Blackwell, 1987. Both the works are very informative especially pertaining to the major ideas of the reformers. He discusses how the Reformation arose from a complex heterogeneous matrix of social and ideological factors.

Scribner, Bob, *The German Reformation*, London: Routledge, 1986. An authoritative work on German developments.

Scribner, R.W., *Popular Culture and Popular Movements in Reformation Germany*, London: Hambledon Press, 1987. Provides a new area of research by examining popular beliefs and behaviour and the reaction of local authorities.

Tawney, R.H., *Religion and the Rise of Capitalism: A Historical Study*, New York: Mentor Book, 1952. Must be read by all those interested in the relationship between religion and capitalism.

Watts, Sheldon J., *A Social History of Western Europe, 1450–1720*, London: Hutchinson University Press, 1984. Comprehensive discussion on the world of supernaturalism, religion and sociability.

Weber, Max, *The Protestant Ethic and the Spirit of Capitalism* (tr. and intro. by Stephen Kalberg, Los Angeles: Basil Blackwell, 2002. A non-Marxist classic essay emphasizing the role of the Protestant ideology in the development of capitalism.

Wright, A.D., *The Counter-Reformation: Catholic Europe and the Non-Christian World*, London: Weidenfeld & Nicolson, 1982. Useful work for the study of the expansion of Christianity.

CHAPTER 5

The Rise of Absolutist States

In the late-fifteenth century, Europe was divided into over 500 decentralized feudal states. The crisis of feudal economy brought about significant changes that were particularly noticeable in the relationship between the structure of changing society and the evolution of state-building. It altered power relations in the cities and in the countryside and subsequently influenced relations with their respective governments. The local coercive power of the lord and his retainers over the peasantry altered and the state began to monopolize the use of force and repressed the economic power of the feudal lords. This period witnessed the rise of strong centralized monarchies, specially in western Europe — France, England and Spain. The form of government came to be called absolutism (in its early stages it was also described as New Monarchy or Renaissance Monarchy).

Absolutism of the sixteenth century did not have a uniform appearance, although its social base remained more or less the same. It emerged out of medieval feudal kingship, where powers were limited by the legislative and judicial rights of vassals, churches, semi-independent provinces and municipal corporations. All these forces were represented in institutions called by different names in different states such as Estates-General in France, Diet in the German states, Parliament in England and Cortes in Spain. Besides, the king depended to a large extent on the cooperation of troops and the administrators, which were provided to him by his vassals and feudal lords. Furthermore, the power of the medieval rulers was severely curbed by episcopal restrictions placed on them by Popes and by the Holy Roman Emperors. The absolute rulers began concentrating all authority in their hands by successfully raising standing armies and by creating royal bureaucracies directly under their own control, collecting taxes independently and formulating independent policies. All these developments transformed the physical, military, administrative and legal aspects of feudal states. The theory of the Divine Right of the king provided moral justification of absolutism, which was supported and legitimized by political theorists like Jean Bodin, Bossuet and Hobbes.

Origins of Absolutism

As regards the origin of absolutism, the initial thrust came from of the crisis of feudalism. The existence of weak feudal states with fragmented sovereignty during the medieval period gave a semblance of stability but in the period of economic and political crises, the solution lay not in the continuation of such frail states but in the absorption and consolidation of smaller units into a strong centralized state. Absolutism was a response to this situation. The conditions favouring the development of absolutism and administrative centralization were almost the same in England, France and Spain.

Gianfranco Poggi lists a number of reasons for the weakening of feudalism. These include increased commercialization, the influx of bullion leading to devalued money and the growing expenditure of the feudal ruling classes. The waning feudalism helped the nascent bourgeoisie and the rulers. The rich bourgeois families purchased some of the official posts earlier monopolized by the feudal nobility. With the introduction of new and costly methods of warfare, the feudal lords lost their military significance. The inter-state politics and some major developments in the technology of warfare made it necessary for the states to maintain a standing army and sometimes even a fleet if they wished to survive. These could only be financed and administered by rulers of bigger states who had the capacity to muster greater resources. This deprived the feudal lords of the power that was needed to provide military leadership. The crunch of economic resources affected the judicial powers of the feudal nobility as well.

During the feudal crisis, the kings faced the problem of controlling the outlying regions with limited means at their disposal.

In the late-fifteenth century, the growing needs of the government forced the rulers to adopt centralized measures for effective governance over the distant provinces, which had enjoyed a fair degree of autonomy. Moreover, along with the monarchy there existed during the middle ages, a land owning baronage, a well-established municipal authority and strong clerical institutions. All these provided a multitude of assemblies and bodies, which eroded the king's authority and led to the formation of a decentralized power structure.

The economic squeeze by the *seigneurs* had led to increased exploitation of serfs and consequently led to peasant rebellions. This not only caused social and political disorders but also resulted in warfare among the feudal lords who were trying to increase their income and power. The feudal nobility proved too factious and incompetent to wield power directly during this period of crisis. The weakened nobility looked to kings to preserve their privileged positions and protect them against threats emanating from below. The kings profited from these circumstances and enhanced their own power and wealth at the expense of the nobility.

There was a long period of feudal warfare (e.g. the Hundred Years War between 1339 and 1453, the Uprising of 1381, the debilitating War of the Roses for the English Crown), which led to a political breakdown of authority, misrule and reduction in royal power. By the end of the fifteenth century, there was widespread support for a strong and effective government to bring internal peace and relief from feudal wars. International rivalry and feudal strife strengthened these sentiments and allowed the rulers to acquire unlimited power.

The rise of absolutist states particularly in western Europe implied the absorption of smaller states by stronger and bigger states. This strengthened centralized governments under single sovereign heads, establishing law and order. Thus absolute monarchs carried out territorial expansion and consolidation, administrative centralization and political integration that made them extremely powerful. The absolute monarchs of France, Spain and England acted as sovereign power in their respective states and were not answerable to their subjects for any institution. Their power increased enormously during the period of the Reformation as they established their own independent authority by destroying or reducing Papal interference. Absolutism required domination over the feudal aristocracy and independence from outside challenges, including the papacy. Yet, absolutism had its own limitations. Absolute rulers raised their standing armies with foreign soldiers constituting the bulk of its force. Many key posts in the centralized bureaucracy were sold to private individuals at exorbitant rates in order to raise royal revenue. Diplomacy was institutionalized through permanent embassies yet matrimonial alliances also prevailed. Thus, in each region, state-building involved imposition on central and provincial elites a complex of linguistic, ritual, social practices to achieve cultural integration. At another level, there occurred a vertical imposition of elite culture on popular culture and made the entire population of the region under central authority distinct from the people in the adjacent states. States with greater power and resources tried to control religious organizations and moral doctrines through the tighter regulation of public and private behaviour of their respective populations.

The Nature of Absolutist States

The form and nature of absolute states has been the subject of diverse opinion. Historians, sociologists, economists and political scientists have all contributed to this debate. Difference of opinion exists not only between the non-Marxists and Marxists but also among Marxist scholars.

Scholars have offered several explanations on the state-building process in medieval and early modern Europe. In his articles Otto Hintze rejects the class conflict explanation of Marxist writers. Instead, he presents a dualist view of the state-building process. According to him, the geographical position of the continental states (those located inland, far from the seas) exposed them to rival states and thus forced them to develop an infrastructure of absolutism and centralized bureaucracy. States like England on the other hand, in the absence of external threats, continued to grow on old lines, leading to a parliamentary form of governance. Hence, a strong link is suggested between the degree of military pressure experienced by a given country and the size and character of bureaucratic apparatus. However, this explanation of the relationship between geographical exposure and absolutism on the one side, and geographical isolation and constitutionalism, cannot be applied to many of the pre-modern states such as Hungary and Poland. They remained geographically exposed yet retained representative institutions that were decidedly constitutional. Spain on the other hand, enjoyed a relatively isolated position but developed a strong bureaucratic absolutism.

Another explanation (of Charles Tilly and Michael Mann) on variations in the state-building process attempts to bring the geographical and economic factors together. This view suggests that the extent and size of the bureaucratic and absolutist structure was determined by the nature of revenue on which the state depended. Where far-flung rural population was the main source of revenue, a strong centralized bureaucratic structure was visible, while the more economically developed states like England, with advanced commercial and trading activities, encouraged a constitutional arrangement, as an elaborate bureaucratic structure was not required. According to Charles Tilly, before 1500, there were two different forms of states in Europe – the urban or the small city states and the states with large territories. The former had a strong mercantile base, dominated by merchant capitalists while in the large agrarian states the landed nobility enjoyed coercive powers and the rulers assumed absolute character. These states had a strong impact on the inter-state system. The other states in order to defend themselves were forced to imitate them and emerged as centralized states. This view also has a few limitations. The assumption that tax collection on land is difficult and requires a vast bureaucratic structure while it is relatively easy to collect taxes on commercial products is not borne out by facts. Besides, it can also be argued that states like Hungary and Poland lacked commercial resources and were almost entirely dependent on agricultural resources. Yet they remained non-bureaucratic and constitutional states.

On the nature of absolutism, the Marxist opinion is equally divided. The controversy seems to have started with the writings of Karl Marx and Engels. At no place can one locate a well-formulated, coherent and sustained theoretical analysis of the absolute states in the writings of Marx, as he had done in the case of capitalism. He made only casual remarks on the existence of centralized monarchy. In fact, Marx never used the term absolutism. His primary concern was the origins, nature and consequences of capitalism. The controversy on the historical nature of these monarchies has persisted ever since. Frederich Engels in a famous dictum on the origins of state (in *Selected Works*, 1968) briefly mentioned that the absolute state was the product of class equilibrium between the old feudal nobility and the new urban bourgeoisie. This description implied that the absolute state was a type of a bourgeois state that acted as a balancing force between the two opposite classes. It also implied that the beginning of the epoch of absolutism marked the decline of the feudal nobility along with its social and political domination. In his famous work *The Eighteenth Brumaire of Louis Bonaparte,* Karl Marx declared: 'The centralized state power, with its ubiquitous organs of standing army, police, bureaucracy, clergy and judicature – organs wrought after the plan of a systematic and hierarchic division of labour – originates from the days of absolute monarchy, serving nascent middle-class society as a mighty weapon in its struggles against feudalism.' On the one hand, absolutism is seen playing a crucial role in maintaining feudalism in a modified form while on the other hand, it appears progressive because it facilitated the rise of capitalism. These views have created ambiguities even among Marxists writers.

Marxist scholars have taken different positions on the nature of the absolutist state. Although they agree that the absolutist state was a form of class power, they disagree amongst themselves on the question of which social class it represented. The traditional view suggests that absolutism developed within the parameters of the feudal state (scholars like Christopher Hill, Takahashi, Porchnev and Eric Molnar). Takahashi considers absolutism as nothing but a system of concentrated force for counteracting the crisis of feudalism arising out of the inevitable development in the direction of the liberation and independence of peasants. Similarly, Hill argues that absolute monarchy was a form of feudal state. Eric Molnar suggests that all forms of European absolutism served the interest of the nobles or landowners who had established their political domination over other classes of society. On the other hand, writers like Étienne Poulantzas (*Political Powers and Social Classes*), and E. Balibar feel that the absolute state possessed a capitalist character. This view suggests that the absolute states acted as a mechanism whereby new productive forces homologous with capitalist relations of production were formed outside the self-perpetuating feudal mode of production. Poulantzas asserts that the absolutist state, which was dislocated with the advancement of the economy, promoted the domination of capitalism. This dislocation enabled the state to carry out the process of primitive accumulation through expropriation of small landowners, investment in industrialization, attacks on seigniorial power and the destruction of internal common barriers. For him, these activities could only have been carried out by the autonomous state, which could act against the interests of the nobility at a time when the bourgeoisie was incapable of advancing capitalism by itself. E.K. Trimberger also considers the role of the state as transformative towards capitalism during the period of transition and she argues that the state acted as an external dissolving agent. Another view (Michael Hetcher and William Brustein) states that the absolute states arose to protect the economic interests of the feudal nobility but in due course the interests of the capitalist class governed them.

Immanuel Wallerstein points out that the emergence of European absolutism during the sixteenth century in the core economies was unmistakably a capitalist phenomenon. It became the chief means by which national groupings of commercial capitalists asserted their interests in the world economy. The strong state in the form of absolute monarchy was seen as a guardian and protector of their interests by the rising capitalist class. The sixteenth century represented a period in which all elements of the capitalist economy combined into a single process to form the modern world. Many historians do not accept this argument of Wallerstein that the strong state structures only existed in the 'core' economies, i.e. the Netherlands, England, parts of Spain and southern Germany. As pointed out by Theda Skocpol, the Netherlands and Germany represented weak state structures and contrary to the Wallerstein model, there were much stronger absolutist states outside the core regions.

However, these views on the nature of absolutism have not gained sufficient popularity among historians. Between these two explanations, there is another view, which lays stress on the autonomy of state structures and suggests that absolutism possessed a political character that was independent from both modes of production – feudal as well as capitalist. The state is presented as a transitional social formation and Theda Skocpol is a prominent propounder of this view. Writers like Hartung and Mousnier (*Social Hierarchies*, 1969), feel that without the profitable business through loans to the state, the raising of taxes, the exploitation of royal domains, expenditure on warfare and on royal courts, commercial capitalism could have never experienced such a spectacular rise in the first half of the sixteenth century.

Perry Anderson most systematically presents the social nature of the absolute state within the traditional Marxist framework. According to Anderson, the long crisis of European economy and society revealed the difficulties and outer limits of the feudal mode of production. The emergence of absolutist states was the political outcome of this crisis. The emergence of centralized monarchies in France, Spain and England was a decisive change from the earlier medieval social formation represented by the pyramidal 'parcellized sovereignty'. While arguing that the rise of absolute monarchies was the product of feudal crisis, Anderson emphasizes their feudal character. He contends that these monarchies may appear to be pre-eminently capitalist as they introduced a standing army, a permanent bureaucracy, central taxation, a codified law and unified markets, yet they retained the feudal character. With the coming of the feudal crisis, serfdom may have disappeared but the feudal structure in the countryside persisted. This structure continued till the emergence of 'labour-power'. For Anderson, the changes in the forms of feudal exploitation were significant because these changes determined the form of each state. For Perry Anderson absolutism was essentially 'a redeployed and recharged apparatus of feudal domination', designed to put the peasant masses back into their traditional social position. The absolutist state for him, was never an arbiter between the aristocracy and the bourgeoisie, still less an instrument of nascent bourgeoisie against aristocracy: It was the new political carapace of threatened nobility.

The feudal social and political organization reflected a form of organic unity retaining the self-sufficient form of natural or subsistence economy while its polity exhibited distribution of political authority into parcellized sovereignty. With the disappearance of serfdom, the class-power of the feudal lords was threatened. The result was a displacement of politico-legal coercion through a centralized and militarized absolute state. This was the reinforced apparatus of royal power whose political function was repression of the peasant masses. This new state machine also had the coercive force to check the powers of the nobility itself. The process of evolution of absolutism was uneven and sometimes reflected sharp ruptures. The political concentration of power under a centralized monarchy at the height of social order led to economic consolidation of the units of feudal property beneath it. The feudal aristocracy was threatened not only by the peasant from below but had to face the challenge of another antagonist – the mercantile bourgeoisie. The feudal nobility in order to survive, accepted the sovereignty of the monarch and in return these monarchs who became absolute rulers, incorporated the feudal nobility in the state's structure. The revival of the Roman law from antiquity gave juridical expression to the absolute nature of political power and provided the basis for the emergence of absolute property, which was an essential precondition for capitalism. The state form under absolutism ensured the basic interests of the mercantile and manufacturing classes. The process of primitive accumulation of capital began by removing internal barriers to trade, external tariff was effectively enforced and colonial and trading companies were established. Thus, the rise of absolutism and the adoption of absolute legal property, although carried out in the interests of the feudal landed class, created preconditions for the emergence of capitalism.

In recent years scholars like John E. Martin and Teshale Tibebu have pointed out certain difficulties in Anderson's conceptualization of the absolutist state. Martin points out that the political definition of the feudal mode of production in terms of parcellized sovereignty and serfdom faces difficulty when it is placed in the context of absolutism representing a decisive break with parcellized sovereignty. Anderson insists on the continuation of feudal character of the state. He does not explain in what form the state retains the feudal character even after the crisis. Second, there is little indication of the manner in which absolutism secures such relations of production, other than through incorporation of the landowning class into the state apparatus. According to Martin, Anderson introduces an 'instrumentalist' view of state where the state functions as an instrument of the ruling class. Third, Anderson does not analyse why absolutism was a form of transitional feudal state. He largely confines his attention to the state's relationship with the manufacturing and mercantile bourgeoisies, rather than analysing its function in relation to feudal domination. These problems, according to John E. Martin, largely derive from Anderson's theory of feudalism. His identification of feudalism with parcellized sovereignty makes it impossible to conceptualize the changes following the feudal crisis. These difficulties were also caused because of Anderson's usage of an internal dissolution theory of transition in which he argues that the dissolution of feudalism began in the late-fourteenth century and, on the other hand, he insists that the feudal character of social formation persisted till the seventeenth century. Teshale Tibebu also questions Anderson's views on conflicting stands on centralized feudalism and the parcellized sovereignty. Tibebu argues that Anderson follows a double standard in identifying feudalism: one is political which he applies to parcellized sovereignty and another is economic which is uses for centralized sovereignty. Rise of absolutism is explained as the demise of political institutions of the parcellized sovereignty, while the continuation of feudalism under absolutism is explained in terms of the continuation of economic relations of parcellized sovereignty. Yet Anderson insists on the feudal character of the state. Tibebu also criticizes Anderson's theory of comparative analysis of western and eastern absolutism in Europe. For him the absolutist state in the west was a redeployed political apparatus of a feudal class that had accepted the commutation of traditional dues. The absolute state in eastern Europe was the repressive machine of a feudal class that had just erased the traditional, communal freedom of the poor peasants. The western absolutism, according to Anderson, was a political apparatus of a more powerful feudal aristocracy ruling more advanced societies and the rise of absolutism here was the product of internal dynamics while it obliged the eastern nobility to adopt an equivalent centralized state machine to survive. Thus, according to Teshale Tibebu, he offers two fundamentally different explanations for the same problem. Eastern absolutism, on the one hand, arose through the consolidation of serfdom by the class of feudal lords by means of eliminating communal right of the peasants (internal cause), but on the other hand he suggests that western absolutism forced eastern feudal lords to organize their own absolutism.

While agreeing with the interpretation of Anderson on the nature of the absolutist state as the hierarchy of parcellized sovereignty, John E. Martin emphasizes the transitional nature of absolutism. According to him the absolute state is unable to prevent the expansion of commodity relations of production and the transformation of feudal tenant-at-will into petty commodity producers. The reproduction requirements (conditions of existence) of the state's structure are to be found in the transitional social formation in both capitalism as well as feudalism. State policies like mercantilism and internal trade regulation, in reality, helped mercantile capital and also enhanced the state's physical revenue. At some stage absolutism became a barrier in the advancement of capitalism as it preserved feudal structure and resisted change. Martin explains the shifting relationship between the state and bourgeoise in Tudor and Stuart England on this ground. In the agrarian field, the policy dictated by absolutism was non-capitalist in the long run. The state generally protected feudal, landed structure against agrarian capitalism because of its reliance on the peasantry for fiscal and military needs. It was the structure of the state that determined the state's agrarian policy.

There are some other views on the nature of the absolutist state. For Maurice Aymard, a noted French historian, the state of new monarchy possessed a war-like character with a heavy fiscal apparatus and unwieldy bureaucracy. For it, war appeared to be the most important mode of expansion of surplus extraction. The territorial expansion of the absolute state provided additional revenue and thus the military element of the nobility furnished social basis to absolutism. Louis Althusser regards the political regime of the absolutist monarchy as the new political form needed for the maintenance of feudal domination and exploitation. Citing the example of the French monarchy, V.G. Kiernan considers absolutism as the highest stage of feudalism, while Boris Porchnav regards the sixteenth century states as feudal instruments to repress and suppress peasant resistance in the interests of nobility. The majority of historians agree with the view that feudal aristocracy constituted the social basis of the absolutist monarchy in western Europe. It continued to dominate society and monopolized power and privileges for their own interests but the concentration of power in the hands of an absolute monarch created favourable conditions for the capitalist development in the long run.

Contribution of Culture to the Ideas of Absolutism

In the courts of most absolute rulers, important figures from the field of art and literature were patronized and given importance. Monarchy was glorified in a variety of forms of artistic and literary representation. The crowns of Europe played an active role in their own propaganda. Court ceremonies were held with pomp and splendour. The monarchs created their permanent seats of government attended by a large number of court officials and surrounded by the important personalities of the time. The idea of a capital city emerged and these centres portrayed wealth and glory of the nation. The Flemish painter Anthony van Dyck painted magnificent images of three generations of Stuart kings of England. He himself was a court painter of Charles I. In Spain, Diego Velasquez became the court painter of Philip IV. His portraits of the Habsburg rulers of Spain elevated their personality. In France, Peter Paul Reubens created paintings from the life of Queen Marie de Médici. One of the most popular French histories of the period had the title *On the Excellence of the Kings and the Kingdom of France.*

The famous English philosopher and scientist, Francis Bacon wrote the history of Henry VII glorifying his rule. A number of playwrights, poets and scholars were attracted to the English court. Ben Johnson was one such important figure who made his mark by writing and staging *masques* – a form of light entertainment – which included acting, dance and music. It is believed that William Shakespeare (1564–1616) also created public interest in the history of rulers who exhibited power and the essence of justice. In his famous plays *Tempest* (1611), *Measure for Measure* (1604), *Richard II* (1597) and *Henry IV*, Shakespeare highlighted the usefulness of a strong ruler while showing how a weak ruler could bring about ruin for the entire state. His plays were viewed by members of all classes in London theaters in which his focus on the character of rulers helped reinforce their dominating importance in the lives of their subjects.

The political theories of sovereignty during the sixteenth and seventeenth centuries provided legitimacy to the rule of absolute monarchs. In France, the most famous propagator of the state's sovereignty was Jean Bodin (1529–96). He was a famous theoretician and his *République* is considered an influential work of political philosophy. He believed that every state must possess supreme authority. The ruler should enjoy the powers of making, forcing and judging laws. While many medieval political thinkers and several contemporaries of Bodin emphasized that the ruler should share authority with the estates, Bodin returned to the Justinian tradition of Roman law and insisted that sovereignty could not be shared and should reside at a central place of authority. His concept of sovereignty went side by side with the theory of the 'divine right of kingship'. For Bodin, 'the King was placed on his throne by the direct command of God'. This divine right of kingship was hereditary and could not be checked or interrupted by the court or church officials. The law-making powers which governed the society, according to Bodin, were guided by God. Thus in *The Six Books of Commonwealth* (1576), he pointed out the essence of a sovereign's power is the right to impose laws on the subjects without their consent. Bodin's idea of sovereignty suited the absolute rulers and it gave legitimacy to their despotic rule.

An important propagator of the theory of divine right was James VI of Scotland, who became the ruler of England after the death of Queen Elizabeth. In his work *The True Law of Free Monarchies* (1598), he advised the leaders of nobility and the church in Scotland to obey the command of the ruler. According to him, in the Old Testament, God had placed kings to rule the earth and it was the duty of the subjects to follow their king. In England, Thomas Hobbes (1588–1679), provided a doctrine of the absolute state in his famous and lasting work *Leviathan* (1651). His hatred of the English Civil War (1642–9) led him develop a political philosophy of absolute state power. He wanted sovereignty to combine secular as well as ecclesiastical powers. His theory was based on the determinist view of human nature. He believed that all human actions are based on self-interest, which makes life 'poor, nasty, brutish and short'. Hence, men need a guarantee of good behaviour from the fellow beings and this could only be provided by a sovereign. According to him the Leviathan, whether one or more, possessed absolute power. He was projected as the sole source of law as well as its interpreter. Unlike the medieval kings, he was not himself subject to civil laws. For Hobbes, Leviathan was the creator of Right and Justice. He accepted that sometimes laws could be inequitable or unnecessary, yet they would remain law as they were the command of the sovereign. The law of nature or the law of God could never be applied against Leviathan, as the latter was its sole interpreter. Defending Leviathan, Hobbes pointed out that it does not mean that Leviathan did not tolerate liberty. Liberty was seen as something that men enjoyed in the silence of law. Leviathan's authority was legitimate because it was based on the consent of the people and it was the moral obligation of each member of the society to obey him. The basis of power of the Leviathan was not the divine right but social contract. Although Hobbes failed to distinguish between state and government, his political philosophy justified the absolute rule of the sovereign.

France

The absolute monarchy in France emerged slowly by reinforcing ties between the government and local administration, by raising taxes through a central policy, by setting up a powerful, elaborate and permanent army and bureaucracy, and by creating an independent judiciary to implement the king's laws. The Catholic Church acted as its ally to cement the social base of royal absolutism. The greatest hurdle in these developments was the political, social and cultural disunity that existed in France.

The unification of France under a centralized rule was a slow process. Attempts at centralization of authority were made in the medieval period but without much success. France in the fifteenth century was a fragmented feudal region that lacked well-defined frontiers and a unified legal system. Even the language of the French people was not common. *Langue d'oil* from which modern French descended, was spoken in northern France while *Langue d'oc* was spoken in the southern region. The eastern border of France was blurred with the Holy Roman empire while the French suzerainty over Artois and Flanders was ineffective.

The Duchy of Burgundy had remained independent of French control and posed a constant source of threat for the French rulers. Charles of Valois ruled Burgundy. He raised the status and influence of courts among the European rulers. It became an important centre of art and culture, where artists, sculptors and musicians from distant regions came and received patronage of the rulers. The court of Burgundy always created trouble for the French monarch. After the death of Charles VII (1477), Louis XI became the ruler and established his control over the duchy of Burgundy. With it started the process of centralization of monarchy. It also marked the beginning of the autonomous authority of the French towns through institutional innovations and reforms, extension of royal bureaucracy, imposition of state taxation and creation of the state army. Although the French kings appeared powerful and absolute, their position remained far from stable and it was only during the sixteenth century that the process of absolutism really set in. By the end of the seventeenth century, France became a model of absolutism for other European states. Between the Hundred Years War (with England from mid-fourteenth to mid-fifteenth centuries) and the Wars of Religion in the second half of the sixteenth century, the foundations of absolutism had been firmly laid.

J.P. Genet points to the problem of genesis of the modern state in the late-medieval and early-medieval periods. He argued that the developments of the twelfth to fourteenth centuries were crucial in the formation of the state in western Europe. It began with the extension of royal justice and was followed by their attempts to raise revenue. The economic and social crisis caused by the Black Death strengthened the hands of the rulers. Perry Anderson suggests that the centralization of authority in the hands of the French monarch began in the fifteenth century. There were three important breakdowns of political order in three separate centuries – the Hundred Years War in the fourteenth and the fifteenth centuries, the Religious Wars of the sixteenth century and the Fronde Revolts in the mid-seventeenth century. The process of formation of absolute monarchy halted each time with the crisis but subsequently accelerated. The ultimate outcome was the creation of royal authority, which had no parallel throughout Europe. According to Le Roy Ladurie, France till around 1460s was poised for a state-formation between unitary and decentralized models. However, the military conflicts of the fifteenth century led to a concentration of power in the hands of the rulers who continued to enjoy the support of the nobility. They transformed the feudal army into a centralized force. In some ways the power was manipulated in the interest of the centralized state. To pay for the regular army which was needed during the war, the monarchy brought taxation directly under its control. A new tax *taille* (1439) was imposed on the French people. The nobility remained exempted from it. This period also witnessed the rise of *parlement* – essentially a judicial body located in the major towns but was generally used as a consultative body because of its representative members. The rise of the *parlement* marked the beginning of a period of centralization. During this period, France underwent a series of territorial changes. The French forces occupied the duchy of Savoy and Calais was acquired from England. But France also lost territories like Flanders, Artois and Tournaisis to Spain. The process of unification began with the annexation of the duchy of Brittany. However, an intense rivalry continued between the two ruling houses within France – the Valois and the Bourbons.

Historians hold divergent views on the nature of French absolutism during first half of the sixteenth century. Questions are raised whether Francis I (1515–47) and Henry II (1547–59) were absolute monarchs. There are two major views on the subject. According to the first, as pointed out by Georges Pagès, the rulers were as powerful as the later absolutist rulers and that it was at the beginning of the sixteenth century itself that absolute monarchy in France had triumphed. The other view, as brought out by Henri Prentout, suggests that if one must use the term 'absolute monarchy', then it can only be applied to the rule of Louis XIV. He preferred the use of the word 'contractual' for the monarchy between 1285 and 1589. Scholars like Lublinskaya and Roger Mettam reject the notion of French absolutism and consider this term hopelessly inadequate. Sharon Ketterings feels that the early modern state bore little resemblance to the model of bureaucratic rationality and that the French government and French society coexisted in a state of constant tension throughout the old regime. On the other hand, J. Russell Major describes the French monarchy of this period as 'popular and consultative'. According to him, it was in the nature of a feudal dynastic structure and its powers were limited. It had to depend on popular support rather than on military strength. Thus, it promoted the growth of representative institutions. Refuting these views, R.J. Knecht argues that Francis I and Henry II never called any meeting of the Estates General – the only national body based on representative principle. Neither kings had faith in this institution and its meeting was kept in abeyance till 1560. Instead a meeting of the Assembly of Notables was called for in 1527.

The powers of the French rulers expanded with the development of administrative, judicial and financial structures during the sixteenth century. The Renaissance monarchy in France developed its machinery with the evolution of the King's Council. A centralized administrative structure had to be created. In 1515, Francis recruited about 5,000 soldiers who were made independent of the jurisdictions of the feudal nobility. The process of judicial reforms had started earlier and a part of the judicial business was transferred to the *Grand Conseil*. It was more like a tribunal that followed the directions of the king. The Council's decisions were turned into law by the Chancery. Its members included notaries and secretaries who enjoyed noble status. They drew up royal enactments. The new members were trained in law and they played an important role in strengthening the powers of the state. These members, after receiving their posts (mostly by purchase through auctions) improved their social standing. They formed the new nobility and came to be known as *noblesse de robe* as against the traditional feudal nobility who had earned their status by contributing through military services, known as *noblesse d'epée*. The judicial system in France was based on the idea that the king was the first and the foremost judge. The lowest level of judiciary consisted of magistrates called *Prevôts* or *Vicontes*. They were placed above the feudal courts and their powers were limited to only simple cases. The smallest unit of local government was the royal *bailliage* which comprised almost a hundred posts. During the sixteenth century, the official in-charge of this unit was called *bailli* or *sénéchal*. They had military duties to perform, summoned the feudal levy and also judged appeal cases from the interior courts and enjoyed important administrative powers. Above the *bailliages* there were *parlements,* of which the most prestigious was that of Paris. There were occasions when the *parlements* adopted an opposite stand from the rulers. On the whole, the rulers of France succeeded in establishing their influence over them by controlling its membership. Although *parlements* judged a variety of cases, it was not really a court of law. It regulated different types of businesses in town such as public hygiene or maintenance of roads. It ensured supplies of corn and fuel and controlled price, quality and weight of essential products. It could also censure books or punish actions against the state. Even the Papal bull had to be registered by the *parlement* before it could be implemented. Similarly, all royal legislation had to be ratified by it. In 1552, the two-tier structure of judiciary was changed into a three-tier one when the *présideaux* were placed between *bailliages* and the *parlement*. Sixty-one such courts were formed with a large number of staff. Although officially it was stated that the purpose of this was to save time and money for the litigants, the real purpose was probably to secure an additional income for the crown through the sale of offices.

The financial structure created by the rulers of France was extremely complex and unsystematic and became one of the reasons of dissatisfaction outside the government. The rulers succeeded in imposing direct tax on the people without consulting the representative assemblies. Contemporaries often highlight this aspect of the French monarchy. An impression is created that the French monarchy enjoyed extraordinary financial powers. This is contrasted with the constitutional limitations imposed on other European princes by their subjects or their representatives. The French rulers had to make compromises at the beginning itself. The royal revenue in France was built on two kinds – the ordinary revenue which the king could collect from his own demesne land while the extraordinary revenue was collected in the form of taxes. The latter was collected with and for a short duration, normally in the war period. By the sixteenth century, it became a regular form of tax imposed on a permanent basis. The government of France exempted the nobles and clergy from it in order to avoid a conflict with them, as they required their support in the continuation of absolutism. The three extraordinary revenues were the *taille, gabelle* and the *aides*. The *taille* was the only direct tax and was levied annually as a land tax on the unprivileged commoners. The amount was to be determined by the King's Counsel but the two centuries of absolutism witnessed a continuous increase in this tax. *Gabelle* was a salt tax that was imposed on the common people in northern and central France. Every household had to purchase salt from the royal granary, and this tax was levied in different ways. In western France it was fixed on the basis of sale price while in south France it was on the basis of total trade. The *aides* were duties imposed on commodities that were sold in large quantities such as wine, beverages or livestock. The taxation structure was inequitable and the common people had to pay all the taxes while the upper classes, who had the capacity to pay these taxes, were exempted from them. With each war, there was heavy imposition of the *taille*. Between 1610 and 1644, the state's exactions from *taille* rose from 17 million to 44 million livres. Total taxes increased by almost six times. By 1654, nearly 63 per cent of all the taxes collected by the state came from extraordinary means. Thus, the combination of state exactions and the collection of seigniorial dues by the nobility became such a heavy burden on the peasants that they were barely able to support their families. The taxation structure in France proved so burdensome for the ordinary people that it contributed to the revolutionary situation towards the end of the eighteenth century, and led to numerous rebellions and uprisings throughout this period.

French absolutism made rapid advances in the seventeenth century despite certain events, which posed a serious threat to it. As brought out by writers like Perry Anderson and J.H.M. Salmon, the rise of French absolutism was the product of the feudal crisis that had resulted in the reformation of the state based on the support of feudal nobility. In France, the feudal ruling classes felt threatened by the revolts of the common people. Ultimately they preferred royal authority rather than social anarchy and were compelled to put aside their fractional struggles and their selfish interests. Instead, they acknowledged royal supremacy. This was the basis on which French absolutism developed and with it came many long-term changes. A comparison is often made between England and France on the development of absolutism. Robert Brenner suggests that while in England, the first step towards consolidation of agrarian capital was taking shape in the seventeenth century, the French developments were moving against it. In England, the feudal crisis during the fourteenth century and the subsequent peasant uprisings, the rising prices and the expansion of markets for the surplus products resulted in the growth of petty commodity production. It gave rise to economic differences within the class of peasants. The emergence of richer stratum of middling peasant and their engagement in small-scale capitalist farming caused the breakdown of village solidarity. These differences sapped the peasant resistance and the new landed class promoted commercial agriculture. In France, despite a brief period of capitalist agriculture, economic transformation in the capitalist direction did not take shape. There was an impoverishment of the seigniorial class. The entry of outside elements into agriculture led to new forms of exactions and caused rural indebtedness. The bulk of French peasantry was driven deeper into poverty largely due to the heavy tax imposed on them in the form of *taille* by the state. This resulted in massive revolts. Peasants appealed to the king against the harsh treatment of the local landlords. The state intervention in this conflict signified a decisive turning point in the drive towards absolutism. Royal officials adjudicated most of these conflicts in favour of peasants. It was done to maintain the tax paying capacity of the peasants who provided the bulk of the state revenue. In the long run, it prevented the growth of capitalist relations in rural France by enabling the poor peasants to cling on to their tiny pieces of land through legal protection and thereby prolonged the continuation of the state feudal structure. It also resulted in the dual exploitation of the peasantry – by the state as well as by the seigneurs.

During the weak rule of Charles IX (1560–74) his minister Michel de L'Hôpital carried forward the work of centralization and reforms. He was the son of a doctor and rose to political fame. After receiving judgeship in the *parlement* through his marriage, in 1560 he became the Chancellor of France. He outlined a programme of reforms at the opening of the Estates-General of Orlean. He considered the pursuit of self-interest and corruption of public morality to be the main evils. He called for suppression of religious passions that he considered extremely harmful for the state. He proposed reforms of judicial and administrative systems. On the one hand he deplored the fact that no meeting of the estates had been called since 1484, on the other, he himself revealed an autocratic bent of mind. He held the view that the Estates possessed no authority to rival the king. He wished to see the magisterial class to act as an effective bureaucracy of the French state and he strongly opposed venality of offices (the auction of the official posts). He faced strong opposition when he tried to control the Paris *parlement* through a direct legislation. He desired major judicial reforms because he felt that the corruption of justice was the real reason for the prevalent troubles. In his *Treatise on the Reformation of Justice*, he proposed the setting up of a national code, an effective system of examining the qualifications of the candidates, an enhanced status for magistracy over traditional nobility and proclaimed supremacy of the crown over the bureaucracy. According to J.H.M. Salmon, the general tone of the entire legislation appeared to be paternalistic. His regime has been known for its plethora of legislation. Several edicts were issued by the *parlements* of Orleans and Moulins which aimed at introducing national law of inheritance instead of local customs, e.g. on the subject of second marriage, on consumption of luxuries and on the rate of interest which was fixed at 8.33 per cent. However, due to the weak personality of Charles IX and an unfavourable climate caused by religious wars, he was not able to achieve a great deal. Yet he did contribute in the process of centralization and unification, which was necessary for exalting the position of the monarchy.

During the seventeenth century absolutism in France was further strengthened. A number of individual ministers contributed to the development of royal power such as Cardinal Richelieu, Mazarin and Colbert. The administration of Cardinal Richelieu (1624–42) was of considerable importance in the growth of royal absolutism. Although Richelieu did not have a well-formulated programme, his practical measures contributed to the building of royal absolutism. He held a feudal vision based on past experience. His methods rather than being innovative, were empirical. He strongly believed in the theory and practice of absolutism and considered the king to be the living image of God. The theory of the divine right of kings had already been strengthened through the writings of Bodin. The Wars of Religion in the previous century had greatly damaged the position and status of the monarchy. The process of repair was going on and the importance of Richelieu lies in the fact that he was aware of the weaknesses of royal power and he tried to re-establish and restore it. He achieved this aim by developing ministerial absolutism in the name of the crown and by strengthening the powers of the bureaucracy. The growing power of the crown was closely associated with the rise of a royal bureaucracy. On the other hand, the traditional institution of *Curia Regis* which was later converted into inner Royal Council. Richelieu developed tighter control over the conciliar system through the king and his few selected ministers. The king's control over the provinces was maintained through the *Conseil des Dépêches*. Richelieu's measures enlarged royal authority over the provinces where the powers of the provincial governors had already been curtailed in 1545. Richelieu went a step further. The crown could dismiss those who resisted royal absolutism or those who assisted plots against it. With the expansion of royal power, it became easier for the rulers to deal with local disorder and maladministration.

The process of elevating a few ministers while reducing the size of the decision-making bodies continued during the seventeenth century. This helped the rulers sustain royal absolutism. The expansion of administration was linked to the power and position of the royal officials called the *intendants*. They played a crucial role in reestablishing the powers of the crown in the far-flung territories of France. They were responsible for raising troops, for supervising administration of justice and implementing royal decrees. By 1637 these officials were posted over most parts of France and controlled provincial subdivisions called as *généralités*. Their powers increased during the period of Mazarin, the successor of Richelieu. He transferred the work of tax assessment and collection to the *intendants*. This was a crucial phase in the history of France as numerous uprisings took place in different parts, such as the Croquants rebellion, Nu-pied uprising, and the most successful and widespread uprising was the backlash of Frondes (1648–53). France's close involvement in the Thirty Years War caused great hardship to the people who resented the ruinous level of taxation. In fact, these wars had made the tax farmers the chief targets of the masses. It was also an inevitable reaction to the growing burden of taxation. The local officials opposed the appointment of royal institutions like *intendants*, etc. The Fronde was against the growing power of the absolute rulers. Royal absolutism received a big jolt but soon after the crisis it emerged more powerful and effective. The *intendants* were reinstated after the Fronde uprising.

One of the important sources of resistance to the growth of royal absolutism was the Paris *parlement*. It regarded itself as the guardian of law and liberty and resisted all efforts of the crown to interfere in its functioning. Richelieu advised Louis XIII to avoid a direct confrontation with it and follow a path of temporary compromises. Yet he was aware of the potential threat of this institution and he consequently concentrated on reducing its powers without destroying it. He created *Chambre d'Arsenal* for the trial of political offenders and thus bypassing the *parlement's* judicial authority. He also tried to deal with the problem of taxation that was far from uniform. Direct taxes were unequally assessed and distributed. He resorted to doubling the *taille* and *gabelle* to meet the increasing financial resources required to deal with wars and rebellions. Like other ministers, Richelieu failed in this task and was unable to overcome the inherent defects of the system. Richelieu's problem was also related to the growing ambition of the nobility. It tried to recover its earlier status and privileges, which had been eroded by the expanding royal authority. The crown could not go against the nobility as it provided the social base to the king's regime. Thus, Richelieu adopted a policy that allowed the nobility to retain its privileges and social status but weakened their political influence by deliberately strengthening the royal bureaucracy and the standing army. This policy was pursued in the later period of Louis XIV, who selected most of his ministers from outside the ranks of original nobility (*noblesse d'épée*). The sale and proliferation of offices enabled members of the bourgeoisie to enter the ranks of nobility.

The zenith of French absolutism was reached during the rule of Louis XIV (1661–1715), when he stated 'I am the state!' He had a strong belief in the unlimited powers of the ruler. His authority was completely enshrined in the concept of the divine right of kingship. The political dislocation caused by the Fronde revolt resulted in greater concentration of authority in the hands of the French ruler. Colbert's reforms further contributed to the process of royal absolutism. Louis XIV benefited from the earlier measures of centralization and administrative reforms of the sixteenth century and the first half of the seventeenth century. He inherited compact and fertile territories (France was the biggest state in western Europe), vast population and cultural leadership that gave the French monarchs an extra range of powers. Strict economic regulation by the state apparatus, commonly known as 'mercantilism', also became an instrument of absolutism. In the reign of Louis XV France had 4,00,000 troops. Law and order had been restored in the country, the legal status of the subjects was redefined and French culture came to be accepted in the outside world.

Louis XIV dominated the first half-century after 1660. He waged wars in all directions. He ensured that no single minister was able to dominate state matters although Colbert continued to work as his principal minister and contributed to the creation of a strong absolutist state in France. Louis himself authorized and supported the extensive reforms of Colbert. The restoration of the authority of the *intendants* with vast powers, who were the main rivals to the traditional governors, marked the beginning of absolutism under Louis XIV. Marc Bloch considers this as a key event. The country's administration was divided into thirty-two generalities headed by *intendants*, which supervised justice, security, lower officials of the administration and the priests, and tried to check the prevailing feudal laws. Besides, they suppressed revolts and collected land taxes. In other words, they virtually destroyed the institutions of local self-governments. The municipalities of the towns were increasingly subjected to royal control. It would be wrong to say that all this was achieved quite easily. There was strong resistance by traditional institutions against the growing centralization, yet the balance was in favour of the crown. No attempt was made to reconstruct the local administrative structures that had been eroded by absolute rulers. Many traditional offices, including the financial posts, were offered for sale. The right of the town councils to elect their own officials was appropriated by the *intendants* through the statute of 1692. In most cases the new royal officials did not replace the traditional provincial functionaries but simply overlapped them. It resulted in a two-tier bureaucracy that impeded normal functioning and brought inefficiency.

The strength of absolutism depended on the extent of centralization. Attempts were made by Colbert to establish a uniform legal system by framing new legal codes, which included the Civil Ordinance (1667), the Criminal Ordinance (1670), the Ordinance of Commerce (1673), the Ordinance of Marine (1681) and the *Code Noir* (1685) for the slaves. Despite all these attempts, France remained a land of local diversity and, in the absence of a uniform law (since Common Law was popular in the northern region while Roman Law applied to the south), absolutism could not create legal uniformity. This could be achieved only after the French Revolution. The policy of mercantilism promoted by Colbert also contributed to the trend of centralization of authority, as *étatism* (statism) was one of the important aspects of French mercantilism. The church was kept close to the monarchy although Louis seemed to stop short of full clerical control. On the one hand he guaranteed the basic gallican liberties (the traditional church) in the Assembly of Clergy in 1682 and secured the passage of Four Articles, on the other hand he prevented discussions on separatism. It demonstrated the extent to which royal authority was prepared to go with the church. It preserved some of the important privileges of the church, especially in matters of taxation (tithe). In return, the church was made to pay a single bloc payment every ten years to the Crown.

According to John Lough, the new form of strongly centralized monarchy that grew up in the 1660s did not fundamentally change the social organization of France. It was superimposed on the existing social structure and political institutions and it did not destroy them. One of the reasons for the success of the French rulers in matters of taxations was the fact that they never summoned the highest representative institution – the Estates-General. It was simply forgotten but was not abolished. The other representative institution, the *parlements,* was not allowed to intervene in state affairs. Louis adopted the practice of keeping the governors at court and in their place the *intendants* performed their functions. Many of them were selected from the bourgeoisie to counteract the influence of traditional nobility.

The secret of the French domination of the European scene, according to Bellof, was largely political as well as cultural. The Grande Court at Versailles became the most artistic and luxurious court among the royal courts of Europe. The French language became the vehicle of French cultural domination and became the symbol of the polite society. Many of the international treaties came to be signed in French and often the rulers of other states took pride in expressing their thoughts in French. The science journals helped in establishing the achievements of the French scientists.

Similarly, the creation of new French writings on political philosophy, and the achievements in the field of visual arts and architecture helped in the spread of French tastes in Europe. Thus the cultural leadership of France also gave the monarchs greater respect among the people.

SPAIN

Spain is situated in the Iberian Peninsula, on the south-west region of Europe. The Pyrenees mountains isolate the peninsula from the rest of the European continent. Despite its separation from Europe, Spain neither remained aloof from the European conflicts nor could it develop strong bonds of unity. The process of geographical unification and political centralization had to be imposed from above through the absolute rule of the monarchs.

The Iberian peninsula in the late fifteenth century faced division on grounds of geography, ethnography and politics. The main problem of this region was the multiplicity of cultures. Although Latin races dominated, there were other groups such as the Basques in the north-west, and Jews and Moors were scattered all over the region. The Moors had established themselves in the kingdom of Granada. Their number was quite large in the southern peninsula. Religion in this region had sharply divided the people. Christians were in vast majority but there were other religious groups, which lived in the Spanish states. After a long period of toleration and peaceful existence, an intense hatred against the Jews and the Moors had developed, which divided the people and caused mutual distrust. There were many other sharp divisions – between the pastoral population and the agriculturists, between the rural and mercantile population and between nobles and non-nobles. One could also notice linguistic divisions in this region – Catalan was the language of the east and the north-east, Castilian was spoken in north, central and southern Spain, Galician and Portuguese was spoken in Galicia and in parts of Leon, Basque in the north-west territories of the peninsula and Arabic was the language of Granada. Many separate states existed in this region such as Castile, which was the largest in the peninsula, Aragon, which included the principalities of

Catalonia and Valencia, besides Navarre and Granada. It is estimated that the population of Aragon was about 2,70,000 in 1495, that of Valencia was also roughly the same in 1510 while Catalonia in 1512 had an estimated population of 3,07,000. There is some disagreement among scholars on the population figures of Castile. The estimate varies from 75,00,000, which is considered too high, to 34,33,000 from figures in the tax registers of 1513. The actual figure could be somewhere between the two.

Aragon and Castile were the two important states of the Iberian Peninsula. The kings of Aragon were involved in the Mediterranean politics and had successfully acquired territories in that region. Unlike Castile, Aragon was less involved in the work of *Reconquista* (acquisition of land by ousting the non-Christian population). By the late-fifteenth century, the Aragonese ruler had established control over the Italian state of Sardinia. Sicily was also ruled by the Aragonese royal family, and later became a base for the future conquest of the kingdom of Naples. Their relationship was based on contractual arrangements. Barcelona was the chief centre of administration and judiciary. Aragon was a volatile but very powerful state. The feudal nobility, military orders and the church monasteries owned most of the Aragonese land. The ruler also owned substantial tracts of land. The hilly soil was not conducive to the cultivation of wheat, which had to be imported from outside. Instead the rulers encouraged sheep farming to promote wool production, which had a vast market in Flanders. They received considerable income from this. Castile, on the other hand, was much larger in size and more populous than other states. Mainly an agricultural region yet it depended on pastoral activities. This is because the Castilian rulers needed a large number of soldiers to wage wars and crusades but their recruitment could only be made from the peasants. Hence agriculture was neglected at the cost of wool production. The demand for food grains was met by imports from Netherlands, Denmark and Germany. Sheep rearing dominated the economy of Castile. The movement of shepherds was regulated by the *Mesta* – a national guild consisting of wealthy landowners. They acted as bankers for the crown and in return enjoyed monopoly rights. The institution of *Mesta* became so powerful that by the early sixteenth century, it is estimated that it had 3.5 million sheep in its possession. The economic power within Castile was divided among those groups who contributed to the Reconquista. Such men who had taken a religious vow to fight the enemies of Christianity created militias. Military orders assumed control of vast lands in the course of the Reconquista. Many nobles also contributed to this and held large stretches of land and virtually became independent rulers. Some of them even encroached on crown lands, when the rulers were weak. In short, the economic power in Castile remained in the hands of the nobility while the monarch enjoyed political power.

The rise of royal power started during the second half of the fifteenth century. The political integration in the fifteenth century was achieved through the marriage of the two ruling houses. In 1469, Ferdinand, heir to the kingdom of Aragon and Catalonia, was married to Isabella, the daughter of the Castilian king. In 1474, Isabella became the queen of Castile and in 1479 Ferdinand assumed the throne of Aragon. The two kingdoms, as mentioned above, were totally different. The union of crowns led to the creation of a unified Spain. This marriage was of great importance in the history of Spain. But the union of crowns did little to unify the two monarchies. The nobles of the two states had a long history of warfare – they had fought over disputed boundaries, over trade duties and against the exploitation of foreign merchants. No treaties existed between them for the extradition of criminals and the people of the two states were reluctant to accept the ruler of the rival state as their own monarch. The process of the rise of absolutism in Spain faced several difficulties. Despite all these factors, the rule of Isabella and Ferdinand had a profound impact on the political life of Spain. The two monarchs showed personal interest in every aspect of administration. They visited different parts of their kingdom, reorganized municipal governments, tried to control the powerful military houses, strengthen the existing institutions to make their rule effective and ignored those institutions from where they faced resistance. The process of centralization began soon after the marriage. The Spanish union of the Hispanic kingdoms later developed into the Habsburg empire or *Monarquia*. The four major kingdoms of Spain – Castile, Aragon, Catalonia and Valencia, besides several smaller states like Galicia, Asturias, Leon, Andalucia formed a kind of loose federation – each state retained its own parliament (cortes), political institutions, law courts, taxation, etc.

The major achievement of the Spanish rulers was their attempt to extend the royal authority in different branches of the government of the federal units. The royal councils were frequently used to create effective control over the nobility, for the appointment of royal officials at the level of local government and to counteract the legislative influence in Aragon and Castile. *Curia Regis* was the great council that had existed in many states of Europe during the Middle Ages. It was an integral part of the feudal administrative system. It consisted of the leading members of the nobility who used to advise the king on state affairs. These medieval institutions were extensively reorganized in Castile (1480) and Aragon (1494). They were converted into two separate Royal Councils with separate territorial jurisdiction. The Spanish rulers were given the power of supervision over internal affairs and justice. This led to the formation of a complex councillor system that governed Spain during the sixteenth century. Ferdinand and Isabella created many other councils such as the Council of Inquisition (1483), the Council of Military Orders (1495) and the Council of Cruzada (1509).

Royal absolutism in Spain had to face challenges from the feudal nobility. In Spain, the majority of the population lived in the countryside, and 95 per cent of them were peasants owning very little land. The great landed magnets controlled almost 95–97 per cent of the land. It was this class that posed a serious threat to the absolute rulers. As this class had played an important part in leading the Crusades against the Moors, they had amassed considerable powers and enjoyed a fair degree of independence. The Spanish monarchs tried to check their powers by promoting the lower levels of nobility. Honours were conferred on them for their loyal service. The collaboration between the two ruling houses of Castile and Aragon led to the reduction in the power of the nobility. On the one hand, the lesser nobility was drawn towards the court, and on the other hand, an attempt was made to stop private wars by putting an end to the construction of unauthorized castles. Most of the

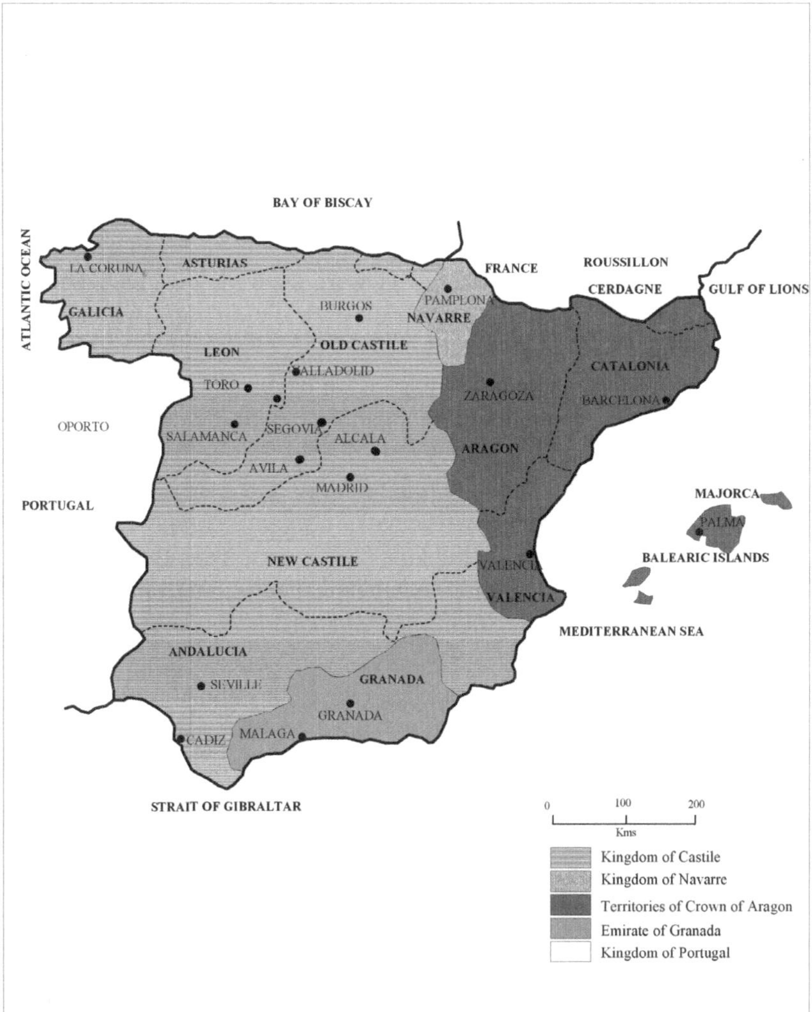

Map 5.1: The Spanish States in the Late-Fifteenth Century

Spanish nobility lived in cities and had developed their own assembly and officials called *Regidores*. The monarchs attempted a policy of compromise. Municipal privileges were not taken away but a new set of officials called *Corregidores* were appointed to share power with *Regidores*. They were given judicial and administrative duties. Another medieval institution, *Hermandad* was used to establish law and order and to suppress violence, especially in the distant provinces. This institution was in the form of a brotherhood, consisting of townsmen and lesser nobles. It was used as a police institution and was assigned the powers to arrest, detain and try the miscreants. *Hermandad* courts were created to punish law-breakers and they played a significant part in reducing lawlessness in the Spanish states.

The biggest casualty in the expansion of royal powers were the legislative institutions in all the Spanish kingdoms who had displayed a peculiar arrogance towards the rulers. The Castile cortes consisted of three estates – nobles, clergy and townsmen, while the Aragon cortes had four estates – nobles, clergy, gentry and townsmen. They had made the kings dependent by controlling the finances of the state. The two monarchs, Ferdinand and Isabella, realized the importance of building financial reserves. They began acquiring alienated lands and property which once belonged to the crown. They also carried out an effective tax collection to reduce their dependence on the cortes. Thus, the monarchs allowed its existence in both Aragon and Castile but their role was gradually reduced. The crown avoided conflict with it but reduced the frequency of its sessions. No session of cortes was called in Castile between 1482–98. Instead, the crown used the *Hermandades* (the local brotherhoods of law officers commanding small forces of police) to raise money. The Spanish crown resorted to heavy taxation to meet the growing demands of the state – its elaborate bureaucratic structure and the vast army. The cost of the army had increased from 20 million *maravedis* in 1482 to 80 million in 1504, while that of the royal court from 8 million to 35 million during the same period. The important taxes of the Spanish rulers included *servicio, alcabala* and *millones*. *Servicio* was the main tax on laymen and could only be increased with the consent of representative institution like the cortes. The Spanish rulers did not raise this tax because they wanted to avoid confrontation. *Alcabala* was a sales tax on all commercial transactions. It was charged at 10 per cent on the sale and purchase of goods. It became the cornerstone of the Spanish royal finance but became a heavy burden on merchants. It was supplemented in 1590 by *millones*. These taxes constituted nearly two-thirds of the Spanish revenue but had a negative consequence on the Spanish economy as it cut the purchasing power of the peasants, wage-earners and the craftsmen. The Spanish rulers also developed supplementary income apart from the taxes. The crown resorted to the issue of *juros*, the interest bearing bonds, which were secured against particular revenue. *Asientos* were contracts in the form of passes which were issued to the German, the Flemish and the Italian bankers for loans usually secured against the king's share in bullion treasure which arrived from the new world. The basic problem of the Spanish revenue system was that in the long run the financial burden became unbearable for the people. According to Ralph Davis, the Castilian revenue of Philip II at its peak in 1519 was ten times that of the English Crown. But it was drawn from a very limited base. The Spanish nobility was numerically the largest among the European states but were exempt from taxes, while the other sections of society had to meet the entire burden. It can be said that the Spanish monarchy permitted the Castilian nobility to be free of financial obligations towards the state and yet allowed them to enjoy most of the benefits of the empire. In return, the nobility conceded their political gains to the monarchy. The church of Spain also contributed an enormous amount of funds to the royal treasury to retain its autonomy. Silver trade provided an additional income to the Spanish rulers. The crown in general received one-fifth of the total silver that reached the Spanish ports of Seville and Cadiz. Another source of income came from the *mesta* sheep farmers who made huge contributions to the state in return for their monopoly over the wool trade. The government concentrated its energies and resources in developing sheep farming in Castile. The crown reduced taxes on sheep in 1476, while the orders of 1492 and 1511 codified the powers of the *mesta*. It was virtually made a department of the state in 1500, when

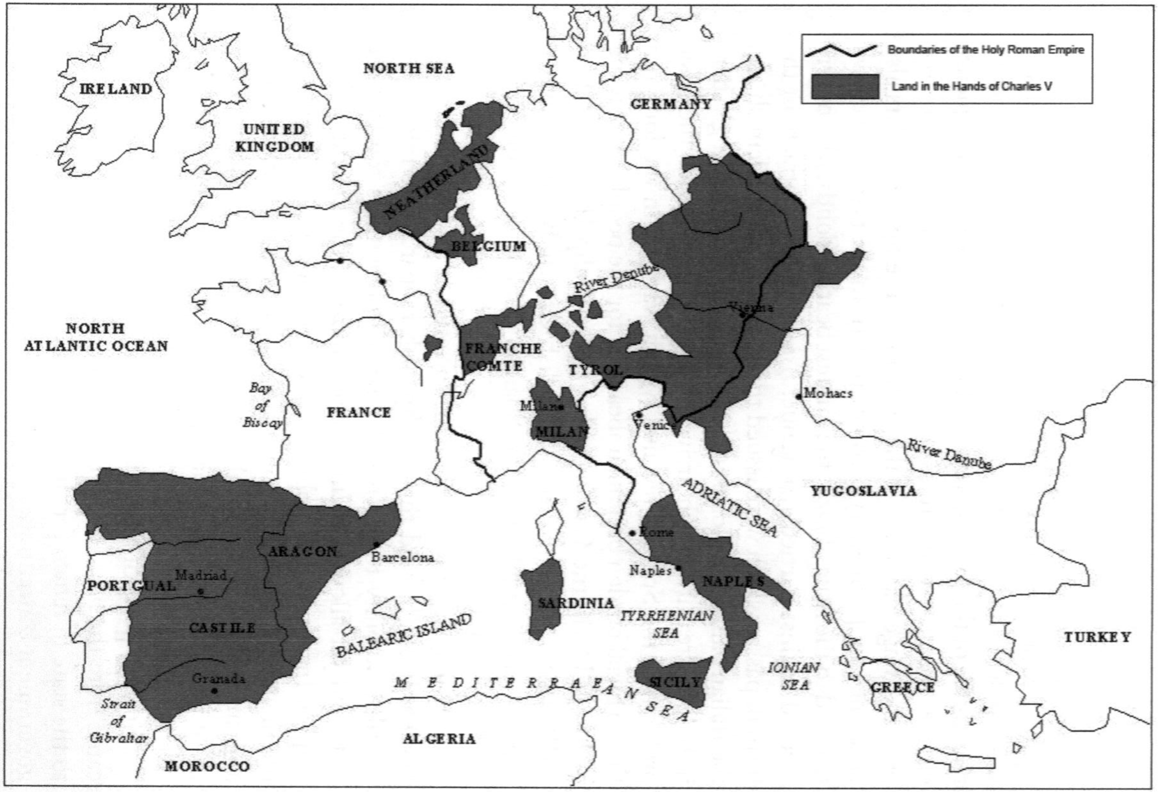

Map 5.2: The Empire of Charles V of Spain after he was Elected as the Emperor of the Holy Roman Empire in 1519

its president began to be appointed from the Royal Council. This had some harmful effects on the Spanish economy because the owners were able to persuade the government to sacrifice cultivation of cereal crops in order to increase wool supply to the Flemish market.

Relations with the Church

The relations between the Papal church and the state greatly determined the progress of absolutism in Spain. Ferdinand and Isabella had supported the Pope in his Italian policy and in return obtained from him the right to nominate bishops and other ecclesiastical officials in their domains. The church in these states had to look to the crown rather than to the Pope for their position. The Spanish rulers could also prevent the implementation of a Papal bull (order of execution by the Pope) in the Italian states of Sicily, Naples and Milan. At one stage, Ferdinand had threatened to break relations with Pope Julius II, when the latter disregarded his authority.

The church remained an important source of income for the Spanish crown. *Fercia reales* was given to the crown of Castile and it constituted a third of the tithes collected by the church in this region. One of the most important powers enjoyed by the Spanish rulers was related to the *Inquisitions*. It became an important instrument for the expansion of state power and was given by Pope Sixtus IV in 1478 to the Spanish monarch. The Spanish monarchs believed that orthodox Christianity was the only real basis for a strong kingdom. Many Christians living in Spain were allies of Jews and Muslims and were called *converso*. The Spanish rulers used the instrument of *Inquisitions* to attack the powerful *converso* families in order to acquire their estates and wealth. In 1492, an order was issued expelling all the Jews from the kingdom within four months. It is believed that over 10,000 Jews left Aragon and an even greater number was expelled from Castile. Many of them moved away to North Africa through Portugal. In 1504, the same instrument was used to expel the Muslims from the kingdom. Between 1482 and 1492, Ferdinand and Isabella concentrated their efforts on the conquest of Granada which had a Muslim majority. The policy of *reconquista* was achieved under the military leadership of Ferdinand. After their final success, the two monarchs received the title of the 'Catholic Kings' from Pope Alexander VI in 1494. Although, this greatly enhanced their prestige among their subjects, the economic and social cost of these measures proved harmful as it led to a large exodus of professional men and merchants who had earlier contributed to Spanish culture and economy. They had successfully brought ideas from the outside world into Spain and helped Europe to remain in contact with new developments. After their expulsion, a new social tension developed between the old and the new Christians.

Spanish absolutism was also dependent to a some extent on its military power. The reign of Charles V saw the imperial expansion of Spain. Its foundation had already been laid through the policy of dynastic marriages. The Spanish ruler successfully contested the Imperial Crown of the Holy Roman Empire in 1519. However, this transformation of the Kingdom of Spain into the Spanish empire created many problems. The ruler of Spain became the sovereign of the largest empire of Europe, which included the territories of Austria, Burgundy, the Netherlands, the Italian possessions apart from the vast colonial empire in central and South America. The territorial responsibilities were enormous and the Spanish crown found it difficult to give sufficient attention to Spanish problems. This is evident from the fact that between 1516 and 1556, Charles could spend only sixteen years in Spain. This vast empire became a huge drain on Spanish resources as it led to the extension of the political and administrative structure. The population of Spain rose by nearly 50 per cent between 1530 and 1580 resulting in an increased demand for food grains that pushed up prices. Silver imports from the New World also contributed to this situation. One finds considerable changes taking place in the Spanish society during the reign of Charles. The number of *hidalgos* or the lesser nobility grew rapidly as trade profits were invested in purchase of noble ranks. This mentality, along with many other factors, checked the rise of capitalist development. The expansion of the state functions led subsequent rulers to utilize the councillor system started by Ferdinand and Isabella, as an instrument of royal power. The Royal Council was supplemented by the Council of War (1517), the Council of State (1522) and the Council of Finance (1523). The Council of State became Charles's inner cabinet. The enormous overseas empire led to the creation of two important councils – the Council of the Indies and *Casa da Contratacion*, to regulate the activities of the colonial officials and to supervise trade. With the expansion of the Castilian government, the bureaucratic structure began to expand to compensate for the absence of the rulers. The role of the legislature was gradually declining and Spanish institutions were increasingly coming under the influence of royal power. With the growth of the Spanish empire, the ambition of Spanish rulers also grew and the Spanish economy and society had to pay the price for the vastness of the empire.

When Charles V abdicated in 1556 he divided his huge empire into two administrative regions, one under his brother that included the Holy Roman Empire, and the other comprising Spain and Burgundy under his son, Philip. The period of Philip II (1556–98) saw the establishment of a permanent capital at Madrid, greater involvement of the crown in government functioning and further extension of the bureaucracy. The council system was taken further with the creation of *Camara de Castilla* and the Council of Flanders in 1588 to stem the Dutch revolt. The Council of Portugal was established in 1582, two years after the Portuguese union with Spain. Philip faced resistance in different parts of the kingdom because of his intolerance of the minorities and his opponents. He used the Inquisition to bring orthodoxy in society but it resulted in a number of rebellions including that of the *Moriscos* in 1568–9 in Granada (it is believed that nearly 80,000 *Moriscos*, the Muslims who had been converted to Christianity, were driven out of their homeland). The Dutch revolted fighting for their independence against Spanish rule from the 1580s and there was revolt in Aragon against the alleged policy of discrimination in 1591. Superficially, Spain under Philip II appeared great and rich because of the huge influx of silver. The fact is that Spain had failed to exploit the advantages of the American market. The natural resources of Spain remained limited and largely undeveloped. The colonial wealth was squandered in waging wars and suppressing revolts. Soldiers often remained unpaid. The ordinary Castilian was totally crushed by the weight of taxation. It is estimated that the burden of tax increased by 430 per cent during Philip's reign while the wages rose only by 80 per cent (J.A.P. Jones). The climax came in 1596 with the royal bankruptcy. After this Spanish fortune took a downward turn.

ENGLAND

Monarchy in England was not a new institution. There had always been reverence for the king but the feudal nobility often replaced those kings who were unfavourable to their demands. In the long period of feudal warfare and political disorder after the Black Death in the mid-fourteenth century, the kings found it difficult to rule effectively. The Hundred Years War was followed by the Wars of the Roses – a series of civil wars fought in medieval England from 1455 to 1485 between the House of Lancaster and the House of York. These wars considerably weakened the powers of the feudal nobility and led to their decline. However, the English ruler still depended largely on the feudal lords who had formed their own rival factions, which were led by members of the royal houses. The loss of Normandy and the failure of the English against the French in the era of feudal wars had caused widespread anarchy. The rival ruling houses of Lancaster and York had become puppets in the hands of feudal lords. The period after the Wars of the Roses marked the beginning of a strong monarchy first under Edward IV, which was further developed with the establishment of Tudor rule under Henry VII (in 1485). Though England was dominated by the feudal order, yet England was different from other regions of Europe in some ways. England experienced the disintegration of the feudal order much earlier than other European states. England was among the first in Europe to develop into a nation state. Monarchy was seen not as a form of despotism, but as a symbol of English unity. England emerged as an absolute state under the Tudors but English absolutism differed from that of France in several ways. Many factors contributed to the success of the Tudors in creating a strong monarchy: Henry had secured his throne by conquest at Bosworth. He needed legal sanction and legitimacy. The parliament acknowledged him as the 'new sovereign'. He then married in 1486 Elizabeth of York, the eldest daughter of Edward IV, thereby uniting the 'white rose' and the 'red'. Henry also succeeded in establishing a strong government in England taking advantage of the economic growth and social and intellectual changes. Late-fifteenth century marked the beginning of population growth that continued in the following century, the export of raw wool gave way to the export of woollen cloth and rural cottage industry had started emerging giving additioal income to the rural population. The steady inflation acted as a tonic for clothiers and manufacturers. This also proved extremely beneficial to the landlords who with high rents and growing market opportunities made them invest in land and on sheep farming. Rise of landed country gentlemen and the middle class had political repercussions. They all favoured political centralization rather than a decentralized feudal political structure causing intermittent wars and anarchy. The gentry and the emerging social classes supported Tudor government in the hope of securing official posts while the merchants desired stability and peace to promote business activities.

It is important to remember that the Tudor government was essentially medieval in character like its counterparts on continental Europe, as far as its economic and social goals were concerned. Its primary aim was to regulate social life of the people and check competition and curb economic freedom in order to maintain stability in society. Yet, its policies of centralization and regulation created conditions that proved beneficial for economic growth and the rise of new social forces.

In the rise of Tudor absolutism, the Privy Council played an important role. The Council had existed throughout the Middle Ages. It functioned primarily in the interest of the feudal nobility to control and check the actions of the ruler. From the fourteenth century, the big landed magnates began to claim greater share in it and started dominating it. The composition of the council was enlarged and it became an aristocratic body. It was becoming virtually independent of the crown. Edward IV made an unsuccessful attempt to revive the lost powers by ruling without the Council, as he feared its interference in his official work. Henry VII could not throw out all its members and had to retain almost half of them much against his wish. Barons formed an important group in the council but their collective power was declining although the individual influence continued. The nobles were outnumbered by the clerics. Among the most powerful members who did not belong to the upper feudal nobility but became Henry's trusted advisers were men like John Morton, Richard Fox and Empson. They were all educated men who looked forward to royal rewards and had no hereditary claims to office or wealth. Henry Tudor assigned new functions to the old Council. The Council was asked to translate the royal will into legislative action. Its membership was not fixed and could vary with each meeting. The inner circle of the Council included permanent officials, peers of the land and lawyers who were full-time administrators. The personal presence of the king in Council meetings gave it cohesion and unity. According to Bindoff, its twin characteristics were its complete dependence on the king and its constant presence under him in state affairs. Its scope of work was enormous. It made no distinction between judicial and administrative business. It also functioned as a court of justice and effectively handled complaints against powerful feudal landowners. Whenever Henry VII's rivals posed a threat to him by organizing plots against him or instigating violence, the Council functioned as a court and decided each case in favour of the king. The Privy Council began to plan and initiate legislative matters that were translated into law by parliament.

Although their rule was essentially based on the support of the landed class, the Tudor rulers enjoyed the cooperation of several sections of the society. Henry Tudor was the first English monarch for over a century who was not surrounded by big feudal lords, whose combined wealth and influence outweighed the ruler. To deal with these strong feudal lords, Henry began summoning members from the lower ranks of nobility. As compared to fifty-three barons and earls in 1454, Henry invited only twenty-seven Barons and six Earls to parliament. In 1487, he asked parliament to pass the Act of Livery and Maintenance. It was an effort to disband the private armies of the feudal lords, which had become a major source of disorder. The execution of royal policy was entrusted to the Privy Council, which was placed above the ordinary machinery of law. Henry did not spare even his loyal supporters, e.g. the Earl of Oxford, who had turned up with an army of liveried retainers to greet him.

Another powerful institution to emerge under the Tudors was the Court of Star Chamber. A series of prerogative courts were created by the Tudor monarchs, which were made independent of the common law courts. Many more such courts were created to deal with specific problems but they helped in expanding royal intervention in England. An notable feature of Tudor despotism was that the monarchs had neither a standing army nor a professional bureaucracy to enforce its will unlike the other absolutist states of Europe. The English ruler had to depend on the cooperation of the natural leaders of society for the execution of his commands. In place of a powerful bureaucratic structure that the rulers of France and Spain had built-up, the English rulers relied on the justices of the peace. They were the agents of the royal government and were selected from the class of gentry or from that segment which had not enjoyed power till now. They were not appointed as professional bureaucrats and did not receive salary from the government. For them, the appointment was seen as a special favour made by the king to elevate their social status. The justices of the peace were placed under the control of the Privy Council and the Prerogative Courts. They formed the pillars of Tudor absolutism. They looked after every detail of parish administration and justice. All edicts of the government were enforced through them. They virtually replaced the sheriff and his shire-court. A personal element in the relationship between the justices of the peace and the monarchial state existed till the rule of Elizabeth. She took personal interest in their appointment and their number continued to grow. With the increase in the prestige and the profit of their office, the institution of the justices of the peace came under intense pressure. The strong cooperation between the crown and the officials that existed in the time of the Tudors began to break. Under the Stuart kings, it became increasingly difficult for the justices of the peace to enforce the unpopular policies of the government. Besides, their social basis began to conflict with the interests of the feudal monarchy and this caused a breakdown in the alliance, which had earlier provided strength to the Tudor monarchs.

The emergence of the absolute state in England in the reign of Henry VIII was closely bound with the Reformation. The English Reformation was a political act of the state made possible by a weak church. The religious crisis of the 1530s marked a significant progress in the direction of national unification and the establishment of royal absolutism. This period has been termed by G.R. Elton as the Henrican or Tudor 'administrative revolution'. A series of procedures were adopted such as a new mode of managing finances, centralization of administration, the use of Privy Council for coordinating various departments, rationalization of the royal household under king's personal control and unlike the rest of the continent, integration of the English towns into a single national unit. The disintegration of Papal church in England expanded the prerogative powers of the ruler. Members of the gentry enjoying royal support used the failure of a dangerous revolt in the northern countries called the Pilgrimage of Grace (1536–7) a pretext to replace the ruling families of the north. The Duke of Norfolk protested against this policy by calling it 'arming small thieves to hunt down the big'. A major feudal uprising in the north led to the creation of a branch of Privy Council at York. It was called the Council of the North, and was there to maintain royal authority in that region. This court lasted over a century and helped in the establishment of a strong government in that turbulent region. A similar council was established at Ludlow for Wales. This resulted in the Union of England and Wales in 1536. Wales was given representation of thirteen members in the English parliament. This example was followed with the other neighbouring states. In Ireland, it marked the introduction of the English system of shire administration to check local liberties and turbulence. However, it was the establishment of royal supremacy over the English church and the breach with Rome that vastly expanded royal jurisdiction in England. The nationalization of the English church brought all

Englishmen under a single authority. This was not an unusual step as many other states of Europe had their own national churches. In the case of England, it gave unlimited powers to the ruler, which had a major impact on the finances of the crown. Before this, the English rulers had to depend on the Pope to control the higher clergy who were also rich landowners. After the Reformation, they became royal subjects losing much of their independence. The Reformation acts forbade any foreigner, be it even the Pope, to intervene in the English affairs. The religious offenders were punished not by the Papal authority but by the crown's officials. During the reign of Elizabeth, the Court of High Commission was created as a prerogative court to supervise and control ecclesiastical courts and was given coercive powers to enforce royal decisions. The results of these measures were far-reaching. In the view of Sir Lewis Namier, religion, in the sixteenth century, became a word for nationalism.

Unlike in France or in Spain, monarchs in England did not face centrifugal tendencies. England achieved a strong unity because of its relatively small size. The Tudor rulers had successfully harnessed the governing class. This class had achieved a reasonably developed national consciousness during the years of wars. The crown utilized some of the traditional institutions, as well as created a few new ones to control the outlying regions. This allowed the king to disregard the common law and ignore normal legal procedures in the name of welfare and safety of the kingdom. The Tudor rulers exercised prerogative powers according to their own judgement in all matters of the state. Although, absolute power did not give any new attributes to kingship, the Tudor kings successfully enlarged the scope of prerogative powers which the early Stuarts tried beyond their realistic limit. This caused arbitrary methods of governance and the king's inroad into public and private spheres through forced collection of taxes without the consent of parliament, caused popular resistance culminating in the civil war in 1642.

John E. Martin suggests that the desire for a strong state existed in England for a relatively short period during the rule of Tudors and early Stuarts. This aspiration had reached its height in the reign of Henry VIII, particularly when Thomas Cromwell, the Earl of Essex was in power. Thomas Cromwell had been a great statesman and advisor to Henry VIII after the dismissal of Cardinal Wolsey. He had served the king as Chancellor of Exchequer, Vicar-General and Lord Great Chamberlain between 1533 and 1540. He worked hard to make the Tudor government effective and efficient. He realized the need to end the chaos of feudal privilege but he could not succeed in the end. His ideas manifested itself in different forms – the proposal for creating a standing army in 1536–7 (attempts for it were made earlier also), the creation of the councils (Council of the North and the Council of the Wales). An attempt was made by the crown to usurp the legislative powers through the Statute of Proclamations in 1539. According to Lawrence Stone, Thomas Cromwell's policy aimed at developing economic and military power. Attempts to create a powerful absolutist regime in England could not succeed as the Tudor state was handicapped by its small size. The rulers had to depend on the landed class to enforce administrative control. Even the French rulers depended on the landed class but they had succeeded in establishing their control through royal bureaucracy. This limitation of the English Crown is reflected in its limited base of fiscal resources and the absence of a professional bureaucracy.

Royal taxation in England proved beneficial for the economy but it also created problems for the state. Peace during the Tudor rule and the absence of a standing army made taxation in England relatively light compared to the continental states. This greatly helped the progress of trade and industry and yeoman farming in England prior to 1640. A narrow fiscal base and a low level of tax collection prevented the Tudors from creating an elaborate bureaucratic structure. Insufficient revenue made the English rulers depend on parliamentary grants. Parliamentary control over revenue continued, which created a belief that the king should live on his normal income. Parliament granted extra subsidy only during times of emergency like a rebellion or a foreign war. Direct taxation was the only means for the royal income. Henry VII through stringent control over expenditure and effective resource mobilization had succeeded in transforming a bankrupt state into a state with a reasonably sufficient wealth. However, under Henry VIII the first financial crisis was seen in 1525 when the parliament refused to grant subsidy for a war waged against France by Cardinal Wolsey. The parliament relented after some persuasion by Henry VIII. This situation was often repeated during the rule of James I and Charles I (1603–42).

Income from crown lands was an important source of royal revenue during the Tudor period, greatly augmented by the acquisition of monastic lands in the 1530s with the dissolution of the monasteries. According to Christopher Hill, the crown sold the monastic lands for £2¼ million between 1558 and 1640. On the other side, the wars with France and Scotland were believed to have cost £2 million between 1542 and 1546, and another one million in the subsequent period. Inflation during that period created serious difficulties for the crown. It forced the rulers to resort to obsolete sources of taxation. One such method was the wardship, the old feudal custom by which the minor heirs of big landed nobles, who died, were placed under the crown as wards. This was turned into a fiscal game by the rulers as they received part of the income from land of their wards. The wardships of rich heirs and heiresses were eagerly begged and bought by the courtiers. The Court of Wards developed as an instrument of financial exploitation. The revenue from this source quadrupled between the 1560s and 1640. Purveyance was another feudal source of revenue. The crown was given the right to purchase goods well below the market price. It was meant only for an extraordinary situation but the Tudors turned it into a regular tax. This caused widespread discontent because it affected production and led to scarcities of several goods. James I raised this tax further in 1610. Custom duties constituted almost half the ordinary revenue of the state and a good part of it was used for the development of the royal navy. The objective of this tax was to protect the merchants from foreign competitors. The Tudor emphasis on navy definitely contributed to the commercial prosperity of England. However, in the absence of an elaborate royal bureaucracy, the collection of customs had to be granted to custom farmers who enjoyed substantial profit from these collections at the government's expense. At the same time landowners generally remained under-assessed as far as taxes were concerned. The crown was forced into a policy of expediency, as the government showed no intention to reform the taxation structure to meet the mounting deficit. In 1610, James and his parliament had almost come to an agreement on a proposal of tax restructuring called the Great Contract but it could not be implemented because of their mutual distrust. Monopolies were created along with a system of regulation. The financial crisis in England resulted in political strain because the monarchs found it difficult to reward loyalty and services in the form of pensions, patronage or grants of privilege. Elizabeth adopted the practice of granting exclusive monopolies to the elite subjects of the crown. It caused resentment among those left out. The reaction became more pronounced under James I. The Office of Lord Treasurer and the titles of peerage were sold for hefty amounts. James I began the practice of selling knighthoods. Between 1615 and 1628, there was a marked increase in the sale of peerages. While the English economy was growing rapidly, the government was unable to receive its share. In the period of steep inflation when average prices increased five times between 1530 and 1630, the royal revenue increased from £2,00,000 to only £6,00,000 annually. The Spanish war and the Irish troubles during the last years of Elizabeth's rule created financial difficulties for the early Stuarts. This seriously affected the position of the Stuart rulers and made their position vulnerable.

One major limitation of the Tudor rule was the lack of substantial military apparatus. The rise of monetized feudal economy caused progressive dissociation of the nobility from the basic military function much earlier than in other places in Europe. The wars in the later middle ages were mostly fought by indenture companies raised by the big feudal lords for the rulers through cash contracts. However, the mercenary troops owed obedience to their own captains rather than to rulers. Tudor monarchs, unlike the French or the Spanish rulers, neither needed nor were able to build a military machine.

In England, a concurrent centralization took place, both of royal power and noble representation within the parameters of the medieval political structure. The rise of centralized monarchy produced a unified assembly representing the feudal ruling class, unlike the three or the fourfold division of legislature representing nobles, clergy and townsmen or burghers as was the case in other countries. In England, from the period of Edward III, knights and townsmen were represented along with barons and bishops in the same house of the parliament. The division of parliament into Lords and Commons developed gradually. Thus, there existed a traditional check on the royal legislative power. It enabled the nobles to exert their influence on the absolute rulers. Therefore, while the executive powers of the medieval rulers of England were much greater than those of the contemporary rulers in the continent, they could never achieve the same legislative autonomy that was enjoyed by the French absolute rulers.

A similar fusion between the monarchy and the nobility existed at the local levels of judiciary and administration. In the continental states, the royal and seigniorial jurisdictions remained segregated. The survival of feudal courts in England provided a common ground on which the two forms could be blended. Sheriffs were the non-hereditary royal appointees, who presided over the shire courts but they were selected from the class of local gentry and did not constitute a professional bureaucracy. This situation did not permit the emergence of the type of professional men like the French *baillis* created by the rulers nor could the baronial form of court be tolerated. Instead, the justices of the peace were created representing a blend of the two. They were the unpaid royal appointees from the aristocratic class. In the Tudor period they consolidated the relationship between the crown and the landed aristocracy at the local level. With the passage of time, the social basis of the court became narrower. The rapid economic growth and increasing commercialization led to a shift in the socio-political balance. Conflicts surfaced between the new economic forces and the feudal policies of the state by the 1590s. Class tensions manifested at the state level. Economic interests of the justices of the peace began to diverge from those of the monarchy resulting in the breakdown of the state apparatus.

The English landowning class was gradually becoming civilian in background, commercial in occupation and commoner in rank (unlike *noblesse d'épée* in France). The feudal crises, the price rise and the expansion of market promoted sheep farming in many parts of England. Economic changes moved in the direction of commercialization of agricultural. During the sixteenth century, there was a drift towards rural cottage industry caused by the growing internal demand. Some sections of the English nobility associated themselves with commercial activity. It contributed to the prosperity of the gentry and increased their political influence as they were actually promoted by the Tudors to counter balance the strength of the peerage. The economic growth and the transformation of social classes in England affected the social foundations of the absolute rulers.

These agrarian changes also caused political and social disturbances and threatened political stability. Such disturbances arose because the English peasants felt threatened by the new developments such as the expropriation of common lands by landlords, rack-renting by the new landlords and the enclosure movement which introduced unfavourable changes in land-tenurial relationship. All these developments were linked to the conversion of cultivable land into pastures and led to depopulation in those regions. It became imperative for the absolute rulers to maintain order and peace. On the other hand, they did not have a standing army to quell the peasant uprisings. The rulers were concerned with the problem of depopulation and saw it as a source of potential disorder. According to John E. Martin, the constraints on absolutism in England had important consequences, particularly on its relationship with the peasantry. The emergence of capitalist agriculture introduced changes that subverted the traditional feudal relations and in turn threatened the state's own survival. It forced the state to adopt an anti-capitalist stance. The transformation of feudal nobility into a new landed class also shifted their priorities and interests. They were prepared to rally behind the state to safeguard their own interests but not when state's own apparatus was threatened. However, political instability caused by internal revolts or peasant rebellions posed a threat to the entire structure including the partnership between the absolute rulers and the landed class. Thus, the agrarian legislation of the absolute state was motivated primarily by its own concern to check depopulation. Selective legislation was carried out from 1515 onwards to prevent peasant depopulation without undermining the position of the landed class. Absolute monarchy in England received the strongest blow in the mid-seventeenth century from the emerging capitalist elements, which were monopolizing the lower house of parliament in their struggle for supremacy.

The English parliament played an important role in placing an outer limit to the powers of Tudor monarchs. England's withdrawal from European politics after the Hundred Years War meant that there was little need to summon frequent meetings of the parliament because there were no financial pressures. The frequency of meetings increased from 1529 to tackle religious issues. The membership of the parliament also underwent major changes; the clergy were replaced by laymen not only in the legislature but even within royal administration. There was persistent financial crisis after 1603 under the Stuart kings. The financial difficulties of Charles I (1625–49), forced him to raise taxes needed because of growing expenses that included wars. The parliament resisted this stubbornly. The renewed external threat, the revival of religious controversies and the issue of royal patronage (including prerogative powers) prepared the ground for a civil war in 1642. The old patronage structure of the feudal state was destroyed after this. As Thomas Ertman states, 'By breaking up the old national patronage networks centered on the Court, it [the civil war] removed a key structural underpinning of the parasitical state which had flourished before 1642.' Under Oliver Cromwell, one of the rebel leaders, the New Model Army was created in 1645. A series of constitutional experiments under him introduced fundamental changes in state administration. The pillars of absolutism – the prerogative powers of the rulers were abolished. The civil war had a profound impact on the relationship between the crown and the parliament. The House of Commons began to influence state policies. Standing Committees were formed to oversee the major departments and subsequently, strict parliamentary control was established over state finances. A few unsuccessful attempts were made to reestablish despotic rule, particularly by James II (1685–8) but the English monarchy was transformed into a constitutional monarchy through the Revolution of 1688. With it the patriarchial features of the English state slowly disappeared. As opposed to this, the French rulers dispensed with the advice and cooperation of the Estates General, which was not summoned even once between 1614 and 1789 and in the absence of any legislative checks the state became a model of absolutism.

Eastern Europe

In eastern Europe the emergence of serfdom and the erection of absolutism were closely linked. According to Perry Anderson, the mode of production in eastern Europe was founded on extra-economic coercion. Conquest was the primary form of expansion and the state depended on territorial expansion and not on commerce. The most important example of absolutism in eastern Europe is Russia. It began with the small principality of Moscow with the state growing around the Muscovite nucleus and transformed into a powerful state. This process had begun in the mid-fifteenth century and continued till the eighteenth century.

The Mongol invasions in the thirteenth century in the present Russian region led to the rule of the Khans of the Golden Horde in lower Volga. The territories around this region consisted of small tribes and principalities. The dukes of the small states required confirmation of authority from the Khans to collect taxes from the local tribes from which they paid tributes to the Tatars. This system continued throughout the fourteenth century. The people were divided into three main categories: the Great Russians, the Ukrainians and the White Russians. Great Russia was cut-off from western Europe. It was broken into a large number of small appanages (units created for the maintenance of young princes). Muscovy was one of the many appanages around which others rallied to form Russia.

The rule of the Tatars was based not on conquest and control, but on frequent raids, in Lithuania and in other smaller states in order to capture booty and slaves. Gradually their power and influence began to decline. Seizing this opportunity the Lithuanian kingdom began expanding at the expense of Russian territories. A rift between Poland and Lithuania provided an opportunity to the Russian dukes to not only recover certain territories but also develop Russia into a centralized state. The Tatar power had broken into three separate *Khanates* which enabled Russia to push for independence.

Intra-dynastic relations governed the domestic politics of the Rus' principalities. With the disintegration of the Golden Horde and a waning Lithuanian influence, the Muscovy princes adopted a vertical pattern of succession, the throne passing to the eldest son instead of going to brothers or cousins. The grand princes, Vasily II (1425–62), Ivan III (1462–1505) and Vasily III (1505–33) not only consolidated their existing territories but incorporated the surrounding independent principalities. Vasily II spent most of his time in countering civil war but he ensured a smooth succession for his son Ivan III. The real foundation of the Russian state was laid by Ivan III (1462–1505).

Territorial Expansion

The reign of Ivan III saw a threefold expansion of the Russian territories. Till then, Russia was still under the nominal control of the Tatars. Moscow was surrounded by numerous small and autonomous states such as the Duchies of Riazan and Tver, city states of Novgorod, Vyatka and Pskov. However, the strongest state in the mid-fifteenth century was Lithuania that ruled the Ukrainian lands along the rivers Dneiper and Kiev. The transformation of the Muscovite state into Russia began with the rule of Ivan III. He was the first Russian duke who did not seek permission from the Tatar Khan for his confirmation on the throne. Under his rule, large territories were acquired. The independent duchy of Riazan was brought under Russian control through a marriage treaty in 1464 and Tver and Vyatka were acquired by force in 1485. However, the most important territorial gain was of Novgorod which checked Lithuanian expansion. The process of acquisition of Novgorod was carried out gradually from 1465 to 1488. It was a major gain for it was an important centre of trade, covered a large territory, had a

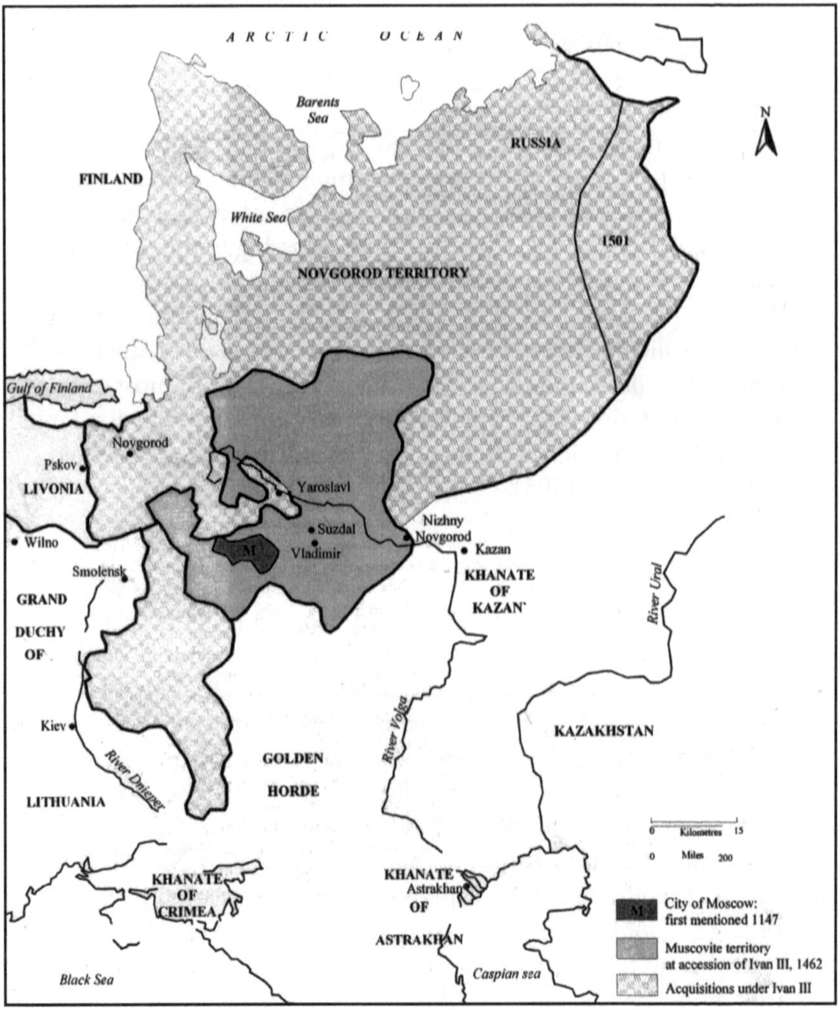

Map 5.3: The Growth of Russian Empire

large population and could consequently provide more revenue to the Muscovite rulers. It fell on the major trade route between Central Asia and the Baltic and it controlled not only the inflow of silver but also had an access to the source of fur, one of the main items of export from that region. However, the greatest significance of this acquisition was that it decided the question of supremacy between Lithuania and Moscow in favour of the latter and marked the emergence of Russia. The Russian subjugation of Novgorod led to a major rebellion in 1478. Once the revolt was crushed, the town was placed under lieutenants who were appointed by Ivan. The Russians also increased their control over the city of Pskov, which ultimately lost its independent status in 1510. When the Holy Roman Emperor Maximilian offered to confer the title of King on Ivan, the Russian ruler rejected it and proclaimed himself emperor. He assumed the title of *Tsar*, meaning a ruler obeying nobody. The success against Novgorod and his claim as an independent ruler made him Ivan 'the Great'. Ivan successfully countered the Tatar attacks in 1481 and again in 1487, when they invaded Muscovy. Finally the Russian ruler annexed the whole stretch of Byelorussia and Ukraine along the western border after he invaded Lithuania twice—in 1492 and 1501.

The rule of Ivan IV was marked by significant territorial expansion. Kazan was brought under Russian control in 1552 and Astrakhan was taken over in 1556. The entire Volga basin was made a part of the Russian empire. It placed the important trade routes through Central Asia under Russian hands and paved the way for Russian expansion in Siberia and to the Pacific region. The third important phase of territorial expansion through wars of annexations was carried out by Peter the Great (1682–1725). The Northern War (1700–9) between Sweden and Russia ended with Russia gaining important territories in the Gulf of Finland, Livonia (Latvia) and Estonia. This pushed Russia up to the Baltic and made her a strong naval power in that region. The Swedish invasion, in the words of Perry Anderson, proved to be the 'Hammer of the East' (Russia is located on the east of Sweden). It had great impact on the formation of Russia as an absolutist state; just as the Tatar attacks in the earlier period had provided the impetus for centralization in the duchy of Muscovite.

The rule of Ivan III and Ivan IV covering a century or more was significant not only for territorial expansion but also for the development of a powerful state structure. The policy of expansion was governed by social dictates as well as demographic considerations. In the newly-acquired territories they destroyed autonomous corporations in the cities and created their own institutions. In this way they were able to establish their control over the towns and the regional autonomous bodies but the structure of state which they created was rather an autocracy than absolutist. In order to strengthen his claim as the successor of the defunct Byzantine empire (once a power controlling the entire eastern Europe and protecting the Orthodox Greek Church), Ivan III married Sophia, the niece of the last Byzantine ruler in 1472. This gave him the claim over the kingdom of Kiev. Sophia was half Italian by birth and this marriage introduced the Renaissance culture in Russia. The queen was accompanied by a number of architects, builders and artisans, who not only built new styles of cathedrals and citadels but they also replaced wood structures with stone buildings. The city of Moscow was fortified and rebuilt. Kremlin became the official court that was built to create imperial splendour. Ivan believed that anything that pleased the prince had the force of law. He set in motion the policy of expansion, which gave certain advantages to the state by turning it into an empire. But it also brought a wide variety of non-Russian population into the empire that created problems of effective governance.

The nature of rule and the character of Ivan IV remains a debatable subject among historians due to paucity of historical documents. Writers like S.M. Dubvrovskii severely criticize Ivan IV for creating a tyrannical system that undermined the productive capacity of the country and pushed Russia towards a crisis by the end of the sixteenth century. On the other hand, Bakhrushin describes Ivan as the 'People's Tsar' whose reforms received their full support as these assured order within the country and defence against external opponents. The writings of the Stalin era (I.I. Smirnov, I.V. Budovnits, etc.) depict Ivan IV as a progressive ruler, a great statesman and a national champion. After Stalin, a reappraisal of Ivan IV started. The new writings emphasize the feudal nature of the centralized state under him.

Church and State

In order to make his position powerful, Ivan III claimed supremacy over the Orthodox Christian inhabitants of eastern Europe and considered himself their protector. He tried to give a sacramental character to his position and showed that he was the true protector of the Orthodox Christians. The church provided legitimacy and ideological basis to the Muscovite rulers. After a prolonged debate, the 'Third Rome Theory' was articulated by Pskov Filofei, a monk, (Janet Martin) which stated that Moscow was heir to Rome and Constantinople and made a strong appeal to the Russian prince to relieve the suffering of the Christian subjects from oppression and tyranny. This theory along with other religious issues was debated by the ecclesiastical scholars and by the church officials. A meeting of the Church Council was held in 1503 that adopted a mid-way approach of maintaining the autonomy of the church on the one hand and supporting and justifying the all-pervading authority of the Grand Prince. In the reign of Ivan IV, the 'Third Rome Theory' was discussed once again. It was elaborated upon in many ways that included preparation of literary texts and holding ceremonies to glorify the Muscovite rulers. These actions justified and legitimized the theoretical claims of the rulers and contributed to state building.

Nobility and the Absolutist Structure

The only social group in Russia that could counter the position of the Tsars were the boyars. They were the itinerant Russian warriors who transformed themselves into landed aristocracy. Many of them descended from the families of princes. They played a dominant role in political, institutional and legal sphere in the provincial territories and controlled the provincial assemblies called Dumas. The political strength of the boyars led to the introduction of serfdom in Russia on a large scale. Free peasants were turned into serfs by force and consequently a rigid form of serfdom came into existence that lasted till the nineteenth century. The rise of serfdom and the emergence of the absolute state went hand in hand in Russia. The influence of the boyars had greatly reduced the powers of the Russian rulers. The boyars had established themselves as the master of land and collected taxes, administered law and justice, and controlled peasants and serfs. The peasants were compelled to pay labour services (*barshchina*) and money rent (*obrok*) to their lords. Ivan III adopted a policy of promoting those members of the gentry who were prepared to render military service to the king and he built-up the *dvoriane* or the service nobility and rewarded them with land grants in the newly-acquired territories. The land–labour ratio in Russia was too low compared to other regions. The prolonged struggle between the monarchs and the boyars came to a head during Ivan IV's rule.

Ivan III made attempts to reduce the powers of the boyars and push for absolutism. Territorial expansion brought about significant changes in land relationship. Not only was the peasants' monopoly of the lord checked, the new financial obligations on them altered their position. A new type of estate called *pomeste* emerged. The landholder, a *pomeshchik* was given the right to collect income from the estate assigned to him in return for military service to the Grand Prince. This system was introduced on a large scale after the conquest of Novgorod. Land belonging to the old nobility in the annexed territories was confiscated. The Novgorod boyars were asked to settle in the north-east. Ivan introduced the principle that boyars could hold land only if they were loyal to the prince and pledged military service to him. He tried to ruin them financially. Kholmsky, a distinguished noble, was arrested in 1474 and later released when eight guarantors stood security for him. He had to sign a similar pledge. Nearly 80 per cent of the private land passed into the hands of the Muscovite rulers. Between 1488–9 about 8,000 boyars were removed from Novgorod, when that region was brought under the Russian rule. This brought an ever-increasing number of men into the service of the Russian ruler. However, the introduction of the *pomestie* system and its rapid growth led to a land crisis. The private domains of the rulers were insufficient to meet the growing demand for land. The Russian rulers started confiscating the land from old nobility from the newly-acquired territories and gave it to the new service nobility. The annexation of Novgorod provided the richest territory to the rulers of Russia to be rewarded among their supporters. About 1,600 to 1,800 men were rewarded with about a million hectares of land in the frontier territories that formed the new landed class of *pomesties*. Conflicts took place between the service nobility and the Boyars. The *Pomestie* system became the primary source of income for thousands of royal supporters in the provinces. It integrated the military men in Muscovite society and gave the rulers full control over them.

The Institutional Structure

The administrative structure of Russia grew slowly from the time of Ivan III. In his reorganization of the administration, army, and land tenure, Ivan contributed greatly to the centralization of authority and established the real basis of Russian autocracy of the sixteenth century. During his reign an attempt was made to revive the Byzantine law and culture in Russia and it was introduced with a renewed emphasis on jurisprudence. This resulted in the framing of a new code of laws in 1497 called the *sudebnik*. It was based on the earlier laws of Kievan *Rus*. Under Ivan IV, fresh laws were introduced to handle cases of crime and to impose punishment through the *sudebnik*. Historians see the reign of Ivan IV or Ivan the Terrible (1533–84) in differing ways. The first picture of Ivan is that of a ruthless political ruler who was totally dedicated to the accumulation of absolute powers. The second view shows him as a mad man, a paranoid, possibly suffering from some serious illness, making him appear over-medicated.

With the death of Vasily III, troubled times followed. The heir to the throne, Ivan IV was too young and the boyars made an attempt to regain their past freedom and power. But with Ivan's coronation in 1547 he regained his power. However, the Boyar revolt of 1553 changed him completely. This experience led him to set up an institution called the *oprichnina*. This was a private court or a private household of the ruler that included only the loyal followers who had committed themselves to the service of the Tsars. In return, they received land grants confiscated from the boyars and other landowners. The *oprichnina* consisted of about a thousand chosen men regardless of rank who were there to check the boyars responsible for the disorders in the state. The *oprichnina* ran parallel to the feudal institution of *zemshchina*. Ivan gave the members of *oprichnina* the license to drive out boyars and even slay them if they so desired. As a result the boyars lost all protection of life and property. The institution of *oprichnina* was something like a state within the state and constituted half of the total territory of the Russian state. Their activities were brutal. When its members rode the country in search of traitors and opponents, they wore dark dresses and attached images of dogs to their saddles. It is estimated that at least 4,000 men lost their lives through the actions of *oprichnina*. Its unpopularity and a fear of a plot forced Ivan to disband it in 1572.

After the Second World War, many revisionist scholars in Russia have stressed the negative aspects of the *oprichnina*. A.A. Zimin, for example, argues that its central organization was responsible for consolidation of feudal elements in the government. Some recent scholars reject the traditional view that the *oprichnina* incited class warfare. It is also suggested that it seriously weakened the institutions of representative government. Institutions like *Zemskii Sober* showed signs of decline from the mid-sixteenth century. Some Russian historians go to the extent of blaming the *oprichnina* for weakening the foreign policy of Ivan, especially in the context of the Livonian War.

The development of the Russian legislature was quite different from that of many other Western states. In England, the parliament had emerged as a junior partner to the Tudor rulers. At the same time it gained prestige and experience by participating in important state matters and the English kings found it difficult to ignore it. The French rulers had completely avoided the summoning of Estates General. In Spain too, the rulers avoided confrontation with the cortes. In Russia, the traditional representative institution was the Dumas (a representative body of the upper nobility enjoying executive and judicial functions). It was an assembly of old boyars which functioned in the territories outside the *zemshchina*, the other half of the country outside the sphere of *oprichnina*. Threatened by external invasion on two fronts and the treachery of the old ruling classes, Ivan IV summoned the *Zemsky Sobor* in 1566. It was an assembly of representatives of clergy, princes, government, bureaucracy and merchants and traders. The Russian rulers invited the representatives of the last category for the first time. It consisted of 374 members and the majority belonged to the service nobility. Ivan IV was keen to get the support of all the classes against the boyars and used this institution like a national assembly to get a vote of confidence. It was Peter the Great, who decided to replace boyars Dumas by the Senate. Dumas virtually became a rubber stamp of the Russian rulers.

In recent years, a fresh attempt has been made to redefine the relationship between the Tsars and the boyars, the service elite. This view suggests that the boyars were deeply involved in the process of governance and that one must discount the assertions about the Tsar's unlimited powers and the so-called autocratic rule because the court included besides the ruler, the service elite – the boyars and the *okol'nichie*. The boyars enjoyed legitimacy as advisers, reflecting to some extent their real power. According to Nancy Kollman, the façade of autocracy was deliberately created and was the product of an entire complex of ceremony and assertions (Daniel H. Kaiser and Gary Marker).

The militarization of the state apparatus was linked to the structure of absolutism along with its relationship with the feudal landowners. The formation of an armed force contributed to the powers of the Russian king. The chief components of the Russian army consisted of a militia, which was provided by the service nobility (*dvoriane*) Cossacks and the private guards of the rulers called *Streltsy*. The Russian rulers organized their basic administrative system to meet the needs of war and territorial expansion. Ivan IV tried to transform the landholding class into service tenure;

thereby making the landed nobility perform permanent military duties for the Russian state. The Russian rulers were constantly engaged in wars with their neighbouring states, including with Swedes, Poles, Lithuanians, Tatars and many others. The early troubles and the subsequent attempts at consolidation carried out by the rulers of the Romanov dynasty (after 1613) strengthened the relationship between landownership and army build-up. In 1556 Ivan IV promulgated an order that made military service obligatory for each landlord. Each feudal lord had to provide a certain number of soldiers to the Russian ruler depending on the amount of land he owned through the crown. Two out of every three male members had to join the army.

Although, Ivan IV initiated the process of building a permanent army, it was effectively implemented during the reign of Peter the Great. Till that time foreign mercenaries constituted over half of the Russian army. Peter developed the first armed force in Russia based on national interests. It was primarily recruited from the ranks of peasantry, built on loyalty, intensive training and discipline. The cost of the army was met from the contributions of the peasants. The expansion of the army encouraged industrialization, although in a limited way. Iron and munitions industries were promoted to equip the army. The strength of the standing army reached an impressive figure of 2,10,000. The traditional guards of the ruler, *Streltsy*, who were the politically active elite corps of the Russian rulers, opposed the military reforms of Peter. Many others revolted against the plans of Westernizing Russia that had been going on for many years. Not only was the revolt crushed but about 1,200 members of the Streltsy were executed and their bodies kept for display for months in order to intimidate potential rebels. The development of the Russian navy also began in the period of Peter the Great. The naval programme was implemented after his visit to western Europe, and by 1725 Russia possessed fifty battleships. Through it, Russia could establish control over the Baltic region and subsequently over the Black Sea. The military and naval expenses formed almost 75 per cent of the state budget.

The policies of the Russian rulers towards the ruling class was closely linked with the development of administration. In the Western countries, the feudal aristocracy was isolated and checked through the appointments of royal officials but in Russia this class was fully utilized in state functions. The expansion of the Russian empire created fresh demand for the new posts. To handle the growing clerical work of the administration, Ivan III drew heavily from the ecclesiastical schools to meet the demand for trained secretaries and clerks. The church became an important contributor to the state bureaucracy. The Tsar appointed the local governors called *voivods*. They were provided a share of the *imposts* for their upkeep, called *cormlenie,* but this was subsequently abolished and the police work was assigned to the district elders called the *starosty*. They worked without receiving any remuneration. They performed a variety of functions like policing, road construction and maintenance and other works that required management. Compared to the officials who were posted inside Moscow, the *starosty* enjoyed greater freedom. The department administration was called *prikazi* that worked with the help of the aristocracy. It held daily sessions that were often presided over by the Tsars themselves. Its business was miscellaneous in character that included legislative, executive and judicial functions. Gradually it was subdivided into about thirty smaller departments. However, its duties were not clearly demarcated, although it was assigned an important role as a bureau of military affairs. Its officials were graded into a hierarchy of ranks, the state bureaucracy was divided into fourteen ranks. The top eight enjoyed hereditary noble status while the lower six were given non-noble status. The feudal rank was merged with the bureaucratic organizations in which the service nobility occupied a central position in the power structure. The Russian rulers transformed the character of feudal aristocracy to a certain extent but could not become independent of it.

The relationship between the Russian state and the peasants also contributed to the development of absolutism. The state legislation played a crucial role by carrying out step-by-step attachment of the peasants to the newly acquired land and correspondingly, an official recognition of the institution of serfdom.

This led the development of a complex obligatory service. The boundaries and frontiers between Russia and Poland remained unclear because of deep forests. Western Siberia and the Volga region of the south-east were the other remote territories, which had not been colonized as yet. Rural migration of the peasants to these regions had increased because of excessive exploitation of the farmers. The Tsars eliminated various categories of nobility and peasantry and laid the foundations of a two-class society that continued till the twentieth century. Peasants had to pay heavy taxes and forced into military conscription and compulsory public works. Below them were the serfs whose numbers multiplied rapidly. Peter I demanded full cooperation from the nobility who had the onus of providing manpower for the expanding bureaucracy and the army. In return Peter gave them a free hand in the exploitation of the peasants. An intense conflict had developed between the service nobility and the boyars, the old nobility. It was not resolved till a stable and powerful centralized state was established. In the reigns of Ivan III and Vasily III, a system called *mestnichestvo* was created in the imperial court. It provided a mechanism by which the new and the old clans could achieve high ranks, wealth and power in the service of the ruler. As to why the subjugation of the Russian peasants was so prolonged, one can trace the roots of Russia's feudal structure to the mutually advantageous bargain made by the Tsars with their nobles at the expense of the peasants during the formative period of absolutism. In the nineteenth century too, the role of the Tsars was crucial in the abolition of serfdom.

The economic and social changes during the period of Russian absolutism were not very significant or noticeable. The state structure that was dominated by the feudal order blocked the bourgios elements from gaining upper hand in political sphere. The nobility continued to prosper at the cost of the serfs while the absence of rapid industrialization and urbanization prevented the emergence of the bourgeoisie.

Moscow was fast emerging as a huge city by late-fifteenth century and the contemporary accounts suggest that it was nearly twice the size of Florence. The other urban centres were Novgorod, Tver, and Nizhnii. Many of the rural magnets and boyars lived in the cities. They created demand for goods like foodstuff, fish, firewood, salt, honey, wax, flax, hemp and leather. The building of Kremlin along with the emergence of a few new towns promoted the timber industry to meet the demand of construction. Like Spain, Russia was expanding in Europe and was creating a colonial empire simultaneously. The major difference between Russia and other European states lies in the fact that the Russian expansion was contiguous instead of lying far away and was closely bound with its own political developments. Ivan IV established trade relations with England, first through the Arctic and later via Norway and the Baltic. In this there was hardly any personal initiative by the ruler, rather, he was afforded with an opportunity in 1553. Richard Chancellor was a survivor of the ill-fated English expedition to the orient. He landed in Russia and through him Ivan succeeded in discovering a trade possibility with England. In 1555 the two countries concluded a trade agreement. Through this Queen Mary of England granted complete monopoly of English trade with Russia to Muscovy Company, a chartered institution of Englishmen while Ivan granted to the English an exclusive monopoly of the northern route. This included the right to trade duty-free throughout Moscow, an exclusive right to trade with Kazan and Astrakhan, and transit through the river Volga. The Russian merchants barring a small group of powerful oligarchs did not enjoy such concessions.

The industrial development in Russia was imposed from above. The metallurgical works at Tulla, were run by foreign merchants. Private enterprise could hardly develop in such an atmosphere and the merchants were deprived of important profits that were reaped by foreign merchants. The absence of big towns and the overwhelming domination of economy by nobility in those places greatly reduced the scope for the Russian merchants. The strengthening of serfdom promoted a self-sufficient rural economy that proved detrimental to the growth of trade, and the forced wage-labour in the countryside and in the state-run industries prolonged the survival of serfdom in Russia till the reign of Alexander II.

According to E.I. Kolycheva, the Muscovite empire was badly affected by a series of crisis beginning in the 1570s. A number of unfavourable factors were responsible for this – ecological (epidemics, bad harvests, etc.) and socio-economic disturbances (wars, ruinous taxation, foreign raids). The Tatars had carried out massive raids and the military failure in the Livonian War revealed the weakness of the Muscovite empire and of the socio-economic structures. The crisis continued till about the 1590s followed by political instability caused by succession struggles. The impact of this on the Russian economy was traumatic. It resulted in depopulated villages, caused a decline in cultivation, fall in food production and reduced the tax base for state. The manufacturing centres were equally affected by the crisis so was trade. Bread prices rose sharply and all this led to political disorder till 1613, when Michael restored stability.

Thus, we find that in western Europe, absolutist states emerged at a time when feudalism reached maturity and had begun to decline. In Russia, the acquisition of new territories resulted in the reformulation of the relationship between the Tsar and the nobility on feudal lines. The rise of Russian absolutism introduced and strengthened serfdom in Russia. The Tsars became both sovereigns as well as proprietors of their kingdom. They converted the free population under their territories into bonded labour. However, the vast territories, mostly isolated because of poor communication and roads, provided space for expansion on the one side but at the same time curtailed the effective rule of the Tsars in those regions. Unlike the nobility of the West, the Russian nobility was turned into a service nobility that depended on the personal whims of the rulers. Its privileges did not go beyond the ownership of serfs and the status of nobility. The nobles were frequently transferred from one region to another or shifted from military to civil duties and they remained at the mercy of the state, though in case of weak succession there always was the possibility to bounce back.

European Rulers in the Period of Absolutism

France	Spain	England	Russia
• Process of centralization began with Charles VII 1422–61, followed by Louis XI 1461–83, Charles VIII 1483–98, and Louis XII 1498–1515. Rise of absolutist rule	• Isabella of Castile 1474–1504 and Ferdinand of Aragon, 1476–1516	• House of York	• Process of centralization began with Vasily II 1425-62
• Francis I 1515–47	• Charles I, 1516–56, became in 1519 Charles V, the Holy Roman Emperor	• Edward IV 1461–83	• Ivan III 1462–1505
• Henry II 1547–59	• Philip II, 1556–98	• Edward V 1483	• Vasily III 1505–33
• Francis II 1559–60	• Philip III 1598–1621	• Richard III 1483–5	• Ivan IV 'The Terrible' 1533–84, became Tsar in 1547
• Charles IX 1560–74	• Philip IV 1621–65	• House of Tudor	• Theodore I 1584–98
• Henry III 1574–89	• Charles II 1665–1700	• Henry VII 1485–1509	• Boris Godunov 1598–1605
• Henry IV 1589–1610		• Henry VIII 1509–47	• Theodore II 1605
• Louis XIII 1610–43		• Edward VI 1547–53	• Vasily IV 1606–10
• Louis XIV 1643–1715		• Mary 1553–8	• Romanov dynasty
• Louis XV 1715–74		• Elizabeth I 1558–1603	• Michael 1613–45
• Louis XVI 1774–92		• House of Stuarts	• Alexius 1645–76
		• James I 1603–25	• Theodore III 1676–82
		• Charles I 1625–49, civil war 1642–9	• Ivan V and Peter I 1682–9
		• Commonwealth and Protectorate 1649-60	• Peter I, The Great, 1689–1725
		• Charles II 1660–85	
		• James II 1685–8	
		• The constitutional Revolution of 1688	

Suggested Readings

Anderson, Perry, *Lineages of the Absolutist State*, London: New Left Books, 1974. This is the best exposition of the Marxist explanation of the origins and the nature of the absolutist states.

Elton, G.R., *The Tudor Revolution in Government*, London: Cambridge University Press, 1953. The focus is on institutional changes that took place under Tudor monarchy.

Ertman, Thomas, *Birth of the Leviathan: Building States and Regimes in Medieval and Early Modern Europe*, Cambridge: Cambridge University Press, 1997. This book not only contains an excellent discussion on recent historiography on the subject but also proposes a new general theory of state-building by taking up the widest range of cases stretching across the continent.

Jones, J.A.P., *Europe 1500–1600*, Surrey: Nelson, 1997. A standard textbook and takes into account recent historical research and contains interesting illustrations.

Kaiser, Daniel H. and Gary Marker, eds., *Reinterpreting Russian History, Readings, 860-1860s*, New York: Oxford University Press, 1994. Section III of the book provides the latest scholarship on the Russian state, including its economy and society.

Kettering, Sharon, *French Society, 1589–1715*, Harlow: Longman, 2001. An interesting survey of the diverse elements in society and Chapter 6 discusses the traditional and the revisionist interpretations of the French state.

Lynch, John, *Spain under the Habsburg*, vol. I, *Empire and Absolutism*, Oxford: Basil Blackwell, 1964. Examines the fundamental problems of the Spanish state.

Mann, Michael, *The Sources of Social Power: A History of Power from the Beginning to AD 1760*, vol. 1, Cambridge: Cambridge University Press, 1986. Complements the arguments of Tilly by bringing together the geographical and economic factors in the rise of modern states.

Martin, John E., *Feudalism to Capitalism: Peasants and Landlords in English Agrarian Development*, London: Macmillan, 1983. Good analysis on the social basis of the absolutist state in England. Focus on class relations.

Martin, Janet, *Medieval Russia 980–1584*, Cambridge: Cambridge University Press, 1995. A comprehensive narrative of the process and emergence of Russian absolutism, along with its weaknesses till the reign of Ivan IV.

Parker, David, *The Making of French Absolutism*, New York: St Martin's Press, 1983. Has a good discussion on the social basis of French absolutism and examines the historiography of early monarchy.

Poggi, Gianfranco, *The Development of the Modern State*, London: Hutchinson, 1978. Gives a good account of the institutional development of modern states.

Poulantzas, N., *Political Power and Social Classes*, tr. T. O'Hagan, London: New Left Books, 1973. Provides an altogether different explanation on the nature of absolutism.

Tibebu, Teshale, 'On the Question of Feudalism, Absolutism, and the Bourgeois Revolution', *Review*, XIII, 1990, pp. 49–152. This long article includes a detailed discussion on feudalism and brings out the theoretical inconsistencies in Anderson's arguments.

Tilly, Charles, *Coercion, Capital and European States; AD 990–1990*, Oxford: Basil Blackwell, 1990. Suggests an alternative interpretation on the origins of the modern state and the reasons for their variations in different parts of Europe emphasizing the role of external threats.

Wallerstein, Immanuel, *The Modern World-System: Capitalist Agriculture and the Origins of the European World Economy in the Sixteenth Century*, London: Academic Press, 1974. Path-breaking but highly debatable analysis on the origins of capitalism and should be read by those interested in this theme.

CHAPTER 6

European Economy in the Sixteenth Century

The sixteenth century in Europe has come to be known as the age of expansion that lasted till the beginning of the seventeenth century when another period of economic contraction and demographic decline set in. During this period the long-distance trade with Asia and Africa and the New World of America resulted in the shift of economic centre of Europe from the Mediterranean cities to the Atlantic coast of north-west Europe.

The economic history of Europe since the Middle Ages has shown distinct phases of growth and contraction. From the age of invasions in about AD 1000, which lasted till the early years of the fourteenth century, Europe experienced a long period of economic expansion. Population increased and with it grew the area under cultivation; a number of towns and cities emerged and this promoted trade. There was an overall growth of wealth during this period. This economic growth was later reversed and the Black Death brought a long period of misery to the Europeans. The last quarter of the fifteenth century saw the burgeoning of the European economy. The sixteenth century is regarded as a time of advancement – economic expansion, prosperity and demographic growth. Sea voyages were followed by the emergence of colonial empires that unfolded a new sphere for the Europeans. Colonies not only transformed the structure of trade but also introduced in the European markets a number of products, including sugar, silver and goods of common consumption on a bigger scale. The total volume of trade attained new heights. It overcame the traditional barriers of low consumption and high distribution costs. The enormous expansion of business activities and commercial transactions brought changes in the structure and organization of trade.

Rural Economy

The bulk of the rural population consisted of people dependent on land. Over four-fifths of the people lived and worked on land to earn their living. The rest consisted of craftsmen, traders, rentiers, nobles and churchmen. The rural workers generally produced goods for local consumption but increasing urbanization encouraged a small stream of rural products to reach towns, which included farm products, food grain, milk items, wool, skins and cattle. The agricultural surplus of the peasants was almost entirely appropriated by their masters through taxes and feudal dues. These masters were the seigneurs – both lay and ecclesiastical lords, as well as the newly emerging absolute rulers in some parts of Europe. The peasants were not left with sufficient income that could be used for land improvements. The only exception was the Low Countries, where some investment was made in land reclamation works by the commercially inclined segment of the population. Drainage and dyke-building made rapid progress along the coast of the North Sea. According to Wilhelm Abel, 44,000 hectares of land was reclaimed in Netherlands, between 1565 and 1615. In the eastern parts of Germany, the area of arable land increased eightfold between 1590 and 1650.

European agriculture did not undergo any significant change in most parts during the sixteenth century, despite an increase in total production. The general impression is that it was an unprogressive agriculture that changed little from the fourteenth century. A large part of cropland was under cereals. Wheat was considered the best bread crop but it was meant only for a very small segment of the population. It needed good soil and was cultivated in the Rhineland, the Limagne, in central Europe and in parts of Spain. A substitute of wheat called, spelt or dinkel was cultivated in southern Europe and in the Low Countries and had virtually replaced wheat in this region. For the majority of the population, it was not wheat but rye that was the basic food crop. It was cultivated in much of western, central, and eastern Europe, but Poland was the chief centre for its cultivation. The higher altitudes of the north as well as the Alpine region specialized in the cultivation of oats. A growing population throughout the sixteenth century pushed food prices up and put pressure on food supply. Efforts were made to increase production by enlarging the area under cultivation and by improving the yield. In areas where land was available in abundance, there was hardly any change in agricultural practices in the yield per acre. However, in some regions more intensive use of land was made, particularly in the Low Countries by relaxing medieval tenurial restrictions. The shortage of manure remained a major limitation in agriculture.

In the Alps, the Pyrenees and the higher mountains of eastern Europe pastoralism was the main occupation. In the territories beyond the corn-producing belt, animal-rearing was the primary occupation. A vast number of animals was supported in Scandinavia, in the plains of eastern Europe, Spain and the grasslands of the Balkan states. Northern Europe adopted dairy production and by the end of the century, milk products were reaching distant markets. Some rural areas in Europe witnessed regional specialization. Sheep and cattle farming became more organized in England, in the French Alps, in some parts of Italy and in Spain. At no other place was the seasonal migration of stock more highly organized than in Spain. Much of the grassland of Castile was turned into pastures for sheep. Their wool was sold not only at local fairs and in Medina del Campo but was sent to Flanders. In certain parts, even the peasant farmers who were generating an increased volume of marketable surplus felt the impact of commercialization. At most places, the farmers used the money from their market sales for buying goods of daily consumption not locally produced or spent it on paying taxes. According to Fernand Braudel, agriculture in the Mediterranean not only assured the people their everyday livelihood but provided a range of expensive goods for export, such as saffron, cumin, raisins, olive oil, besides, raw silk, citrus fruits and wine. However, no definite pattern of agriculture emerged in the Mediterranean comparable to that of the Low Countries. It remained, in the words of Braudel, 'a world of rigid structures' between peasants and landlords, and a large percentage of the agricultural product remained outside monetary economy.

Within the rural framework, the production of wine became a specialized economic activity in the course of the sixteenth century. Earlier, it was produced in scattered regions like the English Midlands, Flanders and Brandenburg but climatically these places were not suited for it. As wine production in southern France and the Mediterranean region was cheaper, it affected the fortune of the earlier centres located in Saxony, Pomerania and Prussia, where grain production for exports was becoming popular. Gradually south-western France, the regions around the Rhône and the Rhine and the coastal islands of the Mediterranean became the largest commercial centres of wine production.

Two factors restricted trade in farm products and commercialization of agriculture in most parts of Europe. One was the growing rural population that caused fragmentation of landholding and poverty in the rural areas. Braudel points out that after the waning of the Middle Ages, there was a progressive deterioration in the condition of the peasants. According to him, the peasants were not left with money to buy anything beyond cereals and consequently, meat consumption declined for a long period. The second factor was that the tenurial conditions restricted experiments and checked conversion of land for commercial produce. It was only in north-western Europe where the bourgeois landowners carried out successful experiments on land that led to beneficial changes in agriculture.

The upward movement of prices, the growing population pressure, the feudal wars of the fifteenth century and the expensive lifestyles of the nobility led to the gradual decline of the manorial system, at least in north-western Europe. The lords suffered as the peasants in the turbulent conditions of the later Middle Ages. Conditions of land tenure were changing rapidly in the early-sixteenth century. At many places, the *demesne* lands belonging to the manorial lords and cultivated by peasant labour, were broken up and leased in small tenancies and labour dues were commuted for a rent in money or in kind. Under new conditions, the form of tenure called *métayage* was adopted on a wide scale. In this system, the lord provided the land, seeds and equipment to the cultivator and in return claimed a part of the crop, sometimes as much as two-thirds. This type of tenure became widespread in France and Italy. In many other places, land was leased for a specific period of time at a fixed annual rent and often with some servile obligations on tenant farmers. In some commercially advanced regions, unfavourable conditions forced the traditional landlords to alienate at least part of their lands. Some of the ambitious members of the peasantry bought land on favourable terms or became tenants on very advantageous terms and on long lease. They later emerged as a class of rich peasants, called yeomen. In some cases, the lands around the cities or market centres were bought by the rising urban bourgeoisie hoping to enter the status of landed gentry.

Most of the landownership at the beginning of the sixteenth century rested in the hands of either the lay aristocracy or the church. There also existed large estates but most of these were acquired through confiscation of monastic lands. In the Protestant states of Germany, in Scandinavia and the Swiss cantons, the ownership of church lands changed frequently and passed into lay hands. On the other hand, land in Spain and particularly in southern Meseta, was concentrated in the hands of the religious orders through the policy of *Reconquista.* Nevertheless, in western and southern Europe with the exception of Spain, the tendency was to break-up large estates for tenant farming and for the conversion of labour services into money rent. An opposite trend can be observed in eastern and east-central Europe. In Poland, Hungary and Bohemia, the labour dues of the peasants increased substantially and their mobility was severely restricted in the course of the sixteenth century. Independent holdings of the peasants were seized by the lords and added to the *demesne* farms. Free peasantry was reduced to the status of serfs and many writers describe this trend as the 'second serfdom'. A number of explanations are provided by historians. Jerome Blum attributes these developments to political and social conditions of this region, particularly the weakness of the central authority and the complete dependence of the rulers in these states on feudal nobility. This enabled the nobles to concentrate all powers in their own hands. Marian Malowist links these changes to growing demands of the west European markets for foodstuff. With the rising prices of agricultural products, a shortage of food supply in western Europe, and a growing population, the profit margin appears to be the determining force behind this trend.

A large number of books on agriculture appeared in Italy, England, France, and Germany in the course of the sixteenth century. Martin Grosser, Johann Coler and Conrad Heresbach in Germany, Olivier de Serres and Jean Libault in France and Anthony Fitzherbert and Thomas Tusser in England wrote major works on agriculture and animal husbandry. Tusser's book went through thirteen editions. This suggests that an enthusiastic readership existed for agronomical writings in the sixteenth century.

Slicher van Bath has studied Dutch agriculture exhaustively. He points out to the three types of crop-rotation that emerged in the Netherlands during the sixteenth century. One form was the rotations of several crops. This led to an end of the practice of keeping the land fallow to the fourth, fifth or even sixth year. The second form was of cultivating grain for two years followed by one fallow year and three to six years of grazing. The third was of crop rotation with fodder crop grown in the fallow year. This foreshadows the English crop-rotation system of the eighteenth century. These forms were gradually adopted in the eastern regions as well. However, the new farming methods could not meet the rapidly growing urban demand for food in the Netherlands and the Baltic grain met this shortfall.

In England, the practice of land-enclosure was being followed in the fifteenth century, which gained momentum in the early sixteenth century. This was associated with a shift from arable farming to extensive grazing. The falling grain prices and the rising expenses of agricultural overheads in the fifteenth century had led to an extensive livestock farming. It is estimated that in the period 1485–1607, on an average 21.1 per cent of the cultivated area in the Midland was enclosed (John E. Martin). However, by the 1550s, the growing profit margin in corn in relation to wool, the popular opposition to the enclosure movement and the government stand against enclosures reversed the trend in favour of corn production (Abel). After the mid-sixteenth century, rents on arable lands rose more rapidly than the rents on meadows and pastures. With this, cattle breeding shifted from England towards Ireland.

For a long time historians concentrated only on the urban crafts in the overall economy but the importance of the non-farming section of the population in the rural economy cannot be ignored. A number of crafts existed in the countryside to meet local demand. Such crafts had existed for centuries but what distinguishes the sixteenth century from the earlier period was the spread of cottage industry in the countryside. Many new towns, for lack of space for industrial production, or for reasons of raw materials or availability of energy (water/fuel) or due to labour problems were shifting production to the neighbouring villages. These included foundries, oil, stone and grain and saw-mills, paper works, refineries, mining activities and many others. Such rural industries were spread across Europe but these were more visible in England and northern Europe. Usually a whole group of rural centres came under the control of urban merchants. These clusters of villages became the chief centres of the new variety of cheap textiles and silk that began dominating the urban markets of distant regions.

Thus, in the words of Ruggiero Romano, agriculture remained 'sensitive to price rises and to demographic expansion'. The price rise secured the increased value of crops and land, while the population growth guaranteed a good market and the labour to increase production. In the absence of technological advancement, this growth of agriculture was obtained by bringing more land under cultivation. European agriculture expanded enormously by utilizing waste lands, marshes, forest lands, and reclamation projects and by intensive cultivation. The expansion of trade encouraged regional specialization to utilize the relative advantages of each area. The situation was not the same everywhere and the gap between regions began to widen from the sixteenth century.

Urban Economy

The early-sixteenth century is considered a decisive period for the expansion of urban industry. There were intimate links between sixteenth-century agriculture and industry. As Coleman points out, much of the industry of the time consisted of the direct processing of agricultural products to meet the basic needs of life. Industries remained labour-intensive rather than capital-intensive. Not many changes can be seen in the system of manufacturing during the sixteenth century when compared with the Middle Ages. Technology remained the same but the structure and organization witnessed slight modification. However, the real transformation had to wait till the last decades of the eighteenth century. Except for mining and to a certain extent, metallurgy, units of production remained small and were more like petty workshops employing a handful of artisans. The ratio of capital to labour was also minimal in most of the manufacturing units.

A steady population growth from the mid-fifteenth century increased the demand for basic commodities although the labour market remained depressed. This was due to the increased availability of labour. In many parts of Europe, wages fell far behind the rising prices and many scholars suggest that the real income of the artisan classes become lower than at any time since the thirteenth century. An abundant supply of labour discouraged innovation and introduction of labour-saving devices. The feudal structure, a steady inflation, problems of transportation and the low purchasing power of the masses were the major impediments in the development of mass industries. Nevertheless, from the point of view of industrial expansion, J.F. Neff refers to the sixteenth century as a period of industrial revolution. He gave three arguments for this: (a) coal production increased fourteen times, from 17,000 tons annually in the 1550s to 25,00,000 tons by the 1680s, which facilitated the growth of towns and shipbuilding, (b) it led to the rise of the iron industry, and (c) it introduced felxible methods and new technologies of production. Most scholars do not accept this view and object to the term 'revolution', as no fundamental change can be seen either in technology or in the organization and processes of manufacturing. There was a phase of vigorous growth from the mid-sixteenth century in certain parts of Europe, particularly in the production of metals and minerals. Iron production expanded enormously with the introduction of the blast furnace and it promoted a number of other industries such as armament, brass and copper ware and glass. Textile production also increased and with it products like alum and dyestuffs. This economic growth began to slow down by the early part of the seventeenth century because of state restrictions in the form of mercantilist policies, declining trends of population and falling prices. In France, the state laws, particularly in 1581 and 1597, prevented the merchants from keeping in stock larger stores of raw materials than what was actually required, controlled the conduct of craft guilds and created monopolies for the manufacture of several luxury products. The southern states of the Netherlands were seriously affected by the war against the Spanish rule and the closure of the Scheldt River. Only in the north of the United Provinces of the Netherlands (formed after becoming independent of Spanish rule), economic progress continued till the late seventeenth century.

The textile industries, with the exception of agriculture, employed the largest number of people throughout the sixteenth century. It also produced goods of greater total value than any other sector of industry. During this period, the industry witnessed some significant trends in organization. As an urban craft, it continued to depend on skilled artisans working in their own homes or in workshops. It was kept under the regulations of the traditional guilds and as such there was hardly any possibility of such workshops adopting new technology or carrying out innovations. Another trend was in the direction of the transfer of textile production to the rural countryside. This organization provided part-time employment to the rural workers. Spinning, thus become virtually a rural occupation even for the urban weavers who began to depend on its supply from the neighbouring villages. It provided an additional income to the rural population particularly in England, Germany and the Netherlands. It helped in bringing about agricultural prosperity. The textile industries of Europe were producing different varieties of cloth such as woollens, linen, cotton, mixed materials and some luxury fabrics.

In the Low Countries, Flanders was an important textile manufacturing centre till the early sixteenth century when the traditional broad cloth industry declined and was replaced by the rise of 'new draperies'. However, around 1540, even this prosperity vanished and from 1560s, the textile industry was completely ruined by continuous warfare. The shrinking market and uncertain political situation were responsible for the collapse of the industry. The decline of the Flemish cloth industry led to the industrial rise of Brabant in the east and Holland in the north. Some of the skilled workers migrated to the new centres at the outbreak of the war against Spain in 1568 and the division of the Low Countries into the United Provinces independent of Spanish control and the Spanish-controlled states in the south led to the rise of the Netherlands. Till this period, the industries in the United Provinces of the Netherlands had been catering only to local demand. The most important textile centre was located at Leiden, which became one of the leading centres of cloth production in Europe by the seventeenth century. Workshops in this city emerged employing up to twenty artisans and spinning Spanish wool. This industry was dependent on imported raw materials and on the export market for the sale of finished products. The rise of a similar industry in England and the English prohibition of wool export seriously affected the serge and worsted varieties of Leiden.

Woollen industries had developed in France and the Low Countries during the Middle Ages. On the other side, linen production was going on in central Europe. During the sixteenth century, immigration of skilled artisans from the Low Countries and state-sponsored policies led to the spread of the woollen industry up to Saxony. However, the real growth took place only in the eighteenth century. In Bohemia and Silesia, linen was manufactured under the old form of organization but from the mid-seventeenth century, this production actually expanded when its organization was taken over by the merchant capitalists.

Northern Italy, Tuscany and Catalonia were the major textile centres of the medieval period. They declined during the fifteenth century and then recovered for a brief period during the sixteenth century before disappearing subsequently. Although Spain produced the best quality wool, the guilds placed serious restrictions on its growth. The Italian city states were known for their cloth industry and had markets all over Europe. The northern regions of Italy had a vast population of weavers and artisans. Silk weaving formed an important part of manufacturing activity and this craft was popular in many parts of Italy and Spain. It was the most difficult branch of the textile industry as silk production was a long and cumbersome one. The silk worm is a delicate creature and needs a lot of care. As the mulberry tree needed a specific climate and required seasonal care only, a huge labour force could not be kept occupied throughout the year. This sector needed capital investment and its markets were small and highly elastic. This industry was confined to only specific parts of Europe. During the sixteenth century, Venice emerged as an important centre but its industry continued to decline from the late-sixteenth century. Outside Italy, Lyons in France and Zurich in Switzerland gained immensely by the arrival of the French Huguenots and refugees from the Low Countries, many of them were skilled craftsmen and entrepreneurs. From here, silk weaving areas developed in other regions like Geneva, Basil, Tours and the northern areas of France. State sponsorship played an important role in the emergence of the silk industry.

There was an expansion of manufacturing and mining activities throughout the sixteenth century but these did not result in the factory system of production. Although the volume of trade had grown, there was a rise in population and a steady increase of prices; Europe lacked the mass demand for manufactured goods as most of Europe was still under the grip of feudalism. There was a shortage of capital for investment and the concept of management remained imperfect. The state structure in most of the states had grown within feudal parameters and at many places, including England and France, the government had placed restrictions on new forms of organization and technology. Capital-intensive methods were rejected and state laws favoured the continuation of guilds. Despite such restrictions, the manufacturing sector tried to escape these regulations by shifting their industrial activities to rural areas, leading to the emergence of rural cottage industry in those parts where capitalist elements began to dominate production. The first signs of industrial transformation could be noticed here.

Sixteenth century in Europe is considered important by economic historians because it marked the rise of the Atlantic economy caused by the shift in the trade belt and trade routes because of the colonial empires. The long established trade routes from Asia to Europe through Constantinople via Genoa or Venice lost their importance with the discovery of new oceanic trade routes thereby favouring the economies of the states bordering the Atlantic coast. The first sign of this change can be observed in the rise of Antwerp in the Low Countries.

The Rise and Decline of Antwerp

According to Fernand Braudel, 'the career of Antwerp, although comparatively brief, nevertheless represents an important and in some ways original episode in the history of capitalism' (*The Perspective of the World*). The rise and decline of the port-cities in Europe was closely associated with the importance of trade routes, which continued to change because of political, economic and geographical factors. The rise of Antwerp is one such example. Antwerp replaced Bruges on the Atlantic coast and Venice on the Mediterranean and later it was itself replaced by Amsterdam, the capital city of the Netherlands. Antwerp was located in the Low Countries (the present Belgium and Holland). With the formation of the Portuguese and the Spanish colonial empires the trade route from the Mediterranean cities shifted to the Atlantic coast. As Antwerp was located at a central position on the Scheldt River, it was destined to play a leading role in the commercial world of Europe.

There were several contributing factors for the rise of Antwerp, which indirectly signified the rise of the Atlantic economy. During the sixteenth century, the city came to be described as the 'commercial capital of the world'. The boom for Antwerp began towards the end of the fifteenth century, when the Venetian merchants lost their monopoly over the spice trade of Asia to the Portuguese. The first sign of this change could be seen in 1501, when the Portuguese ships laden with pepper and cinnamon, reached Antwerp. In 1508, the Portuguese ruler established a branch of Lisbon's *Casa da India* at Antwerp called *Feitoria de Flandres*. The close trading relationship between the Portuguese and the south-German merchants was established at Antwerp. In order to sustain the spice trade with Asia (the Asians showed no inclination for European goods) the European began paying for this trade in gold or silver. The Portuguese needed copper and metal goods from the Germans in order to purchase silver from the central European mines. Thus, the Germans began to exploit the copper mines of Hungary and started financing the Portuguese trade in the Indies. Most of these Portuguese investments were in the hands of the Fugger families (the German bankers) and this has led historians to suggest that 'the age of the Fuggers was the age of Antwerp'. Antwerp became the chief mart for German goods at the beginning of the sixteenth century and it also benefited from its trade with England. The English company of Merchant Adventurers established a staple in the city for its wool, where it was stored and sold in other parts of Europe. The English exports to Antwerp doubled between 1500 and 1540. From the north came the agricultural products, grain from the Baltic, wines from France, cheese from Gouda, fish and seafood from Zeeland, merino wool from Spain and many other products from the American colonies. The markets of Antwerp were bustling with life and the number of foreign merchants constituted almost 15 per cent of the total population. In fact, Antwerp had become an important centre of re-export trade as all principal trade routes met here. The importance of Antwerp prevented the Portuguese capital, Lisbon (despite enjoying several advantages) from becoming the chief commercial centre. Antwerp also gained immensely by being a part of the vast Spanish empire. Spain sent not only wool to Antwerp but also many oversees products such as cochineal from Mexico, American dye-woods and sugar from the Canaries Islands and received through Antwerp, numerous products from northern Europe, like timber beams, tar, ship parts, wheat and other agricultural items from the Baltic and manufactured goods like linen and woollens. The deficit caused by greater imports was met by the export of American silver to Antwerp. Thus the rise of Antwerp took place largely because of the Portuguese and German connections and later because of the Spanish trade.

In its ascendancy, Antwerp gained from its close link with the German traders and bankers. The investment of Germans was at the expense of Venitians as the Germans had started diverting copper and silver from Venice to Lisbon on a large scale. According to van der Wee, as quoted by Braudel, 24 per cent of the Hungarian copper had been sent by the Fuggers to Antwerp in 1502–3, which had gone up to 49 per cent by 1508–9 while the share of Venice had come down to just 13 per cent. The German exports of silver to the Portuguese proved beneficial to Antwerp. A number of German commercial firms had started establishing their branch offices at Antwerp. The Meutings (1479), the Hochstetters (1486) and the Welsers (1509) were the important firms besides the house of Fuggers. The latter made huge profits from its commercial transactions with Antwerp. The wholesale and retail trade was an important aspect of the economy in this city. Many important business firms maintained permanent halls or display centres of their industrial products.

The rise of Antwerp was also because it was an extremely important centre of banking and commercial activities. By the late-fifteenth century, Antwerp had developed two bourses – the old one was called the Wool Street and it dealt primarily with trade in goods and commodities, while the new bourse was built in 1531 chiefly as a financial centre. Here the foreign investors were involved in various types of speculative activities. It was speculation and financial transactions, which drew foreign consortiums to conduct their business. It is estimated that the capital transactions in the mid-sixteenth century averaged about 4,00,00,000 ducats a year. Loans were arranged at short notice and several rulers, including the King of Portugal and Queen Elizabeth of England, borrowed big amounts from Antwerp. The big syndicates and banking houses handled such loans. The cities and provinces of Netherlands also sold bonds. It was not uncommon to see some frauds or bankruptcies caused by the intrusion of fake bankers or financiers, e.g. the case of Gaspar Ducci. In the early part of the sixteenth century, speculation was carried out on pepper and grain trade, which often gave high returns. However, most of the merchants followed conventional and safer avenues for their investments or borrowings. Although Antwerp had not yet developed the modern form of banking, those instruments of credit such as bills of exchange, promissory notes and accounting methods, which were in vogue in the Italian cities, were adopted and elaborated. The European overseas expansion had greatly increased the scope of international trade and stimulated far-reaching changes in business organizations and its methods. These proved favourable for the development of capitalism in Europe.

S.T. Bindoff mentions four main conditions which governed the conduct of international trade at Antwerp: the technique of the trade itself; the conditions upon which the various 'nations' were admitted; the regime of the two town fairs; and the state policy (*The New Cambridge Modern History*, vol. II). The growth of trade promoted finishing industries like the textile industry. In 1564, the clothiers' guild alone had 1,600 masters and apprentices. Antwerp had already adopted business techniques like double-entry book-keeping, credit instruments and the new modes of payment. The city authorities had made the conditions quite liberal as is evident from the terms of entry offered to the English merchants in 1446. In Brabant four market fairs were held annually, each of two weeks duration, later these were increased to six weeks each.

The rise and growth of Antwerp, according to Braudel, passed through three significant phases. The first started with the Portuguese participation in this region. The ruler of Lisbon established close commercial links with the merchants of Germany such as Welsers and Hochstetters, who were in control of silver production in central Europe. The second phase of expansion is attributed to the Spanish participation and the supply of silver from America between 1535 and 1557. The last phase coincided with the return of peace after the Treaty of Cateau-Cambrésis (1559) and the growth of industry in Antwerp and the Netherlands during a brief period from 1559 to 1568. This period marked the withdrawal of the Portuguese, English and Spanish commercial involvement from Antwerp. From this period the focus shifted to industry. Since the capital available was sufficiently large which could not be fully utilized in trade or government loans, it was invested in small workshops. This resulted in the expansion of some industries such as linen, tapestry making and textile. Antwerp had specialized in the finishing and dyeing of cloth, in sugar refining, soap making and in the production of glass and majolica ware. Antwerp was one of the most important centres of printing industry. Plantins was the famous printing house in that period that produced books and pamphlets on a large scale. Unfortunately, the industrial expansion could not last long as widespread disturbances dislocated the economic activities in the Netherlands and directly affected the fortunes of Antwerp.

Antwerp's success story did not last too long. In fact, Antwerp had reached its apogee by the middle of the sixteenth century. It had become the heart of the market economy not only of Europe but also of international trade. No city of Europe had played such a dominant role in the European economic life. Just as the rise of Antwerp was caused by external factors, its decline was largely the result of events taking place outside it. The decline was as sudden as was its rise. Antwerp had certain disadvantages from the beginning but because of the prosperous trade these did not surface in the early part of the sixteenth century. No powerful king ruled Antwerp. A few Aldermen families, who were from landed aristocracy, monopolized power. Antwerp never had a powerful group of merchants of its own, enjoying international status. Throughout the period of its rise, the foreigners such as the English and the Hanseatic traders, German commercial firms and the merchants from France, Portugal, Spain and Italy dominated Antwerp. The city did not have a powerful navy to defend its trade. The rise of this city was closely bound with foreign trade but it was carried out in the ships of Holland, Portugal, Spain, England and Zeeland. It was the melting point of foreign traders that had made her fortune. Antwerp had succeeded in attracting merchants from diverse regions and faiths because of a large measure of toleration on the religious front. However, the rise of Antwerp was succeeded by a major religious turmoil in most parts of Europe, which seriously created disorder and adversely affected the trade routes. There were economic, political and social factors, which contributed to the sudden decline of Antwerp.

While Antwerp was at its zenith by the 1560s, economic problems had already started, which contributed to its rapid decline. In 1549, the Portuguese found that they could get silver more easily and cheaper from Spain and they decided to withdraw their spice monopoly from Antwerp. The Germans on the other hand turned directly to Lisbon and Venice. However, they found the competition from American silver rather tough. The cost of production of maintaining the silver mines in the German region was also proving too high. This was followed by the problems that Antwerp faced from England. The devaluation of silver was carried out in 1550 by the English government. Consequently the Merchant Adventurers exported a record quantity of clothes to Antwerp, which caused a temporary glut in the market. The following year, there was revaluation of the sterling in England, resulting in sudden rise in the price of textile. Antwerp trade could not recover for over a decade and then new types of problems emerged. The Spanish imports also declined because of an economic slump and the war between the emperor (of the Holy Roman Empire) and France in 1552 made the situation difficult. Crop failure in western Europe in 1555–6 led to a rise in grain prices. The European states had to pay three to four times the normal price for imported grain from the Baltic and they fell into massive debts. The war between France and Spain had complicated the situation for Antwerp. By 1557, all the debts were turned into state bonds, called *jeros* by the Spanish government. The French and the Portuguese governments adopted similar measures to postpone the payment of debts. This caused a major European financial crisis and as the economy of Antwerp to a large extent depended on financial trading, the consequences were serious for them. Although commercial and trading activities continued, Antwerp could not fully recover from these events. One of the important reasons for the decline of Antwerp was related to the prolonged war of independence of the Netherlands against the Spanish rule. It started in 1566 and continued intermittently till 1648. The Netherlands rebellions eventually split the country into two halves – the southern half remained under Spanish rule that included the city of Antwerp, while the seven provinces of the north proclaimed independence and formed the United Provinces of the

Netherlands. In course of this long struggle, the mercenary soldiers of Spain twice sacked Antwerp in 1576 and 1583 for not receiving their payments. The worst was still to follow when in 1585 the Spanish forces captured Antwerp and forced the Protestants to leave the city. As the economy of the Netherlands was controlled and run by a large number of Protestants, the exodus of the Protestants seriously hampered the commercial activities of the city. The frequent wars and political disturbances resulted in the closing of the Scheldt and the eventual decline of Antwerp. The loss of Antwerp was the gain of Amsterdam.

In France, the rulers preferred to develop their own commercial centres within the country rather than depend on borrowed money from a foreign city. For this purpose they promoted Lyon, an important city located in central France. In the medieval period, fairs had been organized at Champagne. From the fifteenth century the French kings, particularly Charles VII, decided to develop Lyons as the chief financial and trading centre and granted special privileges and freedom to the city. The French merchants were prohibited from participating in the Geneva fairs and instead were advised to participate in the Lyon's fairs. Every year four such fairs were organized for a fortnight each. Soon merchants from Italy and southern Germany began to participate in the financial transactions and commercial dealings and loans were arranged at the rate of about 10 per cent, which compared well with the financial lendings at Antwerp. The French rulers borrowed money from Lyons and the public from other neighbouring places had started investing here. However, the prosperity of Lyon started declining with the rise of Paris as the new centre of France.

The Rise of England

With the early sea voyages and the formation of colonial empires under Portugal and Spain by the first half of the sixteenth century, the centre of economic activities shifted from the Italian city states to the Atlantic coast. Land trade routes began to lose importance with the expansion of the Ottoman empire in eastern Europe and the new oceanic trade route gained popularity. The centre of economic activities shifted to the countries located on the Atlantic coast, where trade from different parts of Europe converged. This led to the rapid rise of England and Holland as important economic powers.

The second quarter of the sixteenth century witnessed many religious and political confrontations in continental Europe. It caused an influx of people from the main continent to England including the artisans from Flanders, who specialized in textile production and the metallurgist from Germany. They promoted manufacturing activities in England, where the feudal structure had already started declining from the late-fifteenth century. No technical breakthrough was achieved during the sixteenth century nor was the pace of transformation revolutionary, but England witnessed a steady economic growth throughout the sixteenth century except for a brief period of market recession in the early 1550s. The chief areas of economic growth were to be seen in agriculture, manufacturing and trade. The process of change, which had started during the sixteenth century, resulted in bringing about the Industrial Revolution by the end of the eighteenth century.

It is important to note that the shift of the trade belt from the Mediterranean to the Atlantic coast was not the only factor responsible for the rise of England, although she benefited immensely from this change. The dynamics of change in England was located within her economy and society, which had started showing signs of progress and change even before the colonial empires had emerged in the New World and in Asia. The beginning of change can be seen in the demographic growth and the price revolution. Compared to other countries of Western Europe where the population growth was not so quick, the population of England and Wales more than doubled between 1500 and 1700, and almost quadrupled by 1800. The total population of the British Isles stood at about 3.5 million at the beginning of the sixteenth century and reached nearly 16 million by the end of the eighteenth century. The rate of growth was fastest in the late-sixteenth century, which stood at 5.6 per cent increase per decade between 1570 and 1600, 5.5 per cent between 1600 and 1630 and only 0.8 per cent between 1630 and 1670 whereas the mid-seventeenth-century period is regarded as the time of demographic decline or stagnation in most parts of Europe. The growing population itself continued to outpace production and the prices continued to rise. In the early-sixteenth century, only 7 per cent of the population lived in towns with over 2,000 inhabitants. By 1640, the ratio went up to 10 per cent. The debasement of the coinage and the influx of bullion from the New World via Spain contributed to the Price Revolution. Its impact was not confined to England alone but it affected entire Europe. The 1520s saw a sharp rise in prices that continued till mid-1540s. After fluctuating sharply, the prices were 75 per cent above those prevailing around 1475. From the 1560s, there was a fresh burst of price hike and by the beginning of the seventeenth century, food grain prices were almost 500 per cent higher than those prevailing in the early-sixteenth century. The magnitude of the price rise and the steady rise in population set in motion forces of change. It also promoted industrial and trading activities on a new scale. Demographic growth resulted in gradual urbanization, thereby putting pressure on agricultural production and creating a growing demand for consumer products.

Rise of Capitalist Agriculture

The Black Death of the fourteenth century was followed by a steady decline in villienage. The foreign and civil wars along with the gradual complexity of trade became social solvents that brought the disintegration of old social order. At the top of the social hierarchy stood the nobles, the bishops and senior abbots. Below them stood the knights and country gentlemen, who were lower in social order but enjoyed greater numerical strength. The balance between these two had changed after the Black Death. During the sixteenth century, the traditional land arrangement also changed. The original form of direct labour and payments in kind were converted or commuted into money payment. The lower orders gained greater freedom and security over land. The internal wars and the executions carried out by the early Tudor government considerably weakend the traditional nobility. The church also experienced reduced authority and income. The decline of the great magnets was an important change in rural society. It marked the beginning of a gradual but steady rise of yeomen. They had once been villiens and were bound by manorial lords to render labour service and were subjected to numerous restrictions. However, by the late-fifteenth century they all became nearly free and began possessing small holdings of land on payment or by custom of the manor, taking wages for the work they performed and became equal subjects in the king's court. The term cannot be strictly defined but generally yeomen ranked next to gentlemen. Though Karl Marx applied this term to the economic category of 'peasants', it is indicative of the substantive men with some security of tenure. A yeoman was a freeholder and owed no other service except the payment of rent. Most yeomen worked large farms and employed labour as servants or day labourers, and by the middle of the seventeenth century, became more proto-capitalist farmers than peasants, though they were more likely to do physical work on their farms than the gentlemen. They were less educated than the gentlemen but played an important role in the community life of the sixteenth century as churchwarden of parishes, overseers of poor relief, and jurymen. The agrarian changes in the sixteenth century had led to an increase in their numbers and economic strength. In the period of price rise it seems that the farmers, yeomen and the lesser landlords were the first to develop the bourgeois qualities of thrift and their ability to rack-rent, operate according to the market situation and take an interest in profit-making in the agrarian sphere.

Among the lower rungs of rural population, husbandmen constituted almost half the farming section. For several others, such as cottages and labourers, land they owned was not sufficient for them to survive and they had to find alternative ways to supplement their income. Gregory King, a well-known statistician of the late-seventeenth century mentions that their number was growing in the last century and a half and formed over half the farming population. In the early-sixteenth century, their proportion was about one-third of the farming population.

The sixteenth century was a period of commercialization in agriculture. The price revolution created problems for the traditional landlords but offered new opportunities for many of the new landlords and subsistence farmers. There were several factors that promoted commercialization of agriculture in England. The enclosure of land was carried out to enable the landlord to earn profit by evicting peasants and to fully utilize the productive capacity of the land. Many landlords discovered that the price of wool was rising in the European market and they switched from grain cultivation to sheep farming by converting their land into pastures. The rising population had pushed the prices of farm products. According to Bowden, there was a sudden forward leap between 1570 and 1640 in the volume, organization and impact of agricultural trading in the English economy. Increasing demand for food promoted internal colonization in Cumberland, Westmoreland and south-western England. The pressure of demand led to the cultivation of common land and wasteland and even royal forests. Large-scale migrations of surplus labour took place from open villages to forest settlements such as in Gloucestershire and Worcestershire. The expansion of the wool-growing regions in the newly enclosed lands had become a common feature as sheep farming had been encouraged by high prices of wool till the 1620s. As John E. Martin points out, wool had a high value for its weight and it was a cheap commodity to transport and this made sheep grazing especially attractive to many capitalist farmers who were not able to profit from the extra-regional market for grain.

There are divergent views on the rise or decline of different agrarian segments during the sixteenth and seventeenth centuries. R.H. Tawney suggests that the middle and lower members of the landowning class, termed as the gentry, rose to economic significance during this period by their active participation in the land market. It had been caused by the sale of crown and monastic lands during the period of Reformation in the 1530s. This marked the introduction of new capitalist methods in agriculture. The traditional aristocracy declined because their income depreciated in the period of inflation. Trevor-Roper disagrees with Tawney and does not find major differences in the estate-management of the two groups. For him, the possibility of earning large profits from agriculture was not there. Rather, the profits were made due to their close connections with the court. Lawrence Stone suggests that the massive land sales at the turn of the century are reflective of the serious financial difficulties, which the aristocracy faced in the mid-sixteenth century onwards. According to him, during the seventeenth century this group recovered partially because they adopted new methods of estate management and because of their close relations with monarchy and its court. Christopher Hill argues that these were essentially legal and social groups and not economic classes and members from both sections of gentry and aristocracy rose or fell. It was not that the rise of one section led to the fall of another. The period from 1500 to 1640 saw a rise in agricultural prices by almost 600 per cent, and in this many small landowners, such as the gentry and yeomanry adopted new forms of tenure and rent and participated in market operations in order to increase their income. The entry of successful yeomen into the ranks of the gentry provided a solid basis to this group. The sixteenth century offered chances of making money through land investment and production for the market. Those who made significant land purchases after the Reformation became gentlemen. By 1600, the new and the old type of 'gentlemen' occupied a far-greater proportion of land in England than what they possessed in 1530, to the disadvantage of the crown, church, traditional aristocracy and small peasantry. The inflationary situation enabled them to increase their income in numerous ways. Land was increasingly used for market production and thereby it not only transformed the agrarian relations but also contributed to the expansion of manufacturing activities by generating rural income. However, this process of transformation was much more complex and indirect.

From the late-fifteenth century to the 1640s, no important breakthrough had taken place in arable farming methods but it was the scale of commercial practices that brought about the transformation. The possibility of higher profit encouraged some farmers to introduce new crops such as tobacco (from 1571) in places like Gloucestershire and East Anglia and dyestuff in Kent. Artificial grasses, turnips and carrots were increasingly grown as new fodder crops. Potato as a food crop came from America and was actually introduced around 1585 and was later grown on a large scale after the colonization of Ireland. It is difficult to know whether the coming of new literature on farming made any contribution in the promotion of Agrarian practices despite enjoying good readership. No doubt, its contribution appears significant from the second half of the seventeenth century. Probably the first known farming manual was printed in 1523, *Boke of Husbandrye* written by John Fitzherbert. Subsequent literature was based on a detailed observation of experiments carried out in farming practices but it must have had a very limited number of readers. The major success of English agriculture was due to its reorganization in the capitalist direction. It was a movement away from subsistence farming towards commercialized agriculture. Many important regions like the Thames Valley, Kent and Suffolk started feeling the pressure of the growing urban demand. The presence of a large population living in neighbouring towns offered opportunities for agricultural specialization. This was given a further stimulus by the price revolution.

Expansion of Manufacturing Activities

Sixteenth-century England saw people taking greater interest in manufacturing, particularly textiles. An interesting aspect of the industrial expansion was that it was accompanied by comparatively little industrial reorganization. The Tudor kings generally adopted policies which were restrictive and aimed at preventing rapid development of capitalist relations. Nevertheless, industrial development continued in the capitalist direction despite government checks. A law was passed against gig mills in 1551–2. The Weavers Act of 1555 forbade country cloth merchants to own more than one loom, while weavers could not own more than two. The objective was to keep textile manufacturing within the confines of the towns. The Statute of Artificers of 1563 established guild control over the manufacturing sector. This was also an attempt to prolong the old form of urban organization by excluding people from joining the skilled profession unless they had undergone a seven-year apprenticeship. Even the Stuart government continued those restrictions. In 1624, the government carried out the destruction of needle-making machines. In 1633, casting of brass buckles was prohibited and in 1635, orders were issued against the use of windmill for sawing wood. Effective implementation of these policies would have caused serious damage to the industrial development of England but the Justices of Peace, who came from the same social background as the gentlemen and the merchants, did not properly implement these measures. In the absence of a professional bureaucracy in England, the rulers had to depend on the Justices of Peace. Parliament also resisted many government rules, as was the case in 1624 on the question of dispersal of industry to the countryside.

Textiles constituted the most important production and employment generation sector. Although there was no major technological breakthrough, the sixteenth century witnessed a continuous growth in textile production. The most important development was the spread of worsted cloth. It had become the chief occupation of the Flemish industry till the early sixteenth century but it started gaining ground in south-eastern England during the second half of the sixteenth century. This was primarily caused by the coming of Flemish and Walloon refugees. According to Ralph Davis, this change had become necessary, as the quality of wool had improved with the introduction of new varieties. The market for the cheaper varieties of old heavy cloths was lost to these worsteds. However, worsted was not the only fabric that recorded growth. The production of coarse linen of Lancashire increased because of the Irish supplies of flax and yarn made out of it but this product remained heavily dependent on imports. Fustian (thick coarse cotton cloth) was a variety primarily produced in Holland and Germany but it was slowly introduced in England. A major change was seen in the hosiery sector that included the knitting of stockings. The manufacturing sector prospered because knitting had become a source of supplementary income for a large number of rural families. The popularity of this industry in Nottinghamshire encouraged William Lees to invent a knitting frame in 1589. Its introduction in the industrial sector was opposed for the fear of causing unemployment among the rural population. Another invention in the early sixteenth century in the textile sector was the gig mill which probably came from the continent. It was a water-powered device used by a shearer to raise the nap. Many shearers could not afford it because it required heavy capital investment. A strong reaction against it by the shearers led to its prohibition in 1551 and then again in 1633.

According to Wallerstein, the English textile industry had developed two very important features by the sixteenth century. First, it had become more of a rural industry; and secondly it led England to a search for an export market. Marian Malowist suggests that the recession of the fourteenth and the fifteenth centuries had caused a sharp reduction in agricultural income. This led to the creation of the rural textile industry which supplemented the income of the families dependent on agriculture. The creation of rural industries had several benefits. It avoided the high wages imposed by guilds in towns and had the advantage of utilizing cheaper waterpower to run the fulling mills. Rural industries produced cheaper varieties of textiles which were within the reach of the impoverished nobility and other ordinary people. The urban decline was more than compensated by the rise of the rural industry. William Stumpe and Jack of Newbury made attempts to bring the weavers out of their cottages so that they could work at one place like a modern factory. However, they failed and cloth manufacturing continued to be organized on a domestic basis. From the mid-fifteenth century, locally manufactured products in the form of textiles replaced the export of raw wool. Textiles thus became the hub of the English exports.

Some other manufacturing activities also grew during the sixteenth century. While the old industries usually expanded, several new manufactures developed dealing in items such as glass, copper, brass and luxury fabrics. The political stability provided by the Tudor government and the absence of regular wars helped the expansion of industries.

Industrialization was not confined to the textile sector. Change and development was visible in other industrial fields. The best instance of rapid industrial progress was seen in coal mining. From 1540 to 1640, coal production shot up from 2,00,000 tons to about 20,00,000 tons. From an ordinary economic activity, coal mining almost became an industry. The principal reason for its growth was the increasing shortage of wood brought on by population pressure. Coal deposits were located in many parts of England. Since coal is a heavy item, its transportation would have been fairly expensive in the absence of modern modes of transport. In England, this problem was solved to a great extent by navigable rivers like the Thames, Severn and Trent. The discovery of coal deposits not only brought great relief to the English people it also created an important base for the large-scale industrial transformation in the eighteenth century. As mining was a capital-intensive activity, it required heavy investments and thereby created favourable conditions for the growth of capitalism.

Like coal mines, the iron industry also developed on a distinctively capitalist direction. The blast furnace was already known in other parts of Europe, particularly in Germany. It was probably introduced in England in 1496. Although the exact details of production are not available, it can be said with certainty that by 1640 there was a marked growth in the output of English iron. The need for iron increased with increasing warfare, which required weapons. The metal-working trades increased in the Birmingham region. In 1568, a joint stock company was formed in the name of the Society of Mineral and Battery Works. However, the real progress in iron production took place in the eighteenth century with the beginning of the Industrial Revolution. The Mines Royal created at the time of Elizabeth aimed at making England independent of foreign copper.

Expansion of Trade

Export trade underwent significant changes between the fifteenth and the seventeenth centuries. In this period, wool and food grains played a larger role in English exports but from mid-sixteenth century, textiles began to replace agricultural products. The major trade depression in the 1550s brought about this transformation. One aspect of this change was the squeezing out of the alien merchants by the English trading groups, particularly the Italians and later the merchants of the Hanseatic League. M.M. Postan describes this as 'precocious mercantilism'. England's cloth industry experienced several setbacks in the fifteenth century. Scholars like Postan and Bindoff consider these setbacks as an explanation for the creation of a new commercial organization of overseas traders, the Fellowship of Merchant Adventurers of London, in 1486. It monopolized export links with Antwerp. The major difference between the trade in wool and cloth lay in the nature of the market. Except for the exports to the Italian states, the English themselves sold their wool to the continent at Calais, a port, which they controlled. However, it was the foreign merchants who monopolized cloth trade to regions like Prussia, Poland or the Baltic States. These markets remained unprotected and often faced some form of disturbance. By the sixteenth century, England witnessed a spurt in its export trade. Nearly two-thirds of the English exports reached Antwerp while the remaining portion went to France and the Iberian Peninsula. The rise of a unitary state under a strong monarchy also had a beneficial effect on the English foreign trade.

An important factor in the growth of trade was the emergence of a new form of chartered companies. Various companies were created and favoured by the state with grants of monopolies. These included the Muscovy Company, the Levant Company, the Hudson Bay Company and the East India Company. These were either regulated or joint stock companies and they played a crucial role not only in the expansion of trade but also in the creation of English colonial empires.

However, the most important development during the sixteenth century in the sphere of trade was the rise of a new group of peddling traders and middlemen, who not only carried consumer goods from town markets to the outlying regions but also supplied artisans with raw materials. The state and the traditional authorities opposed such middlemen. An attempt was made in 1614 through the Cokayme Project to prohibit the participation of middlemen in the wool trade. The government also tried to stop the activities of those merchants who supplied food to the inhabitants of London. These merchants are regarded as the transforming elements in the economy of England during the sixteenth and seventeenth centuries. The process of change in England reflects a close integration of English agriculture with the manufacturing sector that manifested itself in the growth of trade within as well as outside England.

The Dutch Ascendancy

To many scholars, the rise of Holland appears spectacular and sudden. If one looks at the history of the Netherlands in the late medieval period, then it is evident that the great Flemish towns such as Ghent, Bruges and Pyres had been important centres of textile production and enjoyed extended trade links with many parts of Europe. The duchy of Brabant and the county of Flanders were important centres of industry and trade. These towns experienced a steady decline but the rural textile industry around the small towns of west Flanders witnessed a steady growth. The decline of the Flemish towns had resulted in the rise of Antwerp and by the middle of the sixteenth century it had become the central market of Europe with abundant resources. However, it could never become a major industrial centre.

The supremacy of the Netherlands over other maritime states of Europe was a phenomenon in the seventeenth century but the rise of Holland as an economic power was becoming evident even towards the last decades of the sixteenth century. As Antwerp and Lyon experienced a steady decline, Amsterdam was fast becoming the financial centre of Europe. The rise of Amsterdam was intimately bound up with the ascendancy of Holland. In the late sixteenth century (1566), a struggle for independence against the Spanish rule had started. It was a reaction against the economic exploitation of the Dutch merchants by the Spanish authorities as it was also a religious reaction of the Protestant majority against its Catholic rulers. Although the conflict between Spain and the Netherlands continued till almost the middle of the seventeenth century, the northern states of the Netherlands declared their independence in the sixteenth century under the leadership of men like William the Silent. The result was the formation of the Dutch republic consisting of Holland, Zeeland, Utrecht, Gelderland, Groningen, Overijssel and Friesland. In the course of the war of independence, the Dutch had become a nation but it remained more like a federation than a unified nation with no strong centralized monarchy. It was an extreme form of decentralization in which individual provinces maintained much of their autonomy. The government of the United Provinces of the Netherlands was run by a collective leadership drawn from the prominent merchant families of Amsterdam, and the nobility, particularly the house of Orange. It was the Council of the State called *Raad van Staat* and the States-General (representing ambassadors from different provinces meeting at The Hague) wielded real power. This kind of state governance was peculiar in comparison to the contemporary governments of European states; most of which had strong centralized, absolute monarchies. It was Holland that was able to dominate the rest of the states due to its powerful economic and social base. This made P.W. Klein observe that there was hardly anything resembling a state in the United Provinces of the Netherlands. In fact, the Dutch prosperity hardly owed anything to the state. The positive aspect of this arrangement was that the merchant oligarchy directed the state policies for the promotion of trade and commerce.

Scholars have explained the rise of Holland in different ways. In fact, there has been a debate on this question. Immanuel Wallerstein in his stimulating work, *The Modern World-System,* suggests that the rise of Holland was in the nature of a hegemony that formed the core-status in the world economy. And because of its geographical location, the Dutch established their hegemony and triumphed on all fronts by placing the neighbouring states in a subordinate position. They enjoyed all the benefits of a free market and did not require adoption of a mercantilist policy. There was no need for a strong and centralized state authority that could have proved costly and oppressive, like in France and Spain. The economic and political supremacy of Holland achieved through the city of Amsterdam, was itself sufficient to hold the entire country together and provide a flexible and decentralized structure of government. Not all historians accept this explanation. B.H. Slicher van Bath and J.C. Boyar agree with Wallerstein's theory in general but they add that before attaining the new position of hegemony, the United Provinces had solved to a great extent the main problems, which had blocked the development of pre-industrial economies. Braudel regards this an imperfect hegemony. Schoffer suggests that the shift from an initially unfavourable to the subsequent advantageous position was caused by accumulation in agriculture. This was because of the new international economy shaped by Spanish silver and the creation of a Dutch monopoly over the Baltic grain trade. For Schoffer, the real question was to know how this 'centre' came about that led to this hegemony. Morineau doubts whether any country situated at the centre automatically had the advantage in the acquisition of the surplus. For Neils Steensgaard, the three great Dutch institutions – the deposit banks, the exchange institutions and the Dutch East India Company (VOC) – led to the development of Dutch capitalism during the seventeenth century. According to Maurice Aymard, the United Provinces was the first to benefit from the increased interdependence and economic integration of Europe from the sixteenth century, which was brought about in a large measure by the activities of the Dutch fleet, their merchants, their capital which poured into Amsterdam from different places and by the efficient trade networks created by the Dutch. Aymard points out that although it was still described as a period of commercial capitalism, nevertheless it was a time when the economic space of Europe was gradually being reshaped, with the opening and enlargement of markets and profits through international trade. This was a new aspect of the Dutch supremacy in which the stock market in Amsterdam became the living heart of financial operations.

The rise of Holland began in the last quarter of the sixteenth century when Antwerp and Venice were declining. The Dutch Republic was established in January 1579 when the Treaty of Utrecht formalized the split between the north and the south. The provinces and cities that signed the treaty agreed to form a new political and military union in perpetuity to resist the Spaniards. This new union was named the United Provinces of the Netherlands. The treaty stipulated that each member would remain sovereign in its internal affairs but they would jointly take decision on war, peace and taxation.

Map 6.1: The Dutch Republic in the Seventeenth Century

The religious wars and tensions between the Catholics and the Protestants resulted in a stream of refugees – not only the Protestants coming from France, Antwerp and southern Netherlands but also the Jews from the Iberian region, consisting of prosperous merchants with substantial capital and skilled craftsmen who contributed to Holland's economic rise. They were also instrumental in establishing commercial links between Holland and other regions, including the New World. The contribution of the Jews has been highlighted by a number of writers. Amsterdam was backed by a regional economy that pursued a systematic exploitation of diversified fields. It reached a high level of development in all spheres of economic activity during the seventeenth century.

The Dutch interest in shipping can be located in the mixture of land and water that constituted the United Provinces. The Dutch were a seafaring people and many of them learnt their trade in the North Sea through fishing and navigational activities. For a long period, the Dutch and the fisherman of Zeeland had sailed in the North Sea and fishing had become the national industry. It not only procured numerous varieties of fish but also generated wealth creating modern enterprises. From 1595, the Dutch had started harpooning whales. The monopoly of fishing was granted to a northern company in 1614 covering the coasts of Nova Zemblya to the Davis Straits. Whale fishing provided enormous profit not only to the fishermen but also to the other manufacturers as its oil was needed to light lamps, to prepare soaps and to treat cloth. Hundreds of fishing boats were employed as feeders to large vessels. According to Braudel, during the seventeenth century, 12,000 fishermen caught 3,00,000 tons of fish. The herring trade also contributed to the salt trade as fish could be preserved with salt application. Besides, salt was manufactured near the sea and taken to interior parts for profit. The fishing industry resulted in the expansion of the Dutch pledge. By the 1570s, the Dutch came out with new types of vessels, variously called *vlieboot* or *fluyt* or *flyboat*. These were sturdy, round-sided ships of great capacity compared to the ships from other countries. They could carry much greater merchandise and required fewer crewmen. The success of Holland was intimately connected with the Dutch shipping. By 1636, according to J.L. Price, the Dutch merchant fleet numbered about 2,300–2,500 ships besides 2,000 herring-buses (the specialized fishing boats). The *fluyt* was the most successful merchant ship of that period which was designed to carry bulky cargos like grain and wood. According to Braudel, Dutch naval shipyards exhibited unbeatable costs primarily because they were able to obtain timber, tar, pitch, rigging and other naval stores directly from the Baltic. As the Dutch were expert craftsmen, they used the most modern technology of that time such as mechanical saws, hoists for masts and interchangeable spare parts. Sarrdam was the famous shipyard near Amsterdam. The port of Amsterdam was large enough to handle 4,000 ships and was itself the home of 500 ships. The freight business was an important source of income for its citizens as was the market in second-hand ships. The shipping industry not only provided jobs to numerous fishermen but around 48,000 men worked in the shipyards. The Dutch integrated the economy of the coastal belt with the economies of the interior regions.

The Dutch imported cereals from outside, particularly from the Baltic region, an enormous grain trade they dominated. Like England, the feudal system in the Netherlands had started declining much earlier than the rest of Europe. A solid rural democracy developed in the absence of centralized states. The growth of trade promoted commercialization of agriculture. The large network of trade led to capital investments in this sphere. All these factors considerably strengthened farm economy, which became independent of all constraints, as was to be seen in many parts of western Europe. It drew the peasantry into a system of monetary exchange. Peasant agriculture in northern Netherlands prospered because of the possibility of agricultural profit. In the fifteenth century, the pressure of demand from the urban population resulted in conversion of cultivable land into dairy farming and the introduction of fodder crops and crop rotation. It transformed the northern region into an important centre of dairy farming, providing milk products like butter and cheese to different parts of Europe. The same factors promoted market gardening, especially in the region between Leiden and Amsterdam. These changes had transformed subsistence farming into market farming and agriculture became an important source of income for the Dutch. It formed the nucleus of agrarian capitalism. This kind of activity required heavy capital investment and intensive labour. The capital was available in towns and the absence of banking institutions was overcome in a limited way by arranging funds from these towns. The steady rise in prices throughout the sixteenth century also favoured commercialization.

However, this situation existed essentially in Holland and Zeeland. In contrast the eastern provinces, including Utrecht, hardly changed during the sixteenth century. Most of this region remained confined to subsistence agriculture. Till the middle of the seventeenth century, it suffered heavily due to the war against Spain. Yet some developments had taken place in the late sixteenth century such as land reclaimed through draining. The scale of these changes was relatively small compared to the large-scale reclamation in northern Holland. The capital provided for such reclamation projects came principally from the merchants of Amsterdam. The contrast between the eastern provinces and Holland had become quite glaring by the early seventeenth century.

Trade and Industry

The fortune of Holland was intimately linked with its trade and industry. It was the Dutch hegemony over European trade that contributed to the rise of Holland. This gap between Holland and the other members of the union not only caused jealousy but it also brought a divergence of interest in foreign relations. The Dutch economy was tied up with international trade and supported freedom of trade in international seas. Only Zeeland and Friesland to a certain extent could share the advantages of this trade. It is estimated that in the third quarter of the seventeenth century, the trade of Amsterdam was five times more than that of Rotterdam. The Dutch participation in the war between Denmark and Sweden in 1645 brought favourable advantages to the Republic although the Dutch were not directly involved in the war. The Dutch also gained from the trade with France and southern Europe as it dealt with staple items like grain and flax. The Dutch, in which the

Rotterdam merchants also participated, controlled the trade of French wine and salt through the Atlantic ports. In the early seventeenth century the Dutch were involved in the export of British coal (in 1616, out of 686 cargoes of coal which left Newcastle, 537 were shipped by the Dutch and the French). The Asiatic trade carried out by VOC (founded in 1602) saw the real change in the relationship between Europe and Asia. Steensgaard describes it as a state within a state, because it was an entirely new form of institution based on the modern technique of capital shares. It made the Asian trade lucrative by not only increasing its volume but also by introducing a new form of trade called the 'country' trade. European ships led by the Dutch started participating in the inter-regional trade of Asia. The Dutch wrested the monopoly of spice trade from the Portuguese by establishing their colonies in the Indonesian archipelago. As Denys Lombard points out, the Dutch did not make any innovation in the economic system of the Asiatic world, they simply slipped into the existing channels and patterns.

The biggest province of the Dutch Republic of the northern Netherlands was Holland. It was the most populous province consisting of a little less than half of the total population of the northern Netherlands, i.e. 6,70,000 out of a total population of 14,00,000 in 1622. By 1680, the Dutch population had gone up to 8,83,000 out of a total population of 19,00,000. This population increase is evident from the sixteenth century itself. Between 1514 and 1622, the population increase was about 145 per cent. While the rural population increased steadily, there was great explosion in the big towns like Amsterdam, Leiden, Haarlem, Rotterdam, Delft, etc. This trend continued till the late-seventeenth century.

The expansion of the Dutch industries was quite marked throughout the sixteenth century. Industrial development was closely associated with the scientific exploitation of the two great energy sources of the pre-industrial era – wind and heat energy. These were utilized not only to meet the needs of the two key sectors – boat building and textiles – but were also used in refineries, foundries, breweries, potteries and brick kilns. The textile manufacturers were located mostly in Holland and in Twente, Tilburg,

Leiden and Haarlem. The towns of other provinces could not enjoy the benefits of industrial prosperity. Leiden and Haarlem emerged as the two most important textile centres. They profited immensely from the influx of foreign immigrants, not only capitalist merchants but also skilled artisans. The Leiden woollen industry attracted Flemish textile workers from Hondschoote and these men brought new methods with them, particularly in the manufacture of light cloth. Fresh markets opened up fresh opportunities for the new products. Textile production in this city increased from 27,000 pieces a year in 1584 to 1,44,000 pieces by 1664. However, towards the end of the seventeenth century, serious competition from France and the tariff wars between the Dutch and the English, and subsequently with the French, resulted in a steady decline of this industrial centre. A similar trend could be noticed in the linen industry of Haarlem, known for the bleaching of imported cloth. The industries based on raw materials and half finished manufacturers were called *trafieken*. A great portion of the finished product was exported. Major industrial activities were related to sugar refining, tobacco processing and earthenware. Their survival to a large extent depended on the Dutch supremacy over the seas. The shipbuilding industry was concentrated around Zaandam, north of Amsterdam. This became the biggest centre of shipbuilding in Europe during the seventeenth century and provided employment to a large number of rope and sail makers, dockworkers and sailors. According to J.L. Price, Holland's prosperity was not confined to a narrow section of society but also benefited a large section of the middle and lower middle classes of the towns. This was mainly due to the *rederig* system. Several men of moderate means could participate in the trading and shipping ventures by contributing their small savings in fitting out herring boats, or purchase cargos for trade through trading associations. They received profits according to the size of their share in the venture, as profits were distributed on the basis of one's share.

The most important factor responsible for the Dutch hegemony was the emergence of Amsterdam as the capital market of Europe. The stock exchange at Amsterdam had reached sophistication and refinement through speculative trading. It became a special trading centre of Europe. The bourse or the stock exchange was started in a new building in 1631 and was meant only for the exchange of goods and consumer products, although, the old exchange went back to 1530. Initially, the only stock traded at this new place was that of the Dutch East India Company. Gradually other stocks were dealt with and loans were arranged in no time, making Amsterdam an attractive place for finalizing international loans. With this began the trading in money or shares and the rise of brokers. These brokers were divided into two types – the *rotteries* who were like the bulls, who tried to push up the value of shares through rumours of big dividends or high profits, and the *underminers* or the bears who tried to keep the prices of the shares low by spreading the news of losses and disasters. These two opposite groups contributed to the techniques of speculative business in that period. According to an Italian traveller, the stock exchange of Amsterdam was the busiest even as late as 1782, although Dutch hegemony was on the decline. Another commercial institution was the Amsterdam Bank or the Amsterdam Wisselbank (1609). It was a type of Giro Bank, i.e. it was a bank of deposit and transfer. Its functioning was simple, and included attracting deposits and changing money. Any merchant of Holland could bring coins of different currencies and deposit them in the bank and could enjoy credit facility from the bank. The coins were valued on the basis of their gold or silver content. The smallest sum that could be deposited was 300 guilders. This contributed to the system of account holding although the withdrawal of deposit was not a common practice; instead the bank account was sold to someone who needed it. The bank money enjoyed a slit premium over the cash. The bank deposit in Amsterdam increased from 10,00,000 florins in 1610 to 80,00,000 by 1640. The plan of the Amsterdam Wisselbank was soon adopted in other towns. Another noteworthy aspect of the Dutch economy was the commission trade as opposed to the trading in person. It was known as proprietorial trade, i.e. handling goods on behalf of someone else and charging a commission on it. The person who gave the order (or *commission*) was called the *commettant* and the person who received the commission was called *commissionaire*. Although this system of commission trade had existed much earlier, it was Holland that popularized it through trade. As the Dutch merchants handled trade on a large scale, these methods facilitated its functioning. Another form of business was the acceptance trade, which was concerned with the bills of exchange for payment, transfers, endorsements, discounting, drafts and deposits, which became an important vehicle of credit. It is interesting to learn that Holland experienced a period of credit surplus because of its economic prosperity, as the traders of Europe could not absorb the bills of lading offered by Holland. Through such means Amsterdam was able to establish Dutch supremacy over the financial markets of Europe. The merchants and financiers of Amsterdam did not give any room to the merchants of other provinces.

Decline of the Netherlands

The great expansion of the Dutch lasted till the middle of the seventeenth century. After this period, the Dutch economy began to be seriously affected by the navigational wars and the protectionist measures adopted by the neighbouring states against the Dutch. It was creditable for the Dutch to prosper and expand even during their war with Spain. All these years the Dutch maritime supremacy could not be challenged. However, the naval wars with England in the second half of the seventeenth century revealed the vulnerability of the Dutch trade. The navigation laws passed by the English parliament were aimed at destroying the Dutch fleet and their oceanic trade. These wars gave a hard blow to the herring fisheries and to the cargo trade on which Dutch economic prosperity depended. A similar challenge came from the French. The famous Minister of Louis XIV, Jean Baptist Colbert, initiated a commercial war against the Dutch. The French placed heavy duties on Dutch products and the state provided all forms of assistance for producing goods, which were manufactured in Holland. The navigation laws of France aimed at replacing Dutch supremacy on the sea. Like their neighbours, the French also fought three wars with the Dutch in the late-seventeenth and early-eighteenth century. Although the Dutch Republic had retained much of its economic domination until well past 1700, the Dutch merchants acted as intermediaries of different European states and carried out re-distribution trade for the goods coming from the America and Asia. The share of profit was not evenly distributed among the provinces of the Republic. The Dutch hegemony was also due to its carriage trade. They were transporting several British and French commodities in their ships on regular payment. Dutch transport of wheat grew from an average yearly figure of 4,300 in the 1580s to 28,400 in the 1640s, constituting 58 and 88 per cent of the total wheat exports respectively (J.A. van Houtte). As Danzig was the chief port for the grain trade, the Polish-Swedish war of 1655–60 adversely affected the Dutch trade that had long-term repercussions. The navigational laws reduced their share considerably and by the end of the seventeenth century, the decline was steep. One of the important reasons for the ultimate decline of the Netherlands, was the over-dependence of Holland on foreign trade. Six wars within a little more than half a century seriously affected the trade supremacy. The prosperity of Holland had given rise to jealousy not only of the neighbouring countries but also of the other provinces within the Republic and of their towns against Amsterdam. This resulted in the transfer of commercial supremacy from the Dutch to the English hands.

For a long time it was believed that the British Navigational Laws and the French mercantilist measures marked the beginning of the economic decline of the Netherlands from the mid-seventeenth century. Recent works, particularly those of van Dillen and van der Kooy, not only reject this presumption but also highlight the various stages of Holland's decline by focusing on its economic structure. According to this view, the naval attacks of England and France in the second half of the seventeenth century did not completely destroy the Dutch monopoly. The English laws were riddled by exemptions on license and the Treaty of Breda gave the Dutch some distinct advantages in the Rhineland. It is true that the French tariffs of 1664 and 1667 were aimed at eliminating the Dutch from their role as intermediaries between France and Northern Europe but the Treaty of Nimeguen provided sufficient relief to the Dutch. Later, the Dutch who had strengthened their position in trade, received further concessions. Thus, the attacks on the Dutch world market, according to C.H. Wilson, failed to penetrate their monopoly. The Dutch domination of European transport and commerce remained intact right till about the end of the seventeenth century, because of their geographical advantages, superior organization and technique and the relative economic backwardness of their neighbours. Even in the early-eighteenth century, Amsterdam remained the granary from where the Baltic grain was supplied to the southern states of Europe.

On the question of the decline, recent inquiries reveal that there was no sudden or catastrophic decline like that of Italy. The Dutch decline becomes visible only when their intermediary position in the world trade is noticed. It was slowly slipping down. Economic swings continued till the 1730s. The two visible changes were (a) the average volume of the Dutch grain trade shrank during the eighteenth century, due to harvest failures and because of the decline of Baltic wheat trade as the rising price of bread led to its replacement by cheaper foodstuffs like buckwheat, and (b) increasing foreign competition. Holland was not well placed to counter the economic rivalry of Britain and France for a long period. The English strongly competed with the Dutch in the Russian, the Spanish and the Levant trade. In the Baltic region, the British merchants wrested half the Russian trade that constituted the richest part, from the Dutch. France under Colbert blocked the Dutch trade, especially their import of raw sugar from the French West Indies, seriously affecting the refineries in Amsterdam. Many argue that Holland declined not because her trade volume had shrunk but more because the total volume of world trade had risen dramatically, while Holland's trade remained static. For example, the Dutch share in England's foreign trade fell from 14.6 to 3.6 per cent in her imports and from 41.5 to 12.7 per cent between 1696–7 and 1772–3 (J.B. Manger, *Recherches sur les Relations Economiques entre la Française et la Hollande pendant la Revolution Française*).

There were three general weaknesses in the Dutch industrial sector. Firstly, the textile industries were largely based on exports and dependent on foreign markets. Hence, it could not gain from the protection policy of the state because the domestic demand was too small. By the eighteenth century, the demographic factor came to play a role in Dutch fortunes. While the Dutch Republic had a population of under two million, Britain and France had 6.9 and 20 millions respectively, besides controlling vast empires. Second, as the Dutch industries imported most of their raw materials from foreign lands, they had no effective control over price. Earlier, the Dutch had enjoyed two basic advantages; they themselves dictated freight rates and kept them low and consequently dictated the price of raw materials gaining from the absence of similar industries in the neighbourhood. These advantages vanished once capital generation took place in other regions making the availability of capital plentiful, and the growing ability of England to compete with lower interest rates. Third, the Dutch textile industry faced high labour costs as labour was well organized. High wage-level existed in the printing, bleaching and textile industries. Besides, the Dutch industries were heavily taxed and this raised the cost of production. On the other hand, the protection and subsidies granted to the linen industries in Ireland and Scotland dealt a severe blow to Haarlem by completely ousting Dutch linen from the British markets. After the Treaty of Aix-la Chappell in 1748, a major slump seriously affected the Dutch industry. The Industrial Revolution established the economic superiority of Britain. Many other industries were gradually losing out due to foreign competition. The manufacturing of fine glass lost its lead to England by 1675, while the pottery industry declined in the eighteenth century because of the rise of porcelain in other continental states. The paper industry continued to prosper, particularly after the imposition of heavy duties on French paper.

However, the gradual decline of the Dutch industries was accompanied by a shift from trading and industrial activities to the commercial sphere of banking and finance. The availability of abundant capital made the transition from international trading and commission business to credit banking rather smooth. The stock exchange at Amsterdam was the busiest bourse even as late as 1782, according to a contemporary Italian traveller. As C.R. Wilson puts it, 'In this way, Dutch houses came to act as paymasters, transferring capital from one part of Europe to another.'

The Commercial Revolution

As has been mentioned earlier, the sixteenth century experienced vast economic expansion. This expansion was to a great extent related to the expansion of trade, emergence of colonial empires and commercial prosperity. The demographic growth created demand for consumer goods and increased market transactions. The rigidity of rural life was breaking down and the overseas expansion was widening the commercial world of Europe. To handle these ever-growing economic transactions, the importance of commercial instruments was realized. The sixteenth and the seventeenth centuries witnessed an increased use of commercial instruments in the business world that speeded up the process of modernization and hastened the transition from feudalism to capitalism. Many scholars have described this as the 'commercial revolution'. The effects of the commercial revolution permeated every sphere of urban life and indirectly contributed to the development of capitalism. However, two divergent views exist on the commercial revolution. According to the first (that of Henri Hauser, Richard Ehrenberg, etc.), the sixteenth century was a decisive period in the history of finance. There are many other scholars who contend that such an emphasis on the sixteenth century is misplaced. The crucial financial techniques such as credit, banking and bookkeeping had developed much earlier though these became more common in the sixteenth century. Recent research provides a more evolutionary interpretation in which this century is seen as a period of revived economic and commercial growth after a prolonged period of depression.

Causes

The expansion of trade from the late-fifteenth century was one of the major reasons for commercial advancement. Although the rise in international trade created a contradictory situation in Europe, yet the regions, which were closely associated with the trade routes and with the market forces, experienced significant advancement in the management and organization of trade. Many countries and regions experienced integration because of trade. Till the end of the fifteenth century, the Mediterranean region had been the nerve centre of economic activity. In fact, the Italian city-states had already developed several forms of commercial instruments to handle the trade between Asia, North Africa and Europe. With the emergence of colonial empires of Portugal and Spain, some regions of Europe were linked to the emerging port cities of north-western Europe. Central Europe started sending its mineral products to Antwerp. Sea routes had become popular because of the risks to the internal trade routes caused by increasing religious, political or social disturbances within Europe and the significance of colonial links was now being realized. Shipping was not only cheaper but also faster and easier to handle. The significance of eastern and central Europe began to diminish with the emergence of the Baltic region as the major supplier of food grains to the rest of Europe. The rising population further escalated the demand for food. At this time, countries situated on the Atlantic coast started emerging as the principal centres of trade and commerce. Widening trading relation made trade organizations much more complex. This also brought about profound changes in the structure of European trade.

The growth of European population from the second half of the fifteenth century applied strong pressure on the market economy. In the medieval period, trade was confined to luxury products and the demand mainly came from the nobility and state officials. From the sixteenth century, the rising population shifted this demand to consumer goods. The rise of the middle classes and their growing prosperity changed the pattern of European trade and this in turn stimulated trade and industry. It transformed the nature of commercial economy. Numerous urban centres emerged and the size of towns began to grow. The urban demand for consumer goods and the scale of business required greater skill and expertise. This situation was conducive for greater acceptance of new commercial instruments. The government and the entrepreneurs designed new institutions or neutralized some of older institutions which had been in use in the commercial world of the Italian states. The expansion of global commerce during the sixteenth and the seventeenth centuries was responsible for bringing about the so-called commercial revolution.

A parallel economic movement during the sixteenth century was the price revolution. The demographic pressure and the availability of an increasing quantity of silver resulted in a steady rise in prices. This price rise gave stimulus to business activities and hastened the expansion of money economy. Besides, it opened up new opportunities for large-scale commercial enterprises because inflationary situations always provide possibility of higher profit. The scale of business and the increasing use of liquid money created practical difficulties. The monetary transactions needed different handling to facilitate the growing trade through credit instruments. Business institutions had to be reorganized. Risks had to be covered. Capital was to be made available. All these considerations promoted commercial economy in Europe.

Elements of the Commercial Revolution

Commerce is the organization of trade and it facilitates the transaction of business in terms of payment and organization. Certain special elements of commerce emerged in the common transactions of business during the sixteenth century.

The first basic requirement of the commercial world was the availability of capital. The colonial enterprises in the late-fifteenth century were carried out by the funds supplied by important merchant bankers of that period – the merchant families of the Italian states, particularly the Genoese, the Venetians, the Florentine families and the Fugger families of Augsburg in Germany. The expansion of trade needed capital investments for a longer duration to not only fit out ships in the trans-oceanic trade but also to purchase cargo. The possibility of profit prompted many bankers and entrepreneurs to invest their capital in trading ventures. The commercial enterprises provided opportunities to the capitalist investors, merchants and, on a number of occasions, to the rulers of the European states. In the absence of modern banks, merchant-banker families performed this function of accumulating capital. The Fuggers of Augsburg and the Medici family of Florence were the most notable examples of this. The establishment of new types of banks led to the rise of these houses. They reflected the mercantilist goals of fulfilling the financial needs of the state. However, the rise of modern banking system developed only from the middle of the seventeenth century. Till then, banking operations were performed by private bankers either individually or in the form of family partnership. During the sixteenth century, the domination of the Italian and German bankers was on the wane and several new bankers emerged in France, Holland, Flanders and England. The banking system as a specialized activity had not yet emerged and it was mixed up with commercial business. Gradually some of the firms dropped trade connections to concentrate purely on banking.

The tie-up between government financing and banking was a significant feature in the sixteenth century. A gradual demarcation between private and public banks was taking shape. The first public bank was established during the fifteenth century at Barcelona and Genoa. The abuses and shortcomings of the private banking system resulted in demand for public banks during the sixteenth century. Moreover, the earlier merchant bankers were more interested in investing their capital in state loans (which were often non-productive in nature) rather than in economic enterprises. In the second half of the sixteenth century, the institution of public bank began to emerge. In 1587, the government in Venice set-up the Bank of Rialto. It accepted deposits and transferred money but it was not allowed to loan money. In 1593, a similar bank was established in Milan. A public bank, established in Amsterdam in 1609, was assigned the function of mobilizing deposits and carrying out transfer of funds. Similar banks were created in Hamburg in 1619 and in Nuremberg in 1621. These banks played an important role in attracting surplus money by offering a safe place for deposits and rendered valuable service in the transfer of money from one place to another. The rise of banking institutions facilitated handling of the increasing volume of trade by a better system of payments.

The rise of banking was accompanied by the adoption of different methods of financial transactions. New credit instruments and facilities were important in the coming of the commercial revolution though some of these instruments were already in use in the Italian states. However, from the sixteenth century, the European businessmen not only popularized these methods but also perfected the technique of handling such instruments, which facilitated capitalism. The bills of exchange were widely and commonly employed in handling trade transactions, both in internal as well as in external trade. It had the advantage of making payments without carrying with oneself huge quantities of money from one place to another – something that was not only inconvenient in the absence of proper transport but also very risky. Now a merchant in Antwerp could purchase goods in Lisbon through the bills of exchange issued by a banker in Antwerp. The merchant in Lisbon could obtain his money by depositing the bill of exchange with the agent of the banker in Antwerp. Subsequently, the accounts could be settled between the banker and his agent. The same bill of exchange could pass on to many persons before it was finally deposited, changing hands and settling debts. It was based on the practice of endorsement by the bank where the bill was presented. There were other forms of credit instruments that came into use during the sixteenth century, particularly in Holland, Antwerp and France. These included *promissory notes*, which were made payable to the bearer. These were almost like bank notes. In fact, the practice of issuing bank notes during the seventeenth century started from this. Closely linked to these credit instruments was the device of discounting. This system enabled the 'discounting of the bill'. A certain percentage was deducted from the face value of the bill of exchange or promissory note when it changed hands as product or service charges. It gave the merchant his money ahead of time and it gave income to the banker. Some bankers began specializing in the handling of bills of exchange concerned only with foreign trade while others confined their activities to internal trade. An important feature of these credit instruments was its *negotiability*, i.e. transfer of the bills from one person to another and its conversion into cash. It had several legal problems concerning the responsibilities of endorsement and acceptance but they were slowly overcome towards the end of the seventeenth century. Negotiability of credit instruments was the chief feature of the commercial transaction of the banking operations. The credit trading through the bills of exchange, letter of credit and promissory notes along with the issuance of bank notes as a substitute for currency was of great significance in increasing the volume of trade because the credit resources of the banking and business firms could be increased beyond the actual amount of cash in their possession.

With the coming of the banking system and growing use of credit instruments, the concept of insurance gained ground. The risks of trans-oceanic ventures were enormous. The firms or individuals involved in long distance trade faced not only natural calamities in the course of a voyage but also threats from pirates. This made insurance necessary as a risk cover. Maritime insurance emerged as a commercial practice against risks of oceanic trade and it was managed by merchants or bankers. It is estimated that by 1504, there were about 600 persons in Antwerp alone who made a living out of insurance. Gradually different forms of insurance schemes were introduced, such as fire insurance in German cities like Hamburg.

The trading activities had to depend to a certain extent on improved form of communications. During the sixteenth century, although the system of transport remained backward – poor roads and the dislocation of trade routes during the rainy season and acute winter – the rise of shipping solved some of these problems. River navigation was also becoming popular as it reduced the cost of transportation. However, there were distinct improvements in the system of communications. Trade news began to reach different commercial centres with the introduction of the postal services. By the early-sixteenth century, state postal services were established in Spain, France and England and by the seventeenth century all the major towns of Europe were linked with each other through newspapers and trade journals.

The expansion of European commercial economy brought about changes in the trade organizations. Although the concept of fairs or weekly bazaars remained the heart of mercantile life, permanent markets began to emerge in important commercial cities of Europe.

These central superstructures of exchange were set-up above the markets, the shops and the peddlers, and were handled by expert operators. This was a period of transition from subsistence economy to an exchange economy moving in the capitalist direction. The practice of organizing fairs during the carnival season was a medieval form of trade. The organization of fairs remained a common feature till the eighteenth century in most parts of Europe. Here, trade transactions took place primarily between the producers and the consumers. Slowly the role of traders increased and in important cities the goods started moving from open bazaars to godowns set-up by big merchants. To sell and store goods, the system of auctions and the concept of retail trade gained ground. This resulted in the rise of middlemen who thrived on profits made from this new exchange system.

Commercial expansion on an international scale required changes in the nature of business organization. In the late medieval period, trade was organized either by individuals or in the form of family partnership. Italy had formed business organizations on the basis of partnership like the *commendas* or *societas* but these were short-term organizations. They existed only for a single voyage or for a very brief period. The expansion of trade began to change the scale of organization as well as the form of arrangement. The earlier form of partnerships was subjected to the disadvantage of unlimited liability for its members concerning the debts or losses. These were not capable of facing heavy risks or making huge capital investments. The opening up of overseas territories and the expansion of trade of bulk items created new problems. As the Dutch expanded their trading activities in the Baltic zone, it became quite common for the Dutch firms to appoint a partner at a Baltic port and place him there permanently to handle their business. Similarly, the Spanish firms sometimes placed one of its partners in Seville and another in the American colony as a factor or an agent. Thereby the Dutch, the French and the English merchants through secret partnership agreements with the Spanish merchants were in a position to evade the regulations of the Spanish government, which prohibited foreigners participating in the American trade. Gradually attempts were made to develop more suitable forms of business organizations. One such form was the regulated company.

The origin of a regulated company can be located in the Middle Ages, particularly in England where the Merchant Staplers were created, but not in a fully developed form. The regulated company was partly like a partnership and partly like guild. In some ways it was also like a joint stock company that emerged later. It was an association of merchants to monopolize, exploit and control a specific branch of trade like a common venture. The members agreed to abide by certain specific regulations but they did not pool their resources together. Rather, they agreed only to cooperate for mutual benefit. These companies were chartered and given monopoly by their respective governments. They were regulated companies because they followed the rules laid down for the conduct of their business. They maintained common trade centres abroad and enjoyed monopoly rights. Their respective governments protected them against the 'interlopers' (those who attempted to break into the monopoly). There were many such companies in England like the Merchant Adventurers, the Eastland Company, the Muscovy Company and the Levant Company.

The increasing volume of trade and the expansion of commercial economy transformed the form of organization. The regulated company was changed into a new type of organization called the joint-stock company. It was more compact and wider in scope. Even this form of organization was not entirely new in Germany. The mining activities were organized on the joint-stock basis. Heavy investments in the mining sector prevented individual merchants from carrying out the entire operation alone. Thus, the stock of mines was divided into *Kuxen*, which were owned by several merchants jointly. The chief feature of a joint-stock company was the union of capital rather than of persons. Several people purchased the shares, which were offered to the potential investors. The actual shareholders entrusted the functioning of the company in the hands of selected directors and shared the profit or losses in proportion to the amount they had invested. There were several advantages which a joint-stock company offered. It functioned as a permanent organization and was not subjected to dissolution or reorganization in case of withdrawal or death of one of its members. Moreover, it had much greater resources at hand through the sale of shares. This company could secure much larger capital than any other form of partnership. Its nature of organization and conduct of business was very similar to the modern corporations. The formation of the joint-stock company in the initial years remained a slow and hesitant exercise. Initially, the joint-stock companies, such as the English East India Company and the Dutch East India Company (*Oost Indische Compagnie*), followed the practice of dividing their capital and profits at the end of each voyage. This created confusion among its shareholders. With the passage of time these companies assumed a permanent character. The Dutch East India Company, which was established in 1602, had expected to pay off its investors within the first ten years. However, it was unable to do so. It advised the shareholders to realize their profits by selling their shares to the interested buyers in the Amsterdam stock exchange. From this began the practice of the sale of company's shares in the stock market. The joint-stock companies also enabled ordinary people to invest their savings in these large ventures and earn regular dividends. Although joint-stock companies were mainly created to handle long-distance trade and participate in commercial ventures, they also subsequently organized industrial enterprises. Most of the trading companies were also chartered companies as they received charters from the government concerning their privileges, monopoly and assignment of specific territories where they could operate. In England, two joint-stock companies were organized in 1568 for an entirely different purpose – the Mineral and Battery Works Company to carry out brass founding for manufacturing copper or brass wires, and the Mines Royal Company to carry out silver and copper mining. During the seventeenth century, such companies became more popular, especially because of the mercantilist influence on state policies.

An interesting aspect of the commercial revolution was the formation of a stock exchange in the commercial cities of Europe. The stock exchange centres were also called bourse, which originated in Bruges. According to Braudel, a stock exchange was the meeting place of bankers, merchants and businessmen, dealers and banker's agents, brokers and investors. Although there is no clear evidence of the origins of such exchanges, in Amsterdam the new exchange was founded in 1609 while the old one probably dates back to 1530. The Bruges exchange was created in 1409, Antwerp in 1460, Lyons in 1462, London in 1554, Paris in 1563, Bordeaux in 1564 and the number continued to increase throughout the seventeenth century. By the mid-seventeenth century, according to a contemporary source, almost all the exchanges looked like a place of noisy dealings. However, the stock exchange at Amsterdam made significant advances not only in terms of scale but also in terms of organization. In 1631, a new building was constructed for it where speculation was carried out in a totally modern fashion. The new elements of the Amsterdam stock market were the volume, the fluidity of the market and the publicity received and the speculative freedom of transactions (Braudel, *The Wheels of Commerce*). Through speculations, several investors had a windfall while many lost everything. The chief contribution of the stock exchange was to promote large-scale capitalist ventures by means of sale and purchase of shares and public investments.

The commercial revolution contributed to the growth of money economy. The growth of business and industry accentuated the need for a uniform monetary system and financial stability. To some extent this problem was overcome by adopting a standard form of money by the government. The process of uniformity was far from complete even in the seventeenth century but attempts were made to construct uniform coinage, as had been done in the time of Queen Elizabeth in England and Colbert in France. By popularizing new instruments of credit and commercial transactions, the commercial revolution contributed to the inflationary situation of the late-sixteenth century. It introduced an element of price fluctuation characterized by alternations between booms and recessions. This was added to by feverish speculation, which was clearly demonstrated by the South Sea Bubble in the early-eighteenth century in England which resulted in almost complete crash of the share market. A similar situation also arose in France in the case of the Mississippi Company. It is difficult to answer in what ways the commercial revolution contributed to the rise of capitalism. However, the expansion of trade, the development of credit instruments, the insurance schemes, and the speculative markets certainly created a strong element of competition and more sophisticated organizations. These trends subsequently became important aspects of the capitalist economy.

The Price Revolution

Europe witnessed phenomenal price rise in the sixteenth century. Steady increase in prices continued throughout the sixteenth century. Its cumulative impact was so profound that the economic historians have termed it as 'the price revolution'. Answers to simple questions like what led to the price revolution and when did it actually begin, are rather complex, and on this the expert opinion is far from unanimous. The economic and social consequences of the price revolution has drawn the attention of several historians from different countries and their explanations help us understand the role of economic forces in the social transformation of pre-modern Europe.

'Price Revolution' is a term used for a period of prolonged inflation despite occasional dissent in the use of this term. It is true that there is some degree of exaggeration. The price rise appears revolutionary when the price level of the sixteenth century is compared with the long period of static prices of the middle ages and with the declining or stagnant price level during the seventeenth century. But it looks negligible from today's standards. Although the annual price increase was hardly 2 to 3 per cent, there were price fluctuations for short periods during the sixteenth century and the actual price rise was noticeable from the middle of the century. The cumulative effect of this inflation appeared astonishing to many scholars. It is important to note that the prices of all the products did not increase uniformly and the rate of inflation varied from one region to another depending on numerous factors.

The rise in the cost of living was first noticed when the price of food grains, especially cereals, showed an upward trend. The English, the French and the Alsatian sources indicate that the steepest rise was in the prices of arable farm products followed by livestock farm products. The increase was minimum in the case of manufactured items like textiles or metals. In the southern Netherlands and Norway, the price of cereals escalated faster than that of fish and cheese, and in Sweden between 1460 and 1559 the price of barley and rye went much higher than that of butter, cloves, pepper and iron. In fact, there was a slight decline in the price of lime, brick and cloth. In England, the period between 1550 and 1650 witnessed a fourfold increase in the prices of cereals and wood, while those of meat, cattle, wool and metal doubled. The cost of building material increased less than threefold, and that of textiles even less. In Germany, a phenomenal price rise was experienced in the town of Speyer between 1520 and 1621. The price of rye rose by fifteen times, peas fourteen times, wheat thirteen times, salt six times while the wages had gone up only by two to three and half times. In France, the price of grain from the end of the fifteenth century till the beginning of the seventeenth century had risen ten times and that of cattle eight times. By the beginning of the seventeenth century, the wholesale grain prices had risen five times on an average. In France, it had gone up by seven times while in Spain the increase was even higher. According to Hamilton, the Spanish price level had gone up 3.4 times between 1601–10 compared to a century before; in France 2.2 times; Leiden, the famous Dutch textile centre it was over three times while in Alsace, Italy and Sweden it had more than doubled. According to Brown and Hopkins, if we compare the price rise between 1475 and 1620, assuming the period between 1451 and 1475 as 100 index points, the food index point had gone up to 555 in England, 729 in France and 517 in Alsace. Similarly, the index point of industrial products had gone up to 265 in England, 335 in France and 294 in Alsace. The minimum rise was in the builders' wages, which rose to 200 points in England, 268 in France and 150 in Alsace. The exact extent of the price revolution is extremely difficult to assess, as the data of different products is not easy to obtain. The available evidence is only for certain areas and for particular commodities. Very little information is available on the prices of ordinary commodities. As far as woollen cloth and textiles are concerned, more trade data exists but variations in the quality and size of cloth are not always mentioned in it. Hence, it is almost impossible to compile an accurate price index for the sixteenth century. Statistics are available only for a limited number of commodities and that too, only for a few places. Many of the figures are based on rough estimates and hence it is difficult to interpret them. In the absence of reliable statistical data, the precise nature of the price revolution is difficult to ascertain. Yet on the basis of the available figures provided by the laborious and painstaking research of some historians, a general trend can be deciphered. These figures clearly indicate that the highest price increase was in food grains while the prices of manufactured goods did not show a corresponding increase.

There is general disagreement on the question of the actual beginning of the so-called price revolution. Some scholars believe that it had started from the late-fifteenth century itself, while some others feel it began after 1500. There is also a suggestion that the sixteenth-century price revolution was preceded by a pre-revolution in prices (*The Cambridge Economic History of Europe*). It was characterized by a slow rise in prices, perhaps 1 per cent annually between 1450 and 1500. Sharp cyclical movements interrupted it but the upward movement is clearly evident. This pre-revolution made itself felt at different times depending on the place and region. Except for Spain and probably Portugal, it extended over almost the whole of Europe. However, this movement remained within certain confines. Similarly, on the question of its duration, there is no unanimity among the historians. It probably varied from one region to another depending on the vitality and strength of the economy. The first signs of recession are to be found in Spain in the 1580s. In Italy also there were indications of a similar trend in the last decade of the sixteenth century. In Germany, the recession started around the 1620s. In northern Europe, there are indications of a slow growth in the second half of the seventeenth century, but not of declining prices. Historians feel that the prices followed a cyclical pattern in Europe. The twelfth and thirteenth centuries experienced a rapid rise, the fourteenth and three quarter of the fifteenth century was a period of gradual fall followed by high prices from the 1480s to the 1620s and then another period of recession for almost a century before the prices began to rise during the eighteenth century. Pierre Chaunu suggests that the period from 1504 to 1550 experienced a steady rise in prices followed by a relatively minor recession from 1550 to 1562–3. The next fifty years was a period of expansion and sharp price rise before recession set in. Hence the duration of the price rise varied in different parts of Europe and depended on many factors.

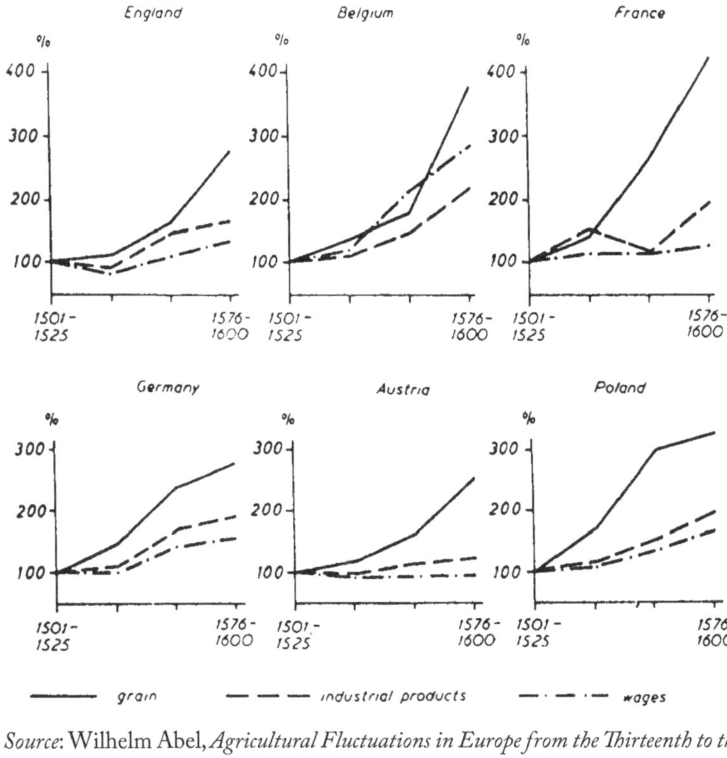

Source: Wilhelm Abel, *Agricultural Fluctuations in Europe from the Thirteenth to the Twentieth Centuries*, 1980, p. 120.

Graph 6.1: Price and wage movements in some parts of Europe from 1501–1600 (25-year averages, starting with 1501–25 with 100 index points).

This graph is based on 25-year averages and the silver content of coinage is placed at 100 index points for the period 1501–25. Each graph indicates that grain prices led the way followed by the prices of industrial products. The gap varied from one country to another. In all these graphs, the wage rise appears to be the slowest. In Austria, the wage-level went even lower than the base points, i.e. 95 per cent of the first quarter of the fifteenth century. The wage rise in England was 131 per cent, in France it was 126, in Germany 157 per cent and it was 165 per cent in Poland.

The fall of real wages or the failure of wages to compete with grain prices has been explained differently by historians. Scholars in France trace the causes back to the mid-fifteenth century when the state authorities levied tax on earnings. But it can be said that a different situation existed in many other countries where severe wage taxation and strict regulations were carried out in the late-fourteenth century and early-fifteenth century, and the wage-level continued to rise. Several explanations have been provided for the wage-lag of the sixteenth century. In England, enclosures were blamed for agricultural unemployment and the lowering of wages. But in Germany there was no enclosure movement and still the wages declined. Schmoller was perhaps the first to emphasize the debasement of coinage to be the major cause for this trend. On the other hand, J.U. Nef argues that the view, which suggests that wages lagged behind the price-level, is highly exaggerated. If wages had really lagged behind prices to the extent as has been claimed, the demand for industrial goods would not have existed. In recent years, scholars emphasize the role of population growth causing surplus labour and consequently the lowering of wages.

Another feature of the price revolution was that the price of animal products did not rise as much as those of cereals. This can be explained on the basis of different elasticity of demand for the two types of product in relation to income. The demand for animal product is income-elastic. This means that in case of price rise or a decline in the purchasing power, the purchaser can turn to cheaper articles of food. This is not the case with grain.

Causes of the Price Revolution

Historians have provided various theories and explanations on the origins of the price revolution. It is one of the most researched subjects in the economic history of Europe. The initial reaction to the price inflation in the sixteenth century was seen as a creation of individual wickedness. Theologians and preachers made scathing attacks on the monopolists and the usurers. The German Diet blamed the Fuggers and other merchant bankers for this situation. The scarcity of food and other commodities was also seen as the result of human weakness such as idleness or greed. Thomas More in *Utopia* blamed 'the unreasonable covetousness of a few' for 'the great dearth of victualles'. He described the sheep as men-eaters as he believed that food was running short because of the greedy landlords who were turning their lands over to sheep to make profits out of the sale of wool. Thomas Starkey also expressed a similar sentiment against the idlers and the ill-occupied people in 1533. In England, the rack-renting landlords and grain merchants became the common targets and were blamed for the price rise. Till now no proper explanation has been provided and all these views are based on beliefs rather than proper analysis.

Professor Martin de Azpilceuta of Salamanca University came out with another explanation in 1556. He suspected a connection between the price rise and increasing availability of bullion. To him money was worth more when and where it was scarce than where it was in abundance. He said that money was scarcer in France than in Spain and he believed that saleable goods and labour became much cheaper after the discovery of the Indies. Jean Bodin further expounded this view in 1568. The two Frenchmen – Bodin and Malestroit – debated the causes of inflation. The latter, an official of the French Royal mint maintained that the so-called inflation was illusionary and he compared the prices of the thirteenth century with those prevalent in the sixteenth century and found no indications of inflation. He believed that whatever slight increase had taken place was due to the debasement of currency. It is a common fact that many European governments had debased their coinage by reducing the silver content to increase the number of coins. This was done to fetch a better price for the products in the international market and to pay their debts that had been mounting because of the growing expenditure of the luxurious courts. The English government debased its coins first in 1520 then in 1546 and 1551. During this period the silver content of one penny was reduced to one-sixth. Between 1543 and 1546, the silver content of a shilling was reduced from 100 to 40 grains. Jean Bodin offered several explanations based on his own observations and among them he focused on the influx of gold and silver causing the price rise. He believed that the currency debasement was an insufficient factor to account for the price rise. Bodin argued that as the rise in food prices was out of all proportion to the extent by which the monies of account had been depreciated, the real reason could only be the influx of American silver. Later Richard Cantillon and Adam Smith also shared this view. In the late-eighteenth century, Adam Smith wrote that the discovery of the abundant mines of America seemed to have been the sole cause of diminution in the value of silver in proportion to that of corn. In the twentieth century, Earl J. Hamilton (on Spain) and Fernand Braudel (on Mediterranean) gave this theory historical confirmation. This has come to be known as the 'Quantity Theory of Money'.

Earl J. Hamilton primarily wrote on the price rise of the sixteenth century in Andalusia and later he applied his observation more generally to western Europe. Hamilton believed that there was a close connection between the imports of American gold and silver and the prices in Andalusia. He observed an upward trend in the prices from 1503–5 until 1595, which he believed was closely linked to the arrival of treasures from America. Thus, the sharpest rise in prices, according to Hamilton, coincided with the greatest increase in the imports of gold and silver. After that period, decrease in the import of bullion resulted in the declining trend in prices. Irving Fisher gave a new mathematical basis to the Quantity theory, when he stated,

$$MV = PT$$

(This equation states that money supply times its velocity of circulation is equal to the price of goods and services times the number of transactions.)

Graph 6.2 provides a glimpse of silver imports from the New World into Spain. The earliest imports can be seen in the 1520s consisting of a paltry volume of 148 kg. It soon picked up in the next decade, and continued to rise till the end of the sixteenth century. The peak was reached in the 1590s when 2,707,627 kg. of

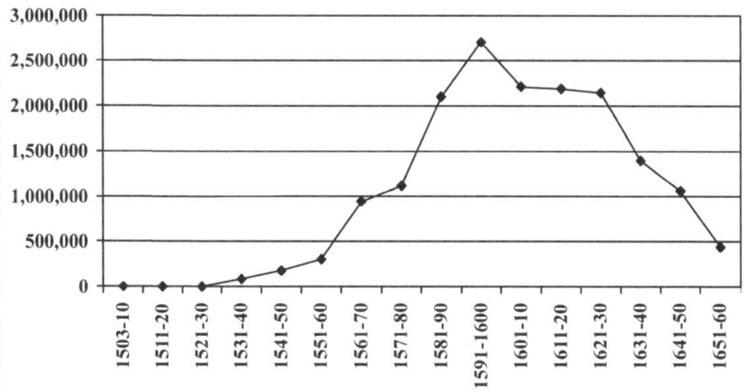

Source: Based on figures provided by Harry A. Miskimim, *The Economy of Later Renaissance Europe*, p. 33.

Graph 6.2: Import of Silver from the New World into Spain 1503–1600 (in kilograms)

silver was imported through official channels. The subsequent decades witnessed a steady downward trend in silver imports.

This explanation of the price rise received immediate attention of many scholars. Comments were made both in favour and against this view. Many historians do not fully agree with this view. The quantity theory of money has been subjected to much attack on empirical as well as on theoretical grounds. Doubts have been frequently expressed whether V and Q remain constant. In a strong criticism of Hamilton, Ingrid Hammarstrom argued that Hamilton had got his sequence wrong. She argued that it was an increase in economic activity that led to an increase in prices. The mining activities in central Europe also augmented the supply of bullion. For her the fundamental question is – to what use was the bullion put to? Y.S. Brenner also supports Hammerstrom and argues that the changes in the commodity price level were caused less from an increase, or lack of increase, in the European stock of metal than from the manner in which this stock was employed. Citing the English example, Brenner suggests that the price rise antedated the arrival of American treasure. Historians such as P. Vilar and Jorge Nadal criticized Hamilton for concentrating only on the town prices and ignoring the rural prices of the local markets. They argue that Hamilton omitted regions like Catalonia and Basque, which were perhaps closer to the European economy than the rest of Spain. They also object to the authenticity of data provided by Hamilton, as it does not indicate the criteria adopted for separating royal income from private income.

Writers such as Miskimin and R.S. Lopez have accepted the role of American bullion in causing price revolution in a general sense. Citing the mercantilists' obsession with bullion, Miskimin suggests that the inflow of precious metals would probably have set men and resources to work and, at the same time, tended to increase the funds available for government finance, thereby lowering the cost of fighting wars. Miskimin also supports the view of Hamilton on the slow rate of inflation till the first quarter of the sixteenth century and feels that the economic growth from 1465 till the period of the Reformation was a process of slow recovery. To Miskimin the gap between the prices of agriculture and manufactured goods does not disprove the quantity theory because there were many factors such as the demographic change, shifts in taste, and divergent elasticity of demand and supply. These can all be comprehended within the quantity equation. Yet, the quantity theory of money has been criticized for not providing an adequate explanation for the price rise. Ralph Davis draws attention to the unevenness of the price rise between different categories of products showing the consistence patterns with corn leading the way while the prices of industrial goods seem to have risen but more slowly. If the increase in prices was caused by the supply of money, the prices of all the commodities would have risen evenly. There is also a doubt over the chronology of the rate of price increase and the volume of bullion imported into Europe. Drawing from the German case Jack A. Goldstone suggested certain improvements to the equation $MV=PT$ by stating that between 1500 and 1650, the population active in the market rose by a factor of three or slightly more and the overall population doubled. This should be multiplied by 50 to 75 per cent increase in market participation. The ratio of V/Q in the monetary equation $P=MV/Q$ could also have increased by a factor of three or more (because V grows as the square of population while in the same period Q grew linearly or slightly less). As this population growth – induced velocity effect, would roughly triple the impact of any increase in money supplies on prices, the population–velocity mechanism was probably the key factor during the price revolution. This population-velocity model derived from the network theory, according to Goldstone, has a force to account for the magnitude of inflation during the price revolution.

According to C.M. Cipolla, the highest average price increase in Italy took place between 1552 and 1560, when the prices rose on an average of 5.2 per cent annually, while the influx of the American silver affected Italy only after the sixteenth century. The reason for the price rise before that period, in the view of Cipolla, was the restoration of peace after a prolonged war from 1494, which was one of the chief causes of the price increase. The price rise had taken place much before the influence of American gold and silver was felt in Europe. The most important reason for the rise of Italian prices prior to 1570, according to Cipolla, was the country's work of reconstruction after the prolonged war. The range of price variation in Italy can be seen from Table 6.1 provided by Cipolla.

This Table indicates that in the case of Italy, the arrival of bullion in Europe did not affect the price rise correspondingly and that there must have been other factors operating on the prices. Cipolla is skeptical of the term price revolution but he agrees that the

TABLE 6.1: PRICE RISE IN ITALY 1552–60 to 1600–17

Period	Average annual movement (per cent)
1552–60	+ 5.2
1560–5	- 1.2
1565–73	+ 3.3
1573–90	- 0.4
1590–1600	+ 3.1
1600–17	- 0.8

Source: C.M. Cipolla, 'The "so-called" Price Revolution: Reflections on the Italian Situation' in Peter Burke (ed.), *Economy and Society in Early Modern Europe*, 1972, p. 44.

American silver bullion inflow created a floor below which the price could no longer fall in the long phases of depression. Michel Morineau suggests that the wheat prices rose or fell in direct response to the harvest situation. Bullion did not raise prices so much as prevented them from falling below a particular point.

The demand for bullion existed even in the fifteenth century when the American mines had not been discovered. In the early period, the silver mines in Serbia and Bosnia were developed and remained an important source till the Turkish invasion in the mid-fifteenth century. From the 1460s, the silver mines in central Europe were exploited rapidly with the help of technological improvements. Silver production between 1460 and 1530 witnessed fivefold increase in Central Asia. The central European silver production reached its peak in the period 1526–35 when the annual production was about 10,00,000 kg. (B.H. Slicher van Bath). The expansion of trade and the increasing scale of monetary transactions made this supply inadequate. The Portuguese began to procure gold from Sudan but silver could only be supplied from central Europe. The trans-oceanic trade further added pressure on silver mines to pay for the unequal trade balance between Europe and the Orient. After 1530, the shortage of silver was considerably eased due to the unexpected discovery of American treasures. After 1580, silver supply increased many folds as the new method of amalgamation of the treatment of silver with mercury, which was earlier devised in Germany, was introduced in the Central American mines. After 1571, this method was adopted in the Potosi silver mines in upper Peru. This resulted in a tenfold increase in silver production. Silver supplies picked up between 1580 and 1630. However, the rise in prices had started much before the arrival of the American silver and in the seventeenth century when the silver imports into Europe were at their peak, a downward trend in prices had already set in. Thus, if the quantity theory of money is to be accepted as the primary cause of the price revolution, then the velocity of circulation and its application in the context of the disparities in the European economy has to be taken into account. The relationship between the influx of precious metals and the rise in prices has to be seen with a lot of caution keeping in mind its limitations. The treasure in itself was not the only factor in the price revolution as prices were also affected by several other reasons.

The demographic explanation has been provided as an alternative to the quantity theory of money. Scholars like Peter Kriedte and Ralph Davis suggest that the growth of money in circulation is, in conditions of economic expansions, more probably a reflection of expansion than its cause. It is, therefore, likely that other non-monetary factors unleashed the price revolution and the Spanish silver only provided a secondary role. The real cause, according to them, is to be located in the demographic factor. The period after the second half of the fifteenth century experienced a steady increase in the European population. It was accompanied by a steady rise in urbanization leading to people moving to urban centres. The rise in population created greater demand for food, fuel and clothing.

The sources available on population figures are very unsatisfactory. There are no census reports or reliable estimates for the whole of the sixteenth century. Whatever statistics are available has been pieced together from the materials such as parish registers, tax returns or muster rolls. All this evidence points to the rise in population from the late-fifteenth century till the beginning of the seventeenth century.

Sixteenth-century European population was still rural in composition and the production process worked mostly within the framework of traditional and a relatively unchanging structure. Most of the expansion had taken place outside agriculture due to the inelasticity in the method of cultivation. In such a structure, population movements became the principal factor in the formation of demand. Although the study of population before the eighteenth century is subject to pitfalls and very few reliable estimates are available, still scholars like Cipolla, Hilton, Peter Kriedte, J.U. Nef and many others have tried to provide some rough estimates based on varied sources. Most of the information on demography comes from municipal records, district or provincial censuses of households, land registers, taxation records and the muster rolls for military recruitment. On the basis of these, it is estimated that in 1500, there were only five large cities in Europe, each with a population of over 1,00,000 inhabitants – Constantinople, Naples, Venice, Milan and Paris. By 1600, seven or eight new cities emerged such as Rome, Palermo, Messina, Marseilles, Lisbon, Seville, Antwerp, London, Amsterdam and probably Moscow. The population of Paris and Naples had crossed over 2,00,000. A number of smaller towns also expanded such as Vienna, Lubuck, Augsburg, Straasburg, Danzig, etc. Treating 1500 as the base year on 100 index points, Peter Kriedte suggests that in northern Europe, the index points had gone up to 163, in north-western Europe to 154, in southern Europe to 132, in central Europe to 130, south-eastern Europe to 123 and in eastern Europe it moved to 125. According to Julius Beloch, the most populous regions in around 1600 were in Germany, France and Italy while Scandinavia and Denmark were the least populated regions. Italy had the heaviest density of about 114 persons per square mile; in the Low Countries it was 104; in France 88; in England and Wales 78; in Germany about 73 while in Spain and Portugal average density was just 44 (F.C. Spooner, *The New Cambridge Modern History*, III). Lombardy was probably the most thickly populated region. All these figures are based on rough estimates and are subject to the methodology used by historians. It is estimated that the population of Europe was between 50–60 million in 1450 but by 1600 it had reached 82–5 million (F.C. Spooner), while some scholars put the figure much higher. An estimate of the population growth during the sixteenth century can be had from Table 6.2 that depicts population figures between 1500 and 1700.

As is evident from this table, the sixteenth century witnessed a steady rise in population in every part of Europe, though the rate of growth varied. It began to place a heavy burden on agrarian resources and led to an extension of cultivable land. Agricultural production increased but without much change in technology. The increase could not go beyond a point because of feudalism. The rise in population hastened the process of urbanization as families became larger, the peasants started keeping back more of their produce for their own needs. This growing demand and an inadequate supply of food grains explain the phenomenon of price increase of agricultural products in which corn led the way. It also explains why the prices of manufactured commodities did not increase in the same proportion. The pressure of a growing urban population can be gauged from Table 6.3.

TABLE 6.2: COUNTRY-WISE POPULATION IN EUROPE 1500–1700

(*in millions*)

Regions and countries	*c.* 1500	*c.* 1600	*c.* 1700
Spain & Portugal	9.3	11.3	10.0
Italy	10.5	13.3	13.3
France (including Lorrain & Savoy)	16.4	18.3	20.0
Benelux countries	1.9	2.9	3.4
British Isles	4.4	6.8	9.3
Scandinavian countries	1.5	2.4	2.8
Germany	12.0	15.0	15.0
Switzerland	0.8	1.0	1.2
Durbian countries	5.5	7.0	8.8
Poland	3.5	5.0	6.0
Russia	9.0	15.5	17.5
Balkans	7.0	8.0	8.0
Total for Europe	81.8	104.7	115.3

Source: C.M. Cipolla, *The Fontana Economic History of Europe*, p. 38.

TABLE 6.3: URBAN POPULATION AS A PERCENTAGE OF TOTAL POPULATION (1500–1750)

	1500	1550	1600	1650	1700	1750
Scandinavia	0.9	0.8	1.4	2.4	4.0	4.6
England and Wales	3.1	3.5	5.8	8.8	13.3	16.7
Scotland	1.6	1.4	3.0	3.5	5.3	9.2
Ireland	0.0	0.0	0.0	0.9	3.4	5.0
Netherlands	15.8	15.3	24.3	31.7	33.6	30.5
Belgium	21.1	22.7	18.8	20.8	23.9	19.6
Germany	3.2	3.8	4.1	4.4	4.8	5.6
France	4.2	4.3	5.9	7.2	9.2	9.1
Switzerland	1.5	1.5	2.5	2.2	3.3	4.6
Italy	12.4	12.8	14.7	14.0	13.4	14.2
Spain	6.1	8.6	11.4	9.5	9.0	8.6
Portugal	3.0	11.5	14.1	16.6	11.5	9.1
Austria/Bohemia/Moravia	1.7	1.9	2.1	2.4	3.9	5.2
Poland	0.0	0.3	0.4	0.7	0.5	1.0

Source: J. de Vries, *European Urbanization 1500–1800*, p. 271, quoted by N.J.G. Pounds, p. 271.

As is evident from this table, Belgium and Netherlands were the most urbanized regions but the former could not sustain the pace and consequently, the percentage of urban population declined. Italy, Spain and Portugal also experienced a similar trend but only after the mid-seventeenth century. In the Netherlands and England, urbanization speeded up rather sharply from the mid-sixteenth century coinciding with the period of Dutch hegemony followed by England's economic ascendancy. However, even the demographic explanation by itself cannot account for the price rise. Several factors must have been responsible for the upward trend in prices during the sixteenth century: the increased volume of money in circulation because of wars; the growing urban population raising demand for agricultural and manufactured goods; economic prosperity, war expenses and the expenditure on reconstruction, and most importantly the rise in population. At the same time, the quantity theory of money cannot be completely ignored. It has to be remembered that every thing that caused long-term upward movement of prices from the late-fifteenth century to early-seventeenth century was interdependent: moneys of account, coinage, state of economy, social structures, demand elasticity, demographic trends and the availability of metals. By money of account, we mean a scale of measurement, or a unit of measurement for gold coins, silver bullion or copper that brings them all into a valid relationship with one another. It is distinct from the currency in every day circulation and is used in settlement of international trade (for more on money of account, see *The Cambridge Economic History of Europe*, IV).

The Impact of Price Revolution

As noted earlier in this chapter, various historians have explained the causes of the price revolution differently. Similarly, the consequences of inflation are the subject of a lively debate. It has been suggested that the price revolution affected the whole of Europe and had important social repercussions. At the same time, it should be noted that its impact was not uniform but varied in different regions.

Earl J. Hamilton is of the view that during the price revolution, wages lagged behind prices causing profit inflation. The increase in profits stimulated business and capital investment and contributed to the capitalist development and economic prosperity. Hamilton asserted that there was not only a price rise but also a wage lag. It deprived the labourers of a large part of the income and diverted this wealth into the hands of manufacturers and middlemen. Rents as well as wages lagged behind prices. This resulted in windfall for some and this provided them an incentive for the feverish pursuit of capitalist enterprises. The disparity between wages and prices becomes evident in the 1530s resulting in discontent among the labourers and occasionally leading to open revolts. J.M. Keynes not only supported this view but also went much ahead of Hamilton when he argued that there was an extraordinary correspondence between the period of profit inflation and profit deflation respectively with those of national rise and decline in the case of France, England and Spain. There are many others who argue that by greatly increasing the money supply, the added bullion contributed much to the use of money. It gave greater mobility to capital, encouraged investments, promoted market activities and resulted in division of labour. These views were expressed with rudimentary simplicity and became the subject of much criticism subsequently. Writers such as J.U. Nef and David Felix do not subscribe to the views of Hamilton and deny that profit inflation automatically contributes to capital formation. Nef observes that whereas the price inflation was greatest in Spain, profit inflation was perhaps greater in France but the economic growth was fastest in England. On the basis of his study of wage rates, prices and industrial technology, he accepts that one cannot disprove the thesis that the price revolution stimulated capitalism but the influence of price movement was much more complex. David Felix also points out that there was no clear sign of profit inflation as suggested by Hamilton and Keynes.

The price revolution led to a few changes in the manufacturing sector in the form of new methods and inventions in the preparation of soap, glass and in the sugar refineries but these were minor industries. The major industries such as textile, shipbuilding and metal processing underwent little change in the course of the sixteenth century. Textile manufacturing shifted from the guild-controlled urban centres to the rural areas to escape municipal control and strict regulations and to utilize cheap labour.

Some scholars have tried to explore and analyse the relationship between prices and wages. Slicher van Bath prepared a series of drafts pertaining to the prices of cereals, population growth and the levels of real wages. In his argument he tries to establish that fluctuations in population exert a strong influence on consumption and thereby affect the course of prices. The price level and price movements, according to him, are also determined by the quantity of money and the rate of its circulation. The swings in prices are not so important because money should be treated as a medium of exchange. According to him, in the second half of the sixteenth century, particularly after 1550, there was a decline in real wages at an increasing rate till the first half of the seventeenth century when it reached its lowest point. While the wage level was rising in the period of monetary inflation, the rate of increase was not in proportion to the rate of increase in prices. The real income of the workers and artisans had reached the lowest level since the thirteenth century. Based on the ten-yearly averages at the 1700–49 level, Mark Overton has prepared a table of prices for England covering different products including wheat, barley, oats, mutton, wool and wages. The price of wheat shows a steady and speedy rise from twenty-two points to hundred by the 1590s. The price of barley also rose rather sharply from seventeen to ninety-two in the same period and wool prices increased from twenty-four to eighty-nine. Wages rose from thirty-two to seventy but the increase was far less than other items. However, the real wages declined by more than half, i.e. from one hundred forty-six to seventy-two points. This is evident from Graph 6.3.

Historians generally agree that the social consequences of the sixteenth-century inflation were immense. Prices went up faster than the wages, generating social tensions in the urban population. It seriously affected the wage earners and salaried sections in the towns. Besides, the price rise greatly increased the costs of administration and created serious problems for many rulers. The

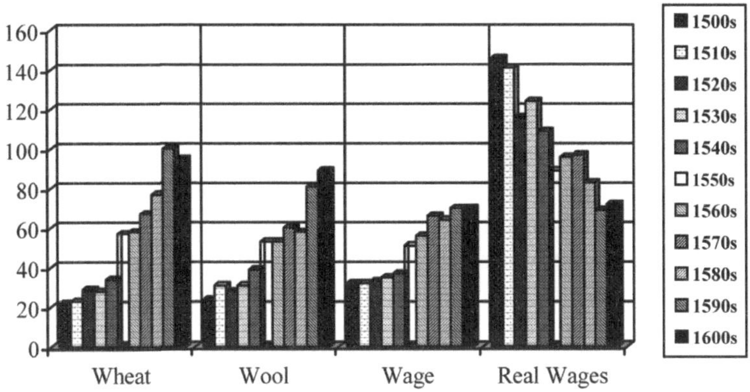

Source: Mark Overton, p. 64.

Graph 6.3: Price Level in England 1500–1600
(with base index of 100 on prices prevalent in 1700–49)

first two Stuart kings of England faced stiff popular resistance on their financial policies leading to the break with their parliaments. The Spanish rulers also faced grave threats caused by their mounting borrowings. The French rulers faced strong opposition on the question of state taxation.

Many historians believe that the price revolution provided a major incentive to economic transformation in western Europe and resulted in partial collapse of the manorial system of agriculture. It was accompanied by significant social changes. The impact of the price revolution was felt differently by different classes and varied according to the regions. It did not affect all market goods uniformly but it brought about major changes in the economic relationship between classes and individuals. The inflation of the sixteenth century brought about a major redistribution of income among the classes and thereby widened the gaps between regions and countries. However, a clearer assessment, especially of the rural society of Europe, is not easy in the absence of sufficient statistical data. A number of scholars have argued that the price revolution brought about the rise of the gentry in England during the sixteenth century, as they were involved in the market structure, reaped huge profits in agriculture and emerged as a strong political force. However, recent studies have questioned this analysis by doubting whether the rise of the gentry was because of the favourable market conditions or because of royal favour.

In France, Spain and Italy, the nobility managed to overcome the serious financial problems caused by the price revolution by raising the rent of their lands or by imposing entry fines. The upper nobility, especially in France, received favours from the crown in the form of pensions, lands or offices in return for military and administrative services. The lesser nobility in France was less successful in adjusting their rents to the economic situations and consequently many of them joined the army or engaged in the wars of religion. In this situation, the younger sons of the lesser nobility suffered. In Holstein and Denmark, the nobles benefitted from the higher prices by acting as middlemen between the peasants and foreign merchants. In Germany, the social effects varied according to the locality and the classes. In western Germany, the nobility found it difficult to raise rents except in Bavaria and Austria, as the ruling princes allowed their claims of raising entry fines. In south-west Germany, the situation was slightly different. The princes provoked unrest among the peasants at several places by substituting the local customs with the autocratic form of the Roman law. They took direct control over the villages and seigneurial jurisdictions by imposing new taxes. In many parts of western Europe, it was seen that peasants whose dues to their lords had been commuted to fixed money payments were paying less in terms of real value than the earlier generations. Conversely these landlords received lower payments because of the diminished value of money. This situation was beneficial for those landlords who rented their land on short-term leases, thus reaping the advantages of the market situation.

The socio-economic impact of the price revolution was considerable in many parts of central Europe. There was a growing market of products like rye, timber and furs in western and southern Europe. Poland profited from this new situation. The landowners started substituting feudal cash rents into service rents. They raised cheap labour to carry out farming work in their *demesne* lands by forcibly tying the peasants to their holdings. Nothing was done by the local princes to check this trend of fresh enserfment because they were themselves dependent on these landowners or junkers as they were called.

The small peasants generally suffered in this period of rising prices, as they were unable to take advantage of the increase in the prices of agricultural products. They produced on a small scale and could not independently participate in the market transactions. The Polish middle class could not profit either from the expanding markets as the nobility exerted greater weight. Capital accumulation of merchants was greatly restricted in the Polish towns because the landed magnates pocketed the benefits of the trade. The high cost of living disrupted the lives of a large number of people. During the price spiral, there were frequent complaints and counter complaints by the merchants and the nobility against each other in the Diet and in the pamphlet war. This situation was not confined to Poland or the German states only but could be seen even in Bohemia. In the years of the anti-Habsburg revolts in the mid-sixteenth century, the nobility not only enserfed the peasants but also actively participated in the grain trade by prohibiting the peasants from sending their produce directly to the markets. Instead they themselves bought this produce on extremely favourable terms and exported it to Saxony and other areas at profitable rates.

Various scholars have seen the impact of the price revolution on land tenurial relationship differently. It is true that not all the people were directly affected by the price rise. The long-distance trade in food items provided profit to the middlemen or to those sections that controlled this trade. Usually it was favourable to the agriculturists because price rise was the greatest in agricultural products. In the case of England, it is no longer accepted that all the peasants suffered in equal degree from excessive rents imposed by the landlords. Most of the time it was the smaller landlords, quite often the recent purchaser of land, who rack-rented their tenants to obtain a share of increased produce from the land. Not all English landlords could break the legal and customary barriers of tenuarial relationship by enhancing the rent in order to raise their own income. The smaller peasants did not have surplus stocks of corn to profit from the rising prices of food grains. They were the chief victims of rent increases. For most part of the sixteenth century, the rents usually lagged behind the prices of corn but between the 1580s and 1620s, the rents rose steeply and many landlords were able to recover their earlier losses to the tenants by enhancing their rents. In many cases land was given on shorter leases to the tenants. However, by this time some of the big landlords were ruined in England and France, particularly those who showed unwillingness to adopt better methods of land management in order to meet the challenge of rising prices. At places, landlords exerted political influence to evict the farmers from their land or to rewrite the lease deals. In England, some of the landlords were fortunate to escape their economic ruin, as they possessed supplementary sources of income in the form of mineral deposits within their estates. These advantages kept them out of bankruptcy.

The social impact of the price rise proved disastrous for some sections of the people. In many parts of western Europe, the number of landless population increased because of evictions by the landlords. The growing population and lack of job opportunities led to a steady flow of population away from agriculture towards the towns. Even in towns, there were few jobs available in the absence of big industries. The powerful guilds in towns and the government legislation on professions prevented them from entering the manufacturing sectors. The falling standards of living of the poorer sections were evident from the growing problem of pauperism, which existed in many parts of western Europe, but was more evident in England. The glut in the market after a period of boom, caused by a series of debasement of currency, resulted in market crisis in the early 1550s, especially in textile items. It intensified the problem of poverty into a serious social concern. People who were forced out of jobs in the textile sector became beggars and vagabonds in many large towns. The Tudor kings found it difficult to solve this problem. A series of Poor Laws were enacted and finally codified in 1601. It also forced the government to adopt legislation against the enclosure movement and to prevent rural depopulation.

Thus, the price revolution set in motion a series of economic and social changes throughout Europe. On one extreme, it contributed to the commercialization of agriculture, expansion of the market structure and promoted manufacturing activities, thereby breaking manorial hold over land, as it happened in some parts of western Europe. On the other extreme, it strengthened the control of the nobility over land and expanded serfdom and feudal order in Central and Eastern Europe.

Suggested Readings

Abel, Wilhelm, *Agricultural Fluctuations in Europe: From the Thirteenth to the Twentieth Centuries*, London: Methuen & Co., 1980.

Aymard, Maurice, ed., *Dutch Capitalism and World Capitalism: Capitalisme hollandaise et capitalism mondial*, Paris and Cambridge: Maison des Sciences de L'homme, 1982. Extremely useful book on Dutch ascendancy, containing writings of many important scholars on the subject.

Burke, Peter (ed.), *Economy and Society in Early Modern Europe: Essays from Annales*, New York: Harper and Row, 1972. Has a collection of essays on diverse themes that includes a short chapter by Carlo M. Cipolla.

Cameron, Enan (ed.), *The Sixteenth Century*, Oxford: Oxford University Press, 2006. Six leading experts discuss this period from political, social, economic, religious and intellectual perspectives.

Cipolla, Carlo M., *Before the Industrial Revolution: European Society and Economy 1000–1700*, 2nd edn., London: Methuen, 1981.

——— (ed.), *Fontana Economic History of Europe: The Emergence of Industrial Societies*, London: Collins, 1975. Cipolla is considered an authority on the European economic history. The book is rich in data and detailed analysis.

Davis, Ralph, *Rise of Atlantic Economics*, Ithaca: Weidenfeld and Nicolson, 1973. Contains useful discussion on price revolution.

Earle, Peter, ed., *Essays in European Economy 1500–1800*, Oxford: Clarendon Press, 1974. Contains some important contributions from Braudel, Kallenbenz, Vilar, Chaunu, Romano, etc., on economy of different regions during the sixteenth and the seventeenth centuries.

Goldstone, Jack A., 'Monetary Versus Velocity Interpretations of the "Price Revolution": A Comment', *The Journal of Economic History*, 51, 1, 1991, pp. 176–81. A well-argued essay on price revolution covering some historiography too.

Kiernan, V.G., *State and Society in Europe 1550–1650*, Oxford: Basil Blackwell, 1980.

Kriedte, Peter, *Peasants, Landlords and Merchant Capitalists: Europe and the World Economy 1500–1800*, Cambridge: Cambridge University Press, 1983. A well-argued work containing detailed information on European economy over three centuries.

Martin, John E., *Feudalism to Capitalism: Peasants and Landlords in English Agrarian Development*, London: Macmillan, 1983. Takes up the issue of agrarian development in relation to social structure.

Overton, Mark, *Agricultural Revolution in England: The Transformation of the Agrarian Economy, 1500–1850*, Cambridge: Cambridge University Press, 1996. Has analysed in detail the European economy of the sixteenth century.

Pettegree, Andrew, *Europe in the Sixteenth Century*, Oxford: Basil Blackwell, 2002.

Price, J.L., *Culture and Society in the Dutch Republic during the 17th Century*, London: B.T. Batsford, 1974. Chapter three briefly deals with the Dutch economic expansion and commercial domination.

Rich, E.E. and C.H. Wilson, eds., *The Cambridge Economic History of Europe*, vol. IV: *The Economy of Expanding Europe in the 16th and 17th Centuries*, Cambridge: Cambridge University Press (1967), 1975. Very good for the demographic studies and an in-depth analysis of price movements and trade statistics.

Romano, Ruggiero, 'Between the Sixteenth and Seventeenth Centuries: The Economic Crisis of 1619–22' in Geoffrey Parker and L.M. Smith, *The General Crisis of the Seventeenth Century*, London: Routledge and Kegan Paul, 1978. The book has a collection of impressive articles mainly on the seventeenth-century crisis.

van Houtte, J.A., *An Economic History of the Low Countries, 800–1800*, London: Weidenfeld & Nicolson, 1977.

vsan Bath, Slicher, *The Agrarian History of Western Europe, a.d. 500–1850*, London: Elward Arnold, 1964. Good for agricultural developments but also contains useful information on population, prices and wages.

CHAPTER 7

Crisis of the Seventeenth Century

The vast expansion that began in the second half of the fifteenth century slowly came to an end in many European regions between 1600 and 1620. Some parts experienced decelerated growth, some stagnated, while the economy of many other regions witnessed a steady decline. During the sixteenth century, the centre of economic activities and the bustling of trade first shifted from the Italian city states in the Mediterranean to the Iberian states of Spain and Portugal and then it gravitated further north towards the north-western states of the Atlantic, particularly Holland and England. This was a clear indication of the decline of the Iberian peninsula and the Italian states – the two prosperous regions of Europe in the early-sixteenth century. The seventeenth century witnessed an overall contraction of the European economy after a century of expansion in agriculture that allowed the boom in trade and industry. After 1600, the commercial and industrial sectors began to lose their drive because of the lack of support of agriculture. Many parts of Europe experienced uprisings, major conflicts and wars and breakdown of political orders. Contemporaries have painted destructive pictures of Europe of this period. Demographic trends suggest downward movement or stagnation in the different parts of Europe. Several scholars describe the seventeenth century as a period of crisis. A debate has been going on among historians on the nature and the scale of the problems that Europe experienced. Though the debate is still alive, the majority of scholars believe that the seventeenth century was a period of crisis. The decline of the Mediterranean states is particularly highlighted in this period of European crisis.

The all-round growth of the European economy in the sixteenth century was arrested in the last decade of the century first in the

Mediterranean region and then in many other parts. The only exception was the north-eastern region of Europe comprising mainly Holland and England. An attempt was made in the sixteenth century to enter the age of modern economy by breaking the barriers of medieval structures but it did not succeed. In fact, the entire growth had taken place within the old mould. Thus, the old feudal mode of production continued, rather strengthened in the course of the crisis in most regions. Europe had to wait till the eighteenth century to depart from the old economic systems and to enter the definite phase of capitalism.

Decline of the Mediterranean Economy

Fernand Braudel described the Mediterranean in the sixteenth century as a *Welttheatre* or *Weltwirtschaft* – a world-theatre or world-economy (*The Perspective of the World, Civilization and Capitalism*). This whole area was stimulated by trade. The Mediterranean region had a certain economic unity despite political, cultural and social divisions. In the Italian peninsula, this unity was imposed upon it by the dominant cities of northern Italy that lasted for over two centuries. Foremost among them were Venice, Milan, Genoa and Florence. According to Braudel, this economic activity went beyond the frontiers of empires – whether the Spanish or the Turkish. The Christian merchants could be found in Syria, Egypt, Istanbul and North Africa, while the Levantine, Turkish and Armenian merchants reached the Adriatic Sea. In this economy, large volume of transactions of currencies and commodities created prosperity. Venice was the centre of this economy directly operating in the Mediterranean by way of intermediaries. The trading network reached the Baltic, northern and western parts of Europe and through the Levant ports in the east to the Indian Ocean and northern Africa.

Since the mid-fourteenth century, some of the Italian cities had become the centre of industries. Venice with an extended network of trade and enormous fleet of trading vessels became the epicentre of world economy. Similarly, the evolution of Spain under the crown of Castile and Aragon as the supreme power of Europe in the sixteenth century was spectacular. In the course of sixteenth century, the importance of Venice waned. The zenith of Spanish hegemony was reached in the 1580s when the Grand empire included Portugal, several states of Italy, the Netherlands, and the Philippines and huge territories in Central and South America. It not only possessed the rich mines of the New World but had become the mightiest military power in Europe. However, by the mid-seventeenth century the domination of the Mediteranean states came to an end and they were pushed outside the main network of world economy. Even Antwerp lost its importance to Amsterdam. To understand this economic transformation, one has to take up the cases of Spain and Italy separately.

Decline of Spain

During the sixteenth century, Spain dominated Europe. Spain possessed an extensive empire within and outside Europe and dazzled the visitor with her vast territorial empire and her formidable force. The vast colonial possessions were the source of her riches and wealth. Silver reached the Spanish ports Seville and Cadiz, in abundance. Trade between Spain and her colonies expanded manifold and so did the Spanish navy and the shipping industry. The Habsburg rulers of Spain ruled a vast stretch of Europe that included the Netherlands, Austria, several German and some Italian states. If the size of the empire was a measurement of power, then Spain appeared to be at the pinnacle of glory in the sixteenth century. However, within this vast empire, several weaknesses existed, which manifested themselves once that phase of glory was over. Historians are intrigued by the fact that almost a century later, Spain came to be considered a second-rate power, much behind England, the Netherlands and even France. Several interpretations, whether this degeneration was the result of internal factors or external causes, needs to be examined.

A discussion on the causes of the decline of Castile can be seen in the works of a group of seventeenth-century Spanish writers called the *Arbitristas*, who influenced historical writings for a long time. An idea of their views can be formed from their writing –

'The Political Programme of an Anonymous *Arbitrista*'. It states,

> I assure Your Majesty that . . . improvements are very necessary, because monarchy has reached the unhappiest condition that is believable, and it is the most decayed and prostrate condition that has ever been seen until today . . . it is now customary for them [ministers], having spent all their early life pleasantly and without working in a university or college, to arrive young at the leading posts in this monarchy and government. And there they are only exposed to excessive luxuries, salaries, and gifts . . . there are at present many incapable, inefficient and unworthy ministers. . . . (Quoted by Gary M. Best, p. 33)

There is no unanimity of opinion among historians on questions like – when did the decline start, was the decline all-pervasive or confined only to a few states, and on the actual causes of the decline. It is much easier to describe the decline than to provide an explanation.

J.H. Elliott suggests that the Spanish decline cannot be viewed in isolation. Much of the seventeenth century in Europe is regarded as a period of commercial contraction and demographic stagnation. For him, certain features, earlier considered Spanish, can now be given a universal character. Criticizing the writings on the decline of Spain, Elliott argues that much of these are written with hindsight, as the end of the story is known. For him, the decline was not a dramatic one because even in the mid-seventeenth-century Spain was the largest military power. Some historians, such as Carlo M. Cipolla and Henry Kamen, reject the decline thesis. For Cipolla the fundamental fact is that Spain never developed to begin with. A similar expression can also be found in the work of Henry Kamen. Arguing that early modern Spain could not have declined, as she had never risen, Kamen calls upon the historians to reject this thesis of decline. Spain's development was hindered over centuries by fundamental economic weaknesses. At the same time it would be erroneous to presume that all the regions of the Spanish empire experienced a similar trend. As to the question of precise period of decline there is no clear-cut answer. It varies with each historian. One view is that the period of expansion lasted till about the 1550s and then decline set in, culminating in the 1640s while another view sees the beginning of decline from the 1620s but in no case before 1598.

The second controversy rests on the argument whether it was actually the decline of Spain or only that of the Castile. Many historians believe that it was actually the decline of only a few states of Spain and not the entire region. For example, J.I. Israel argues that in the state of Valencia, the pattern was one of growth and expansion in the sixteenth century followed by stagnation and decline in the seventeenth century. This was also the case with Castile. Kamen emphasizes that the state of Catalonia showed distinct development during this period and that it was not the decline of Spain but only of Castile.

Monetary and Fiscal Troubles

Emphasizing the role of American silver, Earl J. Hamilton suggests that silver imports played a major role in the rise of Spain and when the volume of imports declined from the 1620s, her decline began. Spain could not have maintained and expanded the vast empire without the American silver. According to him, the illusion of prosperity created by American gold and silver in the age of mercantilism was primarily responsible for an aggressive foreign policy, a love for luxury and extravagance, and a contempt for manual crafts, led to the economic decay of the seventeenth century. Supporting this argument, Dennis O. Flynn contends that mining profits rather than the quantity of silver imports supported the Spanish empire. The increased production of American silver and its arrival in Spain drove down its market value. The cost of production increased leading to mining recession and the colonial possessions came to be described as 'parasitical'. According to this viewpoint, the decline of Spain was primarily because her society had got addicted to the influx of American treasure and could not survive its reduction, as had happened from the 1620s. The huge resources at the command of the Spanish rulers were dissipated in unnecessary wars and expenditure. Spain was involved in prolonged conflicts that included the Habsburg – Valois struggles (between the Spanish empire and the French), punitive measures against the Protestants, a war against England, suppression of the Dutch revolt and crusades against the Turks. The Spanish rulers over-estimated the availability of their resources. In the seventeenth century, the supply of silver bullion declined considerably while the expenditure of the Spanish crown continued to grow. This caused a twofold impact and contributed to the Spanish decline. First, it pushed the Spanish rulers towards bankruptcy and forced them to borrow from outside agencies and this caused the outflow of treasure from Spain to other countries. The rulers borrowed at high rates of interest from the foreign bankers like Fuggers and Welsers by mortgaging future cargo arriving from the New World. The situation turned alarming when the rulers were unable to make payments to the troops fighting for Spain in distant regions. This resulted in mutinies, like the one in Antwerp. Second, the reduced inflow of treasure and the insurmountable debts of the Spanish crown led to increased taxation on the people. The new taxes imposed by the rulers included the *millones, alcabala, centos* and *octrois.* Like many feudal states of Europe, the entire burden of these taxes fell on the peasants and businessmen while the unproductive and rich nobility, which could pay the taxes, were exempted. These taxes adversely affected the commercial and the manufacturing sectors and caused major uprisings like the one in Catalonia. The introduction of unchecked minting of copper currency caused violent fluctuations in prices and bankruptcies.

Social Drawbacks

There are some historians who hold the Spanish society responsible for the decline of Spain. They believe that there was no substantial growth of the middle class in Spain despite a vast colonial empire. In some of the port towns or commercial centres such as Seville, Burgos and Medina del Campo, a small class of merchants did exist but society was contemptuous towards trade. According to Jan de Vries, 'Nowhere was the depletion of the bourgeoisie more disastrously complete than in Spain.' There were many economic factors, according to Lynch, operating against the Spanish businessman in the sixteenth century. The influx of precious metals offered great opportunities of economic expansion but they were not properly utilized nor did it promote the rise of a powerful class of businessmen and merchants. There appeared to be a social prejudice against trade, which existed in many other regions of Europe as well. Trade was seen as an intermediary stage of social hierarchy by the society of pre-modern times – a social feature that was also prevalent in France. The ambition of the prosperous merchants was to be able to join the aristocracy and escape the heavy burden of taxation. This mentality proved ruinous for the state in the long run as it made it economically weak. The cities in Spain, which were the centres of wool and textile trade, became the centres of courtiers, officials, clerics and state functionaries. Unlike the English gentry, which remained linked to commerce and market operations, the Spanish nobility displayed contempt for trade and remained aloof from business activity. Otherwise also, the scale of urbanization remained minimal in Spain and large-scale commercial operations could not take place in a sparsely populated country. According to Ralph Davis, the reconquest of Spain left its rulers with an exceptionally large class of people, the *hidalgos*, who claimed privileges of nobility. The *hidalgos* constituted nearly a tenth of the population in Castile and perhaps even higher in other provinces. The nobility constituted not more than 2 per cent of the total population in France and about 3 per cent in England. In Spain, this class exhibited a strong aversion to manual work. They were almost free from direct taxation, from military conscription and degrading punishment. They were men who had acquired vast lands or *juros* allowing them to leave their original occupation, since the status of *hidalgos* gave them privileges and security.

Economic Decline

Hamilton has been criticized by many scholars for over-stressing external factors, while ignoring the internal weaknesses of the Spanish economy. To most historians, Spain's decline was essentially an economic one although it could have been aggravated by politico-social factors. An important indication of the Spanish decline can be found in the demographic losses which she suffered throughout the seventeenth century. This phenomenon was not peculiar to Spain alone but existed in many parts of Europe. However, Spain had several reasons for the loss of population. The heavy loss of population between 1595 and 1602 was mainly caused by plague which killed nearly one million people. The population losses were nearly made up in the next twenty years or so but fresh waves of famine and epidemics at regular intervals particularly between 1647 and 1652, reduced the Spanish population to nearly 80 per cent of what it was about a century earlier. This must have caused a major dislocation of the economy. Compared to other regions of Spain, the concentration of population was the heaviest in Castile. Since Castile had nearly seven-eighth of the total Spanish population, it must have had general impact on Spain. Interestingly, the population of Catalonia actually grew during this period, and that of Andalusia suffered slightly. The impact of population loss was greatest on the cities such as Seville.

Ascribing some peculiar reasons for the decline of the Spanish population, John Lynch emphasizes the role of not only the natural factors but also the specific policies adopted by the Spanish state. According to him, Spain lost perhaps the most enterprising section of its population because of the policies of religious intolerance adopted by the monarchs to evict the Jews and Moors from Spain. It is estimated that nearly 2,000 Jews were burnt alive and 1,20,000 were forced to leave Spain. A large number of Moors were similarly expelled from the Spanish territories and their property seized by the state. This had a paralysing impact on Spanish economy because the Jews not only constituted a vital element of the community occupying important positions as officials and entrepreneurs but also possessed considerable capital. Similarly, the Moors constituted a large segment of the artisans and agriculturists, and were particularly involved in wool production. Historians like Hamilton deny any major impact of such expulsions on the decline of Spain. They suggest that these were neither carried out on a scale that was announced by the government, nor did it have any impact on wages, prices of agricultural products and labour ratio. These writers also maintain that these expulsion had no hand in the decline of agriculture. Opposed to this view, John Lynch stresses the role of the anti-Jew policy and the negative role it played on agricultural production. It created an imbalanced economy and led to a shortage of food grain, which had to be imported on a regular basis from 1506, the time of large-scale evictions. Henceforth, the Spanish demand for wheat was met by imports. Among the factors that caused demographic decline in Spain, Ralph Davis emphasizes the significance of the expulsion of the Moriscos (Muslims who had been converted to Christianity) from 1609 to 1611 and the fact that a large number of men and women were joining the church and thus remaining unmarried. It is argued that the eviction of Moriscos ruined the rice fields of Valencia, the sugar industry of Granada and the vineyards of Spain. As opposed to this view there are others who suggest that there is no evidence to confirm the negative economic impact of these state policies, that the price stability of most of the commodities earlier produced by Moriscos continued in the period following their expulsion. There is no evidence of any significant change in supply or demand of those products. Jan de Vries and many others stress the role of the military and wartime activities in the decline of Spain. The Spanish government was sending on an average seven million guilders to Antwerp throughout the first half of the seventeenth century to maintain a force of 60,000 to 70,000 in Flanders. According to Dennis O. Flynn between 1566 and 1654, the Military Treasury in the Netherlands received a minimum of 218 million ducats from Castile, while the Crown received only 121 million ducats from the Indies. The large-scale military conflicts, religious wars, naval expenses and lavish expenditures of the state created serious problems once the invincibility of the Spanish forces no longer existed.

Several historians blame the agrarian policy of the Spanish state for the gradual decline of Spain. The picture of Spanish agriculture is not very clear, and it is difficult to say whether this period was a time of agricultural difficulties and decline or a period of continuity. While Ralph Davis sees the seventeenth-century agriculture as a movement away from corn production into export crops and of little or no overall decline, Braudel and some others highlight the shortcomings of the state policy towards agriculture that emphasized sheep farming rather than cultivation of the land which caused a constant shortage of corn. According to John Lynch, the Spanish rulers never adopted a consistent policy towards the agriculturists and had little to offer to the rural masses. Only in Catalonia, a struggle between the feudal landowners and the peasants led to the royal judgement of 1486 by which king Ferdinand converted service rent into cash rent. But in a similar situation in Aragon, the crown lent support to the feudal lords. According to Jan de Vries, the crown established control over grain prices in 1539 that lasted until 1756 and this discouraged production. There was an acute dearth of capital in agrarian sector, except in sheep farming. In Castile, the cultivators were sacrificed to the sheep farmers who were given absolute rights over property. A law guaranteed the pastoral interests of the sheep farmers in 1501. The *mesta* farmers comprising the largest landowning families were given permanent rights over extensive tracks of land. The crown in return received substantial and sure revenue in the form of taxes on the number of sheep and on the sale of wool. This strong alliance of interests between the crown and the aristocracy adversely affected agricultural production. The enclosure of arable land was prohibited because it affected the migratory routes of the *mesta* herds of sheep. From the last decades of the sixteenth century, Castile like other southern European states became increasingly dependent on foreign supplies to meet its food requirements. The government's control of grain prices, the alliance between the crown and sheep owners and the spread of epidemics and famine-like situations during the seventeenth century discouraged viable peasant farming. Compared to the other regions, peasants in Spain were generally not enserfed but their freedom had little meaning as they could not enhance their economic status and they continued to struggle for survival.

Outside Castile the agrarian structure assumed slightly different characteristics. Agriculture in Valencia depended on labour-intensive, market-oriented production that was sustained by the Morisco population. This region specialized in wine, rice, sugar and mulberry. The problems began with the expulsion of the Moriscos in 1609–14 but before the situation could normalize, the market conditions deteriorated by the 1620s. Natural calamities and heavy taxation adopted by the Duke of Olivares to finance wars in Italy and Flanders resulted in long-term agrarian depression. Catalonia was the only region where agricultural growth took place. The presence of urban centres and markets promoted enclosed farms by tenant farmers holding secure leases. Here, the development of agrarian structure encouraged capital investment in land and innovative practices despite depressed market conditions.

The nature of the Spanish economy and its relationship with the colonies caused a negative impact on Spain. The unending influx of silver made the Spanish rulers wasteful and misuse their resources. The limited nature of Spanish agriculture, with all its shortcomings, did not allow Spain to fully exploit the abundant source of silver supply. The real advantage passed on to the Atlantic states of England, Netherlands and to some extent France. The growing colonial demand for manufactured goods could not be met by the limited nature of industries in Spain and hence the shortfall of supply was met by foreign purchases, particularly from the Netherlands and England. The Spaniards found it easier to import articles from other countries using bullion rather than developing their own industries.

Industrial Decline

It would be wrong to presume that Spain did not have industries. The wars and the expulsion of the non-Christian subjects created labour shortage but it is not certain whether it caused industrial decline. Hence, it is difficult to build a case of de-industrialization for Spain. The state promotion of sheep farming contributed to the establishment of the woollen industry but from the 1580s, the Spanish woollen industry began losing its vigour at centres like Segovia, Cuenca and Toledo. Cloth manufacture at Segovia declined from an average of 13,000 pieces annually during 1570–90 to 3,000 pieces by mid-seventeenth century. But the chief demand was for the coarser variety that was made of Spanish wool and largely produced by the Dutch and the English who captured the American markets gradually. According to Ralph Davis, the woollen industry of Spain provided the greatest example of industrial decline.

Another Spanish industry that experienced growth during the

sixteenth century was shipbuilding. This was located at Basque but the Spanish shipbuilding industry was unable to keep pace with the American demand. The Spaniards made attempts to develop shipbuilding in their own colonies such as in Havana in the 1570s, and later at Cartagena and Maracaibo. By the beginning of the seventeenth century, the shipbuilding industry at Basque experienced rapid decline. The destruction of the Spanish armada in 1588 led to the emergence of Holland and subsequently England as the bulk carriers of international cargo. Even the Asturian and Basque iron industries faced stiff competition from Sweden in the 1620s. Much of the craft-works in Seville, Toledo, Segovia, Cordoba and Cuenca completely disappeared. However, those industries, which did not face competition from foreign markets, continued to perform fairly well. There was no major collapse of the home market and industries such as paper, poultry and leather ware continued to gain modest prosperity. Even during the period of expansion in the sixteenth century, the Spanish industries witnessed stunted growth and never reached the 'take off' stage. Communications and transport proved a major hurdle in the development of industries in Spain. Madrid was declared the capital city but it was located at the centre of a rough terrain and had to depend on undeveloped surface transportation. Efforts were made to develop river navigation on the Tagus but these could not be sustained because of conflicting interests.

Thus, the American bullion failed to have a stimulating effect on the Spanish economic development. In the seventeenth century, Spain fell into heavy debt and unrestrained expansion of bureaucratic structure and the expansion of army caused a heavy burden on population. All these factors clearly explain that the sixteenth-century prosperity was an artificial one and that it did not transform the Spanish economy in the capitalist direction.

Spanish Rule and the Revolt of the Netherlands

The Netherlands was the most important possession of the Spanish empire in Europe. It comprised of seventeen provinces including Flanders and Holland. By the early-sixteenth century the port of

Antwerp in Brabant had become the leading economic region reaping benefits from the American colonies of Spain. The Netherlands was rapidly emerging as the hub of trade and manufacturing. The demographic growth was equally impressive. Timber and grain trade between the Baltic states and the Spanish empire provided a fillip to the Dutch shipping industry. The English interests in the Netherlands grew because of their economic ties. All these factors gave advantages to the Netherlands but posed serious threat to the Spanish strategic interests.

Each of the seventeen provinces of the Netherlands had dissimilar political, economic and cultural features. The representative assemblies of these provinces accepted an administrative authority at Brussels in Brabant. The Council of Representatives had members sent by the rulers and it controlled finances, taxation and justice. It was virtually a federation with multiple power centres. The growing burden of taxation imposed by the Spanish government on the one hand and a series of harvest failure and the disruption of the Baltic trade on the other, led to friction between Spain and the people of the Netherlands. The Spaniards monopolized all the important posts by ousting the local nobility. The harsh religious policy of Philip II towards Calvinists and Anabaptists antagonized the townsmen. The urban elite and the nobles were alarmed by the creation of fourteen new bishoprics which were given the right to act as inquisitors. The municipal councils refused to implement the decisions of the Spanish government. A strong resistance developed against the Spanish policy by 1564–5. This transformed into a popular political agitation in several provinces and the rebels converted to Protestantism to express their protest. These were accompanied by food riots. Armed rebels laid sieze to a couple of towns in the southern Netherlands. Philip's half-sister, Margaret of Parma carried out ruthless suppression. In 1567 the Duke of Alba was sent from Spain with 10,000 troops to crush the revolts. His tyrannical acts worsened the situation when he executed almost a thousand rebels. His newly imposed taxes were vehemently opposed. Hundreds of Protestant nobles and townsmen went into exile. Many took refuge in France and other neighbouring states and assembled under the leadership of William of Nassau (from the province of Orange) better known as William of Orange.

The exiled Calvinists captured dozens of towns in the northern region. The local population that had suffered under the Spanish rule welcomed and supported the army of rebels and William of Orange led the noble forces. In the meantime, the troops of Alba sacked and killed the local population of towns and cities. A strong resistance developed in the northern provinces but the Spanish forces preferred concentrating their hold over the southern provinces which were richer and more prosperous. Many issues, privileges of the nobility, religious sentiments, economic independence and oppressive and tyrannical rule, merged to make this conflict a long-drawn confrontation. A series of military campaigns caused large-scale destruction of lives and property and led to an acute shortage of essential goods. The Spanish authorities faced shortage of funds because of the delay in the arrival of American silver and this caused a mutiny among the Spanish soldiers as they had not been paid salaries for over three years. Antwerp was plundered, sacked and over about 8,000 townsmen were killed in 1576. This incident is known as the 'Spanish fury'. The representatives of the southern provinces met with the leader of the northern provinces, William of Orange in 1576, and negotiated the Pacification of Ghent. However, the arrival of Spanish funds led to an improvement in the Spanish position who recovered their hold over the southern provinces. The northern provinces, comprising seven states, declared themselves independent and gained from the naval conflict between Spain and England in 1588 which diverted Spanish resources. These northern provinces called themselves the United Provinces of Netherlands. The fight between Spanish forces and the people of the Netherlands continued throughout 1590s till 1609 when a temporary truce was made. Henceforth, the centre of economic activities shifted from Antwerp to Amsterdam, the capital of Holland. Power came to be divided between the 'Regent', a group of wealthy merchants and the office of *stadholder*, a form of military governorship under the House of Orange. They successfully defended the United Provinces against the Spanish attempts to recapture lost power right until 1648, when the Treaty of Westphalia recognized their independence.

Decline of Italy

The problem of understanding the factors responsible for the decline of Italy is much more complex than those of Spain. Unlike Spain, which was fast becoming a political entity under absolute rulers, Italy was more of a geographical zone and not a political unit. Italy consisted of numerous states displaying a variety of economic levels and political structures. This makes it extremely difficult to explain the process of decline of the Italian states.

As discussed in the first chapter, the Italian city states constituted the most dynamic economic region in Europe till the early-sixteenth century. States like Venice and Florence had flourishing economies, a large number of manufacturing units, a wide network of trade and a substantial population directly involved in manufacturing activities. Many of the Italian states displayed an advanced level of economic organization and possessed some of the pre-capitalist features. The sixteenth century was a period of mixed fortunes for most of the Italian states. Urbanization and economic growth came much earlier to Italy than to other parts of Europe. Consequently, during the sixteenth century many of the Italian city states tried to regain their earlier prosperity rather than strive for positive advancement. Unlike Spain, which remained essentially a rural region interspersed by a few towns, Italy was mainly an urban region with a heavy concentrations of population in cities and towns.

After a period of demographic growth, the Italian population began to fluctuate and Italy declined demographically at least till the late-seventeenth century. The overall population in the whole of Italy shows an upward trend in the second half of the sixteenth century and a decline between 1600 and 1675. In the Republic of Venice it is estimated that the population in 1550 was about 15,90,000, in 1600 it went up to 18,20,000 but by 1650 it had declined to 13,40,000. Similarly, in the Kingdom of Naples the population growth in the same period was 23,73,000 (in 1550),

30,45,000 (in 1600) and 28,13,000 (in 1650). The population of the Duchy of Mantua declined from 1,13,000 in 1600 to 1,06,000 in 1650. The decline was not universal and a few states like Sardinia and Genoa grew demographically but the overall population fell in the first half of the seventeenth century. The factors responsible for this were famines, plagues and epidemics and wars which ravaged the urban population. The Italian towns were more exposed to epidemics because of their higher density of population and the wars caused blockades, invasions and destruction. All these were short-term factors but they had long-term repercussions on the fortunes of these cities and severely restricted economic opportunities and caused de-urbanization. According to Hollen Lees and Hohenberg, inter-regional changes and de-urbanization led to the shrinking of the town population and a growth of rural demography (see Table 6.3). Between 1600 and 1700, the urban population as a percentage of total population declined from 14.7 to 13.4. Even those cities, which were government capitals or centres of administration such as Turin, Naples and particularly Rome, were affected by the economic and demographic decline of other cities. The decline of Venice was much more complex as it also included the loss of overseas possessions to the Turks and the declining social mobility between Venice and its dominions. From 1494, widespread dislocation was caused by persistent wars that continued till 1559. The French rulers invaded Italian states and destroyed their economies. This was followed by the invasion by Spain which led to heavy losses. These conflicts contributed to the political decline of the northern states of Italy. Despite being the most dynamic region of Europe till the sixteenth century, the city states remained incapable of resisting foreign rule.

The demographic decline in Italy had some serious repercussions on the urban economy and caused a major crisis in the early-sixteenth century. The merchant bankers transferred capital from Italy to the safer regions. It also made its impact felt on trade and industry. The industrial centres such as Como, Brescia, Bologna and Milan were destroyed and the population in many other cities declined sharply. According to Miskimin, production fell even faster than population. For example, in Florence the population fell by one-sixth, but the number of wool shops decreased by three-fourths between 1500 and 1540. Interestingly, the Venetian industry prospered at a time when other states were in turmoil. Several neighbouring states faced industrial closure and Venice took advantage of this chaos and Venetian woollen and silk industries grew rapidly. The number of silk weavers increased from 5,000 to 12,000 in the first half of the sixteenth century, and some lesser industries like glass, soap and candle manufacturing also recorded an increase in production. This prosperity proved short-lived and fragile as with the revival of the neighbouring industrial centres, Venice began to decline and the plague of 1575–7 inflicted a severe blow to Venetian economy. It is estimated that nearly one-third of the population perished in this epidemic and although there were signs of revival later, the period of Italian economic domination was already over. Although Italy was shattered and destroyed, the standard of living in the Italian towns even in the seventeenth century was fairly high, though the urban areas constituted only about 13 per cent of the total Italian population. Braudel presents a revisionist view on the decline of Venice. According to him, by the end of the sixteenth century and in particular after the crisis of the first decades of the seventeenth, the wealthy Venetian patricians did a complete turn-around, abandoning trade and concentrating on farming instead. The focus shifted on the cultivation of wheat, maize, hemp and mulberry. The yields were high and so were the profits. For Braudel, the flight away from more risky trade to farming should not be seen as the sign of decline because Venice remained the busiest port throughout the seventeenth century because of foreign shipping (*The Wheels of Commerce*). Besides, he also suggests that the Genoese bankers by their extensive participation in Spain compensated the decline of the Florentine banking houses. Thousands of Genoese financiers, merchants, commission agents and shopkeepers were solidly established in Spain at every level of the economy, in Seville as well as in Granada (*The Perspective of the World*). However, this view is not tenable for the rest of Europe, and even on Venice, most economic historians do not hold Braudel's view.

The cloth production continued to increase steadily from the

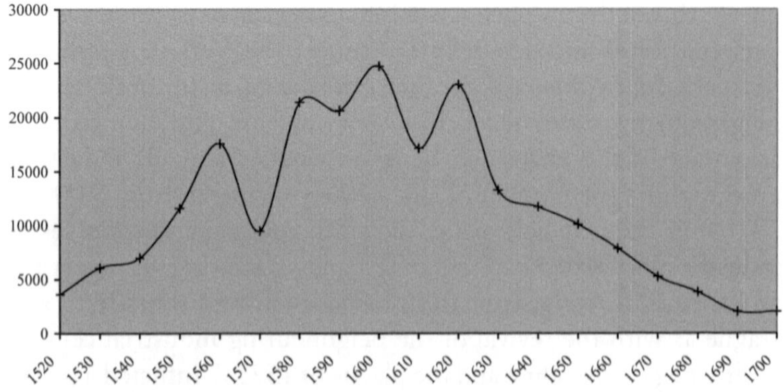

Source: Based on D. Sella's figures given in N.J.G. Pounds, p. 282.

Graph 7.1: Cloth Production in Venice (1520–1700) (in pieces)

beginning of the sixteenth century despite political disturbances and natural calamities. As is shown in Graph 7.1, the total output of cloth increased from 3,639 in 1520 to 24,719 pieces in 1600, except for a brief period in the 1570s when it came down to 9,492. This was primarily due to the spread of plague and political troubles. However, the situation reversed in the seventeenth century and the production began to decline from 23,000 in 1620s to 2,033 in 1700. Cloth production experienced a sharp fall after 1650.

A series of natural calamities during the seventeenth century also had a devastating impact on population, trade and industry. Milan's population declined by almost half due to the plague of 1630–1 while in many other towns the losses varied from 30 to 60 per cent. Many owners of silk and woollen manufacturing units either became bankrupt or had to drastically cut production. Wool production in Milan fell from 15,000 pieces annually in 1600 to just 100 by 1709. Como was left with just four woollen firms out of a total of sixty by mid-seventeenth century, while the production of woollen cloth in Brescia declined from 8,000 to less than 1,000 pieces. In Florence, according to Ruggiero Romano (in Peter Earle, ed., *Italy in the Crisis of the Seventeenth Century*), the total output slumped from 30,000 pieces a year (1560–80) to mere 6,114 pieces by 1641–5. Similarly, the production of woollen cloth in Venice declined from 28,729 pieces in 1602 to 1,721 by 1702. Even in Genoa the number of silk looms came down from 10,000 (1565) to 2,500 (1675). Natural calamity alone was not the only factor responsible for the decline of the Italian city states. The decline had set in during the sixteenth century itself. There were phases of recovery but the earlier economic prosperity pertaining to manufacturing and trade was never restored. The restoration of industries was in the nature of revival of old structures along the traditional lines.

With poor natural resources, Italy's economic prosperity was largely dependent on the capacity of each state to promote exports. The revival of industries in Italy took place at a time when it had already lost its domination in the international market. Its position, particularly in the field of textiles, was taken over by the English, Dutch and the French as they offered textiles at a much lower rate. Their textiles were not only cheap, brightly coloured, although less durable they were more affordable. In contrast, the Italian textiles were lighter, more durable but proved too costly in comparison to the international rates. There were many reasons for the higher cost of Italian products. While the Dutch and the English had successfully reduced the domination of the urban guilds by developing rural cottage industry, in Italy they continued to retain excessive control over the whole manufacturing process and opposed all innovations and improvements in technology and organization. Their domination over production process compelled manufacturers to continue with obsolete methods. Moreover, taxes were heavy and the taxation structure was ill conceived. The taxes were collected from various groups in the form of quotas in approximate terms and assessments were not made regularly. Because of guild control labour costs were high and wages in Italy were too high compared to countries like England or the Netherlands. Braudel points out that the most dramatic problem faced by Italian industry between 1590 and 1630 was competition from the low-priced industrial products of the northern countries. Basing his work on the Venetian experience, Domenico Sella suggests that as the wages had risen prohibitively high, there were three possible solutions: carry out transfer of industries; specialize in luxury products; or develop hydraulically run machines to reduce labour cost. Braudel suggests that all these were tried out but with little enthusiasm.

In agriculture, the relationship between the cities and the countryside from the beginning of the rise of Italy had been one of exploitation and domination. The countryside was virtually treated as colonies of the urban centres, and this relationship was termed as *contado*. During the period of trade expansion and industrial activity, the landed aristocracy lived in large towns and actively participated in political life. Once the phase of Italian glory was over, there was a reverse flow of capital, away from manufacturing and trade into investments in land. The trend, as Braudel describes it, was 'towards re-feudalization of the seventeenth century, an agricultural revolution in reverse'. The Italian nobility now took refuge in the countryside and provided no leadership in either the cultural or economic sphere, something it had done during the time of the Renaissance.

The urban centres of the Italian city-states were importers of food grains because of geographical limitations on the extent of arable land, low yields in the absence of developed technology, and heavy concentration of population creating perennial demand for food. It is difficult to present a uniform picture of Italy as it was not unified and consisted of disparate geographical features. The northern states usually depended on cereal imports from outside while the southern states of Italy supplied food to other regions in times of surplus production or when a constant market demand existed. Even within these two regions, there were several variations. The mountainous terrains and low rainfall in the summer months prevented the introduction of new methods, or even the usual three-course rotation of crops that was common in the other parts of Europe.

The northern plain comprising Venetia, Lombardy and Piedmont, was known for intensive agriculture during the sixteenth century. Apart from producing foodstuff like rice, it provided the neighbouring industries and markets with raw silk, dyestuffs and fruits. Agriculture in this region thrived on a strong urban demand. However, the collapse of industries and the contracting urban population, reduced demand for many agrarian products. Declining prices, heavy taxation and the spread of plague had a negative bearing on the economy of the northern region.

Conditions were hardly better in the southern peninsula. In Naples, the sixteenth-century boom in agriculture had created a class of commercial grain farmers who thrived on loans and borrowings. They took advantage of the inflationary situation but once the prices began to fall, their position worsened and their debts mounted. The ecclesiastical and noble landowners, with their large capital resources, turned their estates into sheep farms. In this situation the ordinary peasants suffered the most.

In southern Italy, the church controlled the largest portion of agricultural land (according to Miskimin, the church possessed about 65 to 70 per cent of the total land, while in northern Italy its share was hardly 10 to 15 per cent). During the same period, sheep farming was also promoted in southern Italy but it did not turn out to be very lucrative. Already intense competition had developed in the European wool market and the Italians found it difficult to compete. Capital flow in agriculture and the confiscation of church property by the city rulers led to real investments in reclamation, irrigation and drainage projects. In some regions the urban entrepreneurs also introduced sericulture. Excessive deforestation, hard weather conditions and soil erosion had made the Italians dependent on food imports.

Italy also declined in the social and cultural sphere. The coming of Protestant Reformation reduced the Pope's ecclesiastical domination and consequently his financial resources. During the Renaissance, the church inspired philosophical, theological, artistic and scientific speculation and creativity. After the Council of Trent, however, it retreated into a baneful intellectual orthodoxy. It imposed censorships on publications and the Inquisition became powerful instrument of coercion for strict compliance to doctrines. The nobility that encouraged innovation in the world of art and letters itself took refuge in the feudal system and began opposing modernization. With this, the pre-capitalist elements in the Italian society began to weaken and almost disappeared.

Nature and Extent of the Crisis

The date and intensity of this crisis varies from one region to another and differs with each historian, but there is a general unanimity that major problems developed in Europe during the seventeenth century that caused social, political and economic dislocations.

As early as 1649, a French scholar Robert Mentet de Salmonet wrote that the century would become famous for the great and strange revolutions that took place in it. Contemporary scholars to prove this argument presented a long list of revolts and upheavals and suggested that it was a period of crisis of urban economy and trade that led to economic depression, a sharp decline in population, social unrest and destructive wars. Supporters of the crisis theory argue that the Eighty Years War (1582–1662) between the rebellious population of the Netherlands and Spain, affected most parts of Europe. The Thirty Years War (1618–48) ruined the economy of central Europe. A number of revolts were led by the peasants. In France, a major insurrection on the question of *gabelle* (salt) tax at Aquitaine province was the beginning of widespread peasant wars. The Croquant peasants uprising in the 1590s and the 1620s were followed by *Nu-pieds* (1639) and the widespread Fronde rebellions (1647–53). The Croquant uprisings recurred in 1594, 1624, 1636–7 and 1707 and covered the same geographical regions. The local population resisted the outsiders who were extracting provisions and contributions. These were political and anti-fiscal rebellions. The most dangerous of these revolts was the one in Périgueux in 1637 where over 30,000 equipped and armed peasants revolted. Equally serious was the revolt of *Nu-pieds* in Normandy. The Frondes was a major socio-political movement that reflected a deeply troubled society and state. For France the Thirty Years War did not end in 1648, much against the wishes of the people but went on till 1659. This long war put heavy strain on French resources and caused steep increase in taxation at a time when there was a major slump in the economy. The Fronde revolt opposed the growing powers of the absolute rulers and some of its programme would have made Parlément almost a sovereign body in France by placing the ministers and the crown's finance under its control. Its failure led to the strengthening of royal absolutism under Louis XIV. Boris Porchnev described the Fronde as a French variant of the English bourgeois revolution which was breaking out on the other side of the channel and a distant prologue of the French Revolution of the eighteenth century. The Revolts in Catalonia, Naples and Portugal caused crisis in the Spanish empire. In Spain, the revolt of the peasants in 1640 swept across Barcelona, drove out the Castilians and killed the viceroy. The townsmen probably supported them. It almost became a secessionist movement. In Catalonia, a popular uprising occurred in 1688-9. It arose from isolated riots caused by the spread of plague and official apathy but soon took a serious dimension. The revolt of Naples in 1647 was the product of the deteriorating economic situation caused by the Thirty Years War. The position of peasants had worsened during this period. The long absence of the king of Aragon, who had withdrawn his seat of power from here leaving a nominated government, made the local barons powerful and unconcerned to popular demands. Like the Fronde in France, the revolt in Naples was the direct outcome of inefficient administration and heavy taxation. In July 1647, the city of Naples was shaken up by widespread popular revolts caused by the shortage of food and continued imposition of an unpopular tax on fruit. The religious celebrations were turned into riots. A young fisherman, Masaniello emerged as the main leader. For a brief time, Naples became a republic under French protectorate before the Spanish ruler reconquered it. In Palermo, the revolt was not directed against Philip IV of Spain but mainly against the local authorities. There were many other uprisings elsewhere like the Swiss Peasants uprisings (1653), Stamp Paper uprisings in Bordeaux and Brittany (1675), Ukrainian revolts (1648–54), Russian revolts (1672), Kuruez movements in Hungary, Irish revolts (1641 and 1689), the English Civil War (1642–60) and the Glorious Revolution of 1688 in England and the Palace Revolution in the United Provinces of the Netherlands. They all form a chain of revolutionary upheavals and political and social revolts. All these events suggest that there were some major problems in Europe during this period.

The concept of crisis can be first located in the writings of the famous French philosopher of Enlightenment, Voltaire in his *Essai sur les moeurs et l'esprit des nations* (1756). He believed that this 'crisis' was not confined to Europe alone. Rebellions and uprisings could be seen in many parts of the world, including Turkey, India and China. However, the idea of crisis surfaced in historical writings only from the middle of the twentieth century in the works of Roland Mousnier, Eric Hobsbawm, H.R. Trevor-Roper, H.G. Koenigsberger and R.B. Merriman. Mousnier in his work *Les XVIe et XVIIe Siècles* (1954) described the period between 1598 and 1715 as one of crisis. These crises manifested themselves in the areas of demography, economy, administration and diplomacy but more so in the intellectual sphere. For Eric Hobsbawm, it was a major crisis of European economy that marked a decisive shift from a feudal to a capitalist order. He also subscribes to the view that it was a 'general crisis'. Trevor-Roper argues that it was a crisis of the 'Renaissance State' and describes the major events as a part of political revolution. The universality of political disturbances leads him to believe that there was serious structural weakness in European monarchies. R.B. Merriman in his work *Six Contemporaneous Revolutions* suggests that all these disturbances could be seen as social and political manifestation of a crisis that had been affecting entire Europe and he compares the various upheavals of mid-seventeenth century in England, France, Catalonia, Naples and Holland. There are other historians who reject the entire notion of crisis. J.H. Elliott argues that there were as many revolts in the 1540s as there were in the 1640s. To him the evidence of economic crisis is inconclusive and the relationship between economic and political crisis is not easy to establish and the idea of crisis is the product of hindsight. The opponents of the theory of general crisis argue that the social or political disorders remained specific to local conditions and these did not coalesce into broader movements. The rebels, except in England, did not challenge the legitimacy of the rulers, and the main demand was the restoration of customary norms. Only in Catalonia and Portugal, the political unrest to some extent developed into a challenge to the government. The local elite used these revolts for their own gains and secured concessions from their respective rulers. To understand the nature of these crises, it is necessary to examine the dimension of the problems.

Some historians object to the use of the word revolution and argue that the era of revolutions or upheavals was not as unprecedented in European history as, for example, the period 1560–75. To scholars like A. Lloyd Moote, the revolt in Scotland leading to the abdication of Queen Mary of Scotland in 1567, the revolt against the Duke of Savoy, the French Civil Wars, the revolt of the Corsicans against Genoa, the revolt of the Netherlands and the northern rebellion in England took place in this short period but they cannot be described as revolutions or termed as a period of crises. Such writers suggest it would be wrong to describe the popular revolts like those at Bordeaux, Naples, Antwerp, Brussels and Palermo of the seventeenth century as revolutions. They had the ingredients of a rebellion but they were not against the basic structure of the regimes. However, the supporters of the crisis theory emphasize that the reversal trend of the economy during the seventeenth century accompanied by socio-economic changes makes the period different from the earlier phase and hence can be seen as a period of general crisis.

As regards the beginning of the period of crisis, for some historians it started in the 1620 while some consider the middle years of the seventeenth century, the 1640s and the 1650s, as the real beginning of the crisis. Peter Clark places the beginning of this crisis in the 1590s. He gives several illustrations to prove his point. For him the crisis could be located in the English sequence of harvest failures along with economic depression (1593–7), Irish crop failures in 1594 leading to Tyrome's Rebellion. In the Low Countries, the destruction and turmoil by the Spanish armies, the ruin of Antwerp and depopulation in the countryside resulting in large-scale migrations from Brabant and Flanders to the United Provinces of the Netherlands and large-scale peasant uprisings between 1594 and 1597 in Austria, all of which were precipitated by severe food crisis and heavy exactions. In Sicily and Naples, there emerged a subsistence crisis in 1590–2. The greatest impact could be seen in Spain, where bad harvests and epidemics resulted in the loss of almost half a million population between 1596 and

1602. In Russia, agriculture was badly affected in the 1590s because of the disastrous wars with Sweden, while famine ravaged Poland, the Balkans and Romania. Scholars supporting the view that the seventeenth century was a period of revolution present the earlier troubles of 1560s and the 1570s as preconditions of revolution and population trends, agrarian structure, political domain and the economy are generally held as the causes.

Demographic Crisis

As already discussed earlier, the sixteenth century witnessed a spectacular growth in European population tapering off towards the last decade of the century. While in some parts there was demographic stagnation, in some other regions the growth continued but at a slower rate. It is true that most of the population figures available to historians are scattered and are not very reliable yet the available data generally indicates a downward trend in population growth (England and Switzerland), except for a few northern states like the Netherlands, Norway and Sweden. Peter Kriedte emphasizes the role of the Thirty Years War, which had catastrophic impact on the German population. It is estimated that the population losses were as high as 40 per cent in the countryside and 35 per cent in the towns. The thickly populated states like Brandenburg, Saxony and Bavaria lost nearly half their population, though the impact was not very severe in the north German states. The population loss was as high as two-thirds in Pomerania, Hesse, Wurttemberg and Palatine, while in Bohemia, which was the centre of warfare, the population declined from 17,00,000 in 1618 to 9,30,000 in 1654. A similar trend could also be seen in Poland. In the same period, Spain experienced depopulation. The Spanish population came down to 50,25,000 from 70,68,000 between 1587–92 and 1646–50 although it recovered to reach the figure of 7,000,000 by 1712–17. In the case of France, the population remained relatively stable but the rate of increase was definitely halted from the 1630s.

As is evident in Table 7.1, the population of southern Europe declined quite sharply and by 1700 it was less than that of 1600.

The population growth was very fast in northern Europe including the Low Countries and England but even here, the rate of increase considerably slowed down in the second half of the century. What led to the decline in the European population is a matter of conjecture. For Peter Kriedte, the demographic decline was a reflection of both Malthusian and social crisis – the growing population during the sixteenth century had put heavy pressure on the fixed ceiling of agricultural output. Thomas R. Malthus had argued that in a natural economy population has a natural growth rate and increases geometrically whereas the natural resources necessary to support that population grows arithmetically. This results in a crisis till it is resolved with a loss of population. The impact of a demographic factors had long-term consequences on family life and birth patterns. The earlier growth of population seems to have created problems of food supply and the shortage of food brought about a change in the reproductive behaviour of the people. Thus, the average marriage age of women rose, for example in Colyton in England, from 27.1 in 1600–49 to 29.4 in the next half century and in Geneva from 24.6 to 25.7 during the same period. This was caused by a control mechanism designed to prevent a further increase in the gap between the size of the population and the availability of food. This resulted in the deterioration of the overall economic situation and enabled the landlords to appropriate a larger portion of agricultural income. However, these

TABLE 7.1: EUROPE'S POPULATION, 1600–1700 (IN MILLIONS) REGION-WISE

Region	1600*	1700	Percentage Change
Mediterranean (Spain, Portugal, and Italy)	23.6	22.7	- 4
Central (France, Switzerland, and Germany)	35.0	36.2	+ 3
North & West (British Isles, Low Countries and Scandinavia)	12.0	16.1	+ 34
Total	70.6	75.0	+ 6

Source: Jan de Vries, *The Economy of Europe in an Age of Crisis, 1600–1775*, Cambridge, 1976, p. 5.

demographic trends had great variations in different regions but they certainly played an important role on the economies of different regions.

Monetary Crisis

Some historians stress the role of money supply in effecting economic changes. Scholars like Earl Hamilton and Pierre Chaunu point to the role of Seville – Atlantic trade in causing the European economic crisis. He suggests that the crisis of the 1620s and its subsequent impact were caused by a failure to finance a growing volume of trade. According to him, the frequent debasement of coinage throughout Europe in the sixteenth and seventeenth centuries were manifestation of a chronic shortage of currency. It was temporarily solved by Spain's silver imports from the New World. The economic growth of the sixteenth century began to diminish once the quantity of silver imports started declining resulting in monetary chaos. E.J. Hamilton also holds monetary factors related to the bullion imports to be the main reason for economic depression of the seventeenth century. He provides detailed figures of world silver production and later Pierre Vilar supplemented these with those for gold. He argues that silver imports from America reached its peak by 1620 and thereafter it started declining. This caused a decline in money in circulation. Hamilton believes that an upward movement of prices would result in surplus profit and encourage capital investment in business and industry. In a reverse situation, the declining circulation of money would reduce the profit margin and cause disinvestments from manufacturing and business sectors. For Hamilton, this situation began to develop in the seventeenth century. Taking up this argument, Ruggiero Romano suggests that the first forty years of the century showed signs of a steady, or sometimes direct, contraction in the issue of money. The intense and sudden fall of the years 1619–22 takes place against the background of this chronic contraction. Romano argues that there was stagnation in minting resulting in a shortage of monetary stock, that the price of money was progressively falling but there was a considerable expansion in credit. For Romano, money, prices, exchange or banking were essentially facts of production and distribution and the prices should not be seen in isolation. Prices only act as a thermometer to gauge trends in trade, production and revenue. The factors of economic reality are so complicated that prices alone cannot explain the entire intricate situation.

Commenting on the nature of the crisis, Jan de Vries questions the role of monetary factors in the long run. He does not subscribe to the view that the economy of Europe rose and fell with the flow of precious metals from the New World though he concedes that the monetary instability played an indisputable role in short-term cycles, especially in the crisis of 1619–22. However, scholars such as Evaraert and Morineau have challenged Hamilton's data. Their own figures are based on the French Consular Reports. Their main argument is that silver coming from America did not stay in Europe for long and it was taken away to the east via the Levant to India and China. Thus, the impact of the silver influx was not so great. Besides, many historians do not accept Hamilton's argument, as it presents a very simple explanation of a very complex economic system. The money in circulation was considerably reduced in the seventeenth century because at many places capital was tied up with land, keeping small farmers dependent on it and making a free sale of property very difficult. There existed perennial problems like disjointed and fragmented holdings and shortage of labour. Attempts by the court officials to amalgamate the land holdings had failed. In places like Poland, the landlords controlled and dictated the small farmers, as they could not work independently. They could not take advantage of the rising prices of food grains. In such a situation, prices were not dependent on demand or on profit margins but purely on the volume of production.

Agrarian Crisis

Several historians have emphasized that declining population had great bearing on agriculture in different parts of Europe. The condition of agriculture was not the same everywhere and reliable information on it is not easily available though some of its basic trends can be observed. European agriculture for the past several centuries had been passing through a cyclic phase, alternating between expansion and contraction. Since agriculture was still almost completely dependent on the forces of nature, the growing population placed serious limitations on its expansion after a time. At a time when technology was stagnant, rising population placed a heavy demand on food grains and consequently the land under cultivation had to be extended. This was the situation in the sixteenth century. Agricultural production received a boost because of demographic expansion and price rise. The price inflation guaranteed increased value of agricultural produce and land, while the population growth ensured a good market and necessary labour for agricultural expansion. In the absence of technological innovation, the expansion meant land reclamation and deforestation. At the same time growing population in many places like Spain and Germany resulted in fragmentation of holdings. After the sixteenth-century European agriculture showed signs of exhaustion.

According to Peter Kriedte, the index of grain prices in France declined from 100 (1625–50) to 50 (1681–90) while in Poland grain prices declined from 100 index points in 1580 to about 87 in the 1650s. The Swedish–Polish War, caused further agricultural destruction and pushed the index further down to 43 by 1660. The result was that many fields were turned into pastures and grasslands. In Germany and Austria there was a continuous downward trend in agriculture that lasted till the end of the seventeenth century. The declining ground rents brought down the prices of property and there was hardly any incentive left to cultivate. According to N.J.G. Pounds, the trend of grain prices varied greatly from country to country. Compared to the price level of 1601–10, the prices continued to rise in England, Belgium and Austria to 147, 150 and 118 per cent respectively. In Germany and the Netherlands they rose till the 1630s to 186 and 148 per cent respectively, while in France, northern Italy and Denmark they stopped increasing from the 1620s. The cereal price in western and central Europe remained high till the middle of the seventeenth century but the circumstances varied. In England and in some parts of France the agrarian boom continued without interruption but in Germany agriculture collapsed despite high prices mainly because of the Thirty Years War. In Flanders, Brabant, Zeeland and Frisia, grain cultivation was greatly reduced and was replaced by flax, hops, rape seed and such other crops. The tobacco boom in central and eastern parts of northern Netherlands came to an end during the seventeenth century. There were reports that villages, farmsteads and fields were being deserted in Germany, Languedoc and Castile. In the Prussian estates, the proportion of land used for agriculture was 57.8 per cent in 1600 but by 1683 it had come down to 32.4 per cent. The average exports of grain from the Baltic, and from Danzig show declining trends. These regions had seen enormous expansion during the sixteenth century but they experienced stagnation from the middle of the seventeenth century.

As far as France is concerned, agrarian decline was not substantial but here agriculture was coming under increasing pressure from above. The French monarchy in order to increase its fiscal interests protected the small peasant proprietors but it led to long-term agrarian stagnation. To meet the growing cost of administrative expansion and to conduct continental wars, the state squeezed the peasants. Between 1600 and 1651, according to Lis and Soly, taxes equivalent to 10.5 million hectoliters of wheat were collected. This was enough to feed 15 per cent of the French population throughout

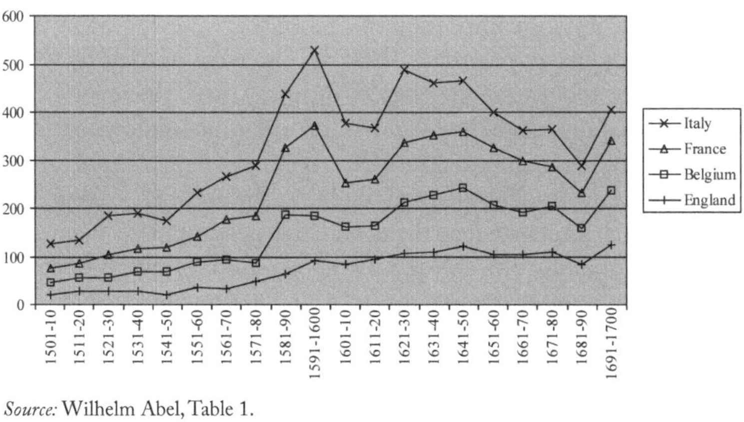

Source: Wilhelm Abel, Table 1.

Graph 7.2 : Price of wheat in different parts of Europe 1500-1700 (10 year averages in grams of silver per 100 kg.)

the year. The nobility also subjected the peasantry to heavy exaction. Similarly, Jan de Vries argues that the maximum exploitation of the peasantry was done by the nobility through their agents and lawyers to increase their incomes as agricultural reorganization was ruled out by the policies of the absolute monarchs. This development checked agricultural investment and technical improvement. Like many other countries, France also witnessed a crisis of agrarian productivity during the seventeenth century, which had catastrophic results for the bulk of French peasants after 1630. Many of them fell into debt, as they were unable to repay usurious loans taken during harvests failure or at the time of tax collection. The peasants were gradually dispossessed of their land during the seventeenth century. The condition of the lowest strata of the French peasantry *manouvriers* and *haricotiers*, who hardly owned any property in the form of land, remained precarious. Though the French population did not increase much throughout the seventeenth century and almost remained stagnant, agriculture did not transform itself as it did in England.

The rural history of France has been studied in much greater detail and with fresh methodology compared to other regions. In recent years, several French historians made intensive study of the rural and urban revolts of the seventeenth century. According to a Russian historian Boris Porchnev, the small peasant rebellions were not necessarily more important in France than elsewhere but they are probably better recorded. These revolts were not led by well-known figures but were the work of ordinary men. The revolts had their origins in crop failure, epidemics, urban unemployment and the heavy burden of state taxation.

The peasant troubles demonstrate that the agrarian system had outlived the limits of feudalism and the peasants had begun to influence urban fortunes. Not only did agricultural supply become necessary to feed the urban population and to provide raw materials to the workers of the cities but it also directly contributed to the urban incomes through rent payments such as state taxes, tithes, seigniorial dues, land rents and other forms of surpluses. All these were unilaterally transferred to the cities directly or indirectly. However, the rural crisis disrupted the flow of rents to the urban centres at the peak of urban prosperity. Thus the urban decline began later but it lasted much longer. In the regions facing intense agricultural crisis, urban centres were hard hit for long periods of time. At the same time it must be pointed out that the seventeenth century was not a time of complete and universal agricultural dislocation and decline. Several parts of north-western Europe, including England, the Netherlands and certain parts of northern France, experienced significant agricultural growth.

The seventeenth-century agrarian crisis in the southern and eastern parts of Europe led to the widening gap between the two extreme zones of Europe. While eastern and central-eastern Europe witnessed an extension and tightening of serfdom, a distinct progress in England and the Netherlands was made away from feudalism on the capitalist lines. Here, a pattern of commercial agriculture made rapid strides. In some parts, the price of animal products rose faster than that of grains. Apart from England and the Netherlands this was also seen in the Swiss Cantons. This resulted in the popularization of forage crops like clover and turnip. The method of crop rotation came to be practised in the Netherlands and England towards the close of the seventeenth century. In England, Norfolk system of four-yearly sequence of crops like wheat, turnip, barley and clover was introduced on an increasing scale. Such methods of crop rotation and specialization vastly improved soil fertility and led to a higher yield per unit of land. This improved the agrarian condition in these north-western countries and to a certain extent led to the partial dissolution of the older types of communal agriculture.

Climatic Factors

To many scholars, particularly from the Annales School, the crisis of the seventeenth century is seen as a subsistence crisis forming a part of *conjocture*, which means a crisis located not in the structures, but in coming together of many short- and long-term factors such as events, contingencies and trends broadly belonging to the economic domain. These short-term forces interact with structures and may help to modify them in the long run yet they remain distinct from them. These forces include prices, taxes, rents, trade cycles and the subsistence level of the people. For these writers, the seventeenth-century crisis involved the coming together of conjunctural factors, e.g. crop failure and high grain prices, which were followed by a sharp fall in prices of food grain, heavy taxation, epidemics and bad weather. This caused in a large number of peasant outbreaks not only in France but also in many other parts of Europe. In the absence of substantial capital investment and new technology, agriculture was precariously balanced. This could easily be broken by natural factors leading to an agricultural crisis. In such situations the peasants were left with little options – either to face death or revolt against the authorities.

An interesting explanation has been provided by the scholars of Annales School emphasizing the role of climatic factors calling it 'Maunder Minimum', which it considers responsible for the agrarian and demographic shifts. Geoffrey Parker discusses the role of astronomical studies in locating the non-human factors in this crisis. Some historians, basing their arguments on the works of scientists such as John Eddy of America, Cassini of France and Hevelius of Poland, described the period as 'the Little Ice Age'. The notebooks of the European leading astronomers, according to A.E. Douglass, reveal an almost total absence of or a sharp decline in the Sun's spots in the period between 1645 and 1715, with a few spells of normalcy in between. G.D. Cassini, Director of Paris Observatory, also observed this in 1676. A similar observation was also made with the *aurora borealis* (the Northern Lights caused by particles from the Sun entering the earth's atmosphere). After 1640, this was also observed in Scandinavia and Scotland. The observers began to doubt whether the Sun's energy was actually diminishing. A decline in solar energy causes increase in Carbon-14 in the atmosphere, thereby affecting all living organisms. Another evidence of these phenomena is provided by dendrochronological evidence (the study of the tree-rings) along with the records of the vineyards, particularly in France. During this period, there was a significant growth in the tree-rings, a phenomenon associated with wet summers and severe winters. Experts also suggest the advance of the glaciers and consequently the reduction of cultivable land at higher altitudes. All these evidences, whether gathered by historians or meteorologists or solar physicists, indicate a period of greater extremes of weather, especially cooler and wetter summers in the temperate zones. Fall in solar radiation by even 1 per cent causes lower summer temperatures and more rainfall thereby restricting the growing season in the farms by three to four weeks. It also has a bearing on river flows because the cold weather would reduce melting of snow. As nearly 80 to 90 per cent of the European population depended on agriculture, such climatic changes were bound to affect vegetation and cereal crops. According to Gustav Utterstrom, the years 1596–1603, 1630, 1649–52, 1675–7 and the 1690s were disaster years because of the climatic fluctuations and demographic losses. W.K. Jordan suggests that the most immediate and pressing concerns of governments was the problem of vagrancy which had its roots in the rural depopulation caused by worsening agricultural situation during the 'Little Ice Age'.

Political Crisis

Neils Steensgaard presents evidence of a marked increase in governmental activity and expenditure during the seventeenth century, most of it caused by wars. Some historians consider the early modern states as military institutions as almost half their income every year was spent on wars. Increasing governmental revenue led to larger armed forces. Inflation led to an increase in the cost of maintaining the army; the cost of each soldier rose five times between 1530 and 1630 and the cost of waging a war increased even more. Almost every country was engaged in wars for most part of the century. To increase its income, the government tried new methods and new sources of revenue collection, an aspect that has been emphasized by historians like N. Steensgaard, I. Schoffer and J.H. Elliott. These new sources included many forms of taxation such as ship money and monopolies in England, *taille* and *aides* in France and *alcabala* in Spain. This was also a period of rising religious passions as is evident in the case of England, Poland, Rhine, Palatine and Bohemia.

The increase in political crises can be located in several countries of Europe and a detailed discussion of the Spanish and the French political crisis has been provided in the earlier section of this chapter. In both countries the bureaucratic structure expanded on the one hand and popular resistance against taxation increased on the other exposing the deep trouble existing between society and the state. The *Fronde* rebellion in France almost developed into a civil war.

An important proponent of the theory of general crisis is H.R. Trevor-Roper. His main argument is that the crisis of the seventeenth century was not merely a constitutional crisis or a crisis of production; rather it was a crisis in the relation between the state and the society. The seventeenth century saw the multiplication of ever-growing costly offices that outran the needs of the states. Originally it was the need that had created officers but later the officers created the needs as all bureaucracy tend to expand. This ever-expanding bureaucratic structure became parasitic; it began to be sustained by using marginal lands and by increasing taxation. Thus, according to Trevor-Roper, the Renaissance monarchies continued to expand in the sixteenth century till their cost and extravagance, their growing bureaucracies, wars and governmental inefficiency caused an intolerable burden to the societies that they dominated. The post-1620 depression coincided with a widespread reaction against the royal courts of the European rulers. H.R. Trevor-Roper attributes all these rebellions to one and the same crisis that developed through the tension between the court and the country but the solutions to these crises were different in different places.

The views of Trevor-Roper have not been fully accepted by many historians. J.H. Elliott has been a strong critic of the theory of political crisis. According to him, the essential difficulties of Spain were not a dislike by the society of an overloaded court but was more in the nature of a struggle between the periphery provinces and the royal authority at the centre. These political problems were among many such episodes in early modern Europe. The French wars of religion and the Dutch revolt of the previous century were much more prolonged and disruptive. He argues that if the economic slowdown and a few simultaneous rebellions were all that could be shown as a crisis of the seventeenth century, then he would prefer words like 'continuity' to 'discontinuity'. To retain and expand the bureaucratic control over its respective society, each absolute state needed a vast military force that continued to grow with the expansion of the court and bureaucracy. This is evident from Table 7.2. Steensgaard also rejects Trevor-Roper's court-country concept as having no European validity and considers the crisis the outcome of a dynamic absolutism, which with its taxation policy, ignored customary laws and posed a threat to the traditional social balance. Linking the political crisis approach to the economic factors like agrarian disturbances and contraction of trade, Steensgaards suggests that there was a shift in demand caused by the transfer of income from the private to public sector by means of taxation. In this way he relates the political upheavals of the mid-century to the response against government taxation, bureaucratic inefficiency and the role of the state in redistributing income. Scholars like Schoffer prefer terms like 'stabilization' and 'shift' rather than 'crisis'.

Economic Crisis

Scholars present several explanations for the economic decline during the seventeenth century. Some historians such as J.H. Elliott, J.I. Israel, Aston, Domenico Sella and Braudel, emphasize that this period was not one of complete economic regression, as suggested by E.J. Hobsbawm, but only of regional decline. On the other hand, there are some writers who consider this a period of industrial crisis

TABLE 7.2: MILITARY STRENGTH OF THE EUROPEAN STATES 1470–1710

Date	Spain	France	England	Russia
1470s	20,000	40,000	25,000	NA
1590s	200,000	80,000	30,000	NA
1630s	300,000	150,000	NA	35,000
1650s	300,000	100,000	70,000	NA
1670s	70,000	120,000	NA	130,000
1700s	50,000	400,000	87,000	170,000

Source: Geoffery Parker and Lesley M. Smith, p. 14.

covering urban manufacturing that also affected trade and commerce. In the Marxist writings the crisis of the seventeenth century is viewed as the crisis of production.

The European economies were quite uneven at the end of the sixteenth century and displayed stark differences among regions and states. The intensity of the crisis varied according to regions and economic setbacks did not necessarily assume uniform patterns. The crisis did not mean a return to old forms of economic and social structures. While some economic centres witnessed an irrevocable change and lost their earlier domination, certain others experienced slower growth and a few regions made rapid strides in the capitalist direction. Mediterranean economy, Germany and the southern half of France experienced rapid industrial decline. This was also true of many other regions. As far as industrial production is concerned, the picture is not very clear. It is difficult to obtain data for products catering to domestic demand. At best some data is available for a few cities which participated in international trade. The decline of a city did not always imply the decay of the entire region but could lead to the rise of an alternate centre as happened in the case of Florence. The industrial decline of Florence was followed by the rise of the textile industry of Prato and Siena. Similarly, the decline in the demand of one product could increase the demand of its alternative. There were distinct signs of decline in certain regions of Europe but in some other regions the situation was not so bad. In fact, in many parts of northern Europe it was a period of industrial growth and economic progress.

Among the important industrial activities were textile production, mineral extraction and shipbuilding. Other industrial activities were organized at the artisan level. Even the textile industry was still dominated by the artisan world of production. Taking up the case of textile production, most historians agree that the Italian cloth virtually disappeared from the export market in the seventeenth century. The rural as well as urban expansion of the previous century of the Flemish wool industry also went into long-term contraction. Many of the French textile centres, such as Amiens, Reims, Rouen, also declined, and even Beauvais stagnated. However, the situation was not the same in Holland and England, where the textile industry had reached a phase of distinct growth with the introduction of 'draperies'. In the seventeenth century, Leiden emerged as one of the most important centres of industrial production in Europe. From just 12,000 in 1582 the population increased to almost 70,000 by the mid-seventeenth century. In England too, the rise of new draperies led to the English domination of the textile market in the Iberian peninsula and the Mediterranean. The English textile industry was located in East Anglia, West Riding and Devon. Here, the producers lowered the prices of their products after 1660 to a level at which the continental producers could not compete. The English exports of wool showed a downward trend after reaching a peak in 1614 when 1,27,215 woolsacks were exported. On the other hand, the export of English cloth increased till 1610, followed by a period of stability, then declined for about two decades. There was distinct revival from about the 1670s. While these regions of textile production witnessed an increase in employment opportunities, in many parts of Europe, including northern Italy, Spain and Germany, the destruction of the textile industry caused not only unemployment of thousands of artisans but also socio-economic dislocation. It caused a prolonged situation of disinvestments from the manufacturing sector. It is estimated that by 1700, the number of wool weavers in the northern towns of Italy had come down to less then 10 per cent of the sixteenth-century figures. The silk industry tried to fight the situation and could not hold on till the end of the seventeenth century.

Germany was an important centre of silver supply till early sixteenth century. Here, the annual production of silver fell from 360 tons in 1540s to just 120 tons during the Thirty Years War but recovered during the eighteenth century. In respect of the shipping industry, Holland stood out as an important centre of Europe. Ship construction in Rotterdam increased from twenty in 1630 to twenty-three between 1630 and 1650 annually but declined rapidly thereafter to eleven in 1673. The Spanish shipbuilding industry at Basque had already declined by the beginning of the seventeenth century. In Amsterdam where no textile industry existed in the middle of the sixteenth century, woollen cloth production was not only taken up but it also experienced reasonable prosperity. However, in most of the regions, as pointed out by Romano, the general economic development was brought about during the sixteenth century by an expansion in agriculture that also caused a boom in trade and industry. However, during the seventeenth century, the commercial and industrial sectors were no longer supported by agriculture because of the agrarian crisis and we find that in this second half of the seventeenth century the pace of industrial and commercial expansion was considerably checked. Two important areas of international trade – Mediterranean and the Baltic – experienced significant changes in its trade-structure. After 1650, the Mediterranean was merely an area that exchanged locally produced goods, mainly raw materials instead of exporting finished products. The French Levant trade also halved between 1620 and 1635 and further sank after the 1650s. The Baltic region, which earlier was the granary of western Europe, had changed its staple exports from foodstuffs to items like timber, metals and naval stores.

During the sixteenth century, we find that European economy tried to break the medieval bottlenecks to go beyond the traditional structure. Conditions were favourable for the capitalist mode of production to emerge on a wide scale because of growing population, increasing manufacturing activities, expanding overseas markets and rising prices. But the obstacles of a feudal social framework prevented direct advance towards modern capitalism. In the absence of technological innovations the growing population pressure led to increased agricultural output but at the end it resulted in diminishing returns, shrinking of grain-exporting regions, food-shortages and famines. The crisis of the seventeenth-century is seen as the manifestation of this feudal crisis. This has led many Marxist historians, particularly Eric Hobsbawm, to maintain that the seventeenth-century crisis existed in many parts of European economy and was basically a crisis in the mode of production. It occurred because the preceding economic growth was still set in a feudal matrix from which it was unable to break out. The old forms of socio-economic relations did not allow sustained economic development. They favoured unproductive investment on luxuries and wars and checked the expansion of home markets, industrial production and division of labour. The Marxist scholars see the crisis as the last phase of transition from the feudal to the capitalistic economy. To Hobsbawm, the crisis revealed Europe's failure to overcome the obstacles created by the feudal structure to reach the stage of capitalism. The crisis was resolved in different ways by different societies. One such way was the creation of new colonial markets, which some Western countries had carved out, in the late-seventeenth and the early-eighteenth centuries, a point that has also been made by Steensgaards in the context of Holland. The expansion of the colonial empire encouraged the growth of the commercial fleet, which increased threefold between 1629 and 1686. The re-exports also increased from 100 index points in 1663–9 to 221 points in 1669–1701. The colonies were becoming emporia of goods for the European nations. Capital investments began to be made in foreign trade through the East India Companies and the African companies.

According to Hobsbawm, the motive force behind at least some of the revolutions was the force of the productive bourgeoisie. He emphasizes that the crisis of production was general in Europe but its solution could be found only in the English bourgeois revolution of the 1640s. To him, this bourgeois revolution was 'the most decisive product of the seventeenth-century crisis'. Although, the crisis was experienced in many parts of Europe, the forces of capitalism could triumph only in England, where the old structure was shattered and a new form of economic organization was established. Within that organization, modern industrial capitalism could achieve astonishing results. Here, the crisis is seen as a form of class conflict – the revolutionaries were the bourgeoisie and the governments they sought to overthrow were the champions of changed but still recognizable feudal class. Another Marxist historian Josef Polisensky suggests that the Thirty Years War was an integral part of the crisis and reflected an aggravation and culmination of the internal contradictions in the structure of the society, at least in some of its components that impacted violently on economic, social and cultural relations. He regards the Thirty Years War as a crisis of at least central Europe if not of the entire continent.

However, there are some scholars who reject the very notion of a seventeenth-century crisis. Writers like Perez Zagorin and Trevor-Roper do not agree with the analysis of Hobsbawm. Zagorin argues that there is complete absence of evidence in Hobsbawm's argument and that he cannot demonstrate the actuality of the 'general crisis' in accordance with his description of the crisis. Similarly, the connection between the English revolution of the 1640s and the crisis in Europe is unconvincing. John Elliott and A.D. Lublinskaya completely reject the notion of general crisis as provided by Hobsbawm, Trevor-Roper and Mousnier. Pierre Goubert suggests that an examination of the localities of France undermines the assumption that any one period was a time of specific economic crisis and that if varied from one region to another. Thus, for all the disagreements and controversies, most scholars seem to suggest that there was a major crisis in Europe during the seventeenth century. Yet the debate remains inconclusive.

Impact of the Crisis

The seventeenth-century crisis brought about significant changes in Europe but its impact was far from uniform. On the one hand it created conditions for a new phase of expansion by removing tensions within the productive sectors and restoring balance between population and food supplies, and on the other it fastened feudal grip over a sizeable population of Europe.

In demographic terms the crisis resulted in high mortality in several parts of the continent. The impact was greater in urban centres. The demographic losses caused extensive dislocation of trade and industry. Military conflict was one of the principal causes of human mortality. Prolonged wars accompanied by natural calamities like plague epidemics and famines, caused extensive disruption of social life. The most catastrophic demographical reversal was seen in Central Europe. Most of the battles in the Thirty Years War were fought in this region. The population losses varied from 25 to 40 per cent. Poland experienced a similar fate. The Danish–Swedish war of 1658–60 reduced the Danish population by about 20 per cent. In northern Italy, the major industrial centre during the sixteenth century, a quarter of its population perished. It took another half century for Europe to recover from the demographic losses.

Military operations, economic disruptions and population losses caused severe strain on government resources. It placed heavy strain on already burdened economies of the European states by increasing the burden of taxation on the lower classes. Except for England, the crisis led to the extension of power of the rulers over their subjects to extract the maximum from all possible sources. The French crown emerged much stronger after the crisis. On the other hand, the decline of certain regions and states proved to be beneficial for other states of the north, like the Dutch republic and England. Not only did England reap economic benefits at the expense of the southern states of Europe, the overthrow of the feudal monarchy by the rising landed gentry and bourgeoisie led to the establishment of a constitutional monarchy and the emergence of representative democracy.

One of the most important developments in the post-crisis period was the shift away from the continental countries towards the sea powers of the north-west. The gap between the eastern and western regions of Europe had already begun during the sixteenth century. It was further widened during the seventeenth century. The share in the international trading system of the eastern and central Europe declined rapidly while the vigorous growth of the trans-Atlantic trade contributed to the industrial and commercial expansion of western Europe. The two countries also gained immensely from the influx of Flemish refugees, particularly those from Hondschoote who settled in Leiden in Holland and near Norwich in England. The French Huguenots also contributed to the paper and glass industry of England. The role of merchants became important in organizing extensive network of rural households to produce for distant markets.

An important consequence of the crisis was the displacement of industry to the countryside and the spread of proto-industrialization in some parts of western and central Europe. This marked the first phase of industrialization. The manufacturers and the merchant entrepreneurs reacted to the seventeenth-century crisis in different ways. Many of them moved manufacturing to the countryside because of the rising labour costs in the urban centres and began to depend on cheaper rural labour. The declining prices turned them towards mass production to reduce unit costs by higher output, thereby increasing profits by means of larger turnovers. This resulted in the manufacture of inexpensive draperies instead of the more expensive cloth. The third means of increasing their profit was to expand the volume of trade with the colonial world to compensate the reduced demand in domestic markets. By the early-eighteenth century, a large part of wool, linen, cotton and blended cloth was being produced in rural areas in England, France, the Low Countries, Switzerland and even in Germany. This trend resulted in profound transformation in urban industrial organizations which now faced competition from rural industries and in the eighteenth century the guilds began losing their economic significance. This proto-industrialization marked an important phase and generated capital and rural labour for production for distant markets.

In France, the ruling class was unable to consolidate their fragmented land units into large holdings because of the protection provided by the absolute state to the peasant proprietary rights. The seigneurs imposed feudal dues in the form of *mortmain* and *banalities*. In Hungary, a similar trend was evident. The peasants were left with nothing and they could not introduce production-related improvements. In Poland, the landed nobility forced the peasants to work on their lands. The small peasants had no freedom to choose even the crops and they lost interest in improvement measures. Despite the possibility of securing higher prices, the nobility could not increase total production because of the inelastic political and economic structure of Poland. It was the improved technology of England, the Netherlands and northern France that enabled them to overcome the problem of low prices and make substantial economic progress. Robert Brenner and P. Vilar emphasize the role of a strong feudal structure in preventing the progress of capitalism. The outer limits of the feudal structure placed limitations on market and restricted the demand for manufactured goods. As labour in lands remained tied up in petty production, heavy feudal exaction and the exploitative role of feudal monarchies played a vital role in prolonging such conditions. The peasants were able to sell only that produce in the market from which they paid feudal rent and taxes, interests on their borrowings and land revenue. They depended on land to get their food and clothing. This situation led to stagnation of technology and kept the market structure extremely limited. For capitalism to develop, it was necessary for the peasants to turn into landless labourers. This situation developed in England where peasant unity had given way to social differentiation consisting of different layers of peasantry but in other places, the absolute monarchs protected small peasants in order to remain in power. Land transfers were few and the consolidation of landholdings in the hands of the entrepreneurial class of landlords did not take place on a large enough scale to introduce capitalist relations of production.

In western Europe the seigniorial class began increasing *demesne* land at the expense of communal holdings and recruited hired labour to produce commercial crops for the market. This led to a sudden upsurge of agrarian capitalism in that region. In Bohemia and in Eastern Europe, the opposite happened. Here too, the feudal nobility enlarged their *demesnes* but not always at the expense of peasant holdings, as had happened in western Europe. This was made possible because during the Thirty Years War, vast tracts of land lay fallow. This war had caused heavy losses in population and land was abandoned in several parts of Germany. The landlords forced higher dues and labour services on the remaining peasants. So in eastern and central Europe, feudalism experienced a fresh twist when landlords increased their reliance on serf labour services. The war had caused enormous increase in taxation. The significance of the peasants as generators of income increased immensely both for the landlords and for the states. In Germany, particularly east of the Elbe, feudalism intensified. The war had created a serious shortage of labour, which was needed to work on *demesne* lands. The demographic losses had made labour very costly. In such situations, the lords instead of hiring fresh labour to work in their private lands, opted to utilize the existing serfs by placing additional responsibilities on them. The landlords procured not only peasant labour services for their *demesne* farms but also successfully altered the obligations of the peasants according to their own needs and thereby serfdom was revitalized. At several places there was a tendency towards transmutation of labour services and dues into money payments. As far as the rise of English agriculture is concerned, it shall be examined in greater detail in context of the English Revolution. Thus, whereas in western Europe the extension of the *demesne* was carried out through the employment of hired labour to strengthen the impetus towards capitalism, in eastern Europe, because of chronic shortage of manpower, it led to strengthening and consolidation of serfdom. Hence the gap between eastern and western Europe was greatly widened after the seventeenth-century crisis. The most important outcome of the seventeenth-century crisis created drive towards the capitalist agriculture and the strengthening of feudal relations respectively.

It is widely believed that the post-crisis period was marked by universal domination of politics, society and culture by the aristocracy. The feudal lords of eastern Europe were able to enserf the peasants and consolidate their class interests at the local and the national level. These lords of large estates had come to dominate the governing institutions. Here, neither royal authority nor the interests of the nascent bourgeoisie were capable of challenging the authority of the nobility. The large-scale turmoil of the mid-seventeenth century had badly frightened the traditional nobility. As T.K. Rabb argues, the period from about 1660 to 1789 was the age of aristocracy *par excellence* – a time when the great landowners and courtiers became secure, confident and relaxed by their supremacy. They were the ones to benefit most from the new situation as they gained privileges, offices, status and wealth.

The Thirty Years War

Seventeenth-century Europe was dominated by the Thirty Years War (1618–48). For a long time it was viewed as a religious war originating in Germany between the Catholics and the Protestants caused by the breakdown of the Peace of Augsberg. There were others who refused to call it a German war. A number of explanations have been provided on the subject of its origins and nature.

Similarly, its impact has been discussed and debated among the historians but the entire controversy remains unresolved. While some scholars minimize the importance of the war by suggesting that it produced no drastic social changes and had no revolutionary impact, most scholars argue that it had a profound impact not only on economic and socio-political lives of the people in many parts of Europe but had a determining influence on the inter-state relationship in the subsequent period.

Background

It is generally accepted that the trouble first started in Bohemia, a German kingdom that was a part of the Holy Roman Empire. Like the Holy Roman Emperor and the ruler of Poland, Bohemian rulers were also elected by the Diet. However, after coming under Habsburg rule (Austria) in 1526, election became an issue of debate. The Habsburg rulers contended that Bohemian kingship was hereditary and election only meant confirmation, a practice developed as a form of compromise, in which the Bohemian ruler proposed his successor who was then elected by the Diet. Bohemia held an important place in the Holy Roman Empire as she contributed substantial amount of material and manpower resources to the imperial armies of the emperor. Densely populated, it was economically an extremely rich kingdom during the sixteenth century with a large number of textile and glassware industries, iron, silver and copper mines. But her fortunes were declining because of the imperial wars. Financial burden was becoming heavy at a time when the economy of Europe was slowing down, profits diminishing and the Bohemian silver mines becoming unprofitable against the competition from the New World.

Bohemia was also the centre of religious troubles even before Martin Luther appeared on the German scene. There was the Hussites movement in the fourteenth and fifteenth centuries. The spread of Lutheranism and other rebellious groups like the Calvinists and Bohemian Brotherhoods had reduced the Catholic religion to a minority, confined to barely 10 per cent of the population. The Protestants began to dominate all the higher posts including the University of Prague and the Bohemian Diet. There was a deep religious rift that had developed between the Catholics and the Protestants in the Holy Roman Empire. Emperor Charles V tried hard to wipe out Protestantism from the empire through Catholic revival but he was forced to accept the Peace of Augsburg in 1555. The Catholic emperor made serious efforts to regain grounds in Germany and Bohemia. Unfortunately, there were conflicting interpretations of the treaty by the Lutherans and the Catholics. The two test cases – the case of Archbishop of Cologne turning Lutheran and his removal by the Pope and Emperor Rudolf II of Austria, and the Donauworth Incident of 1607 in which the city was taken over by the Bavarian ruler Maximilian I and the Catholic religion restored. Thereafter, Bavaria became the centre of Catholic Reformation and the rulers started enforcing all decisions of the Council of Trent. These events marked the regaining of the Catholic control in some parts of Germany. An increasingly aggressive policy was pursued towards the Protestant neighbours of Germany to win them back to the Catholic fold. To resist these moves, the Protestants formed the Evangelical Union in 1608 and the next year, Catholics formed the Holy League under Maximilian I.

Emperors Rudolf II and Matthias followed the Bavarian example in Bohemia. The atmosphere was very tense because of mutual mistrust and animosity between the Protestant subjects and the Catholic rulers. The trouble started with the intolerant and staunch Catholic policies of Emperor Rudolf II (1576–1612) and his brother, Emperor Matthias (1612–19). Along with the Protestant resentment, Czech nationalism combined with many other factors created an open Bohemian rebellion against the Habsburg rule. Apart from the basic struggle between the tyrannical Austrian rule and the Bohemian subjects and the Catholic impositions on a Protestant population, there were several other issues. The urban businessmen faced heavy taxation, economic depressions and the threat of rural nobility, who after enserfing the peasant population began controlling towns and tried to refeudalize society. It is seen as a struggle against the German culture and Catholic religion. This revolt was the immediate cause of the Thirty Years War but the issues sustaining the war continued to change. The Bohemian revolt, which marked the beginning of the Thirty Years War, is seen mainly as a nationalist as well as a religious revolt. The fears of Protestant revolt against the pro-Catholic measures of Rudolf II forced the Emperor to grant the Letter of Majesty in July 1609 which gave some concessions to the Protestants. Matthias became the king of Bohemia and was elected Holy Roman Emperor after Rudolf II. He appointed a council of regency that enforced unpopular religious policies – Protestants could not construct new churches and crown land was distributed to the Catholic Church. In May 1618, as assembly of Protestants tried the royal officials, for the violation of the Letter of Majesty and threw them out of the window of the palace. This incident has come to be called the 'Defenetration of Prague' (fenêtre in French means window). The rebels proceeded to establish their own government and emperor Ferdinand II of Bohemia was ousted by the Czechs. The Bohemian crown was offered to the Calvinist Elector, Frederick V of the Palatinate. He accepted the offer and got the support of the Evangelical Union, that he himself founded in 1608. It included many Protestant German states. The Bohemian Revolt directly involved German states into a war. Spain came to the assistance of Austria and the Bohemians were defeated. It led to the execution of many rebel leaders and mass confiscation of their properties. The ambitions of Ferdinand II in alliance with Spain aroused French apprehensions and led to direct confrontation between the French and the Habsburg rulers. The coming of Spain in this conflict transformed it into a contest for hegemony.

Causes

The traditional view on the origins of the Thirty Years War has been that it was basically a series of dynastic–religious wars, a continuation of the religious conflicts between the Protestants and the Catholics. The religious wars of the sixteenth century that swept across several parts of Europe, particularly Germany, France and the Netherlands, could not be settled and the same issue of religion, continued to divide different sections of society. The Peace of

Augsburg (1555) was an attempt to settle the religious conflicts between the Protestants and the Catholics though it left a number of issues unsolved. It recognized only the Lutheran religion while Calvinism, which emerged later but gained a large number of converts, particularly in Bohemia, was not given any recognition. The rights granted to each ruling prince to decide the religion of his respective state caused further controversies and made the situation in that region explosive. At the same time it is important to note that this conflict brought the two Catholic powers – Spain and France – directly against each other. The religious issues did play a part in the diplomatic aspects of the war as many alliances were formed on grounds of religious affinity. There are two opposite interpretations concerning the role of religion in causing the Thirty Years War. The traditional view emphasizes that the war was primarily religious in its inspiration, inception and development while a more recent view gives the religious element less importance. For them, religion played a part only in matters of diplomacy, particularly in motivating the German states to forge some kind of unity. It must be noted that in the Bohemian Revolt of 1618, many Protestant states refused her assistance only on religious grounds yet the Protestant states were given valuable assistance and later, leadership by the Catholic kings of France.

Some scholars have explained the origins of the Thirty Years War through the 'encirclement of France' thesis. It is argued that during the sixteenth and seventeenth centuries, the French rulers felt threatened by the Habsburg rulers and were forced to adopt aggression to break this encirclement. S.H. Steinberg suggests that the war was the product of French efforts. After the conclusion of the civil war in 1598 that was fought on the question of religion, France decided to break her encirclement, which had been carried out by the Habsburg powers – Spain and Austria. P. Brightwell and J.H. Elliott provide similar arguments although Braudel rejects these views. Another view on the same lines suggests that it was a struggle for the 'natural frontiers' of France. The Treaty of Cateau-Cambrèsis (1559) had brought the Habsburg-Valois struggles to an end but only for a short while. The treaty was an acknowledgement of a stalemate and did not give any distinct advantage to either of the two powers. It could not provide a permanent solution to their contest and it could not dispel the French fears of Habsburg domination. This view has also not gained popularity among historians. Instead many see the war as a struggle between two powerful ruling dynasties – the Habsburg and the Valois – for the hegemony of Europe. This aspect of the struggle manifests itself in the later part of the war. The war is presented as a struggle between European powers. Georges Pagès argues that the prime mover in this war was France as she was involved in it indirectly from 1629 and directly from 1635 and that it was essentially a conflict for supremacy. It was Richelieu who tried to extend the French frontiers further towards the Rhine. A German approach led by C.V. Wedgewood, suggests that the war was essentially a German tragedy born of its own problems. It implies that the war was sparked off by a number of revolts against the Habsburg rule of the Holy Roman Empire in different parts of Europe. The conflict then spread to the German core. Half a century of constitutional and religious disputes had produced two distinct groupings and it drew major powers into a struggle against the Habsburg for dynastic, political and religious reasons. The conflicts represent mixed motives of Olivares in Spain, Richlieu in France and Gustave Adolf in Sweden to achieve their political ambition. Another view presents the Thirty Years War as a part of a much longer struggle against Spain, in which the Netherlands played an early role. K. Griewank considers it as an episode in the Eighty Years War between the Netherlands and Spain that lasted till 1659.

Some attempts have been made to shift the focus to inside rather than outside forces. J.V. Polisensky seeks to redress what he considers an excessively German approach by concentrating on the origins and the initial phase of the conflict and by focusing on Bohemia. He sees the conflict as a political one, which was the logical result of a crisis in the policies of the old ruling classes in various regions of Europe. In Bohemia, this political and social crisis had deep economic roots. M.P. Gutmann provides an alternative approach by re-emphasizing the long-term issues in this conflict. He dwells less on internal and external causes but stresses on the old and new types of extension like those of France and the Netherlands.

He sees it as a struggle between two opposite ways of life. The first representing Protestant values of free institutions, intellectual freedom, tolerance and encouragement of business pursuits while the second is based on the ideas of centralized absolutism, the inquisition, persecution of heretics, a patronizing nobility and enserfment. In central Europe, the authority of the Habsburgs was challenged by the German states and Sweden and the war is seen in the background of changing nature of European society.

Gerhard Ritter asserts that in the second half of the sixteenth century, during a structural crisis, there arose in western Europe 'modern anti-feudal states' (as Braudel describes them) – the Netherlands, England and France. In central Europe, this crisis had not been resolved. Thus, the repercussions of the religious wars of the sixteenth century were delayed and subsequently transformed into a conflict among the great national states of modern Europe. The Thirty Years War was the product of this situation. The war continued with brief interruptions for a considerably long period and as the centre of conflict and its participants continued to change, it is not easy to ascribe precise reasons for the conflict. With each renewal of war, fresh issues came to the forefront, and the interest of the warring parties became complex and quite different from what they were in the beginning. A study of different phases would illustrate this point.

The Phases of War

The Thirty Years War consisted of five important and different stages and issues, and the major participants continued to change with every different stage of the same war. The chief powers in this war included Spain and Austrian Habsburg who remained involved throughout the duration of the war, while the other major states such as Denmark, Sweden, many German states, actively participated or withdrew at different stages. Only France, who joined the war a little late, remained an active participant till the end. The conflict between France and the Habsburg power was probably the most direct confrontation, which continued for a large part of the sixteenth century until the temporary compromise was

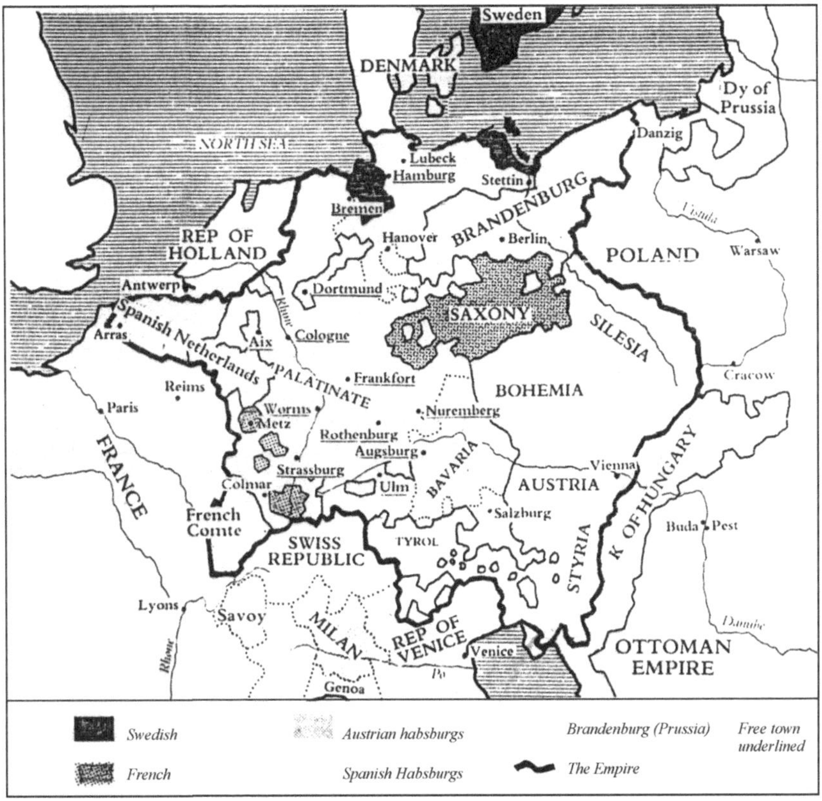

Map 7.1: Central Europe after the Treaty of Westphalia 1648

made under Treaty of Cateau-Cambrèsis. The French Wars of Religion had kept the French government preoccupied in domestic problems and after the Edict of Nantes in 1598 the French renewed their interests in foreign affairs. However, the French did not join the conflict from the beginning in 1618. Instead they subsidized the enemies of the Habsburg and entered the war only in 1635 when the resistance against the Spanish-Austrian forces was failing.

The first stage of this war was short, from 1618 to 1620, and was marked by the Bohemian Revolt. By 1620, the Palatinate, Baden and Brunswick were on the verge of being conquered and occupied by the Spanish troops. The Catholic League that had been formed in 1609 assisted the emperor. Many foreign powers also got involved in the conflict. English interest in this conflict was because Frederick of Palatine who was elected the king of Bohemia, was the son-in-law of the English ruler James I. France was concerned by the Spanish moves in the border principalities, which were of strategic importance for both the powers.

The religious elements dominated the second phase of the war from 1619 to 1623, and it began to spread to the different states of Germany. The Catholics achieved an important victory in 1620 at the Battle of White Mountain. In the third stage from 1624 to 1629, Denmark got involved in the war. The imperial troops swept across northern Germany causing large-scale destruction. Till now the Lutheran states of Saxony and Brandenburg were unwilling to be involved in this war as it was started by the militant Calvinists, but by 1627 the situation had become alarming. The reconverted Catholic states of Germany had become menace to the other Protestant states. Christian IV of Denmark felt threatened as he considered himself to be the protector of the lower Saxon circle. However, he was defeated and in the next stage Sweden because of her strategic concerns, was compelled to assume leadership against the Habsburg. Her chief interest was to establish control over the Baltic. The defeat of Denmark was followed by the Peace of Lubeck in 1629. The presence of Wallenstein's army of the Habsburg on the Baltic coastline forced Sweden to change her policy of neutrality. The Swedish ruler Gustave Adolphus assumed the leadership and formed an alliance with some Protestant states. The initial success of the Swedes against the imperial forces in the battle of Breitenfeld in 1631 led to the entry of Saxony and Brandenburg in the war, which had remained neutral till this period. Gustave Adolphus saw himself as a crusader of the Lutherans. By this time the war had become more complex – the merging of strategic and religious factors with the Swedish ambition as an additional ingredient. Adolphus now aimed to acquire substantial territories in northern Germany along the Baltic seacoast by defeating the Habsburg power. Swedish ambition received a major jolt in 1632 when Gustave Adolphus was killed in the Battle of Lutzen after which Swedish fortunes began to dwindle. The Peace of Prague in 1635 ended large-scale fighting and gave favourable terms to the Catholics. It was a fragile peace that was broken by the French entry. The final phase of the war commenced in 1635 when France led by Cardinal Richlieu decided to participate in it and face the Habsburgs directly. After initial reverses, the French secured a series of successes. The armies of both the groups mainly mercenaries and marauding soldiers, were more interested in plunder, extortion and destruction and were often difficult to control. The soldiers showed no loyalty to the princes who paid them through the hired generals. The war caused widespread devastations and was brought to an end by the peace Treaty of Westphalia in 1648.

The Treaty of Westphalia is considered an extremely important document for a variety of reasons. It decided the territorial claims of many powers like Germany, France and Sweden. Sweden received the western half of Pomerania and the Bishoprics of Bremen and Verdun. She came to control the mouths of the rivers Oder, Elbe and Weser and established substantial control of the German seaboard. The French claims of Metz, Toul and eastern Verdun were confirmed and the acquisition of Alsace gave immense advantage to the French on the upper Rhine.

The Thirty Years War marked a new phase in territorial wars. It marked a transition from men-based offensive to greater dependence on firepower that included artillery and volley power. This method of heavy and continuous shelling to protect field troops was adopted first by Gustave Adolphus. Henceforth, wars became more offensive in nature and a higher proportion of soldiers became gunners. Drill and discipline became important ingredients of the future wars.

Political Results

The settlement led to a long-term peace between the Protestants and the Catholics. After the Peace Treaty of Augsburg the Protestants were given back church properties that were seized. The supporters of Calvin were also granted religious tolerance and given an equal legal standing with the Lutherans.

The Princes of Germany were given a variety of political and territorial rights like the right of forming alliances with each other or with foreign powers. The Treaty led to the emergence of stronger German states at the expense of smaller principalities. The larger states were the Palatinate, Bavaria, Saxony and Brandenburg. The Protestant leadership in this war passed from the hands of Saxony to Prussia-Brandenburg. Prussia emerged as the leading German state in the post-war period. The most important result was the disintegration of the Holy Roman Empire. The political fabric of the empire was much weaker in 1648 than it had been before the war. The empire almost lost its sovereign character and could never function as a unified political unit. On the other hand, the weakening of the empire implied the consolidation of the larger German states. The consequence of this was the rise of northern Germany as a major military power to counterbalance the traditional power of Austria in the southern region. There were several fairly large German states which operated in the international power structure after 1648. Austria and Brandenburg-Prussia emerged as the two strong states of central Europe. Outside Germany, the Swiss Confederation and the Netherlands became sovereign states. The Thirty Years War also increased the prestige and influence of France. The French success in this war enhanced her prestige and led to the rise of powerful absolutism that became a model for many other states. Prior to the war, Sweden had been pursuing an expansionist policy through territorial acquisitions towards the Russian borders, Baltic and central Europe. This policy of Sweden was soon checked because of her failure in the Thirty Years War. The political map of

Europe was somewhat changed after the war and had significant political consequences on the European states.

The Peace of Westphalia was an important achievement, for it signified the beginning of the modern concept of European Congress. The only sovereigns who did not participate in the peace deliberations were the rulers of Russia, England and Turkey. In fact, there were two separate congresses – one for the Protestant Swedes and Germans at Osnabruck, and the other at Munster, where the French and the German Catholics negotiated. The discussions and resolutions took three years before the Peace of Westphalia was announced. Its decisions formed the basis of the international law of Europe till the Napoleonic wars.

Socio-economic Consequences

Historians are divided on the subject of the social and economic effects of the Thirty Years War on Europe, particularly on Germany. One set of historians argue that the war had disastrous consequences on the German people and it alone caused the decline of Germany. Those who subscribe to this view belong to the 'disastrous war school'. In recent years, many historians have rejected this view and have come out with the argument that the war's impact was not as catastrophic as had been presented for many years and that the decline of Germany was not caused by the war alone. The decline had started in the sixteenth century itself. The second group of writers is called the 'Revisionist School' or the 'earlier decline school' – a term expounded by Theodore K. Rabb.

For a long time historians argued that the Thirty Years War had a devastating effect on Germany. Gustav Freytag argued that when the war ended, little remained of Germany, and that the German nation had been utterly devastated by the conflict. Other scholars such as David Ogg and William Durant, also highlight the destructive aspect of the war and its short-term impact by citing demographic losses and the destruction of trade and manufacturing. The war was fought on such a massive scale by the mercenary and the para-mercenary armies long used to violence and pillage that the civilian population in many places were brutalized and killed on a vast scale. Attacks on towns and cities by Commanders like Tilly and Wallenstein and the movement of troops brought chaos and destruction because they were unable to impose discipline on the mercenary army. As the war covered almost every part of Germany and lasted thirty years with changing participants, the destruction was bound to be massive. The city of Magdeburg was besieged ten times and such frequent destructions caused immense losses to the people. It is argued that a large number of cities were destroyed in the course of the war and the revival took a long time, while in some cases some cities could never recover.

The impact of the war on the German population was terrible. Most of whom who died were military casualties caused by the new methods of warfare which brought greater accuracy and higher destructive potential. At Breitenfeld, 8,000 out of 31,000 imperial troops were killed. The Swedish losses were as much as 50 per cent while 60 per cent of Saxon and imperial forces were killed at Wittstock. Civilian losses are difficult to establish for lack of authentic sources. It is believed that the population of the Holy Roman Empire declined from 21 to 13.5 million, that of Bohemia, the main centre of warfare, from 3 to 0.8 million, Augsburg city was left with only 21,000 people in 1650 from 48,000 in 1620 while in the violent sack of 1631, Magdeburg lost 25,000 out of 30,000 inhabitants. In the other regions like northern Brandenburg, parts of Rhineland, Bavaria, the Palatinate and Pomerania, the population losses were extremely high, up to 80 per cent in some parts. It is estimated that the population of Germany as a whole declined from about 16 million to 10 million in the course of the war. It is believed by writers of the 'disastrous war school', that the impact of the war on the whole of Germany was long-lasting and completely dislocated the economy.

It is difficult to evaluate the impact of the war on German economy and society. Long-term destructive consequences can be observed not so much in material terms as in structural changes and reduction in economic activity. F. Lutge has emphasized the long-term damage that the war caused to the domestic and international economic relationships. According to him, studies of the local regions reveal that this war affected trade and industry operating in an well-developed urban economy. The war blocked the normal trade routes and led to the shift of old economic centres and trade routes which affected the export-oriented textile sector. Countries like England, the Netherlands and France curtailed their trade with central Europe. The Treaty of Westphalia handed over control of the river outlets of Germany to foreign powers, e.g. the Netherlands got control of the mouth of the Rhine while Sweden established her domination over the mouths of the Weser, the Elbe and the Oder. Hence in matters of trade, the advantages passed into foreign hands. Another victim of the war was the Hanseatic League, the famous trading association of north German states. But it can be argued that the decline of this commercial union had started in the sixteenth century. The rise of Sweden and her control of the Baltic ports greatly destroyed its trading sphere.

As opposed to the writings of the 'disastrous war school', many recent writers have denied the role of the Thirty Years War in the decline of Germany. An important revisionist writer is S.H. Steinberg. He refutes the long-standing assumptions that the war was a disaster for Germany as made out by Freytag, basing his arguments on two important contemporary sources – *The Conditions of the German Empires* by Pufendorf and *Simplicius Simplicissimus* by Grimmelshausen. They present harrowing details of torture and killings of peasants and reveal a picture of civilian sufferings. Many other sources like diaries, paintings and engravings depict the destruction of the war. Steinberg is skeptical of the worth of these sources and suggests that Fredrick William, the Great Elector, needed to justify the tough policies he had adopted after 1648 towards the peasantry, the estates and the town's people. According to Steinberg, the dark picture painted of the war years was meant to highlight the magnitude of his political, economic and cultural success. He thinks that the evils of the war have been highly exaggerated and that Germany suffered much less than what is generally believed. He thinks that the loss of population was small; there was no significant damage and hardly any economic losses. The war damages were soon recovered with the reconstruction of economic life. Germany was neither better nor worse off than what she was in 1609, but different from what it had been half a century before. Steinberg argues that the national income, productivity and standard of living were higher than before, as the economy had reached the limits of growth (the rising population of the earlier period had begun to play a negative role on the German economy). Shailagh Ogilvie suggests that the Thirty Years War with all its devastating effects did relax the pressure of population on food resources and released the Central European economy from the 'Malthusian trap'. There is no doubt that the seventeenth-century depression was long and damaging but the first signs of recovery were seen earlier in Germany in the 1690s, whereas in France, Belgium, Denmark, England and Poland, the agrarian depression continued and at times grew worse till the mid-eighteenth century.

Several scholars like F.L. Carsten, A.J.P. Taylor, Henry Kamen and V.H.H. Green argue that the decline of Germany had already started before the war. Carsten raises a question whether it was a national decline of Germany or merely a transfer of economic activity from towns to the countryside. A.J.P. Taylor believes that the war caught the empire during a period of weakness, and it was not the cause of German decline. The impoverishment, the dwindling of the cities, the decay of culture and material standards had been happening for almost a century before the Thirty Years War broke out. On the other hand, Steinberg finds a remarkable continuity in cultural achievements. For example, the lyrical poetry and the *baroque* style, which earlier was considered an anathema, found a place in history.

Henry Kamen argues that there was no single economic and political unit called Germany, rather there were several economic regions. Therefore, the decline was only of a selected few regions of Germany – some may have suffered long-term factors of decay, while others were annihilated by the war. The old commercial and financial centres were already on the path of decay by the end of the sixteenth century. The rise of the English and the Dutch trade had hastened the decline of the Hans. The German princes were politically eclipsed by Spanish imperialism and many of the important towns were well on their decline. Kamen believes that the currency manipulations in the 1620s played a part in producing commercial dislocation that affected the entire trading zone of

Europe. It was a crisis in currency, commerce and agriculture, accompanied by high mortality and depopulation caused by war. According to Kamen, the most interesting feature of these demographic reverses was not the death rate but the birth rate that declined. In many German towns, the birth rate fell below the pre-war level that caused a decline in population. He believes that the war was not universally destructive and that the disasters were spread unevenly. Cities like Lubeck, Bremen and Hamburg even increased their population because of immigrants. The population of Hamburg had grown from about 54,000 in 1620 to 75,000 in 1675. The decline of Magdeburg was accompanied by the rise of Hamburg as the most prosperous city in Germany. While the Rhine and southern Germany witnessed stagnation in trade, new centres of trade like Bremen and Hamburg brought huge profits to the merchants through trade in war materials. Businessmen from outside, including the Netherlands, were investing their money in its enterprises.

Finally, the war impacted both the peasant population and the class of nobles. In the countryside, the demand for food grains to feed large armies helped a section of the peasantry that had access to the market. In the southern and western Germany, particularly in Bavaria and the Palatinate, the war hastened the decline of feudalism. The demographic loss, particularly of the peasants, reduced the number of tenants and thereby improved their bargaining power with the nobility. On the other hand, in the northern and particularly eastern regions of Germany, the nobility was too powerful and the decline of the peasant population led to the tightening of feudal obligations through fresh regulations. The rulers were dependent on the nobility and acted on their advice by issuing legislation to strengthen feudal regimes. In some parts of Germany the position of the nobility suffered during the war and they became dependant on the rulers. In states like Bavaria, the nobility entered the state's employment. The Bohemian nobility underwent qualitative change after the Battle of the White Mountain. The new nobles had little connection with land and owed its position to the Habsburgs. In Brandenburg they began to join the army and the bureaucracy. These two institutions became the 'twin-pillars' of Prussian autocracy during the eighteenth century. There was also a trend of manufacturing industries, especially textiles, shifting to the countryside, promoting proto-industrialization in certain parts of Germany.

Important Events in the Seventeenth-century Crisis

1599–1600, 1605, 1623–5, 1630, 1635–6, 1648–9, 1655, 1664	Plague epidemics in Castile, France, Spain, Italy, Amsterdam and London.
1618	Bohemian revolt against Habsburg, Defenetration of Prague
1621	Truce between Spain and the Netherlands expires, war begins
1623	Financial and monetary crisis
1624 & 1636–7	Croquant uprisings in France
1626	Imperial forces defeat armies led by Christian IV of Denmark
1629	Peace of Lubeck; Sweden takes up the leadership in war
1635	Peace of Prague, final stage of the war begins
1637	*Nu-pied* revolt in France
1640–68	Revolt of Portugal against Spain
1641 & 1689	The Irish revolts on religious issues and crop failure
1642–9	The English Civil War, also called the bourgeois revolution
1647	Revolt in Naples and Sicily
1648	Peace Treaty of Westphalia and the official end of the Thirty Years War; Cossack revolts, the Fermo War in Rome. Treaty of Munster ended the Dutch rebellion and led to the recognition of independence of the United Netherlands.
1648–53	The Fronde revolts in France
1648–54	The Ukrainian revolts
1652–3	The Swiss Peasant War
1658–60	The Danish-Swedish War
1675	The Stamp Paper uprisings in Bordeaux and Brittany
1688–9	The Glorious Revolution in England, the Catalonia uprising in Spain
1693–4	The period of severe winters and wet summers

Suggested Readings

Aston, Trevor, ed., *Crisis in Europe 1560–1660, Essays from Past and Present*, London: Routledge & Kegan Paul, 1965. A collection of essays in which the idea of the 'general crisis' is interpreted from various perspectives. Includes an article by Hobsbawm, pp. 5–58.

Braudel, Fernand, *The Mediterranean and the Mediterranean World in the Age of Philip II*, 2 vols., New York: Harper & Row, 1973. A brilliant work and provides a new perspective by bringing out the role of geography in determining the course of human history.

Burke, Peter, ed., *Economy and Society in Early Modern Europe: Essays from Annales*, New York: Harper & Row, 1972. Collection of some brilliant essays by reputed scholars on this subject. Particularly good for the Price Revolution and the crisis.

Davis, Ralph, *The Rise of the Atlantic Economics*, Ithaca: Cornell University Press, 1973. An extremely useful book from the point of view of Iberian peninsula, Atlantic trade and the emergence of colonial empire.

Elliott, J.H., *Imperial Spain 1469–1716*, London: Edward Arnold, 1963. Masterly work on Spain and her decline.

———'The Decline of Spain', *Past and Present*, 20, 1961, pp. 52–75.

Hamilton, E.J., 'The Decline of Spain', in E.M. Carus-Wilson, ed., *Essays in Economic History*, vol. I, London & New York: Edward Arnold, 1963. An important essay on the subject which led the debate on the role of monetary factors in the crisis.

Flynn, Dennis O., 'Fiscal Crisis and the Decline of Spain (Castile)', *Journal of Economic History*, 42, 1982, pp. 139–47. Takes up the role of financial problems of the Spanish state in the decline of Spain.

Forster, Robert and Jack P. Greene, eds., *Preconditions of Revolution in Early Modern Europe*, Baltimore & London: John Hopkins, 1972. The book is a product of talks by experts on the subject and includes Lawrence Stone, J.H. Elliott, Perez Zagorin, Ruth Pike, Roland Mousnier, etc.

Israel, J.I., 'The Decline of Spain: A Historical Myth', *Past and Present*, 91, 1, 1981, pp. 170–80. One of the contributors to the debate on Spanish decline.

Kamen, Henry, 'Decline of Spain–myth or Fact,' 81, *Past and Present*, 1978. An important contributor on the concept on Spain; he calls it the decline of Castile.

Kriedte, Peter, *Peasants, Landlords, Merchant Capitalists: Europe and the World Economy 1500–1809*, Cambridge: Cambridge University Press, 1983.

Parker, G. and L.M. Smith, eds., *The General Crisis of the Seventeenth Century*, London: Routledge & Kegan Paul, 1978. An extremely important work on the subject and should be read by all scholars on this subject.

Polisensky, J.V., *The Thirty Years War*, Berkeley: University of California Press, 1971. A well-written work based on Marxist interpretation.

———, *War and Society in Europe 1618–1648*, Cambridge: Cambridge University Press, 1978.

Rabb, Theodore K., *The Struggle for Stability in Early Modern Europe*, Oxford: Oxford University Press, 1978. Contains a good review of the historiography, particularly Chapter III that discusses the main proponents and critics of the crisis.

Rich, E.E. and C.H. Wilson, eds., *The Cambridge Economic History of Europe*, vol. IV: *The Economy of Expanding Europe*, Cambridge: Cambridge University Press (1967), 1975.

Ruggiero, Romano, 'Italy in the Crisis of the Seventeenth Century' in Peter Earle, ed., *Essays in European Economic History*, Oxford: Oxford University Press, 1974.

Steinberg, S.H., *The 'Thirty Years War' and the Conflict for European Hegemony 1600–1660*, London: Edward Arnold, 1966.

Trevor-Roper, Hugh, 'The General Crisis of the Seventeenth Century', *Past and Present*, no. 18, 1960, pp. 160–70. This volume contains the articles of J.H. Elliott, Roland Mousnier, Lawrence Stone, E.H. Hobsbawm on the same theme.

Vries, Jan de, *The Economy of Europe in an Age of Crisis, 1600–1750*, Cambridge: Cambridge University Press, 1994. Very useful and substantive work on agricultural, urban and capitalist developments.

Wilson, C.H., 'Economic Decline of the Netherlands', in E.M. Carus-Wilson, ed., *Essays in Economic History*, London: Edward Arnold, 1963. Contains some very important articles by known writers on European economy of the sixteenth and seventeenth centuries.

CHAPTER 8

The Rise of Modern Science

The seventeenth century witnessed a great change in man's perception of the universe. It created a new intellectual climate as the centuries-old earth-centered concept of the universe gave way to a new picture in which the earth was seen only as one of the many planets orbiting the sun. It was discovered that sun itself was one among millions of stars. It resulted in the demystification of the universe and by the second half of the seventeenth century, a mechanistic view of the world was created. With it the intellectual crisis in Europe was resolved. It led to a re-thinking of moral and religious matters as well as man's ideas on nature. The process, by which this new view of the universe and the knowledge of science came to be established, is termed as the Scientific Revolution.

The origins of modern science can be seen in the process of constant interaction between man and nature. By the seventeenth century, scientific learning and investigation began to increase dramatically. Attention was paid to an examination and understanding of the physical realm. The subsequent creation of scientific method proved crucial to the evolution of science in the modern world. The rise of science, which was called natural philosophy in those days, was associated with spectacular intellectual triumph in mathematics, astronomy and physics. Observation of natural phenomenon, formulation of laws or principles on the basis of experiment and conclusion were the chief features of the scientific revolution. The scientific and intellectual changes of the seventeenth century were vital in the creation of the modern world.

According to J.D. Bernal, the period of Scientific Revolution can be divided into three phases. The first was the phase of Copernicus when the geocentric view of the universe was replaced by the heliocentric concept. In the second phase a scientific basis was provided to this view by thinkers like Tycho Brahe, Kepler and Galileo. The third phase was the period of Isaac Newton and René Descartes in which the scientific societies were formed and science was becoming an institutional part of European society.

Origins

The beginning of science goes back to the ancient world. The Greeks had shaped knowledge of science for a very long time. The view of Aristotle in the field of physics, Ptolemy in astronomy and Galen in medicine had dominated European thought for centuries. In the medieval period, theologians studied the world, especially astronomy, based on the conclusions of the ancient Greeks. Aristotle believed that all heavy bodies fall toward the centre of the universe and rested there unless propelled by a mover in some other direction. Earth was seen at the centre of the universe. This explanation of the universe created difficulties in understanding natural phenomena. In the fourteenth century some scientists tried to provide a new explanation to the problem of motion by suggesting that a moving body possessed impetus, which keeps it in motion. Another ancient scholar, Ptolemy held that a concentric series of transparent crystalline spheres revolved in an ascending order of purity around man's corruptible earth. The moon, the sun, the planets and the fixed stars and the *primum* mobile (the outermost sphere that drove the entire system) revolved in perfect circles. Beyond this lay the purest region where heaven existed. Even in the field of life sciences, Galen's theories were based on incorrect information of the human anatomy. He was the most famous Greek physician after Hippocrates and lived in the second century AD. He was one of the first to show the existence of muscles and the importance of the spinal cord. He wrote many treatises, mostly on medicine. Galen's most famous work was his book *On Anatomical Preparations* that remained a standard text for over fourteen centuries. He based his work on animal anatomy which when applied to the human context proved wrong. Galen believed that the liver was an extremely important part as all the veins entered it. He argued that it was the liver from where one kind of blood ran through the veins to all parts of the body supplying nutrition, while a different type of blood, mixed with a sort of spirituous substance called pneuma, flowed out through arteries, which kept men alive. All these ideas had survived the Middle Ages with some changes. Historians no longer believe that medieval Europe was a period of scientific darkness. Medieval scholars continued the study of astronomy and medicine. They had succeeded in preserving and continuing the knowledge of Greek science while adding something of their own. The Europeans of the middle ages acquired knowledge of mathematics through the Arabs. They also dwelt on Platonic speculations and tried to develop the ideas of Hippocrates that every disease had a natural cause. Aristotle's system came under serious attack in the medieval period from a number of intellectuals. In the mid-fifteenth century, a famous theologian, Nicholas of Cusa, argued that the universe was infinite and uniform both in its substance and in the laws governing it. However, he could not develop a coherent alternative system of cosmology. In this period, the focus was on assimilation of knowledge rather than experimentation. It was a period of intellectual activities primarily in the universities of Europe but the study of natural science was largely based on the works of ancient Greeks.

Another factor, which engaged the intellectual interest in the late medieval period, was 'magic'. There were various sides to magical enquiry. Alchemy was seen as a secret formula of nature while the theory of atomism suggested that all matter was made up of tiny particles whose composition could be changed. A famous alchemist, Paracelsus, propounded his theory of medicine that suggested that diseases were separate entities with lives of their own. Astrology was another field that attracted the attention of medieval scholars. They claimed that the natural phenomena were understandable and predictable if the planetary movements were properly interpreted. Hermeticism was a school of thought that believed that all knowledge existed in the mysterious and philosophical writings that could be obtained through right approach and intelligence. With it a complete insight into the structure of the universe could be obtained. Cabala was a system of Jewish thought suggesting that the key to the universe consisted of magical arrangements of numbers that could be understood and used to explain the mysteries of the world. However, irrational these ideas may be, they created an interest among medieval scholars in the unexplained happenings of nature. The mechanized picture of the world was created after years of search in the domain of the mysterious. Besides, the Scholastic stress on human rationality tried to rationalize the authority in theology and emphasized all branches of human learning. At the same time, Scholastic activities proved unfavourable to the development of modern science because of their conception of finality – God's wish being the ultimate truth. For a long time these ideas continued to exist side by side with the ideas of modern science.

Some writers suggest that the origins of modern science are related to two events – the discovery of the New World and the Renaissance. The conventional assumptions were broken in the sixteenth century by the discovery of the New World and the realization that the earth revolves round the sun. The search for new territories and the long-distance voyages created a genuine desire to develop the science of navigation. It created interest in science and technology. The search for ancient Greek texts by Renaissance scholars brought European thought to the threshhold of modern science. Many scholars suggest that not only did science develop during the Renaissance, but that there was a definite relationship between the two and that this was a crucial age in the history of modern science.

In the fifteenth and early sixteenth centuries, improvements were made in the knowledge of machinery and technology. Water wheels were introduced in mining activities. The undershot wheel and the overshot wheel were used for damming rivers and metal processing, as well as in the paper mills. This period witnessed improvements in metallurgy (smelting and processing), military equipment (firearms and cannons), navigation and shipbuilding and in the printing industry. A serious study of nature based on observation and experiment was carried out as the great contributors of Renaissance wanted to find explanations for natural phenomena. Burckhardt, in his famous work *Civilization of the Renaissance*, argued that the Renaissance of the fifteenth century was not merely a revival of classical studies but also a renewal of close painstaking research. In his arguments, Leonardo da Vinci is often cited. Everyone admired the genius of Leonardo, a man of wit, a singer and a poet, an excellent painter, sculptor and architect, a mechanic, military and civil engineer, a natural philosopher and a pioneer in many realms of science. He can also be seen as an anticipator of Galileo, Newton, Bacon and Harvey. Although known for his paintings and masterpieces of sculpture and architecture, Leonardo da Vinci spent most of his time in the study of mathematics and cosmography during his stay in Venice. In 1502, while working for Cesare Borgia, he prepared accurate maps as chief engineer and was regarded as a marvel of scientific cartography. He anticipated the use of steam and sketched a steam cannon and designed paddles for ships. He was also the originator of the science of hydraulics, the camera obscura, and was the first to study the structure and arrangement of flowers and foliage. Santilla, though, considers Brunelleschi, the famous Renaissance architect, as the real revolutionary from the way he used science in his creations. Butterfield suggests that 'the Renaissance witnessed an upsurge of ability that was scientific and pre-scientific age'. Solutions to the problems of nature provided the elements of modern science during the age of Renaissance.

The contribution of the Renaissance to modern science can be seen in several fields. One of the famous scholars of that period, Masaccio, learnt geometry from Brunelleschi who was taught by the greatest mathematician of that period – Paolo Toscanelli. As Kenneth Clark suggests, the basis of all the theories was the assumption that painting was concerned with the accurate representation of the visible world and this was the scientific basis of Renaissance naturalism. Alberti believed that no painter could paint without a thorough knowledge of geometry. He believed that the knowledge of nature could be improved on with the aid of the mathematics and for this end he advocated the use of mathematical system of perspective known as the focussed system. In every work of composition, whether painting or architecture, the role of geometry remained important. Many of the artists seemed to lean on science to attain perfection. Leonardo had argued that experience and experiment are the only path to certainty. Piero della Francesca, an intellectual painter, revealed a great passion for geometry and planned all his works on mathematical principles. Different historians have emphasized different aspects of the Renaissance as contributors to modern science. While Clagett believes that the spatial world of the seventeenth century had its origin in the new departures in perspective that came about as a result of Brunelleschi's work, Randall considers the logic school of Italian universities as the 'House of Novelty' while Koyre regards Platonic tradition as the decisive factor in the rise of science. According to Koenigsberger, the Italian artists in the fifteenth century developed the theory and technique of linear perspective (the presentation of reality as it appears to the eye from one specific point of view) which allowed more penetrating presentation of reality. Almost all the great artists of the fifteenth and early-sixteenth centuries attempted to incorporate mathematical principles and mathematical harmony in their paintings, with realistic perspective as a specific goal. Artists like Signorelli, Bramante, Michelangelo and Raphael were all deeply interested in mathematics and were aware that art is subject to laws. The application of geometry to the theory of perspective and the art of representing three-dimensional space were all the result of prolonged experiments and intelligent use of the knowledge of geometry. Herbert Butterfield thinks that the scientific attitude to art can be seen in the accurate and detailed knowledge of the structure of the human body. A number of anatomists at Padua University created their own school which became famous for its work in dissections and direct investigation into nature. In medicine, Belgian physician Andreas Vesalius dissected cadavers and discovered many secrets of the human anatomy. Many leading contributors to the scientific revolution received training in methods of experiments and observation at this centre. Renaissance scientists carried out the study of nature through observations and experiments, to understand natural phenomena. The knowledge of mathematics and geometry was used to ensure correct proportions in the field of art and architecture.

In the sixteenth century, European society needed the skills and services of scientists. The practical needs of every city state consisted of fortification of towns, greater utilization of minerals and commercial gains, systematization of accounts, accurate preparation of maps, and improvements in artillery. Besides, greater sea voyages required more knowledge of navigation and the skill of cartography. The most significant contribution of the Renaissance to science was the introduction of the concept of the universe as an independent entity. However, despite all these significant developments the Renaissance did not create a scientific revolution.

The rise of modern science in the seventeenth century was a product of intellectual growth in which the observation of nature led to the formulation of laws based on experiments. Experiments were carried out during the Renaissance, but there was no formulation of general theories. This could only develop when scientific study was applied to physics, mechanics and astronomy. These constituted the real scientific developments. The developments of the Renaissance created skilled artisans and engineers but they did not create true scientists. The Renaissance was in fact the work of artists and artisans, not that of scientists. The period up to the sixteenth century was concerned more with the technological aspects, like the mechanical clock, microscope, telescope, barometer and air pump which did contribute to the rise of modern science.

Social Context of Modern Science

There are alternative approaches explaining the origins of modern science. Marxist writers generally argue that the developments of the Scientific Revolution arose in direct response to the needs of early capitalism, especially trade and navigation. R. Hooylass argues that the process of discovery started by the Portuguese navigators culminated in the discovery of the New World. The knowledge of new lands in Asia, Africa and America, their plants, animals and people, created a fresh interest in the natural world. He rejects the notion that the progress and achievements in the field of science was confined to the domain of science alone. He insists that in order to understand the rise of modern science, one needs to examine factors which created favourable climate for it ranging from theological issues to the rise of new social classes. Scholars have opposing views on the relationship between the social climate and the rise of modern science. For some, the rise of science was the product of society and there was a direct relationship between the two, while some others argue that scientific development was independent of society in which individual's qualities played a decisive role.

Scholars, who discount the relationship between social needs and the rise of science, include A. Koyre, Arthur Koestler, etc. For them each event in the development of modern science was independent of society and was unrelated to it. The development of modern science was the product of individual genius. Herbert Butterfield uses phrases like 'an epic adventure' or 'a certain dynamic quality' to describe the scientific events. For him the Scientific Revolution was ultimately inexplicable and it could not have been predicted. He points out to the wider changes in the world that affect man's thinking or even alter those conditions under which this thinking takes place. He emphasizes the part played by technology in the development of scientific movement. He believes that history of science would become imperfect if regarded too exclusively as the history of scientific books. Alexander Koyre gives credit to the unparalleled insight of individuals. According to Koyre, it is difficult, rather impossible, to define the Scientific Revolution. For him, its achievements were based on an admixture of genius, insight, delusion and error. He thought that scientific developments were more accidental and considered the Scientific Revolution as almost the personal creation of a single man – Galileo. Arthur Koestler, in his book *The Sleepwalkers,* suggests that the scientific development was essentially a sketch of great individuals whose achievements were governed by individual qualities rather than the demand of the society.

Some scholars like A.C. Crombie and M. Clagett emphasize the progressive aspects of science. According to them, Galileo and other scientists owed their success to the intellectuals of the ancient and medieval periods. For them, the Aristotelian views were not a hindrance; rather they were important factors in the development of science and deserve credit for this. According to this view, the history of science takes an evolutionary character. They thought that the Scientific Revolution was not so unusual or revolutionary as was made out to be. Crombie, in his book *Robert Grosseteste and the Origins of Experimental Science* (1953), points out that modern science owed much of its success to the use of the inductive and experimental procedures, constituting what is often called the experimental method. The philosophers of the West created a part of the qualitative aspect of this method in the thirteenth century. They transformed the Greek geometrical method into experimental science of the modern world. Charles Webster also emphasizes the vast scope of science and says that by ignoring religious, political, economic and intellectual movements from the study of science, the scope of science could become extremely limited. This would drastically reduce the scope of history.

Marxist writers have provided social interpretation to explain the development of modern science. Boris Hessen links the scientific development to the needs of the bourgeois class. In his work, *The Social and Economic Routes of Newton's Principia,* he suggests that Newton's work was related to the needs of the English merchant class. Marxist scholars argue that the rise of modern science should be seen in context to the contemporary social change. As F. Engels wrote in 1894, if society had a technical need, that helps science move forward and performs the role of more than ten universities. He argued that there was no place for unique genius in the materialistic interpretation of history. He also believed science to be a product of social needs. Edgard Zilsel is one of the important contributors to the idea that modern science was the product of changing society. For him, the origin of science should be recognized as a sociological phenomenon. In Europe, according to Zilsel, the beginning of science was greatly influenced by the achievements of ancient mathematicians and astronomers and medieval Arabic physicians. Illustrating this point he gives the example of the period of transition from feudalism to early capitalism, he relates the emergence of science to the needs of the capitalist society. He argues that the emergence of early capitalism was connected with a change in both the setting and the bearers of culture. In a feudal society, the castles of knights and rural monasteries were the centres of culture. In the period of early capitalism towns became the cultural centres. The spirit of science could not have developed in the rural setting of feudal knights or clergymen, rather it emerges only in towns and cities. The introduction of new technology and technical inventions were related to the demands of production and warfare. In medieval society, the individual was bound to the traditions of the group to which he belonged. In early capitalism, economic success depended on the spirit of the enterprises and competition, something unknown in feudal society. The individualism of the new society is a presupposition of scientific thinking. The critical scientific spirit could not have developed without economic competition. Moreover, tradition and custom ruled feudal society while capitalism is governed by rationalism. Urban society needed the knowledge of mathematics for keeping accounts, calculations and to understand the laws of mechanics. So, a capitalist society provided the necessary condition for the rise of scientific spirit. Machinery and science could not develop in a civilization based on slave labour. The development of most rational of sciences, i.e. mathematics, is closely related to the advancement of rationality in a society. Zilsel's sociological interpretation thus emphasizes the three distinct strata of intellectual activity between 1300 and 1600 in which universities, humanism and labour contributed to the rise of the scientific spirit.

A.R. Hall also emphasizes the contribution of diverse individuals to the rise of modern science during the sixteenth and seventeenth centuries. He believes that this great diversity of men who contributed to the growth of scientific literature, were essentially professionals, including amongst them university teachers, professors of mathematics, anatomy and medicine, men of applied mathematics, various practitioners such as physicians, surveyors, mariners, engineers, opticians, instrument makers and many others. Although there was wide divergence in their social origin and intellectual attainments, yet they held positions in the scientific hierarchy. They all contributed to the development of science. Christopher Hill in his many articles and books, particularly *The Century of Revolution*, reinforced the sociological interpretation of the Scientific Revolution by placing modern science within the ambit of social history. In Hill's work science is treated as a general social phenomenon linked with the rise of Puritanism and the rise of the bourgeoisie. He included science among other factors that were responsible for the English Civil War. Christopher Hill elaborates his argument by citing the examples of Gresham College and Francis Bacon, the great contributors to the modern science. According to Hill, the merchants of London established Gresham College to promote the study of science. Similarly, Francis Bacon emphasized that the development of science should be based on experiments on a cooperative basis involving different scientific perspectives working for the common benefit of society. According to Hill, Bacon's two works – *Advancement of Learning* and *Novum Organum* gave a blue print to 'forward looking' merchants and artisans of the early Stuart period. These self-taught men tried to come to terms with the new picture of the world provided by Copernicus and Galileo and increasingly rejected the authority of the traditional church and the feudal state. The court, the clergy and the universities looked to the past, accepted authority uncritically and were skeptical of future progress through new ideas. For Hill, 'the civil war was fought between rival schools of astronomy, between Parliamentarian heliocentrists and Royalist Ptolemaics' (*The Century of Revolution*). Hill contends, that in 1628, Harvey used anatomical analogies to support theories of absolute monarchy. In his text, Harvey compared the heart to a prince in the commonwealth and in an elaborate dedication of *de Motu Cordis* (*Anatomica de Motu Cordis et Sanguinis in Animalibus*) to Charles I, the English ruler; he compared the king with the heart. But in his second letter written in 1649 to Riolan after Charles' execution, according to Hill, Harvey dethroned the heart and spoke no more of the sovereignty of heart but the prerogative and antiquity of blood. This 'somersault' in Harvey's political ideas was due to the changing political scenario. Thus, Hill argues that we cannot separate a thinker from the social climate – a view that is countered by scholars like W. Pagel and G. Whitteridge.

One of the important contributors to this debate is H.F. Kearney. He argues that there was no direct connection between economic and scientific developments. The rise of Commercial Revolution in the sixteenth century and the subsequent Scientific Revolution were not necessarily linked, as there is no valid body of evidence to suggest that. The revolutionary discoveries in science had no practical application. The mathematical world of the new science was as abstract in its own way as the world of Aristotelian metaphysics. However, in his conclusion, Kearney does not rule out the possibility that social change did have some effect in making the Scientific Revolution. In the seventeenth century, new wealth was acquired by a greater number of scholars who could afford more leisure than before. More men attended the universities than at any time before, which meant that a greater number of men were receiving training in abstract thought, particularly mathematics. Social change of this kind, according to Kearney, could be a decisive factor in the rise of modern science. Most scholars of social sciences now agree that the rise of modern science was the product of social needs and historical progress.

Major Developments

The scientific developments after the Renaissance may be divided into two categories: (a) micro cosmological and (b) cosmological.

The micro-cosmological field consisted of different branches of medical science such as anatomy, physiology, pharmacology, pathology, etc. In the field of biology, Conrad Gesnar wrote a voluminous work, *History of Animals,* while Otto Brunfels, Jeromebock and Leonard Fuchs made contributions to the field of modern botany. Guillaume de Rondolet produced an excellent account of marine life. The chemists also contributed in many ways to the new ideas. They included skin diseases (Roilau 1648, Willis 1670), rickets (Glisson 1650), apoplexy (Wepfer 1658), diabetes (Willis 1670), gout (Sydenham 1683), and tuberculosis (Morton 1689). Of all these branches, the best founded was anatomy. It studied the arrangements of bones, muscles and organs. The same period also saw greater and better use of chemical remedies and of exotic drugs. Modern physiology is usually associated with Harvey, who discovered the circulation of blood. It was published in 1628. It was an extremely important discovery but it remained unknown for quite some time. It was a major contribution in the field of science and was based on the scientific method as emphasized by most scientists. Vesalius wrote *The Structure of Human Body*, which was published in 1543. However, it was essentially based on the physiological theories of the Greek scholars, Hippocrates and Galen. Eustachi made significant studies of the ear and throat and the tube connecting the throat with the middle ear. He also made important observations on the vocal cords. However, it was Malpighe, who was able to show the flow of blood with the help of a microscope and turned belief into fact. Stephen Hales carried out important studies on blood pressure in animals using hydrostatic apparatus. A more advanced view of mechanical physiology was provided by Albecht von Haller, who showed that the body acted as a kind of filter by which the appropriate nutritive particles were either added to the blood stream or leached from it whenever necessary. On the basis of this, he proved the function of the kidneys. Yet, one can say that there were hardly any revolutionary changes in the fields of biology and chemistry as neither of these subjects had developed rational methods. Though biology as a subject was witnessing new trends, chemistry emerged as a part of modern science much later. Robert Boyle (1627–91) became the leading experimentalist and theorist in the field of chemistry but the revolutionary developments in the subject began through the works of Lavoisier in the eighteenth century. The discoveries and observations of diseases and remedies checked the mortality rate in Europe and prepared the ground for the rise of medical science.

In the field of cosmology (pertaining to the theories of the origin, creation and evolution of the universe), important contributions were made in the sixteenth century, creating an intellectual climate for subsequent scientific developments. Vieta had developed algebra and trigonometry which speeded up calculations and contributed to the field of mathematics. In 1568, Stevin introduced the decimal system, which was represented in fractions. It is common knowledge that Europeans had immensely gained from the mathematical knowledge of the Arabs. In 1614, Napier introduced logarithms that facilitated the work of mathematicians and made difficult calculations much easier. It was the new arithmetic based on Arab notations, which helped in the adoption of new knowledge in the field of commerce and industry. Together with double-entry bookkeeping, it transformed the commercial computations and methods. The solution of the cubic and quartic equation, gave great impetus to the scientific studies.

Nicolaus Copernicus (1473–1543) made one of the earliest breakthroughs in the field of modern science leading to the Scientific Revolution. His actual name was Niklas Kopprnigk and he was born in what is now north-central Poland. His father was a copper dealer but at the age of ten he lost his parents. His uncle, Lucas Waczenrode became his guardian and this proved to be the turning point in his career. Lucas was a great scholar and had received a doctorate of canon law from the University of Bologna. Realizing the importance of learning and with a sufficient financial backing, Nicolas could pursue his academic career in canon law, astronomy and mathematics, as well as philosophy, Roman law, medicine and Greek in the universities of Bologna and Padua. His first love was astronomy. He was appointed as a canon at Frauenburg Cathedral. He revealed a keen intellectual interest and came in contact with the Humanist ideas of Italy. Part of an intellectual elite, he was requested by Pope Gregory XIII to prepare a reformed calendar for the church. That was produced in 1582. The old calendar called the Julian calendar, was not very accurate and had existed for the last fourteen centuries. It counted century years as leap years and thus added extra days that pushed Easter further away from its normal occurrence in late March. It was necessary to reform the calendar that led Copernicus to carry out a thorough study of the universe. He was a known mathematician and did not agree with the planetary movements that were accepted since the time of Ptolemy. It was Ptolemy who had suggested that the planets and the sun were attached to transparent crystalline spheres and they revolved round the earth. Copernicus was influenced by new Platonic ideas and he argued that the sun was the most splendid celestial body and was the centre of a harmonious universe. This work, *On the Revolutions of the Heavily Bodies* was published in 1543 and created a great stir in the courts of Europe. It overthrew the Aristotelian system of the universe which had existed for centuries together. Although the planetary system of Copernicus was no less simple than that of Ptolemy, it demolished the traditional views concerning the world. It was nothing less than an intellectual revolution but the impact of the Copernicus theory was felt much later. It was the great Danish astronomer Tycho Brahe (1546–1601) who made a major contribution by plotting the paths of the moon and planets every night but the only theory with which he came out was a compromise between the Ptolemaic and Copernicun systems. He remained unconvinced that the earth moved around sun as suggested by Copernicus. At the same time, Tycho Brahe had produced a rich data on universe through his painstaking observation and his elaborate and costly instruments that he had

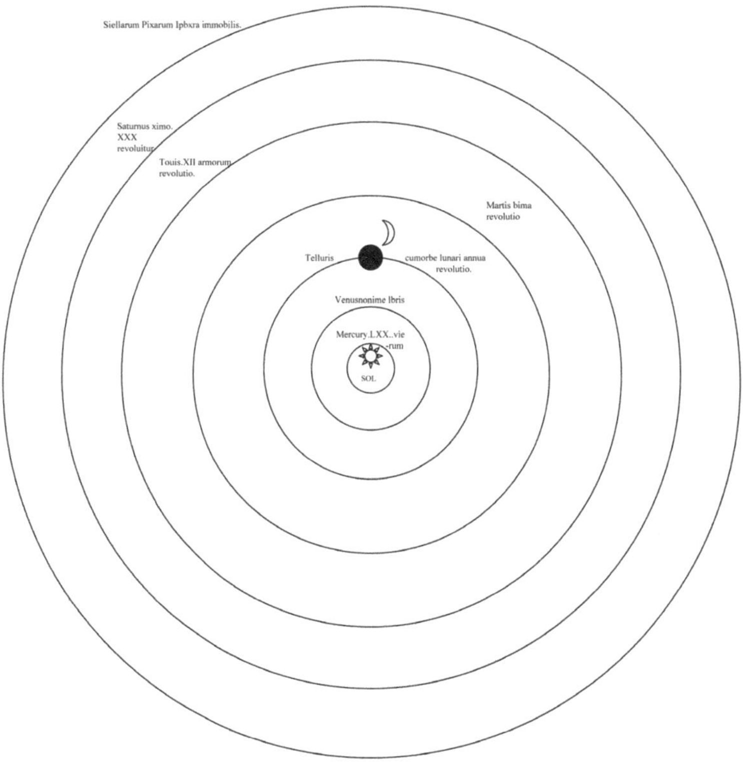

The Copernican System based on the idea that the Sun and not the Earth was at the centre of solar system.

himself devised. He spotted a 'new star' or nova and later a comet. It was seen as by the superstitious people as a bad sign. Aristotle had earlier explained them as atmospheric events taking place within the realm of the earth, between the earth and the moon. Tycho proved through his calculations that the comet came from the realm beyond moon and followed an elliptical path. His observations defied to certain extent the prevalent notions of heaven and earth. It was his German disciple Johannes Kepler, who provided solutions to the problems in the field of astronomy.

Johannes Kepler is considered one of the chief contributors to the Scientific Revolution. He strongly believed in the value of mathematics to determine the movements of the planets. He was convinced by Copernicus's conclusion confirming the heliocentric theory (sun-centered), which had been partially supported by Tycho Brahe also. Kepler's three laws of planetary motion not only gave

Johannes Kepler

substance to Copernicus's speculation of the earth's movements around the sun but it also opened a new chapter in the study of astronomy. The first law stated that the planets moved round the sun in an elliptical orbit. Copernicus and others accepted it but could not prove it with mathematical precision. According to the second law, a line always sweeps across the same area in any given time from a planet to the sun. When a planet moves farther from the sun, its speed also decreases. This destroyed the traditional view on the motion of heavenly bodies. The third law took a long time to be formulated and concerned an entirely different area. It deals with the relationship of the movements among the planets. It stated that the square of the time taken by a planet to complete its orbit bears a constant ratio to the cube of its mean distance from the sun. This law of Kepler reflects his mathematical skill and was an important discovery. However, it did not have great immediate impact and it was Newton who used it in his construction of a new system of the heavens. Kepler's other achievement was the publication of *Rudolfine Tables* in 1627, named after his patron Emperor Rudolf II. He combined the observations of planetary positions observed by Brahe with his theories of planetary motion which made it possible to predict the movements of celestial bodies more accurately than before and was of great help to navigators. Although the followers of Ptolemaic cosmology continued to oppose these new ideas, they lost support rapidly. The new theory of planetary motion gradually gained acceptability.

One of the prominent scientists of that period was Galileo Galilei. He was a contemporary of Kepler. He perceived a connection between the earth and planetary motions. His chief contribution was in the field of astronomy, which was based on his study of mathematics and physics. He created a new understanding of the universe and received widespread attention. He is regarded as one of the first modern scientists because of his concern for technique, argument and evidence. Galileo's major success lies in his total rejection of the Aristotelian concept. Aristotle believed that the commonly noted characteristics of an object – its composition, quality, colour, smell and value – had major relevance to the problem of its motion in space. Galileo rejected this concept and instead argued that only those qualities, which were measurable, e.g. mass, weight, speed and acceleration, could form the elements of the science of mechanics. Aristotle held that a body is naturally at rest and needs to be pushed constantly to keep moving. This view dominated the study of dynamics. Kepler believed that some steady force emanated from the sun, which maintained the motion of the planets. Galileo developed a new explanation of physical laws. He himself built a telescope to study the heavenly bodies. He devised pendulums rolling down inclined surfaces to verify his theories and finally arrived at a new principle of inertia. Galileo's contribution not only undermined the long-held views of Aristotle but it gave a new scope to the field of physics as he proved through his experiments that only mathematical language could explain the principles of nature.

In 1610, in his publication Galileo stated that Jupiter had satellites and that the moon has mountains on its surface. Both these discoveries gave further jolt to the traditional beliefs that held that the earth is changing and imperfect while the heavens are unchangeable. It showed that other planets had moons just like the earth and that Jupiter had four larger moons, that there was a ring around Saturn and the dark patch on the sun called the 'sun spots' often causing electrical disturbances on heavenly bodies. He even calculated the height of mountains on the moon by using geometric techniques. In all these cases, Galileo attempted to establish that the earth was like any other planet and was part of a uniform universe. Later he became famous for creating new grounds in the study of astronomy and for confirming the views of Copernicus, which had caused major shocks in the academic circles of Europe. Although Galileo established himself as a great scientist, he stood on dangerous ground. He was severely criticized by the religious and academic men for his views on the moon and rotation of the earth. Staunch religious critics argued that in the Bible, Joshua made the sun stand still. Galileo reacted with scorn saying that observations and proofs carried greater weight than beliefs. He suggested that one should begin with a sense experience rather than the authority of the scriptures. The intense rivalry between Protestantism and the Roman Catholic Church began to take serious note of what was being said about religion. Galileo's sarcastic comments on religious beliefs greatly antagonized the Jesuits and Dominicans. After his publication of *Letters on Sunspots*, he came under attack of religious authorities. He countered this by questioning the claims of biblical authority to decide matters of astronomy. This implied not only a demand for the separation of theology from science but an evaluation of the work of theologians. It was a direct challenge and the church took action against him in 1616. The Inquisition forbade him to teach the heretical doctrine which stated that the earth moves round the sun. In 1623, he published a masterpiece in Italian language, *Dialogue in the Two Great World Systems*. It was written in Italian rather than in Latin because he wanted his work to reach the widest possible audience. This was perhaps the most important work for popularizing the Copernican theory. Galileo was tried for heresy in 1633 though he was given a light sentence of house arrest on the personal intervention of Pope Urban VII. Despite his persecution by the church his works were widely read and discussed in the scientific societies that were flourishing at that time.

It was Isaac Newton (1642–1727) who brought the Scientific Revolution to its logical culmination after the steady progress made by earlier contributors like Copernicus, Kepler, Galileo and Descartes. Newton was a versatile scientist who made great contributions in the field of mathematics, physics, astronomy and optics. Newton broke the dichotomy between Bacon and Descartes's approach to modern science by uniting laboratory experiments with mathematics. He was the true genius and the greatest scientist, although he had many unattractive traits of personality. Isaac was prematurely born on 25 December 1642. His father died before his birth and he was handed over to his grandmother's care. He remained a lonely child who kept himself busy making gadgets. He showed general curiosity in the natural world and had fascination for alchemy. His uncle was a member of Trinity College, Cambridge University. He was instrumental in sending Newton there in 1660 although he was forced to leave Cambridge in 1665 for his home farm in Lincolnshire because of an outbreak of bubonic plague. This proved to be the most fruitful period of his life as he

Isaac Newton

developed keen interest in mathematics and scientific experimentations. He laid foundations of modern calculus, that revolutionized the method to handle complicated equations.

Newton's greatest achievement was his formulation of the laws of universal gravitation, expressed in his monumental work in Latin – *Principia Mathematica* (Mathematical Principles of Natural Philosophy) (1687). It was written to refute the much-admired French school, the Cartesian approach to science as propounded by Descartes. While rejecting Descartes's emphasis on the powers of the mind or deductive approach, Newton relied on mathematics to prove his experiments, a branch of science, which even Descartes also stressed. In his *Principia*, Newton propounds the mathematical laws of mechanics, which were valid on earth and throughout the universe. He held that the force of gravity kept moon in orbit. This was a direct rejection of Aristotle's view that earth and heaven (meaning universe) operated on two different sets of laws. Most crucial of his findings was the solution to the problem of motion, which had engrossed the attention of thinkers of material philosophy since ancient times. Newton explained his system in three laws: first, in the absence of force, motion continues in a straight line with uniform velocity; second that the force acting on motion determines the rate of change of momentum (mass times velocity), including friction; and the third, considered the most important, that every action has an equal and opposite reaction. These laws were explained through the concepts of mass force in relation to velocity, inertia and acceleration. These laws together with the law of gravitation became the universal tools applicable to the planets as well as the earth. The structure of the solar system was now comprehensible through the laws of matter and motion. Newton's fame rests on his fundamental work on light through optical experiments and the invention of the infinitesimal calculus which was a mathematical procedure specifically used to calculate the rates of change in motion. He was the first to distinguish between the mass and the weight of an object. His contribution to dynamics and explanation of tidal waves related to lunar movements and his work of light *Opticks* (1704) made him a celebrity. Till then, people assumed that white light was the absence of colours. Using a prism, Newton successfully revealed that light could be separated into different colours. He also reconstructed white light by combining these colours.

The application of mathematics to the treatment of mechanical problems represented the greatest achievement of the seventeenth-century science, which created a mechanized picture of the world. At the same time, like many earlier scientists, Newton propounded the concept of absolute infinite space in theological terms, which was fundamental to his cosmology. He stated that space existed eternally and was not created, while the existence of matter in space was contingent on God's will and was the arena of divine activity. The greatest accomplishment of Newton was to weave Kepler's laws of planatery motion, Galileo's law of falling bodies and the concept of inertia, Descartes' views of science and his own concept of gravitation into a single mathematical-physical system. Many scientists like Christian Huygens (1629–95), Christopher Wren (1632–1723) and Edmond Halley (1656–1742) continued to build on Newton's work to come up with a Mathematical formula that accounted for a circular orbit around the sun. In the twentieth century, the great scientist Albert Einstein resolved many of the queries that were left unresolved by Newton's physics.

Historians hail his *Principia* as the greatest work as regards originality and authority of knowledge in the whole history of science. It inspired and guided future generations of scientists because he brought about a fundamental re-conception of the physical universe by rejecting supernaturalism. The long controversy of the seventeenth-century over the relative superiority of ancient and modern writers, which was well brought out in one of the famous poems *The Battle of the Books* by Jonathan Swift (1710), ended in favour of modern thinkers and this was the triumph of Newton.

Newton's views gained ground when he proved that there is celestial mechanics like the one that operates on earth. He became an idol in his own time. The educated middle class and the gentry openly acclaimed his achievements. In 1703, he became the President of the Royal Society and he was the first scientist to be knighted in 1705. When he died in 1727, he received a hero's burial in Westminster Abbey. The famous French philosopher, Voltaire, when he visited England was amazed to see the respect in the hearts of Englishmen for a mathematician who was treated like a king.

The Formulation of Scientific Method

The creation of a new scientific method played an important part in promoting modern science in European society, particularly in England. Two thinkers – Francis Bacon and René Descartes – made major contributions by highlighting the form of scientific study which should be adopted to promote scientific learning. The two great thinkers suggested contrasting methods of scientific studies.

Francis Bacon (1561–1626) was born in London where his father Nicholas Bacon held the position of Lord Keeper of the Great Seal to Queen Elizabeth. Francis Bacon possessed one of the finest intellects and exhibited an inquiring mind. In the three years Bacon spent at Trinity College, he developed a strong contempt for the narrow medieval university learning of the day and began to plan his great philosophical work. When it came out, it made him famous and immortal. Although Francis had lived in the atmosphere of the court, he never neglected his academic interests. He was advised by his father to enter the field of diplomacy and went to France in 1576 and was placed under the care of Sir Paulet, the British Ambassador in Paris. Three years later his father died, and he was forced to return to London. There he studied law and qualified as a barrister and in 1584 entered the British parliament. After Elizabeth's death, he rapidly scaled political heights. In 1613, he became Attorney-General and in 1618 he became the Lord Chancellor and Baron Verulem. The successes in his political career never came in the way of his intellectual pursuits. He was not a scientist by profession but his writings paved the way for scientific literature of an extraordinary quality. He had been publishing essays since the beginning of his career and in 1605 he produced one of the most remarkable academic works, *Proficience and Advancement in Learning.* It examined the state of existing knowledge and criticized the errors and absurdities of his times. In 1620, his famous work, *Novum Organum (New Logic),* was published. By 1621, he had reached the pinnacle of glory and success. *The Great Instauration and New Atlantis* of Francis Bacon was the new philosophy that contained the seeds of scientific method. In this, he claimed to have provided an outline of comprehensive encyclopaedia of natural philosophy. By instauration Bacon meant a recovery of unknown wisdom that could be procured through an entirely new scientific method. He advocated the advancement of learning through cooperative effort and empirical experiments for useful knowledge and the betterment of human life. He is regarded as one of the pioneers of the scientific method – the method of inductive reasoning from observations and verification by experiments (Stuart Andrews). After 1621 Bacon's political career came to a sudden ruin as accusations of receiving bribes were established against him and he was removed from his official post. He faced severe financial hardship but continued his primary interest in writing. He became famous through his powerful works and created a special name for himself in the world of science. The Royal Society of London, which was founded in 1660 to promote the natural knowledge of science, was dedicated to him.

Another famous personality associated with the world of science was the French philosopher René Descartes (1596–1650), who spent most his time in the Netherlands. Like Bacon he believed that all past knowledge should be discarded and one should begin afresh with every new problem. However, there is a vast difference between the two in their approach to science and they formulated two different methods for its study. For Bacon, it was empiricism or the study of science based on experiments. He himself propounded the method of inductive science. Descartes, on the other hand, was a rationalist and an advocate of mathematics as an instrument of modern science. In his *Discourse of Method* (1637), he emphasized that nothing should be accepted as truth and everything should be doubted till it is proved through deductive logic. His principle of doubt undermined the traditional assumptions. He made rationality the point of departure in his philosophical exercise. He reconstructed the universe on the basis of speculation that differed in every way from the universe created by the Greeks. He believed that natural processes often consisted of such small parts that they could elude our senses and so everything could not be empirically verified. He deducted two principles: (a) since the idea of perfection was by man, an assuredly imperfect being, the idea may have come from a perfect being, i.e. God. Therefore, God exists; and (b) since the mind cannot be doubted but the body and the material world can be, the two must be radically different. From this second principle followed an absolute dualism between mind and matter. This concept played an influential role in European scientific and political thought. It meant the world was a pure mechanism, governed by its own physical laws and without any intervention of God. God was like a watchmaker who stopped interfering in its daily functioning once the watch was created. Thus, Descartes created a philosophy of dualism, maintaining a sharp distinction between the body and the soul. God created only these two kinds of reality: mind belonged to man alone while all else was matter. He argued that beyond man, physical laws governed all forms of existence, both organic and inorganic. It meant that the entire universe could be studied objectively without the help of theology or appeals to the occult. He believed that the pursuit of science should be dispassionate. He also believed that activity of the mind was the vital element in the search for truth. In *Meditations,* Descartes cited the personal crisis that made him doubt everything except the existence of God and his own capacity to think. In what came to be known as 'Cartesian Dualism', Descartes suggested that while humans are detached from the world yet they can be objective observers of the world. The real radical aspect of Descartes' thought was the changing role of God from being an active controller of the world to the guarantor of Knowledge. Many alleged that he encouraged atheism but he remained a faithful Roman Catholic and accepted the existence of God.

Descartes contributed in other areas as well. In physics, he made a distinction between mass and weight while in mathematics he applied for the first time algebraic notations and methods. He developed a liking for mathematics because of 'its certainty of proof and the evidence of its reasoning'. His most important work was on geometry that laid foundations of analytical geometry. He showed that geometric problems could be put into algebraic forms. In this way he introduced a system that could solve problems of space by numerical calculations based on algebraic and arithmetical methods.

The followers of Descartes were known as Cartesians, who showed greater orientation towards mathematics and philosophical speculations that comprised of his contemporaries as well as his immediate successors. They include his friend and disciple in Holland, Henri de Roy or Regius (following Descartes in physics and the derivative sciences but departing from his views in metaphysics), Johann Clauberg in Germany, Malebranche, Simon Foucher, Rohault, Claude Clerselier and Pierre-Sylvain Régis in France. They carried out more or less self-conscious efforts to supply what they found lacking in Descartes's work on human knowledge, each providing his own explanation, often disagreeing with each other. The Cartesian view of mechanistic physics was based on the views of Descartes, as presented in his *Principia Philosophica.* He argued that matter consist of myriads of tiny particles or corpuscles which fill the universe. These particles, which God had provided are in a state of constant motion. He considered the universe to be full of continuously rotating particles and totally rejected the idea of a vacuum. At the centre of each vortex is a sun and it is the motion of these infinite sum of vortices that carried the planets and other heavenly bodies through space. He claimed also to have deduced the properties of the whole universe using similar mechanical principles that were involved in the design of machines.

The mechanical philosophy of Descartes not only made ontological claims (metaphysics concerned with the nature of existence) about the world and the things that exist on it but also epistemological claims (theory of knowledge) of what constituted real knowledge. It insisted that an explanation of physical process has to be provided in mechanical terms. He thereby rejected Aristotalian views, the occults and the magicians. The mechanical presentation of the world meant that all natural bodies consist of nothing but particles of matter acting upon each other that comprise our sensory organs. Later, numerous other views developed within the Cartesians, debating whether movement was in a vacuum or in a *planum* (a plane or flat surface), or whether matter, wholly inertor, has spiritual elements in it. The segregation of mind and matter in Cartesian dualism had tremendous impact on psychology and philosophy. Modern biology springs from the model of *bête-machine* described in 1637 by Descartes. He suggested that if it were not for his power of communicating his complex thought by means of speech, man would have been indistinguishable from automation. Molecular biology explains the interaction of complex molecules (e.g. enzymes) based on the method mentioned by Descartes in *Discourse on Method*, part V. Cartesian philosophy also had some impact on the women's consciousness. The old Christian concept suggested that a woman possessed a distinctly female nature which was mostly sinful. The Cartesians, on the other hand, suggested that sex-differences are secondary, bodily and indeed, mechanist in type. Men and women are the same basic human forms with a few differences of machinery. In Descartes' dualist philosophy, mind and body are quite separate and that made, one of his followers to declare that 'mind is without sex'. Poullain de la Barre lent strong support to feminism and female education in his two works published in 1673 and 1674 in French. He went to the extent of calling women superior to man by virtue of her motherhood (*Égalite des deux sexes* and *De L'éducation des dames*). He thereby suggested gender equality, as woman is in all essential respects identical with man in respect of mind and soul. Another scholar of the early eighteenth century, G.E. Stahl talked of the organic unity of soul and body and claimed that women have sensibility that is as much physical as mental. These arguments were later picked up by Rousseau, Bordeu and Roussel in their own ways.

However, by the eighteenth-century Newton's ideas achieved ascendancy over Descartes's physical theory, the duality of mind and matter. Cartesian influence nevertheless, has been wide and pervasive over European philosophers. His mathematics and skeptical method provided a base for modern science and his views on mastering mind and matter has influenced contemporary thought.

Bacon and Descartes provided two paths for the study of modern science, and the scientific methods governed the course of scientific developments in subsequent periods. The Baconians in England stressed the role of empirical science based on experiments. Bacon's idea of research as a collective enterprise was aimed at providing practical benefits to entire society. He made a strong impact on many scientists, especially the founders of the English Royal Society. This experimental method was adopted by important scientists such as William Harvey (1578–1657), a well-known physician who discovered the circulation of blood, Robert Boyle (1627–91), a renowned chemist who formed Boyle's law on temperature and gas pressure, Robert Hooke (1635–1703), a famous biologist who used the microscope to discover the cellular structure of plants. In France, Blaise Pascal contributed to the research in conic sections that help in the foundation of integral calculus, discovered barometric pressure and invented a theorem, and Pierre Gassendi worked on atomic theory within the Cartesian tradition. The principles of scientific inquiry and the methods of science began to receive serious attention from the intellectual community not only in England and France but throughout Europe. In Newton's time science gradually became an institutionalized feature in some societies of Western Europe.

Several contributors of science, such as Gilbert (magnetism and electricity), Kepler (astronomy), Harvey (physiology), Galileo (dynamics) and many others promoted the climate of academic sciences. The foundations of several new branches of science were firmly laid by the mid-seventeenth century. Many academic societies in different countries were also established to promote and diffuse science in their respective societies. In London, Greesham College became a centre for scientific discussion and research. In Paris, Martin Mersenne (1588–1637) created a network of extensive scientific exchange that cut across state boundaries. He also translated Galileo into French. There were many people from different professions, members of the aristocracy, merchants and scholars and thinkers of natural philosophy who contributed to the formation of such societies. Perhaps, the first academy dedicated to scientific works was created in Naples in the 1540s. It was a secret place of work, Acadèmia Segreta, as the name suggests. This was followed by the Acadèmia dei Lincei at Rome, created in 1603. Galileo was associated with it from 1611. The first formal organization was the Accademia del Cimento at Florence (1657). It was followed by the creation of the Royal Society of London (1662) and the Académie Royle des Sciences in Paris (1665). All these institutions came into existence because of the interest of their ruling houses and were supported by financial grants. Among the earliest members of the English Royal Society were William Petty and Robert Boyle who became famous through their contribution to mechanical or agricultural innovations and scientific studies respectively. The Royal Society was formed under the patronage of Charles II, the English ruler and reflected the growing interest in science in England. The members came from diverse social backgrounds and included Edmond Halley, an astronomer, the philosopher John Locke, founder of British empiricism and Christopher Wren, a talented and renowned architect. The intention of the Royal Society was to encourage ingenious and enlightened tradesmen as well as philosophers and physicians. The *Philosophical Transactions* of the Royal Society published some of the important works of its members, particularly in the field of mathematics. It began to collect information about agricultural practices in the country in order to select the best and make it popular, but the real objective was to promote pure sciences and bring scientific contributors to a common platform. In this society, new scientific outlook was defended purely on intellectual grounds and not because of its usefulness. In this process technology as a branch of science did not receive sufficient attention and its promotion only took place during the eighteenth century with the coming of industrialization.

Scientific subjects like matter and motion, vacuum, magnetism and the components of colour were also debated and studied under the famous natural philosopher Margaret Cavendish, the duchess of Newcastle (1623–73). This 'Newcastle circle' became a gathering of distinguished scholars and scientists. In Paris, the Académie des Sciences was the creation of the famous mercantilist and minister Colbert under the patronage of Louis XIV and served as a department for scientific and industrial research. It was a product of mercantilist thinking and its objective was to promote useful inventions, to survey the natural resources of the land and to make them useful to the state. It also aimed to raise the level of technical proficiency to increase foreign trade and accumulate bullion. The Paris observatory was also established to conduct research in the field of natural philosophy. Both in England and France, the scientific activities flourished around the national societies in order to make scientific research more useful. As mentioned earlier, both the societies failed to promote technological studies, which had a direct bearing in the field of crafts and industries.

Science and Religion

There has been an important debate on the relationship between the Protestant reformation and the rise of modern science. Some of the scholars argue that the experimental science was the product of Protestant ethics. There are many others who suggest that the development of modern science was not confined to the Protestant societies, rather it originated in the Catholic countries, especially in Italy.

Among the scholars who argue that the rise of modern science was closely associated with the ideas of the Protestant religion and believed that the experimental science developed by the seventeenth century because of the new ethical considerations provided by the Protestant thinkers, we can include the names of Max Weber, R.K. Merton, S.F. Mason and Christopher Hill. According to Weber, the Protestant religion, particularly Calvinism, created a favourable atmosphere for experimental science. Linking Weber's Protestant Ethic thesis that considers Protestant Reformation promoting the rise of Western capitalism, an American sociologist Robert K. Merton in his work, *Science, Technology and Society in Seventeenth Century England*, emphasizes that those factors which promote active life and scientific experimentation, were to be seen in the Protestant ethics and religion. He considers the role of Puritanism as crucial to the emergence of modern science. While comparing scientists with religious reformers, he suggests three important elements of the relationship between the two. First, the early Protestant ethos was expressed in a scientific thought. Second, Calvinism emphasized good deeds, which the scientists also considered important hard work and experimentation. Third, Merton suggests that there was a definite combination between the minute details of the political doctrines of Calvinism and the principles of modern science. According to Merton, we must turn to the religious ethos and not theology to understand the integration of science with religion in the seventeenth-century England. He argued that Protestant religious values, particularly those of the Puritan and Piest sects, created an intellectual atmosphere that helped scientific development. Merton believed that a godly involvement in the worldly affairs would also encourage science. Citing examples from the seventeenth-century England, he argued that the social utility of both science and technology was increasingly recognized by Puritan values. Merton tried to provide evidence to his argument that Protestants played a major lead in the Royal Society of London. He cites the names of Theodore Haak, Denis Papin (a French Calvinist expelled from France), Thomas Sydenham and Sir William Petty. Yet his thesis does not ignore the importance of socio-economic forces. He never implied that it was the sanction of science by religion that led to the discoveries of Boyle or Newton and that Protestant religion was the primary variable on which science was based. Merton suggests that the Puritan values helped to create an audience that was receptive to programmes for the improvement of man's life.

S.F. Mason is another contributor to this debate on the relationship between science and reformation. In his work, *The Scientific Revolution and Protestant Reformation*, Mason ascribes a variety of factors to the growth of scientific movements. He points out that the new technical problems in the field of industry, navigation and war were caused by economic stimulus, the religious drive by the Puritans towards performing good work and many other factors. Mason suggests that throughout the sixteenth century, science was closely connected with mercantile enterprise. Robert Recorde and John Dee were technical advisers to the Muscovy Company and the Cathy Voyagers. The merchants promoted science through the translation of scientific works and sponsorship of lectures on mathematics. Sir Thomas Greesham contributed to the promotion of science as he in his will wished three out of seven chairs at Greesham College to be devoted to scientific subjects. Mason points out that during the early seventeenth century, English science remained connected with navigational and mercantile problems. William Gilbert and Francis Bacon stressed the value of science for the promotion of industry and the building of a new world-view. During the Civil War this college became the meeting place of a group of scientists who termed themselves the 'Philosophical College', which became the immediate precursor of the Royal Society. However, such factors were essentially practical and could account only for specific branches of science such as magnetism, mechanics and astronomy but not the structure and pattern of new theories of early modern science, i.e. the ideological theories of which the theology of Calvin was most important in England. Mason suggests that the preponderance of Protestants over Catholics among the important scientists of modern Europe could be ascribed to three main factors. First, concordance between the early Protestant ethos and the scientific attitude by which the medieval world-view was overthrown by the Protestant reformers and the scientists; second, the use of science to highlight the basis of Christian thought by the later Calvinists, particularly the English Puritans; and third, there existed some congruity between the more abstract elements of Protestant theology and the theories of science. Giving the example of Swiss and German reformers, Mason points out that the new religious thought implied that man should reject the guidance and authority of the priests and should seek spiritual truth through his own experience. Similarly, modern scientists turned away from the systems of ancient and medieval philosophers to search for scientific truth through their own empirical and theoretical experience. According to Mason, Thomas Sprat, a Calvinist, expressed a similarity of aim between early modern science and Protestantism. For him, the Anglican Church and the Royal Society may place equal claim to the word Reformation, the one encompassing it in religion and the other revealing it in philosophy. Mason also points out that early Lutheranism appears to be in accord with the scientific attitude because the earliest technical study of the Copernican theory of the world came from the scholars of the University of Wittenberg in Germany, an important centre of German Reformation.

While establishing the relationship between English Puritans and scientists, Mason argues that the Puritans emphasized the religious duty of performing 'good works' and they placed scientific activity among the good works that was sanctioned by Puritan ethic. This view dominated the first generation of the members of the Royal Society. The anti-authoritarianism and individualism was common to the early Protestant and modern scientists. The main centres of scientific activity passed from Catholic Italy and Lutheran Germany to the territories which were under the influence of Calvin, such as England, Holland and France. Thus the impetus to scientific activity was given by the religious ethos and this, according to Mason, was the single most important element that integrated science with religion in the seventeenth-century England.

One of the most important contributors to this debate is Christopher Hill. In his two major works, *The Century of Revolution* and *The Intellectual Origins of the English Revolution*, Hill argues that scientific development was an ordinary social happening along with the rise of Puritanism and the bourgeois class. Hill concentrates on intellectual movements related to the English Revolution. He suggests that the groups involved in this conflict laid the foundation of organized experimental science between 1640 and 1660. Their intellectual growth was based on Puritan social values. Hence the Puritan revolution in England had a strong scientific element. He also emphasizes that Puritanism, modern science, merchant class and the skilled artisans had a close relationship, which is reflected in the establishment of Greeshan College in 1579. According to Hill, this college was the creation of the merchants and traders of London and it had a number of scientists on its faculty. It was not an ordinary college like the one that existed before. It taught numerous subjects. During the Civil War, it became associated to an increasing degree with the Puritan movement and became the meeting place of a group of scientists who were the immediate precursors of the Royal Society of London.

There are a number of writers who do not subscribe to the above views and refute the argument that the rise of modern science was related to the spread of Protestant Reformation. Among the important critics, are of M.M. Knappen, M.H. Curtis, J.B. Cannot, T.K. Rabb, T.S. Kuhn and H.F. Kearney. T.S. Kuhn in *The Copernical Revolution,* suggests that both religious groups, the Catholics as well as the Protestants opposed Copernicus. Martin Luther, John Calvin and Melantchot, all ridiculed his views whereas the Popes who were against the Reformation welcomed such views. They were interested in upgrading the old lunar calendar.

H.F. Kearney refutes the arguments of Christopher Hill for treating the Scientific Revolution too narrowly. Kearney emphasizes that it was a European movement rather than English and that Hill should have attempted a sociological interpretation on a European scale. Hill feels that merchants and craftsmen played a decisive social role. For Kearney, the patronage for mathematics did not come from a single source of prosperous merchants. For him, the essence of the relationship between Puritanism and science cannot be established because the term Puritanism is extremely ambiguous. In the end, Kearney submits that it is possible that a more critical attitude towards religious authority created a climate of opinion that was scientific in approach. Parallel to the Protestant

Reformation, there was a rival movement taking shape throughout the sixteenth century, which included important disciples from both Catholic and Protestant faiths. Among them were men like Lipsius and Montaigne and perhaps scientists like Galileo and Kepler and even Francis Bacon. Thus, Kearney concludes that there was no clear connection between Puritanism and science but he does not rule out the alternative theories of a relationship between religious radicalism and the pursuit of science. Casting doubt on Merton's arguments, Lotte Mulligan has shown that the number of Puritans in the Royal Society was very small. R.K. Merton's thesis of English Puritanism has come under scathing attack from many sides. His evidence from the pre-revolutionary period fails to support his conclusions. Another critic of Merton is George Becker. He rejects the idea that there was compatibility between religious and scientific ideas.

T.K. Rabb criticizes some of the arguments of Hill and others and suggests that it is not easy to find any neat statistical connection between Puritanism and the rise of experimental science. The relationship is not clear at least till 1640. He points out that Catholic Italy was the only centre of scientific experimentation in the early period of modern science. Almost all the contributors to the Scientific Revolution had lived in Italy for some time or studied at the important centres of learning. Copernicus was a priest and held strong religious views. Galileo and Descartes wished to stay within the religious fold and Kepler, though he was a Protestant, had to depend on Jesuits for astronomical experiments. Rabb criticizes Hill for taking only those aspects of Puritanism which were favourable to his arguments, and confining his entire concept of Scientific Revolution to the case study of England. However, Rabb concedes that after 1640, the Puritans did contribute to modern science. This cannot be said of the period before 1640 because till this period the Puritans were involved in religious education rather than science.

William Ashworth in 'Catholicism and Early Modern Science' suggests that the Jesuit scientific enterprise was first such effort based on collaboration. Many Jesuits had a keen sense of the value of precision in experimental science, a trait not seen the contemporary societies of Europe. They practised science on a wide scale, they were able investigators, made many important discoveries and inventions, and encouraged others in these activities. Yet, according to Ashworth, Jesuit science was somehow deficient. There was a total lack of discrimination and reliability of evidence. Besides, there was no philosophy of nature and as a result no Jesuit could come close to the stature of Descartes, Galileo or Pascal.

Toby Huff presents another interesting view. Without emphasizing religion, Huff gives a culturist interpretation of the rise of modern science. He argues that till the fourteenh century, China and the Arab world were far ahead of Europe in the field of science but in subsequent centuries the situation reversed. For Huff, this was because of the dramatic cultural differences and the key to European progress was the legal revolution that emphasized rational study of nature based on criticism. The Arabs and the Chinese lacked the autonomous legal corporate bodies that were needed for the free and objective investigation of nature. The establishment of a large number of universities in Europe encouraged independent learning and free thought. However, it can be said that it was not the cultural but economic differences that prevented further progress of the Arabs and the Chinese. The rise of modern science should be placed against the dramatic shift from feudalism to capitalism that was taking shape from the sixteenth century.

The achievements of the seventeenth century brought about a new independence of scientific inquiry. Francis Bacon warned the experimental philosophers that they should not be diverted by metaphysical considerations. Though John Locke and Issac Newton were both devout Christians and had faith in Trinity, they argued for a 'rational religion' that was independent of miracles and mysteries contained in the Bible. These rationalists subscribed to physio-theology, an attempt to explain God's natural world rather than seeing him through the Bible. By the early eighteenth century, *deism* (based only in belief of God) arose but was soon replaced by *pantheism* (belief that God and nature are identical).

Although the debate remains inconclusive, more and more scholars are accepting the view that the Reformation contributed to the atmosphere of intellectual activity, though a direct relationship between the Reformation and the Scientific Revolution is difficult to establish. The rise of modern science was the product of urban society yet individual contributions also played a significant role in this process. With the changing economic and social conditions, both the Protestants as well as Catholics had to adjust to a new reality. As the centre of economic activity shifted from southern Europe to north-west Europe, the scientific activities increased in the latter region.

Thus, scholars on this subject say that the Scientific Revolution marked a triumph of mind, underscoring the essential link between liberty of thought and intellect with democracy. Many sciences underwent fundamental reorientation both in their conceptual foundations and their component. The concepts and practice of many individual sciences like optics and kinetics were transformed and new philosophies of nature. Science began to occupy a permanent place in European culture and society. Most importantly, new conceptions of nature were formed and man's relationship with it was formed. Seventeenth century science created and imposed its concept of nature based on a regular mechanical order and universal laws. With this, as Roy Porter says, God became more remote and Nature less sacrosanct.

Important Events of the Scientific Revolution

1543	Copernicus's *On the Revolution of Heavenly Bodies* published.
1560	Italian physicist Giambattista della Porta (1535–1615) established the Academy of the Mysteries of Nature (*Nutura Magick*), the first scientific association but it was short-lived.
1576	Construction of Brahe's observatory started.
1582	Gregorian calendar adopted.
1591	Galileo comes up with the law of falling bodies.
1600	William Gilbert publishes *De magnete.*
1609	Kepler constructed third law of motion.
1610	Galileo, *The Starry Messenger* (that helped in the study of Jupiter, four moons, Venus and sunspots).
1620	Francis Bacon comes out with *Novum Organum* or the Scientific Method.
1627	Kepler's book of planetary tables published.
1628	Harvey's *On the Motion of the Heart* published.

1632	Galileo's *Dialogue on the Two Chief Systems of the World* published.
1633	Galileo condemned by the Papal Church.
1637	Descartes' *Discourse on Method* published.
1660	Boyle's *New Experiments Physico-Mechanical* published.
1660	The Royal Society of London founded.
1666	The Royal Academy of France established by Colbert.
1686	John Ray of England publishes the first of the three volume of the classification of plant species.
1687	Newton's *Principia Mathematica* published.

Suggested Readings

Bernal, J.D., *The Social Function of Science*, London: George Routledge, 1939. A classical Marxist approach to modern science that places it in context of social environment.

Butterfield, H.J., *The Origins of Modern Science 1300–1800*, New York: Macmillan, 1958. A standard and authentic work on the subject.

Brooke, John Hedley, *Science and Religion: Some Historical Perspectives*, Cambridge: Cambridge University Press, 1991. Treats the two fields of science and religion in historical context as separate developments and focuses on the separation of science from religion.

Cohen, I. Bernard, *The Newtonian Revolution*, Cambridge: Cambridge University Press, 1983. Brings out the achievements of Newton's ideas.

Goodman, D. and C.A. Russell, eds., *The Rise of Scientific Europe 1500–1800*, London: Hodder Arnold, 1991. Good discussion on the rise of modern science that includes scientific societies, education and Copernican and Newtonian revolutions.

Hall, A. Rupert, *From Galileo to Newton*, New York: Dover, 1981. Good introduction on the history of science.

———, *The Scientific Revolution, 1500–1800*, London: Beacon, 1956. A well-written explanatory account of the Scientific Revolution.

Kearney, Hugh, *Science and Change, 1500–1700*, London: Weidenfeld and Nicolson, 1971. A readable presentation of the social perspective of the Scientific Revolution.

———, *Origins of the Scientific Revolution: Problems and Perspectives in History*, New York: Barnes and Noble, 1969. An extremely useful book containing all the major views and relevant documents.

Koyre, Alexandre, *The Astronomical Revolution*, London: Methuen, 1973. He argues that it was not the experiments of the scientists but change in perspective and the theoretical outlook towards the world that led to the Scientific Revolution.

Kuhn, Thomas S., *The Copernican Revolution*, New York: Random House, 1957. Lucid explanation of Aristotle's world and a good presentation of the revolution in astronomy.

Mason, Stephen F., *A History of the Sciences*, rev. edn., New York: Collier Books, 1962. Covers a vast period from the origins of science in the ancient period till the present time.

Merton, R.K., *Science, Technology and Society in Seventeenth Century England*, New York: H. Fertig, 1970. An important contribution to the debate.

Oster, Malcolm, ed., *Science in Europe 500–1800: A Secondary Sources Reader*, London: The Open University, 2002. Contains articles by leading scholars on the subject.

Porter, R. and M. Teich, eds., *The Scientific Revolution in National Context*, Cambridge: Cambridge University Press, 1992. In this volume, leading scholars argue the importance of national contexts for understanding the transformation in natural philosophy between Copernicus and Newton.

Past and Present journal has published a number of articles on this subject including the debates in volume numbers 27, 28, 29, 31 and 33, covering the views of Christopher Hill, H.F. Kearney, Theodore K. Rabb, etc.

Shapin, Steven, *The Scientific Revolution*, Chicago: University of Chicago Press, 1996. He denies the view that there was a 'Scientific Revolution'.

CHAPTER 9

The English Revolution, Social Change and Constitutional Developments

The dynastic change from Tudor to Stuart, after the death of Elizabeth in 1603, in England was relatively a peaceful affair. There were some weak contestants for the throne such as Lady Arabella Stuart and Lord Beauchamp, but they did not pose a serious challenge. The first Stuart king, James I, already the ruler of Scotland was the son of Mary Queen of Scots and came to the English throne after Elizabeth. Described by his critics as 'the wisest fool' or 'impractical king', James found it extremely difficult to manage the English parliament, the way the Tudor monarchs had done. The next four decades saw the first two Stuart kings – James I (1603–25) and Charles I (1625–49) facing growing tension in state affairs. Under their rule, England drifted towards a civil war that broke out in 1642 and continued till 1649 with the defeat and execution of Charles I. Historians have described it as a period of revolution and the debate on the causes and nature of the English revolution has been going on ever since the event took place over three and a half centuries ago and its roots are traced to the economic, social and intellectual changes.

Before analysing this event, it is useful to first study the sequence of events that led to an open rift between the king and the parliament. The social climate in England had been changing rapidly in the sixteenth century because of the economic, social and religious developments and this change was quite evident at the time of James I's accession to the English throne. It is not that Elizabeth in her long rule of forty-five years did not face parliamentary opposition. The clouds of change had started appearing in the last years of Elizabeth's rule, perhaps even earlier.

However, its real impact could be felt only with the coming of the Stuarts. In Scotland, James had been on the throne since he was thirteen months old and by the age of nineteen, he had taken effective charge of running his own government. He was thirty-seven when he became the ruler of England and strongly believed in the 'divine right' of kings. He faced many problems with various factions within the Scottish nobility, with both Protestants and Roman Catholics and with the leaders of Presbyterian Church but eventually prevailed over them. However, the situation was quite different in England. His Scottish background appeared to be a handicap as Scotland was regarded as a much poorer and economically less developed region. He was an educated and learned man and was a theological scholar as well. Holdsworth comments that 'he could criticize a theory, but he could not judge a man'. Some of the writers have gone to the extent of arguing that King James I tried to put back the clock by resisting the wishes of the House of Commons. However, the reality was not so simple and the causes of the English revolution cannot be analysed on the basis of the individual character of the king.

When James I was coming from Edinburgh to London in 1603, he was presented the Millenary Petition by a group of puritan clergy to redress the several abuses in the English church. The English Church Settlement in 1559 under Elizabeth was a cautious compromise in which Calvinist and Catholic elements were blended (as discussed in Chapter 4). However, the extreme elements were trying to pull it in the opposite directions. With the coming of a new ruler, both groups expected not only concessions but also some changes in the settlement according to their own faith. James got a chance to show his knowledge of theology by organizing the Hampton Court Conference in 1604 but abandoned it when his mood and temper changed. However, one good result of this conference was that the king authorized a new translation of the Bible and when it was completed in 1611 it became a magnificent work of English prose. Its publication gave a new impetus to the Bible-reading Puritan movement. The negative result of the conference was to agitate the religious passions which created problems for his son and successor Charles I.

The Commons Apology of 1604 marked the first sign of the conflict between the parliament and the Stuarts. It was the first striking document presented by the House of Commons to James I. In form the document was extremely respectful but in essence, it was a lecture given to a foreign king on the constitutional customs of the realm. It declared that the privileges and liberties of the Parliament was their right through due inheritance, and that they could not be withdrawn, denied or impaired without causing harm to the whole realm. This free and outspoken expression of the Commons was resolutely maintained in the subsequent period. James, during his rule, called four parliaments but every parliament presented signs of growing disharmony. Some of the major issues of discord were related to taxation, prerogative rights of kings, religion and foreign policy. The foreign policy of James I resulted in the mounting debt of the monarchy and a serious political crisis. While James wanted peaceful relations with Spain, the Puritan members of the Parliament clamoured for war in support of the Bohemian rebels against the Spanish forces. The growing distrust of the parliament over the intentions of the king created unending controversies. The parliament did not trust the ministers appointed by the king. The two most unpopular ministers of that period were Earl of Salisbury and George Villiers. The issue of parliamentary grant was raised, as the parliament insisted that royal subsidy would only be provided if the parliament had faith in the minister who was likely to spend it. Also raised were the issues of royal taxation and the prerogative powers of the king.

The antagonism between king and parliament was revealed in the first parliament itself in Francis Goodwin's Case. The disclosure of the Gunpowder Plot in 1605, organized by the Catholic conspirators under Robert Catesby, made the new ruler more suspicious. In 1606, John Bate opposed the imposition of higher duties on import and a legal battle between the king and his subjects took place, in which the king's prerogative powers became the subject of dispute. Although the court decided in favour of the king, the issue of legal supremacy between the prerogative and the common law was initiated for the future. They failed to reach an agreement on the 'Great Contract' over financial arrangement in which the crown had agreed to surrender some feudal taxes like purveyance and wardships in return for a bulk amount provided by the Commons. This led to an abrupt end of the first parliament. The second parliament in 1614 called 'the Addled Parliament' sat in protest and passed no act because of its misgivings of the king's policies. No parliament was called in the next seven years as it opposed the pro-Spanish policy of the king. In 1621 the third parliament was summoned when England decided to support the Protestant son-in-law of James, Fredrick the Elector of Palatine in the Thirty Years War. The parliament granted a subsidy after demonstrating its anger against the king's minister and his policy of granting monopolies. The Lord Chancellor, Francis Bacon and a monopolist Giles Mompesson were impeached by the parliament. The parliamentary interference in the rights of the ruler and the king's refusal to allow the House to 'meddle with deep matters of state', led to the dissolution of the parliament. The parliament started asserting its right to be consulted on all questions of state policies, not only on grants of money, and heralded of future conflicts. The English failure in the foreign policy and the inability of James to handle his last parliament in 1624 brought an end to the first phase of the changed relationship between the crown and the parliament. It would be wrong to presume that the entire parliament held unanimous view and that both the houses of parliament jointly opposed the policies of the crown. There were several members in both houses who had sided with the king.

Under Charles I the relationship between the crown and the parliament finally broke down. He was a total novice in matters of politics. Compared to his father his approach was less flexible. He was governed by the advice of persons who were far from popular and had been opposed by the vocal section of the parliament. His first parliament broke down in 1625 on the question of parliamentary grant. England was involved in a disastrous war and Charles was in desperate need of money to wage a war against Spain with the help of the French and the Danes. The parliament made a limited grant of tonnage and poundage only for a year and the money voted was just one-seventh of what had been asked for. It also vigorously attacked his close advisor and minister, the Duke of Buckingham and Charles dissolved the parliament in anger. The second parliament proved more uncompromising than the first. There were many issues of conflict. Apart from Buckingham's disastrous foreign policy, Charles had promoted the Arminian clergy and had relaxed some of the laws against the Catholics. He had imposed Forced Loan and when Chief Justice Crew refused to confirm its legality, the king dismissed him. Seventy-six men refused to pay forced loan but they were all imprisoned. This led to the famous Five Knights case or Darnel's case (1626) in which the King's Court declared their arrest lawful. Another important event was the passing of the Petition of Right in 1628 by the parliament, which forbade arbitrary imprisonment, non-parliamentary taxation, billeting and the imposition of martial law. This act became one of the most important constitutional documents of England. The same year Buckingham was assassinated and the next parliament turned out to be quite volatile. The speaker was forced to sit on his chair while three resolutions were passed condemning non-parliamentary taxation and religious changes. This marked the first phase of the conflict. For the next eleven years no session of the parliament was called and the period is described as one of personal rule of Charles I. In the absence of any parliamentary grant, the foreign wars could not be continued and peace had to be signed with France and Spain.

The church measures under Charles became serious issues of strife. The Puritans were opposed to Arminians, a branch of Protestantism patronized by Charles I. They held opposite views on predestination and clashed over forms of worship. The Arminians stressed royal authority over the Church of England because they were dependent on it. Their views seemed to favour royal absolutism, an idea bitterly opposed by the Puritans. The king's blind espousal of Arminianism led to an unrestrained influence of William Laud (1573–1645). Laud and his minority Arminian clergy were given undue promotion and were allowed to impose their decisions on the majority of the population. He was made the Primate of England in 1633. The Puritans viewed all his measures with suspicion and firmly believed that he was secretly working to make Catholicism the established religion of England. In the nonreligious sphere, another advisor of Charles I was Thomas Wentworth, who was later made the Earl of Strafford. He adopted a paternalistic policy on the self-governing communities of England by enforcing the Poor Laws, Enclosure Acts and wage assessments which were framed under the Statute in Artificers in 1563. The state used several methods to enhance its revenues: Tunnage and Poundage continued to be collected without parliamentary approval, monopolies were granted and Ship Money was imposed in 1634 first on merchants living in port towns and later extended to inland territories. This led to the famous litigation known as the John Hampden Court case in 1637. The crown won the case but only by one vote which exposed its weakness.

The Laudian regime during the rule of Charles I had aroused strong resentment against the crown. The revival of feudal devices of enhancing state revenue caused widespread opposition, particularly among the Puritans. Many Puritans began to migrate to America and contributed to the process of colonizing America. The imposition of the royal policy by Laud over Scotland, primarily Presbyterian, resulted in a major revolt. The Scots felt threatened by the new ceremonies introduced by Laud, which were considered papist. Four committees called the 'Tables' seized the Scottish government and the revolt assumed a national dimension. The English attempts to suppress the revolt led to two wars against Scotland, popularly called the 'Bishops' Wars'. Between the two wars, Charles was forced to summon the parliament in 1640. John Pym, the famous parliamentarian, led the opposition in the parliament. This opposition forced Charles to dissolve the parliament once more and caused widespread riots in London. But by November 1640, he was left with no alternative but to call another parliament, called the long parliament by historians. Its members insisted that the Constitution of England and the relations between the crown and the parliament be redefined before it resumed its proper functions. The parliament also decided to punish all the ministers responsible for non-parliamentary rule. Wentworth was impeached and Laud was sent to prison. The *Triennial Act* laid down that parliament must be summoned at least once every three years. The parliament also abolished Ship Money, Knighthood and insisted that Tunnage and Poundage could not be levied without parliamentary approval. The most radical act was to abolish all the prerogative courts like Star Chamber, the Court of High Commission, and the Council of the North and the Council of Wales – the instruments of royal power under the Tudors. These acts destroyed royal absolutism and brought about a new relationship between the crown and the parliament. Before a solution to the conflict could be found, a major Irish revolt began in 1641. These widespread insurrections of the Irish Catholics and the killings of many Protestants created a fresh rift between the English ruler and the parliament. The Irish rebels claimed that they were acting for the king. It had great repercussion in England as it created a deep cleavage within the parliament and led to the formation of the King's Party. The parliament led by Pym produced a document called *The Grand Remonstrance*. Although it was passed by a thin majority of only eleven votes, it divided the English leaders into two hostile groups – Roundheads and Cavaliers. The chief issues centred on the reform of the church and the limitation of executive powers. The situation had become volatile and Charles decided to attack the parliament with 400 soldiers on 4 January 1642 to arrest the five opposition leaders and the civil war thus commenced. It culminated in the defeat of Charles I and his execution in 1649. A tribunal appointed by the House of Commons consisting of 150 members carried this out.

Causes

Historians writing on the causes and the nature of the English revolution find this subject extremely complex. One way of understanding the causes is to see how different historians have explained this major event. In 1913 R.G. Usher rightly observed that the English revolution of 1640 was considered an enigma at that time. One can add that it remains the same even today. Was it a 'Great Rebellion' staged by dissident members of the landed classes, the last and the most violent of the many rebellions against unpopular kings, as suggested by Clarendon? Was it merely an internal war stemming from particular political circumstances? Was it a Puritan Revolution, as suggested by S.R. Gardiner, or a clash of liberty and royal tyranny that put England on the road to parliamentary monarchy, as Macaulay argued? Or is it possible to treat it as the first bourgeois revolution, as the Marxist writers contend, in which progressive and dynamic elements in society struggled and emerged victorious against the feudal order? It is also presented as the first revolution for modernization. There is no unanimity on any of these views and the scope of interpretation remains wide open.

The historiography of the English Revolution has undergone major changes since the writing of S.R. Gardiner, a great historian of the Victorian period. He provided a political narrative of the civil war in eighteen volumes under the title *History of England 1603–1656*. It was a work of great scholarship written with meticulous care. His view that the civil war was a Puritan revolution, in which the driving force behind all the controversies was religion and ideologies, has come under scathing attack from Marxists. The Marxian theory suggests that the first major shift in European society from feudal to bourgeois phase occurred in England during the seventeenth century. Engels presented a broad explanation of the bourgeois revolution and placed the English revolution in that framework. He included the aristocracy and the gentry in the class of bourgeois landlords that opposed the feudal order. Marxist writers such as E.J. Hobsbawm and Maurice Dobb, call it a revolution that was aimed at destroying the feudal structure in England and in its place build a capitalist organization. It has been seen as a bourgeois revolution – a conflict between the rising social forces of the bourgeoisie and the decaying feudal classes. In this, the progressive and dynamic elements struggled to break the feudal shackles to become independent. As the feudal structure hampered the economic activity of emerging social classes with its obsolete, wasteful and restrictive production system, it assumed the character of a class-war. Thus, the English revolution is shown as the crucial 'breakthrough' to modern capitalism. By the third quarter of the twentieth century, serious works on the subject have come out. Writers such as R.H. Tawney, Trevor-Roper, Lawrence Stone and

Christopher Hill have provided a series of explanations. Together, these are called the social interpretation of the English revolution.

The genesis of the English revolution is located in the socio-economic changes that preceded the revolution for almost a century. One school of thought appears to suggest that the revolution was caused by the rise of the gentry in the century before the 1640s (R.H. Tawney). According to this view, the civil war was fought to restore the balance of property which had been upset because of the redistribution of land in the century before 1640, a view somewhat shared by Stone. In this change in the ownership of property, the old type of landowners decayed while a new class of gentry rose to the top. He attributes this change to the difference in the adaptability in estate management because of rising prices, new agricultural techniques, new outlets for market and also partially to the presence or absence of non-agricultural sources of wealth. Tawney regards the events of 1640 as a shift in the political structure to accommodate the power of the new gentry. He supports this argument with massive statistics. Lawrence Stone elaborates this interpretation with some new arguments. He believes that the rise of the gentry and the decline of the traditional landowners were not because of the inefficient land management by the latter but because of their over-expenditure. He provides data to prove the growing indebtedness of the old landed aristocracy. He emphasizes the importance of social change by which the aristocracy lost its control of military power, their territorial positions and their prestige. Their real income declined and this left the crown and the church isolated. This explanation suggests that the expansion of trade and the Price Revolution provided the original impetus to the capitalists' development. Commercialization of rural economy and the rising prices of foodstuff affected the old feudal class and the nascent bourgeoisie in totally different ways. A new urban and a rural class of entrepreneurs consisting of gentry and yeomen, took advantage of the market opportunities and sticky rents and became rich and more powerful while the feudal class was unable to respond to the changing conditions. The civil war was an attempt to transform the political structure in accordance with the socio-economic changes.

H.R. Trevor-Roper severely criticizes this viewpoint of Tawney and instead proposes a rival interpretation. According to him, there was no substantial rise of the gentry and they suffered a massive decline, primarily because of the inflation in the sixteenth century. Those who actually rose in the social ladder were the yeomen (a yeoman was a prosperous farmer who cultivated his own land and sometimes held the position of a lesser official in a royal household or in a noble's domain). According to him, those sections of the gentry or nobility who practised trade or law – the so-called 'mere gentry', formed the country party. The real profits in the century prior to 1640 were made not by farmers but by those holding court offices. According to Trevor-Roper, it was the mere gentry (the mere gentry was the rural or country gentry as different from the town gentry, and consisted of small or middling landowners and had a vastly different interests from those attached to the king's court) that tried to overthrow the court system in the 1640s and emerged as the radical leaders of the New Model Army. They pursued independent policies designed to bring about a decentralization of authority and the destruction of the old financial system. They made several desperate attempts to make their way into the court. These include Essex's revolt in 1601 and the Gunpowder Plot in 1605. J.H. Hexter criticizes both the views of Tawney as well as Trevor–Roper, and argues that the aristocracy declined, lost control of the military and over the greater gentry and that the political leadership shifted from the House of Lords to the House of Commons.

Christopher Hill finds Trevor–Roper's analysis of the civil war rather unconvincing. He objects to Trevor–Roper's inclusion of lawyers in the category of courtiers, who, he believed were in opposition to the 'mere' gentry. Hill argues that Trevor–Roper wrongly equates the court gentry (including the lawyers) with the royalists in the civil war period, whereas the evidence suggests that a large section of the common lawyers had supported parliament. Hill traces the origins of the English revolution to the socio-economic consequences of the Henrican Reformation. According to him, the Reformation was an act of state and the Protestantism in England was a consequence and not a cause of the Reformation. The church lost its economic and political power during the rule of Henry. The removal of abbots from the House of Lords in the parliament reduced the clerical vote from absolute majority to a minority. Besides judicial profits, the church lost about £40,000 annually in the form of 'first-fruits' and 'tenths'. It also shifted wealth and economic influence away from the church into the hands of the crown. These developments led to long-term as well as short-term consequences in England. Hill argues that there was nothing revolutionary about the land transfers of the Reformation era. There was a shift in the balance of property but it remained within the landed ruling class, benefitting those who were politically influential at the time of the dissolution of monasteries. Two-thirds of the peers were either granted monastic estates or they bought it themselves. Thus, the main recipients of the new landed wealth were the peers, royal officials and the state servants. According to Christopher Hill, it was not a social revolution. Yet, it marked more than a mere shift of landed property along with its power and prestige, from clerical big landowners to lay big landowners.

The court of Henry VIII had many new men, who were members of the lesser gentry. According to Hill, sections of the old aristocracy were out of sympathy with Henry's policy and this was clearly visible in the Pilgrimage of Grace, the famous revolt. There was a shift of power within the ruling landed class – from the big feudal families towards the ambitious men from the gentry who depended on royal favour. The Statute of Livery (1487) and the dissolution of monasteries contributed to the declining influence of the old aristocracy. It also expanded the prerogative powers of the English monarch. At the same time, the Reformation did not permanently strengthen the monarchy. In fact, the church property was soon dissipated. The newly acquired wealth was spent on constructing a naval fleet and on war with France. Elizabeth had to sell almost the rest of the monastic lands in order to pay for the Irish war. English taxes were relatively light compared to the tax-structure in other countries and the men of property gained both ways. It is indeed one of the many paradoxes of the English Reformation that in temporarily solving the economic problems of the ruling class, it gave a stimulus to ideas, which were ultimately to overthrow the old order (Christopher Hill).

The dissolution of monasteries contributed to the pace of social change but it did not cause a social revolution. The latter was taking shape independently. Social change was related to the rise of capitalism caused by an enormous expansion of trade (internal as well as foreign), manufacturing activities and changes in agriculture. The gentry took economic initiatives and many of them purchased estates that they were already farming. Several outside elements also entered the land market in order to make profit through resale. In the ultimate analysis, land came in the hands of moneyed men who also exhibited a spirit of enterprise. The acquisition of new land enhanced the prestige of the owners but in order to recover their investment in land, they adopted better methods of land management. In some places, the value of landed property began to soar. At St Albans Abbey, the value went up eighty times in just one century after the dissolution. There were many families such as the Herberts, Cliffords and Lilburnes, who were able to increase their wealth by the discovery of coal or iron deposit in their lands. Such purchases stimulated economic development.

Towards the close of the sixteenth century, while the gentry and yeomen strengthened their economic position, the aristocrats faced financial difficulties. To face the new challenges the aristocrats looked to monarchy for support. The latter created court offices for the old aristocrats and conferred on them the rights of commercial and industrial monopolies. The expanding economy gave advantages to those men who were associated with manufacturing activities. As a result, the bourgeoisie, including the gentry fought for commercial freedom and parliamentary rights to guard their material interests. This precipitated a political crisis and brought about a contest between the rising groups against the absolutist state and the feudal aristocracy.

For Christopher Hill, the English Revolution of 1640–60 was a great social movement like the French Revolution of 1789, and was a bourgeois revolution. In his earlier writings he described it as a class war in which the reactionary forces like church and the conservative landlords defended the despotism of Charles, while the parliament got the support of the progressive forces like the gentry, yeomen, trading and manufacturing classes, etc. Hill's views changed gradually with his numerous publications. The Civil War involved conflicts over material interests of the two rival forces but in his *Intellectual Origins of the English Revolution* Hill points out that the conflict developed not only because of material interests but ideas and values also played a crucial role. Hill also uses the term 'Puritan revolution' for the civil war but not in a narrow sense. He suggests that the term Puritanism should not be seen in strictly religious sense, rather it conveys the new political, social and intellectual concepts of the so-called 'the middling sort' comprising merchants, artisans and yeomen. Puritan ideas motivated the seventeenth-century revolutionaries towards radical experiments between 1640 and 1660.

The chief limitation of this social interpretation is that it has not been able to specify the distinct feudal and capitalist classes. It does not explain which feudal classes gained from the new economic conditions and transformed into capitalist mould or which classes created obstacles in the path of emerging capitalist structure. It also does not explain adequately why the traditional feudal lords did not try to change and transform their households despite economic pressures and sufficient opportunities. Moreover, while those tenants who received long leases in the early sixteenth century did gain immensely at the expense of the landlords from rising prices and greater profits. The position reversed by the end of the century when the grant of long leases virtually ended. Besides, it is very difficult to bring out specific distinctions within the category of large landowners. Even the distinction between 'nobles' and 'gentry' was not very clear any more.

Social interpretation fails to provide enough evidence to prove that feudal and capitalist classes took divergent economic paths and reached a stage of direct confrontation in 1640. It is argued by its authors that most big landlords did not suffer economic difficulties before the 1640s; rather they enjoyed significant economic improvements. In fact, this period witnessed a rise and not a decline of the aristocracy and big landlords. The time between the 1580s and the 1640s was one of rising rents and food prices. Those nobles and gentry, who had ceased to be military lords and transformed themselves into commercial landlords dependent on markets and were the chief instruments in determining rents, must have done very well. The widespread socio-economic changes contributed to the major transformation of the landed class as a whole, marking the emergence of a capitalist-oriented landed class. It also brought about a homogenization of aristocracy with hardly any social or political distinction between the top layers of the landed class representing a large number of peers and the big untitled landlords. They held top political positions in government, in the court and in parliament. The difference between the English landed class and its capitalist farmers was not unbridgeable. This gap existed in many other countries as well. Leading nobles and great landowners were divided in their alignment between the crown and the parliament, though Brenner argued that leading nobles and other big landowners led the parliamentary legislative revolution from 1640 against the increasingly politically isolated king, supported by dependent courtiers, the upper level of ecclesiastical men, merchants the magistrates.

Religion

Religion and taxation are considered two important issues of conflict. The era of Mary Tudor and Elizabeth revealed the potential threat of aligning with the Catholic religion. A large majority of the parliamentary members began to consider a theologically orthodox Protestant religious settlement as absolutely necessary for protecting English interests. It implied the independence of the English monarchy from foreign direction and the autonomy of the English church. The construction of an independent state was carried out by adopting an autonomous church on the lines of Calvinism, free from Papal and Spanish threat. Historical ties had bound the greater landed classes with Calvinist Protestantism since the Reformation period. During the seventeenth century, the position of Protestantism had become precarious, both outside England with the Spanish dominance in the Thirty Years War and inside England by the policies of Laud in the reign of Charles I. The Protestant cause was raised in parliament against the Papal antichrist and Catholic Spain. It became the reason for calling Parliament after eleven years of personal rule by Charles I. The factors behind this were not constitutional but religious. The Scottish reaction to Laud's religious policy had forced Charles to summon parliament to discuss this national issue. Nor that many supported an alliance with the Protestant Holland, but the pro-Catholic policy of the Stuart rulers caused concern to many leaders in the parliament. The rise of Protestantism after Henry's Reformation also created conditions for change. The famous sea voyager and naval hero of Elizabethan times, Sir Walter Ralegh, wrote in his *History of the World*, 'let us build upon the Scriptures themselves and after that upon reason and nature'. The Puritan movement in England had a sound literary base and was further strengthened by the writings of men like William Prynne, Henry Burton, and many others. The failure of the Hampton Court Conference had forced the Puritans to use parliament as a stage to push through their reforms. Archbishop Richard Bancroft and William Laud, the two important advisers of the Stuart rulers intensified the Puritan movement, which was sustained by the support of the House of Commons. The Stuart policy drifted away from the late Tudors on the question of religion. It provided an occasion for conflict, giving an opportunity to the parliamentarians to interfere in policy-making decisions of the crown. The issue of royal taxation without parliamentary consent added fuel to the contest in which legal issues like royal prerogatives and parliamentary liberties surfaced. Thus, the monarchy and the parliamentary classes tended to formulate divergent principles to explain and justify their actions.

The Stuarts can hardly be blamed for believing that they had 'divine rights' to rule the country based on unquestionable 'prerogative powers', a claim that every European ruler made in that period. Every ruler had demanded military and financial aid from his subjects. The Stuart claims of patrimony over the state subjects were in tune with the time. Active parliamentary involvement in state matters, especially from the time of the

Reformation, had given parliament enhanced strength and realization of its position. The un-parliamentary taxation of the crown was seen as a threat to the security of private property.

Taxation

A major irritant between the crown and the parliament was the financial issue. Under Tudor rule, the taxes remained relatively light by the standards of the continent. The crown did not require spending heavily on army or bureaucracy. This fact is collaborated by the flourishing state of trade and industry. The rise of yeoman farming in the century before 1640 owed much to this light taxation. The most important component of royal revenue was the income from crown lands. It had greatly increased through the acquisition of monastic lands in the 1530s. It was soon dissipated in Henry VIII's wars against France and Scotland. The steep inflation during the sixteenth century had made the situation difficult for the crown. The Tudors had developed other means to supplement their income. One such device was the wardship – the right to manage the estate of a ward during his or her ministry. The Court of Wards become an instrument of generating income. Sometimes the courtiers bought the wardships of rich heirs. Revenue from this source had grown four times from the accession of Elizabeth (1558) till the beginning of the civil war. An attempt was made in 1610 between the crown and the parliament to end it but mutual distrust prevented any decision.

The government was unable to tap the growing wealth of England caused by the expansion of economy, particularly the business sector. Royal income was not able to keep pace with the price rise. Royal revenue did increase from about £2,00,000 a year in the 1530s to about £6,00,000 in the 1630s. However, the price rise was much more and hence the real costs of government continued to increase. Sale of crown lands could not solve the financial problems of the rulers as the Irish troubles and the Spanish War proved too costly for the state. The new types of weapon, larger ships and the cost of the royal court required much greater income. This could have been possible by reorganizing the tax structure through realistic assessment. But this raised the question whether the crown had the right to tax the subjects or whether the Parliament enjoyed this power. Besides, the vested interest groups opposed any such attempt of altering the system of taxation. The richer landowners were greatly under-assessed and were powerful enough to resist new proposals. The increase in custom duties helped the Stuart rulers financially but antagonized the merchants. Loans from different sources caused further difficulties. The sale of peerages between 1603 and 1629 brought roughly £6,20,000 but the distribution of gifts and favours had cost at least £3 million (Lawrence Stone). The breaking point in financial matters was reached in 1637 on the question of ship money.

The economic regulations in the reign of Charles generated friction. The state imposed rigid guild regulations from above on many crafts and trades. The much-despised monopolies were strictly enforced. The royal inspectors imposed harsh conditions on manufactures in the name of quality while the breakers of anti-enclosure laws were fined heavily. The climax against the crown's policies was reached in the famous Ship Money Case in 1637. The anti-royalist feelings were clearly expressed by the merchants of London when the Civil War actually broke out.

In the 1620s, an alliance was formed between the new merchants and the colonial aristocratic groups to exploit commercial, colonial and private opportunities in America. They sought to oppose the Spanish Atlantic fleet and the Spanish colonies in the West Indies. They also opposed Laud's religious measures. They were in support of parliamentary rights and opposed un-parliamentary taxation. On the other hand, the company merchants were foregoing ties with the crown to exploit the Levant–East India trade. They paid un-parliamentary duties in exchange for exclusive privileges and had replaced the old Merchant Adventurers Company. However, this alliance could not last long as the crown faced increasing financial pressures, particularly because of the Scottish revolt. The crown not only failed to honour its commitments, it also placed greater demands on its allies. The elite element within this merchant community became victims and faced loss of privilege and property.

Revisionist writers like John Russell and John Morrill suggest that the failure of some of the parliamentary leaders to understand the financial and administrative needs of the state remained a central underlying cause of the inability of the crown and parliament to find a mutually satisfactory solution.

Two themes have been given prominence in recent interpretations of the Stuart monarchy: taxation and the interpretation of constitutional documents. Revisionist writers (like John Russell, J. Morrill and Kishlansky, etc.) emphasize the role of conflicting issues pertaining to constitutional interpretation and religious beliefs along with state policies in the pre-civil war period. These struggles were consistently articulated in terms of principles to rationalize personal, factional or local short-term interests. On the part of monarchs, they followed such foreign policy or carried out wars that were not approved by the Parliament. This brought to surface questions of constitutional and religious importance pertaining to parliamentary powers, liberties of the subjects and Protestant ideas. John Russell suggests that powerful parliamentary pressures were exerted to restrict taxation, which can best be traced to the MPs' close dependence on their constituents, rather than having any desire to shackle the powers of the crown. A fundamental incompatibility had developed between the institutions of parliament and that of monarchy. Any solution would have meant radical modification of one institution or the other. Once these issues had been settled by the civil war and through revolutionary settlements, future conflicts on these subjects were avoided. However, these revisionist writings have not replaced the social interpretation in understanding the causes of the English civil war. There is no denying the fact that the transition from feudalism to capitalism had a formidable impact not only on the nature of aristocracy but also on the evolution of the English state. The capitalist development and the rise of the new landlord class influenced the process of state formation. In this change the relationship between the capitalists landed class and the patrimonial monarchy became antithetical and ultimately became the source of fundamental conflict.

It would be wrong to presume that the rural gentry and the nobles in the parliament were deliberately preparing for a revolution.

Most of them were moderates in their political and religious outlook. But their opposition to royal policies forced them to adopt radical language. It was only from 1647 that deliberate effort was made to arouse public opinion through pamphlets and emotional speeches, raising the issue of legitimate authority in public debates. Hobbes described this situation as 'boiling hot' while Henry Parker presented a theory of sovereignty in which the source of political power was vested in common consent and wishes of the subjects (implying parliamentary supremacy). As the conflict deepened, the role of ideas and public expression became quite evident. The next two decades witnessed several ideologies surfacing – radical, revolutionary as well as conservative. The Grand Remonstrance to the king, a statement of reforms that parliament had achieved, was passed with a thin majority – 159 votes in favour and 148 against. Some moderates like Falkland, Hyde and Waller feared that the reforms had gone too far. However, it was the king's refusal of the 'Nineteen Propositions' that marked the beginning of the war as these proposals suggested the idea of parliamentary supremacy. The big cities and the prominent financiers of London, along with eastern and southern England supported the Commons. The king enjoyed support mostly among the rural population of the north and west of England and nearly the whole of Wales. No social group including the gentry was entirely on one side – they were divided in varying proportions between the king and parliament. The split between the royalists and the parliamentarians was an even one. Many of them remained neutral. According to Lawrence Stone, the crisis of the 1640s was not a crisis within society, but rather a crisis within the regime. However, the class conflict nature of the revolution cannot be rejected completely. At least in the early stage of the conflict, there was a clear tendency among the country yeomen and middling groups in the urban manufacturing centres and towns to associate themselves with the parliament while many old aristocrats and most of the merchant oligarchies sided with the king. No doubt the social base of the two rivals was rather complex in terms of classes, orders and status groups. It depended also on ideologies, personal gains, group interests, religious faith and differences in political or constitutional outlook. The rapidly changing society and economy created disequilibria and led to the flow of new intellectual currents. The state apparatus was unable to respond to those changes. The crown was not powerful enough to defend itself as the crisis developed in the absence of two instruments – a standing army and a professional state bureaucracy.

Fermentation of Ideas

Lawrence Stone stresses the role of the alienation of the intellectuals from royal favour in the period of educational expansion. The Puritan ministers and teachers, professors and lawyers, they all increasingly found themselves cut-off from government institutions. The civil war and the subsequent experiments in political field raised hopes of numerous intellectual groups who came forward with their own schemes of governance. Among the major intellectual movement, one can include the names of the Puritans, the Levellers, the Diggers, the Fifth Monarchy Men, the Republicans and the Royalists.

Puritanism as a socio-political movement can be traced to the period of Edward VI. Although it is difficult to clearly define this term because it had several shades of opinion, yet it contributed to the development of an important ideology that dominated the early part of the civil war. In Elizabeth's time, the Puritans took a radical view of the Reformation. For the moderate members of the English church the Reformation meant not only removing the abuses from the church but for the Puritans it was also a question of establishing a new church. It not only aimed at removing corruption but also many catholic elements such as holy days, kneeling at the altar, vestments, the ring exchange, etc., on the ground that Bible did not advocate such practices. In the early phase of Puritanism in the 1560s, it mainly concentrated on opposing certain rituals. Elizabethan religious settlement imposed strict discipline and forced many moderate Puritans into obedience. However, the hard-core elements moved towards a more radical position. Within church organization, the Puritans led by Thomas Cartwright demanded the creation of a full-fledged Presbyterian form of church government. In many parishes, informal preaching spread and an underground 'shadow Presbyterian church' within the church of England developed. They had their synods and provincial and national assemblies. Some Puritans entered parliament and raised issues that were not tolerated by Elizabeth. With the coming of Stuart dynasty their activities resurfaced. Elizabeth was able to suppress this revolutionary movement by forceful police action through Archbishop Whitgift. But by crushing this organization it drove the movement deeper into English society. It continued to grow and spread and became extremely active in the period of the civil war and brought about a split in the religious lives of the English. The success of Puritanism was primarily due to the shortcomings of the established church, particularly under Laud. As Christopher Hill points out, 'Protestantism, patriotism, parliamentarism and property all worked together against Laud's attempt to reverse history'. The spiritual weakness and their educational and organizational shortcomings contributed to the Puritan success. Several Puritans began participating in provincial corporations. Public preaching became a strong weapon of Puritanism. Puritanism not only became an ideology but also a way of life that promoted scientific thinking, political democracy in certain ways, social egalitarianism and was particularly popular among the small merchants, shopkeepers, manufacturers and artisans. The doctrines preached by the Puritans suited the economic interests of the emerging new classes. The crucial element in the success of this movement was the role of the landed nobility and gentry that provided patronage and political weight through Parliament. Puritanism had become popular in the urban centres where it acted as a strong stimulus to radical political thinking and was directed towards political action. Several historians in the past have emphasized the role of Puritans in pushing the conflict towards a civil war. However, the excesses of violence and disharmony weakened the Puritans as a political force after the restoration of the English monarchy.

Another very prominent ideological group consisted of the Levellers. Theirs was a radical movement that flourished in London and within the army, particularly after the defeat of the king. It was the most advanced democratic group that appeared on the political stage of Europe. The name Levellers was given to them by their enemies and was earlier applied to anti-enclosure rioters (who levelled hedges and palings). John Lilburne and John Wildman, leaders of this movement became popular heroes in the time of Laud. These two men provided an intellectual content to the movement by formulating a radical and democratic programme. Levellers appealed to the small proprietors in towns and in the countryside and to the vast majority of the population. Their radical plans were aimed at protecting small entrepreneurs and their arguments were based on the law of nature rather than on any precedent or religious authority. They made use of historical illustrations from the Anglo-Saxon past and presented a concept of the natural rights of man. They projected themselves as the recoverers of ancient rights and fused Biblical and political theories together. For them all men were the sons of Adam and they were all free and equal under God.

The Levellers produced their programme under the name of 'Agreement of the People', a concept of modern democracy. They stood more or less for households' suffrage, though not for every adult male and were certainly not for women's suffrage. Yet it was an idea far ahead of its time. They also believed that the parliament, though a sovereign institution of the government, should also be bound by certain fundamental laws. These included religious liberty for all Protestants. They were against military conscription and opposed all forms of trade monopolies and corporate privileges. It was a direct response to the parliamentary claim of sovereignty during the civil war. The Levellers demanded a constitution that would guarantee equality, equal electoral constituencies, annual elections and abolition of property as a qualification for voting. However, they neither attacked inequality of wealth nor the institution of private property. Some historians see this movement as the natural culmination of the popular and democratic tendencies that were inherent in the Protestant religion. Even John Lilburne was a radical Puritan before he became a Leveller. This group was despised and abhorred by the most orthodox Puritan group, the Presbyterians. Marxist writers have described the concept of democracy as propounded by the Levellers a 'bourgeois democracy'.

In the initial period, Lilburne had accepted the views of Edward Coke, a famous lawyer of that period, that the Magna Carta embodied the Anglo-Saxon liberties but later he came to the conclusion that neither the Magna Carta nor a common law guaranteed those liberties. While Coke wanted to establish the supremacy of the Common Law made by the judges, the Levellers wanted Common Law to be made the jury. The judges were to be drawn from the ruling class and were therefore to be closely associated with the government. It can be said that democracy was not the goal of the Levellers but they tried to provide an opportunity for economic independence that ought to be made available to all. The Levellers constituted, according to Hill, the first grass root political party in English history. They organized demonstrations and processions in order to mobilize the public.

Another interesting and colourful group of religious men were the Fifth Monarchy Men, who participated in the political experiments during the revolutionary period. It was a radical religious movement that was active in the early 1650s and represented the aspirations and grievances of the same social order to that the Levellers had addressed. However, instead of democracy they believed in the rule of 'saints'. They genuinely believed that the four temporal monarchies of the world had passed away based on *Daniel* and *Revelations*, in the ancient period in Babylon, Persia, Macedon and Rome. They argued that the fourth monarchy was continuing in the form of papacy, also called anti-Christ and that its end was numbered before the fifth monarchy began as the reign of Christ. It was not a peaceful sect, as they believe in direct military action to hasten the arrival of the fifth monarchy. Many of these constituted the nominated members of Barebone's parliament (July–December 1653). These members themselves dissolved the Parliament disappointing Oliver Cromwell, who had made an attempt to bring about 'a Godly reformation' to establish an honest and ideal rule in England. The Fifth Monarchy Men exerted influence on not only Cromwell in 1653 but they also caused anxiety to the government after the Restoration in 1660.

Among the radical groups of that period, the Diggers also came out with drastic solutions to contemporary problems. The Diggers were a small group led by an ex-textile merchant, Gerrard Winstanley. They appeared on the political scene in 1649 but they probably existed before. They believed that feudal tenures and copyholds obstructed the development of agriculture. They suggested direct appropriation of unused common lands, to be cultivated collectively by the people and this meant a step in the direction of common ownership of the means of production. They believed that redistribution of political power was not enough as it ended in exploitation and oppression. For them true freedom consisted in the evolution of private property. In his book *The Law of Freedom* Winstanley blamed most human selfishness to the institution of private property. His vision of society was a form of Utopia in which no class distinctions, property or money existed and where the community exploited land. Although they were also called the 'True Levellers', the Diggers had a social base below that of the Levellers. The Rump government of Cromwell was alarmed by their ideology and decided to intervene. However, the force led by Fairfax to suppress this movement found the Diggers harmless cranks. They never emerged as a serious political force like the Levellers.

Besides the Levellers and Diggers, there were some smaller groups which surfaced during the period of the civil war. The most important among them were the Quakers. They were too radical in their outlook and posed a direct challenge to the authority of the church and to the formal religious institutions. Though most did not tolerate them Cromwell appeared to be more liberal towards them. The Quaker movement based its authority on revelation and their founder leader George Fox rejected the doctrine of a formal ministry and instead organized group meetings for worship. These were conducted without any formal service and in which members of congregation spoke openly. The Quakers denied many of the ideas of existing social order. They refused to take off their hats in the presence of anyone – a practice that was followed by the English upper classes. They also refused to take oaths that were practised in legal proceedings. They appeared to be the only sect during the revolution that totally denied the right of civil authority. However, the Restoration in 1660 led to an increasing repression of these independent ideas. The Quakers displayed an unusual passive obstinacy and many of them went to the New World in North America. The period of civil war was thus a very fertile era in which numerous independent ideas sprang up and some of them influenced political activities.

The political writings of these various groups, particularly those of the Levellers, are of great interest because they present the complaints of the common people. These groups had a positive aspect as most of them tried to provide their own solutions to the social and economic problems of that period. However, most of these solutions were either too ahead of their times or too idealistic to be implemented in that tense social climate. This period is also of great significance for the history of political philosophy. Two important works were published during this time, which influenced contemporary and subsequent political thought. One was written by Thomas Hobbes and the other by James Herington. The two did not agree in their political philosophy but they provided new ideas on political power. Hobbes gave a materialistic outlook on life and society. He wrote that universe is material as all that is real is material and what is not material is not real. His idea of sovereignty was based on concentration of authority under the state. His theories created an all-powerful and all-embracing state that had genuine strength of will that could impose peace and prosperity in society. It also marked a new view of state formation in which the concept of divine right was replaced by the notion of social contract. On the other hand James Herington's *The Commonwealth of Oceana* (1656) was dedicated to Cromwell and gives a glimpse of socialist idea. His theory was based on the concept of a balance of property. He believed that a stable society depended on a direct relationship between the distribution of property and political power. His state was founded on an agrarian law laying down that no one should possess land above the value of £2,000 in England and £300 in Scotland. He also believed in equal distribution of property among children. He wished to establish an aristocratic republic based on socialist division of property. By keeping power in the hands of a stable agrarian community, he believed that an extreme form of democracy could be avoided. He also suggested a senate of property owners that could frame laws while an assembly based on universal suffrage would vote on them. They were many other writers who enriched the English literature and political thinking by their intellectual creations. One such important writer was John Milton, a great Puritan poet, one time Presbyterian apologist and an enthusiastic supporter of the execution of the king.

Commonwealth and Protectorate

The Royalist army faced a tough challenge from the parliament's army in its bid to capture London. The New Modes Army that fought for parliament was the creation of Oliver Cromwell, who emerged as the main leader during the civil war. He was an outstanding Puritan general and was responsible for the defeat and execution of King Charles I. He created an army-controlled republic and made various efforts to give it a constitutional form but could not succeed. This period (1649–60) turned out to be an era of intense political activities and constitutional experiments that had never been seen in English history.

Cromwell belonged to a yeoman family which had gained land and gentry status under the Tudors. He had undergone a conversion to Calvinism. From a back-bench MP he rose to become the great commander in the parliament army. His New Model Army gave him a power base that made him the strongest man by 1649. As an independent MP he worked in parliament to prevent the 'Presbyterian members from disbanding the Army and from establishing a Presbyterian church. He worked with the parliament to legitimize his own power base. Despite his efforts, the parliament and the army kept drifting apart. He demonstrated a peculiar mixture of oratory skill, tolerance and brute power. He tried to bring about a moderate settlement with the king, called the *Heads of the Proposals* (1647) but Charles rejected it. Cromwell created a General Council of the Army and forced the Army to withdraw its proposal of a settlement called *Agreement of the People*, which had been greatly influenced by the Levellers. He had to suppress a mutiny by force before waging a final assault on the king. He then cleaned up the parliament by dispersing all the MPs except sixty members belonging to the radical wing of the 'Independents'.

A 'Commonwealth' then ruled England between 1649 and 1653. This was a ministry of the House of Commons of the long parliament, consisting of about sixty members. The parliament ruled through an elaborate system of Committees since the beginning of the war. These committees had mixed members from MPs and local counties and even from autonomous bodies. The coordinating agency was the Council of State elected by the Commons. Its membership included civilians as well as some army men. The purged parliament came to be known as the 'Rump'. It was a single chamber parliament as the House of Lords was abolished in the course of the civil war. The execution of the king shocked many moderates in England and Scotland. The legitimacy of the Commonwealth government was always in doubt because of its narrow political base and it became difficult to formulate policies and implement them effectively. A majority of the reformist gentry had been excluded and purged from the parliament, as were the Levellers. The power rested with army and hence Cromwell wanted to give his rule a constitutional colour. During this period, the Irish and the Scottish revolts were crushed and about two-thirds of the land of the Irish landowners was confiscated.

The Rump faced a serious crisis in April 1653 when it was dissolved by Cromwell. The Rump faced religious problems from the Presbyterians, Independents and the radical Puritans of the army who were in collision with the other members. As Rump parliament had not achieved much in the form of reforms and Cromwell was keen to have his position strengthened by proper legislative support, he wanted an elected house carrying great legitimacy. He was forced to take swift action because of the problems created by the Scots and the Irish, the outbreak of a war against the Dutch brought on by the passing of the Navigation Act and the growing opposition that was developing against him. His decision to dissolve the Rump was taken suddenly and it appears that there were no clear plans for the future of England. At this time there were two sources of power but they were both in constant opposition to each other. The first source of power emanated from the gentry that was still active in politics and held strong influence over local government. The minor gentlemen had been elevated politically with the displacement of the senior members. Most members of the Puritan gentry wanted civilian control over the army, the rule of law, parliamentary control over taxation and a settled constitution to regulate the power at the top. The second source of power was the army that had several aims. They were suspicious of civilian hostility and wanted a supreme authority to protect their interests. Some of the members of the command like Major General Harrison had sympathy with the radicals like the Fifth Monarchy Men. Cromwell tried to bridge the two conflicting interests. He had a paternalistic approach towards the people and wanted to bring stability and good governance for England. It was with this intention that Cromwell decided to create a parliament of nominated members as a Protectorate in December 1653. The members were chosen from the independent and Baptist congregations. It was described by the contemporaries as an 'assembly on Saints', also called the 'Barebone's Parliament' named after one of its members. This experiment did not last long as it came to be dominated by a large number of Fifth Monarchists and they tried to achieve too many things without any plan. They did bring same reforms such as reduction in legal fees, improvement of prison conditions and introduction of registration of civil marriages. The moderate members felt threatened by the radicals and voted their own dissolution.

The Protectorate (1653–1660)

The failure of earlier experiments made Cromwell frame a new constitution. It was prepared under the guidance of Major General Lambert. It was called the Instrument of Government in which Cromwell acquired the office of Lord Protector, a clearly defined constitutional position. The real power was to be shared between the Lord Protector and the Council of State containing both civilian and military members. A parliament was also created representing elected members from England, Scotland and Ireland. It was given the powers to frame laws and taxation. It was the first written Constitution in English history and the first united parliament of the three independent states. The most important aspect of this experiment was the franchise reforms based on the ownership of property. The Protectorate produced little change in economic policy but the government was always prepared to regulate the economy. The Puritans received sympathy but the radical groups like the Fifth Monarchists and Quakers were imprisoned. This parliament could not function normally not only because of ideological divisions but also because of the disputes between the Protector and the members concerning his control over the armed forces, financial provisions and the issue of religious liberty. Cromwell had to dissolve this parliament in 1655.

To counter the threat of the Royalists who were reviving their plots to support the exiled king, the country was put under Major General's rule. The entire country was divided into eleven regions, each under a Major General and a penal tax was imposed upon the Royalists to pay the cost of the militia. It would be wrong to suggest that Cromwell acted as a military dictator as his main concern was to prevent future disorder. It was a period of severe repression placing strict censorship on newspapers and public opinion. As Cromwell had thrown England in a war against Spain he realized that it was not possible to raise money without the help of the parliament. Hence the second parliament was called under the Instrument of Government. At this point, the members of the parliament presented him 'Humble Petition and Advice' that included the proposal of making Cromwell the king of England under a new constitution. Cromwell rejected the proposal of becoming the king but accepted other suggestions that included the creation of another house. This experiment also ultimately failed as the Royalists dominated the parliament causing problems for Cromwell as well as for the republicans. The Spanish war became increasingly unpopular as the government ran into debt and found it difficult to get fresh taxes voted by the parliament. It was in these circumstances that Cromwell died and his nominated successor, his eldest son Richard Cromwell was unable to control the situation. This made the return of Charles II possible in 1660.

From a constitutional angle, the commonwealth rule established the supremacy of the parliament based on popular sovereignty, but narrowed it down to parliamentary domination. The limited powers was used to reform government administration and the system of law. After his fifth conquest of Ireland, colonization was implemented more thoroughly than had been done earlier under the Tudors and early Stuarts. The English ruling class was imposed on the Irish people. Similarly, the Scots were defeated in 1651 and this led to a union of parliament between England and Scotland, sometimes described as a 'shot-gun marriage'. The final union of the two states could only be achieved in 1707. The period of commonwealth protectorate was marked by many constitutional experiments. It was for the first and the last time that England was ruled in turn, by a written constitution, by a united parliament and by the army. For the first time, the idea of parliamentary representation was tried. The state itself adopted measures to control social and moral life of the people by introducing civil marriages, registration of births, marriages and deaths, and better treatment of lunatics. In the new franchise, the freeholders (tenant farmers holding copy of court roll) were deprived of their rights but the copyholders (tenants enjoying rights of land by inheritance or for three lives according to the nature of grant and could make leases for one, sometimes three years with Lord's license) and the leaseholders were given better treatment than was given by the Reform Act of 1832.

Economically there were certain important changes. This was a period of large-scale transfers and sale of land that had started since the mid-1640s. Church property that belonged to the bishops, deans and the other officials, was confiscated and sold. Although most of the lands of the crown were sold some officers and soldiers also became the recipients of these lands in lieu of arrears in pay. Many Royalists were compelled to sell their land to pay for the heavy fines and faced serious economic difficulties. It is believed that the purchase of church, crown and Royalist lands by officials, London merchants, lawyers and land speculators implied the emergence of a new landowning class. There are many historians who refute this view because much of this change in landownership under the republic was reversed in 1660.

The importance of privilege was greatly reduced in favour of careers open to talent. The privileges of private property were made more secure. Political subversion or religious dissidence that could cause public disorder was harshly suppressed. Commonwealth rule ended any hope of Episcopal or Presbyterian rule and instead established a mild form of tolerant religion.

In foreign affairs, the Commonwealth encouraged commercial investment and expansion and reorganized the East India Company. It also aimed at establishing English mercantile domination, and the destruction of the Dutch mercantile strength through Navigation Acts (1651) and promotion of colonial development. The naval voyages of Robert Blake and George Aysene (1650–1), the Convoy Act and a war against the Dutch gave fullest protection to the English merchants. The acquisition of Jamaica gave a strong fillip to the English rule in the West Indies and turned it into a base for slave trade. The Navigation Act brought about the subordination of colonies to parliament and thereby it made possible the formulation of a coherent imperial policy. It also led to the monopolization of colonial trade for the English ships. The act was modified in 1660 and laid the basis of English colonial policy for the next 150 years. As Lewis Namier points out, trade needed more positive state action than was the case with the landowners for agricultural labourers and this was provided from the revolutionary decades. This period also marked the dismantling of the Dutch control of the overseas trade in sugar, slaves, tobacco, furs and cod fish. Besides, this period marks the beginning of English territorial power in India and the opening of the Chinese trade.

The critics of Oliver Cromwell suggests that the only legacy he left behind was a permanent hatred among Englishmen against standing armies and a broken and totally discredited Puritanism. At the time of his death the army had disintegrated. However, his constitutional experiments were of greater significance despite their failure. These constitutional reforms were delayed for several generations because Cromwell had tried to achieve them by the sword. He was an idealist without any clear-cut theory of his own. He was an impatient democrat but he distrusted popular demands. The disunity among his supporters strengthened the position of the Royalists and his weak successor could not prevent the restoration of the Stuart dynasty.

The English civil war had some momentous repercussions. In

this brief period, a series of experiments were carried out, many of them were too radical for the age. The restoration of the old arrangement revealed that Englishmen were basically conservative though the old structure could never be restored. Subsequently, a new political system began to emerge based on continuity rather than a break with the past. The old feudal monarchy could not be revived and the royal absolutism built on prerogative powers came to an end despite the attempts of James II (1685–8) to resuscitate it. The end of the civil war marked the beginning of party and cabinet system in England. It also marked the complete defeat of the Puritan republic and the restoration of Anglican orthodoxy. The Clarendon Code placed severe restrictions on Puritans and asked the state to adopt a series of repressive measures against them. The Puritan groups held many secret congregations to organize resistance but stern measures of the restored government compelled many of them to migrate to the new World, helping in the rise of the American colonies. The acquisition of Trinidad in the West Indies also led to rapid commercial expansion and the rise of overseas trade.

Restoration of 1660

The kind of absolutism that England experienced under the Tudors and the early Stuarts, came to an abrupt end during the civil war period. After almost two decades of intense political activity, England returned to the old form of monarchy. Charles II, the new ruler was placed on the English throne and he pledged himself not to rule as a despot, to respect parliament and follow the spirit of the Magna Carta and the Petition of Right. He did try to strengthen the monarchy and make it relatively independent but the parliament was alert and watchful and immediately opposed any such attempt. So much had happened in the last twenty years that the monarchy could never be the same as it was prior to the civil war. Thus, English monarchy after its restoration presented quite a contrast to the French absolute rulers.

The restoration of 1660 was not merely the restoration of the king. As G.M. Treveleyan points out, there were in fact two restorations. The first was carried out by the convention parliament that restored the monarchy, the parliament with two houses and the non-military state dominated by the hereditary upper class. The second restoration was brought about by the new parliament called the cavalier parliament which restored the Anglican Church in England.

The restored monarchy differed from Tudor monarchy. Before he fled from London, Charles I had given his assent to all the Acts of parliament that included the curtailment of powers of the crown. The prerogative powers of the king to govern through his institutions and raise money without parliamentary consent had all been abolished. So the restoration of the king did not re-establish those prerogative courts such as the Star Chamber, Council of the North, Court of High Commission, etc. Unparliamentary taxation such as ship money and forced loan stood condemned. The criminal jurisdictions of the Privy Council also disappeared. The members of parliament could no longer be arrested on the king's order without showing the cause for their arrest. The parliament had been rather lenient in restoring rest of the traditional powers of the king, as most of the members were royalist in their outlook. The king was left with his right of royal veto – the power of summoning and dissolving the parliament. The Triennial Act of 1664 only states that a parliamentary session must be called at least once in three years and that the summoning and duration of parliament was a matter of royal discretion. Charles II took full advantages of this clause and retained the same parliament from 1661 till 1679 as it favoured him. The convention parliament also tried to solve the problem of the king's finances to avoid future conflicts. The parliament granted a fixed amount of revenue to the king. A committee after studying the financial aspect of the crown in the pre-civil war period reported that the royal revenue was about £9,00,000 of which £2,00,000 was raised by unlawful means. The normal expenditure was about £2,00,000 more. So the king was awarded £12,00,000 as ordinary revenue and another £1,00,000 in place of feudal dues. The effect of these changes was to put a relatively greater financial burden on the poor and on some business people while the landowners had to bear a much lighter burden.

The proposal of a regular tax on landed property was rejected. To pay the crown's army expenses, the Hearth Tax (according to the number of fire places in peoples' home) was imposed which hit the poor relatively hard. However, subsequent rulers, in order to manage parliament adopted bribery, patronage and manipulations.

The restoration of the English parliament was on traditional lines as the House of Lords that had disappeared during the civil war was restored, along with the House of Commons. Consequently the bishops also bought their right back to sit in the House of Lords. The number of peers also increased under the later Stuarts. However, the members of House of Common had acquired vital experience during the civil war and were no longer afraid of the king. Although it would be absurd to suggest that the ultimate sovereignty had passed from the crown to the parliament, one can definitely state that the relationship between the crown and the parliament had undergone significant change. The crown was careful and sensitive to the wishes of the parliament and neither were keen to create a situation which they had experienced in the 1640s. In 1672 Charles issued the Declaration of Indulgence granting full toleration to all religions by claiming his right to 'suspend' any law or 'dispense' any individual from its operations. The parliament strongly opposed it and Charles had to withdraw the Declaration. However, the parliament did not have any machinery to impose its will on the king except exerting pressures on financial matters. Its attempts to exclude James, the brother of Charles II from the English throne did not succeed and the Exclusion Bill could not pass the House of Lords after receiving acceptance of the House of the Commons. It was this issue that led to the dissolution of the parliament after a long session of eighteen years. After 1660 the parliament was accepted as a regular part of the government. Unlike his father, Charles II was on a very different footing. His position as a king was strong but he lacked the machinery to reestablish a Tudor form of conciliar or absolute monarchy. The friction on non-parliamentary taxation had almost ended. The king was left with some discretionary powers but he could not use them against the wishes of the House of Commons. The king began to influence the members of the Commons by different means. At election time patronage was used in the form of government and court appointments to get the supporters of the king elected. Those who wanted to oppose king's policies had to organize themselves in the same way, thus leading to the formation of political parties in England.

Religion had been an important source of division during the civil war and it continued to pose a tough challenge even to Oliver Cromwell. The elections of 1661 had brought a large number of Royalists with Anglican and Cavalier sympathies to the parliament. They passed a series of Acts and together these Acts came to be known as the 'Clarendon Code'. It constituted a series of repressive measures against dissenters and aimed to prosecute Puritans who were responsible for the civil war. The Corporation Act (1661) excluded all those men from municipal bodies who refused to announce the Covenant and take the Sacrament according to the rights of the Church of England. They had to swear not to resist the king. The Act of uniformity insisted that the clergy who did not prescribe to the new liturgy must give up their posts. It is estimated that nearly 2,000 ministers lost their livelihood and that this was a far more sweeping change than the one brought about in the civil war. The Five Miles Act (1665) forbade the non-conformist preacher from living or visiting any place within 5 miles of the town. Thus the spread of Puritanism was official curtailed and it increasingly became the religion of a single social class, primarily the middle class. It almost ceased to be a socio-religious movement of different classes. How far this code was enforced is not very clear. The royal administration in the countryside depended on the justices of peace and local gentry for the enforcement of its Acts. They were usually sympathetic to the non-conformists but the latter suffered civil disabilities as they were excluded from the universities and official posts.

Charles II showed great disposition towards the Catholics, while his brother James II was an open convert to Catholicism. The first attempt of Charles in being tolerant to all non-conformist Protestants, including Catholics was not accepted by parliament. In 1678, Charles had made a secret treaty (Treaty of Dover) with the French crown about which even his ministers did not know.

He had promised to re-establish Catholic religion in England and in return Charles was offered substantial financial and military help. By the end of his reign, he had almost become financially independent of parliament because of the secret subsidies from France and the enhanced revenue from overseas trade. The succession of James II (1685–9) generated high tempers and tension on religious issue. The anti-Catholic feeling had united all the Protestants. Although James never imposed Catholicism on England, he issued two declarations of indulgence in 1687 and 1688 in which Catholics were given not only religious toleration but they were appointed at crucial posts. This pushed the members of parliament into a situation where they had to oppose James by appointing his daughter Mary and her husband William of Orange as the joint rulers of England. This came to be known as the glorious revolution of 1688.

The restoration of 1660 also attempted to restore the land belonging to the Royalists. The land settlement was of great significance as it was an attempt to undo the changes that had taken place during the Commonwealth Protectorate. Crown and church lands were confiscated from the purchasers who were not given any compensation. Some of the men holding ecclesiastical property was given the option of becoming tenants of the restored owners. Those lands, which had been confiscated from leading Royalists, wielding political or court influence, were also given back their land. Yet it was not a complete restoration of land. Many Royalists had been compelled to sell their land through commercial transactions in order to pay the heavy fines and taxes placed on them by the republican government and did not receive their lands after restoration. They failed to enact any parliamentary measure to get such lands back and many of them fell into debt. In Ireland, the supporters of Cromwell had acquired a large chunk of property from the Roman Catholic Irish owners during the rebellion of 1652–4. Most of these Protestant landlords retained their land and thus formed the big landowners who exploited Irish peasants. Thus a religious divide that created a war-like situation in Ireland accompanied the economic division and caused immense damage to the Irish people. The Irish problem surfaced soon after the revolution of 1688.

Socio-Economic Changes

Changes in Agrarian relations culminated in 1646 with the abolition of feudal tenures and the Court of Wards. Indirectly it implied that feudal relations of the medieval period had come to an end and this was confirmed in the 1660 restoration. According to Christopher Hill, its importance was manifold. Landed property was greatly consolidated after the Restoration with the removal of several restrictions. It led to the end of dependence of landowners on the crown. While the government could no longer benefit from the lucrative perquisites for courtiers, the landowners gained absolute ownership of their estates. Land became free from various restrictions like the death duties and wardships. This made possible a long-term planning as well as capital investments in estate management. This settlement helped the landowners to survive periods of economic troubles without selling their lands. This was one of the chief reasons for the rise of the Whig oligarchy in the early-eighteenth century. It enabled the younger sons of the landed families to look for new careers in different fields such as the army, navy, business, and the civil services. The lesser gentry was pushed down as the defeat of the radicals proved to be a decisive factor for future development. Another important feature of this period was the abolition of feudal tenures at the upper level. The Act of 1660 had clearly stated that it did not intend to alter or change any tenure by copyhold. As such, the copyholders obtained no absolute property rights in their holdings and continued to remain completely dependent on their landlords and were subject to the old death duties. The Act of 1677 in fact completed the process by which the property of small freeholders was no less insecure than those of copyholders unless it was supported by a written legal title. Thereby most of the hurdles on enclosure were removed and agrarian changes of the late-seventeenth and eighteenth centuries resulted in the benefit of big landowners and capitalist farmers. It did not help the peasant proprietors who faced increasing poverty. They continuously lost ground in the face of rack-rents, heavy fines, taxation and did not have the financial resources to compete with the capitalist farmers. Finally, it is also argued by scholars like Hill that after the abolition of the Court of Wards, the king was compensated not through land tax but from an excise mainly paid by consumers and not by the prosperous landowners. This also proved beneficial to the large landlords. A number of lesser gentry that included many ancient families began to disappear while the process of land agglomerations took place. Land transfers and heavy taxation resulted in a significant redistribution of wealth in which many others, such as lawyers and bankers as well as merchants and government contractors, also derived benefits. Many of them had accumulated quick gains through their speculative investments.

The restoration further consolidated agrarian capitalism and with it began the period of agricultural improvement. The smaller landlords and land proprietors were trapped between falling prices and rising taxes. The big landlords pushed many of them out. In a period of increasing competition more efficient and often larger farmer tenants were able to prevail upon the smaller ones as the competition for markets intensified. Though the new trend created problems for many small landowners, agricultural improvement provided for the increasing population as well as for the industry. Thus during the restoration, the English landlord class became firmly rooted in agricultural capitalism. Its control over the English parliament also grew along with certain commercial groups which became a powerful force in foreign trade.

The restoration also marked a rapid commercial expansion in overseas trade, a process that had started earlier. Some groups of merchants experienced vertical growth by penetrating the newer areas of commerce. In the post-1660 period, English trade in new draperies came to be controlled by foreign merchants. The Levant Company merchants enjoyed extraordinary success through royal monopoly, and a new set of merchants acquired elite status by participating and profiting from the Levant trade. However, the most notable gains were reaped by the merchants in the long-distance trade with Asia, West Indies, North America and Africa.

The great success of the East Indian trade led to an increasing number of interlopers agitating for monopolies of the chartered joint-stock companies. The elite merchants provided strength to the Tory leadership and also backed the monarchy for future gains. The American and West Indian trade in sugar and tobacco doubled in less then half a century. The various barriers to the expansion of trade and commerce were brought down and the re-export trade increased even more rapidly. The revolution of 1688 brought about the consolidation of certain long-term socio-economic patterns of development that had began in the early modern period.

The Revolution of 1688

Religion remained a divisive issue for the nation for most part of the seventeenth century. The restoration of 1660 had sought to address the threat of revival of royal despotism. However, the later Stuarts tried to take advantage of unclear aspects of the settlement by increasing royal powers. Charles II was practical enough to avoid the path of confrontation with his parliaments but James II remained adamant in his beliefs and his policies. This was seen as an attempt to restore a despotic and unparliamentary rule against the spirit of restoration. Religion added fuel to this, as most of the members of parliament were alarmed by the zealous Catholic stance of James II. James alienated his Tory supporters (the advocates of monarchial rule but staunch upholders of Anglican religion) and suspended the penal laws against Catholics and dissenters. He appointed mediocre men on the basis of their religion and his personal liking which aroused widespread reaction. His personal adherence to the Roman Catholic religion threatened the English constitutional structure and the people who had advocated the restoration of the monarchy. James' high-handed religious changes rapidly transformed the situation and brought about the so-called 'Glorious Revolution' of 1688.

The first signs of James' brutal and repressive policy was evident from the manner that Monmouth's rising called the 'Bloody Assize' was suppressed. The people regarded its severity as rather excessive and unnecessary. It was also made obvious that the government, in order to achieve its political ends, was using the judges. In government appointment his friends and Catholics replaced the moderates, even those Tories who had always supported the king. James had granted religious toleration to the dissenters but they hardly cooperated with him because everyone knew that it was done mainly for the Catholics. In the seventeenth century religion, social relations and politics were closely woven and this isolated James II. His interference in local groups and universities threatened the interests of the landed aristocracy and middle-class intellectuals and was seen as an attack on their rights and privileges. His religious policy resulted in a famous constitutional battle between the king and the church of England, called 'the Seven Bishops'. Seven bishops were arrested for not carrying out the religious orders of the king but in court they were acquitted and proved innocent. As Aylmer states, this case 'marks the emancipation of the judiciary'. It led to tremendous jubilation in London and was seen as a moral defeat for the king. The birth of a male child to the queen precipitated the crisis, as the people feared another Catholic successor. A strong opposition arose and the leaders of the two political parties – Whig and Tory – decided to invite Mary, the Protestant daughter of James II and her husband William of Orange, the chief executive of the United Provinces, to come with their army to restore religious and political freedom in England and become their rulers. William was already involved in forming a continental coalition against the French expansionist policy. James fled and parliament declared the throne vacant and placed William and Mary as the joint rulers of England. William assumed the English throne in a bloodless coup. This came to be known as the Glorious Revolution because it took place without bloodshed and it brought an end to half a century of conflict. This was followed by a series of Acts passed by the parliament to formulate constitution arrangements based on English historical experience as well as to rectify the shortcomings of the restoration arrangement. The threat of a civil war ended because the new settlement successfully defended parliamentary prerogatives and brought about a political accord in tune with English traditions.

Issues like religion and taxation, the expanding sphere of the powers of the monarchs were common to most states of Europe but in England it exploded into a constitutional conflict. This was primarily because of the emergence of parliament and those well-developed institutions that enjoyed legitimacy of popular support. The English parliament was more involved in political matters, much more then the representative institutions in other countries. But the real reason of conflict lay in the socio-economic transformation of English society into a capitalist one. The newly emerging capitalist relations within society could effectively challenge a feudal monarchy to bring about a constitutional readjustment.

Constitutional Settlement

The final settlement that brought about a redefinition of the relationship between the crown and the parliament consisted of several Acts, which were passed between 1689 and 1701. It consisted of the Bill of Rights, the Mutiny Act and the Toleration Act, all passed in 1689, the Triennial Act (1694) and the Act of Settlement (1701). It also included the financial settlement to regulate the future functioning of the government. There seems little that was so dramatically new in these Acts to consider the settlement a turning point in English history. Yet the revolution brought about significant and irrevocable consequences in the constitutional history of England.

The revolutionary settlement was the work of the English parliament, which had been deeply divided in two political groups, Whig and Tory. The former was the advocate of parliamentary supremacy and limited powers for the monarchy, while the latter supported the institution of monarchy as the constitutional head with all the traditional powers. The two also had differences over matters concerning religion and the supremacy of the church. The Tories believed that God instituted the king's place in a society and resistance to royal authority was a political as well as a religious offence. Rebellion against a legitimate monarch was seen as a sin. By contrast, the Whigs believed that a government was created to serve human ends and a legally constituted authority should normally be obeyed but if a government endangered the rights of its subjects, it could be overthrown. With these differences, it was not easy to bring about a constitutional settlement acceptable to all. It was made possible because of the behaviour of James II and the disillusionment it caused to his supporters. When James II fled England, the parliament decided to invite his daughter and son-in-law as the future rulers. The very fact that the new rulers were placed on the throne by the wish of the parliament became an Act of constitutional importance. In order to get the support of the Tories, the Whigs brought a moderate solution. The greatness of the revolutionary settlement lay in the fact that it displayed an extremely lenient and moderate spirit towards monarchial powers and it hardly possessed any revolutionary element, as the name suggests.

The declaration of rights set out some of the main grievances of the English parliament against the government of James II and listed the reforms that parliament insisted upon. William and Mary became the king and the queen only after accepting these conditions. The Bill of Rights was more in the nature of restatement of the rights that the subjects of England already possessed through the Petition of Right (1628) from the time of Charles I. The 'Suspending powers', which had been used by the later Stuarts, were abolished and 'Dispensing powers' were condemned. The parliament swept away the Ecclesiastical courts and condemned levying taxes without parliamentary consent. There was hardly anything new in all these except one – the power of the king to keep a standing army during times of peace was destroyed. This power came to be based on a statute. Besides, it became impossible for a king or his wife to be a Roman Catholic. The Bill of Right also exhibited the Whig concept of monarchy. The king was given the throne through a contract between him and the parliament, but this did not make it a Whig revolution.

The Mutiny Act tried to solve the controversy over the king's control of the standing army. The Mutiny Act defined the special obligation of military discipline and stated that military discipline be maintained through court-martial. The parliament recognized that a standing army was necessary because of the war in which England was involved. Hence parliament decided to control the army through financial settlement. Instead of voting a substantial lifetime revenue to the king, as had been done in the cases of Charles II and James II, parliament decided to make annual grants and it also 'appropriated' particular taxes for this purpose, thus ensuring parliamentary control over the main departments of the government. This led to annual parliamentary sessions. The Toleration Act was also passed the same year and this was equally modest in its approach. It gave freedom of worship to all those who accepted thirty-six of the thirty-nine Articles. This Act also remitted many of the punishments inflicted by Clarendon Code, but the Catholics did not get freedom to carry out private worship till 1828. Those who refused to take the oath of allegiance were liable to pay a fine or could be imprisoned. Thus although called Toleration Act it did not grant full toleration to all English subjects.

The Triennial Act of 1694 and the Freedom of Press Act were the supplementary Acts brought about by the whig parliament. It ensured that parliament should meet at least once every three years. This Act in practice became unnecessary as annual parliament to maintain the standing army had become a common practice. The Act of Settlement was the product of the English experience of a foreign ruler who had drawn England in a foreign wars and had made appointments of outsiders in the English administration. Hence this Act proved to be most far-reaching of all the Acts because it stated that the decision of the Privy Council could not be evaded, and that crown officials were not eligible to be members of the House of Commons or judges. There was nothing innovatory in these measures except that England was not to be involved in a war without parliamentary consent in territories not belonging to England, that foreigners were prohibited from becoming members of the Privy Council and the royal pardon was not to be applicable in cases of impeachment. Thus the revolutionary settlement decided the constitutional relationship between the crown and the parliament for the future. Its glory rested in its conservatism. It made the king and the parliament partners and neither alone was supreme. As David Lindsay Keir (*The Constitutional History of Modern Britain, 1485–1937*) writes, that in practice the Revolutionary Settlement had set up a constitutional monarchy by prescribing the limits within which the king could work.

Consequences

For most Englishmen of the eighteenth and nineteenth centuries, the revolution of 1688–9 was indeed 'glorious'. It ensured the failure of James II's attempts to establish a Catholic absolutism and made possible the continuation and extension of the great English traditions of parliamentary government and the rule of law. The most important statement on the significance of the revolution came from Lord Macaulay, who saw the seeds of every good and liberal law enacted in the next one and a half centuries in this event, while Trevelyan suggested that the Revolution gave to England an ordered and legal freedom and through that it gave her power. In recent years there have been divergent opinions on the real significance of this Revolution. Much of the misconceptions concerning the Revolution stemmed from the writings of John Locke, published barely a year after the Revolution. In his *Two Treatises of Government,* he justified the revolution and in his *Second Treatises,* he tried to provide an analysis of it. Locke considered those men rational who saw political societies as a means of achieving individual and collective benefits. Only such societies were capable of creating a framework of laws to resolve disputes (pertaining to property, etc.). The formation of such political societies was possible only because its members had agreed to give up some of their rights and liberties to form a common set of laws. These laws could be amended or extended by a legislature and were to be enforced by an executive which should be a part of legislature but which could not dominate it. If the same people dominated the two institutions, it could lead to tyranny. John Locke had not clearly spelt out the nature of the contract between the ruler and the ruled. He stated that a contract gave the ruler rights and obligation and he was expected to serve those particular ends. In his second work he carried out an extreme restatement of patriarchal view and denied anybody exercising to rule only authority as a right. The right of governance had to be vested in the political community as a whole. Similarly, the concept of a trust also remained unclear though he insisted that authority could be taken away if it was not used for the common good. Hence, whether a ruler was elected by the legislature or by the whole community and whether he could be removed by force or through a popular opposition, was not made clear by Locke. His views were presented in an abstract theoretical form and were subject to different interpretations.

The evolution of the English constitution after the revolution was less due to the Bill of Rights than to the new reality of the crown's financial weakness and the impact of the French wars that caused unprecedented administrative, financial and political strains. Consequently, in these new conditions the relationship between the crown and the parliament developed in a way that could not be foreseen by the participants of the revolutionary settlement. The influence of the crown extended not through prerogative but by monetary favours. Under George I and II the crown's patronage was skilfully used to manage the parliament. The war situation led to an enormous growth of armed forces and administrative departments. The war transformed finances and eventually turned Britain into a world power. It is estimated that the disbanded army of Charles II in 1680 consisted of about seven to eight thousand troops whereas William III's army stood at nearly one hundred thousand. In 1683, the ordinance office had about sixty officers but by 1704 the number had gone up to 450 (according to H. Tomlinson). There was also the expansion of revenue administration in which corruption and large-scale bribery of politicians was done to establish the crown's control and as a form of political patronage.

While most historians consider the Revolution of 1688 an important event in English history that marked the beginning of changes leading to the creation of modern Britain, there are some who challenge this viewpoint. Christopher Hill challenged the Whig interpretation of Macaulay and Trevelyan. Karl Marx also saw the Revolution of 1688 as no more than a mere 'palace coup'. Marxists historians generally ignore this event rather than challenge it and consider the events from 1640 to 1660 of greater importance in the socio-economic development of England. So the Revolution of 1688 is seen as the culmination of the events of the seventeenth century, bringing a solution to a long period of conflict and not merely an isolated episode.

In recent years, historians have tried to reexamine the importance of the events of the 1680s in relation to socio-economic and constitutional developments. It is argued that it was not in 1660, rather in 1688–9 that some solutions to the constitutional problems were found. The importance of the Glorious Revolution, according to John Miller, lay in what it prevented and what it brought about. It prevented the restoration of absolute rule and the royal prerogatives and it also prevented the Catholic revival. As far as the second is concerned, there was a difference between the intentions of the men who brought about the settlement and what consequently happened. For most people, the intention was to carry out a restoration rather than innovation – patching up the old constitution and making it workable. The revolution was neither a populist one nor a radical one. One of the revisionist view is (scholars like Jonathan Israel) that the revolution was brought about from the outside as a successful invasion, accompanied by much larger forces than those at the disposal of James II. It was motivated by strategic and diplomatic European consideration and not the domestic English one. The unpopularity of James II and his policies provided the pretext for the invasion, and it took a superior army to drive out James. This view also suggests that the Glorious Revolution did not solve all the problems encountered by the Stuarts. Its immediate effects on Britain are presumed to be deeply divisive. It provided the longest struggle on the question of royal succession. Moreover, according to this view, the years after 1715 did not mark a steady progress towards a constitutional monarchy. The Whigs paid only lip service to the revolutionary principles. Besides many of the gains of the revolution were lost in the period of George I who was one of the most inflexible and authoritarian rulers of that period. He created a one-party state and controlled Parliament through his ministers.

The second view agrees that the settlement was not revolutionary in character, yet it marked a period of transformation and brought about a permanent solution to the constitutional struggle. G.E. Aylmer argues that in many other respects the revolutionary events were of great and lasting importance. The settlement led to the restoration of upper-class supremacy that was already experienced in the Restoration of 1660. The peers and gentry, who formed the ruling oligarchies in the towns, were able to control local government and the militia and corporate privileges were restored. Although not mentioned in the settlement the annual sitting of the English parliament became a permanent feature. The revolution also brought about, though in a limited manner, the principles of religious tolerance based on liberal and progressive ideas.

Thus we find that the Revolution of 1688 and the subsequent legislations placed the unified state of England under parliamentary control and ended the oft-repeated threat of absolutism. The crown and parliament were made mutually dependent in sharp contrast to the political structure of France, where patrimonial monarchy had achieved an advanced degree of authority by completely ignoring the national representative institutions. The English parliament, particularly the House of Commons, by formulation of precise appropriate clauses, established control over the money it voted to the king. This destroyed the independence of the monarchy in financial matters, including taxation. By its own legislation, the parliament had expanded its own sphere of influence.

The defeat of absolutist attempts of the English monarch resulted in the domination of English capitalist aristocracy. As opposed to a patrimonial administrative structure, the class of capitalists landlord as a whole helped in the formation of a bureaucratic structure. Parliamentary rule was consolidated through control of taxation and it helped in the creation of certain basic conditions for the establishment of an institutional framework for the commercial and financial revolution. In matters of trade and chartering of commercial companies, parliament assumed a central position. It created conditions for greater mobilization of capital in overseas enterprises by chartering the New East India Company in 1694 at the expense of influential merchant oligarchies linked with the crown. The exclusive privileges of the Hudson Bay Company were taken away in 1697, the monopoly rights of the Royal African Company were destroyed in 1698 and the Russian company's control of tobacco re-export was taken away in 1699. The London merchant groups associated with long-distance unregulated trade and closely linked with the Whigs began to enter, enlarge and transform the new commercial enterprises. In short, the Revolution of 1688 and the subsequent settlement were able to realize the original objectives of the parliamentary capitalist aristocracy by early-eighteenth century.

The late-seventeenth century is also considered important for the emergence of rudimentary political parties. Although the contours of modern political party system were still to emerge, political groups appeared to control the members of parliament. The major line of division was between the supporters and the opponents of the church and the king. Those who supported these institutions were called the 'court party' while their opponents came to be known as the 'country party'. The formation of rival groups into political parties were more noticeable after the Exclusion Bill was passed in the House of Commons to exclude James II from the throne. Since not all were in favour of exclusion, the lines of demarcation were redrawn and were becoming more noticeable. Later they were called the Tory and the Whig parties. These terms were used more in the nature of criticism of each other. Those who supported Shaftesbury and who wanted to exclude James from the English throne, were called Exclusionists and as in the absence of parliamentary session they organized public meetings and sent petitions, they were also called the petitioners. The supporters of the court who were prepared to follow the king's solution and abhorred encroachment on royal prerogative, produced rival manifestos and came to be known as Abhorrers. Their opponents gave them derogatory nicknames. The petitioners were called Whiggamores, named after Presbyterian guerrilla fighters in the south-west of Scotland. This was shortened into Whigs. On the other hand, the pro-crown group was named Tory after the Irish Catholic guerrillas fighting in the hills of Ireland. The two groups played an extremely important role not only in bringing about the revolutionary settlement but also in the subsequent period. The Tories came to be the upholders of the church of the England and of the royal prerogative while the Whigs wanted limited royal prerogative. Queen Anne (1702–13) trusted the Tories more and selected almost all the ministers from that group while the subsequent Hanoverian rulers showed greater confidence in the Whigs. This led to Whig supremacy and a virtual rule of the Whig oligarchy after 1714. The formation of political parties subsequently helped in the emergence of other constitutional institutions such as the cabinet system and the institution of the prime minister.

Intellectual and Cultural Trends

The Restoration of 1660 and the revolutionary era of the later seventeenth century was significant for the emergence of the modern world and new cultural trends. It marked the rise of the modern science, particularly in the fields of mathematics and physics. It was the period of experimental science, a method put forward by Sir Francis Bacon and Robert Boyle which discarded Aristotle's idea that chemistry was based on four elements. The formation of the Royal Society of London took place soon after the restoration. The scientific and mathematical discoveries of Newton established new grounds for modern knowledge and research and helped the cause of scientific activities by preparing a suitable atmosphere for it. These were the years of scientific exchanges and formulation of new laws. The publication of Newton's *Principia* in 1687 brought a new epoch in science. This also had a profound impact on the public attitude towards superstitions and probably caused a decline in the practice of witchcraft.

Like in science, the period after restoration is seen as a turning point from medievalism to modernity and it influenced music and art as well. The process of change can be seen during the Commonwealth when music and art in England became secular subjects, though the Restoration did bring about a revival in church music. Before the civil war, English music mainly consisted of madrigals. After the Restoration, changes began when the first public concerts took place. Violin was introduced as a musical instrument and the first popular English opera was written by Henry Purcell, a man of extraordinary qualities and extremely versatile. The period of Charles II witnessed a change in English drama and literature. The Puritans had suppressed theatre and drama and most of the theatres had been closed down. After 1660 a new period began. Scenery was introduced on stage with audience participat-ion. Women actresses starting taking part in bigger numbers and began replacing boys who had earlier performed female roles in Shakespeare's time. Plays were particularly popular among the courtiers. The themes included tragedies and melodrama, tales of love and passion written by famous writers like John Dryden, Thomas Otway and William Congreve. The most famous work was *The Conquest of Granada* by Dryden. Writers like Sedley, Wycherley and Shadwell wrote some comedies of manners. The most marked characteristic of literature of that period was satire. The Duke of Buckingham wrote a wonderful piece named *The Rehearsal.* English prose of this period was concerned mainly with politics or religion and newspaper journalism became popular as an accepted means of reporting events and spreading political ideas. The *London Gazette* was an important newspaper of that period. This period also witnessed the creation of political theory of aristocracy by writers like Milton, Marvell, Sidney and Henry Nevile. These writings had great bearing on England and America during the eighteenth century. However it was John Locke who was recognized as the greatest political thinker of the seventeenth century. Thus we find that whereas seventeenth century England was a time of political breakdown, it was also an important time of significant political and cultural changes which led to the creation of modern England – the basis on which industrialization and a modern parliamentary system could evolve.

Some Important Events of the Civil War and Constitutional Developments

1603–25	James I's rule.
1603	Millenary Petition.
1604	Hampton Court Conference seeking moderate religious changes.
1605	Gunpowder Plot.
1610	The proposal of Great Contract.
1614–15	The Cockayne Project, failure to reform custom revenue.
1614	Addled parliament.
1624	Monopolies Act, declaring grant of monopoly illegal.
1625	Accession of Charles I.
1628	Petition of Right against non-parliamentary taxation and arbitrary imprisonment.
1629–40	Personal rule of Charles I

1640	The work of long parliament begins.
1642–9	The period of civil war ending with the execution of Charles I and the abolition of monarchy.
1649–60	Period of Commonwealth and Protectorate, constitutional experiments of Oliver Cromwell.
1660	Restoration of monarchy, traditional Parliament and Anglican religion. Charles II comes to the English throne.
1661–79	The cavalier parliament, emergence of party and cabinet system.
1678	Habeas Corpus Act to protect individual liberty.
1679–81	The Exclusion Crisis.
1685–8	The reign of James II, attempts of reverting to absolutist rule and Catholicism.
1688–9	The Glorious Revolution, the replacement of James by William III and Mary.
1689–1701	The Revolutionary Settlement consisting of several Acts of parliament leading to the system of constitutional monarchy.

Suggested Readings

Aylmer, G.E., *The Struggle for Constitution*, London: Mentor, 1963. A brief analytical presentation of the major trends of seventeenth-century England.

Brenner, Robert, *Merchants and Revolution: Commercial Change, Political Conflict and London's Overseas Traders 1550-1653*, Cambridge: Cambridge University Press, 1993. Contains a very important discussion on economic transformation of England and its repercussions on the ruling classes and the state.

Caine, T.G.S. and Ken Robinson, eds., *Into Another Mould: Change and Continuity in English Culture, 1625–1700*, London/New York: Routledge, 1992. Examines social, political, cultural, religious beliefs of that period that includes painting, sculpture and the political ideas.

Carlin, Norah, *The First English Revolution*, London: Socialist Party Press, 1983.

Clark, J.C.D., *Revolution and Rebellion: State and Society in England in the Seventeenth and Eighteenth Centuries*, Cambridge: Cambridge University Press, 1986. Places revolutionary and political changes in context of the socio-economic changes.

Cruickshanks, Eveline, *The Glorious Revolution*, London: Macmillan, 2000. Presents not only a good narrative but also recent views on the subject.

Hill, Christopher, *A Century of Revolution: 1603–1714*, New York: Nelson,

1982. Discusses the English developments by stressing economic and social trends. A valuable survey.
———, *The Collected Essays of Christopher Hill*, vol. III, *People and Ideas in 17th Century England*, Brighton: Harvester Press, 1986.
———, *Change and Continuity in 17th Century England*, New Haven: Yale University Press, 1991.
———, *The World Turned Upside Down: Radical Ideas During the English Revolution*, Harmondsworth: Penguin, 1984.
Miller, John, *The Glorious Revolution*, London: Longman, 1983. Brief but analytical presentation with a few short documents.
Morrill, John, *The Nature of the English Revolution*, London: Longman, 1993. An extensive collection of twenty essays on the issues of the civil war.
Plumb, J.H., *The Growth of Political Stability in England, 1675–1725*, London: Macmillan, 1967. A well-researched work on political trends in England in the formative stage.
Russell, Conrad, *The Crisis of Parliaments: English History, 1509–1660*, Oxford: Oxford University Press, 1971. An analytical account of the English political developments and maintains that the role of the Parliament in bringing about the civil war has been overstated by scholars.
Smith, Alan G.R., *The Emergence of Modern State: The Commonwealth of England 1529–1660,* London: Longman, 1984.
Stone, Lawrence, *The Causes of the English Revolution 1529–1642*, London: Routledge & Kegan Paul, 1972. Provides a social analysis of the English Revolution in a judicious way.

CHAPTER 10

Ideas and Practice of Mercantilism

With the discovery of new trade routes and trans-oceanic empires, the volume of trade started growing from the late-fifteenth century and international shipping expanded with it. The influx of large quantities of gold and silver from the New World and the luxury products from the east, began to change the fortunes of European states and their populace. The operations of the merchants and the manufacturers slowly helped to transform the face of Western European society through the introduction of new goods and manufactures. This had a direct and indirect influence on state policies. Emerging states like Britain, France and Netherlands, attempted to bring together economic thought and state policies. A close link was gradually established between the ideas of economic writers and thinkers with the legislative acts of the European governments. This merger of ideas and policies focusing on economic strength of the state came to be described as 'mercantilism'. The term usually applied to the policies and measures which the European states adopted between the fifteenth and eighteenth centuries to acquire wealth and power.

It is difficult to define the exact meaning of mercantilism because none of the European states adopted identical policies. The economic policy of the European states did not have any coherence and their actions were governed by different circumstances. This problem led T.W. Hutchinson to suggest that historians and economists should get rid of the word mercantilism altogether which he described as 'one of the vaguest and most irritating "isms" in the language'. Henri Chambre wrote that 'there are as many mercantilisms as there are mercantilists'. Despite variations in definitions, the term mercantilism is usually adopted to describe the policies of economic nationalism that were followed by the rising states of modern Europe.

Several definitions have been provided to describe the term mercantilism. For example, according to the *Oxford English Dictionary*, mercantilism was a system of economic doctrine and legislative policy based on the principle that money alone is wealth. When we apply this definition in the historical context, it appears inadequate and unacceptable. Similarly, in UNESCO's *Dictionary of Social Sciences*, the term mercantile denotes the principles of a mercantile system, sometimes understood as the identification of wealth with money; but more generally, the belief that the economic welfare of the state can only be secured by government regulation of a nationalist character. The concept of mercantilism has not been given much importance in Marxist writings. For Karl Marx, it was the ideology of monopoly trading companies. Maurice Dobb describes it as a system of state-regulated exploitation through trade and considered it essentially an economic policy of an age of primitive accumulation. Numerous other definitions have been provided by scholars, but the most appropriate one is by Cole and Clough who state that mercantilism is the name given to that group of ideas and practices particularly characteristic of the three hundred years from 1500 to 1800 by which the nation state acting in the economic sphere sought by methods of control to secure its own unity and power.

There are two different interpretations of the 'mercantilist system'. The first, by classical economists, is based primarily on economic evaluation. They generally condemn the basic principles of mercantilism. German historical economists have provided the second view. They deflect it in the direction of state power and approve it.

A prominent classical political economist was Adam Smith. This British economist in his famous work, *Wealth of Nations*, published in 1776, coined the term mercantilism or mercantile system. Economic historians like Gustav Schmoller of Germany and Eli Heckscher of Sweden also use this term. Heckscher wrote two volumes titled *Mercantilism*, which were published in 1931.

All these authors used the term to describe government policy on economic matters based on a set of ideas. The word 'system' implied that these ideas were followed by a number of states at roughly the same time. While Adam Smith and Heckscher's works are extremely critical of mercantilist policies, Schmoller had great admiration for the system and many others such as J.M. Keynes, another British economist, appreciated the ideas of mercantilism. For Schmoller, 'mercantile system' implied the relationship between political institutions and national prosperity and power. Economic and political interests, according to him, went hand in hand. His account of the central features of mercantilist thought and his description of the apparatus of legislation and policy enforcement had some similarities with those of Adam Smith. But while Smith condemned it, Schmoller applauded it. To understand the ideas and practice of mercantilism, one has to keep in mind the context of the time when they were developed and the local variations in different parts of Europe. As G.N. Clark points out, the explanation of mercantilist attitude seems to lie in the commercial conditions of the time, and especially in the needs of traders for 'capital in a solid and ponderable' form. It is true that the practice of mercantilism varied from one state to another and even the ideas were not exactly the same everywhere. State policies were at times influenced by practical reality. But at the same time, there was always the influence of pamphleteers, authors of treatises and policy makers. None of them called themselves mercantilists because they did not belong to any specific school of economic thought. They were only making suggestions or writing on specific local economic or political predicaments.

Origins

The mercantilists adopted policies of economic nationalism in many European states. These policies had their roots in the scattered acts and beliefs of feudal and municipal authorities in the medieval period and were by no means new ideas. There was very little intellectual element or logic within it. Most of these ideas revealed distrust of strangers, peculiar reverence for the special merits of gold and silver and gave significance to institutions based on corporate bondage such as guilds. These were based on restrictions, imposition of authority and regimentation. Mercantilism of the sixteenth century transformed these earlier concepts of the smaller economic units of towns or guilds to the level of the entire state. It did not represent a complete change but gave clear indication that thinkers, administrators and the government of the new states in Europe had brought some coherence to their ideas on economic subjects. With the expansion of trade and the declining revenues of the feudal states, with the emergence of centralized monarchies and larger and more luxurious courts, the emerging states realized the value of trade that brought wealth and greater revenue for the state. It was believed that the wealth of the subjects was the wealth of the kings. This led to active government intervention in economic and political matters and became the central feature of all mercantilist ideas. The chief task of the government was to regulate the economic life of the subjects according to their own ideas. However, the policies adopted by different states varied according to the economic and social conditions prevalent in each state. For mercantilist ideas to succeed, a reasonable development of trade and commerce was necessary. Hence, it can be said that the mercantilist policies and practices could only be adopted in states that had strong governments and a reasonably well-developed trade. It was aimed at strengthening the centralized state structure by weakening and regulating the semi-independent local authorities. It is for this reason that Richard S. Dunn observed 'that mercantilists were always patriots'. In the beginning, the policies of the mercantilist State revealed a wave of nationalism – a desire to defend the frontiers by customs tolls. In the fourteenth century, Castile forbade the exports of grain and livestock (1307, 1312, 1371, 1377 and 1390). France placed an embargo on grain exports in 1305 and 1307; Aragon introduced navigation laws that aimed at controlling foreign trade, while the English placed restrictions on the import of iron in 1355. According to Braudel, 'there was nothing new about the major decisions of classic mercantilism'.

The Chief Ideas of Mercantilism

The mercantilist ideas emphasized government stimulation, supervision and protection of the state's economy. It was an attempt to increase the power of the state and the efficiency of the national government. The mercantilist ideas held that a state's power depended on the actual and calculable wealth, which could be described only in terms of gold and silver bullion. For that the national state required unity and power. This was described as *étatism*. Most of the states sought to gain their strength and power by organizing armies and navy and by waging wars against weak neighbours. Economic *étatism* implied search for control. The states tried to regulate industrial commerce, control taxation and made economic regulations which were earlier carried on by the town, the province, the feudal lords or by the church. In other words, it was the transfer of authority from the lower level of administration to the state level. Wealth was not seen as an economic concept but as a means to reinforce the strength of the state. The mercantilists aimed at protecting the merchants and manufacturers against foreign competition. Even the merchants supported the state although at times it hampered or restricted their activities. Every mercantilist state had its own brand of mercantilism – the Portuguese mercantilism was based on spice trade, Spanish mercantilism was directly related to the bullion trade of America, the Dutch concentrated on shipping and cargo trade, the English focused on manufacturing and colonial regulation while the French paid great attention to their industries, commerce, colonies and navy.

Bullionism was one of the most important tenets of European mercantilism. The importance of gold and silver increased with the discovery of new lands. As the Spanish empire expanded and dominated Europe after its conquest of the New World and reached its pinnacle of glory in the sixteenth century, it was believed by most economic writers and policy makers that the real reason behind the Spanish success was the availability of bullion. As Daniel Dessert says, for the mercantilists, metal money was the only true measure of all things. In fact, the conquest and subsequent plundering of the American colonies by Spain is the best example of mercantilism at work on a large scale. The vast supply of silver to Spain was regarded as a major windfall and many European governments wished to follow the Spanish example in their search for new colonies. A number of treatises were written on this subject. The most famous was that of Antonio Serra's *Brief Discourse on a Possible Means of Causing Gold and Silver Abound in Kingdoms Where There are No Mines* (1630). Serra was convinced that the poverty of Naples was, to a great extent, due to the scarcity of specie. To overcome the problem of metal deficiency, Antonio Serra suggested large-scale export of manufactured commodities, which would bring gold and silver into the kingdom. In many states the export of coins and bullion was not encouraged. In France, Jacques Coeur was severely criticized for allegedly sending money out of the kingdom. French writers also criticized the papal authorities for taking money out of France, because as a *cahier* stated in 1484 money in the body politic is what blood is to the human body. This drain of silver from England also became a major subject of debate between the supporters and opponents of the English East India Company.

An important idea emphasized by the mercantilist states was the balance of trade. It became the leading theme of several writers. As gold and silver were the chief wealth for the mercantilists, the European states tried to retain it in their own territories by controlling the import-export exchanges. Those countries that had no mines at home or in their colonies adopted specific measures to build-up exports and reduce imports so that the money could be used for commerce. In its more developed form, it came to be known as the doctrine of balance of trade. It held the view that only by a surplus of exports over imports could a state amass wealth and power. Subsequently, it resulted in the idea of balance of payments that took into consideration not only the sale and purchase of commodities, but also the amounts spent on freight, insurance, tolls or travel expenses. Numerous memoirs and treatises were written on the subject of balance of trade. In England, Gresham observed that according to the custom calculations in the period of Edward III, exports had exceeded imports. Later, William Cholemeley, a London grocer argued that the exports were far less than the imports and that treasure was being drained overseas as a result. There was a constant pressure on the state to adopt legislative measures to regulate the flow of goods outside and inside the state. Adam Smith's severe criticism of mercantilism was against the policy of rigid control of foreign trade.

Emphasis on mines, manufacturing and industry was universal among the European mercantilist states. Policies were formulated by each nation to achieve self-sufficiency and produce all that it required and to have a surplus of export. To be self-sufficient, it was believed that a country must produce every kind of manufactured goods. It must nurture and protect its industries and start new industries by giving concessions and favours to those who contributed in their objective. Foreigners with industrial skills were to be offered incentives as had happened in the case of Holland where skilled artisans were invited to come and settle from different regions. Agriculture was given importance primarily to encourage the production of raw materials, such as wool, flax, silk or hemp, for the industries.

The mercantilists also laid great stress on the role of colonies. In fact, mercantilism to a large extent developed as a result of the colonial empires. The mercantilists had discovered the South American silver and the Caribbean sugar industry as the chief source for new wealth. For a mercantalist, colonies were important for several reasons. They provided market for the manufactured products of the country and produced raw materials that could not be produced at home. Colonies also became a source of employment and an important basis for trade. They added to the prestige of a country and hence we notice that a large number of European countries from the sixteenth century constantly endeavoured to create their own colonies by reaching out to new lands. Mercantilist ideas and practices resulted in a series of colonial wars among the European powers. The three naval wars between England and Holland and another three wars between France and Holland were primarily caused by mercantilist ideas. Closely associated with this aspect was the importance of sea power. To send goods to foreign markets and to control distant regions, a country required a large number of merchant ships. Moreover, to implement tariff regulations and to protect sea trade against foreigners and pirates, a powerful navy was considered important to threaten opponents, to open up new markets and to enhance the prestige of a country. The French ministers, Richelieu and Colbert made special efforts to develop the French navy during the seventeenth century. It was with this navy that France was able to challenge English supremacy over the seas throughout the eighteenth century.

Mercantilism in the European States

As mentioned earlier, every European state had its own concept of mercantilism and it followed a mercantilist policy in accordance with its own economic strengths and needs. The beginning of an effective mercantilist practice can be seen in the case of Italian states, particularly those of Venice and Genoa. The Venetians had established powerful control over trade which came through the eastern land route. The Venetian government placed strict control over the luxury products passing through the Mediterranean Sea. Foreign merchants were not permitted to participate inside the state and state monopoly was created over the trade. The Venetians also developed a vast fleet of small ships and no European power could challenge their supremacy. However, towards the end of the fifteenth century, the Portuguese activities in the sea and the discovery of new regions led to the eclipse of Venetian power.

The economic interest of Portugal was related to Africa and Asia. The Portuguese under royal supervision had carried out sea exploration for new trade routes to the east. The trade was carried on by the royal ships or by merchants who were given license by the king. The new spice trade, along the sea route became a royal monopoly supervised by royal officers. The king strictly controlled the pepper trade, and the capital and the resources were provided by the crown. This monopoly enabled the king to buy pepper at a very low cost and to sell it to the merchants outside Portugal at an exorbitant price. Although Portugal remained under Spanish rule from 1580 to 1640 and the Portuguese interests were subordinated to Spain, the Portuguese trade ventures continued, though later Portugal lost its monopoly in the eastern seas. During the sixteenth century, the crown monopoly remained effective, which resulted in the creation of the first overseas empire by a European state. To retain control over the sources of luxury trade, the Portuguese used naval gunnery and kept all knowledge of sea navigation a closely-guarded secret. The early success of the Portuguese directed by the crown opened the way for other European powers. It must be noted that the Portuguese mercantilism remained exclusively commercial in which the state played a crucial role in formulating trade policy and the king became the symbol of the nation. To run this eastern trade, the Portuguese kings often resorted to large-scale borrowings from the German and Italian banker merchants and the money market of Antwrep.

According to Richard S. Dunn, the Spanish empire of the sixteenth century was the first great mercantilist state and, at the same time, it was the last great Catholic crusading state. In Spain, certain mercantilist tendencies could be noticed from the thirteenth century itself. Their ruler, Alfonso X, placed restrictions on the export of gold and silver in 1268. This was continued in the fourteenth and fifteenth centuries also. Death penalty could be awarded to a person for sending bullion or coin out of the country by a law of 1471. In the early-sixteenth century, several state regulations were issued to check the illegal export of money. However, despite legislative measures the efforts of the state failed because the Spanish crown remained financially starved and borrowed from outside sources at high interest rates, which drained money from the country. The state adopted some other measures, which reflect mercantilist practices. Castile placed restrictions on the import of wine in 1390. In 1491, Ferdinand and Isabella imposed state order which provided that all those merchants who brought goods to be sold in Spain must export an equivalent amount of Spanish goods within a period of twelve months.

The Spanish crown adopted strict mercantilist legislation to retain monopoly control over the American colonies. This in fact was the best illustration of mercantilist ideas and practices. The crown faced extreme difficulty in administering such a vast territory in the New World, which was several times larger than the actual size of Spain. All the colonies were divided into different categories to be ruled directly or indirectly by Spain. The royal council of the Indies was created to supervise the distant colonies and *Casa de Contratacion* (House of Trade) was founded in 1503 to regulate colonial trade. The twin objectives of protecting and monopolizing colonial trade and the state decision to ensure that bullion reached Spain directly, led to a series of restrictive policies and a rigid system of controls. All colonial trade had to pass through a single port of Cadiz till 1503 and after 1717, while between 1503 and 1717 Seville was the only port to receive colonial goods. A merchant's court was also created in 1543 called *Consulado*. Although the trade restrictions aimed at safety and control, it cramped colonial development. The government imposed *alcabala* (sales tax), which was collected by the crown. Even products like wine, vinegar, meat and oil were placed under excise tax. It is generally argued that such restrictions adversely affected the economic growth of Spain and prevented the accumulation of capital in the hands of merchants. However, the Spanish shipping industry had grown enormously because of colonial requirements. But it was not able to manage the colonial trade by itself, despite the crown monopoly and the foreign merchants benefited from this situation. In another mercantilist measure the Spanish government promoted wool instead of cloth-making. It entrusted monopoly rights to the *mesta* farmers who appropriated all the rights concerning the production and sale of wool and the government assisted them in the export of wool and *mesta* sheep farmers enjoyed royal favour till 1836. But the Spanish economy was the loser because the monopoly to the *mesta* wool farmers ultimately affected agriculture adversely as lands for crop cultivation were converted into pastures and that made Spain dependent on foreign supplies.

English Mercantilism

England emerged as a reasonably unified state at the end of the fifteenth century. Its central government enjoyed power over the cities and localities and thus in England national regulations on the mercantilist lines were enacted at an early date. The salient features of English mercantilism continued to shift from the end of the fifteenth to the late-eighteenth centuries. These included emphasis on bullionism and balance of trade and commerce, regulation of domestic industries and manufacturing activities and from the second half of the seventeenth century, the mercantilist emphasis shifted to navigation laws and colonial regulation. Thus, every aspect of economic life was stimulated and regulated by the central government.

From Henry VII's time, the first Tudor king, the government tried to enrich the royal treasury through trade and bullion. The subsequent rulers continued this policy more vigorously. To control manufacturing activity and make the country prosperous, and promote industry a set of complicated regulations were carried out. The Statute of Artificiers in 1563 was implemented by bringing together a number of earlier laws to regulate employment and check transfer of industry to rural districts. It also tried to provide proper training to the workers to enhance the quality of English products. Earlier, the Weavers' Act of 1555 attempted to check the putting-out system. It was a system in which the merchant provided the raw material to the workers working from their homes and then received the finished products after paying for the labour. The aim of the merchant was to bypass the cumbersome and rigid guild system. No merchant clothier was allowed to control more than one loom and two apprentices. Each weaver was to compulsory serve an apprenticeship of seven years. To maintain the quality and to prevent fraud, checks on weights and measures were introduced and the justices of peace in every region were asked to supervise them. Plans for new industries like linen manufacture and the cultivation of crops such as hemp and flax, which provided industrial raw materials, were introduced. All these measures were closely tied to the idea of reducing imports and boosting exports. Export of wool and leather was forbidden in 1559. In 1605, the English woollens were placed under the state's authority and quality dimension inspected by officials. The next year, the use of gum was forbidden for dyeing silk to prevent deterioration in quality. In 1613, royal inspectors were appointed to control the production of silk. One important feature of English mercantilism like French and the Spanish was the importance given to monopolistic institutions.

Seven monopolies were granted for the production of specific products or to carry out trade in specific regions to selected group of merchants or associations. Under Elizabeth, her minister Burleigh aided the formation of the joint stock Mines Royal Company (1568) to exploit the copper and iron mines of Northumberland and Keswick. Monopolies were also granted to strengthen some industries and also to steer profits to court favourites. Charles I gave monopoly rights to select merchants to manufacture soap, salt, wine and to coal dealers. However, a strong political opposition was already developing against his rule and parliament opposed it and these monopolies had to be withdrawn. A famous project called Cockayne project was prepared on mercantilist lines that tried to forbid the export of undyed cloth. However, the real object was to help the Eastland merchants who were trading in the Baltic region and faced competition from other places. To encourage the export of English products, treaties with foreign states were signed. It began in the time of Henry VII when two important treaties – *Malus Intercurses* and *Magnus Intercurses* – were signed with Flanders, one of the chief manufacturing centres of Europe, specializing in woollen textiles. These enabled English merchants to sell their products on preferential treatment without paying duties.

The Tudor government also passed a number of Poor Laws to check the increase of undesirable elements in the towns. A series of laws passed in 1536, 1563, 1572, and 1576 which were combined into an important Act in 1601. The Act declared that a tax or 'poor rate' was to be assessed and collected in each locality by the parish authorities. Able-bodied poor were to be provided with work. Bridewell in London was the famous poor house where all persons who refused to work were sent. At times, they were whipped until they changed their minds. Pauper children were given training in some useful trade. The Privy Council issued orders in 1586 directing the authorities to provide good quality grain to the poor at reasonable prices during bad harvests. All able-bodied men were to pursue some trade and poor relief was strictly supervised only for those who actually needed support. At the same time, the government also tried to control the entry of outsiders into specific crafts to prevent the decline in the quality of manufactured products. No labourer was to be hired till he possessed a letter of recommendation from his last employer. The Justices of Peace were given the authority to fix the pay of workers. Although these rules were not implemented effectively at all the places and there were some irrational enforcement of laws, these measures reflect the mercantilist trends in state policy.

Bullionist regulations were also enforced based on the general mercantilist ideas. In 1581, parliamentary law forbade the export of any coins or bullion. The Tudor laws also insisted that English goods should be shipped only on English vessels. It also stated that the goods brought in foreign ships had to pay higher duties so as to give English ships a notable advantage. Such measures also contributed to the strength of England by helping her to develop a powerful navy. England asserted itself as a maritime and colonial power by opposing Spain at the end of the sixteenth century, Holland in the seventeenth and France in the eighteenth. From the seventeenth century, the English government began showing interest in colonial expansion. The English East India Company was created in 1600 based on a charter from Queen Elizabeth. Soon the company acquired a number of trading posts in India, in the Indian Ocean, in Persia and several other places. The foreign trade of England continued to grow rapidly and the production volume increased, particularly that of coal. The expansion of manufactures like glass furnaces, forges with large hammers, paper and alum works and textile centres, helped in the rise of the bourgeois class. The fortune of this class was closely associated with the expansion of trade and manufacturing. They needed encouragement and protection of the state, which was reflected in mercantilist ideas.

In 1621, Thomas Mun's *Discourse on English Trade with the East Indies* reflected the mercantilist spirit and emphasized the importance of foreign trade in this work. In *England's Treasure by Foreign Trade*, Thomas Mun wrote on the value of foreign trade and stressed that it provided great revenue to the king and brought honour to the kingdom. It helped the merchants and the schools of arts, satisfied English wants, provided employment to the poor and brought improvement in economy. During Oliver Cromwell's time mercantilist policies were followed with greater vigour. In 1651, the first Navigation Act was implemented to establish English supremacy over the neighbouring waters. This Act insisted that European goods could be only transported on English ships or ships belonging the importing country. This implied that goods from colonies could only be carried in English ships, as the colonies did not possess their own ships. The second and third navigation Acts led to a naval war that destroyed the commercial supremacy of the Netherlands. Eighteenth-century England witnessed increasing regulation over the English colonies. Under Walpole, the English government introduced a series of legislations to regulate and exploit colonial commerce. As France was pursuing a similar policy, it resulted in a series of colonial wars between the two countries and hastened the process of colonization in different parts of the world. The American independence was also the result of this rivalry to a great extent. It was under the guidance of Sir George Downing, who is at times called the architect of the English mercantile system, that trade between England and the colonies was strongly enclosed, protected and channellized in English shipping. Instead of a direct ban on the export of treasure, as seen in the old attempts, the emphasis now shifted to increasing the volume and value of exports, reducing the volume and value of imports carried in foreign-owned ships and by receiving income from freights through British ships as far as possible. Thus, we find, the emphasis in English mercantilism changed with the passage of time and with the economic development of the country. It shifted from bullionism and strict internal supervision to the sphere of foreign trade and colonies.

Mercantilism in France

It was in France that a close relationship between mercantilism and absolutism was established, which continued to have a direct bearing on each other. Resistance to mercantilism also took anti-absolutism character. Thus, reaction against absolutism was at times also an attack on certain tenets of mercantilism. Hence, mercantilism in France received a lot of attention from economic thinkers and scholars.

The idea of a national policy as it developed in pre-modern France had certain similarities to those of England. Though there were significant differences between the two states because of their divergent political institutions and varied economic circumstances, the French mercantilist thought developed as a supplementary force to royal absolutism because it served royal interests. The national size and wealth of France and its geographical location also influenced certain elements of French mercantilism. There was a constant interaction of actions and ideas between French rulers and economists and scholars, who believed that despite various limitations, France was potentially capable of European hegemony. This politico-economic thought had started influencing the official mind from the mid-fifteenth century itself and from the mid-sixteenth century, these ideas gave rise to a corpus of legislation aimed at national self-sufficiency and systematic effort to increase national production. Thus we find the French mercantilism developed slowly from the late-middle ages and in pre-modern period the national economic policies of the state showed concerns on different subjects and they never centered in a single phase or subject.

Like other states of Europe, the French monarchy tried to regulate, direct and control the economic life of the people through mercantilist methods. In the fifteenth century, regulations were made to attract and retain gold and silver in the country. In 1462, Louis XI sought to make Lyons an important centre of trade by promoting an annual fair. French mineral resources were also developed by the official order of 1471. Repeated measures were taken to check the exports of precious metals from France. There was general feeling that the import of luxury goods caused money outflow and hence the government placed restrictions on the consumption of luxury goods and the Edict of 1485 followed by several other laws banned common people from wearing gold or silver cloth and silk. Almost a century later, the Estates-General suggested that the French should produce their own clothes in order to save unnecessary outflow of bullion. It was a mercantilist idea to become self-sufficient by developing a country's manufactures. Sixteenth-century rulers in France conferred honours and granted tax exemptions, privileges and money subsidies to those who set-up new industries. Import duties were raised on silk to encourage the home industry. The manufacture of woollen cloth was regulated by the Edict of 1571. According to this, the sizes and the qualities of various cloths were fixed and were to be inspected. To keep the standards up, the woollen clothes were marked. Similar regulations were also issued for leather goods and textiles. The ordinance of 1581 provided for the organization and supervision of guilds in all types of industries and commerce. However, due to qualitative troubles and foreign wars, these measures were not effectively implemented. Yet, these various measures established mercantilist trends in France, which were effectively adopted in the course of the seventeenth century. Most important was the mercantilist idea that the king had the right to enact laws in the economic sphere that would make France self-sufficient, prosperous and strong.

French mercantilism was well expressed by Montchretien at the beginning of the seventeenth century. He insisted that the wealth of the state required the wealth of the bourgeoisie, and that public prosperity was indivisible from prosperity of the treasury. This meant the inseparable relationship between economic and political elements, which he presented in his work *Treatise on Political Economy* (1616). Montchretien summed up his views of mercantilism in one phrase 'we must have money, and if we have none from our own production, then we must have some from foreigners'. To carry this out, he recommended encouraging national trade by preventing foreign merchants from exporting bullion out of France, regulating the economic professions, creating trade workshops and promoting production through privileges and concessions. Richelieu and Colbert worked out these policies subsequently.

Another person in France who propounded mercantilist measures was Laffemas. The Commission of Commerce was created in 1601 through his efforts. He became its President and this Commission stimulated the economic life of France. It held meetings and discussions on every commercial and industrial subject. From mining to linen manufacturing, from manufacturing glass to horse breeding, this Commission was involved in all aspects of economic growth. The Commission's most important measure was to promote mulberry cultivation – raising silk worms to promote the French silk industry. Laffemas invited Flemish tapestry artisans to help in the Gobelins tapestry manufacture in France. Skilled craftsmen were encouraged to settle in France and they were provided with all facilities. During this period, commercial treaties were also signed with Turkey (1597), England (1606) and Spain (1604).

It was Louis XIII's (1624–42) Chief Minister Richelieu who effectively applied mercantilist ideas and France saw the rise of absolutism in this period. Richelieu adopted a strict line of mercantilism in his policy towards commerce and manufacture. He believed that royal edicts were the best methods of stimulating growth. He differed from his colleague, another mercantilist – Sully – because while the latter laid emphasis on the development of agriculture, Richelieu concentrated on commerce, which he considered the new generator of wealth. As a superintendent of navigation and commerce, he wanted a strong France with a high reputation as a sea power. His desire for French colonies did not come to pass as his energies were taken up dealing with the opposition within the court and suppressing political uprisings caused by the taxation policies of the state.

The French mercantilism achieved its glory under the famous Minister of Louis XIV, Jean Baptist Colbert. As a mercantilist, Colbert followed an orthodox line. On the one side, Louis XIV's rule is described as the epitome of absolutism and on the other it was a significant period for French mercantilism. Mercantilism in France reached its highest point from 1663 to 1685. This period is described as the period of 'Colbertism', a term used to describe classical mercantilism in France. Colbert firmly believed that it was solely the monetary wealth of a state that determined its greatness and power.

Colbert, as Controller General of France, provided effective direction, based on mercantilist ideas, to the French economy.

Although things never worked the way Colbert wanted – he did not have the king's complete confidence, suffered rivalry and open hostility of his colleagues, e.g. Louvois, and France was still coming out of a major political crisis caused by the Fronde revolt – he adopted an impressive set of measures to remedy the major ills of the French economy, so that France could be a prosperous country with abundant wealth and a prosperous population.

Behind Colbert's views on trade, lay his ideas on bullion. He was greatly impressed by the wealth of Spain. He wished to obtain and keep the silver supplies circulating within France and believed that foreign trade alone could attract bullion. Like the English and the Dutch mercantilists, he also looked upon trade with Spain as the greatest potential bullion earner. He followed Vodin's protectionist principles and vigorously pursued it for the benefit of French industry. Colbert considered manufacturies to be not only a source of wealth but also of social stability. This he executed in his mercantilist policy with unparalleled vigour. No aspect of industrial life was left untouched and the chain of authority, which he created, assumed the form of a pyramid. Minute details of this can be seen in his policy measures not only for the manufacturers but also for the officials. For example, the manufacturers of Dijon and Chatillon were to ensure that the fabric contained specific number of threads.

In England, the mercantilist regulations were essentially policy regulations, while in France, mercantilism implied minute and detailed regulation of the industry. The aims of this intervention appear to be (a) to ensure quality and (b) to impose social discipline. The Code of Commerce was drawn up with the help of Savary and covered every aspect of the industry. It also formed the basis of the French commercial law. In this field, monopolies were also granted to the well-connected merchants as had happened in the case of England. Several French industries like Govelin's furnishings, laces, ribbons, mirrors, porcelains, faced foreign competition, particularly from Italy and England. These industries continued to flourish even after Colbert's death. Many of these industries contributed to French exports and, more significantly, reduced imports. Colbert's economic system grew slowly with the passage of time. He believed in a policy which provided extensive state control. For Colbert, the trading companies were the armies of the king and the manufactures of France were his reserves. In the first phase, Colbert adopted defensive measures by imposing tax on foreign ships, introducing protective tariff between 1664 and 1667 and then developing production. To encourage commercial expansion, he established several royal companies, which were directed by the state. These included the French East India Company (1664), the West India Company (1664), the Northern Company (1669) and the Levant Company (1670). These companies helped in the creation of French colonial empires in different parts of the world.

Colbert also increased the scope of state intervention in the economic sphere, and directly participated in the manufacturing activities by forming a series of *Manufacturers Royals*. The state government under Colbert took keen interest in industrial activities. A well-known figure of that period, Van Robais, was lured from the Netherlands to establish a state-sponsored textile-manufacturing unit at Abbeville to produce cloth that was already manufactured in England and Holland. A company was set up and given subsidies to produce serges in Burgundy; Languedoc industry was given bounty to encourage exports to Levant, and the silk industry at Lyon was promoted by royal orders. The iron industry was given state protection against the competition from Swedish iron. The state foundries were also created to manufacture cannons and armaments. He did not hesitate to reduce the large number of religious festivals, which interfered in production and reduced working days. To improve the quality of industrial goods in France, minute instructions were issued and regulations were carried out to guide the preparation of raw materials, and inspectors appointed to control the quality of production. To protect new industries against foreign competition, tariffs were imposed on imported goods. New tariff rates were announced in 1664, which were doubled in 1667. He concentrated on shipbuilding to improve shipping and have been control over distant colonies. It was because of Colbert's efforts that France emerged as a strong naval power and competed with England on equal terms throughout the eighteenth century till the time of Napoleon. Colbert was aware of the problem of internal communications. Colbert encouraged the construction of the famous canal, called *Canal des Deux Mers* that linked the Atlantic with the Mediterranean. Like England, France also carried out three major naval wars against the Dutch to maintain its supremacy in trade.

Colbert's policy focused on the development of effective administration. New legal courts were introduced – Civil Ordinance in 1667 and Criminal Ordinance in 1670. An Ordinance of Commerce was issued in 1673 and that of Marine in 1681. Colbert was aware of the French disabilities in trade and industry. He knew the difficulties in communications and internal custom barriers, the existence of diverse laws on weights and measures, and the lack of enterprise among the French traders and merchants. He also knew the consequences of capital lying unused by the prosperous classes and the crushing burden of taxes on the French economy. He not only tried to improve the financial situation of the government but regulated every sphere of economic activity.

Despite mercantilist measures, French industrialization failed. Colbertism imposed industrialization from above and the French bourgeoisie was hesitant in taking risks and was reluctant to invest capital in the industrial sector. The official posts and the acquisition of noble status through land purchase held greater attraction to them than profit through industrial or commercial activities. Without their support, industrialization could not achieve a definite success. The focus of the state mercantilism was on luxury products that had higher value than the products of mass consumption, which remained neglected in the mercantilist scheme of things. Mercantilism in France did not develop into an academic discussion holding debates on policy matters as had happened in England. Hence, diverse interests did not converge because of the absence of major economic debates. Even the trading companies, which had been created by Colbert, were state-sponsored and state-directed. These lacked the spirit of enterprise and failed to attract public savings through the sale of public shares. In short, the financial base in French mercantilist ventures remained weak and fragile.

Mercantilist projects were successful only as long as Colbert was at the helm of affairs.

Mercantilism in the Netherlands

Compared to other states of Europe, the economic condition of Netherlands was quite different. Whereas most states had basically agricultural economies with some industries emerging upon resources locally supplied, the Dutch had developed essentially as brokers, exchangers, shipowners and had a well-balanced economic structure. Like the advanced economic centres of the Italian city states, the Dutch merchants were basically practitioners of arts and commerce. Unlike other states, bullion accumulation was not emphasized in the Netherlands. In fact, the Dutch mercantilists advocated freedom of the seas. Along with this, the Dutch emphasized monopoly trading in the colonies, supported by political power. The war of independence against Spain brought out Dutch nationalism as well as elements of mercantilism. Dutch mercantilism is difficult to typify which has led H. Kellenbenz to question whether Holland ever engaged in any form of mercantilism. Although the Netherlands was reasonably prosperous compared to other states, and excelled in shipbuilding, trade and financial institutions, the significance of bullionism was not there in mercantilist thought. At the same time, it was difficult for Holland to escape the spirit of the times and Braudel has pointed out that Dutch advocacy of free trade was only skin-deep. All her economic activities required the creation of monopolies, which was an important element of mercantilism. Even in their overseas empire, the Dutch behaved like other colonial powers.

The Dutch mercantilist policy is reflected in the work that was first published in 1662 titled *The Interests of Holland*. The Dutch statesman John de Witt and a famous Leiden merchant Pieter de la Court are believed to be its authors. The *Maxims* as they were also known, is considered the standard account of the Dutch economy and their political occupation. De la Court was mainly concerned with the welfare and prosperity of the Dutch provinces and he sincerely believed that this policy of economic welfare would be beneficial for the whole federation. He emphasized freedom from persecution, taxation, monopoly, regulation and dynastic rule. But the most important of these was the freedom from religious control. As the Dutch were dependent on international trade, the heavy taxes adversely affected the people and the economy. Hence, the Dutch demanded that the traders and manufacturers should be left free to create wealth, and that they should not be placed under either church's restrictions or state regulations. De la Court considered the merchant community a dynamic factor in the economy and saw the presence of a strong centralized power as a major threat. This explains why mercantilism in Netherlands assumed a different character. As their focus was on commerce and universal freedom, import and export duties were kept low so that the French merchants could bring foreign goods for reshipments and earn through carrier trade. Bullion export was permitted with hardly any restriction although there were mercantilists who objected to the outflow of gold and silver. While one section of the mercantilists criticized the state policies for encouraging the outflow of wealth, another section believed that it was the commercial freedom of Holland that was the chief source of the country's economic success. However, in the seventeenth century, the two emerging neighbours – Britain and France, destroyed the Dutch commercial power. These countries adopted strict mercantilist policies based on shipping and colonial interests and clashed with the Dutch claims of supremacy; it resulted in wars – three each against the two countries. Six naval wars in nearly half a century led to the end of the Dutch supremacy in the North Sea.

Mercantilism in Prussia and Austria

Mercantilism in Prussia had long roots stretching to the period of the Thirty Years War (1618–48). The principles of mercantilism were adopted rebuilding the country after the war. A strong state apparatus was required to implement the ideas of mercantilism, and it could only be implemented in the Germany region by Prussia and Austria. The economic theory of mercantilism was modelled on the absolutist doctrine. It was assumed that the state would enjoy absolute directional powers in the economic sphere. The chief objective of the mercantilist policy was to create a favourable balance of trade. The wealth of the state, specially precious metals and money were considered essential requirements for political power. The Imperial Diet issued a large number of economic ordinances but the states implemented them only if they served their own individual interests. These ordinances aimed at pushing through economic growth by all possible means. For this a dirigist system (state control of economic and social matters) of state support and state regulation had to be created. The chief aspect of German mercantilism was the carefully planned population policy that prohibited emigration and encouraged immigration. Frederick II of Prussia stated that 'the true strength of the state was manifested in a high population'. It was considered desirable for political, military and economic reasons. This policy was evident in the programmes of regulated workforce to exploit all possible reserves of labour.

Although Prussia never developed a powerful mercantilism as noticed in the case of France or England, the ideas of mercantilism could be seen in the writings of a school of scholars called *Cameralists*. The word is derived from *Schatzkammer* (that means treasury, *camera* in Latin). Chairs of Cameralists were created in the German universities, first in Prussia, and state recognition was given to these scholars. Cameralist studies appeared in the curriculum of German universities as a branch of the science of government and a theory of benevolent absolutism. Some historians regard Cameralism as the German variant of men and ideas borrowed from the English and French examples. Even Karl Marx alleged that German political economy was a readymade commodity imported from England and France and handled by German professors who remained no more than scholars. However, there are other historians who do not put the Cameralists in the category of 'mercantilists'.

In the narrow sense 'Cameralism' assumed a form of treatises on taxation. In the wider context, it related to the economic welfare of the state, and related to every aspect of trade, industry and agriculture. It suggested training state officials to increase efficiently managed state revenues, and promoted the interests of the state that had been adversely affected in the period of destructive wars.

The Cameralist teachings imbued diverse activities related to economy and state revenues. The most influential of the early theoretician of the Cameralists was Veit Ludwig von Seckendorff. In his book *Teutscher Fursten Staat* (1656) he opposed the outflow of money if it was used for importing luxury goods. He supported the evolution of guilds, whose activities, he believed, promoted economic growth. He also stressed that bureaucrats and state servants should be well-educated.

Towards the end of the seventeenth century, the so-called 'Vienna School' of Austrian Cameralists emerged which advocated a wide-ranging economic programme that unified all the postulations of mercantilists like Johann Joachim Becher, Philipp Wilhelm von Hornigk and Wilhelm Schroeder. Becher (1625–85) is regarded as the father figure of the Austrian school. He denounced those merchants who imported goods from abroad that could have been produced at home and called them *propolists* (usurious merchants), and gave credit to those who were willing to invest in native industry, calling them 'virtuous pillars of society'. He advocated that all foreign manufactures be prohibited even though domestic industries were not fully developed. Schroeder did not advocate orthodox mercantilism by concentrating on the balance of payments. Instead, he laid stress on social demands in determining state policy. He believed that it was not the import and export of money but the balance of different trades that contributed to the wealth of a country.

In the age of enlightenment, the chief exponents of Cameralism were J.H.G. Justi and J. von Sonnenfels. They advocated the concept of social contract in which individuals were expected to surrender their rights to the state because of economic necessity. Thus a combination of mercantilist doctrine and the practical policies of the enlightened rulers provided an intellectual base for the programmes of modernization in many German territories. German mercantilism was neither original nor universal. Although many German writers borrowed their ideas directly or indirectly from the writings and pronouncements of English and French mercantilists, the Germans adopted them according to their needs, purely in practical terms suiting the state demands of their region.

The division of the country into small states accentuated Prussia's economic problems. Each state tried to adopt its own peculiar type of mercantilism which led to economic tensions among them. It was only Brandenburg Prussia where an effective mercantilist system could be developed. However, the practical aspect of mercantilism developed towards the end of the eighteenth century when mercantilism was beginning to be rejected in other parts of Europe. As Prussia was not in a position to develop a navy or its own colonies, there was little emphasis on foreign trade. The Prussian industry was protected by high tariffs and prohibitions were imposed against imports. Minute regulations were carried out through official decrees and the state bureaucracy implemented the policies. A few new industries were created under royal patronage while the old ones were reorganized. Subsidies and monopolies were provided as encouragement. Skilled manufacturers and artisans were invited to come and settle in the country, especially the French Huguenots. The state prohibited the export of raw materials and agriculture was encouraged by all means. Like Laffemas in France, the Prussian ruler, Frederick the Great, introduced schemes to encourage mulberry cultivation to start silk production in the country and encourage the cultivation of potatoes. Although the scale of mercantilist activities was not so wide as in France or England, Prussian mercantilism contributed to the economic recovery after a period of prolonged warfare.

Sweden

In the seventeenth century, Sweden emerged as a strong expansionist state. Naturally, when the ideas of mercantilism were sweeping across the European continent, Sweden could not remain immune from its influence. As a result, the state adopted a policy of tariff protection and granted privileges to those who served the state's interests through economic activities. During Gustavus Adolphus' rule, subsidies were given ship owners to construct armed ships, a few trading companies were founded, but most of them remained unsuccessful and trade in tar was converted into a monopoly. The mercantilist policies did not succeed much because Sweden remained in a state of war for most part of the century and could not concentrate on economic measures. The only significant Swedish mercantilist writer was J.C. Risingh, whose *Tract of Commerce* (1669) was based on the old-fashioned views of bullionism.

Rejection of Mercantilism

By the eighteenth century, people no longer accepted the ideas of mercantilism emphasizing intervention and regulation of economic affairs by powerful states. Several scholars and writers began to have reservations about such policies during the eighteenth century. The historiography of the mercantile system since then has been strongly condemned, though there are some who appreciate the mercantilist ideas as typical products of the age of commercial capitalism.

It is not that mercantilism had no critics before the eighteenth century. Throughout the long period of mercantilism, there were groups advocating freedom of trade and there were the staunch supporters of monopolistic institutions. The adherents of bullionism had strongly criticized the creation of the English East India Company, a monopolistic institution responsible for the outflow of silver towards Asia. The two major branches of trade – the East India and the Baltic – where the bullion export was constant, created a lot of bickering. Trade could only be defended on grounds of high profitability through re-exports. But the Baltic trade could not be defended on the ground of re-exports that would ultimately bring bullion, as was the case in Asia. The expansion of the world market and advent of a system of international lending and credit, and of multilateral payments reduced the anxiety over bullion resources. This began to happen during the eighteenth century. Nicholas Barbon in his two important works, *Discourse on Trade* (1690), and *Discourse Concerning Coining the New Money Lighter* (1696), contested that it is not important to have a large supply of bullion but rather a great stock of useful goods because the value of money lies in its utility as a medium of exchange and not because of its intrinsic value. At the same time in 1693, Sir Joshua Child in his work *A Discourse on Trade* (1693) stated that a low interest rate was much more important for national prosperity than bullion. While emphasizing the need for maintaining the monopoly of the East India trade because of the peculiar difficulties attached to it, Child advocated freedom of commerce for other regions. He also disapproved of certain mercantilist legislation describing these as 'a heap of nonsense complied by a few ignorant country gentlemen'. Another important person was Charles Davenant, who had served as Inspector General of Exports and Imports from 1705–14. He strongly criticized the Whig government for restricting trade with France, but he defended the Navigational Acts and the export of bullion by English companies. He considered money to be a 'serviceable counter'.

France experienced similar criticism of the theory and policy of mercantilism in the eighteenth century. The Council of Commerce, representing various cities, approved the mercantilist system of Colbert but raised a few objections to government policy. The deputy representing Nantes made a scathing attack on the monopolistic commercial companies and advocated the opening of trades for all the free merchants. Merchants started demanding freedom of oceanic trade so that they could also gain from it and some began to denounce the high import duties. One of the most important form of criticism came from the writings of Pierre le Pesant de Boisguilbert. In his *Le Factum de La France* (1707) and in *The Political Will of M. de Vauban* (1712), Boisguilbert demanded freedom in pricing and freedom of foreign trade. He emphasized that consumption was as important as production, and that the former was severely blocked by heavy taxation. He strongly criticized the idea of bullionism and treated gold and silver not as wealth but as a medium for acquiring wealth. He declared that 'the richer a country is, the more it is in a position to do without specie [silver bullion]'.

The waning influence of mercantilist theory can be divided into two phases. The first began in the middle of the seventeenth century and could be seen in the nature of attacks and criticism of certain specific mercantilist views and policies, particularly the idea of bullion. In the second phase in the eighteenth century, came the earliest criticism of mercantilism by positive economic ideas. Two important economic ideas emerged during the eighteenth century – the idea of *laissez-faire* in England and a group of scholars called the physiocrats in France. These new ideas on economy played a crucial role in the ultimate enfeeblement of the mercantilist system in Europe.

The physiocrats valued agriculture, and agricultural labour. François Quesnay, Mirabeau and Dupont de Némours were among the prominent physiocrats of the eighteenth century. They believed in the 'rule of nature' and argued that the produce of the land was the only true form of wealth and anything that shackled it was inimical to the community. Industry merely combined things that had already been produced and commerce merely moved them around, and hence both were sterile. But in agriculture, the producer received *produit net*. For physiocrat it was proprietors of land who created wealth and state policies should be directed towards increased production from land. They suggested that solution to food problems lay in free movement of agricultural produce and that there would be a proper relationship between the producer and the consumer. Artificial regulations merely produced artificial societies. They recommended ample capital be used in new and better techniques, that common land be divided and placed under individual owners, and new land should be brought under cultivation and feudal dues on peasants abolished. They encouraged internal consumption and favoured those industries that used large amounts of raw material. They favoured the removal of all restrictions on internal commerce in grain and other agricultural goods and even supported exports of raw materials for the sake of agriculture. In short, they wished to secure a good market for agricultural products. Greater production from land would ultimately stimulate industry and commerce and with it, the economy would also expand. They seemed unaware of the fact that the process could be reversed – that wealth accumulated in industry and commerce by better means of banking and financial facilities could develop the full potential of the land.

Quesnay, one of the most important contributors was born in a family of well-off farmers, received good education and became a surgeon. He published several medical works and became the general physician to the king. As France was mainly a rural and an agricultural country, which had lagged behind Holland and England for failing to adopt new methods of cultivation, agriculture drew his attention. The heavy taxes on agriculture became a matter of concern for him. He wrote an article entitled 'Farmers' for the *Encyclopedia* (1757) and in this he established the superiority of tenant farming over the traditional *métayage* system and the advantages of horse over the ox for ploughing land. He held that the revenues collected from agriculture were the product of lands and that productivity was exclusive to the earth. He rejected the policy of increasing wealth through the balance of trade. His entire focus was on proving that land is the real generator of wealth. He was in fact a promoter of agrarian capitalism. One of the important ministers of that period, Turgot, was greatly influenced by physiocratic thinking. While attempting to promote manufacturing capitalism, he also wished to develop agriculture. Turgot opposed planned economy and protectionism and extolled economic freedom. It was under the influence of the physiocrats that mercantilism came under increasing criticism. In this context, the debate between Abbé Mollet and Necker on the undesirability of continuing with the French East India Company as a monopolistic institution holds special place. The company was abolished in 1769 and the Asian trade was thrown open to private merchants.

Like the physiocrats in France, in England, a school of political economists who based their theories on the concept of *laissez-faire* developed in the second half of the eighteenth century. Two important thinkers of this school David Hume and Adam Smith, were advocates of the freedom of trade. Smith wrote a classic, *An Enquiry Into the Nature and Causes of the Wealth of Nations* (1776). It was probably he who first coined the word 'mercantilism'. He was a harsh critic of this concept and saw it as a discreditable conspiracy of the traders against the nation. For him, mercantilism symbolized a confusion of ideas in which money was falsely identified with wealth. He believed that under mercantilism, fruitless care for money was replaced by fruitless care over the balance of trade. He strongly opposed the regulations created by a clique of vested interests, who used the state for their own benefit. For Adam Smith, mercantilism was a 'system'. It had benefited the rich and powerful at the expense of the poor.

Adam Smith's contribution to economic thought is given great value and is regarded as a masterpiece in the field of economics. He synthesized the economic ideas of the French and the views of David Hume. His work ran into several editions and was translated into many languages soon after its publication. It is true that Smith did not fully understand the ideas of mercantilism and judged it primarily in the English context. His criticism of the mercantilists for their preoccupation with bullion reflects his misunderstanding of their ideas. As Keynes commented in his *Notes on Mercantilism*, the classical school of economists has been unfair to the mercantilist writers. For two hundred years they had given peculiar advantage to their nations by means of favourable balance of trade. Yet the work of Adam Smith brought about an immediate dismantling of mercantilist views and it was abandoned at several places.

Adam Smith's main charge was that the mercantile system was the product of a partnership established between princes, nobles and country gentlemen who knew nothing about trade and tradesmen. This situation varied from one state to another as the ideas and practices of mercantilism were not identical throughout Europe. In England, there existed a partnership of merchants and officials from where the English mercantilism derived its intellectual and administrative strength. Important men like Mun and Child influenced many mercantilist views through their writings. They were both merchants and important writers on mercantilism. It is true that the merchants did not penetrate deep into the decision-making sphere of the government but their influence and advice occasionally shaped state policy. In France, the merchant community was sometimes consulted but more often the state officials ignored their views. In England, the mercantile views were probably heard more as the merchants had some influence on the parliament, where state proposals were discussed and scrutinized. In France, the influence of the merchants could not be exercised to that extent as the representative institutions were hardly consulted by the absolute state. In Holland, state intervention was minimal. Similarly, Adam Smith regarded the Navigation Acts as an instrument of power rather a means of prosperity. However, the contribution of these navigation acts to the British commercial economy cannot be ignored. Adam Smith failed to see any dynamic element in the mercantilist thought. He believed that the ideas behind the mercantile system were misguided, its ends were unjust, its administration was corrupt and its existence was seen as irrelevant. Thus, under the influence of the new economics, mercantilism began losing its significance. The changed economic reality was also responsible for this because trade and the merchants were no longer at an infant stage and had matured in the course of over two centuries and hence did not require the kind of protection and regulation as they needed in the beginning.

Suggested Readings

Anderson, M.S., *Europe in the Eighteenth Century 1713–1783*, London: Longmans, 1975. A brief but good discussion of mercantilism as practised in the eighteenth century.

Andrews, Stuart, *Eighteenth Century Europe 1680–1815*, London: Longmans, 1965. An elaborate discussion with a broad perspective.

Blitz, R.C., 'Mercantilist Policies and the Pattern of Trade, 1500–1750', *Journal of Economic History*, 27, 1967, pp. 39–55.

Clough, S.B. and C.W. Cole, *Economic History of Europe*, 3rd edn., Boston: Heath & Co., 1952. Discusses the subject in great detail, dealing with each country separately.

Coleman, D.C., ed., *Revisions in Mercantilism*, London: Methuen & Co., 1969. An alternate perspective to the one provided by Adam Smith.

Davis, Ralph, 'The Rise of Protection in England, 1689–1786', *Economic History Review*, 19, 1966, pp. 306–17.

Heckscher, Eli F., *Mercantilism*, New York: Macmillan, 1955, 2 vols. Regarded as a classical work on the subject.

Magnusson, Lars, *Mercantilism: The Shaping of an Economic Language*,

London/Yew York: Routledge, 1994. Discusses the chief Tanets of mercantilist theory and practice.

Rich, E.E. and C.H. Wilson, *The Cambridge Economic History of Europe*, vol. IV, Cambridge: Cambridge University Press, 1967. Provides a comprehensive view of the economic developments of the pre-modern Europe with a focus on trade and industry.

CHAPTER 11

Overseas Expansion and the Colonial Rivalry between Britain and France

The global expansion of trade and conquests by European powers marked the beginning of modern colonialism. The shift of the economic centre from the Mediterranean to the Atlantic was finally consolidated by the eighteenth century through the efforts of the British, the Dutch and the French. The objective of pre-capitalist colonialism was direct extraction of tribute from the subjects through political control. With the rise of industrialization, the focus began to turn to economics. The commercial activities of the European states were closely associated with their colonial trade and it gave rise to intense rivalry. The importance of colonies in the process of modern state building was amply demonstrated by the mercantilist ideas and policies. The aim of controlling as many colonies as possible in order to reap huge profit resulted in a prolonged struggle among these rival powers in the seventeenth century. In the eighteenth century, Britain and France emerged as the two strongest colonial powers who contested their colonial claims and remained engaged in intermittent wars till Napoleon's defeat in 1815. This rivalry between them led to the economic hegemony of England not only in the colonial world but also over Europe.

By the eighteenth century, the importance of colonial trade had been well established. The countries located on the Atlantic coast had immensely gained from the trade with the different colonies. Colonies held a special place in mercantilist ideas. They were areas where imperial power could develop trade and become powerful. These regions were a source of raw material and profits and later a market for the finished products. All colonial powers, particularly

France, Britain and Holland, gave a legal base to these ideas by passing laws and ordinances, so as to fully exploit the newly-acquired territories and transform them into their colonies.

The concept of colonies continued to change with the emergence and decline of the ideas of mercantilism through the transformation from pre-industrial to an industrial society in the respective countries. A constant search for new markets led to the colonization of the newly discovered territories. The importance of the colony was governed by the potentiality of new products, the demand by the native population for products from the mother country, the volume of trade from that colony and its geographical location. Some of the colonies were used as transit points in the long-distance trade and some were strategically located to control and protect other territories. The structure of the market also determined the position of the colonies in different parts of the world. All the imperial powers embodied their objectives in a complex set of regulations to make the colonies complementary and subordinate to their own economies. Colonial rule has been described in different ways. In 1738, a British pamphleteer J. Bannett wrote that every British settler living in the West Indies contributed twenty times more to the national wealth than an Englishman in England by way of labour and taxes. The importance of Africa was recognized because it was the chief supplier of slaves on which the plantation economy of the Western world depended. Similarly, the significance of the West Indies lay in its plantation economy. The English king, George III had once stated that the West Indies must be defended at all costs because it had sugar islands for the additional cost of military and naval operations could easily be recovered through the sale of its sugar. He believed that Britain would not be in a position to continue the Seven Years War (1756–63) if she lost the sugar islands of the West Indies. Throughout the eighteenth century such views were presented in different ways, both in Britain and France. The archives of these countries have hundreds of memoirs expressing the value of outside territories and suggesting their respective governments to acquire them to gain economic or strategic advantage. Colonies were seen as the suppliers and providers of goods for the mother country. As late as

1765, the French officials saw the colonies purely as trade centres and sources of profit. The French realized the importance of these colonies when they lost some of their North American colonies in the Seven Years War and the English realized this when they lost the American colonies (1776–83). Such views ultimately determined the official policies of the state.

The colonies of the early-eighteenth century were not empires in the real sense. They were only expressions of economic imperialism because the political mechanism of control had not fully developed. European states adopted conservative mercantilist principles towards their respective colonies, which included creation of monopolies of the trading institutions, state-controlled institutions, strict regulation of trade and industry, and control over shipments. Holland, which had been pursuing the free trade policy, also implemented these mercantilist views towards the Asian colonies.

One important element of the colonial policy was the Navigation Code, which was implemented by Britain in 1651 under Oliver Cromwell. Subsequent governments framed similar rules which were passed by the British parliament in 1660, 1662, 1663 and later in 1673 and 1696. These enactments were prepared to regulate the colonial trade and to promote the English Navy. These regulations sought to protect profits and monopolise the colonial market. The French attempts to establish and control colonies were more planned and regimental. The French crown implemented numerous measures to encourage search for new territories to settle. In the late-seventeenth century, Colbert made the crown directly responsible for the colonial administration. Strict regulations were issued and monopolistic institutions were created to handle colonial commerce and Letters of Patent were issued in 1717 and 1727 for this purpose. Several monopolistic companies were established by the state and each company was assigned a specific region of operation. During this period the role of the colonies had been over-emphasized by the mercantilist states. The chief tenets of mercantilism were a favourable balance of trade, inflow of bullion and to make the metropolis achieve self-sufficiency.

The continuous and increasing import of slaves in the West

Indies was beginning to change the social balance. By 1789, the blacks constituted nearly 89 per cent of the total population in Saint Domingue, the whites formed 6 per cent and the free and mixed coloured people (called Mulattos) were 5 per cent. The Caribbean colonies were virtually transformed by this rapid expansion of slave trade. The French government under Lovis XIV had published a 'Black Code' or *Code Noir* in 1685 to regulate slavery. A set of conditions were imposed on slaves and their owners regulating their public and personal lives. This gave a direction to the French colonial settlements.

So long as industrialization in Europe had not gained momentum, the colonies were seen purely as profit centres. In the second half of the eighteenth century, economic thinkers propounded new ideas giving rise to the concept of *laissez-faire*. There was growing criticism of the mercantilist doctrines by new economic writers, and mercantilist institutions were attacked on different grounds. Between 1750 and 1753, the monopolistic trading rights of the African company and the Levant company were withdrawn. In India, the Regulating Act (1773) and the Pitt's India Act (1784) restricted the powers of the English East India Company and gave constitutional structure to the British Indian possessions. In 1791, the administrative structure of Canada was reorganized. These new ideologies were legitimized by the writings of economic thinkers like Adam Smith. In France, a similar trend is discernible in the late-eighteenth century, where Richard Cantillon, Francois Quesney and many others wrote in favour of economic liberty. The tirade against the French East India Company (Compagnie des Indes) resulted in its abolition in 1769, although another company had to be formed later in 1785 to conduct trade relations between France and Asia. It is interesting to note that the new economic thinking insisting on freedom of trade concerned only the European states. As far as the colonies were concerned, these new ideas were not applied to the colonial affairs. In the case of Britain the colonies were integrated and absorbed within the British economic system. In France, the colonies remained essentially a source of profit and were not completely integrated as had happened in Britain. Most of the French colonial products were re-exported to other regions within Europe.

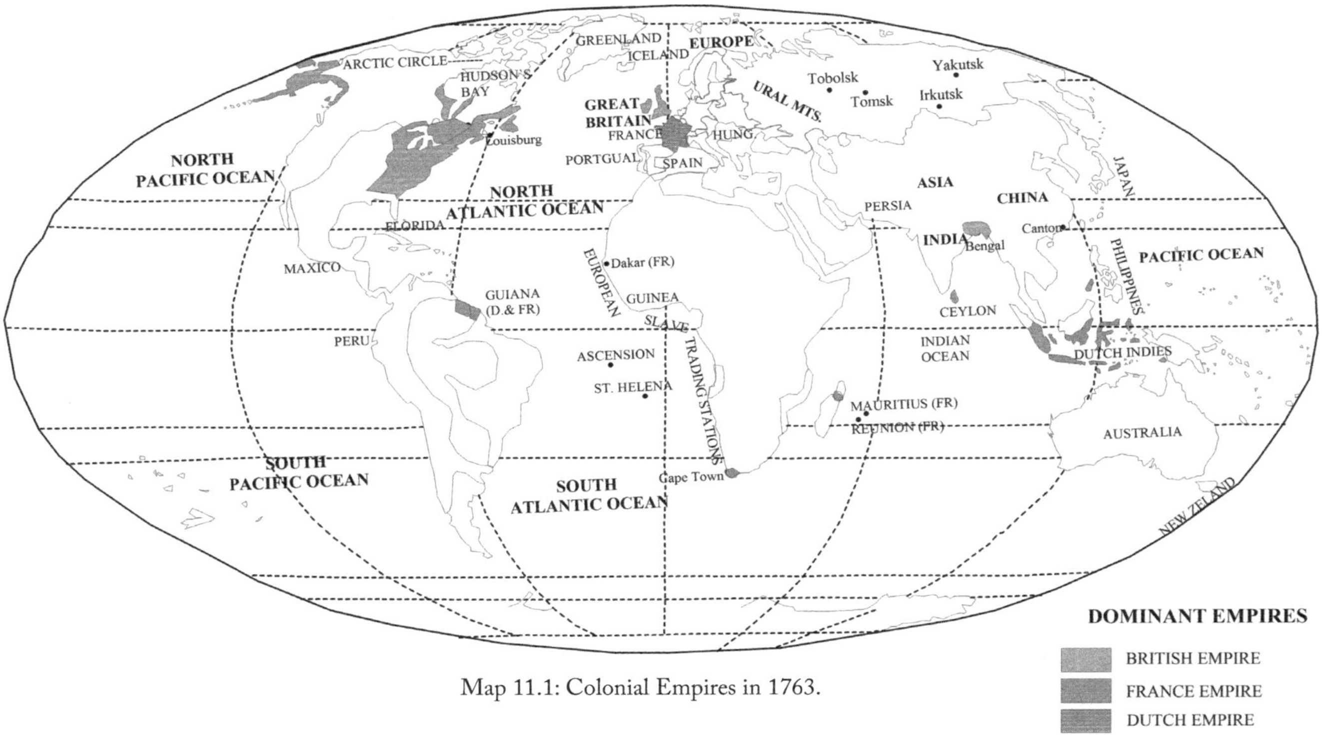

Map 11.1: Colonial Empires in 1763.

In the seventeenth century, the Dutch had emerged as an important maritime power and remained active in the field of shipments and financial market. Most of the Portuguese products from Brazil were brought in Dutch ships and in 1621 a monopolistic company was established in the name of the West India Company to find a place in the growing trade of the New World. The Dutch remained involved in Brazil and neglected the possibility of establishing settlements in the Caribbean islands. By the time the Dutch realized the significance of these islands, the English and the French were firmly settled in this region. Later the Dutch started procuring slaves from the African coast and began to supply them to the Portuguese and the Spaniards and even to the English and French West Indies. They reaped huge profits from their trading activities.

In Asia, the Dutch succeeded in establishing their colonies primarily in the Indonesian archipelago, known for spices, and created small settlements along the Indian sea coast. The Asiatic trade that was earlier dominated by Asian merchants was taken over by the Dutch. A company (VOC) was given monopoly rights by the governments to conduct the Asian trade. Thus, in the first half of the seventeenth century, the Dutch emerged as a commercial power outdoing all its rivals as a trading and carrying nation. The Dutch had also monopolized the Baltic grain trade which was an important source of profit. Their rise was suddenly halted in 1651 when their long phase of expansion ended. The English Navigation Act in the same year had serious political and economic repercussion on the fate of the Dutch. They had not only to fight three important wars with the English on the question of naval supremacy but also had to face French hostility. France aiming at destroying Dutch navigational activities and their shipping power, adopted a similar policy. The Navigation Acts of the English and the French aimed at excluding the Dutch from trading with the American colonies and giving a severe blow to its financial prosperity. By 1654, the Dutch were expelled from Brazil and a decade later their trading base at New Amsterdam was taken away by the English and renamed New York. The economic future of the Netherlands was greatly curbed by the prolonged wars with the French. These wars

(1672–8, 1689–97 and 1702–13) greatly cripped the Dutch shipping services. Several other factors were responsible for the decline of Holland, which have been mentioned elsewhere.

By the beginning of the eighteenth century, with the decline of Holland, Britain and France became the principal contenders for colonial supremacy, a rivalry that lasted almost the entire century. This conflict had started towards the end of the seventeenth century. The two powers fought a long war when William III and Queen Anne and Louis XIV ruled England and France respectively. This war greatly affected the British empire in the subsequent period. It was brought to an end in 1713 through the Treaty of Utrecht. The victory in the war enabled the British to extend its colonial empire in different ways. In North America, they acquired Nova Scotia and Newfoundland and rights over the slave trade in America. This Treaty further strengthened the British position in North America although the French domination over Canada continued. Newfoundland gave the British immense profits through the cod fish trade and the fur and leather trade of Hudson Bay. The further acquisition of Acadia made the English more entrenched against the French. Yet the British control was far from complete in this region. The British and the French remained strong opponents in the War of Austrian Succession in 1740 that continued till 1748, and in 1756 they were again at loggerheads in an intense war that came to be known as the Seven Years War. The American War of Independence saw the two powers in the opposite camps. The war came to a close in 1783 through the Treaty of Versailles, but soon after the French Revolution in 1789, a long period of rivalry commenced that centred on the question of colonies.

Extent of the Colonies and Trade Pattern

The colonies of Britain and France were scattered in both the western and the eastern hemisphere. The reason for the rivalry was that their colonies were situated in close proximity to each other and they traded in almost similar products. The chief centres of colonial rivalry were located in North America, the West Indian islands, western and eastern coast of Africa and in Asia primarily the Indian subcontinent. The two powers revealed major differences in their methods of building colonial empires. The French absolutist state created a centralized structure and the crown uniformly controlled its colonies. Military governors or royal officials ruled distant regions. Even the settlements adopted regimental schemes and were directed by the state. The British North American colonies developed more independently and state regulations were imposed much later. Most of these colonies had developed a tradition of self-government despite the presence of a governor appointed by the British Crown.

At the beginning of the eighteenth century, the English settlements in North America were confined to Newfoundland and a group of twelve colonies located on the narrow strip of coastland between the Allegheny mountains and the Atlantic. On the other hand, the French had established themselves firmly in the valley and estuary of the St Lawrence in Cape Britain Louisiana, Quebec and Montreal. They had a series of forts, mission stations and trading coasts and they controlled two great water bases that passed through the heart of North America. The French efforts to establish their colonial power in this region was state sponsored and well planned. It was the fur trade of this region that occupied the French attention. Samuel Champlain founded Quebec in 1608. The attitude of the French to their colonies was dominated by her trade policy which was a coherent theory of economics in which the self-sufficiency of the colony was the central theme. Barthélemy de Laffemas, a famous mercantilist and a minister in France, showed interest in North America and promised support so that a new France could be raised there, the local population converted to Christianity, and where French manufactured products could be sold and raw materials procured. For this purpose Compagnie du Canada was formed under Henry IV which was later changed into company of New France for Canada. Louisiana was named after King Louis XIV after La Salle had explored the whole basin of the Mississippi River. The French expansion in this region was carried through government-planned acquisition. The French colonial system was based on a hierarchy of military officials appointed by the crown.

The French colonial empire in North America was based on the fur trade, riches from the wilderness and forest resources, whereas the English colonies were based on the exploitation of agricultural lands and manufacturies. In North America the French did not settle in large numbers, as the products procured from this region needed hardly any labour or large-scale settlements. Moreover, the extremely cold climate of this region did not attract many people. The profit was unusually high from the trade. The French settlers were outnumbered ten to one by the British. While the British were divided into many independent colonies without any machinery for common action, the French were all placed under a single unified control of the French government. The French position was weakened by the presence of the British at Newfoundland and Nova Scotia in close proximity of the French. The population of Nova Scotia consisted of people of French origin and the French government tried every possible means to stir them up against the English. The French tried to prevent the westward expansion of the English by building forts and encircling the British. In 1754, the English Ohio Company tried to carry out settlements in the Ohio valley with English men but they were driven out by the French who constructed a fort there by the name of Fort Duquesne. The outbreak of the Seven Years War destroyed the French position in North America while the English colonial empire immensely gained from this war. Unlike the French, the English colonies in North America had a vast population engaged in plantation, trade and manufacturing. The English strength lay in the dense population. Not all the settlers were English in origin and most of them had come to escape religious tyranny or political prosecution or in the quest of making a fortune. The French colonial expansion in this region was largely political in nature, acquiring places of strategic importance through well-planned policies, while the English expansion was primarily governed by considerations of trade. The English colonists were never allowed to compete with British manufactured products and were forced to purchase products produced in England. The products of North America – tobacco, indigo and cotton – were used in England as raw material for manufacturing. The British settlers exploited the timber in Maine and Nova Scotia for the shipping industry and in the southern colonies, rice and tobacco were produced on a large scale. Hence the British enjoyed a stronger position in North America. The French on the other hand exploited resources which were exhaustible in nature. Small populations and isolated settlements made the French presence relatively weak. In the Seven Years War William Pitt blocked the French settlements and prevented them from establishing links with the West Indies. The French were forced to surrender the whole of Canada to the English except two small islands of St Pierre and Miquelon. Exactly two decades later, the French had a sweet revenge when all thirteen North American colonies declared their independence against British rule. The French actively supported the rebels and arranged for the treaty negotiations held at the French court of Versailles in 1783.

The islands of West Indies were of considerable importance for both Britain and France. The colonization in this region had started when the Portuguese pushed the French out of Brazil and introduced the plantation system in the tropical lands in the Caribbean. The first shipment of African slaves was made as early as 1503. Spanish possessions and shipping in the Caribbeans fell constant prey to French privateers like Dieppe, Jean Ango and Jean de Fleury while the British sea voyagers like Hawkins and Drake performed similar acts. In the seventeenth century, the English joined the French settlers and the migration of population increased. The English and the French settlers came into nearly uninhabited lands. Unlike Spanish conquerors who lived idly by exploiting the labour force of the local inhabitants, the English and the French West Indian settlers had to bring slave labour to work on their sugar plantations. In the initial period, the settlers faced insurmountable problems, as they had to face disease and starvation and had to live in unfamiliar lands. The disease took a very heavy toll. However, the plantation economy offered economic incentives to the immigrants. With the extension of land and production of new crops such as tobacco, cotton and indigo, the West Indian colonies attracted a new wave of settlers and the population started soaring. The development of plantation economy directly affected the volume of slave trade. The slave trade gained importance not just for the profits but because the Caribbean islands would have remained largely undeveloped without the slaves. In the eighteenth century, the West Indian trade constituted a sizeable portion of the colonial trade of both Britain and France.

Both Britain and France had powerful vested interests in the West Indies. Their colonies were located fairly close to each other and they dealt in almost the same products. There was intense commercial competition between the two. In the early-seventeenth century, the Dutch received a charter in 1621 to develop trade and commercial settlements in this region. They neglected this of settlement and instead concentrated on the slave trade. They became the chief suppliers of slaves to not only the Spanish colonists but also to the French and the English. The British settlements in this region included the Bahamas, Jamaica, Leeward – Charibee Islands, St Kitts, Montserrat, Bermuda and Barbados. They also laid claims to certain other islands which were under French control. The French colonies included the Lesser Antilles, Martinique, Guadeloupe, St Kitts, St Domingo, modern Haiti and western Hispaniola. The West Indian goods were first placed under enumerated list because of their profitability (these goods had to be first taken to England). Goods like sugar, tobacco, cotton, indigo and dyewoods could not be transported to any place directly and had to be carried in the ships of the mother country and then trans-shipped to the actual destination. The French plantation economy matched equally with the British. The Caribbean trade was firmly integrated with the English economy as it served the economic needs of the British manufacturers. The West Indies sugar plantations contributed to the setting up of a number of sugar mills in Britain, the tobacco brought from the new world was cut and packed at Liverpool while Glasgow, Lancashire became an important centre of textiles which met its need of raw materials from the colonies. The woollen industries of Yorkshire were fed by indigo and logwood from the New World. The French West Indies were also important for France but the colonial commerce was not so well integrated in the French economic structure as her industrialization was not as advanced as that of England. The French reaped immense profits from the West Indian trade through re-exports to European countries. Although the Seven Years War was fought to destroy French commerce in the West Indies, the English were not completely successful and the French were able to regain their losses. The French imports from American and Caribbean colonies constituted one-third of the total imports in 1776 (136/369.6 million livres). But in the total French exports the value of exports to the colonies constituted a very small proportion (42/328.2 million livres). This vast imbalance between exports and imports was compensated by the slave trade and led to dramatic rise of many ports such as Nantes, St Malo, La Rochelle and Bayonne.

Throughout the eighteenth century, sugar was the real base of the economy for all West Indian islands, whether under the British or under the French, although several other products such as coffee, ginger, indigo and cotton were available in these islands. These products needed slave labour on a large scale and to fully exploit and utilize the resources of these colonies, the import of slaves continued to rise. The West Indian colonies were responsible for creating a triangular trade linking Africa, Europe and the West Indies. The French and the English had developed not only economic but strategic interests in this region. This trade was regulated through navigational laws. After the Treaty of Utrecht, Jamaica became the chief centre of illegal trade and piracy. Goods were sent from here to Spanish colonies. In 1730, Jamaica had an annual trade turnover of £3,62,000. The English trade grew continuously throughout the eighteenth century and the Seven Years War made the British supremacy quite effective. On the other hand, this war had serious economic impact on the French colonial trade and the French privateering activities were greatly reduced. The colonial commerce needed a large concentration of capital that could not be afforded by very few individuals. Thus the number of smaller entrepreneurs in colonial commerce continued to decrease. The American War of Independence had a great bearing on the fortunes of the West Indies as they had direct trade relations with the North American colonies, and it provided the French an opportunity to recover some of the losses. Thus, the French continued to resist the English and thwart their efforts of establishing their supremacy in the West Indian region. Their economic strength and the extent of colonies of the two powers matched evenly in this region.

The West Indian islands became the focal point of the 'triangular trade'. Some of the English ships left Europe with manufactured goods like paper, knives, woollens and blankets for North America. They exchanged the goods for fish, timber, oil and foodstuff for Jamaica or Barbados and took back home, apart from many other products, sugar to feed the British sugar refineries. Another route of the 'triangular trade' was to Africa with European goods like rum and textiles, which were exchanged for slaves for the West Indies and the American settlements. Both Britain and France succeeded in profitably super-imposing their own colonial structures on the existing European trade.

The colonial empires in the Old World of Africa and Asia were greatly different from the western trade of North America and the West Indies. In the western hemisphere, there were a large number of settlers from Europe but as Africa and Asia were well populated, few Europeans settled here. The presence of a huge white population in the New World created a demand for British and French products. However, in Africa and Asia the demand for foreign goods hardly existed. The kind of market provided by the Caribbean and the North American colonies did not exist in the Old World. The most important difference between the two zones was in the mode of operations. The chartered and monopolistic companies had failed in the New World but in Africa and Asia these companies remained the main instruments for trade. From Africa the rival powers acquired gold, ivory, timber, dyewood, gum, wax, leather and many types of the cheaper spices. In the initial period, the colonial empire developed in the states located between Senegal and Gold Coast along western Africa. The Portuguese started the African trade in the late fifteenth century. Subsequently, the Dutch tried to replace the Portuguese. The Portuguese had maintained their monopoly for centuries but the Dutch began to force their way into new trading spheres. Later, the English and the French began to create their own colonies. The French settlements in Africa were divided between the Department of

Senegal and the Department of Guinea. Senegal was better known for gold and gum rather than slaves. Andrégrue tried to dislodge the British in this region but failed. The French also made efforts to settle in Madagascar in 1675 but they failed and only annexed this place almost a century later in 1768. Madagascar developed into an important base for sea pirates and slave traders.

An official company that had been created when Richelieu was in power carried on the French trade in Africa. However, this African company was unable to manage this enormous trade and satisfied neither the planters in the West Indies nor the government. It was then thrown open to private traders in 1716. John Law made serious efforts in 1720 to develop a triangular trade and he united all the small companies into the West African Company but it failed. The slave trade was now again in private hands and the merchants of Bordeaux, Nantes and St Malo actively participated in it. Between 1786 and 1788 about 3,000 slaves were annually exported from Africa to the New World. The value of each slave was about 1,300 livres. France exported to Africa goods valued at 180 lakh livres. Of this, goods worth 100 lakh livres came from outside and the rest from French agriculture and industries.

The British African colonies had developed seven important forts on the Gold Coast and also developed bases at Ganvia and Whydah. The English, like the French, never tried to create settlements in this region. Climatically it was not suitable to the Europeans to come and settle in large numbers. Moreover, this region was known for its slave trade but was considered a risky venture and unsafe for the Europeans. Although the British government had created the Royal African Company to conduct trade with Africa, an informal empire had emerged which represented the interest of the private traders and merchants. Every company in Africa faced the problem of insolvency and capital shortage. It remained a common problem for all of them. The English Royal African Company was abolished in 1750, and instead a loosely knit body of private traders was created. With this English Royal African Company trade increased by almost 400 per cent in the next twenty-five years. African colonies constituted an important place in British and French foreign trade. The slave trade helped the shipping industry of both states. New England's rum industry was sustained by slave labour while the region also offered a vast market for the coarse variety of Indian textiles.

Asia was another arena which witnessed intense colonial struggle between the French and the British. The Portuguese had reached India and developed their colonies in Asia without undertaking any large-scale territorial conquests. In the early part of the seventeenth century, the Dutch companies (DOC) established footholds in certain parts of Asia and began challenging the Portuguese domination over the Asian trade. They broke the Portuguese monopoly to a large extent and established their own colonial empire in Indonesia. The Dutch also participated in the regional trade and monopolized the profit of the 'country' trade. The English involvement in Asia began with the creation of the East India Company in 1600. They established their first settlement at Surat in India which remained the headquarters of the English company till it was replaced by Bombay in 1687. The English also developed some settlements on the Coromandel coast and a factory was founded at Masulipatam. Later a fortified factory was created at Fort St George which later developed into the town of Madras. In the east, the English first established their settlement in Balasore and later established a factory at Hughli. By the eighteenth century, the English East India Company had established three principal settlements at Calcutta, Madras and Bombay. By this time the Dutch were losing their hold while the French emerged as important rivals to British supremacy. The two powers were evenly balanced till about 1740. But the Austrian War of Succession and later the Seven Years War turned the tide against the French. The French had two principal settlements located close to the English Presidency towns of Calcutta and Madras – Chandernagor and Pondicherry in Bengal and on the Tamil coast respectively. Their trade continued to fluctuate, sometimes showing signs of spectacular revival till 1793.

The Asian colonies were economically well developed and specialized in manufactured items which were much in demand in different parts of the world. The two companies often brought Chinese luxury products and Indian calicoes and fine variety of textiles which enjoyed enormous popularity in Europe. The Indians also manufactured coarse fabrics which were needed by the New World to clothe the slaves. With a reasonably well-developed economy and populated lands there was hardly any scope for the English and the French to come and settle in large numbers in Asia. It was the French governor Dupleix who showed the path to gaining political power. He acquired important centres of production in the 'northern circars' by supporting the existing ruling families against the English. Under Robert Clive the English brought Bengal, Bihar and Orissa under the East India Company's rules, participated in political intrigues and later were openly involved in wars against the Indian rulers. The wars between the French and the English in the second half of the eighteenth century altered the political balance in favour of the English and the French had to survive in India in small pockets surrounded by the English. With a limited trade from Pondicherry the French colonial effort shifted in two directions – towards Indo–China where they failed, and in the islands of the Indian Ocean where they successfully created their colony at Mauritius. In Eastern Asia, Christian missions such as the one led by Pierre Joseph Pigneau also contributed to the French efforts to establish colonies there. He made genuine attempts to establish French control over Vietnam–Cambodia. From there the French could retain and control their colonial possession on the east African coasts.

The chief reason assigned for the failure of French colonial efforts was its weak navy. It is true that the French government started taking interest in naval expansions much later than the British but the efforts of Choiseul, Richelieu and Colbert cannot be ignored and it would be wrong to presume that the French failed solely because of their naval weakness. In fact, France had contested the British on equal terms till Napoleon's time. It is more fruitful to locate the causes of French failure in the respective socio-economic structure of France and Britain. The French foreign trade had grown enormously but the colonial trade had not been properly integrated within the industrial organization. The process of industrialization in France remained artificial as it was created through mercantilist measures. The French bourgeoisie was not prepared to take risks and invest in industrial ventures and preferred safer investments such as in land and the purchase of official posts. On the other hand, the British foreign trade was more balanced and the British export to the colonies grew rapidly. The colonial trade was well integrated with the internal economy of Britain. The British financial structure, including the institutions of banking and credit, forms of business organization and entrepreneurial spirit showed greater maturity and a higher level of development. The French government concentrated all its efforts and investment in the West Indian islands, and in the process never realized the potential of other regions like India till it was too late. Private mercantile interests of the British traders and officials were more powerful compared to the French and the former succeeded in creating an unofficial empire based on trade interests and thus proved to be more lasting and effective.

Impact of Empires on Colonists

Colonial society in America and the West Indies began to take shape from the 1660s. American cultural life by the mid-eighteenth century was woven of many ethnic strands with people coming from England, Ireland, Holland, France and Germany. Many colonies were composed of people of non-English stock. They made invaluable contribution to the economic and cultural life of the American colonies. The Swedes in Delaware were gradually absorbed by the English culture and lost their language and national customs. On the other hand, the Dutch made a lasting impact on the lives of the people inhabiting New York and the territories along the Hudson and New Jersey through their culture, architecture and customs. A large number of immigrants from Ireland and Scotland created Presbyterian Church while many from Wales who had settled in Pennsylvania were Quakers. The revocation of the Edict of Nantes in France in 1685 caused an exodus of the Huguenots into the colonial lands. Later the French intellectual influence through the writings of Montesquieu, Voltaire, Diderot, etc., gave a liberal tinge to the colonial society. The introduction of black slaves brought about a sharp division in society between the colonies of the north and the colonies located in the south in North America. The southern states of North America had developed an elaborate plantation economy specializing in cotton, sugar and tobacco cultivation and hence based on slave labour. It reflected a semi-feudal structure which made the society vastly different from that of the northern states. There were complex elements involved in the formation of colonial society. Because of the isolation of the early settlers family life, domesticity became a dominant aspect of social life. Art and architecture developed within humble households unlike Europe where they developed in the grand *maisons* or palaces.

The eighteenth century witnessed the growth of colonial culture. Roads and waterways brought isolated colonial units together and promoted greater exchange of visits and information. Many social, intellectual organizations were established and they had definite influence in forming public opinion. Several clubs, such as the Irish Club, the French Club in New York, and the Philosophical Club at Newport were formed. Besides, as in France and England, numerous lodges of Free Masons came into existence promoting Americanism. The social and intellectual boundaries among the thirteen settlements began gradually to disappear. 'The Republic of Letters' was formed on the European model which established scientific and intellectual correspondence with the outside world. The periodical press grew rapidly because of better roads, and expanding trade. The *Boston News Letter* which at one time represented the entire periodical press of the colonies was followed by new publications like *New England Courant* in Boston (1721), *Pennsylvania Gazette* (1729), *The Virginia Gazette* (1736). Many others promoted the newspaper press and literacy in North America. The success of the newspapers reflected the growing interest in popular literature, science, trade and political doctrines such as social contract or the balance of power. It also revealed that the notable feature of the colonial society was the extreme diversity of ecclesiastical situation. In the mid-eighteenth century music, theatre, painting and sculpture emerged in the American colonies in which associations like Orpheus Club of Philadelphia (1753), Saint Cecilia Society at Charleston (1762) and orchestra groups in

New York (1753) made significant contributions. An exhibition of colonial art was held in New York in 1757.

The division of the colonies into a dozen independent governments provided flexibility to colonial institutions, permitting experimentations and adoption of new ideas. Events in Europe affected the colonies in many ways. The English Revolution in 1688–9 brought about changes in the suffrage laws of many colonies. Similarly, the ideas of Enlightenment in France were well received in the American colonies and greatly influenced the American constitution. Democratic processes had already started much before the American independence, as the lower house of legislature in almost every colony was an elected forum.

The economic life of people living in the colonies was regulated by a series of laws. Under the Navigation Acts, all manufactured articles had to be imported from the mother countries. In the direct trade between the northern colonies and England, the balance was heavily against the colonies while the southerners because of their dependence on agriculture and plantation, had plenty to offer to the mother country. Although, inter-colonial trade was considered a source of profit with great possibilities for capital accumulation, the stringent regulations deprived the colonists from earning substantial profits. They had to function within the framework of navigational laws. The English West Indies with an estimated population of about one hundred and fifty thousand, of whom nearly one hundred and twenty-two thousand were slaves, needed large quantities of general provisions, household items, horses and timber from the continental colonies and the latter received in exchange sugar, molasses and bills of exchange. The stock of colonists in this trade was increasing but the restrictions imposed by the English government prevented them from making profits. The 'Molasses Act' of 1733 placed a prohibition on the import of foreign molasses. This was aimed at preventing all trade with the French West Indies. The colonists felt that their legitimate trade and future expansion had both been sacrificed. The American colonies faced a prolonged period of business depression and heavy losses because of the European wars particularly the Anglo–French wars, mounting debt and increasing taxation. The common grievances and the feeling of being exploited united the people of North American colonies together and a spirit of nationalism grew.

The English and the French West Indies, like the English South American colonies, were dominated by large-landed estates and needed huge capital investments which led to the creation of plantation conclaves. The sugar plantations were started by the Dutch after their failures in the Brazilian venture. The West Indian agricultural economy took two different forms – one depended on slave labour while the other was subsistence agriculture dependent on family labour. The latter ultimately gave way to the large-landed estates with the advent of slave labour from Africa. With this, tobacco and coffee cultivation in many parts gave way to labour and capital intensive sugar plantations. The withdrawal of the Dutch West India Company brought the other European nations in direct contact with the West Indies. By the beginning of the eighteenth century, the English and the French colonists had appeared on the Caribbean islands and started acquiring land for sugar plantations. Concessions were granted to the white population and its number increased rapidly and thereby intensifying the process of colonization. The Seven Years War, impacted severely the French colonial trade but the French West Indies were not badly hit. The sugar islands of the West Indies remained reasonably prosperous and most planters took personal interest in the procurement of sugar and sale of their products right up to the port where the goods were loaded for export. Yet the profit from the exports went into the pockets of privileged merchants who were close to their respective governments. This social group greatly influenced colonial policies in which the landed aristocracy of the West Indies hardly had any say.

A large proportion of the population in the West Indies were slaves brought from Africa. The original inhabitants of the West Indies were greatly reduced with the passage of time and outsiders constituted the major portion of the total population. An interesting feature of the West Indian population was that neither the European managerial staff nor the African workforce was self-sustaining. Growing plantations and the need for an even larger labour force along with the net national decrease in the native population resulted in continuous immigration. The agricultural pattern in the West Indies developed quite differently from that of Europe. The plantation economy had many feudal features. On the one hand the owners of the landed estates enjoyed vast legal, administrative and police powers and reserved the right to punish all types of crimes and settle disputes. On the other hand, the plantation complexes produced specialized products and catered to distant markets. Its huge capital investment came from Europe and made the West Indian aristocracy greatly dependent on the European investors.

In Africa, the English and the French established several conclaves along the coast during the eighteenth century. The European trade with the West Indies was based on slave traffic. The impact of the slave trade has been debated in recent years. There were some who tried to justify it on the ground that the trade proved beneficial for the slaves as they came in contact with the civilized world and the Christian religion. It was also suggested that the export of slaves led to the economic development of distant lands like the West Indies and southern America. It is not easy to make a general assessment of the impact but it can be said definitely that the disastrous consequences of the slave trade varied from one part of Africa to another. During the eighteenth century, the rival European Powers like Britain and France had not gone into the interior of Africa and mostly operated along the coastal conclaves. The impact of the large-scale trans-shipment of Africans caused the small village societies to disappear completely, while some other areas were indirectly affected. Though located on the 'slave coast' some regions like the kingdom of Benin between the Igdo in the east to Yoruba in the west did not participate in the slave trade. The destructiveness of the trade must have also varied with the forms of enslavement. Wars were carried out to capture slaves in which the very old and the very young were often killed and the rest were shifted to unknown destinations. In the political warfare in Africa, the slave trade emerged as a by-product but it proved extremely destructive. Even for the captured slaves, death while in transit to the coast, while in confinement awaiting shipment and in the course of sea journey to America or the West Indies was quite common and the losses were probably 30 to 50 per cent.

Asia in the eighteenth century witnessed constant wars among the European powers, most of which were totally unrelated to any event in Asia. The rival companies trading in this region actively participated in political intrigues. The basic objective was to control the chief centres of production. The French took the lead during the Carnatic wars in the mid-eighteenth century. The English company under the leadership of Clive succeeded in establishing political authority in the eastern parts of India. At the beginning of the century, the Dutch company had acquired small territories from where they carried their Indian trade. Their position was already well established in the Indonesian islands. The impact of the European rivalry was felt in eastern India. The English promoted merchant associations to eliminate the competition from other European powers. As Asia did not require European goods in large quantities and as it was not conducive to large-scale white settlement all attempt was towards the control of the existing trade and political domination over the manufacturing centres. The Dutch had established a lead in the mid-seventeenth century by establishing a silk reeling unit at Kasim Bazar in Bengal. The impact of the Europeans on the Indian trade is seen differently by different scholars. K.N. Choudhury suggests that the presence of Europeans increased the volume of trade and contributed to the export-based textile industries while others consider that European presence led to the decline of the Indian textile sector. From the middle of the eighteenth century, the assumption of political power by the English company altered the entire basis of trade. The English acquired the right to collect revenue and this made their position supreme. The land revenue began to be used as a major source of investment in the company trade. Thus agriculture in the eastern region was now sacrificed to the commercial interests of the company. The competition among the European companies had a great bearing on the fortunes of the Indian artisans, weavers and merchants. The English openly forced weavers to manufacture textiles only for the English company. The Dutch resisted the English move in 1759 by sending an expedition against the English but suffered complete defeat and were obliged to recognize English domination. The French also resisted the English. Though they failed in Bengal but could retain their hold on the Coromandel coast. The old traditional system of making advances called *dadni* was replaced by the *gumashta* system – where agents worked directly under European supervision. The independence of the Indian weavers and merchants was reduced considerably. The Europeans slowly replaced the Indian agencies participating in foreign trade. In Ceylon, the English acquired unlimited rights not only over cinnamon but also over other products which were exported from that region. The French presence in Pondicherry also affected the local society in that region. The two powers in their private capacities were involved in the slave trade (young Indians were taken to the islands in the Indian Ocean particularly to the rice producing territories in Mauritius as slaves labour) and in the transfer of funds to Europe through illegal channels. The European companies during the eighteenth century in South Asia had different impact on different regions. In territories where the competition was relatively free and the English political domination was absent, the presence of the European merchants generated increased economic activity. With the emergence of the English East India Company as a political power in Bengal, the process of economic exploitation and the decline of Indian handicrafts began.

Impact on Europe

A question that is often raised is the role of colonial trade in industrialization, particularly in Great Britain. A number of scholars argue that it was through colonial commerce that Britain accumulated much of its wealth. While the triangular trade involving slaves provided high profits, it also needed huge investments as the lengthy voyages blocked capital for extended periods. Traffic in slaves consequently promoted concentration of capital in the hands of slave traders. Equally important, was the growing demand in the later part of the eighteenth century, for the cheap European finished products in the colonies and the increasing volume of colonial trade providing raw materials for the newly emerging industries. Although the colonial trade may not have activated industrial activities in France to the extent it had in Britain, it certainly promoted economic prosperity in the coastal belt of France. Colonial trade became the most dynamic sector of France. Except for the brief period of Seven Years War, it grew twice as fast as external commerce and doubled every twenty years. The French external power in the eighteenth century reveals an impressive growth. The most significant element of that was her trade with the colonies.

Many present-day scholars have refuted the claims of earlier historians that the colonies played a crucial role in bringing about the Industrial Revolution. For them, the Industrial Revolution happened not because of external factors but because of the decline of feudalism and the emergence of capitalist forces from within the economy. No doubt colonial commerce could not have created the Industrial Revolution but neither can its role in the Industrial Revolution be denied entirely.

The plunder and the exploitation of the colonies intensified in the eighteenth century. Sugar produced by African slaves was an important source of wealth for the English in Barbados and Jamaica just as it was for the French in Santo Domingo, Martinique and Guadeloupe. However, it was the slave trade that became an important source of wealth for the Europeans. As Pierre H. Boulle points out, the slave trade was a risky business but a profitable one too. The profits existed in the multiple exchanges undertaken during the slave ship's circuitous route from Europe to Africa to the West Indies and back to Europe. Indirectly it also involved the Indian trade consisting chiefly of textiles needed for the slaves, cowries, liquor and several manufactured products. In the West Indies, the slaves were exchanged for vast quantities of sugar, cotton, indigo and cocoa. These required a large fleet vessels. There is a disagreement among scholars on the profits made in the slave trade. Not only did the price of slaves continue to fluctuate but also the long sea journey were hazardous because of pirates and bad weather. Communications were slow and voyages became more hazardous if war broke out in Europe as the news could not be communicated to those at sea leaving the voyagers with insufficient warning. There was a constant risk of epidemics breaking out on ships during the Atlantic journey caused through overloading and poor sanitary conditions. This caused heavy mortality among the slaves. However, for most European slave traders, the profits outweighed the risks involved in this trade.

In the seventeenth century, the Dutch dominated the slave trade from Africa to the New World. The English and the French were not serious contenders. Once the demand for slaves increased, the English interest rose rapidly. The Royal adventures into Africa were charted in 1660 but the English preoccupation remained with gold rather than with the slave trade. The company, while holding its chartered privileges, farmed out licences to private merchants engaged in the slave trade. It was not the Royal company but the private traders who penetrated this profitable trade. The French island in the West Indies also regulated the demand for slaves. After the War of Spanish Succession, the French slave trade was organized under Compagnie des Indes. It issued licences to the French merchants but their trade fluctuated during the eighteenth century. Despite such fluctuations, the slave trade continued to expand and there was growing resistance by the free merchants and individual shippers against the domination of the company. The possibility of reaping huge profits brought the French and the English into frequent conflicts. The expansion of this trade affected public investments from which this trade was to be financed. The French company of Angola was a joint-stock venture, although the role of the individual merchants working through licenses remained significant. The Atlantic slave trade had its outlets from

TABLE 11.1: ENGLISH EXPORT OF SLAVES FROM AFRICA

Years	Number of slaves exported
1751–60	2,50,400
1761–70	2,50,400
1771–80	1,96,000
1781–90	3,25,500

Source: Philip D. Curtin, *The Atlantic Slave Trade*, London: University of Wisconsin, 1969, p. 136.

different ports of Africa. It included Gambia, Senegal, Sierra Leone, Liberia, Gold Coast, and the Bight of Benina. In England, Liverpool became the chief port, which handled the British slave trade, handling 89.8 per cent of the total slave trade in 1802.

The areas from where slaves were brought from in Africa changed with the passage of time. No single region supplied more than a third of the British slave exports. Initially it was the Gold Coast and the Windward Coast that provided the greatest numbers. Later, Central Africa and the Bight of Biafra contributed the major portion. The French traders and the company procured substantial supply from Senegambia in the beginning but later Angola and Guinea, which became the chief suppliers. The French chief port town of Nantes was an equivalent of Liverpool of Britain. The slave trade of France was smaller than that of Britain but its importance was no less significant.

French commerce expanded enormously during the eighteenth century, in fact, it grew faster than that of Britain till the Seven Years War (1756–63). The total external trade of France increased five times from 1715 till the beginning of the French Revolution. But it was the colonial trade which grew nearly ten times despite wide fluctuations. According to Arnould, the average annual colonial commerce was 35.2 million liveres between 1715–20 while the total foreign trade of France was 203.1 million liveres. During

TABLE 11.2: IMPORT OF SLAVE TRADE

	Slaves Exported from Africa	
Period	Estimated Numbers of Slaves taken from Africa	Approximate Annual Average
Up to 1600	3,30,000	2,200
1601–1700	15,60,000	15,600
1701–1810	75,20,000	68,400
After 1810	19,50,000	32,500
	1,13,60,000	

Source: J.D. Fage, *A History of West Africa: An Introductory Survey*, Cambridge: Cambridge University Press, 1969.

1781–9, the average annual colonial commerce reached 327.6 million liveres while the total French foreign trade went up to 1,002.6 million liveres. The most important element of the colonial trade included the West Indian and West African slave trade, constituting over half of the non-European trade.

The rise of Nantes as a principal port of France was closely associated with the slave trade. As Gaston Martin points out, Nantes witnessed an unbroken increase in commercial activities throughout the eighteenth century. The merchants of this port created for themselves advance methods of trade and new capitalist combination. Thus, Nantes was the first French city to develop a genuinely modern commercial and industrial organization. This transformation was geared to the slave trading enterprises. There was a prosperous slave market in the West Indies for African slaves. The two important islands Saint Guadeloupe and Martinique received numerous slaves in the early part of the eighteenth century. As time passed and sugar cultivation reached a saturation point, their place was taken over by Saint Domingue and the English colony of Jamaica. African slaves fetched huge quantities of sugar, cotton, indigo and coco. Slave trading required huge capital investment and the vessels leaving Nantes usually returned after over a year. It took a long time before the assets could be liquidated and the profits distributed. It was not unusual to see capital blocked (sometimes as much as one million liveres) for over two years. The chief advantages of the slave trade over the more traditional sources of income, according to Pierre H. Boulle, were two – the profits were larger compared to other maritime commodities and the capital could be reinvested more easily. As regards the margins of profit in this trade, Wilson and Pilard suggest that it was over 200 per cent while writers like Gaston Martin argue that it varied between 50 and 100 per cent. The profits can be estimated from the huge increase in colonial imports during the eighteenth century. By the time of the French Revolution, it is estimated that 7,000 vessels manned by about 80,000 seamen were involved in this trade. Almost two-thirds of the French investments were involved in Saint Domingue, which was the biggest sugar island. It is not very clear where this profit from the slave trade was actually invested.

According to Boulle, the slave traders formed an oligarchy of closely-knit families who preferred to invest their profits in land and venal posts to enhance their status in the society and that no family continued trading in this field for over two generations. From this it appears that the wealth accumulated through the slave trade was not spread equally among the French bourgeoisie. The colonial trade, particularly of the West Indies, contributed directly or indirectly to the industrialization along the Atlantic coast. Sizeable industrial complexes developed along the Atlantic coastline during the eighteenth century.

As already mentioned, Nantes became one of the most important port towns of France. Lorient was given a privileged status by the government to conduct the trade of the French East India Company. It became the chief centre for oriental products, including spices, which were re-exported to other parts of Europe. Bordeaux and La Rochelle became the godowns and distribution centres for West Indian products. Le Havre and Marseilles (on the Mediterranean coast) developed the shipping industry and participated in the African and West Indian trade. Marseilles was the chief Mediterranean port of France which gained immensely through its trade with Levant. Numerous sugar refineries were established providing employment for French labour. The cotton obtained from the colonies partially replaced the locally grown hemp in the textile sector. In the first half of the eighteenth century, trade with Canada provided immense benefit to the French merchants. Bordeaux was particularly active in this trade because large quantities of food and spirits, including flour and wines constituted the major part of shipments to the American colonies and these items were available in the surrounding regions. In the inter-war period, on an average twenty-seven ships of 4,200 tons were sent to New France every year while La Rochelle sent fifteen ships annually. Bayonne also had active ties with Louisbourg and Quebec. The French fishing industry had grown sixfold because of her trade links with Newfoundland. They had manufacturing industry in Le Havre and Rouen thrived on the Canadian furs and gum from Africa imported from Senegal. Tobacco was procured from the West Indies and Lousiana and was processed in Dieppe, Morlaix and Bayonne.

TABLE 11.3: OFFICIAL SUGAR IMPORTS TO THE EUROPEAN COUNTRIES

(*annual average in 1,000 tons*)

	France	England	Portugal	Total
1741–5	65	41	34	140
1766–70	78	74	20	172

Source: Richard B. Sheriden, *Sugar and Slavery: An Economic History of the British West Indies, 1623–1775*, University of West Indies Press, 2000, p. 25 (based on data provided by David MacPherson and John MacGregor).

Nantes and Rouen became important textile centres because of the demands of the slave trade and because of the cheap imitation of Indian textiles. Lyons began to depend heavily on colonial raw materials, particularly the dyes. It was the principal textile and silk centre of France and depended on the export market. However, luxury textiles could be purchased only by the aristocracy in the West Indies. The colonial commerce also substantially contributed to the shipbuilding industry in Bordeaux and St Malo. The impact of the colonies went beyond trade. The largest centres of sugar refining were also the principal colonial ports. By the late-eighteenth century, France reflected two contrasting economies – the coastal economy which was moving towards a capitalist organization and the interior regions of France which still remained feudal.

On the issue of importance or insgnificance of the role of colonies in the economic growth of the mother country, Edmund Burke and Adam Smith stood at opposite poles respectively. Many writers suggest that it was through colonial commerce that Britain acquired much of the capital, specially from the triangular trade. This trade gave enormous profit needed to sustain the industrial process. The British colonies not only provided raw materials for the industries that had started developing in the second half of the eighteenth century, but also created demand for the finished products from these industries. Although it will be wrong to assume that the Industrial Revolution was caused by the colonial empires, the role of the colonies cannot be dismissed. There were many factors which contributed to the rapid industrialization such as population growth within Britain causing increased demand for manufactured goods, the rise of the bourgeoisie because of economic prosperity, increasing rent resulting in commercialization of agriculture and the rise of the tenant class, etc. At the same time, one cannot ignore the contribution of the French oceanic trade in the industrial expansion. There was rapid expansion of the colonial trade of Britain during the eighteenth century. In 1715, trade with North America and the West Indies constituted 19 per cent of the total British foreign trade and it went up to 34 per cent in 1785. Even for France this trade was important as it constituted 28 per cent of her total trade in 1785. The British trade with Africa and Asia also grew rapidly and constituted 19 per cent as against 7 per cent at the beginning of the century, while the French trade with these regions showed a marginal increase from 5 to 6 per cent. Frequent wars and colonial losses may have contributed to this.

The population of the English North American colonies had grown ten times between 1700 and 1774. Almost the entire colonial population spent some part of their export earnings to purchase goods manufactured in Britain. The farmers of sugar cane or paddy, whether in the English or the French West Indies, spent a large part of their income on purchasing foodstuff, timber and horses. The British colonists were increasing their share of trade in the Atlantic region. However, the Navigation Acts placed restrictions on their trading activities and prevented them from purchasing cheaper goods from non-British states or their colonies. Apart from sending sugar, rice, coffee, dyewoods and tobacco, the colonies were meeting the British demand for raw materials in many key sectors. The British West Indian colonies provided about 20 per cent of the homeland's total imports between 1714 and 1773 – much of it was re-exported at substantial profits while it also acted as the main source of absorption of slaves. Bristol and Liverpool competed with each other to dominate the greater share of the slave traffic in the mid-eighteenth century but in the end Liverpool emerged as the principal slave centre, controlling nearly two-thirds of the total British slave trade. It also became the principal textile centre and remained so till the rise of Manchester in the second half of the nineteenth century. Liverpool also emerged an important centre of the tobacco industry. Tobacco, which was produced in the American colonies, was brought, cut and packed here, generating employment to the English. The black population of Africa and the West Indies became the chief consumers of rum of Britain. Yorkshire and Glasgow became the main centres of woollen industry depending on the supply of indigo and dyewood brought from the tropical colonies. Several sugar refineries were set up along the coastal belt of south-west England. The colonial demand also promoted export industries such as cotton, wool, silk, nails, paper mills, chinaware and pottery.

Eric William argues that profits made from slave trade made it possible to finance the industrial revolution, a view no more tenable. Yet, as Hugh Thomas brings out, those who became rich through slave trade, often put their profit to greater use, e.g. John Ashton of Liverpool financed Sankey Brook Canal between Liverpool and Manchester, Rene Montaudoin became a pioneer of cotton manufacture in Nantes and James de Wolf in Briston. Similar investments were made on shipbuilding, rope industry, production of guns, rum, brandy and sugar production and on insurance.

According to Immanuel Wallerstein, the evolution of world capitalism passed through four stages. The first stage reflected Europe's early luxury trade with China and India. In the second stage, there was geographical expansion but only moderate evolution. One of the chief features of this period was the intense rivalry between England and France and England's attempt to destroy Holland's hegemonic position. Economic issues resulted in wars among these nations in which the Dutch republic lost its power and ceded economic dominance to the English and the French. This period till 1763 was a time of unbroken rivalry over the questions of colonial territories, markets and supplies of tropical and semi-tropical products and slaves. By the end of 1763, England emerged as the dominant nation in the world economic system. Sugar and slavery were the two important elements which contributed to the colonial expansion. After 1760, according to Wallerstein, the capitalist world economy experienced a dramatic transformation. This was the introduction of mechanization leading to the Industrial Revolution and this period (1760–1815) was the last crucial phase of Anglo–French contests for hegemony in the world economy. The British triumph was achieved largely because of superior strength of its state machinery and military power. It was the Anglo–French rivalry and the colonial wars between the two countries that gave a tremendous advantage to Britain.

Thus, a period of worldwide supremacy opened up for England and it was on an enlarged territorial base that English capitalism developed its markets, extended its domination and organized accumulation. The colonies were developed by the European states for this purpose only.

Suggested Readings

Anderson, M.S., *Europe in the Eighteenth Century, 1713–1783*, London: Longmans, 1975.

Chaudhuri, K.N., *The Trading World of Asia and the English East India Company 1660–1760*, Cambridge: Cambridge University Press, 1978. A thorough work on the English trade in Asia.

Chaudhury, Sushil and Michel Morineau, eds., *Merchants, Companies and Trade: Europe and Asia in the Early Modern Era*, New York: Cambridge University Press, 1999. Contains some very useful articles on the subject.

Curtin, Philip D., *The Atlantic Slave Trade*, London: University of Wisconsin Press, 1969. Rich in statistical details and narrative.

———, *Cross-Cultural Trade in World History*, New York: Cambridge University Press, 1984.

Fage, J.D., *A History of South Africa: An Introductory Survey*, Cambridge: Cambridge University Press, 1969. An outline history of the region from AD 900 until the end of the colonial period and discusses the political development, the European scramble for colonies and the slave trade.

Furber, Holden, *Rival Empires of Trade in the Orient 1600–1800*, Minneapolis: University of Minnesota Press, 1976. A well-researched authoritative work regarded by many historians as a masterpiece.

Parry, J.H., *Trade and Dominion: The European Overseas Empire in the Eighteenth Century*, London/New York: Praeger Publishers, 1971. A standard work on the subject with explicit discussion of events.

Sinha, Arvind, *The Politics of Trade: Anglo-French Commerce on the Coromandel Coast 1763–1793*, New Delhi: Manohar, 2002. Takes up the trade structure of the rival powers in India and the consequences of the rivalry on the Indians.

Thomas, Hugh, *The Slave Trade: The History of the Atlantic Slave Trade, 1440–1870*, London: Picador, 1997. A thorough discussion on the origins, nature and results of slave trade is provided.

Williams, G., *The Expansion of Europe in the Eighteenth Century: Overseas Rivalry, Discovery and Exploitation*, London: Blandford Press, 1966.

CHAPTER 12

Enlightenment and Enlightened Despotism

Eighteenth century was a period of material expansion and prosperity in many parts of Europe. It was accompanied by a marked rise in literary production. The cultural sphere, although still dominated by aristocratic tastes, drew new audiences from the non-aristocratic classes. National culture was becoming cosmopolitan by crossing political boundaries through literary and scientific activities. The Enlightenment emerged as an important dimension of the European cultural life. The Enlightenment was not a coherent body of ideas but was broadly a collection of philosophical views in vogue among the intellectuals during the eighteenth century. Originating from classical times and the Renaissance, these ideas were developed by scientific thinkers and philosophers like Renè Descartes, John Locke, Isaac Newton and many others. These were based on rationalism and humanism. However the pattern of Enlightenment ideology tended to vary from one country to another and it changed according to the peculiar circumstances of each country. Yet most of the thinkers definitely shared the new intellectual environment that was based on observation rather than tradition and obscurantism. Its intellectual content proved crucial to the development of modern society.

Most Enlightenment thought had originated from certain basic premises. Firstly, it was proved by the scientists that natural rather than supernatural forces governed the entire universe. Secondly, it was based on rigorous application of 'scientific methods'. And thirdly, it was presumed that science could help the human race achieve infinite improvement. Isaac Newton had ably demonstrated that all motion in heaven and earth were predictable and that nature was governed neither by divine nor mysterious intervention but by humanly perceivable universal laws. This did not mean that Enlightenment thinkers rejected God and that they were Atheists. Most of them were Deists and believed that once a perfect universe was created, there was no more divine intervention.

Generally speaking, the Enlightenment passed through three distinct stages. Its first phase was the early eighteenth century that was greatly influenced by the Scientific Revolution. The second phase was the period of 'high Enlightenment' that began with Montesquieu's *The Spirit of the Laws* in 1748 and lasted till the era of Voltaire. The third phase began after 1778 and was dominated by Rousseau's ideas.

Chief Ideas

It was the Scientific Revolution of the seventeenth century that created conditions for the emergence of the Enlightenment movement in Europe. The Enlightenment philosophy stemmed from the scientific method as suggested by Bacon and Descartes. This method was based on dispassionate, empirical observation of specific phenomenon in order to arrive at general laws. The Scientific Revolution had greatly encouraged research for new studies. This was not confined to abstract and philosophical studies but applied to human affairs as well. These thinkers believed that the world of human nature could be mastered by scientific means. Thus, Kepler's formulative laws on celestial bodies and Galileo's laws on terrestrial bodies provided mathematical precision to the experimental methods. Newton's gravitational laws laid emphasis on observation, application and formulation. He clearly stated that knowledge alone is not sufficient; its application should be based on empiricism. The ideas of Enlightenment also borrowed from the philosophy of intellectuals like John Locke. He was not only an influential philosopher but also the propounder of an important theory of knowledge, which he presented in his famous work *Essay Concerning Human Understanding*. The Enlightenment thinkers concluded that everything is determined by the environment. These scientific ideas were bound to undermine the traditional political ideas on which the authority of the absolute rulers was based, e.g. the divine right of rulers.

During the eighteenth century, the ideas of the Enlightenment were further developed in France and publicized throughout Europe. There was a sudden outpouring of highly critical literature and ideas of governance. This became the new philosophy of the Enlightenment. This critical spirit did not occur in an intellectual vacuum. The empirical method was adopted for the secularization of political thought. Political activity was to be judged not by supernatural or mystical order, rather by observable facts of political life. The political philosophy of Enlightenment was constructed without reference to divine revelation. The scientific spirit was used against superstitions, inhumanity and irrationality of the existing governments. Most political thinkers of that period lived in France were directly or indirectly influenced by the existing state of affairs. While analysing the inefficiency and autocratic nature of the state, the philosophers were immediately confronted with the problem of privileges, religious tolerance and the basis of royal authority. Tradition had taught the Europeans that the social order based on privileges was necessary for the efficient functioning of society. The political philosophers focused on the exploited elements of these privileges, as these were considered to be against the laws of nature. For a society to be based on national laws and justice, on rationality and on knowledge, many of the existing ideas had to go. It was an attempt to replace arbitrary rules with rules based on reason and the political and administrative structure of the *ancien regime* in France came under scathing attack. The Enlightenment thinkers considered the church to be the most privileged and wealthy body enjoying unlimited power. Individual critics had protested earlier against the absolute powers of the church but for the first time the national laws on the universe gave a powerful weapon to the followers of the Enlightenment.

Enlightenment in France was accompanied by several intellectual trends which were against customary laws as well as the theory of Divine Rights by providing a new basis for the origins of legitimate political authority. Most thinkers regarded the social contract as the true basis of state formation. With it, the functions of state and its obligation to society were redefined. Some French intellectuals formed a group and called themselves physiocrats. It included a number of luminaries such as Turgot (the Finance Minister of Louis XVI who seriously condemned religious intolerance and believed in the beneficial effects of the diffusion of knowledge) Quesnay and Dupont de Nemours. They believed in an all-embracing society based on natural order to protect the right of self-preservation. For them the right to property was a goal to be realized in a civil society and the ruler's activities in this sphere ought to be restricted. They suggested that all artificial control over land use should be brought to an end to free productive capacity and allow independent flow of produce to the market. By artificial restrictions, they meant the feudal and seigniorial system. The physciocrats believed that the best government was that which interfered least. However, this view was not shared by most Enlightenment thinkers. Another group consisted of scholars called encyclopaedists led by Diderot. He strongly believed in the spread of knowledge and for that purpose he laboured day and night to prepare encyclopaedias based on classification of knowledge. These writers also played their part in preparing the ground for modern Europe.

During the seventeenth and eighteenth centuries, a Republic of Letters was formed by a self-proclaimed community of scholars and literary figures. These group of men transcended national boundaries. The members of the Republic of Letters exchanged ideas and knowledge through letters, visits and correspondence. They exchanged ideas across state frontiers with each other. Historians debate the relationship between the Republic of Letters and Enlightenment and whether the Republic of Letters and the Enlightenment as distinct and separate.

It is commonly believed that the Enlightenment as a movement was confined to France alone. France became the main centre of the Enlightenment and its major exponents came to be called *philosophe*. It included not only the French philosophers but even outsiders who wished to reform the society in which they lived by popularizing the new scientific interpretation for a host of existing problems. Their writings included major works of philosophy as well as literary and critical pieces in the form of pamphlets. It was because of their writings that French became an international language respected in the major courts of Europe. Important philosophers of the Enlightenment included Montesquieu (*De l'Esprit des Lois*), Condillac (*Essai Sur l'Origine des Connaissances Humaines*), Voltaire (*Dictionnaire Philosophique*) and Rousseau (*Contrat Social* and *Emile*). There were many other popular intellectual figures – Jean d'Alembert, the mathematician, Marquis de Condorcet, a political figure during the French Revolution, statesman Jacques Turgot and the social scientist and philosopher Claude Adrien Helvetius and Baron d'Holbach. All of them emphasized that reason and observation were the basis of knowledge and not same ancient authority. They believed that human behaviour followed laws that could be discovered by reason and observation and that laws could be applied to morality, government, economy and social order. They also believed that the Enlightenment focused attention on ways to make human life better. In political theory they believed that power is a trust from the community. In certain places this doctrine encouraged resistance to absolutism. These Enlightenment thinkers had different solutions to the problems of human exploitation, political misgovernance or governmental tyranny.

Among all the philosophers, Voltaire exerted the greatest influence on some of the contemporary rulers because of his style of writing, his wit and radical but practical solutions. No doubt France had become the nursery for influential thinkers but the movement had emerged elsewhere too. Outside France, there were many other thinkers like Edward Gibbon, David Hume and Adam Smith in Great Britain, Gotthold Ephrain Lessing, the famous playwright and critic as well as Immanuel Kant in Germany, the Marquis of Beccaria, an Italian economist and legal reformer from Milan, and Benjamin Franklin and Thomas Jefferson the famous American philosopher-statesmen. They fought for the freedom of expression and advocated political reforms by battling against entrenched authority. Their fight was not only against traditional church authority but also against the state and its apparatus, its censorship and oppression. The fact that some of them wrote anonymously or under pseudo-names makes it obvious that strict censorship prevailed at that time. Some of them saw their publications confiscated as had happened in the case of Voltaire and Diderot. They were both imprisoned in the Bastille, the famous prison for political offenders. However, repressing their works made them popular figures and their literary works were much sought after. Their struggle and the quality of their works gave them a permanent place in history. The contributions of these intellectuals were not confined to one sphere but were path-breaking in various disciplines – in the style of history, commentaries, wit and satire, science, politics, psychology and philosophy. These thinkers also stressed the role of an independent judiciary and well-publicized laws. They spoke against torture, capital punishment and favoured public trials, equality before law, prevention rather than punishment. They also advocated complete separation between the judicial system and regular political administration. While Montesquieu insisted on the need for representative intermediary authorities, Rousseau rejected representative democracy. Most of them were not so concerned with imposing restrictions on the ruling authority or in attacking it, rather to assign a new role or certain positive tasks to it.

The definition of the Enlightenment remains difficult. Many new interpretations and assessments have emerged questioning past views. The famous German philosopher Immanuel Kant wrote an article in 1783 in a Berlin monthly journal, 'What is Enlightenment?' Since then, there have been diverse assessments on its origins, its philosophy, politics and ethics and its legacy as well as its relationship with modernity. Ernst Cassirer (*The Philosophy of the Enlightenment*) has described it as a united and self-reflexive intellectual movement concerned with understanding the very process of thought. For him, its philosophical positions and the views of its thinkers constituted 'an essentially homogeneous formative power'. It enjoyed a unity that was based upon a pre-occupation with reason, descriptive natural science, empiricism, tolerance and civil rights. Cassirer's work almost entirely focused on the writings of the philosophers and not on the wider social contexts. Equally influential was the writing of the German philosopher Jurgen Habermas. He, along with Michel Foucault and Robert Darnton, has widened the scope of the Enlightenment by including social practices and culture. In *The Stuctural Transformation of the Public Sphere: An Enquiry into a Category of Bourgeois Society,* Habermas sees the emergence of a 'public sphere' during the eighteenth century. By this term, he means publications like novels, the press, and the places where the new ideas were read and discussed such as family homes, salons, coffee houses, societies and clubs – all such places that used 'reason' in public. He argues that the literary focus of the people became a 'training ground for critical public reflection' in the political public sphere that initiated the process of democratization. A political consciousness developed in the public sphere of civil society, which in opposition to absolute sovereignty articulated the concept of and demand for general and abstract laws based on public opinion as the only legitimate source. Placing the rise of modern public sphere in the context of the rise of capitalism, Habermas suggests that during the mercantilist phase the traffic in commodities and news demonstrated their revolutionary power. The rise of capitalist society introduced new features in the state structure and eliminated estate-based authority. The public sphere emerged outside the feudal and royal courts which was free from royal control. 'Public' in a narrow sense was regarded synonymous with state. The emergence of the new democratized public sphere is called sphere of 'bourgeois sociability' by Habermas, which was independent of the absolute state and provided a platform for public criticism. Peter Gay in his work *The Enlightenment: An Interpretation*, calls the *philosophes* a loose, informal, wholly unorganized coalition of cultural critics, religious skeptics and political reformers. But they all united on a vastly ambitious programme of secularism, humanity, cosmopolitanism, freedom of aesthetic response and the freedom of a moral man to make his own way in the world. Among the more recent writers, Dorinda Outram (*The Enlightenment* in 1995) and Thomas Munck (*The Enlightenment: A Comparative Social History, 1721–1794* in 2000) present the movement as a set of debates, stresses and concerns formulated in response to the new ideas, opinions and the interaction of social and political structures during the eighteenth century. There are some scholars like Jonathan Israel and Margaret Jacob who reject the French-centred perspective.

Another approach to the Enlightenment is provided by the so-called post-modern writers such as Jean-François Lyotard (*The Postmodern Condition: A Report on Knowledge* in 1979) and Michel Foucault (*Madness and Civilization* in 1965 and *Discipline and Punish* in 1977). According to Foucault, the notion of reason under Enlightenment instead of promoting liberation became an instrument of control – silencing unreason. He neither supports the movement nor criticizes it but sees it as a shift crucial to the development of an attitude of modernity. In the nineteenth century, writers of the Romantic movement highlighted the excessive rationalism of the Enlightenment that had led to exploitation and persecution. The feminist movement of 1970s presented critiques of gender bias of the male dominated writings which ignored the needs of women. The postcolonial writings are critical of Enlightenment thought for its culture-specific approach and double standards adopted towards the European societies and the outside world.

Among the chief features of the Enlightenment as a social movement was its stress on universal laws, thereby rejecting supernaturalism. Without denying the existence of God, the advocates of the Enlightenment condemned all forms of religious intolerance. Scientific method was advocated for studying human activities as well as natural phenomena. It was an attempt to free the human mind from superstitions. Human conduct was seen as something which could be changed and not something immutable. Historians looked for evidence to explain the laws that governed the rise or decline of human society and nations while those interested in politics compared the institutions of government and forms of constitution to develop universal laws applicable to political systems. The concept of liberty, citizenship and forms of government became very popular themes in the writings of Enlightenment thinkers. The rule of law was seen as an instrument to protect individual citizens against the possibility of arbitrary excesses by the ruling powers. The laws were to be in conformity with reason and were to be administered impartially. The Enlightenment thinkers constantly emphasized the significance of the rule of law.

The ideas of the Enlightenment effectively eroded the authority of religion and instead promoted secular thinking. The imagery of superstition and rituals was ridiculed. They did not object to religion or belief in God but rejected the concept of miracles. However, scholars of this period strongly argued in favour of religious tolerance. In France, Pierre Bayle in his work *Critical and Historical Dictionary* placed religion to the test of critical reason. Traditional Christianity was seen as promoting and imposing orthodoxy, fanaticism and intolerance. He was himself a staunch Calvinist but he argued for full toleration. For him ethics existed in every religion. There were many more critical tracts on Christianity that had been circulated privately. They emphasized the role of religion in causing bloodshed and hysteria. However, the real antagonist of Christianity was Voltaire. His ideas on religion appeared in the form of sharp satire, and his brilliant and witty books became quite popular and were widely read. The church as an institution of religion was projected as a promoter of tyranny though he propagated Deism and religious tolerance. Even Diderot condemned Christianity, which he described as fanatical and unreasonable. As he grew older, his attacks on Christianity became more bitter and stronger. He became an atheist and many of his works were not allowed to be published, such as his *Supplement to the Voyage of Bouganville.* The attitude of most of the Enlightened thinkers was not to abolish religion but to 'enlarge and liberate God' from incorrect beliefs and create a more tolerant society. They rejected the concepts of hell and predestination that had ruled the European masses for centuries by nourishing superstition and ignorance. God was placed by the laws of nature.

The *Philosophes*

The French intellectuals came to be known as the *philosophes*, a term used by their critics to ridicule their pretensions but these intellectuals accepted this term with a sense of pride. They were conscious of their efforts to reform society by making popular, through their writings, the new scientific interpretations of the universe and applying the scientific method to various contemporary problems. David Hume and Immanuel Kant were the real philosophers in the sense they wrote original but obscurantist thoughts. The *philosophes* espoused views on nature, mankind, society, government, and the value of freedom. They challenged some of the fundamental tenets of the past including slavery and the divine right of rulers, and the doctrinal authority of the established church and sought to replace them by secular institutions.

A well-known name among the *philosophes* was François Marie Arouet, who became popular by the name of Voltaire (1694–1778). Several European rulers held him in high esteem. Described as the personification of the Enlightenment, he wrote on an enormous range of subjects in a variety of literary forms. In his early years he was exiled to England as a punishment for insulting a rich French nobleman. Voltaire returned after three years and was well received in the literary and social circles. He became a great admirer of Francis Bacon and John Locke. In his *Philosophic Letters On the English* (1733), he showed great fascination for English social life and the respectful attitude of the Englishmen towards merchants, scientists and literary men, as well as their freedom of press and liberty of expression. He was also impressed by the existence of religious tolerance in England. Subsequent writers agree that Voltaire had exaggerated the extent of freedom, as it existed in England but by such example he was able to draw the attention of his contemporaries to the many ills of French society that included oppressive rule under royal absolutism, lack of religious tolerance and the absence of freedom. When he left for England he was a playwright but his stay in England had made him a philosopher and a staunch critic of the French society of his times.

In France, Voltaire could never live with freedom. He spent several years in Switzerland and even made a short visit to Prussia. There he wrote an endless number of letters, plays and novels and even history. In the course of his writings, he picked up themes which had a direct bearing on the lives of the French. Although he wrote on various themes, he is especially known for his strong criticism of traditional religion and his firm belief in religious toleration. In the 'Calais Affair' Voltaire published strong letters to arouse public opinion against state oppression and advocated religious toleration in his *Treatise on Toleration*. He was also a known spokesman for civil liberties. He suggested that all forms of 'infamy' should be crushed. By infamy he implied all forms of fanaticism, bigotry and repression. He considered all those persons monsters who prosecuted others because they did not hold the same opinion. Voltaire considered religious bigotry to be a curse, as it was based on superstitions, and as superstitions led to fanaticism, it caused misery to all. Voltaire was also against all forms of arbitrary power and described those acts of the state as criminal when they resulted in unnecessary wars. While earthquakes and storms caused devastations, wars and rapacity by misguided human passions caused even grater devastation. Voltaire exercised great influence in the spread of Enlightenment ideas in his time.

Another famous figure of that period was Charles de Secondat, known as Montesquieu (1689–1755). He came from a noble background and had diverse interests. His marriage to a wealthy Protestant young lady made him financially sound and he spent most of his life in study, travel and writing. He had a classical education in his early days and then undertook university learning

Charles de Secondat, Montesquieu

in law. He revealed interest even in science and conducted experiments on the effects of temperature changes on animal tissues. His most famous work, considered a masterpiece of the Enlightenment was his *Persian Letters*. In this he created a dialogue between two persons from Persia, travelling in western Europe and sending back their impressions of what they saw and experienced. In reality Montesquieu was making his attack on contemporary French institutions, the Catholic Church and the monarchy. It was a clever way of revealing the evils that existed in traditional French society. Like Voltaire he also advocated religious toleration. He denounced the institution of slavery and suggested the use of reason to liberate the human mind from its prejudices. This work brought Montesquieu in company of the leading intellectuals of that age. He visited England and travelled to many other countries. Everywhere, he received a warm welcome. He wrote another famous work, *The Spirit of the Laws*, in 1748. In this he enunciated the concept of the 'separation of powers'. It was a treatise of comparative study of governments in which Montesquieu tried to apply the scientific method to social and political fields in order to ascertain the 'natural laws' on which social relationship depended. It has been described as a great work of political sociology. Montesquieu suggested that the form of political and social institutions depended upon numerous factors such as climate, geography, size of the state, its culture, customs and traditions and its history. He applied the principles of scientific experimentation and formulation of laws to the social and political foundations of states. He believed that there were three kinds of government – republics, despotisms and monarchies. He considered the English monarchy as the best example of political rule and that the English Constitution immensely contributed to political thought based on the idea of checks and balances and separation of power of executive, legislature and judiciary. He believed that a balance between these state institutions would prevent autocratic rule and oppression and thereby provide the greatest freedom. Although his understanding of the English Constitution was not totally correct, the translation of his work into English influenced a large number of American leaders, including American *philosophes* such as Benjamin

Franklin, James Madison and Thomas Jefferson. The American Constitution-makers incorporated the idea of separation of power and their final Constitution clearly reflects these principles. Montesquieu came to be known as a great political thinker but his view on the formation of government according to regional variations suggested that external conditions force human beings to behave in different ways and that the political system of a region is influenced by its historical traditions and environment.

One of the most pragmatic philosophes of the Enlightenment was Denis Diderot (1713–84). He was radical in his ideas and his staunch attacks on religion led him to solitary confinement. This did not deter him from making constant onslaughts on all forms of oppression and censorship. Like Voltaire Diderot wrote on a variety of subjects and was probably the most versatile of all the philosophes. He was described as one of the founders of modern psychology for his works on the blind and the deaf. His deep interest in science and his publications in this field made him one of the important propagators of the organic theory of evolution. He wrote a number of novels in which the conflict between an individual and society was brought out. His plays, such as *The Natural Son,* provided refreshing treatment of the lives that existed in the lower sections of society. He is also credited with creating modern art criticism in France through his essays on art. He presented art and literature in social terms and was among the first European writers to do so. His various essays clearly reflected his interest in the Enlightenment. Like others he also strongly condemned Christianity calling it fanatical and unreasonable. However, the greatest contribution of Diderot was his 28-volume *Encyclopaedia* (1751–72). It was a classified dictionary of the Sciences, Arts and Trades, which he described as the great work of his life. In this work he subordinated religion to a minor position. It was questioned and put to reasoning much to the discomfort of the orthodox and religious man. Modern science occupied the central place in his *Encyclopaedia*, and he laid great stress on the technological side of science. In his work, Diderot elevated the contribution of the mechanic, engineer and artisan. He clearly stated that handicrafts and technology constituted an important area of knowledge that could be compared to pure sciences such as physics and mathematics. He also highlighted the field of social science in which the theories of social organization, and the economic policies and their positive and negative implications were brought out. Some of the portions of the *Encyclopaedia* appeared to be non-conformist for the state and as such its publication was stopped periodically. It was seen as contributing to the destruction of royal authority and promoting the spirit of independence and revolt. Diderot continued this work by going underground and receiving financial help from private individuals. After publication, this work was reprinted several times and had a brisk sale. The purpose of this work, according to Diderot, was to change the general way of thinking and it did precisely this by promoting a critical spirit against the traditional society of France. The *Encyclopaedia* does not appear revolutionary now but for its times it was certainly so.

There were many other known philosophers in and outside France. One of them was Marquis de Condorcet (1743–94), a young contributor to the *Encyclopaedia*. He is also described as one of the last philosophers but became a victim of the excesses of the French Revolution. He started his career as a promising mathematician but he became well known as a great exponent of progress through Enlightenment. His major work was *Outline of the Progress of the Human Mind* (1794) and he was one of the rare thinkers of that period who advocated political rights and education for women.

Outside France, one finds other philosophers, particularly in Great Britain and America. John Locke (1632–1704) tried to link the Scientific Revolution with the Enlightenment thought. He believed that like astronomy, philosophy could be subjected to the rigours of scientific method and critical enquiry. He suggested that the scientific method should be applied to the study of human society. In *An Essay Concerning Human Understanding* (1690), he rejected the notion of ability based on birth and instead recommended that the basis of secular laws of society should be laws of nature. Locke argued that every individual has a right to life, liberty and property (although he excluded the American slaves from this). He argued that monarchies should be based on a social contract between the ruler and the ruled. The rights and liberties of individuals are derived from the laws of nature. Locke advocated educational reforms, freedom of press, separation of political powers and religious toleration. Edward Gibbon (1737–94) became known for a historical masterpiece – *Decline and Fall of the Roman Empire*. It became a classic work of history. He considered Christianity as the greatest calamity of that time which philosophy and science with servitude. David Hume (1711–76) was a Scot and a very respected figure in England. He was a great philosopher and like the other thinkers of the Enlightenment, he adopted the weapon of skepticism. He was essentially a social scientist. In his *Treatise on Human Nature*, he made an attempt to introduce the experimental method of reasoning into a moral subject. He believed that a careful examination of human experience would promote knowledge of human nature and that it could be formed into a possible science. His approach to ethics was utilitarian. He attempted to provide a definition to value judgement in pragmatic terms. It raised the question of moral philosophy, i.e. whether any human values were absolute and eternal. Another Scottish philosopher was Adam Smith, who made a scathing attack on the mercantilist restrictions in his *The Wealth of Nations* (1776). It was the best enunciation of the doctrine of *laissez-faire*. He argued, like the French physiocrats, that economic progress required that each individual be allowed to pursue his own self-interest rather than be directed and regulated by the state. It was Immanuel Kant who brought harmony between traditional philosophical idealism with the Enlightenment.

Although the Enlightenment ideas were not so widespread in other regions of Europe, there were some other *philosophes* such as Cesare Beccaria (1738–94), a well-known jurist from Milan, Gotthold Lessing (1729–81) and the most famous and one of the greatest philosophers of that time Immanuel Kant (1724–1804) from Germany. They all faced stiff resistance from the church authorities, state censorships and smaller audiences, as the number of educated middle class was relatively small. Beccaria opposed the arbitrary powers of all those institutions that placed restrictions and oppressed humanity. His major work *On Crimes and Punishments* (1764) reflected the typical French spirit of Enlightenment. He criticized the existing view of judicial punishments that reflected a vengeance on the malefactor. He believed that unless a useful purpose is served, no person should have the right to punish another. He advocated much greater leniency in punishment because the Enlightened humanitarians believed that man should not punish another man any more than what was absolutely necessary. He also opposed the death penalty, a common feature in the European society. His work became very popular and was translated into several languages and had great influence on the legal code of many countries by 1800, where torture was abolished and the death penalty was sparingly awarded. Gotthold Lessing was a great German dramatist and literary critic and strongly believed in the value of tolerance. In his play, *Nathan the Wise* and a critical essay *On the Education of the Human Race*, he tried to highlight the greatness of different religions. Another German scholar and philosopher was Mendelssohn (1729–86). He wrote the history of Judaism and advocated the spirit of tolerance.

Among the later generation of philosophers and promoters of the Enlightenment, one can include the names of Jean Jacques Rousseau and Baron Paul d'Holbach. Coming from a German aristocratic background, d'Holbach (1723–89) lived in Paris. He advocated a doctrine of strict atheism and materialistic philosophy. He wrote the *System of Nature* in which he ascribed everything in the universe to matter in motion and believed that human beings were merely machines. It was the human mind that created God, theology and revelation. Reason and not morality was important in human lives. His views shocked many people as it meant materialistic determination and atheism.

The greatest French political philosopher of the Enlightenment was Rousseau (1712–78). Son of a watchmaker, he came from a humble background. He was a self-educated man and was introduced to the world of philosophy by Diderot. He felt the 'haute' society of Paris quite artificial and hence often spent his time in solitude. He was probably the most critical and original thinker of the Enlightenment but he is also considered one of the originators of romanticism, a cultural movement of the nineteenth century. His major works reflecting his political beliefs, the *Discourse on the*

Origins of Inequality and the *Social Contract,* made him a celebrated thinker. In the first work, he held private property as the root cause of inequality that was responsible for crimes, wars and murders. People accepted government order and laws to protect their property. Quite often, excessive authority comes in the way of liberty which made him declare that man was born free but everywhere he is in chains. He regarded governments a necessary evil. In *Social Contract* (1762), he tried to establish a balance between an individual's liberty and the institution of government. He propagated the concept of 'general will'. It could exist in an egalitarian republic where the government would determine and act in accordance with the 'general will' of the citizens. It was not a majority opinion but the true will of each individual at the highest level. Rousseau rejected the ideas of institutional brakes on state authority as suggested by Locke and Montesquieu. He held a radical view of democracy in which representative institutions were not recognized. Since everybody was responsible for framing the general will, the power of delegation could never be delegated to a representative body. The 'general will' was seen as a collective decision of all the citizens rather than a majority decision. He considered it not only political in nature but also ethical. It was the will of the entire community and was for the highest good. In his *The Social Contract*, Rousseau held that the interests of the individual and the state are one and the same, and it is the responsibility of the state to implement the 'general will'. This view led to contradictory tendencies in the application of general will. During the French Revolution the radicals justified democratic politics as represented by the Jacobin republic, while it is also believed that Rousseau's ideas led to the formation of totalitarian states of the twentieth century.

Another major work of Rousseau's was *Emile* which made a major contribution to the ideas of the Enlightenment. It was written as a novel but in fact it was a treatise emphasizing the importance of education to man. He believed that education should promote a child's natural mistakes rather than restrict them. He sought a balance between the heart and the mind, between reason and sentiment. His stress on heart and sentiments makes him a precursor of Romanticism, an intellectual movement that merged in Europe during the nineteenth century. However, his views on women and their education remained old and traditional. It is interesting that while Rousseau considered education and virtue as necessary in citizens for the larger political vision, he assigned a subordinate role to women, suggesting that they should strive to be good wives and mothers.

The thinkers of the Enlightenment and particularly the Encyclopaedists focused on knowledge and scientific reason as means of liberating man from traditional bondage. Most scholars assigned women a lower status and confined them within the domestic sphere. Few ever propagated gender equality, although some argued that this inequality was not because of women's own deficiencies but it was customs and laws that kept them away from education and true knowledge. They argued for natural equality between men and women and challenged the views of John Locke that separated women from the public world. After the French Revolution, some men and women began advocating citizenship rights, equal property rights and a proper education for women. Women like Mary Wollstonecraft in England and Olympe de Gouges, Etta Palm d'Aedler strongly propagated women's rights. They criticized the Enlightenment thinkers for their failure to present ideas about women with the same skepticism and rationalism that they revealed in other subjects and for presenting negative assessment of women's capacities.

Is difficult to assign a place to Immanuel Kant (1724–1804) within the parameters of the Enlightenment as some of his writings went far beyond the standard Enlightenment assumptions. Yet some of his views furthered the cause of the Enlightenment. He was undoubtedly the greatest German philosopher of the eighteenth century. He was an intellectual who lived away from the French Enlightenment atmosphere in the Prussian city of Konigsberg, bordering Russia. Two of his famous works, *The Critique of Pure Reason* (1781) and *The Critique of Practical Reason* (1790), criticized the idea of skepticism, a popular theme during the Enlightenment and advocated by David Hume. He believed in the existence of an absolute reality that could not be doubted but remained unknown to human beings. His belief of this absolute but unknowable truth opened up philosophy to mystery and his views became quite influential on the writings of his successors. These writers came to be known as 'Idealists'. However, most of his philosophy was also closely related to the Enlightenment. Contradicting Hume's view of skepticism, Kant suggested that although everyday knowledge commenced with sense experience, its data was ordered by the rational minds in the world of space and time and in such a way as to provide men with reliable knowledge of appearances or as he calls it 'phenomena'. Thus Kant believed that human beings could acquire sufficient truth through their experience of everyday happening through a combination of sense and reason. Like Voltaire, Kant also insisted that men should use their learning faculties to enquire about nature and to improve their knowledge through reason. Kant avoided taking extreme views on ethics. He maintained that reason could neither prove nor disprove the existence of God but that practical reason informs us that in the idea of God, the concept of moral perfection, exists and all human beings must strive for it. This 'categorical imperative' leads to a universal law of nature. Kant's views thus reconcile with the basic assumptions of the Enlightenment that universal laws rested on humans instead of supernatural determinants.

Though the Enlightenment was a movement primarily related to society it had its impact on political policies as well as on the structure of government. Almost all the thinkers spoke of natural laws based on rationalism, humanism and the application of scientific knowledge. It was believed that knowledge alone is not sufficient and that it had to be supplemented by observation, experimentation and application. As Diderot emphasized, everything must be examined, everything must be shaken up without exception and without circumspection. Even for Turgot, the finance minister of Louis XVI, the moving impulse of the Enlightenment was his belief in the beneficial effects of diffusion of knowledge and its comprehensiveness was to be demonstrated by empirical method.

The social background of the philosophers varied greatly. While Montesquieu was from an aristocratic background, Diderot and Rousseau came from the lower middle class. However, the appeal of the Enlightenment remained confined to the upper sections of the society consisting of the aristocracy and the *haut bourgeoisie* living in big cities. Ordinary people from humble social backgrounds had hardly anything to do with it.

The ideas of the Enlightenment were propagated through the publication and sale of books, treatises and through the patronage provided by a few rulers from central and eastern Europe. The emergence of public literary sphere independent of state authority showed that judgement and literary practices were not controlled by the royal court or state institutions, and that the gradual decline in the authority of the court to regulate aesthetic norms of society created greater space for a public literary sphere to emerge in the salons, cafés, libraries and lodges. The salon emerged as one of the most important means for spread of Enlightenment ideas among the literate elites of European society. The salons were very popular particularly in Paris and represented the new public that was literate and fashionable. Salons were the elegant drawing rooms of the wealthy people living in cities and towns and were organized by rich and intelligent women. They became the principal form of sociability, bringing people from the world of fashions and literature together. In the salons of Paris, women hostesses selected topics for discussion and presided over the discussions. As John Merriman writes, 'Women thus became mediators of changing culture. They invited philosophers and guests from different spheres of life, including a few foreign travelling academics. These gatherings engaged in intellectual discussions and witty conversations, concentrating primarily on the new ideas of the philosophers. There were many famous women such as Marie-Thérèse de Geoffrin, Mme Tencin, Marquise du Deffand and Julie de Lespinasse and many others. They tried to attract as many celebrities as possible in their salons. Among the prominent guests to these salons were Voltaire, Montesquieu, and David Hume. Holbach himself organized his own salon. One of the most famous salons was that of Mme Geoffrin, often called the unofficial godmother of the Encyclopaedists. When her husband died, she donated her property for academic cause and helped the Encyclopaedists complete their work. Salons played some part in spreading new political culture and bringing together people of means – nobles and bourgeoisie for social and academic interaction. Here, the guests could discuss the work of philosophers without any fear of state prosecution. Although, such salons were concentrated and remained very active in Paris, similar salons existed in London, Berlin, and Vienna and in some smaller provincial towns. Some complained of feminine influence on French political affairs as some of the powerful women in these salons successfully influenced or recommended for their friends and acquaintances for official posts and thereby enabled an entry into the world of power.

Apart from these salons, the ideas of the Enlightenment were also made popular among the upper sections of society through cafés, reading clubs and public libraries. The French and some Italian academies also fulfilled a role in diffusing the ideas of the Enlightenment by bringing together a literate upper class audience interested in science and philosophy. Unlike salons, these academies played a more formal role as educators and advisers to the rulers. In several towns of Europe, hundreds of new societies sprang up. The Dutch had developed *Het Nut* – societies which worked with charitable works, libraries, and organized lectures.

The Freemasons, a secret society also played a role not only in France but also in England and in part of Prussia and Italy. Masonic lodges extended the geographical range and social penetration of the Enlightenment. These associations began perhaps first in Scotland and attracted freethinkers and the opponents of the church together. Later, these lodges spread to other parts of Europe. By the end of the eighteenth century, there were nearly 50,000 such societies in France alone, comprising almost one-twentieth of the urban population. Members took secret oaths, followed rituals and held regular meetings that included women members as well. Freemasonry was an exclusively urban phenomenon, spreading along the main trade routes and the seacoast. There was a distinct impulse towards egalitarianism, although it was confined to its members alone. They insisted on elections and rejected venality (sale) of official posts. A large section of its membership came from the Third Estate in France – 74 per cent in Paris and about 80 per cent in provincial cities. Freemasons preferred men with time and money so that they could devote more energy for the lodge's activities. A balance was maintained between egalitarian principles and exclusivity. Rather than equality, it was the emphasis on the relationship between morality and politics that gave Freemasonry its secret and critical power. They undermined monarchial order by presenting a new set of values based on ethics. All these associations promoted a critical and rational spirit that created favourable atmosphere for reforms.

The Enlightenment ideas led to a decline in religion in the eighteenth century. The growing influence of the middle class in many countries began to slowly transform cultural life. Publishers fed the growing appetites of readers by providing information on other places. Novels and histories were becoming popular with the literate population. The spread of reading circles and 'home libraries' popularized private reading habits.

The philosophers sought freedom of expression not only for writers but for artists as well. Some of the salons held art exhibitions and critics helped shape public opinion. The secularization of society could be seen in the development of rococo art – a new secular decorative style which had evolved through the highly ornamental baroque style of the post-Renaissance period. The rococo style was very popular with the French nobility and is often called Louis XV's style. This style reflected flowing curves, elegant decorations, and drew elements from nature. It was used to decorate pamphlets and book covers. The French artist Jean Antoine Watteau transformed the art style by making it more secular. It became equally popular in Germany and Italy. Similarly, the music too was influenced by changing popular tastes. It started moving away from the constraints of court and religious dictates into popular operas. The works of Wolfgang Amadeus Mozart reflects this gradual shift away from the dependence on court and noble patronage towards public concerts.

An important question that has been raised concerning the practical aspect of the Enlightenment movement is whether the philosophers had any influence on the masses as most of them were from an elite background and catered to the tastes of the upper sections of society. It is true that the immediate audience of the philosophers consisted chiefly of aristocrats, government officials, prosperous merchants, lawyers and educated men, including the higher clergy. As a majority of the population lived under the influence of the conservative Roman Catholic Church with strict forms of censorship, the views of the philosophers hardly reached them. Also, the masses were usually illiterate or semi-literate and could not understand the writings of the philosophers. The philosophers views hardly percolated down to the masses, yet in the long run their ideas did affect popular belief. Their views cannot be called utopian but they all sought to reform society in cooperation with the ruling authorities and by promoting fresh knowledge based on scientific principles. The American Revolution and the framing of the American constitution was a distinct victory for the Enlightenment because the source of inspiration for the new political system of the United States of America did come from the ideas of the Enlightenment.

Relationship between Enlightenment and Enlightened Despotism

It was probably Diderot who first used the term *despotisme éclaire* (enlightened despots), implying those rulers who were prepared to reform the administrative structure and formulate policies based on the chief ideas of the Enlightenment. Enlightened despots is a term applied usually to some rulers of the second half of the eighteenth century, who continued to develop absolutism rather fortified by the theories of the Enlightenment. Their motives were quite explicit and practical. They wanted to strengthen the power of their governments in order to check anarchic tendencies at home and to provide security against foreign dangers. Stephen J. Lee describes the relationship between despots and the Enlightenment as a marriage of convenience. Just as the Enlightenment was not a coherent body of thought and was essentially a collection of ideas which were in vogue among the thinking men of the eighteenth century, the relationship between the Enlightenment and the despots varied from state to state. It was a shrewd way to survive by providing a new dimension to absolutism in a period of crisis. The economy of many parts of Europe underwent a transformation in the eighteenth century. England had already taken the lead over other European powers and the economic gap between the eastern and western European states had widened after the seventeenth century crisis. The old alignments were breaking up and the rulers required a new social base. They needed to tap new sources of revenue and hence they laid emphasis on trade. They wished to check and control the powerful aristocracy and at the same time they never meant to promote democracy or desired people's participation in government. Thus in the name of Enlightenment, some of them tried to provide new definitions to absolutism and they got a chance to regain lost power.

The monarchs of central and eastern Europe implemented some of the preachings of the philosophers into practice, but they often acted on purely pragmatic grounds. Their claim of implementing the ideas of the Enlightenment provided a confused picture because few of the policies of these enlightened despots were truly novel. Most of these rulers carried out policies which were common such as centralization of government, subordination of the church to the state, dissolution of religious orders, encouragement to new technology in agriculture and industry, incentives to immigrants for the development of economy, construction of roads and canals, removal of internal tolls, standardization of weights and measures and patronage to arts, science and education. Thus, as M.S. Anderson points out, there was nothing new about such policies and whatever novelty there was could hardly be ascribed to the influence of the Enlightenment. Apart from their intrinsic intellectual values, the reforms suggested by the Enlightened thinkers proved useful for these rulers. Lefebvre rejects the whole concept of 'Enlightened despotism'. For Karl Marx it was an attempt to keep alive, by exploiting bourgeois doctrines and achievements, the control that was earlier exercised by the feudal class. On the other hand, writers like Fritz Hartung describes Enlightened Despotism as a form of benevolent kingship. Such rulers governed as servants rather than as masters of the state. The secularization of the state, the disestablishment of the church, a reduction in aristocratic and other special privileges, a deep concern for the general welfare, respect for the natural freedom and rights of the citizens, a broadening interest in economy and improvement in the efficiency of government administration were popular characteristics of 'enlightened despotism'.

The so-called 'Enlightened despots' needed to increase their power, as they required larger armies, more sophisticated weapons, great luxurious courts and a large number of officials. In a period of inflation, they were compelled to search for fresh sources of income. Since there was an outer limit to the amount that could be squeezed from the peasants and common townsmen, the obvious solution for the rulers was to end the tax exemptions that had earlier been granted to the nobles and clergies. They needed control over the church and its property. These rulers wanted to realize the commercial and industrial potential of the country and they needed to destroy the privileged status of guilds. To attract the skilled and wealthy immigrants to carry out the development of the state economy, religious toleration was necessary. They believed that protecting them against exploitation by the feudal lords could increase the paying capacity of the peasants. So there was the need to abolish serfdom or at least to weaken it.

To implement these reforms, the rulers required a professional bureaucracy, paid by the state, who were dependent not on the feudal lords but on the rulers. To prepare these civil servants with sound knowledge, a radical reconstruction of the educational system based on practical application of knowledge was required. With this, the administrative structure also needed to be overhauled. A further corollary to all these changes was judicial reforms to remove the confusion that existed between the regular political, administrative and patrimonial jurisdiction that had been exercised by individual nobles. Thus it is possible to suggest that most of the policies which were commonly regarded as being characteristics of Enlightened despotism were based on *raison d'état* rather than inspired by the Enlightenment. It is also argued that a number of French writers like Voltaire, the Encyclopédists and Physiocrats found themselves out of favour with the French administration and their writings were suppressed. They were disgusted with the existing oppressive state of affairs created by the absolute rulers in France and so they turned themselves to the rulers of Prussia, Russia and Austria. They not only received great sympathy from these rulers but also adulation and admiration. Some of these rulers found the Enlightenment ideas a useful source for justifying their new reforms and policy decisions. Not all reformers among the European rulers could be called enlightened despots because the basic requirement for the purpose of identification of enlightened despotism was a connection between kings and philosophers. Some of the reforms of these rulers were carried out in the name of the Enlightenment and the edicts of the rulers used the jargons of philosophers of the Enlightenment. Most of the legal reforms, particularly the codification of law, were carried out in the name of the Enlightenment and to a certain extent reflected the aspirations of the philosophers. However, it is difficult to establish any direct link between the Enlightenment and the practical policies of the monarchs. The relationship between the enlightened despots and the great thinkers of that period is discernible through the correspondence that existed between the rulers and the thinkers. The chief among the enlightened despots were Frederick the Great of Prussia, Catherine II of Russia, Maria Theresa and Joseph II of Austro-Hungary. The most enlightened rulers were often least successful, as was evident in the case of Joseph II.

Prussia

There had already developed in Germany by mid-eighteenth century a political awareness concerning the theory of enlightened government. It discussed the issues of rationalism, traditionalism and organization of community as part of a wider European discussion on these subjects. A body of thinkers had developed a 'rationalist' theory of organization and opposed to it were the critics of rational politics. These two groups had been carrying out a propaganda war against each other. A group of writers, who came to be known as 'cameralists', desired an absolutist government based on the principles of the Enlightenment. It included Seckendorff, von Hornigke, and two very important theorists of enlightened absolutism – J.H.G. von Justi and Joseph von Sonnenfels. The theory of enlightened government was basically a political theory based on rationalism and derived many of its ideas from the eighteenth-century Enlightenment. The task of politics was to determine the means to achieve the end. They believed that the purpose of man and hence of government, was the achievement of 'happiness'. Politics should be related to this single objective and should be achieved through reason. The individual's natural rights could only be surrendered if it led to the promotion of general happiness and social welfare. The sovereign was presented outside the machine of the state, holding a unique position which could exercise general control of the machinery. It was these ideas that probably influenced Frederick the Great.

The process of state building had already commenced in the time of Frederick William I (1713–40). It was in his time that Prussia began its ascendancy as a powerful state. He treated every activity of the state as official business. He reduced the court's massive expenses drastically to become financially strong. He personally supervised every aspect of state functioning. He concentrated on building military power and increased troops from about 38,000 to 83,000, which made Prussia the fourth largest military force in Europe. He was aware that almost one-third of his military force consisted of foreign mercenaries, and so he began conscription from the peasant population. He forbade his subjects to serve in foreign armies and disciplined his forces. He hardly participated in any foreign wars and thus he could leave a strong military force for his son and successor Frederick II. Along with building his military, he also took steps to centralize the power of the state. A super-agency of the government was created in 1783 under the General Directory. It consisted of Finance, War and Domains under one central administration and was an attempt to establish an autocracy at the top and collegiality below it. Frederick William I saw education as a service to God and to the country and so he made education compulsory for all children in areas where schools existed. In those areas where there were no schools, he instructed local communities to establish schools. Interestingly he never cared for higher intellectual education and during his reign, the universities gradually declined. He distrusted his bureaucracy and assigned limited powers to it. He also expected absolute obedience because he considered himself to be the state and sovereign. The father and the son appeared to be poles apart in their interest and in their outlook. The son, Frederick II holds a special place among the enlightened despots of the eighteenth century.

While Frederick William I was totally committed to the business of the state and remained busy in state building, his son Frederick II had a very different temperament. He was more interested in the world of culture and was keenly involved in learning philosophy, history, poetry, music, mathematics and science. He was often seen reading and taking notes late in the night and entered the world of the Enlightenment by corresponding with Voltaire and d'Alembert. He spent hours at his desk reading and writing and even published *Works* and *Political Correspondence*. He composed symphonies, over a hundred sonatas and concertos for the flute. He himself was a competent flautist. His interests became a subject of worry to his father and by brute force and terror; his father groomed him so that he could be a strong king. His father was a God-fearing Protestant and a proud German while Frederick II was a deist and greatly admired French culture and looked down on anything that was German.

Frederick's interest in the Enlightenment remained active while he was free from state responsibility. Once he became the ruler, he was left with no time for his academic pursuits. He still played host to Voltaire and d' Alembert on a number of occasions. As the years passed his relations with Voltaire became cold but they continued to grow with d'Alembert. Frederick's fascination with French culture is evident from his involvement with the Prussian Academy which he transformed into the Academy of Science and Literature in 1786. Only five out of its eighteen members were German. As a ruler, according to Blanning, Frederick the Great was perhaps the first European absolutist ruler to publicize his belief in the contractual theory of state. His celebrated description of the monarch as 'the first servant of the state' symbolized a subtle shift in the theoretical basis of absolutism, as was practised in France and elsewhere. Although the period of divine right was over, very few rulers explicitly recognized the social contract theories. In his letter to Voltaire after becoming the king, he suggested his order of priorities. Those were to enlarge the army, to create a cultural academy and to encourage industry and commerce. At another point, he wrote in his letter 'since the loss of my father I have come to believe that I ought to devote myself entirely to my country' (Frederick II to Voltaire 27 June 1740). After assuming the throne, Frederick was prepared to lead Prussia in a ruthless struggle for power and territory. He claimed undivided power for the ruler not because he possessed divine qualities but because it was the only form that could bring results. An enlightened monarch, according to him, could lead his people into a more rational and moral existence.

It was rather surprising to see a ruler who was so closely associated with the cultural activities of his time, to adopt an aggressive foreign policy. He began his reign with a sudden attack on the Austrian empire. His aim was to conquer the extremely rich and prosperous province of Silesia over which Prussia had no legal or territorial claims. As Austria was engaged in a war of succession among the various claimants, Frederick swiftly attacked and acquired this province. He justified his action by stating, 'the fundamental rule of governments is the principle of extending their territories'. This principle was used throughout his rule and he built Prussia into a powerful and large state which earned him the title of Frederick the Great.

The foundation of the centralized state had been laid by Frederick William I. Frederick II established his personal control over the entire machinery of the state. He found that the collective responsibility of the General Directory delayed decision-making and so in 1742 he created the ministry for Silesia and in 1746 the military administration, new ministries responsible directly to himself. He tried to be the master of every department of government and stated that a coherent system of government must spring, like Newton's Law of Gravity, from a single agile mind (Stuart Andrews). Frederick spent ten hours a day on state affairs of which four hours were spent on study and writings. He recruited his civil servants through public examination and used his father's institution of *Fiscals* or secret inspectors to keep an eye on the bureaucrats. He developed his own political philosophy according to which a well-conducted government was based on a coherent system so that the various branches like finance, police and army were coordinated to the same end, i.e. the consolidation of the state and increase in its power which could only be achieved through the sovereign. His government was based on the concept of stratified classes and each class was assigned specific functions – the Junkers or the nobility was assigned administrative functions of the state, the bourgeoisie was inchange of providing wealth and the peasants were there to provide soldiers. In fact, his entire administrative system relied heavily on the Junker class and he could never afford to antagonize them. According to G.P. Gooch, Frederick's system formed a bridge between feudalism and the modern democracy, although the latter could never flourish in Germany.

The administration of justice in Prussia suffered from a number of defects. It was mainly in the hands of manorial courts and Frederick William I's attempt to bring about moderate reforms failed. The Chief Justice in his period, Samuel von Cocceji, prepared schemes to create a single centralized judicial system with a standard procedure to replace the hereditary powers of the nobility. He suggested full-time, properly trained servants to carry out justice. The aim was to codify Prussian law under a single list. Frederick showed interest in this and by 1750 important reforms had been introduced. One central court was created for each province and the judges were appointed on state salaries and not permitted to take fees and fines. The nobles were advised to reform the conduct of the manorial courts. However, it took much longer to prepare a new code of civil procedure. It was finally achieved in 1781 and issued as the *Prozessordung*. The civil code was prepared only in 1794 after Frederick's death and was called the Prussian *Landrecht*. It remained in force till 1900. The Preamble to the 1791 version of the new code spoke the voice of the Enlightenment. Frederick succeeded in abolishing torture and prohibited his subjects from participating in the slave trade.

Frederick was tolerant in the religious sphere. This is often regarded as a measure of his Enlightenment thinking. In his political testaments written in 1752, he compared himself with the Pope and the Lutherans but clearly stated that he was neutral in his approach between Rome and Geneva. He wanted to diminish religious animosities and strove to unite people of all religions, as he looked upon them as state citizens. This policy of toleration was based on the Prussian tradition of encouraging the immigration of hard-working and skilled men irrespective of their religious beliefs. He was prepared to accept even Muslims if they proved useful to the state. According to him, the dictates of reason and humanity demanded religious toleration. His treatment of Catholics was quite liberal for that age.

Frederick did very little to develop higher education and never abolished censorship completely. On the other hand, he refused to suppress the Jesuits like other rulers probably because the Jesuits were good teachers and there was a demand for them. The universities continued to decline and nothing substantial came out from his scheme of national education. Besides, lack of funds prevented further reforms. He was not wholly convinced of the advantages of universal education and primary school education of Prussia remained backward.

Frederick's economic policies were criticized even in his lifetime, although he did make attempts to improve the economy. He followed rigid mercantilism based on the French model and owed nothing to the contemporary economic theories of the physiocrats or the concepts of *laissez-faire*. He continued to sponsor trading companies, created state monopoles and told his officials to observe two important things – to acquire bullion from foreign countries and prevent Prussian money from going out. In agriculture, he pursued the policy of internal colonization on a scale that had never been attempted before. It is estimated that as many as three lakh immigrants were allowed to settle in his dominion. He welcomed religious refugees, whether Protestants or Jesuits and encouraged peasants from neighbouring states to settle down in the devastated regions. He tried promoting the cultivation of turnips, potato and even sugar but his suggestions were not taken seriously as the conservative peasants were suspicious of the new ideas.

Frederick set-up rural schools to train spinners and weavers and encouraged the setting up of cotton mills. He wanted the immigrant spinners to develop the Prussian cotton industries. The silk growers were paid bounties and given all forms of assistance. This was the period of rising silk exports. The government constructed warehouses to store silk. The exports of woollen products had grown in Brandenburg. The porcelain industry had also emerged and metal wares on the dining table were replaced by porcelain crockery. After the Seven Years War (1756-63), state schemes were undertaken to foster iron production in Westphalia and mining in Silesia. State monopolies were created in salt, sugar, porcelain, tobacco and coffee. These were all based on Colbert's views on mercantilism, i.e. promoting home industries by high tariff and simultaneously encouraging internal trade by abolishing tolls. To promote industry, several new ministries were created such as Commerce and Industry (1741), Mines (1768), Forestry (1770). However, the state interest in promoting these industries was only to treat them as a source of state revenue and the taxation structure did not correspond to the policy of economic growth. According to William Roscher, a nineteenth-century writer, Frederick's views on economic matters lacked originality and it changed very little during his long reign. He lacked proper understanding of economic problems and never cared to study and adopt the new principles of economics that were advocated during his rule. In many ways his economic policy was misconceived. However despite these limitations, Prussia was able to achieve spectacular progress through territorial expansion. The expansion of the army created great demand for articles of daily consumption and thereby contributed to industrial progress.

Frederick was never such an idealist as to sacrifice his political gains at the altar of the Enlightenment. He used some of the ideas in his plan of legal reforms and through his Academy of Science and Literature. He maintained strong links with some of the philosophers in the earlier part of his career but the dictates of *realpolitik* made him adopt a pragmatist approach rather than experiment with the theories of natural law. He contributed to the strengthening of the Prussian economy by adding valuable and rich territories to his dominions, where mines, plants and factories were located. He remained in constant touch with his subordinates through correspondence and travels. But at no point of time did his reforms mean greater political freedom for the masses.

Russia

To Voltaire, the monarchy seemed the best possible instrument to curtail church influence, introduce legal codes, remove hinderances to economic activity, promote educational and scientific knowledge and create a reasonable and just society. For Voltaire, one of the best enlightened ruler was Catherine II of Russia. She proved to be one of the most able and powerful rulers of imperial Russia and displayed a rare combination of intelligence, scholarship, pragmatism, accountantship, vision and ambition.

Catherine the Great (1762–96) as she was often described in her own lifetime, was born at Stettin in Pomeranian. She was the daughter of Prince Christian August, Governor of Stettin, and Johanna Elizabeth of Holstein-Gottorp. She received Lutheran education and got deeply involved in European Enlightenment. She took keen interest in the study of French thinkers and later developed strong personal bonds with some of them. She was married to Peter III of Russia in 1745. After her marriage she discovered that her husband was not only hostile but an uncivilized person. She spent most of her time in solitude, reading the works of French scholars. She was a stranger to the Russian way of life and did not know the Russian language. She found her husband, Peter, quite repulsive. She once wrote in her *Memoirs* that he was mentally backward and that she found the dullest book a great delight than his company. Within months of his accession to the Russian throne, Peter III was forced to abdicate in a palace coup believed to have been organized by Catherine with the help of the Orlovs and their supporters in the guards. Later Peter was poisoned and Catherine was coronated in 1760 as the Empress of Russia. In the thirty-eight years preceding Peter, as many as six rulers had changed in Russia because of the dynastic turmoil. The Russian nobility had reasserted itself and had become very powerful and had wrested back its privileges from the rulers. Russia needed political stability at that juncture to escape political disintegration and Catherine was able to provide that through her ambition, intelligence and political guile.

Catherine regarded herself a sincere pupil of Enlightenment thinkers and made special efforts to participate in the intellectual activities of that period. She maintained corresponded regularly with Voltaire for many years till his death in 1778. Their correspondence began in 1763 but she had been reading his works since 1746. While Catherine showed great admiration for him, he was full of praise for her reforms and was keenly interested in her achievements. He was keen to visit St Petersburg, the Russian capital, but Voltaire was seventy-five years old. Catherine dissuaded him from undertaking the journey. On his death, Catherine ordered for a hundred copies of Voltaire's works for distribution. She believed that this would 'foster a thousand talents'. How serious she was in her action one is not certain because with the coming of the French Revolution, these works were removed from the Royal Gallery. Catherine also corresponded with Montesquieu and Diderot. She admired the *Encyclopaedia* of Diderot, which she described as an 'excellent work'. She was keen to get it published in Russia but could not convince him. He visited Catherine in 1773 and Catherine was immensely impressed by his oratory skill. Their relations were also very warm. She herself wrote plays, began writing the history of Russia and published a digest of William Blackstone's commentaries on the laws of England. It was her active interest in intellectual activities, wide reading and personal contacts with the stalwarts of Enlightenment that made her an Enlightened Absolutist. However, there was a big gap between her aspirations and her real achievements in promoting Enlightenment policies. According to Stephen J. Lee, Catherine's reign opened with the prospects of extensive reforms but ended with unrelieved reaction. The reason for her absolutism at the initial stages was to introduce certain ideas of the Enlightenment but it ended in the preservation of *status quo*.

The process of centralization begun under the direction of Peter I (1682–1725) but this was seriously checked by the political turmoil under his successors. He had tried to replace the old aristocracy by the new, based on state service. He had also created a national army and carried out administrative reorganization. Peter III issued an edict in 1762 that freed nobles from rendering the state obligatory service. However, this measure was in fact a recognition of the independence the nobles had already acquired in the last few years. The permanent institution of the Russian government was the Senate with the crown appointing its members. Catherine reduced its membership and assigned it a less significant role. Her main administrative reforms were in the sphere of local government.

The administration of Russia was decentralized through the Law on the Administration of Provinces of 1775. It further expanded the administrative structure of Peter I. The entire administration was divided into eighteen units, each under a governor called *guberniia*. Each unit was further divided into provinces or *provintsiia*, each of which was again divided into districts or *uezda*. By the end of Catherine's reign there were about fifty governments and about 360 districts while the provinces almost disappeared. The powers of the central colleges were transferred to the head of each government called the *gubernator*. The judicial system was rearranged to separate criminal and civil justice and to form three district hierarchies of courts for the nobility, the town-dwellers and the peasants. Boards were created at each level and were manned partially by locally elected men and some nominated members. This administrative structure survived till the Soviets came to power. The chief weakness of the system was that its bureaucracy remained small. The charter of the cities in 1785 divided the town people into six separate guilds, graded according to wealth. A six-man urban committee based on an elected municipal council was formed to run the town administration instead of professional bureaucrats. The territorial expansion of Russian into Ukraine, the Baltic provinces, Finland, Siberia and Poland-Lithuania led to the formation of governorships and districts under Russian control favouring the nobles at the expense of serfs.

Catherine's legal reforms drew the attention of contemporary rulers and she received praise from some of the famous Enlightenment thinkers. She wanted to give a uniform legal system to Russia, manned by state bureaucracy. The legal system outside Moscow and St Petersburg had suffered from many defects. Not only did it lack uniformity and was primitive, it had placed the people at the mercy of all-powerful governors called *voevody* who remained independent of central control. Catherine called a Legislative Commission in July 1767 that represented all social groups except the serfs, but in reality the nobility dominated it. Her dependence on the nobility shackled her legal innovations. The objective of the commission was to re-codify the law which had been prepared in 1649 in the reign of Alexis. Based on the ideas of Montesquieu and Beccaria she issued instructions to the commissioners called *nazak*. Before undertaking the legal reforms, Catherine consulted Voltaire and other philosophers on her project. She spent two years in writing it. It consisted of 655 paragraphs of which 250 came directly from the writings of Montesquieu. The completed document reflected Catherine's hard work and personal control. Voltaire described it as the 'finest monument of the century', while Frederick the Great made her a member of the Berlin Academy. Within four years it appeared in twenty-four foreign languages. However, the French government forbade its publication and stopped its entry into France.

The Instructions were intended to guide the legal reforms to be made by an assembly. This Legislative Commission consisted of 564 members of which 161 represented the nobility and 208 came from the towns. The rest of them came from the nominally controlled regions. These representatives brought grievances from different segments of the population, and each group brought its own complaints. Catherine's Instructions opened with an uncompromising assertion of absolutism. She declared the sovereign to be the absolute ruler and argued that the extent of the Russian empire necessitated absolute power. Later articles asserted that all men are equal before law and the object of administration should always be to prevent rather than punish a crime and that capital punishment should be sparingly given. The document appeared to be liberal in many respects but also reflected the realities of the Russian political situation. Article 13 of the Instructions stated, 'What is the true end of monarchy? Not to deprive people of their natural liberty; but to correct their actions in order to attain the supreme good'.

The Instructions of Catherine made no efforts to abolish or limit serfdom. She stated that serfdom ought to be rare and could only be justified by state. Yet she believed that it would be dangerous to free all serfs. Rather, she strengthened the hands of the feudal nobles. It is interesting to know that her Imperial Free Economic Society organized an unnecessary competition on the condition of peasants in Russia but forbade the publication of the winning essay as it suggested peasant proprietorship of land. The legal subjugation of peasants in serfdom was extended to the newly acquired areas, as a matter of state policy so that she could secure the allegiance of landholders. Serfdom was actually promoted not only in territories of White Russia and the Ukraine, but also in the crown lands which were assigned to her favourites. Historians are skeptical of the actual intensions of her legal reforms and see them more as a propaganda stunt to receive praise and glory from outsiders. On the pretext of the Turkish War in 1768, the Legislative Commission was suspended after nearly 200 sittings. Not a single law was framed or introduced during this period. However, some of the sub-committees continued to be in session till 1775. The judicial reforms included separation of civil cases from the criminal, and separate jurisdiction was provided to courts to render justice to nobles, town-dwellers and the peasants of crown lands. The positive aspect of this entire episode was that the meetings and the publication of the Instructions introduced educated Russians to the west European ideas and promoted the spread of political consciousness. The commission provided a place for airing general grievances.

Catherine's reign helped the nobles consolidate their powers. The Charter of the Nobility of 1785 raised the status of the nobles and relaxed the power of aristocracy over them – a trend that had started after Peter I. The Charter guaranteed the existing rights of the nobility and gave them some more. It provided them legal safeguards against arbitrary power and allowed them to form corporations in their regions and districts. But unlike the national assemblies in western states, the Russian nobility as a class could not resist the crown. Seniority was the criteria for promotion and Peter's Table of Ranks that opened careers to talent, ceased to exist. Political authority in Russia came to the exercised at two levels –

one in which the *dvoryane* (landowners and officials enjoying hereditary rights) established tyrannical control over the serfs, while in the other, the *chinovniki* (the lower ranks of bureaucrats) ruled the lives of the peasants belonging to the state and the church. The serfs suffered more in the new set up. Peasants of the Volga were forced to render free labour to the state. Catherine as an Enlightened ruler, may have favoured emancipation of the serfs on humanitarian grounds against the interests of *dvoryane*, but she was incapable of executing the reforms because she was dependent on the support of the latter. There was growing frustration among the masses that resulted in a major revolt in 1773 called the Pugachev rebellion. Soviet historians describe it as the fourth peasant war. Emelian Pugachev was an ex-member of the Russian army and a Cossack rebel leader and he issued his own manifesto that offered freedom of religion, land and ownership. He was joined by diverse groups of discontented elements including serfs, peasants, workers, Cossacks and tribes. The Imperial army suppressed this revolt. Pugachev was captured, brought in an iron cage, dismembered and burnt. This savagery was committed to warn others against future revolts. This event brought the nobles closer to the crown.

In matters of religion, Catherine subordinated church to the state. The church was plundered and subordinated to the state dictates. In 1764, she confirmed the decrees of Peter III nationalizing all land belonging to the churches and monasteries and brought them under a new department called the College of Economy. The monks and clergy were now paid salaries by the state. A large number of peasants of the church lands now directly came under the state and were thus available to Catherine to render labour as serfs and were later given to the nobles who supported her. In the 1790s, the church boundaries were redrawn to match the administrative boundaries to have a better control over the church. However, her religious policy was one of toleration. The partition of Poland brought a large Catholic population under Russian control. She allowed these new subjects religious freedom. When the Society of Jesus was dissolved in 1773, she did not insist upon the expulsion of Jesuits. She even tolerated the Jews who were given permission to join municipal offices. Whether it was because of practical needs of the time or the influence of the Enlightenment, it is not easy to answer.

Catherine's contribution to culture and education was much more than that of Frederick II. She was aware of the value of education. Her plan of education was state-sponsored. She separated the Academy of Fine Arts in 1764 from the Academy of Science to better supervise all branches of art in the whole of Russia. The Academy of Fine Arts' function was to provide classes in painting, etching, engraving, metal work, architecture and mechanical instruments. For the daughters of noblemen, Smolny Institute was founded and a college of medicine was established in 1763. She volunteered herself to be inoculated against smallpox when others were reluctant to experiment. This is regarded as a great action in the spirit of the Enlightenment. Her enthusiasm for fine arts could be seen even in the naval academies where courses in dancing, theatre acting and painting were introduced. A commission was sent to England to study the university and school education there and though she accepted its recommendations of a national system of primary education there was hardly any action taken on it. Most of the free primary schools of Russia were in the towns, while the rural schools continued to be run by the clergy and private schools continued to cater to the needs of the nobility. There was a strong bias against education for the children of peasants.

Catherine's reign was dominated by foreign wars and territorial aggrandizement. Poland was wiped out from the map of Europe by three partitions in which all the so-called enlightened despots shared the gains. Wars against Turkey – the first in 1768–74 and the second in 1787–91 were caused by Russian aggression. Russian expansion towards the Black Sea continued and Crimea was annexed in 1783. Catherine's reign saw the Russian empire increasing by nearly 2,00,000 sq. miles with an additional 7 million new subjects.

Thus, Catherine as an enlightened ruler began her career with great enthusiasm for reforms. The two most important pieces of domestic legislation in her reign were the administrative reorganization of 1773 and the Nobles' Charter of 1783. Her Legislative Commission aimed at strengthening the foundation of her rule and not for greater participation of the people. She reformed the administrative system, subjugated the church, liberalized the economy, strengthened the nobility at the expense of the peasants and the serfs and introduced Western culture amongst the Russian elite. However, by the time the French Revolution broke out, she had almost withdrawn from the path of reforms and returned to traditional Russian policy of suppression at home and expansion abroad. It is difficult to say whether she considered the Enlightenment as a window dressing for her policies or whether she was frustrated in her aspirations by harsh political realities.

The Russian economy was growing during the eighteenth century. Catherine adopted a liberal policy to increase the state's income to manage the growing army. She continued the policy of Peter III's decree of abolishing many state monopolies and permitting free participation in trade. Industrial activities were also opened up by the decree of 1762 and by another decree of 1775, men of all ranks except serfs were given the liberty to participate in setting up industries. Catherine encouraged trade and industries in the villages instead of towns and placed them in the hands of nobles and peasants rather than merchants or townsmen. The merchants were prohibited from owning serfs and this placed a serious check on their participation, as without this form of labour, they could not compete with the other classes.

Russian merchants remained an unprivileged class and most of the Russian trade was in the hands of foreign merchants. As far as agriculture is concerned, the total output increased but it was not due to any improved methods of farming, but because of the extension of cultivated areas. Russian boundaries constantly expand under Catherine and a vigorous policy of colonization was followed in the Ukraine and the steppes right up to the Black Sea. The population also grew with the territorial extension, thereby broadening the base for military recruitment. The pace of urbanization was far slower than the growth of population. In trade and commerce, export duties were abolished on some products while it was increased on others like hemp, flax, skin, fur and naval stores – for which a huge demand existed in England. Several commercial treaties were concluded with European states like Poland (1775), Denmark (1782), Turkey (1783), Austria (1785), Naples, Portugal and France (1787). Catherine's reign began with liberal economic measures but towards her last years, she returned to the common mercantilist policies. The Russian foreign trade during Catherine's rule increased from about twenty-one million roubles to nearly 96 million roubles (Stuart Andrews). However, the proportion of manufactures was very small in her exports.

Thus, the so-called 'enlightened reforms' in Russia had hardly any impact on the lives of the masses. It certainly benefited the state and nobility at the expense of peasants. They were more firmly bound to their lands and became more dependent on the lords.

Austria

Enlightened reforms in the Habsburg empire started with Maria Theresa and lasted till the end of Leopold's brief reign, i.e. from 1740–92. During this period, the Enlightenment inspired not all reforms and the real impact of the intellectual movement could only be seen in the policies of Joseph II. However, the outbreak of French Revolution and Austria joining the first coalition war against France in 1792 marked a sudden shift to a conservative, rather a reactionary era.

Maria Theresa's accession to the Austrian throne was amidst internal chaos and a prolonged war of succession (1740–8) but it led to an internal reorganization of the empire. She headed the disintegrating Holy Roman Empire and ruled Austria till 1780. Her son Joseph II became the co-regent from 1765 and became the monarch in 1780. The empire of Habsburg rulers was vast and included besides Austria, Belgium, Croatia, Slavonia, Transylvania, entire Hungary, the Duchy of Milan, the Grant Duchy of Tuscany, Naples and Sardinia. The Austrian forces suffered military humiliations despite such a vast empire. The biggest loss was that of Silesia, the richest and the most prosperous province, to Prussia. The loss of this richest region, consisting of over a million people, and which had contributed nearly one-fourth to the Austrian revenue, forced the rulers and the important political men to look for the causes of the failure. The real failure was located in the internal organization of the empire. This empire had a variety of population from different races, religions and backgrounds and spoke as many as ten different languages. There was complete lack of unity and the only political unity seen in this empire was the allegiance of the subjects to the dynasty. The task of imposing unity was a formidable one. Maria Theresa had been seated on a throne of miserable inheritance. She was only twenty-four years old and was devoid of political experience and most of her ministers were too old to bring about any radical reforms. The young empress displayed extraordinary courage in an adverse situation. She finally found in Count Friedrich Haugwitz and Prince Wenzel Anton Kaunitz, two very competent and dedicated advisors. They were determined to pull Austria out of its domestic and external troubles. They were aware of the fragmented nature of the empire and the relative backwardness of their military and material resources. The failure of Austria against the much superior Prussian force in the war of succession led to the first period of *Rétablissment*. The emphasis was placed on improving the revenue of the state and to develop the economic resources. The Seven Years War (1756–63) clearly brought home the fact that the Austrian military and administrative machinery had failed again. There was an immediate need for radical reforms after the Prussian army, half the size of Austrians, defeated them at the battle of Leuthen in 1757. This led to the second *Rétablissment*. The first step was the creation of the Central Council of State (*Staatsrat*) in 1760. It was presided over by the dynamic Chancellor of State, Prince Kaunitz. It was a purely advisory body and drew up plans for future reforms. It retained control and supervision over other official bodies. Kaunitz had advised Maria Theresa to depend on this institution because he believed it was the only means of saving the state and preventing its disorder and decay. This marked the beginning of widespread reforms.

The reforms in Austria took place in two stages. The first stage under Maria Theresa, reforms were strictly practical in character, generally averse to the principles of a radical enlightened measure. In the second stage, Joseph II's, doctrinal zeal for reforms became evident. Joseph was so much swayed by the idealism of the Enlightenment that he tried to push Austria to modernity from above which antagonized conservatives and raised an unrealistic hope for the radicals. He had to finally withdraw his programme.

Maria Theresa's programme of governance was pragmatic and did not have any major ideological roots. This was because of her conservative character and her religious devoutness. She was too strong a Catholic to approve of Voltaire as she had been isolated from the intellectual evolution in the West. If her political programme owed something to the Enlightenment ideas, it was only to Montesquieu because she had read his works. In all the various stages of her reforms, it is very difficult to decipher any significant influence of the Enlightenment. Austrian defeat at the hands of Prussia provided the original impetus while the military and fiscal needs of the state also contributed to the era of reforms. The demand of a unitary state was not based on any opposition to the principle of privileges but because Austria did not want to lose any other region. It is true that men like Haugwitz and Kaunitz had admired the philosophers but no direct relationship between the administrative reforms and the intellectual current can be established. Maria Theresa remained aloof from these new ideas. Thus we find that whereas there was personal absolutism under Frederick the Great in which the views of the king were of paramount importance, the Habsburg monarchy emerged as a product of ministerial absolutism. Despite her strongly held views and prejudices, Maria Theresa was susceptible to the influences of the Enlightenment, to the people who surrounded her, and wished to translate some of their principles into legislation. It was Joseph II who found the conservative views of his mother oppressive and he remained an impatient idealist. He was a great admirer of Frederick for amalgamating the principles of the Enlightenment with practical policies. Although he did not meet Voltaire, he showed keen interest in his writings.

The Habsburg rulers initiated the process of reorganization of provincial administration. As a result, Bohemia ceased to be an independent state. The impact of their administrative reorganization was the gradual ascendancy of the centralized government over basically feudal institutions. The victory was not completely achieved in their reigns, particularly in Hungary. While the process of centralization greatly destroyed the power of the feudal estates, the superstructure of feudal order persisted. The reforms based on the Enlightenment curtailed the powers of the estates and strengthened absolutism. The social outlook of the government widened, as it had to shape the interests not only of the ruling class but of the subjects as well. Besides, the politico-military dictates also contributed to the financial innovations. The economic dictates had led the Habsburg rulers to impose taxes on the estates of the nobles and the church. Although the chief motivation for administrative reforms was mainly the efficiency of the government, the humanitarian factor could no longer be ignored. The shift in perspective was seen soon after Joseph began to control the realm of the state. Earlier he had a limited sphere to control. He believed that the service to God was inseparable from the service to the state. By this he implied military service, which he imposed on his subjects. After completing education, three years of unpaid compulsory service was introduced. He was strongly against the court's pageantry and he was the first ruler to forbid the kneeling before the emperor (1787), regarding it as against the dignity of man. Joseph as a reformer and enlightened despot was a striking personality because of his uncompromising manner of expressing and applying the ideas of the Enlightenment. His administrative reforms were aimed at improving the efficiency of the government but were also accompanied by humanitarian ideals.

The agrarian situation within the Habsburg empire was complex and varied. There was virtually no important legislation in this sphere to serve as a legal precedent for the rulers. Maria Theresa was probably aware that so long as the social conditions of the peasants, who constituted the bulk of rural population, were miserable the empire would not prosper. At the same time any radical solution was not feasible. During the eighteenth century, peasants in this region generally belonged to two categories – tenants who had a contractual relationship with the lords but were not excluded from personal services and the rusticalits, who constituted a much larger group consisting of the hereditary bonded peasants belonging to the lords. However, the real situation was much more complex. The tenants, although enjoying a better position than the serfs, were always insecure. In theory, a tenant enjoyed freedom of movement and freedom of marriage for himself and for his children, and the right to learn a craft with the lords' consent but in reality these rights hardly existed. Maria Theresa was prepared to grant to her peasant subjects the status of free tenants with freedom of movement, of marriage and choice of occupation but she was not in favour of granting freedom from service to the lord, as long as the peasant held manorial land. She feared anarchy in case it was granted. She desired to restrict serfdom and struggled to achieve it despite all odds. A clean demarcation of the extent of peasant land and manorial land was made for the first time, and this prevented future arbitrary seizures of land by the lords. The arbitrary fees imposed by the lords could not be abolished but at least it was standardized. The Urbarial Commission was set up to control excesses of the robot system (compulsory labour service). The Robot Patent of 1775 restricted robot to render free labour between one and three days a week. There was strong opposition to this by the lords, particularly in Bohemia. Maria Theresa was not deterred by this, and continued with her endeavours.

The attempts at centralization towards a unitary state remained incomplete in Hungary. Maria Theresa compromised and avoided direct confrontation with the Magyar Nobles and tried to transform them into court nobility. Her policy was largely a failure. Joseph's agricultural policy in the first phase was a continuation of his mother's reforms. In Hungary, he found greater scope for his reforming energies. In 1780, Hungary appeared to be almost an independent state. The Hungarian constitution was very old and favoured aristocratic rule. At the top stood the parliament, called *Reichstage* with two houses. The first represented the 300 noble families while the second represented a large number of gentry families while other classes had no representation. Though the big magnates enjoyed vast income, the gentry exercised political power. Maria Theresa avoided convening parliamentary sessions after 1765, and used instead the power of the gentry. Joseph was keen to bring about a comprehensive plan of administrative reforms that began in 1785. The country was divided into ten provinces on the basis of population. Imperial commissars replaced the old officials appointed by the nobility. An ambitious plan of land service was prepared and implemented all over the Habsburg dominions in 1782. Next year, all occupants of land were equally liable to taxation, irrespective of their status. He expected the service to be completed within six months but it took almost four years to be completed. In 1789, a single land tax was introduced that was to be collected in cash. He did not abolish serfdom in one stroke but in name of reason and humanity, he abolished the personal dependence of peasants on lords. The peasant subjects of Joseph could now own land, marry freely and take up new professions. This law was first applied to Austria, Bohemia and Transylvania in 1783 and Hungary in 1785. The Patent of 1781 introduced a system of arbitration between the lords and the peasants. Whenever peasants could not afford the cost of litigation, governmental lawyers would represent them.

The industrial and trade policies of the Habsburg rulers was a mixture of liberal and strict mercantilism. Joseph II's legislation concerning the guilds was of great importance for economic expansion. In 1776, Maria Theresa's ministers had prepared a comprehensive plan to break the stronghold of guilds but little could be achieved. Joseph provided the missing zeal. He knew very well that if all the guilds were abolished in a single stroke, his empire would face a serious crisis of production. Hence, he adopted a series of piecemeal measures. Guild property was confiscated and utilized on public works and their monopoly of trade was also broken. In 1781, some professions such as tanning, leatherwork and the sale of grain were made free. The guilds lost all their power of impending and restricting commercial activities and Joseph was able to allow choice of profession to his subjects. Anyone qualified in his field could carry out the trade of his choice without the restrictions of guilds.

Although mercantilist influence on the Habsburg regime was not so rigid as one finds in Prussia or in the last years of Catherine, yet protectionism was evident in the economic policy. On the whole, the cornerstone of Joseph II's economic legislation was the protectionist system, as introduced in 1784. It strictly excluded the import of all foreign-made goods, materials and agricultural products which could be produced within the Habsburg dominions, or for which substitutes were available. It adversely affected the interests of all those who were dependent on foreign trade. At the same time, it provided a powerful stimulus to increase production for homemade goods. At the same time, favourable trade agreements were concluded with states like Morocco, Turkey, Russia and the newly formed United States of America. Within the empire, the Tariff Union of Bohemia, Moravia and the Austrian duchies in 1775 formed the largest free trade area in Europe.

The commercial policy of the Habsburgs were governed by financial considerations. A series of financial reforms attempted for the first time to impose a tax on property and income of the nobility and clergy. However, the financial burden on the peasants remained very heavy due to their poverty and the government continued to be in debt because of uncontrolled expenditure and insufficient income.

The loss of Silesia was a grave economic setback for the Habsburg kingdom. This loss led to the emergence of Bohemia from the 1770s as an important manufacturing centre. It marked the beginning of the spread of proto-industrialization. The flax industry alone employed nearly 2,00,000 workers, mostly women. The textile factory at Nova Kydna had about 1,400 spinners and about 100 weavers though few worked under one shed. The textile industry in Bohemia and in Lower and Upper Austria expanded significantly. A new textile factory was set up in the western Alpine region. Glass industry in Bohemia, iron mining in Styria, mercury mining in Carniola, lead in Corinthia and leather and jewellery in Vienna were the other major industrial activities. The results though, were only notable not extraordinary. There was no major breakthrough in industrial production and Hungary hardly saw any industrial development. The region remained a source of cheap raw materials for Austria and Bohemia and the low cost of Hungarian labour sustained Austrian industrialization. Joseph was interested in promoting trading activities but his attempt to form an East India Company at Trieste failed.

The judicial reforms of Maria Theresa's regime remained inconspicuous. The reforms started by her were given a definite direction and velocity by Joseph II. In 1740, the judicial system under the Habsburgs was diverse and extremely complex. The customary law had taken centuries to evolve but it reflected the dominance of corporate groups in the provinces. There were too many institutions such as the ruler, church, towns and guilds, besides individual landowners which exercised jurisdiction of some form. Procedural matters lacked uniformity. The system of appeal was incomprehensible while no distinctions existed between civil and public law. The reforms under Maria Theresa tried to provide a modern notion of legal sovereignty. A distinction between public law from that of civil law was introduced by separating the two, so that subjects were to have some form of protection from the despotic acts of the rulers or individuals.

The emphasis on utility and belief in rationalism prompted reforms in the existing penal system. One of the major influences on the legal reforms was Cesare Bonesana Marguis de Beccaria. The first step in the direction of legal reforms was taken in 1749 when a Supreme Court was created, separate from the highest administrative body. In 1753, a commission of lawyers (The Compilation Commission) was appointed to collect information required for the new Civil Code but after accumulating vast information, it advised against introducing a new comprehensive code at a single go, as it would cause chaos. It did not suggest any change. A new Criminal Code was prepared and introduced in 1770 but it had not abolished torture as a form of punishment. This could only be abolished in 1776 at the instance of Joseph and Kaunitz. The *Codex Theresiana* published in 1766, was a compromise between the empress and the vested interest groups, and was attacked not only by the conservatives but also by men like Kaunitz, Martini, Sonnenfels and Riegger. Joseph strongly believed that his mother had not pushed the reforms properly and soon took up the subject of legal reforms. Yet under Maria Theresa, the chief gain of her modest reforms was the drastic reduction and restriction of the patrimonial courts of the liege lords. Hundreds of town courts, which exercised the right to impose capital punishment, including death sentence, lost their privileges.

An important influence on the reform programme was Cesare Bonesana, the marquis of Beccaria (1738–94) an Italian philosopher and politician, and was known for his *Treatise on Crimes and Punishments* (1764). He was from Milan but served Habsburg Austria as an important adviser. He had read all the prominent philosophers of his era and strongly believed that the main task of the state was to protect society and respect the dignity of its people. He wanted standard procedures for criminal trials irrespective of social status. He promoted the idea that unless proved guilty, an accused remains innocent. He also argued that the punishment of a crime should not be linked to the concept of religious sin but should be determined according to social dictates. He rejected death penalty except in extreme cases and opposed torture to extract confessions.

Under Joseph, the separation of administration from justice was further extended. The practice of appointing qualified judges was introduced and a regular system of appeal in civil litigation from magistrate's court to the *Landrecht* was started. The number of courts in criminal jurisdictions was reduced to one in each administrative district and one court of appeal in each crown land. The modern notion of jurisprudence was well understood by Joseph. He introduced a new order of criminal procedure in 1788. Joseph's humanitarian approach was accompanied by strict utilitarianism. His Code of Substantive Criminal Law (1787) replaced capital punishment with life sentence of hard labour, giving the government the benefit of the criminal's labour. At the same time, the new code had an egalitarian character and severe punishment was inflicted even on nobles. It thus helped in breaking the class character of Austrian justice. Reforms in civil procedure were carried out in between 1782 and 1784. Joseph did not survive long to see the enactment of the drafts of the planned Austrian Code of Civil Law which was promulgated in 1811 and considered a masterpiece of Austrian judicial legislation. The most noticeable reform related to marriage. It was brought from the jurisdiction of ecclesiastical to civil courts and demoted from its sacramental status to a civil contract. A new law of inheritance was introduced along with the admission of divorce on grounds of adultery, impotence, conviction or desertion. Joseph's achievements in the sphere of civil jurisdiction compared favourably with that of Frederic the Great. It was shortage of trained personnel that robbed much of the impact of Joseph's reforms.

Both Maria Theresa and Joseph were for educational reforms, though both had reservations concerning higher education but for different reasons. Maria Theresa was opposed to the revolutionary ideas of the Enlightenment. Joseph believed that uncontrolled free research would interfere from utilitarian vocational goals required for training administrators and professional men. He was supportive of education only to the extent that the material benefits for society were demonstrable. Maria Theresa was tolerant towards educational reforms, so long as they did not affect the traditional sense of value of her subjects. This danger hardly existed in elementary and intermediate education for the masses, while it was much greater in the sphere of higher education. Consequently, she laid stress on the elementary and intermediate level education, almost ignoring higher university education.

The main credit for the reforms of elementary and general intermediate schools goes to Johan Andreas Felbiger from Prussian Silesia. He was called into the Austrian governmental service in 1774. His reforms pertained to the hereditary lands of Bohemia. His plan introduced three types of institutions: (a) The one-year elementary or trivial schools were meant for small towns, markets and larger villages. It included instructions in reading, writing and arithmetic and attendance was generally made compulsory and its teachers were trained in state institutions. (b) A main school (Hauptschule) was established in every district where besides some vocational training, history, geometry and drawing were taught. (c) In the capitals of the individual crownlands, 'Norman Schools' were created for the children of the urban upper-middle class and also training institutions for teachers for elementary education were set up. Part of the cost of education had to be shared by the parents.

A faculty of medicine was created in Vienna and some distinguished appointments in the law school of Vienna proved useful in judicial reforms. The overall policy of Maria Theresa was to limit the advancement of higher education. Yet in 1749, the Maria Theresa Academy in Vienna was created to train young nobles for higher administrative positions in the government. Other institutions created were the Military Academy in Wiener Neustadt (1752) to train officers, Oriental Academy in Vienna (1754) and Commercial Academy (1770). The Habsburg rulers considered schools as political institutions while universities were seen as a training ground for civil servants.

Throughout the reform era from 1740–92, the problem of church–state relationship was tackled through state control and centralization. The beginning of reforms in purely ecclesiastical matters of the Catholic church was made under Maria Theresa. The reforms of Joseph were focused primarily on the status of non-Catholics and on the monastic institutions.

Through ecclesiastical policy, Maria Theresa tried to establish state superiority over the church but she did not want to dismantle its establishment or its religious practices. As a supporter of mercantilist ideas, she adopted measures to prevent the church income going to Rome. Hence, the financial transactions of the church were strictly scrutinized by the state. Export of bullion to Rome was checked. The church was weakened following the tax reforms after 1748, which abolished the tax exemptions which the church enjoyed. The number of religious holidays were regulated by the state so that the working days were not affected. Religious processions and pilgrimages were reduced as well.

The Patent of Toleration granted full toleration to all except atheists and Deists. Irrespective of religion, the Austrian subjects were given the right to hold property, build schools, and enter any profession and could enter political or military profession. The Patent gave civil equality and freedom of worship to Lutherans, Calvinists and orthodox Christians, so long as their services were held discreetly. The church establishment was reorganized. Foreign bishops lost their power inside Austria. Large dioceses were divided up and now parishes were marked out so that no person had to walk for more than an hour to reach a church.

Joseph's policy towards religion was one of toleration. His attitude presents a sharp contrast to that of his mother. She always hesitated to interfere in any way with the supremacy of the Catholic religion. Joseph, on the other land declared, 'I stand for freedom of belief in so far as I am prepared to accept everyone's services in secular matters, regardless of denomination. Let everyone who is qualified occupy himself in agriculture or industry. I am prepared to grant the right of citizenship to anyone who is qualified, who can be of use to us, and who can further industrial activity in our country'. The Patent of Toleration was published in 1781. Jews were subjected to all kinds of discrimination in the Habsburg empire, as was the case elsewhere. In various ordinances issued in 1781 and 1782, Joseph removed their worst disabilities. His attitude towards the Jews was in sharp contrast to his mother's and was governed by humanitarian concern, as taught by the Enlightenment. However, other elements prevented him from establishing complete parity between the Jews and the Christians.

Joseph was seriously concerned with the lack of economic development of his territories. He held monasticism in abhorrence because it deprived the economy of much badly needed capital and prevented useful citizens from writing for the state. Through a series of decrees, he made himself the sole authority of the human and material resources of the monasteries. Numerous monastic buildings were converted into factories, warehouses, granaries and residences and monastic lands were sold off in the market. The property acquired through the suppression of monasteries led to the creation of a Religious fund of 60 million florins, with which a wholesale reorganization was carried out, including the training and education of the clergy. Thus the church was reorganized and regulated to eliminate waste. One can easily decipher economic motives behind his Patent of 1781. By the Edict of 29 November 1781, he ordered state take-over of all Carthusian monasteries and other religious orders of males and females which neither ran schools or looked after the sick or engaged in academic pursuits for he considered them entirely useless. Economic and philanthropic motives seem to have prompted Joseph to adopt such measures as the proceeds from the suppressed orders were used to establish in

Vienna alone three hospitals, a medical academy and a home for the deaf and dumb.

Joseph's reforms, though genuinely aimed at the welfare of his subjects, were very paternalistic. He was principally interested in creating a unified, well-run state that would be respected in Europe. But his foreign policy aim of aggression abroad did not go down well. His campaigns against the Turks were largely unsuccessful and he failed to acquire Baroria in exchange for the Austrian Netherlands (called Belgium now). Joseph's attempt to impose a blueprint from above proved disastrous. The clerics joined the opposition that was fighting against the destruction of their privileges. His high-handed policy and complete disregard of local privileges and traditions led to much discontent and brought the region on the brink of rebellion at the time of his death. Belgium was lost because of policies imposed on it while Hungary was saved through concessions. Thus rebellion and retreat marked his last years as military failure was accompanied by poor harvest and economic depression.

The outbreak of the French Revolution made Joseph retreat from the path of reforms. He himself was now in extremely poor health but was forced to lead the military campaign against the many rebellions. The middle classes, because Joseph's reforms had aroused their political aspirations, began to make fresh demands that he found excessive. He increased censorship of the press and created a secret police to find out whether there was any discontent so that he could suppress it in the bud if there was a rebellion. But Joseph's rule demonstrated that 'enlightened absolutism', to be successful needed a strong staff to execute the reforms. As his programmes conflicted with the interests of the nobility and the bureaucracy – (that section of the society on whose support its success depended). Joseph was the only monarch of that age to risk a frontal attack on the privileged order. On economic as well as humanitarian ground, he made an attempt to raise the status of the peasants. Naturally the nobles and the clergy condemned these proposals and obstructed its implementation in their estates. The peasants resisted many of his plans as they were badly informed of his intentions. In Hungary, he cancelled all his decrees except those granting toleration, church reform and the abolition of serfdom. When Joseph died, the empire faced disorder and it was left to his brother and successor, Leopold II, an enlightened but pragmatic ruler, to restore order by granting real concessions like cancelling the single land tax, restoring tithe and bringing back the *robot*. The chief problem of Joseph was that his enlightened despotism was rooted in policies and intentions that had a theatrical foundation and he believed that his enlightened measures could be achieved only through absolute rule, to be applied by his subordinates without questioning them. It was the haste and impatience of Joseph II, his tactlessness, lack of administrative cohesion and lack of any preliminary information, consultation and uncompromising attitude that led to his failure. Though aware of the benefits of the Enlightenment, he was basically an inflexible autocrat. But it was his reforming efforts and the policy of centralization along with that of his mother, that transformed Austria from a dynastic expression into a political unit that helped Austria survive not only the Napoleonic wars but hold a place in the European power structure till 1918.

Outside Austria, Prussia and Russia, the concept of enlightened despotism can be seen in the policies of some Italian princes during the eighteenth century. The chief feature of enlightened despotism in the Italian states was that it was tied to monarchial forms and depended greatly on foreign source for inspiration. One such state was Naples that had been ruled by Spain for over two centuries followed by a brief rule by Austria. Naples became an independent kingdom in 1734 under Don Carlos, the eldest son of Philip V and Elizabeth Farnese, who assumed the throne in 1735 as Charles III at the age of eighteen. The concept of enlightened despotism can be located in the rule of Charles III (1735–59) and Ferdinand I (1759–1825). Charles had high notions of his prerogative and his independence and considered himself an absolute monarch. Like other despots of his time, he was knowledgeable but obstinate. Bernardo Tanucci, was the chief adviser of Charles and had served as a Minister of Justice in the 1730s and later became the Minister of Foreign Affairs. He initiated reforms based on the principles of the Enlightenment. He attempted to make law more rational and less barbarous, curb bribery and improve the judicial system. His attempt to codify the Law of Naples failed miserably.

The nobility in Naples was very powerful and controlled four-fifths of the people, exercised influence over municipal government and could block any tax proposals at any time in the parliament. Charles had concluded a Concordat in 1741 with Pope Benedict XIV, that allowed him to tax church property, reduce jurisdiction and privileges of the clergy. Tanucci was strongly against the Jesuits and took repressive measures against them. He did not subscribe to the policy of religious toleration as propounded by the philosphers. In fact, he had ordered a ban on Voltaire's works. Charles III on the other hand was even prepared to welcome the Jews to settle in Naples but could not carry it out because of popular outcry. Charles' contribution in promoting the ideas of the Enlightenment was definitely there but not in a tangible form. He provided encouragement to the opera and the San Carlo Opera house was opened in 1737. This was followed by the creation of the Neapolitan Academy of Art that attracted a number of artists. In 1755, the Royal Herculaneum Academy was set up to promote archaeology and was regarded as an important centre of education. In 1755, the first lecture in Europe on political economy was delivered by Abbé Antonio Genovesi and he also lectured on Montesquieu and d'Alembert. The University of Naples began to promote subjects like experimental physics, astronomy, botany, chemistry, etc., in place of jurisprudence and theology. However, not all efforts of reforms contained the ideas of the Enlightenment.

In 1759, Charles III of Naples became the ruler of Spain. Here the spirit of Enlightenment was missing in his policies probably because of the total absence of academic atmosphere. Initially, Charles tried to introduce reforms at a brisk pace but he faced strong opposition. A measure to reform the revenue collection, by introducing a single tax based on wealth, met bitter opposition of the nobility and some priviledged groups. Similarly, the attempt to control the prices of Five Major Guilds of Madrid antagonized the rich bankers and merchants. The policy of increasing the Power of the crown over the ecclesiastical courts and increased clerical taxation led to the opposition of the clergy. The pace of reform measures slowed down after 1766 when major riots broke out in Madrid and in other cities. It is not clear whether the riots were organized by nobles and clergies.

Tuscany was another Italian state that could hardly be called modern before the accession of Leopold, the brother of Joseph II. Leopold had a similar intellectual background as both brothers were introduced to the world of the Enlightenment and the philosophers by their tutor, Karl Anton Von Martini. Leopold subscribed to the Italian editions of *Encyclopaedie*. At the young age of nineteen, he had formulated his plan for reforms and he showed a will to implement them. There was a small group of energetic men and supporters of the Enlightenment who helped Leopold to adopt a programme of reforms – men like Pompeo Neri, Angela Tavantiorian, Francesco Maria Gianni, etc. Their chief plan included reforms in the structure of the local government abolishing local administrative variations and special privileges enjoyed by a particular group and unifying the fragmented state.

The church in Tuscany was quite powerful. Leopold adopted the Jansenist programme of dissolving the monasteries, enforcement of strict laws, that destroyed papal jurisdiction over the Tuscan church, and abolishment of the lay brotherhood. Leopold adopted a pragmatic approach for his reforms and sought the approval and cooperation of his subjects. Unlike Joseph, he welcomed criticism and consulted both officials and subjects. He was averse to personal absolutism and remained engaged in a project of constitutional reforms. In his drafts of the proposed constitution, he made frequent reference to the scholars of the Enlightenment like Turgo, Mirabean, Rousseau, Montesquieu, and Abbé de Saint-Pierre. He was fully aware of the terms of the newly-prepared American Constitution. He opposed the tripartite division of legislature into nobles, clergymen and common people, as existed in the European states, and instead proposed representation of owners of real estates, professional men and artisans. Unfortunately this new Constitution envisaging a constitutional monarchy could not be introduced because of the opposition of the privileged classes, the political unawareness of the people and the cold response of the officials.

Still, Leopold carried out reforms in other fields. The feudal courts were subordinated to the centre's control, the revenues of the church officials were subjected to state taxation and financial reforms were introduced (tax farming and internal tolls were abolished). The legal reforms brought to an end torture and the death penalty and a uniform criminal procedure was started. The alarming situation in Austria forced him to leave for Vienna where he improved the situation from the mess which Joseph had created but could not do much as he died two years later. Thus, from a feudal state, Leopold turned Tuscany into one of the best-governed states in Europe with a modified administration and rationalized tax structure.

A form of Enlightenment could also be noticed in Sweden and Denmark. A Swedish historian describes the period after the death of Charles XII and the beginning of Gustav III (1771–92) as the 'Age of Liberty'. This period was one of political confusion and diplomatic humiliation, though a time of intellectual and artistic growth. The Academy of Science (1739) and the Royal Academy of Painting and Sculpture (1768) were created in this period. The Swedish Opera was inaugurated in the 1770s. Gustav's period saw the growth and maturation of these cultural trends. The Academy of Belles-Lettres, created in 1753 was revived in 1786 with additional fields of History and Antiquities. The Swedish Academy was created to promote the Swedish language. Reforms of paper currency and of coinage were smoothly carried through. The physiocratic principles in the form of land enclosures and freedom of trade in corn were introduced but the principles of mercantilism were practised in the industrial sphere, particularly in iron production. The constitution of 1772 was framed on Montesquieu's model. The aggressive designs of Russia and Prussia made Gustav demonstrate his strength, particularly against Russia. He called a session of the *Riksdag*, the representative institution, to handle the foreign threats effectively. When the nobles opposed him, he immediately formed an understanding with the commoners and imposed a new constitution on Sweden, called the Act of Union and Security in which the king was given full legislative freedom. The council became an intermediate body and the official posts were thrown open to all subjects. The only effective control the *Riksdag* had was over financial matters. Thus Gustav brought about major changes in Sweden for which a revolution had to be carried out in France.

The Danish rulers, Frederick V (1746–66) and Christian VII (1766–1808), cannot be compared to Gustav but some of the ideas of the Enlightenment can be seen in their reforms. Struensee, the German physician of the king (and the queen's lover), introduced these reforms. He exercised tremendous political power. The reforms programme included confiscation of church revenue, freedom of worship, end of press censorship, establishment of hospitals and some legal reforms, including the abolition of torture. However, a strong reaction against his programme developed as these reforms were seen as an attempt to Germanize Danish society. Struensee was executed but Crown Prince Frederick carried his reforms forward though more cautiously.

Major Works of Enlightenment

1733	Voltaire's *Philosophical Letters*
1738	Voltaire's *Elements of the Philosophy of Newton*
1746	Diderot's *Philosophical Thoughts*
1748	Montesquieu's *Spirit of Laws*
1749	Rousseau's *Discovery on the Arts and Sciences*
1749	Condillac's *Treatise on Systems*
1751	First volume of *Encyclopaedia* by Diderot
1753	Voltaire's *Essay on Manners*
1756	Holbach's *Christianity Unmasked*
1758	Helvétius's *On the Mind*
1758	Quesney's *Economic Tableau*
1759	Voltaire's *Candide*
1762	Rousseau's *Social Contract*
1762	Rousseau's *Emile*
1764	Voltaire's *Philosophical Dictionary*
1772	Last Volume of *Encyclopaedia*
1776	Adam Smith's *The Wealth of Nations*
1781	Immanuel Kant's *Critique of Pure Reason*
1784	Immanuel Kant's *What Is Enlightenment*
1790	Immanuel Kant's *Critique of Practical Reason*

1791	'The Declaration of the Rights of Women and the Female Citizen' by Olympee Gorges
1792	Mary Wollstonecraft's *A Vindication of the Right of Woman*
1793	Condescet's *The Progress of the Human Mind*

Enlightened Despots

1740–86	Frederick the Great of Prussia
1762–96	Catherine II of Russia
1740–80	Maria Theresa of Austro-Hungary
1765–90	Joseph II of Austro-Hungary
1759–66	Charles of Naples
1766–88	Charles III of Spain
1771–92	Gustavus III of Sweden

Suggested Readings

Anderson, M.S., *Europe in the Eighteenth Century, 1713–1783*, London: Longmans, 1975.

Andrews, Stuart, ed., *Enlightened Despotism*, London: Longman, 1967. Contains a number of passages from the original writings on the subject concerning various aspects of the policies of enlightened rulers.

Blanning, T.C.W., *Joseph II and Enlightened Despotism*, Essex: Longman, 1984. A sound analysis of the term and also includes a brief list of documents besides assessing the achievements and failure of Joseph II.

Chartier, Roger, *The Cultural Origins of the French Revolution,* New York: Duke University Press, 1991. Represents recent interpretation on the role of cultural factors in creating conditions for the French Revolution.

Evans, R.J.W., *Austria, Hungary, and the Habsburg: Central Europe c. 1683–1867*, Oxford: Oxford University Press, 2006. Takes up the entire period as a whole and demonstrates continuities and aspects of evolution towards modern statehood as well as the crisis of ancien-regime structures.

Gay, Peter, *The Enlightenment: An Interpretation,* 2 vols., London: Weidenfeld & Nicolson, 1966, 1969. A detailed and highly researched work providing a fresh interpretation elucidating a coherent philosophy from the writings of *philosophes*.

Hyland, Paul, ed., *The Enlightenment: A Sourcebook and Reader*, London:

Routledge, 2003. A useful guide on the subject that bring together the works of major Enlightenment thinkers.

Jacob, Margaret C., *The Enlightenment: A Brief History with Documents*, Boston/New York: Bedford, 2001.

Merriman, John, *Modern Europe, from Renaissance to the Age of Napoleon*, New York: W.W. Norton & Co., 1996. A very good discussion on diffusion and the legacy of the Enlightenment in Chapter 10.

Munck, Thomas, *The Enlightenment: A Comparative Social History, 1721–1794,* London: Arnold, 2000. Places this movement in its social context.

Porter, Ray, *The Enlightenment*, London: Macmillan, 1990. A useful historiography on the subject.

Outram, Dorinda, *The Enlightenment*, Cambridge: Cambridge University Press, 1995. Has a brilliant introduction to the historiography of the subject with a fresh interpretation.

CHAPTER 13

Economy and Society in the Eighteenth Century

The eighteenth century was a period of growth, expansion and transformation in agriculture, trade, commerce and industry. The European economy showed signs of progress after decline and stagnation in several parts of the continent in the seventeenth century. Population grew beyond what Europe had ever seen before. Mercantilism had intensified competition among the European states. Production was restructured and came out of the bonds of feudalism. Governments actively encouraged agriculture, industries and commerce. The process of industrialization gained momentum and by the second half of the eighteenth century, England was already on the road to Industrial Revolution. Rapid industrialization radically changed the economic and political relationship between industrial Europe and the non-industrial world of Asia, Africa and southern America. Britain became the first and the most industrialized nation and the most dominant imperial power, at least till the other European nations caught up with her in the late nineteenth century.

Demographic Growth

The demographic growth started around 1730 after a prolonged stagnation. The population growth was clearly marked in western Europe. In England, it rose from about 5 million in 1700 to more than 9 million in 1801, the year when the first British census was conducted. There are different figures of population provided by experts according to different methods of counting adopted by each one.

TABLE 13.1: POPULATION OF THE BRITISH ISLES

(*in millions*)

	England and Wales	Percentage of increase per decade
1603	4.1	+ 5.5 (1600–10)
1701	5.8	+ 2.7 (1701–11)
1731	5.9	- 0.3 (1731–41)
1751	6.1	+ 7.0 (1751–61)
1781	7.5	+ 6.8 (1781–91)
1801	9.2	+ 11.0 (1791–1801)

The population of Scotland and Ireland also grew rapidly during the eighteenth century. Strong demographic increases were common in most of western Europe. France was a populous region and its territories had expanded from about 480,000, sq. km in around 1580 to 5,20,000, sq. km in 1780. France's population had risen from about 16 in 1715 to about 26 million or perhaps more by 1789. She had an estimated 18 per cent of the total European population in 1750. According to Parker and Wilson, the French population in the 1690s was 1,93,52,000. In 1787, it went up to 2,50,65,000. Statistical data of the French population between 1690 and 1780 shows two trends. First, there were enormous differences in the demographic growth of different regions; second, the overall growth was relatively small and the principal gains were registered in the frontier regions, which had earlier been devastated by the wars of Louis XIII. In the interior regions, the growth was not significant. The French proportion of the European population continued to increase till the time of Napoleon and after that it fell steadily. In Russia, a similar growth could be seen much later in the nineteenth century. Spanish demographic growth during the eighteenth century was also quite marked, perhaps from 7 to 10 million. Prussian population also rose from probably 1.7 to 3.1 million after a disastrous phase in the seventeenth century. Germany too, recorded a rise from approximately 10 to 12 million in 1650 to around 17 million by 1750, though the figures are not very reliable. The number of towns increased sharply. The Low Countries had an unusually high degree of urbanization with a considerable number of small- and medium-sized towns. The population density here was very high, not matched elsewhere.

What were the reasons for the rapid growth of population? One view is that the development of modern science accounted for a fall in the death rate. In more recent years, historians talk of two types of 'checks' or controls that limit population growth. The first, described as 'positive', consists of epidemics, famines and wars that cause a large number of deaths. The second, called the 'preventive' controls meant reduction of births within marriage or delayed marriage. This usually happens where there is a fall in the real wages, as the workers cannot afford to support a family and hence postpone their marriage. It was a self-regulating system. The rise in food production in the late-seventeenth century and the growth of the industrial sector in the eighteenth century also saw a corresponding growth in population. The economic expansion promoted urbanization and the increasing number of people created demand for manufactured goods.

Agriculture

Agricultural expansion immensely contributed to the rise of industry. It generated wealth for investment in industry and infrastructure. The accumulation of wealth in the hands of the landed class generated demand for manufactured goods. It also made the rich agriculturists invest in better seeds, and on fertilizers, canals, roads and on the new methods of cultivation. The introduction of an efficient form of cultivation not only provided more food for the growing population but the growing population provided the labour force for the urban factories and the mining sector.

Agriculture in Britain

The English revolution in the mid-seventeenth century introduced significant changes in agriculture. It brought an end to the feudal tenures and marked the advent of capitalist agriculture. It promoted a rational and scientific attitude towards agrarian problems and led to greater organizational and technological changes. The English agriculture transformed itself by the first half of the eighteenth century. A large part of the English population continued to depend on agriculture but the proportion steadily declined. In 1700, nearly 80 per cent of Englishmen and women lived on agriculture but by 1800 it had fallen to approximately 40 per cent. Still the declining number of agricultural force was able to feed the growing population of England. This resulted in a big shift of labour and resources to industry. As E.J. Hobsbawm points out agriculture held an important place in England for two reasons. First it was the indispensable foundation for industry. The second reason was that the 'landed interest' dominated British politics and social life. Landownership was the price of entry into high politics as the new landowners dominated the parliament.

According to Phyllis Deane, there were four salient features of the British agrarian revolution. It involved farming in large consolidated units instead of the medieval practice of open-field cultivation in discontinuous strips. Secondly, it involved the extension of arable farming over heaths (an area of open uncultivated land), and commons and the adoption of intensive livestock husbandry. Thirdly, it signified the transformation of a village community of self-sufficient peasants into one of labourers who depended more on the condition of national and international markets than on local factors. Finally, it involved a big increase in agricultural productivity. These developments became evident by the eighteenth century.

A decisive shift in agriculture had already begun in England in the sixteenth century. The English ruling class, according to Robert Brenner, was the most highly self-organized one in Europe and was able to exploit the peasantry efficiently. In the long run it implied that by the eighteenth century, they were able to dispossess the peasantry by bringing in enclosures of land effectively. It was the retention of property rights that proved decisive as it enabled the lords to undermine the customary rights and copyholds of the peasantry in the late-sixteenth and seventeenth centuries and allowed them to farm their holdings on capitalist lines.

Improvement in agricultural technology greatly helped in the scale of change in England. The chief problem in any agricultural system till that time was the loss of fertility of the soil from constant use of the land. European farmers followed the practice of leaving a part of their land fallow under the two or three field system. It helped restore nitrogen to the soil. Manuring the fields heavily was not possible, as poverty did not allow the farmers to keep enough animals to provide manure. Thus till the late-seventeenth century, English agriculture had largely remained traditional as far as technology was concerned. One of the first innovators in the field of agricultural productivity was Jethro Tull, an agriculturist himself. He conducted experiments that proved extremely beneficial. He designed a horse-drawn hoe and a mechanical seeder. His invention allowed farmers to saw in straight lines that also made it easier to harvest crops. Lord Townsland demonstrated the value of using turnips, clover and other field crops in rotation and so it became possible to cultivate land throughout the year. Later, Thomas William Coke wrote several tracts on the use of field grasses, new fertilizers such as oilcake and bone manure, and the principles of efficient estate-management. Robert Bakewell introduced improvements in breeding and greater specialization in the methods of livestock raising so that land that was unfit for crop cultivation could be used to raise cattle and sheep. Arthur Young popularized new agricultural ideas through his *Annales of Agriculture* in 1784. He also established farmers' clubs and organized competitions among the farmers. King George III was himself stimulated by these efforts and established his model farm at Windsor where Merino sheep farming was introduced. During the eighteenth century, scientific farming became fashionable, in which several landowners, including the king, took keen interest. Norfolk in the east of England earned a special name for its techniques of 'high farming'. Orchards and hop fields were developed in East Kent and Worcestershire, while the West County produced cider (drink made of crushed apple). Sussex and Surrey became known for geese and capons (domestic fowl fattened for eating).

The enclosure movement was another distinct feature of the agrarian change. The system of cultivation followed varied forms place to place. The continuation of open fields or its conversion to enclosed ones depended on several factors like the quality of soil, the nature of the product and its distance from the marketing centre. In the eighteenth century, about half of the arable land in England was still held in intermixed open-field strips.

Enclosures

To use new methods and to make agriculture profitable, the farmers required consolidation of their landholdings. Like in many countries, the open-field system had dominated the English countryside from the Middle Ages. Even the biggest landlords had scattered landholdings that were usually in elongated strips that were interspersed with the land of their neighbours. The owners of such scattered strips were forced to follow the traditional form of cultivation. It was impossible for any landlord to raise grass for his cattle when his neighbour was cultivating wheat. In such a situation, the village as a whole decided on the selection of crops and the number of cattle each member could graze on common meadows. Even the quantity of wood that each could take from the forest was determined by the village community. Thus the open-field system was a great hindrance to the new technology. Any landlord who wished to form a compact farm and adopt new methods of agriculture could not function in this old system. Enclosing the landed property was necessary.

Private enclosures were carried out in England since the late-fifteenth century. It was only in the eighteenth century, through the Acts of parliament that enclosures became the common method of consolidating landholdings. The Tudor government did not encourage enclosure of land as it created political and social problems for the state. The government's interest lay in keeping the peasants tied to their land while the enclosures caused large-scale eviction of the peasant population. Hence the process of land enclosures was considerably checked till the late-seventeenth century. Besides, both common law and the cost factors also ruled out fencing the long narrow strips. For it to be profitable it required the enclosure of all village land. It was also necessary to have the agreement of all its members, including the very poor farmers.

Voluntary enclosures thus became nearly impossible to attain. An Act of parliament provided the alternative. Parliament showed, as a general principle, its willingness to pass the necessary Act as long as the owners of four-fifths of the land and of the ecclesiastical property supported the petition. The views of copyholders, current leaseholders and even of small freeholders were usually ignored and the commissioners appointed under the Act transmuted their existing holdings and rights into single consolidated farms of supposedly equivalent value. Parliament usually passed the Enclosure Act in response to a petition, and enclosure of a village was carried out despite the opposition of some of its members. The process of land enclosure was difficult and expensive. The lands of the village had to be surveyed and redistributed in compact blocks among its members in proportion to their earlier holdings. Quite often roads had to be constructed to provide access to the fields. The first Act of parliament that carried out the enclosure of a village was registered in 1710 but the process was quite slow in the beginning. It was only after 1760 that the number of such Acts increased. Between 1750 and 1760, parliament passed 156 Acts of enclosure while the number had gone up to 906 by 1810. According to Lis and Soly, between 1761 and 1815 no less then 600,000 hectares of waste and common lands were enclosed by Acts of parliament.

It is generally believed that enclosures enforced through Acts of parliament formed the most dramatic aspect of agrarian change in England. It should be noted that the enclosure only accelerated the process of expropriation, which had been at work since the sixteenth century. The major change was the involvement of parliament in this process of land reorganization. Historians have debated the importance of enclosures in the economic and social history of England. One view considers it a precondition to industrialization in the cities. It is argued that by the middle of the eighteenth century, there was a distinct improvement in agrarian organizations and in husbandry techniques that gave England a decisive advantage over other European countries. English agriculture was able to meet domestic needs and even produced a significant surplus for exports. After 1750, favourable conditions, including a steady rise in food prices accompanied by demographic expansions stimulated capitalist farmers and landlords to raise agricultural output by extending arable land and by more intensive use of land. The new conditions stimulated them to adopt technical improvements to raise productivity. The increasing profits from land utilization led the landowners to raise rents but at the same time the tenants also enjoyed the security. They knew that if they functioned efficiently and spent part of their profits to improve stock and equipment of their farms they would continue to retain their tenure.

TABLE 13.2: WHEAT EXPORTS: ANNUAL AVERAGES IN THOUSAND CWT

1700–9	105
1710–19	109
1720–9	116
1730–9	296

The importance of the spread of the enclosure movement should not be over-estimated. Although enclosures might have been necessary for improving agriculture, it was not a sufficient factor for progress. Generally it removed the restrictions on technological change, but it did not always ensure the welfare of the village. In fact, the enclosure movement caused the destruction of rural society. It undermined the traditional peasant economy since agrarian improvement went hand-in-hand with concentration and consolidation of farms. The small landowners and copyholders with legal property rights were slowly eliminated. Some of the smaller farmers received land under the Enclosure Act but they were rendered too poor by the legal and fencing costs in which they were involved against their own wish. They were forced to invest in land improvements much beyond their capacity. Most of them were left with tiny and unprofitable plots and many of them were forced to sell their holdings to their richer neighbours and seek employment as landless labourers or migrate to urban centres. Phyllis Deane argues that the standards of food consumption deteriorated for the rural poor in the second half of the eighteenth century. Their diet was reduced to mainly bread and cheese because the system of enclosures had taken away their pasturage and the land where they collected the fuel for cooking their meals. Even the ponds from where they collected their fish were placed under closed lands of big landowners who invoked savage game laws and protected their enclosures with man-traps and spring-guns.

The social landscape and the physical appearance of the English countryside underwent a major transformation. The villages acquired a new appearance that continues till today with large and verdant fields and neat hedges and walls. It led to the virtual disappearance of peasant cultivators working in their fields. The English countryside of big landlords boasted vast estates, each with its huge manor house, gardens, and parks. Many of these families of landlords had come to the countryside by investing their wealth made in trade and commerce and were different from the old landed noble families. Throughout the eighteenth century the number of men who owned such estates continued to increase. Men from cities and from professional groups moved to the countryside for various reasons, including with the objective of entering parliament, which was dominated by prosperous landlords in the eighteenth century.

Agriculture provided material for a number of industries. Wheat, e.g. passed from the farms to the corn millers, then to bakers, distillers and subsequently to starch makers. The launderers, papermakers and textile workers also used wheat starch. Stationers, bookbinders, linen printers, trunk makers and paperhangers also used flour. Barley was sent to the distilleries. Sheep provided wool and cattle provided hides for tanners and leather for a variety of products. Soap boilers and candle makers used cattle fat in their products. These examples demonstrate the impact of agriculture on the manufacturers. The enclosure movement made many peasants landless. These people provided cheap labour for the factories and transformed the self-sufficient peasants into urban consumers of manufactured products. In other words it transformed a rural England into urban and industrialized society.

Agriculture in France

France was territorially a much larger state than England; almost four times its size and could be divided into two prime geographical zones – northern France specializing in cereal production and the wine-producing zone of the south. France stood astride both the Atlantic and the Mediterranean. The possession of colonies in Asia, Africa and in the West Indies had led to urbanization and economic growth of the coastal belt. However, hardly any change took place in the interiors of France. The disparities within France had become glaring in the eighteenth century. Louis Dermigny stresses the geo-political circumstances, including the location of Paris and the size of the country that caused economic unification lag far behind political centralization.

It is difficult to know whether the real agricultural output of the eighteenth-century France increased substantially. Seigneurialism was still a vital and dominant fact of agrarian life and was the foundation of rural-social relations. As P.M. Jones states, the seigneurial system was an integral part of the social and economic fabric of the ancient regime.

Peasants themselves constituted a stratified social group in France. Most French peasants were extremely poor and formed the semi-proletarianized group and were variously called in different regions by the name of *journaliers, manouvriers* or *travailleurs de terre*. They owned very small parcels of land and had to work on the fields of others. They performed unremunerative tasks and in the event of any crisis they were pushed to the ranks of wage earners. They represented the exploited section of the feudal order in France. The level of economic exploitation varied from one region to another. The middling sort of peasants called *haricotiers* formed the next social scale. They were slightly better off and worked with mule or some livestock. The wealthiest and the best equipped in the French rural society were the *gros fermiers*. They were the substantial peasant-farmers, who owned vast lands and lived comfortably. When the government took steps in 1763 and 1766 by exempting cleared land from taxation, *gros fermiers* were the first to respond to the challenge. They were accused of land *engrossment* (amalgamation of land) at a time when grain prices rose inexorably in the second half of the eighteenth century. Landowners of all types sought to cash in as rents rose rapidly and seigniorial obligations were exacted with greater efficiency. Profits accruing from speculation in basic foodstuffs were used to purchase more land at the cost of the lesser peasantry. Two forms of *engrossment* caused strong reaction – firstly, the proprietors stealthily enlarged their estates by absorbing adjacent holdings either through purchase or foreclosure and secondly, at times they acquired scattered farms one by one. The feudal structure in France had remained strong and was protected by the absolutist rulers. The rural society was clearly divided between the feudal aristocracy and the toiling masses. The economic and social structure of French agriculture was still dominated by small, individual peasant producers. The seigneurial surplus extraction by extra-economic coercion prevented any major breakthrough in the French agriculture. The agrarian transformation in France was brought to an end in the late medieval period when the peasants' right to land property was protected by the state. This established a check on the transfer of landed property to the big landlords and ensured a wide base for the state taxes by keeping the peasants within their villages. However, during the eighteenth century some changes in rural France were discernible in the land clearances, contraction of fallow land, increase in yield ratios, introduction of new agricultural techniques and changes in agrarian organization. But these changes were slow and limited to specific areas. There was no agrarian revolution of the English type. Perhaps the pressure of a growing population had contributed to increased production but it did not alter the productivity and technology. This makes Michel Morineau comment that the expansion of French agriculture in the eighteenth century was a 'development within stagnation'. Certain areas such as the Paris basin and the Seine valley, known for their fertile soil, responded to the pressure of the neighbouring market by better methods of cultivation. Capitalist forces began to emerge at such places and the productivity of soil increased with the introduction of new methods and greater use of fertilizers.

Another important change was the rise of professional 'managers' or the *fermiers généraux*, who rented all the estates of one or more landlords and in turn hired them out. These were the capitalists who generally functioned as collectors of seigneurial dues and ecclesiastical tithes and sometimes controlled the disposable produce of several estates. We do not come across any other movement in France on a large-scale similar to that of the enclosure movement in England. Most of the French peasants worked on the land under a system similar to the open field arrangement, called *vaineapature*. This required the owners of land to follow the same routines of cultivation as their neighbours and it was the village that determined the rights of its members on common land. From the middle of the eighteenth century some individuals approached the state demanding enclosure of their land and the division of communal properties. The French monarchy did not adopt enclosure as a national policy. Yet some individuals carried out *engrossment*. These amalgamations reduced peasant tenures while piecemeal acquisition was generally accompanied by ousting the original owners and tenants. In these places the new landlords with their financial power and entrepreneurial flair adopted scientific methods of farm management. It was not uncommon to find them owning a dozen or more farms in one region. This change became evident after 1760 when grain prices began to rise steeply. Lefebvre describes them as rural bourgeoisie. They were different from the traditional seigneurs because they had appropriated surplus land in order to profit from production whereas the seigneurs were primarily feudal lords who were only interested in increasing their exactions from the peasants. According to A. Soboul, it was the persistence of land property rights that prevented proper restructuring of the French agriculture.

Increasing food grain prices and the growing population pressure led to a seigneurial reaction. This period marked an intensification of feudal obligations. The lords imposed harvest dues, which turned out to be most burdensome on the peasants. Casual taxes on property transfers were introduced in the form of *lods*, *ventes* and *rachets*. However, there was an extreme unevenness of seigneurial surplus extraction. As Lis and Soly point out, the eighteenth-century peasantry had to surrender a significant part of their net production to a small minority of feudal lords that constituted about 25 to 30 per cent of their net income. From 1730s the big landowners gained from an upward trend in rents. Between the 1720–9 and 1780–9, the rent increased by 142 per cent while agricultural prices rose by 60 per cent. After the deduction of all forms of dues and taxes, the *manouvriers* (small peasants) were able to retain hardly half of the total harvest while the *métayers* (share-croppers) were left with hardly a third of their produce. It had serious social consequences as small peasants were dispossessed of their lands. In most parts of France during the eighteenth century, three-fourths of the peasants possessed less than five hectares of land, considered the minimum to retain economic independence. Nearly 25 per cent of the farmers had only 1 hectare of land to cultivate. The number of smallholdings and the surplus extraction prevented the introduction of improvements in land management and technology to raise productivity. The condition of the peasantry worsened with the new concentration of landholdings in the hands of *fermiers*. By renting extensive properties of several units, they were able to obtain much better terms of tenancy than other producers. The *fermiers* also made all attempts to appropriate the holdings of subsistence peasants and demanded exorbitant fees from the peasants to plough a small piece of land. As a result, *manouvriers* at several places were either forced to dispose of their land or sell their labour to the *fermier*. It appears that the total number of rural proletariat and semi-proletariat had increased during the eighteenth century. According to Lis and Soly, in Andance, the number of rural day-labourers without property rose from 12 per cent in 1696 to nearly 23.3 per cent by 1789. As the pace of industrialization in France was too slow and hardly existed, it must have cost immense suffering to this section of the population. This explains why Pierre Goubert commented that a French peasant worked on the field with one eye always on the price of bread. The condition of the peasant was one of the factors that contributed to the French Revolution.

There is a disagreement among historians over the economic and social evolution of the French countryside in the second half of the eighteenth century. The main subject of this controversy is whether agricultural production increased or stagnated during this period. On the one extreme, Jean Claude Toutain argues that there was undoubted increase in agricultural production between 1750 and 1790 at an annual rate of 1.4 per cent. On the other hand, Michel Morineau rejects this viewpoint. Toutain believes that agricultural production had risen by 60 per cent despite famines while Emmanuel Le Roy Ladurie argues that there was hardly 25 to 40 per cent increase in the decades between 1700–9 and 1780–9. Ladurie argues that there was no agrarian revolution in France and that though the production increased there was no change in productivity. Productivity should be measured in terms of new crops, new techniques and improved yields per hectare and that there was hardly any change in these areas. The increase in production was based on traditional lines. The domination of small peasant proprietors prevented any major agrarian transformation because they rarely had the resources to adopt new techniques and the growing number of them obstructed new efforts. The French small farmers remained vulnerable to various factors, including the violent movements of food prices and harvest failures.

Germany

The agrarian situation in Germany was almost the same as had existed in France before the Revolution. Like the French, the German nobility was severely criticised by the bourgeois enlightened critics, though it did not lead to any radical change in its social position. The pace of agrarian reforms was gradual and the so-called reforms to bring about 'peasant emancipation' did not bring about the end of feudal agrarian relationship. The real turning point came only in the nineteenth century.

There were signs of economic and social developments in Germany, which contributed to a slow transformation of the agrarian society. An increase in population growth was recorded in the eighteenth century from about 1700 and the pace increased markedly after about 1750. There was also a spurt in industrial production. German agriculture was stimulated because of a constantly rising demand for grain and raw materials. The external market also widened because of a rising population in many parts of Europe. The emergence of towns and urbanization brought pressures on the rural economy. The diverse and concentrated urban environment gave greater possibilities for the growth in the long term.

The process of agrarian change in the German region was

associated with the growth of population, as had happened in England. However, the change came much later, perhaps from the middle of the eighteenth century. Increasing population in many places brought unutilized land under cultivation. Agrarian reforms during the second half of the eighteenth century led to considerable increase in agricultural production and was usually carried out through state initiatives based on the programmes of the Enlightenment. The introduction of 'improved three-field system' and the spread of alternative crop rotation increased yields per acre. This was needed to feed the rapidly growing population. Among the new crop plants that were introduced to supplement the traditional food supplies, the most important was maize that was now cultivated in Baden, the Palatinate, and Wurttemberg. The introduction of potato cultivation by the authorities was strongly resisted by the peasants but it proved greatly beneficial in the regions like Mittelgebirge which were unsuited to grain cultivation. As potato could easily be cultivated even on infertile soil and under unfavourable climatic conditions. It turned out to be a life-saver in 1770–1 when the grain harvest failed. As in England, German agriculture also contributed to industrialization. There were many commercial plants and specialized crops such as flax and hemp, chicory, tobacco, hops and wine grapes. Hemp was increasingly grown in Baden, Westphalia, Hesse, Wurttemberg, etc., as raw material for making ropes and was also used in coarse textiles of common use and for obtaining oil. Flax, was used for making finer textiles, and was produced on an increasing scale in Silesia, Westphalia, Hanover and Bohemia. Chicory was cultivated as a coffee substitute in some parts of Germany while tobacco cultivation was forced by the state but did not achieve much success. At the same time it is important to note that till the end of the eighteenth century none of these areas had achieved the scale of specialization that would give the Germans an edge in the international market.

An interesting feature of German agriculture was the expansion of meadows in many parts of central Europe in the second half of the seventeenth century. It led not only to increased animal husbandry but also provided larger amounts of manure. In the second half of the eighteenth century, many innovations were carried out such as planting of fallow land with nitrogen fixing plants, and better care of meadows and animals. These practices made significant improvements in land productivity and grain cultivation. The most noticeable development in agriculture was in land utilization during the eighteenth century. Though the results of these measures were not seen in the eighteenth century itself and could be observed only in the nineteenth century, they brought about important changes in the law concerning the use of the land and property–tenancy relations. The three-field system was on the verge of disappearance and the introduction of clover, legumes and root crops like potato or turnip were bringing an end to the concept of fallow land. This also led to the reclamation of marginal lands. At the same time, although the privileges of the nobility were curtailed by the policies of the enlightened despots without completely dismantling the traditional feudal powers of the nobility, some forms of enclosure had emerged. In Schleswig-Holstein it was called *verkoppelung* and in Swabia it was known as *vereinodung* as it attempted to rationalize and consolidate scattered holdings and occasionally it involved dissolution of common land. Some of the feudal landlords began to distribute *demesne* land to peasants so that they could increase their revenue. Thus we find that the market that had played so decisive a role in English agriculture also began to influence agrarian developments in many parts of Germany. However, it did not transform the character of the nobility till the nineteenth century as the government had to make various compromises with the powerful nobles. At the same time a gradual difference emerged between the agrarian systems of Germany in the east and the west of river Elbe. Commercialization and intensification of agriculture was limited in the western region. In England, the big landlords themselves played a major role in the structural change, while in Germany this change was imposed from above. The German nobility, in the words of Sheilagh Ogilvie, remained imprisoned within the boundaries of social estates. On the one hand this protected it in the changing situation but on the other hand it was an obstacle to the path of capitalist market society.

Netherlands

Apart from England, the landlords in the Netherlands were able to resolve their agrarian problems during the eighteenth century by adopting new techniques and methods of farming. Most significant of these were the 'enclosures' of open fields and crop rotation. Southern Netherlands was regarded as the chief centre of agronomic experiments. Flanders and Brabant had attained the highest yield ratios in Europe. These were achieved by high labour-intensive farming, improved techniques of fertilization, well-developed methods of crop rotation and the cultivation of fodder and commercial crops for industrial use. By the mid-eighteenth century, southern Netherlands exported 5 per cent of the yearly average of grain harvest.

Cereal cultivation was adopted in almost all parts of the Netherlands except in Holland. Rye was the main crop because it could be used for gin and for making bread. In times of food shortage, it could be mixed with oats or cereals to make bread. The first half of the eighteenth century saw an increase in the consumption of wheat bread. When the prices began to rise, wheat imports from the Baltic started declining and wheat consumption also declined except in Holland. The growing demand for wheat in the earlier years had led the peasants in Zeeland to cultivate wheat. Elsewhere, rye cultivation continued. Towards the close of the century, other foodstuffs like buckwheat replaced bread and by 1798 its consumption constituted 17 per cent of the total cereal consumption in Holland (J.A. van Houtte). Another crop that gained rapid popularity was potato. Its cultivation spread to Brabant, Zeeland, Utrecht, Overijssel and Friesland. Its popularity actually increased because of the high cost of grain during famines. One of the reasons for cultivating potato was that it was exempt from the *tithe* and remained unaffected by excise which was charged on grain milling. Cash crops like flax, hemp hop and tobacco were grown in Zeeland, Brabant, Flanders and Austrian Netherlands. However, the decline of the textile industry affected the cultivation of flax which began to lose ground after 1750.

Flanders' achievement appears remarkable because it presented highly fragmented landholdings and a high density of population.

Crop rotation contributed to intensive cultivation in this region, an idea that England had borrowed from Flanders. Flanders had shown the agronomists the value of intensive cultivation through crop rotation. It spread to other parts of the Netherlands around Antwerp, Campier and northern Brabant. It was adopted in the small farms directly tilled by their owners or in the lands belonging to its proprietors who had to pay taxes even if the land was not utilized. The size of the farms varied according to its utilization. The arable farms were smaller than those on which stock was raised. The poor quality lands were used either for stock farming or potato cultivation. Another possible reason for the spread of potato cultivation was that its cultivation required smaller units of land. It was also affected by the pattern of land tenures. Small- or medium-sized farms were usually farmed directly. The small peasant proprietors frequently increased their farmland by renting other farms. In 1711, the proportion of the small farms (less than 1 hectare) was 49 per cent. By 1790, it had gone up to 66 per cent (Lis and Soly). Rents remained generally high for smaller farms. The main reason for this phenomenon was perhaps the spread of proto-industrialization in the preparation of linen when the major textile towns had either declined or stagnated and the manufacturing activities had increased in the countryside. The peasants in many parts of Flanders faced disruption of the traditional order as the landlords began raising rents seeing the demographic pressure while the merchants and manufacturers kept the wages low. An increasing number of Flemish peasants began to depend for their livelihood exclusively on spinning and weaving. The figure shot up much higher in those areas which were close to industrialized centres.

Spread of Proto-Industrialization

Economic historians have provided two models for the transition from the pre-industrial stage to the Industrial Revolution covering growth, structure of organization and labour force:

a. The Marxist model of primitive accumulation and manufactures
b. The model of proto-industrialization

Both these models attempt to conceptualize the economic and social structures of the period. They both concern a large number of countries and regions. They also focus on the relationship between agrarian change, commercial capitalism and the growth of handicraft industries.

Karl Marx suggested the model of primitive accumulation of capital. He described it as the necessary pre-historical phase of capitalism that brought about capital-labour relations. According to Marx, the process which divorces the worker from the ownership of his own labour brings about two transformations – the social means of subsistence and production are turned into capital, and the immediate producers are turned into wage-labourers. The primitive accumulation is, in the first instance, associated with agrarian changes and the enclosure movement that fitted well with the decline of the English peasantry. However, this view did not bring out the association between the spread of domestic industry and primitive capital accumulation. Marx wrote little on it. He suggested that only through the destruction of the rural domestic industry could an adequate market for domestic goods be provided for the capitalist mode of production. He accepted that such domestic crafts did not simply disappear before the emergence of large-scale industry. For historians subscribing to the 'Primitive accumulation' model, it meant separation of labour from the means of production but it did not necessarily mean removing the labourer from the countryside. This stage in the development of the capitalist labour process was termed as 'manufacture' by Marx – a phase of handicraft workshop industry. It preceded the phase of modern machine production and remained under capitalist control carrying out one or a variety of tasks. The introduction of new technology resulted in the division of labour. Marx hinted that 'manufacturing' could take two distinct forms. First a heterogeneous manufacture or the mechanical assembly of independently made components of the final product, e.g. watches. The second was the organic manufacture involving a series of connected processes such as needles. By these ways, the capitalist relations could enter rural production. Manufacture is credited with giving the capitalist rather than the worker, control of the product, while the control over production process itself was achieved through the factory system.

In recent years several historians like Frankline Mendels, E.L. Jones, Maxine Berg, P. Hudson, J. Schlumbohn, M. Sonenscher, Peter Kriedte and many others have identified rural putting-out with a distinct historical phase. Their chief argument is that the world market for mass produced goods grew at such a pace from the sixteenth century that traditional urban manufactures could not efficiently respond as they were hampered by guild restrictions and high labour costs. The rise and spread of an under-employed mass of landless or nearly landless country dwellers as cheap workforce formed an essential precondition to the development of rural domestic industries. Thus an under-developed peasantry in pastoral regions became the basis for expandable and self-exploiting industrial labour force and the industry improved the seasonal employment of the labourers. It released the traditional limits placed on population growth by the size of landholdings. It also provided a major source for capital accumulation. Proto-industrialization is credited not just with the sources of labour and capital but also with the entrepreneurship, technological and organizational changes that led to the first major increase in productivity before the coming of factory. The exponents of the theory of proto-industrialization identify three essential features – the economic and social symbiosis between agriculture and industry across the seasons, the urban merchants coordinating industry and the dependence of proto-industrial activities on distant markets. It is seen as a distinctively regional phenomenon. When during the eighteenth century, the peasantry faced progressive impoverishment in many areas, particularly because of population growth and the enclosure movement, the demand for manufactured goods rose more than ever before. Thus, there was a growing tendency towards concentration of labour and the growth of industrial output. It was carried out primarily by the expansion of rural manufacture within the family economy. Jan De Vries considers proto-industrialization a crucial link between pre-industrial agrarian world and the growth of large cities in the nineteenth century. Wrigley also relates structural and demographic changes in the eighteenth-century Britain to proto-industrial activity. However, it must be remembered that proto-industrial activities were not confined to England and Flanders alone but also spread in parts of France, Germany and Switzerland. Most of the industrial areas specialized in the production of particular commodities. These regions emerged as the centres of proto-industrial activities because of their trading linkages, concentration of labour and the availability of raw materials.

Unrestricted rural industry was a direct response to the constantly growing demand of new markets emerging from regional, national and international commerce. Many merchants acted as entrepreneurs and took advantage of the putting-out system to meet the growing demand for manufactured goods. This activity was usually free from guild regulations. These merchants bought up a stock of raw materials like wool or flax and then 'put-out' or supplied to rural workers for combing the fibres and spinning. The workers spun yarn and these were collected by the merchant capitalists and handed over to rural weavers to be woven into cloth. The bleaching, dyeing and processing was also done by a separate set of workers within the countryside before they were collected and supplied to the wholesalers or retailers by the merchant entrepreneurs. The putting-out system had several advantages for the rural workers. It was a means of staving off poverty particularly in the period of poor harvests. The work involved the entire family including the children and the women and gave them extra income. They could adjust their labour in accordance with their farming work. Though they had to work within their cottages in cramped spaces, they were free from the close and constant supervision of urban masters.

Though proto-industrialization spread on a large-scale in the textile sector, it was adopted in many other crafts, including metal-works, clock making or coal production.

Germany

During the eighteenth century a larger share of industrial production took place in the countryside. It was caused as much by urban decline as by fast rural growth. Landlords within the feudal system regulated economic activity in the rural areas. Landlords and rural feudal communities remained powerful in most parts of Germany even in the second half of the eighteenth century compared to those in Flanders or in England. Germany had two different agrarian systems – *gutsherrschaft* in the eastern region with powerful landlords and strong bonds of serfdom, with heavy feudal dues and vast *demesne* farming, and *grundherrschaft* in western Germany with fewer serfs, weaker landlords, rents replacing feudal dues and fewer *demesne* lands. Landlords in eastern Germany, particularly in the fertile tracts, prevented the spread of rural industries. The rural industries spread in the less fertile territories as it provided alternative income and those landlords, who expected to gain from this, allowed their subjects to work in these industries.

It is usually assumed that wherever landlords enjoy vast feudal powers, industrial expansion does not take place easily, as they do not allow the rural people to participate in industry. This happened in many parts of northern and eastern Germany. If the rural workers in these fertile tracts participated in industrial activities, it was mainly to escape extortion by landlords. In many parts of Germany, proto-industrial activities arose within the feudal parameters. In central and eastern Germany, the landlords exploited their institutional powers in the industrial sector as well. The *demesne* economy did not disappear. Instead it expanded to include other activities like mining, smelting, glass-making, spinning and weaving besides farming on the *demesne.* The feudal landlords allowed industries to grow because it helped them expand their extra-economic powers by extracting revenue through loom fees, monopoly rights to supply foreign merchants, forcing peasants to purchase flax grown in *demesne* above market rates, reclaiming their lost land and by using feudal obligations to recruit 'forced wage-labour'. Silesian and Bohemian export industries were able to compete at the international level primarily because of the low labour-cost which were forcibly maintained through the extra-economic coercive powers of the landlords. In the long run, this artificial condition created obstacles to industrial development in these regions. The growing English competition could not be met by forced labour and cheap flax but by the technological changes, better industrial organization and mass production. The Silesian landlords vehemently opposed new technology and compelled the state to place legal prohibitions on new practices. The limited powers of the landlords in the eastern regions under *gundherrschaft* provided long-term advantages to industrial expansion. Serfdom was not able to constrain labour markets, the use of land was more flexible, and capital was not flowing to landholdings as it happened in the feudal east, commerce was more developed and the rural markets were less restrictive. Thus places like Saxony, the Rhineland, Wurttemberg, etc., gained in this situation and export-oriented industries rose. In Thuringia, rural guilds dominated all stages of production and were quite widespread. They had control over the workers of small iron goods, the gun manufacturers, toy-makers, knife-smiths and those knitting stockings, etc.

Thus we find that the rural industries in Germany, particularly in Westphalia, the Rhineland, Silesia and Bohemia flourished to a fair degree. Linen manufacture came to be concentrated in Westphalia. By 1800, nearly 70 per cent of the rural population in Minden-Ravensburg consisted of cottages and day-labourers depending on the international linen market (Lis and Soly). Textile and the metallurgical industry had developed in the Rhineland and the population upsurge led to the spread of proto-industrialization in these regions. The number of flax spinners in Bohemia in 1772 was believed to have been about 2,30,000, while in northern Bohemia, nearly 5,00,000 people earned their living from spinning and weaving. Silesia also witnessed a similar trend during the eighteenth century. According to Hans Medick, proto-industrialization was shaped by increased exploitation of the total family labour force that included women, children and the aged. It was this internal dynamics resulting in self-exploitation that made rural industry grow quickly.

Switzerland

In Switzerland, cottage industries quickly developed into an essential part of the rural economy. Cotton production expanded from the beginning of the eighteenth century in the cantons of Oberland and Zurich. An interesting feature of the Swiss agrarian life was its divergence. The plains in central Switzerland with fertile soil remained confined to agriculture, strong village communities and under the control of municipal authorities that protected the inhabitants from outsiders. The textile industry flourished in the mountainous regions. By the end of the eighteenth century, nearly two-thirds of the rural population in Oberland consisted of spinners, weavers and dry-labourers. The swift demographic growth was fuelled by immigration of outside workers and industrialization. Zurich witnessed spectacular growth in population and industry. Twenty districts in the province of Overijssel became known for its linen industry. The region consisted of a vast number of poor cottagers owning on an average 1 hectare of land. Between 1675 and 1723, the total population grew rapidly while the number of peasants remained roughly the same. Lis and Soly ascribe this demographic growth to the spread of proto-industry.

France

In France, the impoverished *manouvriers* were able to secure work through the spread of the rural textile industry. Woollen manufactures in Languedoe had spread into hundreds of villages. In Champagne too, there were over 30,000 woollen workers towards the close of the eighteenth century and the textile production more than doubled. The silk industry around Lyon employed nearly 1 lakh of rural workers. Even the linen industry expanded rapidly near Rouen. The number increased from about 43,000 in 1730 to 1,88,000 workers on the eve of the French Revolution (Lis and Soly). In Nord, nearly three-fourths of the villages were involved in cottage industry and the linen production tripled between 1746 and 1788. This region had seen a steady rise in population density. Maine was another rural region that employed perhaps 1,50,000 people in the local industry. Cotton spinning in Maine and Alsace and pin-makers in the Pays d' Ouche had grown almost tenfold during the eighteenth century. Ironware was an important occupation for the rural workers of St Etiénne. The overwhelming majority of proto-industrial workers who were 'put-out' during the eighteenth century were dependent on merchants directly or indirectly. A small number of capitalist merchants dominated the entire production. In Ronbaix, the great manufactures employed nearly 30,000 spinners in Artoix and Picardy besides 10,000 weavers in the town. A famous merchant capitalist Bernard Scheibler in the Linburg region, employed nearly 6,000 rural workers in 1762. Another very large textile factory was established in Abbéville employing about 1,800 workers. Apart from this, the textile industry depended on another 10,000 rural workers in the environs.

England

As we have seen before, how English agriculture had undergone profound changes during the seventeenth century. We have also studied in the earlier chapters that the rise of the cottage industry in England had already taken place in the sixteenth century. There were significant regional variations in social structures, some promoting industrialization while others did not. Joan Thirsk believes that the rise of domestic industry should not be seen as a product of demographic growth but should be linked to certain types of farming community and social organization. Industrial by-employment in England had a long history particularly in the mining sector. The rise of the rural industry, according to Maxine Berg, was not because of entrepreneurship, easy supplies of raw materials or even market demand but rested on the economic circumstances of an area's inhabitants. Capital investors were mainly interested in those areas where weak manorial system provided surplus labour, where there was a possibility of immigration because of small landholdings of cultivators. The last factor was important because the small size of farms forced the peasantry to take up industrial work to supplement their meagre agricultural incomes. However, there were many other factors that determined the spread of proto-industrialization. Many industries emerged within a pastoral economy but there were others, which grew into towns. The best quality knives were made in the town of Sheffield but the lower and cheaper quality was manufactured in the nearby villages. Similarly, the woollen and worsted stockings were made in the countryside while jersey stockings were manufactured in Norwich and London. England had a wide range of industries that constituted a part of the proto-industrial activity such as the manufacture of starch, needles, pins, cooking utensils, lace, soap, vinegar and stockings. Leather works, textile factories using flax and wool were scattered throughout England. The rural industries flourished till the seventeenth century but their fortunes varied during the eighteenth century. While the proto-industrial activities persisted and ran parallel to the modern factory form of industrialization till the early-nineteenth century, in many parts of England it had started declining.

Historians in recent years have confirmed Clapham's argument that the factory system and new techniques spread across the British industry very slowly till the early-nineteenth century and that the traditional forms of organization and labour-intensive methods persisted even after the coming of the Industrial Revolution. Thus, we find that during the eighteenth century, the British industries grew as much within the old rural structure as through new factories and mechanized workshops. We have evidence to believe that a number of traditional domestic industries declined during the eighteenth century but the causes for this are not very clear. One view emphasizes the role of modern factory organizations in the decline of the rural industries but it is not very acceptable to recent scholars. Sidney Pollard argues that the extending of mines, discovery of cheaper alternatives, location shifts and improvements in transportation deprived certain regions of specific advantages. Norfolk suffered from the competition of Indian products brought by the East India Company that resulted in riots against the Indian textiles. Then it faced a strong challenge from worsted goods from Yorkshire and finally had to face the growing manufacture of cotton textiles in many parts of England. Throughout the century, Norfolk experienced phases of decline throughout the century interspersed by short periods of recovery in the 1750s and 1770s. The cloth industry of Essex also declined sharply by 1800. The rural weaving industry almost disappeared in the beginning of the eighteenth century. Spinning activity, however, continued in the countryside employing a large number of women. The fustian and cotton industry also drew a large number of small peasants who grew a particular variety of wood that was needed for the preparation of natural colours. By the end of the century, its need ended as chemical dyes were introduced. In the West Country, the textile industry lasted till the early-nineteenth century but its fortunes continued to fluctuate. The severe depression in 1783–4 in Gloucestershire led to its final eclipse. Some historians believe that water power and new methods of coal extraction led to industrial activities shifting north. Clapham rejects this explanation. E.J. Jones focuses on the comparative advantage factor that led to a shift in capital investment from one sector to another and from one industry to another. Mechanization also cannot be seen as a chief factor in the decline of the rural industry because the experiences of Essex, Norfolk and Berkshire suggest that decline had set in even before the coming of mechanization.

Urban Industries

The pace of industrialization remained painfully slow in most parts of Europe during the eighteenth century. Almost entire Europe remained within the fetters of feudal order and urban industrial activity remained confined to a few regions in major countries. To understand the factors responsible for the rapid industrialization in England, it will be fruitful to examine the economies of the German states, Russia and France. These were relatively more developed regions of Europe.

In the German urban centres, the emergence of modern industries was delayed because of several reasons. The widespread destruction caused by the Thirty Years War had dislocated the economy in many ways. The second half of the seventeenth century witnessed reconstruction and revival of economic activities. However, the powers enjoyed by guilds and merchant companies delayed the process of modernization and factory production. The post-war recovery phase was a period of economic stagnation and the steady rise of population resulted in surplus labour. The continuation of guilds tended to place restrictions on economic transformation. A limit was placed on the number of masters and outsiders joining any specialized field. This excluded healthy competition and checked entrepreneurial and technical innovations. The Imperial Handicrafts Decree of 1731 forbade strikes, journeymen associations and collective wage demands. The rulers avoided any action against the guilds or their outright abolition as they found it useful to control the industrial sector through them. There are many cases of guilds putting obstacles in the use of new techniques intended to increase industrial production. In the eighteenth century, the Remscheid Scythe's guild prevented the introduction of water-driven scythe hammers. The guild resisted new technology as it was afraid of losing its monopoly (Sheilagh Ogilvie). In Saxony, the same trend was seen during the seventeenth century, which ultimately caused the linen industry to shift to the countryside. The state was prompted to put a ban on ribbon mills by the urban ribbon-makers guild in Lusatia. When this ban was lifted in 1765, it was followed by a swift expansion of the industry. The merchants were forced to shift away from linen to cotton production. The town guilds in Saxony had monopolized the trade of rural industrial products. The rural producers were compelled to sell their products through the merchant guilds of towns and cities throughout the eighteenth century. The linen industry of Westphalia could not achieve any breakthrough in industrial production because of the special status enjoyed by urban guilds.

Eighteenth century saw a steady spread of the putting-out system, particularly in export-oriented industries such as the small-scale iron smelting in Bergland and Saureland, the arms produc ts in Thuringia and the glass production. The putting-out system was fairly widespread in the region between Swabia and Saxony especially in the textile manufacturing. According to Rudolf Vierhans, the spinning factories were greatly influenced by the bleaching manufactories which received material from distant regions. Linen weaving and manufacturing in the Silesian Bergland, Westphalia, Hesse and the Low Rhine was emerging as a major industry in the eighteenth century. In 1763, the Krefeld silk manufactory at Leyen employed about 2,800 workers (Rudolf Vierhans). Division of labour slowly came into force and a distinction was made between skilled and unskilled labour. The unskilled included women and children. In such factories, the inmates of orphanages, workhouses, poor homes and prisoners were often used as cheap labour. The Lenz Wollzesce was probably the largest factory, employing over 1,000 master weavers and nearly 4,000 journeymen in 1786. It had come under state management in 1754 (Vierhans). The Berlin Lagerhans or warehouse for the production of uniforms was another big factory. However, the economic and political climate was not very favourable at times and very few big manufactories could survive into the early-nineteenth century.

The rise of modern industries in Germany was hampered by a number of factors. Communications and transport facilities were poor and the absence of political unity among the German states was a major obstacle in the emergence of a unified market. The region had a multiple coinage system and innumerable customs barriers which affected the flow of trade. The chief obstacle to industrialization was the persistence of the feudal structure in many parts of Germany. The absence of colonies deprived this region of the advantage of colonial markets. All these factors did not permit a free and sustained industrial development till the end of the eighteenth century.

In Russia, the state played an important role in economic affairs, especially in the period of Peter the Great (1682–1725). It encouraged individuals to participate in industrial development, but the results were negligible. The government announced interest-free loans and subsidies to individual manufacturers to encourage new production. Monopolies were granted and tax exemptions given on imports of materials or tools. Some of the state factories in early-eighteenth century were among the largest in Europe. The sailcloth factory in Moscow employed 1,162 workers (M.S. Anderson). The Urals became an important centre of new metal industry where iron and copper was produced in large quantities. M.S. Anderson mentions the name of Nikita Demidov as one of the first successful industrialists of Russia. He began his career as an illiterate artisan in Tula but later set up many foundry buildings from 1716. Industrial development in metal works in the early-eighteenth century, was greatly stimulated by the growing demands of the armed forces. Sailcloth was another industrial product. However, industrial progress in Russia faced numerous problems. The biggest was the persistence of a strong feudal order in the countryside that prevented the rise of wage-labour. This problem was overcome by conscripting peasants as 'ascribed' factory labour by force. A common Russian procedure was the 'ascribing' of groups of peasant villages to the service of particular factories. Sometimes soldiers were utilized but most factories functioned on the labour of criminals, vagrants, beggars, and often on state peasants employed in such industries. Russian industrial development remained retarded because of poor communications, shortage of capital, neglect of the merchant class at the cost of foreign merchants, shortfall of sufficient labour, technological backwardness, lack of technological knowledge and the absence of popular participation in the industrial field. Most of the industrial ventures were promoted by state sponsorships but these enterprises were very few. The vast stretches of unpopulated land and the persistence of a powerful feudal organization were strong impediments to industrialization in Russia.

France, with a potential for rapid industrialization, is often compared with England in economic growth during the eighteenth century. That France lagged far behind England by the late-eighteenth century has led historians to speculate the possible factors that retarded the French industrial growth. One set of scholars suggests that her economy was stagnant and did not move in the direction of industrialization, while the other argues that France enjoyed spectacular growth throughout the eighteenth century, particularly in foreign trade. France could not achieve a breakthrough like England because of the low level of capital accumulation, absence of banking and her obsolete political structure.

The eighteenth century witnessed tremendous growth of French external commerce. Several historians like Labrousse, Pierre Leon Francois Crouzet and Pierre H. Boulle argue that commerce grew more rapidly in France than in Britain until the Seven Years War (1756–63). External trade reached five times its 1715 value at the outbreak of the French Revolution and colonial commerce made even better strides, despite wide fluctuations, growing nearly ten times in the same period, as is evident from Table 13.3.

It is quite evident from this table that French foreign trade grew quite rapidly. It had tripled from 1726 to 1774 despite sharp reverses in the Seven Years War. There were some 1,800 French vessels on the eve of the Revolution. The trade of Languedoc cloth from Marseilles to the Middle East rose from 30,000 pieces annually to nearly 1,00,000 pieces in the course of the eighteenth century (Pierre Goubert). The export of manufactured products rose by 221 per cent and other goods by 298 per cent. The ports of Bordeaux and Marseilles enjoyed spectacular growth. There were many branches of international trade in which the French secured or retained a dominant position. They remained the chief suppliers of manufactured goods to Spain and the Spanish American empire. France had effectively utilized the West Indian colonies through slave labour and had developed a vast and fast-growing re-export trade to Northern Europe. The Levant was an important buyer of the French products. In contrast, most of the goods from the British colonies were used up within Britain to supply the raw material for

TABLE 13.3: AVERAGE YEARLY VALUE OF FRENCH EXTERNAL TRADE 1715–88

(*in million livres*)

Years	Total colonial trade			Total French Foreign		
	Import	Export	Total	Import	Export	Total
1715–20	22.3	12.9	35.2	87.3	115.8	203.1
1721–32	29.3	23.8	53.1	109.4	140.5	219.9
1733–5	39.5	24.5	64.0	116.5	155.5	272.0
1736–9	54.4	35.7	90.1	158.3	181.1	342.4
1740–8	49.9	34.7	81.6	173.4	234.7	407.8
1749–55	85.4	52.5	137.9	260.2	322.3	582.5
1756–63	20.9	16.5	37.4	185.9	251.7	437.6
1764–76	128.1	19.2	177.3	314.8	369.8	681.6
1777–83	103.5	57.7	161.2	326.4	319.0	615.4
1784–9	214.4	113.2	327.6	536.2	466.4	1,002.6

Source: Arnould, *Balance du commerce*, III (quoted by Pierre H. Boulle, 'Patterns of French Colonial Trade and the "Seven Years" War').

domestic industries. Colonial trade was better integrated within the British internal market.

The French urban industrial growth was not spectacular but neither it was negligible. Attempts to promote industrial activities in France can be seen in the last years of the seventeenth century, particularly under Colbert but Francois Crouzet considers his policy of industrialization as nothing but a desperate effort to counteract the declining economic trend. It was undertaken in an unfavourable situation when the prices were falling, the income and consumption levels were going down and the economy was in a state of deflation. It was not the French bourgeoisie but the state that played the major role in the early phase of industrialization. However, the general public lacked confidence in such enterprises. Only a few of the industrial enterprises of Colbert's times survived. One of them was located at Abbéville and was run on capitalist lines. Crouzet argues that England outdistanced France despite her relatively fast economic growth during the eighteenth century. The textile industry in the older cloth manufacturing centres witnessed slow progress, although linen production in Cambrai, Rouen, Lavel and Voiron increased three times in the course of the century. The imitation of Indian textiles, the dyed cotton fabrics also began. Some manufacturers like Jean Boyer Fonfrède made attempts to organize cotton mills on the British pattern but failed because of inadequate infrastructures. Around the period of the French Revolution, there was a spectacular rise in the number of new industries around Paris and eastern France; one example of this was the Oberkampf Textile printing works. There were several industrial cities like Amiens, Lille, Rheims and the most important silk and textile centre – Lyons. Commercial expansion was one of the major factors in the growth of industry. According to Jean Merczewski, the gross product of the French industry and handicraft increased from an annual average of 385 million livres in the first decade of the eighteenth century to 1,573 million livres annually for the decade 1781–90. It was a fourfold increase or an annual growth rate of 1.91 per cent. Crouzet thinks that the growth rate was much lower, probably around 1 per cent. On the other hand Pierre Lion suggests that, the woollen industry in France grew by about 60 per cent during the eighteenth century. He also argues that the silk looms in Lyons increased by 185 per cent between 1720 and 1788. The French linen industry made rapid progress employing a large labour force. However, information on mining and metal industries is not very reliable because of insufficient data. France produced less coal, metals, ships and cotton goods than that produced by Britain but the French maintained leadership in wool, silk, linen and iron, at least in the first half of the eighteenth century.

French made better industrial progress in the first half of the century than in the second. However, the English lead in coal production and its relative value in other industries gave her a decisive lead over France in the industrial sector. Ernest Lacrosse has provided statistical data to prove that the industrial growth slackened from the mid-eighteenth century and after 1770 it almost stopped growing and at many places it declined. The French industry according to historians like Pierre E. Levasseur, was imprisoned in the double straitjacket of guilds and regulations that acted as an obstacle in its progress. Recent studies have shown that the guild system was neither very powerful nor widespread in the French towns during the eighteenth century. The process of deregulation is quite evident in the second half of the century. At the same time it should be noted that state protection sustained the French textile industry against British competition and the Commercial Treaty of 1786 with Britain had a destructive impact. Large-scale industrialization in France was delayed till the coming of railways in the 1840s. The local and the fundamental characteristics of feudal France rapidly disappeared. The railways helped in the formation of a national society and national market by destroying rural isolation – both physical as well as psychological.

France was a large and diverse country and despite political centralization at the top, a single national market had not fully emerged. Instead it was a conglomeration of regional markets. Roger Price emphasizes the inadequate communication as the main factor that restrained innovations in pre-industrial France. The long distances between commercial centres within the country raised the transportation cost. Roads remained in a backward state while some attempts were made to improve the waterways. The Picardy canal linked the Somme and Oish rivers in 1738. In the late-eighteenth century, the Burgundy canal and the central canal works were undertaken to facilitate foreign trade. Road construction activity was undertaken on a massive scale under the guidance of Philibert Orry in 1738. The parish populations of France had to render heavy corvée for building and maintaining roads.

The government also set up a School of Bridges and Roads (Écoles des Ponts et Chaussées) in 1747. It prepared a corps of civil engineers with special training. However, the benefits of such schemes began to be realized only from the turn of the century. The heavy burden of taxes – taille, gabelle, seigneurial dues, tariffs and tolls – adversely affected the economic growth and inhibited commerce. The multiplicity of rules, legal systems and weights and measures severely affected the emergence of a unified market and trading activities. The attachment of the French farmers even to small parcels of land led to regressive labour supply as the worker was reluctant to move away from his traditional way of life. The expansion of output with the putting-out system was hampered by rising marginal costs caused by the vast territorial network and poor mode of transport. The presence and availability of a vast labour force in the countryside prolonged proto-industrialization and did not create immediate need for technical innovations. This also raised the question of capital resources, social structures and maintenance as these set limits to the possibility of change. The problem of generating capital for the mechanization of industries was not very serious as commercial capital had been generated by trade profits. The real factor was the absence of proper channels of investment. It is alleged by a number of historians that the French lacked a spirit of enterprise and that the prosperous traders and bourgeoisie preferred to invest in land or venal offices (saleable posts) to enhance their social status in order to enter the rank of nobility. However, instead of listing a series of causes it would be more appropriate to locate the entire problem in the persistence of feudal structure in France and the feudal state apparatus that created obstacles in the path of modern industrial activities and capitalist ventures.

Origin of Industrial Revolution in England

In England, the putting-out system had existed much before the eighteenth century. However, towards the second half of the eighteenth century, the English economy began to transform rapidly leading to factory-type industrialization in which the workers worked under one roof as wage-labourers brought about by the application of mechanical power in production. Historians commonly describe this change as Industrial Revolution. The term industrialization is not clearly expressed by Karl Marx and Engels but the concept does exist in their writings. Marx distinguishes between 'Modern Industry' or 'The Factory System' or 'The Machinery System' from the earlier forms of production, often described as 'Manufacture'. It is obvious that in modern industry machinery plays the pivotal role. According to Marx, as soon as tools are converted from manual instruments of individuals into implements of a mechanical apparatus, production takes a different form based on machine power. He mentions two stages in the development of the machinery system. In the first, a simple cooperation or a conglomeration of similar and simultaneously functioning machines takes place, using a single power source. In the second, a complex system of machinery exists in which the product goes through a connected series of detailed processes carried out by interlinked chain of machines. The system is said to have reached the stage of factory or machinery production when it is carried out in a complex form under a perfected process in which workers exist merely as attendants and deprived of their personal tools and implements. The beginning of this system can be seen in England during the eighteenth century and it spread to the Continent in the course of the next century.

Arnold Toynbee used the term 'Industrial Revolution' in a series of lectures in Oxford, that were published in 1883–4. Since then the term is commonly used to describe certain identifiable changes in the methods and characteristics of economic organization in the second half of the eighteenth century and the first three decades of the nineteenth century. It marked a gradual and irrevocable change from proto-industry, based on family economy, to the factory system with concentration of labour and mechanized production.

The origin of the Industrial Revolution is still one of the most controversial themes of socio-economic history.

Before discussing the plausible factors contributing to the Industrial Revolution, it is important to know why the term 'Revolution' is applied. Revolution is usually referred to fundamental changes in a short span of time. The Industrial Revolution stretches over a period of more than half a century. Moreover, it is also pointed out that industrialization was not completed within that time span; rather it is still continuing. It is seen as a stable and beneficial process. Some historians refer to British industrialization in 'evolutionary' rather than 'revolutionary' terms. One group sees it as the unspectacular climax of an evolutionary growth. For W.G. Ashley, it was the agrarian revolution that paved the way for industrialization. According to J.U. Nef, 'The rise of industrialization in Great Britain can be more properly regarded as a long process stretching back to the middle of the sixteenth century and coming down to the final triumph of the industrial state towards the end of the nineteenth, than as a sudden phenomenon associated with the late-eighteenth and early-nineteenth centuries.' (E.M. Carus-Wilson, *Essays in Economic History*, 1954, I). Charles Wilson argues that the turning point in the economic growth was 1660 rather than 1760 in which mercantilism in alliance with state power was changing the face of the old agrarian customary economy.

Other writers consider the period after 1760 or 1780 (according to their views on the precise beginning of Industrial Revolution) as revolutionary in terms of the economic changes. Gibbons believed that the change was sudden and violent as the great inventions were all made in a comparatively short space of time. W.W. Rostow considered the Industrial Revolution as a 'decisive breakthrough' and the last two decades of the eighteenth century as the 'take-off' stage. More recent interpretations of economic historians depend on heavy statistical evidence and focus on the rate of economic growth. These writings take a long view of this event from the mid-eighteenth century or perhaps earlier to the end of the nineteenth century dividing industrialization into stages. For them, there were revolutionary changes in the structure of the economy, in the labour organization and in the distribution of employment, in the per capita production, and marked a general economic growth of a wide number of sectors. Within the group of historians who argue that the Industrial Revolution marked a general change affecting the whole of the economy, there are two views – (a) the leading-sector theory suggest that one sector or a small number of sectors were the growth points (e.g. textile industry or coal production) and (b) the aggregate – growth theory that suggests growth took place across the whole economy because of a change in some variable which had widespread effects.

While focusing on the revolutionary aspect of industrialization, David Landes provides a description of a bold sweep of technological advancement based on the new machinery, new sources of power and new types of raw materials. He stresses on the cotton industry that was reinforced by the development of steam power and the expansion of metal industries. J.H. Clapham sees the Industrial Revolution as a slow motion. While the factory system and new techniques spread across British industry, one can see the persistence of traditional forms of organization and labour-intensive techniques well after the inauguration of the factory age and steam powered machinery. According to Maxine Berg, industrialization showed a very uneven pattern, both over regions and sectors of economy. The British industries in the eighteenth century grew as much within the old framework of home and artisan manufacture as within the more industrialized and mechanized factories. There are several reasons for describing the economic changes from the late-eighteenth century as Industrial Revolution. Phyllis Dean suggests that there was widespread application of modern science and empirical knowledge to the process of production for the market. Economic activity was directed towards production for national and international markets based on specialization and division of labour and a shift from primary products to manufactured goods and services with intensive and extensive use of capital resources. It brought about a profound change in the mode of production accompanied by the use of new technology. All these were revolutionary changes as these marked the emergence of new social, occupational classes determined by ownership of the means of production, or having a different relationship to them, and to capital as different from land. As Hobsbawm argues, the Industrial Revolution is not merely an acceleration of economic growth but an acceleration of growth that brought about economic and social transformation, a transformation thorough capitalist economy based on the pursuit of private profit that led to technological innovation.

Causes of the Industrial Revolution

England was the first country to experience the Industrial Revolution that set the process of modern economic growth. Historians and economists have provided their own analyses of the causes of the Industrial Revolution, expounding or criticizing a particular theory of growth. Each explanation consists of a list of relevant factors or forces for the industrial growth.

Natural, Political and Social Factors

There have been a number of explanations for the Industrial Revolution. Theories have been presented citing climatic and geographical factors. It is argued that England had geographical advantages like a vast coastline and a number of ports that facilitated the expansion of foreign trade. The presence of a number of rivers made transportation of heavy goods easier and reduced the cost of the product. England's moist climate was conducive to textile manufacturing. The most important factor was the location of coal and iron mines in close proximity to each other. It led to the concentration of industries around them. Britain's coal reserves have been particularly highlighted. Whig historians stressed the role of the Glorious Revolution of 1688–9 in creating a favourable political climate for industrialization. It is argued that it marked the triumph of individual liberty and greatly enhanced the political influence and social prestige of the commercial and industrial classes. Men from these classes promoted rational economic values. The development of political theory promoting the right to property and its protection by law, as suggested by John Law, ensured the success of individual enterprise and led to the control of civil society by men of property. Such men provided political support to industrial activities. Social scientists emphasize the role of the Protestant Reformation in creating and promoting the spirit of capitalism. It is argued that Protestantism changed the economic attitude and instilled a spirit of competition. However, such arguments cannot be rejected outright but these cannot be considered as exclusive or primary explanations. If geographical or climatic advantages were important factors, then industrial revolution should have come to England much earlier than the end of the eighteenth century. Similarly, if coal reserves were enough to ignite industrial transformation, then why did the rich Silesian coalfields not produce a similar industrial outcome? If the moist climate of Lancashire is held responsible for the concentration of textile industries then the other humid regions should have undergone a similar experience. As far as political support to industrial activity is concerned, then almost all the major states of Europe provided that but revolutionary changes took place only in Britain. As far as the role of Protestant Reformation is concerned, not all Protestant regions experienced revolutionary changes in their respective economies. As Hobsbawm explains, the climatic factors, geography, the distribution of natural resources operates not on their own, but only within a given economic, social and institutional framework. Hence, the causes of the industrial revolution have to be located in other fields and areas.

Role of Agriculture

Economists still debate whether an agrarian revolution is a necessary prerequisite of the Industrial Revolution and whether agriculture can be considered a driving force in economic growth. In most European countries, industrialization was usually preceded by a rise in agricultural production, and the growth of agricultural and non-agricultural sectors was intimately linked in a process of general economic growth. Robert Brenner has demonstrated that the beginning of capitalism in Britain was located in the agrarian class relations that paved the way for industrial capitalism. In recent years, historians have stressed on the magnitude of the agrarian changes and link these up with the industrialization process.

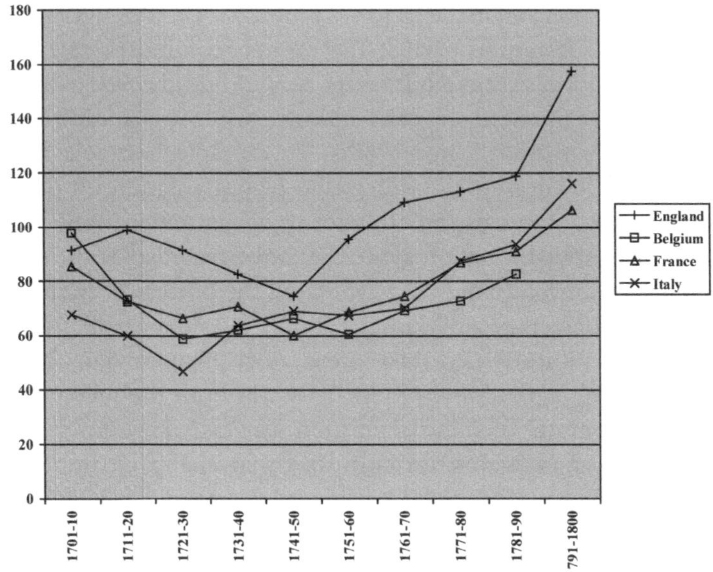

Source: Willhelm Abel, Table 1.

Graph 13.1: Price of wheat in different parts of Europe 1701–1800 (10 year averages in grams of silver per 100 kg)

We have already seen in this chapter that agrarian changes in England after the Restoration had a profound impact on the British economy. Historians generally accept that the British Industrial Revolution was associated with an agrarian revolution. The enclosures led to changes in farming practices and large-scale consolidation of land units. It extended the arable lands over heaths and commons. It increased agricultural productivity dramatically. Most important, it transformed the village community of self-sufficient peasants into agricultural labourers and freed many peasants for industrial activities and linked the agriculturists to the national and international markets. Growth of population, urbanization and industrial activities had widened the market for agriculture produce and created a favourable climate for innovation. A favourable agricultural condition generated surplus incomes that could be spent on manufactured goods as the purchasing power of the common man had increased in the course of the eighteenth century. This created the solid home market that justified large-scale production and made factories profitable. Besides, agriculture provided a substantial part of the capital required to carry out industrialization. Although it is not easy to find the exact sources of funds that financed the early industries, but it is a known fact that most of the early iron-works, for example, were originally built by landowners. Rich farmers also played a significant part in improving roads, canals and other forms of communications. Thus, agricultural transformation alone cannot be regarded as the cause of industrial revolution; but it facilitated the process of industrial growth. Writers like Paul Mantoux and W. J. Ashley emphasize the role of agriculture as necessary 'preparatory changes'. For Ashley the increasing agricultural productivity was both the prerequisite and the promoter of industrialization just as A.H. John regards the key to change was agriculture. By arousing an increased demand for consumer goods, agricultural developments stimulated industrialization.

Role of the Market

Historians are not unanimous in their views on the role of foreign markets in the rise of British industrialization. Historians like Paul Mantoux, J. Cunningham, Witt Bowden, E.W. Gilboy have given importance to the role of the market. There are two schools of thought on this subject. One lays stress on the role of only internal market while the other emphasizes the significance of foreign or export market. A. Redford argues that the fundamental stimulus to industrial change and technological innovation in England during the seventeenth and eighteenth centuries was certainly because of the widening markets following geographical discoveries. It had a stronger impact on England because the country was rich in coal and mineral wealth and was endowed with an adaptable and enterprising people. In view of Bowden, the increasing wealth at home and abroad had enhanced demand beyond the limits that the traditional system of production could supply. The manufacturer, the trader and the farmer felt the pressure of demand alike. According to him, the home market was so large and the overseas market controlled by Englishmen so extensive, that their requirements could not be met without new methods of production. Writers like Ephraim Lipson and T.S. Ashton, while accepting the role of the overseas trade with a far-flung commercial empire in America, India, Africa and West Indies link them up with a combination of other factors.

It is speculated by a number of writers that the capital for the Industrial Revolution flowed from the overseas empire – from the slave trade, from the organized looting of India and from the profits of trade. T.S. Ashton suggests that the early iron industry of South Wales was largely the creation of tea-dealers and other traders of London and Bristol. The industrial equipment of the Clyde Valley was due to the investments of Glasgow merchants dealing in tobacco trade. However, it is not easy to establish a direct link between foreign trade and the Industrial Revolution. Yet the foreign trade certainly generated capital and resources. According to E.B. Schumpeter, the total foreign trade of England and Wales (that included imports, exports and re-exports) had an annual average value of £31 million between the years 1784–8. British trade with the European states was quite limited. She supplied manufactured goods to the Portuguese and the Brazilian markets and dominated the Italian and the Levant markets. British goods did not penetrate the European market on a large scale till the 1780s because of the protective tariffs on the Continent, but after that the low prices of products of the modernized British industries could not be resisted. The English commercial expansion was almost entirely because of her dominance over the colonial trade. The importance of this colonial market was that it provided a rich range of products and raw materials that the English merchants could sell in Europe – spices and silk from the east and sugar, tobacco, cotton, indigo and dyewoods from the West Indies. Thus, in the first half of the eighteenth century, the English re-exports had gone up by 90 per cent and it doubled in the next half of the century (Phyllis Deane). It greatly increased the purchasing power of the British. It also made London the pivotal point of a complex worldwide network of trade. A new market for British products developed in North America in the second half of the eighteenth century. Thus, historians like H. J. Habakkuk and P. Deane consider the role of foreign trade to be of great significance. The foreign market demonstrated a dynamic and expandable character. It is argued that mass production depends on a wide market as the organization of large-scale industry cannot depend entirely on the domestic market which is less flexible than the external market.

There is considerable debate on the significance of national markets in the early phase of industrial growth. Fernand Braudel suggests that though Holland had a commercial revolution and Spain enjoyed extensive colonial trade, neither country progressed to the stage of an Industrial Revolution as they both lacked a purely national market. The rising population and the commercial revolution stimulated industrial development by creating demand for manufactured products. Daniel Defoe's picture of England suggests that the growing population was absorbed in rural industries and inland trade reflected growing prosperity. Unlike France, where the state was directly involved in setting up industries, the most important of them were the luxury industries, in England, the industrial expansion was through private initiative and for goods of mass consumption such as textiles. The Industrial Revolution was an example of economic growth and its basic characteristic was an unprecedented and sustained increase in the rate of growth of goods and services. In the eighteenth century, when population was growing rapidly, the translation of population growth into effective demand provided the market with opportunities for continued investment. The rise in demand widened the range of consumer goods and substituted many older products with new machine-made goods (Hartwell). Hobsbawm also points out the contribution of the domestic market that was large and expanding. He argues that the market could grow in four ways but of this three were not very rapid. These were the increase in population, a transfer of people from non-monetary to monetary incomes leading to more customers, and an increase in income per person. The fourth way of expanding market was important for immediate and substantial change – substituting industrially produced goods for older forms of manufacture. Arguing on the same grounds, M.W. Flinn says that for most individual industries and certainly for all industries put together, home demand predominated and therefore exercised a more decisive influence on output. The home market provided a major outlet for capital goods. The swift increase of coal and iron production was chiefly to meet the internal demand. Steam engines were the product of mines. These two sectors witnessed revolutionary transformation with the coming of the railways. Historians also emphasize the role of non-conformist groups like the Quakers whose members had been depositing their savings within a family or sectarian group. The Quakers made special contributions to brewing industry and the market because of their far-flung connections from London to Norwich, Midlands and other regions. They felt secured in investing in business and industrial sectors with potential markets. Thus, both foreign as well as domestic markets contributed to the intensification of industrialization in Britain.

Development of Transport

Transport and communications formed one of the essential prerequisites for industrial and agricultural growth as well as market expansion. Till the middle of the eighteenth century, like the rest of Europe, the condition of roads was poor. Transport by road was expensive. As Christopher Hill points out, one horse could draw eighty times as much in a canal barge as by cart on a soft road. The sea had become the chief highway of the English throughout the eighteenth century. Apart from the ships of the Royal Navy and the merchants engaged in overseas trade, a large number of small crafts were used in English waters. River navigation had long existed in England but faced increasing difficulties with dams erected by corn-millers and the fishermen's garths caused hurdles for the barges. However, there were some rivers like Savern, which were navigable between Bristol and Welsh Pool transporting coal, salt and grain. The Thames, despite having several barriers, was used for transporting goods from London to Oxford, Reading and Newbury. The Dutch provided the inspiration for canal construction, canals which could be used for transporting goods. Phyllis Deane stresses the role of 'social overhead capital' providing basic transport facilities like harbours, road bridges, canals and railways, which were generally developed by private initiative.

In England, road building efforts intensified through the

parliamentary acts in the second half of the eighteenth century. It was not till the nineteenth century that scientific road-making measures were adopted on a large-scale as developed by the great engineers like Metcalf, Macadam and Thomas Telford. They revolutionized the technology of road construction. Till that time the cheapest way of transporting bulky and heavy goods was by water and Britain enjoyed great advantage in this field. Although no revolutionary change took place in this, inland navigation of rivers was a spectacular development. The canals provided a reliable, low-cost and high-capacity transport system that enabled British entrepreneurs to overcome transportation hurdles. There were two important phases of canal construction; the first in the 1760s and the second after the American War of Independence in the 1790s. It is necessary to know that the efforts had started, though slowly, from the late-seventeenth century. The rise of large-scale industry hastened the process of canal construction towards the end of the eighteenth century. Canals virtually halved the price of the coal that had earlier fluctuated violently in times of bad weather. In most cases, it was the product of corporate and private initiative led by local landlords or businessmen and supported by local shareholders and bankers as well as city corporations. The name of the Duke of Bridgewater as an inveterate canal builder is well known because he was responsible to a great extent for the construction of a network of waterways and turnpikes that linked provincial towns with London. The canals made possible enormous savings in terms of manpower and horsepower at the cost of heavy preliminary outlays of capital. It immensely facilitated market unification and thereby, as Deane suggests, made a massive contribution to the first Industrial Revolution and was a worthy forerunner of the railways. The new roads and canals achieved a huge reduction in the costs of heavy raw materials and enabled the commercial and industrial entrepreneurs to economize in their stock-holdings.

Role of Capital

Early historians of the Industrial Revolution did not pay much attention to the financial aspect. It was presumed that there was an abundance of capital that was invested in new machines and large factories during the eighteenth century and that capital accumulation was the decisive factor in the Industrial Revolution. Mechanization was seen as more intensive use of capital. A study of the financial aspects of industrialization by economic historians has brought out various aspects of capital formation and its limitations. The role of capital formation has become the subject of a great deal of discussion. An important question raised by the recent studies is where did the capital for the Industrial Revolution come from? It is also asked quite often whether capital accumulation can be regarded as an independent initiating force.

One view is that a large portion of the commercial capital that had been accumulated through foreign trade was invested in industrial entrepreneurs. Eric Williams argues that a large portion of the capital that financed the Industrial Revolution came from the profits of the slave trade. Thus, the capital accumulated by Liverpool from the slave trade supplied part of the huge outlay for the construction of vast plants at Manchester. Between 1700 and 1780 British imports of raw cotton increased from one to five million pounds and by 1789 to 32.5 million. The exports of cotton goods increased ten times between 1750 and 1769. The production of broad cloth in Yorkshire mills increased from an average of 34,000 pieces in 1731–40 to 2,29,400 pieces by 1791–1800. The wealth generated through trade, it is argued, generated capital resources. J. Lord stresses the role of fixed capital as a vital component of the Industrial Revolution. The floating and circulating capital from the commercial field turned into industrial capital and fixed capital respectively with the development of machinery, especially steam-powered machinery.

Another view that has not gained much support is that of Earl J. Hamilton, later substantiated by J.M. Keynes. It suggests that the price revolution directly contributed to the progress of capitalism as wages lagged behind prices and this caused enormous profits and prepared the way for industrialization. He argues that the rapid rise of prices brought huge profits to industrialists and widened the margin of earnings that were reinvested in industrial enterprises, thus overcoming the scarcity of capital and stimulating savings.

The main argument is that inflation not only created forced savings by putting a windfall into the hands of potential investors but continuous rising prices created an incentive for industrialists to go on investing. Francois Crouzet rejects this view and suggests that during the second half of the eighteenth century, prices of manufactured goods rose less than money wages and much less than agricultural prices, and it was not cost inflation but profit-inflation that probably exerted pressure on industrial fortunes. M.M. Poston argued that there was no shortage of capital on a nationwide or aggregate basis as there were enough rich people in the country to finance the modest industrial activities. However, the imperfections of the capital market did not assist such new enterprises. England had no reservoir of national savings. Rather there was a multiplicity of small-disjointed pools with little connection with industry. Herbert Heaton also stresses the role of family ties in providing the capital needs of the industrial masters of the eighteenth century. However, the data about the rate of aggregate capital accumulation in the eighteenth century is meagre and impressionistic.

In recent years historians have shifted focus to the relationship between investment and growth. Adam Smith had suggested that the fundamental determinant of growth was the rate of capital formation and this rate was proportional to the rate of investment. Some writers have argued that that the Industrial Revolution was nothing but acceleration in the rate of capital formation. At the same time, doubts have been expressed on the question whether capital accumulation necessarily leads to growth. The pertinent query is the extent to which capital is indispensable for growth. Writers like W.W. Rostow suggest that the ratio of capital formation doubled during the Industrial Revolution. For Rostow, a decisive shift in capital formation took place in the take-off stage which, according to him, was between 1783 and 1802. However, later historians maintain that Rowtow's hypothesis is applicable more to the period of coming of the railways when capital formation reached 12 per cent of the national income. Throughout the eighteenth century, it was much less, about 6 per cent in the most prosperous years but generally between 5 and 6 per cent on a long-term average. According to Phyllis Deane, it hardly exceeded 3 per cent in the early part of the century and rose steadily to about 5 or 6 per cent before the American War. It increased faster subsequently to reach about 10 per cent per annum. Most of the recent writers agree that on the basis of available evidence, there is little theoretical or historical justification for assuming that the Industrial Revolution was the result of any noticeable acceleration in capital accumulation. Recent research supports the idea that Britain carried out most of her Industrial Revolution with modest investments at least till the coming of the railways.

Since the Restoration, English economy showed signs of reasonable prosperity and steady growth. The economy tended to generate a surplus that was available for investment. A good deal of investment took place in overseas shipping, in buildings and other construction activities, in agricultural improvement and in the construction of canals. On banking, one group of historians believes that despite the creation of the Bank of England in 1694, the system of banking was not properly organized. Thus the bank tended to concentrate its activities only for the benefit of the government. It was not the notes issued by this bank that was much in circulation in the commercial markets but the bills of exchange that formed the medium of exchange. It was not till 1760 that private banks emerged. In 1793 there were about 400 country banks that increased to about 900 by 1815 (T.S. Ashton). In 1760, there was hardly anything that could be called a capital market. Lending was still largely a local and personal transaction. The second view suggests that at the time of the first Industrial Revolution, Britain had the advantage of a developed system of money and banking. However, the second view appears to be valid for the period of early and mid-nineteenth century rather than of early-eighteenth century. The limitation was greatly overcome by private houses and family firms operating as agents of lending and deposits.

Many writers observe that the distribution of income in eighteenth-century Britain was favourable to saving, as it was highly unequal. A large share of income went into the pockets of upper-income groups described as the 'automatic savers' by Crouzet. Unlike France, where the nobles squandered their incomes mostly on unproductive expenses, the upper class in England did invest part of their income productively, especially in agriculture and transportation, while the rate of saving was high even among the mercantile and professional classes. The general view among economic historians is that England suffered neither from an absolute nor relative shortage of capital and savings that could threaten economic growth. Capital needs of early industrialization were modest and that the Industrial Revolution was not the result of any significant acceleration in capital accumulation. A long period of steady and constant economic growth was a far more important factor.

Technology and Innovations

Capital accumulation or demographic growth causing a series of changes cannot fully explain the coming of the Industrial Revolution. Equally important, was the role of technology. One view regards technology as the product of a scientific movement which flowered during the Renaissance. It was the process of a stable and civilized change, according to writers like J.C.D. Clark and J.V. Beckett. As opposed to this, writers like Max Hartwell insist that it was the period of Industrial Revolution when great changes in technology took place.

Before the onset of the industrial age, the chief sources of power were human and animal labour, wind and water. All these forms of energy had limitations varying from capacity to reliability. For example, wind energy was subjected to weather conditions while human labour was conditioned by physical factors. None of these was capable enough to support a modern industry. The invention of the steam engine in England was a major breakthrough and marked a rapid growth in industrialization. Two of the important components of industrialization were coal and iron and, according to Christopher Hill, they constituted the major bottlenecks holding back the advance of industry. Machinery could be produced on greater scale only when obstacles to the use of coal for mass production of iron had been overcome. According to Phyllis Deane, the iron industry played an important role in the English economy

The demand for coal and iron and extensive transport and capital facilities on the one hand and in the reduction of costs for a wide range of manufactured goods promoted industrial enterprises.

A major breakthrough in iron production was achieved in 1709 when the Darbys started smelting with coke at Coal Brook Dale. However, the new process was adopted on a larger scale only after about half a century. From the mid-eighteenth century, cast-iron began to be produced on a large scale at lower cost and thus replaced wood in running machines. The new methods of making iron-mould boards and all-iron ploughs during the 1770s greatly helped the agrarian sector. Although the statistics on the output of iron is unreliable, yet the available figures clearly reveal the trend and magnitude of change. The production of pig iron was hardly 25,000 tons in the 1720s. It increased to 61,000 in 1788 and 1,09,000 in 1796. By 1806, it had reached 2,27,000 tons. However, the role of iron appears much greater in the nineteenth century. As far as coal production is concerned, J.V. Nef was the first historian to stress the importance of its increase in England after 1540. It led him to suggest that England had already undergone an Industrial Revolution in the sixteenth century. Early adoption of mineral fuels gave an impetus to inventiveness and a substantial lead to England over continental powers like France. In fact, the steam engine was first used to pump out water from the coal mines. As coal began to be extracted from deeper levels, the problem became more difficult. In 1712, Thomas Newcomen invented a steam-operated water-pump (it was the first practical device to harness the power of steam to produce mechanical work). It came into use immediately. James Watt considerably improved this device and, as a result, steam began to replace water and wind-operated devices. The use of this system spread beyond England into Europe and America. The invention of the steam engine led to centralization of the workplace, as it became convenient and common to carry out the entire process of production in a central factory by employing workers on regular wages to run the machines. This caused a dramatic change in the organization of the workforce and productivity leading to mass-production of goods at cheaper rates. Its greatest impact was to be seen first in the textile and mining sectors. It also transformed the transport system with the introduction of steam navigation and steam locomotives.

The rise of modern science during the seventeenth century is also given the credit for creating a scientific atmosphere. Francis Bacon had stressed the role of experimentation in serving the needs of society. Newton was equally emphatic on the role of empiricism. However, the science that developed in the seventeenth century was pure science and not applied science. The Royal Society of London did not fulfil Bacon's vision and instead pushed abstract mathematics to new heights. In the eighteenth century, the real scientific advance came from those societies established in the Midlands and the north of England, from craftsmen and industrialists like the Lunar Society of Birmingham. These brought science and society much closer and encouraged new technical devices.

The impact of technological changes was first felt on the cotton and iron industries that made England the 'workshop of Europe'. It is generally assumed that the cotton industry was the prime mover as the largest number of technological innovations happened in the textile sector. Historians like Rostow and Schumpeter regard the cotton industry to be the leading sector in the first take-off. The textile sector had dominated English economic life for over two centuries. It was the woollen industry that formed the bulk till the eighteenth century. The cotton industry found it extremely difficult to compete with Indian calicoes and muslins in either quality or price. The English were producing linen warp and cotton weft but the quality and productivity was poor. The ban on the import of Indian textiles by the English parliament on the demand of the English producers proved beneficial to the English cotton industry. Though the first of the revolutionary inventions in textile production – Kay's flying shuttle in the 1730s – was related to the woollen textiles, it was equally applicable to the cotton industry in the 1750s. The carding machine of Paul (1748) was introduced in the Lancashire cotton industry and these two devices transformed spinning process. The flying shuttle speeded up the weaver's operations. The shortage of yarn led to serious attempts to improve the technology of spinning. The remedy was found through

Hargreave's spinning jenny (probably 1764). It revolutionized the process of preparing yarn as it was eight times faster than a weaver's speed. The number of spindles increased from eight in 1770 to eighty by 1784. By saving labour, it reduced the cost of production. Wool was virtually replaced by cotton. Arkwright's water-frame in 1769 produced a strong variety of cotton yarn that served as warp as well as weft and brought out a new product called British cotton. The water-frame was powered by water and later by steam. In a few years time, Crompton's mule (1779) combined the principles of jenny and the water-frame and began to produce a fine and smooth variety of yarn that successfully competed with the Indian textiles, and was produced on a mass scale and ousted it on grounds of cost. A new system of production had became feasible opening up the path to the modern factory system. By 1815, cotton textiles constituted almost 40 per cent of British exports and by 1830, it accounted for almost half the value of exports. Between 1780 and 1800, there was about an eightfold increase in the import of raw cotton (Phyllis Deane) thus opening up new markets and expanding the existing ones for British products. The biggest advantage of the cotton industry was that it was labour-intensive.

R.M. Hartwell emphasizes the role of a favourable economic climate for innovations. Taking into consideration the physical and human resources of the economy and the flexibility of the market, he suggests that English society and economy was freer in the eighteenth century than other European economies. Property and enterprise had greater security and England experienced greater social mobility. The rise of modern society appeared more favourable to change and innovation. The rise of modern science in the seventeenth century was not directly related to industrial technology but it certainly promoted experimentation and broadened social attitudes and also made English society more receptive to new ideas. Englishmen turned to risk-taking and profit-making ventures to make use of economic opportunities. The emergence of 'pushing' entrepreneurs with 'disruptive innovating energy', according to Hartwell, was the result of social forces, of changes in English society that rationalized and secularized human attitudes.

Thus, the Industrial Revolution was the product of a combination of conditions such as favourable endowments, which England possessed along with economic, commercial, demographic growth and a changing society. All these factors preceded and accompanied industrialization. Technical advances and innovations in economic life pushed up industrial production. Breakthrough in one field affected many other sectors. Increasing use of machinery and new technology started affecting the organization and management of labour and capital that in turn hastened improvement in transport and market organization. Hence, instead of treating each factor in isolation, it would be useful to coordinate various spheres of English economic and commercial life to form an integrated picture in order to understand what led to the Industrial Revolution.

Major Innovations and Discoveries in the Agrarian and Industrial Revolutions

1701	Jethro Tull invented the seed drill
1708	Abraham Darby's use of coke in blast furnaces
1712	Thomas Newcomen's steam operated water pump
1733	John Kay's Flying Shuttle
1759	Duke of Bridgewater's canal between Worsley and Manchester
1760	Carron iron works coke blast furnace
1764	Spinning jenny by James Hargreaves
1769	Richard Arkwright's waterframe
1776	James Watt develops steam engine operated machinery
1779	Samuel Crompton's 'mule'
1782	John Wilkinson's steam-hammer
1784	Charorine gas for bleaching textile by Clande Berthollet
1793	Eli Whitney's cotton gin

Suggested Readings

Abel, Wilhelm, *Agricultural Fluctuations in Europe: From the Thirteenth to the Twentieth Centuries*, New York: Routledge, 1980.

Berg, Maxine, *The Age of Manufactures 1700–1820*, Glasgow: Fontana Press, 1985. Particularly good for the Proto-industrialization and the textile industries in Britain.

Brown, Richard, *Society and Economy in Modern Britain, 1700–1850*, London/New York: Routledge, 1991. Provides good explanation of economic change in different sectors of economy.

Crafts, N.F.R., 'The Industrial Revolution in England and France: Some

Thoughts on the Question "Why Was England First?"', *Economic History Review*, 30, 1977.

Crouzet, F., ed., *Capital Formation in the Industrial Revolution*, London: Methuen, 1972. A very useful work for those working on the economic background.

Deane, Phyllis, *The Industrial Revolution*, Cambridge: Cambridge University Press, 1967. Comprehensive discussion of different sectors of economy in separate chapters.

Flinn, M.W., *Origins of the Industrial Revolution*, London: Longman, 1966. An analytical discussion highlighting pre-condition of industrial development.

Floud, R. and D. McCloskey, eds., *The Economic History of Britain Since 1700*, vol. I: *1700–1860*, Cambridge: Cambridge University Press, 1981.

Hartwell, R.H., ed., *The Causes of the Industrial Revolution*, London: Metheun & Co., 1967. Contains many important chapters by reputed scholars but the one by F. Crouzet is very useful.

Hobsbawm, E.J., *Industry and Empire: An Economic History of Britain Since 1750*, London: Weidenfeld and Nicolson, 1968. Excellent analysis of the origins of the Industrial Revolution although, most of the book is concerned with nineteenth-century developments.

Landes, David, *The Unbound Prometheus: Technological Change and Industrial Development in Western Europe from 1750 to the Present*, Cambridge: Cambridge University Press, 1969. Provides a lucid and systematic and inter-related account of the development of technology and culture.

Mathias, Peter, *The First Industrial Nation: An Economic History of Britain, 1700–1914*, New York: Charles Scribner & Sons, 1969. Argues that Britain achieved her domination because of a combination of factors that were unique to her.

Mathias, P. and M.M. Postan, eds., *Cambridge Economic History of Europe*, vol. 7, part 1 & 2, Cambridge: Cambridge University Press, 1978. An authoritative work comprising chapters by well-known scholars on the subject.

O'Brien, P.K., 'Agriculture and the Home Market for English Industry, 1600-1820', *English Historical Review*, 100, 1985.

Ogilvie, Sheilagh C. and Markus Cerman, *European Proto-Industrialization*, Cambridge: Cambridge University Press, 1996, Provides not only a detailed discussion of the concept of proto-industrialization but takes up its progress country-wise.

Okey, Robin, *Eastern Europe 1740–1980*, London: Hutchison, 1982. This book provides a detailed discussion on the economy of the eastern states.

Overton, Mark, *Agricultural Revolution in England: The Transformation of the Agrarian Economy 1500–1850*, Cambridge: Cambridge University Press, 1996. A standard textbook providing survey of English agriculture that combines new material and an analysis of the existing literature.

CHAPTER 14

Transition from Feudalism to Capitalism – A Debate

One of the most lively academic debates in recent times relate to the question of what led to the decline of feudalism and the emergence of the capitalist mode of production that led to the creation of the modern world. This is commonly called the 'transition debate'. It is the outcome of divergent explanations offered on the nature of feudal relationship and the moving forces responsible for its decline and the connection this decline had with the birth of capitalism. Not only has a controversy arisen on this issue between the Marxists and the non-Marxists, there is also complete disagreement even within the Marxist group of writers. There is no single Marxist theory on the transition from feudalism and capitalism. These scholars have some fundamental differences over the concept of feudalism and capitalism and on the causes and the nature of transition from one mode of production to another. Somewhat diverse Marxist approaches exist representing different historical analysis, and often competing with each other. This unending controversy began with the publication of Maurice Dobb's stimulating work – *Studies in the Development of Capitalism* after the Second World War. Another Marxist scholar, Paul Sweezy vehemently challenged the thesis of Dobb. Later, the debate drew the attention of many Marxist and non-Marxist scholars who either supported one of the views or presented their own models of interpretation.

Maurice Dobb argued that the decline of feudalism was the result of inner contradictions within the feudal mode of production. His views are strongly supported and elaborated by scholars such as Rodney Hilton, Boris Porchnev, Christopher Hill, Kohachiro

Takahashi, and many others. They not only substantiated Dobb's arguments but also made their own contributions in this debate. This explanation is commonly referred to as the 'inner-contradiction model' or the 'property-relations' perspective. This view is strongly challenged on a wide range of issues by Paul Sweezy. He contends that the decline of feudalism was primarily due to the expansion of commercial economy that was directly related to the growth of trade which acted as an external dissolving agent. This interpretation is usually termed as the 'market' or 'commercial' model or the 'exchange-relations' perspective. Immanuel Wallerstein makes a significant contribution in this approach. His world-trade perspective is also supported by Janet Abu-Lughod, Andre Gunder Frank and Ekholm. A non-Marxist explanation emphasizes the role of demographic factors in the decline of feudalism. This view is led by scholars like H.J. Habakkuk, M.M. Postan and Emmanuel Le Roy Ladurie. This interpretation is termed as the Malthusian model or the 'demographic model'. Another Marxist scholar, Robert Brenner, reactivated the 'transition debate' in the 1970s and the 1980s. His explanation resembles Maurice Dobb's in some ways but he considers the nature of class-relations to be of paramount importance in the transition towards capitalism. All these explanations assigning different reasons for the decline of feudalism have their strength as well as weaknesses in their arguments. However, the first question that needs an answer is – why such divergent approaches exist even within the Marxist school.

One major reason for the debate is the theoretical ambivalence in Karl Marx's account of transition from feudalism to capitalism. Everyone knows that the chief interest of Marx and Frederich Engels remained in the study of capitalism and transition was never a major preoccupation for them. Transition in their writings (in *German Ideology, Communist Manifesto* and in their brief notes in *Pre-Capitalist Economic Foundations*) was episodic and incidental. They were more concerned with themes such as historical materialism, capitalist mode of production and class conflict as a historical process of change. Hence, they paid scant attention to the transition. Another reason that has given rise to transition debate is the variety of ways in which scholars have used the terms 'feudalism' and 'capitalism'. The explanations of the origins of transformation from the feudal to the capitalist mode of production depend upon the way these terms have been defined and presented. Whether 'true' capitalism began with the coming of the Industrial Revolution in England in the second half of the eighteenth century or with the maturity of merchant capitalism during the sixteenth century, are some of the issues that have been raised in the course of the transition debate.

As stated earlier, Marx does not provide any particular generic theory of transition. On this subject, he shifts away from his stated position in the 1840s where he emphasized the 'productive force' or the 'technical determinism' as the crucial factor in the process of social change. Karl Marx provides two alternative routes to capitalism. In the first, he emphasizes the corrosive effect of mercantile activity, the expansion of market and the growth of cities on feudal systems. He suggested that mercantile capitalism within an autonomous urban sphere provided the initial thrust towards capitalism. The second route, as mentioned in his *Capital* he focuses on the producer and the process by which the producer becomes merchant capitalist. For Marx, this was the real revolutionary path towards capitalism. He explains the preconditions that allow some producers to become capitalists and the separation of the vast majority of producers from the ownership of the means of production turning them into propertyless wage-labourers. The expansion of mercantile activity may turn products into commodities but it does not indicate how labour power becomes a commodity. Hence, Marx lays stress on social relations of production. For him, the commoditified labour is the only source of the captalist's surplus value. He suggests that in western Europe capitalism does not emerge before the sixteenth century and its industrial form not until the late-eighteenth century. According to him, industrial capitalism depends on three factors – private ownership of the means of production, the rise of the bourgeois class and the existence of wage-labour. These formed the basis of production and profit accumulation in the long run. Thus, Marx's explanation of the emergence of capitalism is primarily concerned with the establishment of the structural preconditions rather than with the detailed mechanism that created these preconditions.

Inner-contradiction Model

Maurice Dobb provides the first major explanation for the decline of feudalism representing the classical Marxist approach. This explanation is generally described as the 'property-relations' perspective or the 'inner-contradiction model'. For Dobb, there are two chief elements related to the transition from feudalism to capitalism. The first is a system of production resting on serf-labour or 'subject peasantry' while the second is based on hired wage-labour. These represent two separate phases of transition. What were the historical motive-forces, Dobb asks, that caused disintegration of the feudal system of exploitation, and led to a virtual crisis in the feudal society of the western Europe and brought its end. He suggests that this question has to be answered by taking into account the unevenness of the process as well as the chronological differences between various regions and the factors that led to the introduction and extension of serfdom over previously free cultivators. Secondly, the disintegration of feudalism has to be explained in relation to the rise of wage-labour under the bourgeois or the capitalist method of production. Thus for Dobb, the development of capitalism falls into a number of stages, characterized by its level of maturity. As a specific mode of production, it cannot be dated back to the first signs of the appearance of large-scale trading and the emergence of a merchant class. The capitalist period has to coincide with the changes in the mode of production – the direct subordination of producer to a capitalist. Dobb disagrees with Henri Pirenne who dates the beginning of capitalism to the twelfth century. Nor does he accept fourteenth century as its beginning, when there was the rise in urban trade and guild handicrafts. Instead, Dobb locates its beginning in the later half of the sixteenth and the early part of the seventeenth centuries when capital began to penetrate production on considerable scale. This development was either in the form of reasonably matured relations between the capitalist and the wage earners or in the less-developed form of subordination of domestic handicraft workers to a capitalist through the so-called 'putting-out system'.

On the question of what led to the decline of feudalism in Europe, Maurice Dobb first defines feudalism as a system of self-sufficient natural economy. He treats it primarily as a socio-economic system in which trade and money dealings were not totally absent but occupied a relatively smaller place in the economy. According to him, feudalism is a system under which economic status and authority are associated with land tenure and according to law or customary right, and the direct producer is under obligation to provide a certain portion of the produce or his labour to his superior. Dobb regards this system almost identical with serfdom. He insists that under the feudal mode of production an obligation is always placed on a producer by force and independent of his volition, to fulfil certain economic demands of an overlord. This demand may take the form of services or dues, in money or in kind or in the form of gifts. The coercive power may be because of the military strength possessed by the feudal lord or because of social custom backed by the force of law. The production is generally for the immediate needs of the household or for the village community and not for the wider market. According to Maurice Dobb and many others like Rodney Hilton, Kohachiro Takahashi and Eric Hobsbawm, it is the internal relationship of the feudal mode of production that determines the system's disintegration or its survival. Evidence indicates that it was the inefficiency and incapability of feudalism as a mode of production that failed to satisfy the material demands placed upon it and the growing need of the ruling class for enhanced revenue that was primarily responsible for its decline. The low and the stationary state of labour productivity and hardly any margin from which surplus product could be extracted, makes the system inefficient. The absence of technology, low productivity of the manorial economy, the attempts by lords to augment taxes, an increased need of revenue for wars, brigandage and crusades, and the extravagances of the nobles through costly displays and lavish feasts all combined to act as a special drain on feudal revenues and this pushed feudalism towards a crisis.

Supporting the views of Dobb, Kohachiro Takahashi also insists that serfdom is the existence-form of labour in the feudal mode of production. Its essence was the transference of the labour of the peasant family (which was surplus to what was needed by the family's subsistence and economic reproduction) to the lord. The surplus labour could be used directly on the lord's *demesne*, or it could be transferred in the form of rent in kind or in money (Hilton).

The beginning of the crisis in the feudal economy was evident in the fourteenth and the fifteenth centuries resulting in the serious fall in feudal income. The size of *demesne* lands of the lords began to shrink as some portions were given on lease to the peasants. Some parts of the marginal lands like forest or mountainous regions were also encroached upon to meet food and revenue demands. These were all the symptoms of a crisis infeudalism. Dobb argues that the need for additional revenue placed an increased pressure on the producer and gradually reached a point where it became unendurable. The economic misery provoked mass migrations. The response of the feudal nobility to the feudal crisis varied in different parts of Europe. In some parts like France, the lords were forced to give concessions to attract or retain labour. This meant mitigation of servile burdens and at the same time, substitution of contractual relationship with money payment. Elsewhere, the feudal response was in the form of tightening of feudal burdens and the adoption of firm measures of attachment of serfs to feudal estates, recapture of fugitives, re-imposition of servile obligations, as it happened in Eastern Europe.

Maurice Dobb describes the period beginning with the emergence of feudal crisis in the late-fifteenth century, till the triumph of capitalism associated with the coming of the Industrial Revolution, as the period of transition. Eric Hobsbawm supports and elaborates the arguments of Dobb. He points out that the transition from the feudal to the capitalist mode of production was a highly uneven development and was not a straightforward process. The capitalist elements within feudalism have to become strong enough to burst out of the feudal shell. The crisis of feudalism also involves the most advanced section of the bourgeois development within the feudal system (Hilton). For Hobsbawm, the definite triumph of capitalism is reflected through the Industrial, American and the French Revolutions. In this, the relations between Europe and the rest of the world were decisive at various crucial stages.

Rodney Hilton lends full support to the 'property-relations' perspective of Maurice Dobb. He agrees that the growth and decay of feudalism was the result of the factors operating within it and he considers feudal rent to be the prime mover. Hilton provides an explanation of the inner workings of feudal society. He suggests that the fundamental law of feudal society was the tendency of the exploiting class to realize the maximum rent from the labour of the direct producers. This conflicted with the necessities of social growth resulted in a contradiction within the exploiting class itself. The members of this class strove to increase the feudal rent in order to maintain and improve their position and began competing with others to establish their domination. Thus, it was the struggle for power and land-control that ignited the crisis in which feudal rent became the prime mover. Kohachiro Takahashi strongly defends Dobb's arguments. He maintains that that it is the nature of social existence of labour power that is the basic or decisive factor in the various models of production.

The Market-centric Explanation

Paul Sweezy and Immanuel Wallerstein bring out the role of market and exchange economy in the decline of feudalism and the rise of capitalism in somewhat different ways. This explanation directly conflicts with the views of Dobb and others who endorse the 'inner-contradiction' explanation. As opposed to this, Sweezy adopts a market-centric approach called the 'market' or the 'commercial model'.

Sweezy objects to Dobb's identification of feudalism with serfdom as interchangeable terms. Dobb had defined feudalism by revealing the characteristics of serfdom – an obligation placed on the producer by force and independent of his own volition to fulfil certain economic demands of an overlord.

Dobb saw feudalism as an economic system in which serfdom was the predominant form of social relations of production, organized in and around manorial estates. In such a system, he contends, markets may not be absent but they played no determining role in the purposes or methods of production. The 'exchange relations' perspective of Sweezy defines capitalism as a system of production for profit through market exchange that depends on an international trade-based division of labour. He argues that since feudal society was a system of production for use, there existed no internal dynamic that would stimulate long-term growth and expansion, leave alone the capability of transforming into capitalism. According to him, the rise of exchange economy that led to monetization of relations between feudal lords and the peasant mass somehow signalled the dissolution of feudalism. Sweezy asks Dobb to explain why feudalism remained stable or static despite facing chronic instability and insecurity. He charges Dobb for not explaining the change-resistant character of Western feudalism, nor does he probe deep enough into the effects of trade on feudalism. He finds Dobb's concept of feudalism defective and he contends that some serfdom can exist in systems that are not feudal. In fact, Sweezy finds Dobb's description of feudalism too general to be immediately applicable to any particular region or a social system.

Dobb had brought out some important characteristics of feudalism two features of which, according to Sweezy, existed throughout the whole period – disregard for the interests of the serfs and war and brigandage. If they became more intense with the passage of time, this requires an explanation. He also questions the evidence of Dobb's theory that there was a growth in the size of the parasitic class of nobility. However, he agrees with Dobb that the flight of the serfs from land was an important cause of the feudal crisis. Dobb assumed that the crisis was internal to feudal system as it stemmed from oppression. For Sweezy, the fundamental question is that the serfs could not simply desert the manors unless they had some place to go. Sweezy maintains that Dobb's theory of the internal causation of the breakdown of feudalism could still be rescued if he had shown that the rise of the towns was a process internal to the feudal system. Since trade can in no sense be regarded as a form of feudal economy, it cannot be that the rise of urban life was a consequence of internal feudal causes (Sweezy, Hilton).

Sweezy believes that even the most primitive economy also requires a certain amount of trade. The local village markets and the itinerant peddlers were props rather than threats to the feudal order. As long as the expansion of trade remained within the forms of what may be called the 'peddling system', its effects remained slight. Once it outgrew the peddling stage, and localized trading and trans-shipment centres were established, a qualitative new factor was introduced. For him, the important conflict is not between 'money economy' and 'natural economy' but between production for market and production for use. It is necessary to uncover the process by which trade engendered a system of production for the market and its impact on the pre-existent feudal system of production for use. Sweezy explains that the manorial organization of production was inefficient in contrast to a more rational system of specialization based on the division of labour. Manufactured goods could be brought much cheaper from the outside centres as they had higher form of specialization based on the division of labour than anything known to manorial economy. These were powerful pressures which brought the feudal estates within the orbit of the exchange economy. He suggests that the very existence of exchange value as a massive economic force tends to transform the attitude of producers. Riches were sought not in perishable goods but in the mobile form of money. Thus, not only traders and merchants but even the members of the feudal society developed a business-like attitude towards economic activities. The expansion of commercial economy promoted demand for new products as fresh tastes were created for food, dress, household items and weapons. But the most important impact of the expansion of trade and the rise of towns was that they opened up new opportunities to the servile population of the countryside. All these factors, according to Sweezy, were sufficiently 'pervasive and powerful' to ensure the breaking up of the existing system of production. He, however, agrees with Dobb that the triumph of exchange economy may not always and automatically bring the liquidation of serfdom. While discussing the uneven character of the decline of feudalism,

Dobb points out that in some regions the progress of trade was accompanied by intensification of serfdom rather than a relaxation. But Sweezy calls them temporary and partial reverses which should not obscure the overall trend – that of the steady replacement of *demesne* farming based on serf labour by tenant farming using either independent peasant labour or hired labour.

The rise of the towns, according to Sweezy, was fairly general throughout western Europe, and not only attracted serfs from the manors but altered the social relations in the countryside by showing the remaining population a better quality of life. The urban demand forced changes in the production methods and the mass of customary rules and regulations that were obstructing fuller exploitation of rural resources. Thus, a changed economic order forced the adoption of new forms of production relations and organizations to meet the new requirements.

On the subject of divergent trends between western and eastern Europe, Sweezy suggests that the limited development of town life and lack of urban centres offered little alternative to the agricultural workforce in eastern Europe. Limited market structure checked the rise of capitalism there.

On what came after feudalism in western Europe, Dobb's answer is that the period of two hundred odd years between the end of feudalism and the beginning of capitalism were transitional in character. It implied that this period was not a simple mixture of feudalism and capitalism; the chief character was neither feudal nor capitalist. For Sweezy, it was the period of the 'pre-capitalist commodity production' in western Europe. He suggests that it was the growth of commodity production that first undermined feudalism and later prepared the grounds for the success of capitalism. According to him these constituted two distinct phases.

Thus, the 'exchange relations' perspective defines capitalism in terms of production for profit through market exchange as opposed to the near subsistence economy of feudalism. Capitalism emerges through forces such as trade and the international division of labour, which are seen as external to feudalism. This external agent dissolved feudalism. Sweezy's thesis is opposed not only by Dobb but others like Takahashi and Hilton. In his rejoinder, Dobb clearly disagrees with Sweezy's contention that the conservative and change-resisting character of western European feudalism needed some external force to dislodge it. He accepts that feudal economy was extremely stable and inert but it also had a tendency within to change. In fact, the feudal period witnessed considerable changes in technique. Dobb also defends his definition of feudalism and maintains that feudalism and serfdom is the same thing.

The fundamental difference between Dobb and Sweezy is on the question of trade and urban centres – whether these existed within the feudal structure or outside it. Dobb reiterated his stand that trade exercised its influence to the extent that it accentuated the internal conflicts within the old mode of production and the growth of towns was a process internal to the feudal system. He also discounts Sweezy's contention that there was a co-relationship between feudal disintegration and the 'nearness to centres of trade'. He cites the example of the backward north-west region of England where serfdom in the form of direct labour services disappeared first, but in the more advanced south-east region, situated closest to town markets and trade routes, the labour services survived much longer. Similarly, in most parts of eastern Europe, the intensification of serfdom in the fifteenth and sixteenth centuries was related to trade. Dobb says that the system of production on which Sweezy focuses attention is more concerned with the sphere of exchange than with the relations of production and ignores the transition from coercive extraction of surplus labour by estate owners to the use of free, hired labour. The critics of Sweezy raise a question mark on his view that the monetization of feudal relations signalled the dissolution of feudalism. England had developed money rents in place of labour services in the fourteenth century, yet she had to wait for several centuries for the emergence of capitalism. Besides, the pattern of rent forms varied enormously and did not follow a linear trend. According to John E. Martin, money rent coexisted with labour rents as far back as the tenth century in some parts of England, parts of northern France, the Rhine valley and in central Italy. Takahashi also argues that the belief that the emergence of money rent was somehow incompatible with feudal economic relations is not borne out by evidence.

Takahashi rejects Sweezy's thesis and suggests that the contradiction between feudalism and capitalism is not the contradiction between 'system of production for use' and 'system of production for the market' but between feudal land-property (serfdom) and an industrial capital (wage-labour system). The fundamental processes of the passage from feudalism to capitalism are, therefore, the change in the social form of existence of labour power consisting in the separation of the means of production from the direct producers. The essential cause for the disintegration of feudalism is not trade or market itself, though it accelerated the process of differentiation among the petty producers. The structure of market is itself conditioned by the internal organization of the production system.

An important contributor to this debate is Imannuel Wallerstein. Like Sweezy, he too stresses on the changing character of the market structure. Although he has presented his arguments within the 'exchange relations' perspective, yet his arguments are different from those of Sweezy. Sweezy had followed Henri Pirenne's line that had emphasized the importance of the growth of trade in items of daily consumption like food and manufactured products unlike the trade in luxury goods under feudalism. This led to a division of labour in the market centres. The decline of feudalism, for both Pirenne and Sweezy is caused by the dynamics of expanding exchange relations, acting outside the feudal system.

Immanuel Wallerstein in his provocative work *The Origins of the Modern World System* does not accept the view that capitalism was a 'mature' set of social relations of production existing within the nation-states. Instead, he defines capitalism as a world system. Unlike the empires of the older world, which were tied by political relationships, the capitalist world system is based on international division of labour and a universal market exchange relations. The emergence of free wage-labour in a particular national setting in Europe involves an interplay of market economy between different regions. For Wallerstein, capitalism emerged as a world-economy rather than a world-empire. A world-empire coordinates the whole system through a centralized political and military structure while a world-economy is held together by economic production and exchange relationship. His discussion of capitalism involves three major components, described by him as 'zones'. The *core* represents the most developed region. It has the capability to exploit the available resources through world market and therefore, forms the economic power within the entire capitalist world-economy. The capitalist entrepreneurs of this region have the capability of exploiting the surplus value produced within the system, both inside the core and in other regions. The core enjoys the most advanced technology in the manufacturing process and has the power to control wage-labour. The *periphery* in the world-economy consists of those regions or societies that are technically and economically least developed. It is economically exploited by other regions, particularly by core areas. The periphery specializes in the production of raw materials, agricultural products and minerals with the use of forced labour. Wallerstein uses the term 'coerced cash-crop labour' for it. This generally assumed the form of serfdom in eastern Europe or slavery in Hispanic America (exercised through powerful institutions like *encomienda* in the Spanish ruled colonies of south and central America or *donatarios* in the Portuguese-controlled Brazil). These regions were not only economically least developed but politically and militarily weak. The third area mentioned by Wallerstein is the *semi-periphery* zone. It forms an intermediate zone between core and periphery, with an intermediate level of technology and economic development as well as political and military power. It exploits the periphery but is itself partly exploited by the core. Its production includes both raw materials as well as finished and manufactured goods. Hence, it has wage-labour as well as coerced cash-crop labour.

Wallerstein sees the emergence of capitalism in that long period from the 1450s to the 1640s, what he calls the sixteenth century (although it predates and postdates the century). According to him, the first capitalist states were Spain and Portugal with their vast colonial empires that they exploited. But soon they lost their core status and slipped into the semi-periphery level. The true core status was achieved first by the Netherlands, and subsequently by England and northern France. This argument of Wallerstein is not acceptable to many scholars. It is argued by his critics that he fails to explain those set of factors that made some states into cores. The origins of the modern world-system needs greater explanation because it cannot have come into existence until unequal exchange relations had developed between a powerful core and a weak periphery. The internal dynamics of a society is virtually ignored by him. The main criticism against the market-based model is that it underestimates the extent to which trade and commercial expansion is compatible with feudalism. Wallerstein's model reveals weakness on empirical grounds, as is shown in the studies of Paul Bairoch and Patrick K. O'Brien. Their works point out that even as late as the 1790s, hardly 4 per cent of Europe's gross national product was exported beyond the national boundaries. The core-periphery trade hardly contributed to the total volume of trade, as claimed by Wallerstein. Moreover, for Wallerstein, the emergence of European absolutism in the core economies was a distinctly capitalist phenomenon. It was the chief means by which national groupings of commercial capitalists could assert their interests in international economy. Wallerstein's equation of core region with the existence of strong state structures, his critics point out, does not correspond to reality. His identification of core regions with the Netherlands and England is not acceptable to his critics. These states, on the contrary, had comparatively weak state structures, while countries outside the core, such as Prussia, Sweden, Austro-Hungary, etc., had a much stronger forms of absolutism.

Demographic Explanation

The decline of feudalism and the rise of capitalism is placed by some writers on demographic factors. They suggest that major shifts in demographic patterns caused the disintegration of the feudal economy. M.M. Postan and H.J. Habakkuk are among the first to stress the role of population in the long-term changes in the economic structures. This demography-centric interpretation, also called the 'Malthusian model' as it is based on the population theory of Thomas Robert Malthus (1766–1834), an English classical political economist. This theory has been constructed in opposition to Sweezy's model that views trade and market as a determining factor in the decline of feudalism. Some other writers like W. Abel, A.E. Verhulst and Le Roy Ladurie have all endorsed the importance of population in their studies of pre-modern Europe. Postan asserts that in the medieval period, the market force was far from automatic in bringing about the dissolution of serfdom. Rather, it may actually coincide with its intensification. He cites the case of the seigneurial reaction in the thirteenth century to the powerful pressure from the world market of grains. Instead of leading the path towards capitalism, it tightened the bondage on peasants, although in western Europe, it facilitated the capitalist development.

The Malthusian model assigns an exclusively determinist role to population. The main argument is that European feudalism underwent significant economic and demographic growth from about the eleventh till the end of the thirteenth century. The steady growth led to overpopulation and a conflict between material resources and population developed. A constant pressure on agriculture and other natural resources caused declining returns, lowered productivity, fragmentation of landholdings, shortage of food grain, lowered wages and increasing rents. It forced the people of many areas to use marginal lands for food production. All these developments emanating from population changes created conditions of an agrarian crisis since the scope of increasing production in a natural economy was not feasible. This Malthusian crisis, the problem of growing demand and limited resources, had its own cure. Famines, malnourishment and natural calamities like the Black Death epidemic caused a sharp decline in population. This trend began to reverse after 1450s. This model has, as Brenner describes, a built-in mechanism of self-correction which determines automatically its own change of direction. Habakkuk applies this model to the entire period between roughly eight centuries starting from the tenth century. The demographic crisis of the fourteenth century caused severe shortage of labour and a sharp fall in incomes of the landlords. This shifted the earlier social balance away from the aristocratic class towards the peasants. The nobility responded to this situation in different ways. Some placed new forms of bondage on the populace; some transformed feudal dues into money rents while some others appropriated the land belonging to the peasants or the common lands and turned them into pastures for sheep farming. The latter landlords were showing trends towards capitalist farming. This also was the period that saw the emergence of wage-labourers, while a few tenant farmers transformed into yeomen, a trend more common in England. The proponents of demographic theory suggest that a similar crisis surfaced in the seventeenth century, implying a cyclical process of demographic and economic progress and regression. This cycle of growth, crisis and solution keeps repeating so long as the economy remains dependent on natural factors as opposed to commercial production.

The importance of population changes in the working of an economy has been highlighted by some historians. While Postan assigns an endogenous role to demography in bringing about the crisis when demand outpaced supply, W. Abel assigns it an external role, when the prices fell in the fourteenth, seventeenth and eighteenth centuries as a result of stagnation or reduction of population because of epidemics and wars. Abel suggests that the trend towards commercial production and trade in farm products was restricted by an increase in the rural population and because of the self-sufficient character of peasant agriculture. Emmanuel Le Roy Ladurie in his formidable work *Les paysans de Languedoc* not only supports the 'demographic model' but also provides statistical data to the hypothesis and also introduces climatic factors in it. He argues that 'it is in the economy, in social relations and even in more fundamentally, in biological facts, rather than in the class struggle, that we must seek the motive force in history'.

The 'demographic model', one of the explanations in the transition debate, has been criticized on various grounds. Robert Brenner directly confronts the Malthusian model for introducing a level of orthodoxy that is dependent on 'built-in-mechanism of self-correction'. This model seeks to replace the market-centric approach with a cyclic dynamic trend as a key to the long-term economic change. The disharmony between rapidly growing population and declining food supply due to constant use of soil becomes a fundamental problem and leads to natural occurrences such as disease, high infant mortality, famine, war. These are called the Malthusian checks. This situation of the growing population outstretching primary food resources and the consequent crises keeps repeating. The end of crisis marks a fresh beginning in the growth of economy. Brenner highlights this orthodoxy and criticizes the demographic explanation for several reasons.

According to Brenner, the Malthusian model runs into difficulty with respect to long-term trends in income distribution which this model does not address. For Brenner, any explanation of the progress of income distribution in the late-medieval and early-modern period should be able to interpret not merely the changing distribution pattern of local produce but also explain the question of distribution of property between lord and peasant and the direct applicability of force in the rent relationship. Brenner regards them as fundamental questions of class relations and class power, determined relatively autonomously from economic forces (*Brenner Debate*). He feels that the demographic interpretation runs into even more serious problems in explaining the general trends of total production, economic growth or stagnation. No real account is provided for as to why such conditions persisted. Brenner is not satisfied with Ladurie's explanation that the economic process is essentially the direct result of apparently autonomous processes of technical innovation. Instead, he suggests that it could be explained only through the structures of class relations. He also questions the demographic theory of comparative analysis. He notes that different economic and social outcomes proceeded from similar demographic trends at different times and in different areas of Europe. While in one region, the Malthusian crisis led to the disappearance of serfdom, in another region a counter-tendency could be observed. Ladurie's argument implies that increasing population during the sixteenth and the seventeenth centuries in much of France led to fragmentation of holdings, rising rents and declining productivity but a parallel population growth in England led to larger units of landholding, and the rise of large tenant farmers utilizing wage-labour in agricultural production.

Guy Bois accepts the role of demography in feudal crisis but he criticizes the demographic school of writers for ignoring the role of many other factors like the evolution of the seigneurial and royal levy, the tendency towards accumulation, the transformation of the means of production into free commodities and the political, institutional and moral dimensions of the crisis of feudalism. Bois rejects the notion that economic mechanisms alone were responsible for the demographic regression. He thinks that it was the fall in seigneurial revenue that started the acute phase of the crisis in feudalism that brought about a reorganization of the relations of production. According to him, the old mode of production had not sunk but all its cogs were corroded. Rent and profit mingled inextricably. New economic patterns were taking root. The weight of industrial and commercial activities suddenly rose and reacted strongly on the agricultural sector. Within feudalism, a foreign body was growing, fed by the process of accumulation. Its growth had a disintegrating effect on the feudal system (Guy Bois).

The Class-relations Model

Robert Brenner has gone some distance in redressing the shortcomings of Dobb's account of the origins of capitalism and in consolidating and extending the property-relations explanation. Brenner has confronted the existing theories of transition through a critical synthesis. Like Maurice Dobb, he rejects the characterization of capitalism as a trade-based division of labour and stresses on merchant capital being the catalyst for capitalism. Similarly, he finds limitations in the demographic model as it fails to explain two major problems – (a) the decline *versus* the persistence of serfdom, and (b) the emergence and predominance of secure small peasant-property *versus* the rise of landlord or large tenant-farmer relations to land. For Brenner, it is the structure of class relations that determine the manner and degree to which particular demographic or commercial change will affect long-term trends in the distribution of income and economic growth, not vice versa.

Robert Brenner explains that class structure has two unified aspects – (a) the relations of the direct producers to one another, to their tools and their land in the immediate process of production – called the 'labour process' or the 'social relations of production', and (b) the inherently conflictive 'relations of property' that is always guaranteed by force, i.e. the extraction of surplus from the producers by different means called the 'surplus-extraction' relationship. Brenner contends that the fundamental classes in a society are based around the second aspect. The different class structures, especially the property relations once established, tend to impose strict limits and possibilities on society's long-term patterns of economic development. The class structures, as a rule, are not shaped by or altered by changes in demographic or commercial trends. Therefore Brenner insists, that to understand long-term economic developments, growth or regression, it is critical to analyse the relatively autonomous processes by which particular class structures, give rise to conflicts.

On the question of decline of feudalism, Brenner tends to agree with Postan that demographic crisis was inherent in the medieval economy but he insists that the crisis did not emanate from demographic factors. The major problem was the inability of a serf-based agricultural economy to innovate in agriculture even under extreme market incentives. Surplus extraction by the lords left the peasant without the funds that were necessary to maintain a holding and to prevent long-term decline of productivity. Surplus was thus not ploughed back into production and was squandered on military expenditure and luxury goods.

As regards the origin of capitalism, Brenner goes beyond the views of Maurice Dobb by incorporating 'political factors' such as state formation in his explanation. These form essential elements in his views of production-relations and economic development. For him, a 'fusion' between the 'economic' and 'political' was a distinguishing feature of the feudal class structure and system of production. Brenner uses a particular term, 'political accumulation', as one of the key features of feudal dynamics. Through comparative analysis, Brenner explains how different class structures and their historical developments determined specific historical outcomes in transition to capitalism. By comparing the agrarian class-relations in England and France, he highlights the role of the state. Here, their respective states influenced the balance of class forces between landlords and peasants. In the case of France, the centralized state appears to have developed in large parts, feudal class character. The absolutist state protected rural communities for its own benefit and competed with the landed nobility. The turning point was, at least in the Paris region, some time in the thirteenth century when the monarchical state placed itself against the landlords. By the early modern period, the consolidation of peasant property in relationship to the development of the French state created a very different form of class structure in France from that of England. The state was able to increase its power by intervening between peasants and landlords to ensure peasant freedom, hereditability and fixed rents. This policy of the French state not only made the rulers independent of parliamentary taxation but also helped in perpetuating small peasants and at the same time prevented rural differentiation and agrarian transformation. The state was able to extract considerable surplus from the peasants, though it was spent on non-productive expenditure. In England, according to Brenner, monarchical centralization developed from the late-fifteenth century with ultimate dependence upon the landlord classes. The English peasantry had become free to a large extent by the fifteenth century through their resistance and flights. But they failed to establish freehold rights on a large scale. In England, monarchical centralization could not assume an absolutist and peasant-based form as had happened in France. The state support enabled the English landed aristocracy to raise rents and fines to such levels that small tenant farmers were forced to leave. The enclosure movement also undermined peasant property, thereby introducing differentiation in peasant population and opening the path to agricultural capitalism. The English landowners were able to defeat peasant resistance and undermine peasant proprietorship and helped in the rise of agrarian capitalism based on free wage-labour and large units of production during the sixteenth and the seventeenth centuries. Brenner insists that it was not the rising population or markets and grain prices but the productive use of agricultural surplus that was the key to England's economic development. Thus, it is the structure of class-relations that determines the direction of change towards or away from capitalist development.

Historians have often discussed and explained the divergent trends in historical development – the intensification of serfdom in eastern Europe in relation to its decline in the West. The 'exchange-relations' perspective locates the reasons for the divergent trends, particularly the rise of serfdom in eastern Europe, in the weaker development of towns in this region. This made the whole area more vulnerable to seigneurial reaction. It is argued that because the towns were smaller and less developed the nobility could easily overwhelm them. This restricted independent outlets of flight for the servile population of the countryside. Brenner rejects this explanation and he suggests that the contradiction between the development of peasant production and the relations of surplus extraction that defined the class relations of serfdom tended to lead to a crisis of peasant accumulation, of peasant productivity and ultimately of peasant subsistence (*Brenner Debate*). The crisis was accompanied by an intensification of the class conflict inherent in the existing structure leading to different outcomes at different places. According to Brenner, the previous evolutions of rural society provide the explanations of the divergent socio-economic paths taken by eastern and western Europe. Citing the example of western Germany, Brenner argues that throughout the later middle ages, by protracted struggles at village levels, the peasants had organized themselves through local village institutions as a powerful line of defence against the incursions of landlords. These institutions provided economic regulations, ensured rights of inheritance and fixed rents and at times installed their own village magistrates. He points out that in eastern Germany the situation was quite different. The village institutions representing peasant class interests had not developed much and so the peasants of this region appear to have been less prepared to resist seigneurial attacks and control. Brenner applies the example of the success of peasant communities in western Germany to most parts of western Europe and contends that the peasants were able to considerably limit the claims of the aristocracy and consequently helped the process of the dissolution of serfdom. Thus, according to him, economic backwardness of eastern Europe cannot be the result of its dependence upon trade in primary products to the West. Rather the dependence on grain exports was a result of backwardness and unequal distribution of income that was rooted in the nature of class structure.

Brenner's explanation of the rise in capitalism based on class-relations approach represents an important advance over the earlier Marxist interpretations. His confrontation with the scholars of demographic model and those supporting the exchange-relations perspective has led to the revival of another intense debate, commonly called the 'Brenner debate'.

A number of scholars supporting the demographic explanation point out their main objections to the Brenner thesis. Patrica Croote and David Parker consider his explanation of contrasting developments in England and France unsatisfactory. They also reject his lord-centric approach. Heide Wunder finds flaws in Brenner's study full of factual inaccuracies as it was based on secondary literature and not on original research. His presentation of class-structures in Germany suffers from similar problems.

Brenner's first article was rather harsh on the demographic explanation and a strong reaction by its supporters followed. M.M. Postan and John Hatcher insist that Brenner's class-relations model cannot sufficiently replace their own model and they counter Brenner's criticism by insisting that they never assigned an all-determining role to the demographic trends in medieval society at the expense of social factors. They charge that Brenner has certain misconceptions of the Malthusian model. Their reason for emphasizing demographic factors is to relate periodic movements and economic fluctuations to long-term historical trends. They contend that the shortcoming of Brenner's argument is not only confined to his logic but also to historical evidence, particularly with respect to Germany. His exclusive concern for surplus-extraction relations of serfdom distorts his view of the landlords and the peasants. He exaggerates the importance of rent and its elasticity.

Many critics of Brenner consider his rejection of the Dobb-Hilton explanation of East–West differences, and his own interpretation highlighting the contrasting features of rural class structures and the nature of peasant resistance in the two regions as thoroughly overdrawn. Guy Bois, generally agrees with Brenner's criticism of the Malthusian model and his stress on the decisive role assigned to the class struggles in the long-term evolution of capitalism, but he disagrees with his methodology. The hypothesis of Guy Bois differs from that of Brenner on two counts. Firstly, he believes that the birth of capitalism is a by-product of the socio-economic functioning of the feudal system as a whole and not confined to regions, as brought out by Brenner. Secondly, the idea of inequality of development within the whole system is fundamental to the process of historical development under feudalism. It is the inequalities in the world of feudal production which are at the root of divergence. Bois describes Brenner's Marxism as 'political Marxism'.

Another criticism made against Brenner is his belief that the development of capitalism is based on large-scale units of production. Dobb and Hilton had emphasized on the complex process that led to rural social differentiation in which even some small peasant-proprietors could become capitalist farmers over a long period of time. Patrica Croote and David Parker argue that the real agricultural revolution was a long-term process of good husbandry involving new techniques and crops. In this way the peasants, instead of being obstacles to economic development, may actually have provided impetus to it. They talk of the innovations made among small producers rather than the medium-type landowners. Though Brenner in his rejoinder cited the examples of large-scale units of production in many parts of England, he hardly addresses Croot and Parker's concerns.

Croote and Parker appreciate Brenner's comparative analysis but point out the shortcomings in it. Their main criticism is that in the process of making a number of important observations, he telescopes long-term economic trends and therefore misses out on crucial stages. Besides, they find Brenner's contrasting developments in England and France unsatisfactory and too general. In France the position of the peasantry is misunderstood by Brenner, and hence he exaggerates its independence. Similarly, in England he provides a 'lord-centric' explanation and misses out the role of 'customary-tenants' and 'short-term leaseholders'. He inflates the role of landlords at the expense of peasants. Brenner seems to suggest that the emergence of capitalism in England was essentially a lord-centred initiative rooted in the long-held powers of the English aristocracy. However, critics of Brenner point out that the most spectacular growth of agrarian capitalism took place after the

English Revolution but many of the capitalist farmers emerged from the category of traditional aristocracy. By associating the emergence of capitalism exclusively with aristocratic initiative, it is argued that Brenner's explanation short-circuits the entire process.

Finally, according to Emmanuel Le Roy Ladurie, Brenner's explanation of agricultural and capitalist development is far too unilinear. There is sufficient evidence to show that transition from the feudal system to capitalism is possible without the disintegration of small farmers. Ladurie cites the cases of Holland, Belgium and parts of France and Japan. In these regions small farming catered to the working population of the new industrial capitalism. The destruction of the peasantry and large-scale farming on the English model could be another route to capitalist development, states Ladurie, but not the sole path.

Apart from the major explanations already discussed, another viewpoint worth studying is that of Perry Anderson. His approach in the discussion of transition from feudalism to capitalism is sometimes called 'Marxist eclecticism'. It presents a synthesis of non-Marxist themes like the Malthusian notion of cyclic phases of imbalance between population and food supply, and the more conventional Marxist approaches focusing on production relationship and the study of class structures. Like Dobb and Hilton, he also believes that changes in social relations preceded the development of productive forces in the emergence of capitalism. But he does not propose any simple evolutionary theory of change within feudalism based on class struggle resulting in feudal crisis. Like Brenner, Anderson also assigns a role to political factors in the transition from feudalism to capitalism. He partially accepts the importance of towns and international trade. In his study of the rise of absolutism in Europe, he lays great stress on 'superstructural' peculiarities of the absolutist states of western Europe. For Anderson, the primary element in the eventual emergence of the capitalist absolute property rights was the incorporation of Roman law into the feudal system. This helped the process of centralization and brought about a fundamental transformation in feudal property relationship. Its relative absence in eastern Europe retarded the emergence of capitalist property relationship. For

Anderson, the juridical traditions played a determining role in the transition to capitalism, first in England, then in France and later in other regions.

In Brenner's arguments, the primary concern has been to delineate the origins of capitalism based on the different patterns of class relations in pre-industrial Europe. The rise of capitalism is explained through the process of state-formation and the concept of 'political accumulation'. Perry Anderson provides a far more 'eclectic' framework in the transition to capitalism by assigning a role to the superstructure, including the legal system.

In recent years, the decline of feudalism and the rise of capitalism have been generally explained outside the classical models, and on line with the world-system approach. Andre Gunder Frank rejects the notion that there was any qualitative shift from feudalism to capitalism in the sixteenth century. He in fact rejects terms like feudalism or capitalism as distinct modes of production. For him, the process of capital accumulation had been going on since 3000 BC. Janet Abu-Lughod follows the world-system approach and suggests that the rise of the capitalist world order began not in the sixteenth century but as early as about AD 1250. She argues that this system was truly global but instead of describing Europe as the core region she considers Asia, or more specifically China as the core zone and Europe as the periphery. She objects to the Euro-centric approach and finds nothing special in it during this period. It was the economic decline and withdrawal of China and the breaking up of the oriental link that gave the West an opportunity to expand. These writings highlight the importance of world-trade networks. There are some other writers who give credit to the nation-states for the rise of capitalism. Like Anderson, they also suggest that the rise of nation-states rationalized law, freed land for market speculations, removed internal barriers, established standardized taxation, uniform currencies and brought about redistribution of incomes. However, these views have still to gain ground and the debate on transition remains unresolved.

Suggested Reading

Anderson, Perry, *Lineages of the Absolutist States*, London: New Left Books, 1974. Provides a wide-ranging perspective mainly within the Marxist school of writing but often transgresses the limits.

Aston, T.H. and C.H.E. Philpin, eds., *The Brenner Debate: Agrarian Class Structure and Economic Development in Pre-Industrial Europe*, Cambridge: Cambridge University Press, 1985. This book includes a number of articles including Robert Brenner's, besides those of Guy Bois, Patrica Croote, David Parker and Rodney Hilton.

Bois, Guy, *The Crisis of Feudalism: Economy and Society in Eastern Normandy, c. 1300-1500*, Cambridge: Cambridge University Press, 1984. A provocative work that faced some criticism for placing considerable stress on demographic factors.

Dobb, Maurice, *Studies in the Development of Capitalism*, London: Routledge and Kegan Paul, 1963. Represents the classical Marxist approach, this work marks the beginning of the 'transition debate'.

——— *Papers on Capitalism, Development and Planning*, New York: International Press, 1967. Defends his earlier stand by elaborating some of his arguments.

Hilton, Rodney, ed., *The Transition from Feudalism to Capitalism*, London: Verso, 1984 (4th edn.). It briefly covers the entire debate between Maurice Dobb and Paul Sweezy with critiques of many other scholars including those of Kohachiro Takahashi, Christopher Hill and Eric Hobsbawm.

Kaye, Harvey J., *The British Marxist Historians*, London: Polity, 1984 (rpt. 1995, Macmillan). Chapters 2 and 3 deal with the transition debate while chapter 4 discuss the English bourgeois revolution.

Postan, M.M. and H.J. Habakkuk, eds., *Cambridge Economic History of Europe*, Cambridge: Cambridge University Press, 1966, vols. 4–6. An authoritative work based on thorough research.

Sanderson, Stephen K., *Social Transformations: A General Theory of Historical Development*, London: Blackwell, 1995. A brief presentation of the entire debate with remarkable clarity.

Mielants, Eric, *The Origins of Capitalism and the Rise of the West*, Pennsylvania: Temple University Press, 2008. A recent view in the transition debate which disputes Brenner's view of agrarian capitalism and instead locates the rise of capitalism in the city states of Medieval Europe.

Index